Victor Henry

A short Comparative Grammar of English and German

As traced back to their common Origin and contrasted with the classical Languages

Victor Henry

A short Comparative Grammar of English and German
As traced back to their common Origin and contrasted with the classical Languages

ISBN/EAN: 9783337059545

Printed in Europe, USA, Canada, Australia, Japan

Cover: Foto ©ninafisch / pixelio.de

More available books at **www.hansebooks.com**

A SHORT COMPARATIVE GRAMMAR

OF

ENGLISH AND GERMAN

AS TRACED BACK TO THEIR COMMON ORIGIN AND CONTRASTED

WITH THE CLASSICAL LANGUAGES

BY

VICTOR HENRY

Deputy-Professor of Comparative Philology in the University of Paris, Doctor of Letters, and Doctor of Laws

AUTHOR OF "A COMPARATIVE GRAMMAR OF GREEK AND LATIN"

TRANSLATED BY THE AUTHOR

London

SWAN SONNENSCHEIN & CO

NEW YORK: MACMILLAN & CO

1894

PREFACE.

The French edition of this work, published in November, 1893 (Paris, Hachette), was reviewed shortly afterwards in the *Academy* (no. 1131), in so friendly and sympathetic a spirit that I feel bound to express my gratitude to the anonymous critic, both for the valuable suggestions he made, and for the praise he gave to my book. Of the former I have, as he will perceive, availed myself as far as possible, and have deferred to his opinion in almost every case. There is, however, one point on which he appears to have misjudged me; he evidently missed the note on page 23 (p. 21 of this translation), and was therefore led to suppose that I had stated as a fact that an *r*-vowel actually existed in English. The confusion is only apparent; for the sake of brevity I thought it advisable not to separate the English final *r* from the other English and from the German final liquids and nasals, but at the same time I reminded my French readers that the *r* in this position had become an untrilled vowel, and I referred them for further details to a subsequent section. And I am still inclined to believe this course the best for my purpose, especially when we take into consideration the fact, of which there is hardly any doubt, that as recently as two centuries ago the *r* was no less trilled in *mother* than it is at the present day in *raven*.

A few words are necessary in regard to the terminology adopted in this work. Since the words "phonèmes" for "sounds" and "apophonie" for "vowel-gradation" were not adopted by the skilful translator of my *Comparative Grammar of Greek and Latin*—of which the present book is a symmetrical counterpart—I did not think it right to introduce them here: convenient as they are, I have tried to do without them. But as the term "metaphony" for G. "Umlaut" has no exact equivalent in scientific language, I have ventured to introduce it to the notice of English scholars and teachers in the belief that, when once naturalised, they will find it a serviceable and almost indispensable acquisition. "Pregermanic," though a somewhat loose translation of G. "Urgermanisch," is at any rate brief and unmistakable, considering that the notion equivalent to "Vorgermanisch,"—which in the present state of our knowledge is scarcely distinguishable from "Indo-European"—never occurs in my work, and, when occurring elsewhere, may easily be expressed by some such unobjectionable term as "Ante-Germanic." Lastly, I have retained the term "deflected grade," which Mr. Elliott adopted in his translation, for the *o*-shade of an Indo-European syllable containing an *e*, seeing that the only reason which can be urged against it is that *it means nothing*. And this indeed is precisely the reason why I adopted it many years ago and still adhere to it, since, as it means nothing, it suffices to represent the fact we desire to express, without introducing any misleading connotation. We know what a "normal" syllable is,—namely, one that is accented,—and what a "reduced" syllable is,—namely, one that is unaccented,—but we are quite unable to account for the fact that, in certain derivations, the *e* of the root or the suffix is regularly changed to *o*. Such terms as "nebentonige Hochstufe," besides being rather cumbrous, are merely fitted to conceal our own ignorance and to prejudge the solution of a question which had as yet better remain unsettled, and which indeed may never receive a complete and satisfactory answer.[1]

---

[1] The theory that the deflected grade of the root has any connection with the primitive accentuation becomes more and more improbable or, at any rate, impossible to demonstrate. See Henry, *Muséon*, III. (1884), p. 502, and now Streitberg, *die Entstehung der Dehnstufe* (1894), p. 62.

The present work, as my friendly critic points out in the review already referred to, is intended to introduce the comparative method to students who have already some knowledge of both the English and German languages. An English reader will find it accessible if he has mastered the general outlines of the grammatical structure of German. So much indeed is necessary—for the comparative method does not pretend to teach the rudiments—but at the same time it is amply sufficient; and I venture to emphasize this point at the outset, lest the student should fear to be unequal to the task and should decline to undertake it for lack of knowledge, which, far from being required beforehand, is presented to him as it becomes necessary in each chapter of this Grammar. He must, too, bear in mind that the comparative study of the Germanic languages forms an independent whole in itself and does not necessarily presuppose a knowledge either of Sanskrit, or Greek, or even Latin, and that all the instances quoted in the following pages from foreign languages are intended to aid those who are already acquainted with them, not to disconcert those to whom they are unfamiliar. It must further be remembered that, while a teacher may sometimes be compelled to enter into minute details in order to provide for the wants of more mature students, the beginner may very well pass these over, or at any rate need not remember them. He must use his own tact and judgment in making a choice between the facts and ideas suggested to him, in dwelling upon those which will aid his memory and in overlooking such as might encumber it, and, in a word, in limiting his researches to the objects he has in view,—according as he intends merely to compare German and English, or to obtain a general idea of the complete history of the Germanic languages, or even to glance at the primitive features of the Indo-European mother-tongue.

The student should also beware of too readily accepting conclusions without understanding the evidence on which they are based, nor should he wait to examine one subject thoroughly before passing to another. This fragmentary method of learn-ing, although of great practical utility, must necessarily seem rather discouraging to the linguistic student, since he will know nothing of the goal to which his steps are leading him, and when he at length reaches it he may have forgotten the road he has traversed. Hence I should advise him, in the first place, to read the book as a whole, omitting nothing, of course, but without waiting to consider specially any passages which at first sight may appear difficult or obscure. It must, for example, be confessed that pure phonetics have little charm for the uninitiated reader; it almost requires a special sense to admire a beautiful correspondence of vowels or consonants, no less than a neat formula in mathematics. Word-formation itself, especially when confined within the narrow limits which a primer imposes, seldom appears sufficiently clear and cogent to compensate for the inevitable dryness of its main statements. It is not until he comes to grammar proper, that is, to the study of declension and conjugation, that he will find himself quite at home. Here, at any rate, nothing is unfamiliar to him, and he may even verify for himself facts of which he has hitherto remained ignorant. He will now begin to understand the reasons for the phonetic and etymological processes which may have at first proved bewildering. Were he now to re-open the book after this first perusal, he would find a new and unexpected light cast upon most of the points which he had wisely reserved for further examination. In this second reading he should avail himself, to a large extent, of the numerous references given in the notes at the foot of the page; he should, for instance, associate the theory of final *s* with the study of plurals and genitives, or that of medial *s* with the formation of German plurals in *er*, or vowel-gradation with the classification of the so-called Germanic strong verbs; in short, he should take a broad survey of the vast tract of knowledge into which a sound method has led him step by step.

In the next place, I would recommend my readers to make frequent use of the indexes of words which are given at the end of the book. The examples have been purposely multiplied, and, though of course the most typical among them must occur several times in different places, constant care has been taken to vary them as much as possible, in such a way as to include nearly all the important words of both languages, and thus to supply the student with a double etymological vocabulary, reduced to its simplest elements. He will find it advantageous to take cognate words, and to compare them with each other, vowel for vowel and consonant for consonant, and so obtain a clear idea of the correspondences or phonetic discords they disclose. He may then turn for verification to the complete and detailed dictionaries in which Prof. Skeat and Prof. Kluge have displayed so much erudition and industry.

Finally, although the immediate object of this work is the comparative study of Modern English and German, I may perhaps indulge in the hope that for some students it may also serve as a primer of the earlier languages, and enable them to translate, without further help than that of an appropriate glossary, such easy texts as may be found in an elementary chrestomathy of Middle English or Middle High German, of Old English or Old High German, or even of Low German or Gothic. This, for a tolerably experienced student, is by far the most valuable of all trainings, and he would hardly be likely to meet with any serious difficulties, apart from the variable and arbitrary character of many old transliterations; but if he has once been informed, that Otfrid, for instance, still writes everywhere *th* for initial *d*, or that Notker, in certain well-defined positions, replaces *b*, *d* and *g*, respectively, by *p*, *t* and *k*, or that the Old English texts spell as *eá*, *eó*, etc., the diphthongs which were actually sounded *ēa*, *ēo*, it will only require a little care and attention on his part to triumph over these obstacles. Whatever languages he chooses for study, I should advise him in any case to begin with the Gospels, which are usually translated word for word, so that the difficulties of syntax are avoided; here, too, it is easy to verify and compare. Other texts, for more advanced students, are mentioned below in a bibliographical note.

It is perhaps almost superfluous to add that this is by no means a servile translation of the French. Besides silently correcting errors which were pointed out by my critics or discovered by myself, I have introduced into it some slight modifications which seemed convenient in a book intended for the use of English students and teachers, and, as a matter of fact, if the two texts are compared, few pages will be found the same. For any further suggestions from English critics— supposing they find the work in its new shape worthy of their attention—I shall be truly thankful. I must also express my indebtedness to Mr. D. B. Kitchin, M.A., late of Trinity College, Cambridge, who has been good enough to revise my manuscript and to polish my rough continental English;—to Messrs. Swan Sonnenschein & Co., who undertook the publication of this translation and entrusted me with its completion without any other guarantee than that of my name;—and, finally, to the printers, whose skill, judgment and care have overcome the difficulties of their task and enabled the work to attain at least the material accuracy which the reader expects and the author desires.

V. HENRY

Paris, *May 1st*, 1894.

TABLE OF CONTENTS.

	PAGE
PREFACE	v
TABLE OF CONTENTS	xi
TRANSLITERATION	xvii
CONVENTIONAL SIGNS	xxiii
BIBLIOGRAPHICAL NOTE	xxv
(1) INTRODUCTION	1

FIRST PART.
SOUNDS 15

(8)		
(9)	CHAPTER I.—THE ELEMENTS OF PHYSIOLOGICAL PHONETICS	18
(10)	Section I.—*The Production of Sounds*	19
(11)	Section II.—*Classification of Sounds*	23
(12)	§ 1.—Vowels, Semi-vowels and Diphthongs	23
(13)	§ 2.—Consonant-Vowels	25
(14)	§ 3.—Consonants	26
(15)	CHAPTER II.—VOWELS AND DIPHTHONGS	29
(16)	Section I.—*Vocalic Laws in English and German*	29
(17)	§ 1.—Recent Vowel Change	30
(20)	§ 2.—Shortening and Lengthening	39
(21)	§ 3.—Old English Vowel-Breaking	42
(22)	§ 4.—Metaphony (Vowel Mutation or Modification)	43
(24)	§ 5.—Pregermanic Compensatory Lengthening	49
(25)	Section II.—*Primitive Vowels and Diphthongs and their Evolution*	51
(26)	§ 1.—Short and long *e*	52
(27)	§ 2.—Short and long *i*	54
(28)	§ 3.—Short and long *u*	55
(29)	§ 4.—Diphthongs of short *e*	57
(30)	§ 5.—Short *a* and *o*, and their Diphthongs	59
(33)	§ 6.—Long *a* and *o*	62
(34)	Section III.—*Vowels in Final Syllables*	63
	§ 1.—Final Vowels	64
	§ 2.—Non-final Vowels	65

xii TABLE OF CONTENTS.

		PAGE
(35)	CHAPTER III.—SEMI-VOWELS AND CONSONANT-VOWELS	66
	Section I.—*Semi-vowels*	66
(36)	§ 1.—Semi-vowel *y*	66
(37)	§ 2.—Semi-vowel *w*	68
(38)	Section II.—*Consonant-Vowels*	69
(39)	§ 1.—Nasals	69
(41)	§ 2.—Liquids	72
(43)	Section III.—*Indo-European Vowel-Gradation (Apophony)*	74
(44)	§ 1.—The Principle of Vowel-Gradation	75
(45)	§ 2.—Germanic Vowel-Gradation	77
(46)	CHAPTER IV.—EXPLOSIVE CONSONANTS AND THEIR SUBSTITUTES	82
(47)	Section I.—*The Second Consonantal Shifting*	83
(48)	§ 1.—Labials	84
(49)	§ 2 – Dentals	88
(50)	§ 3.—Gutturals	91
(51)	Section II.—*The First Consonantal Shifting*	98
(52)	§ 1.—Grimm's and Verner's Laws	100
(54)	§ 2.—Primitive Voiceless Explosives	104
(56)	§ 3.—Primitive Voiced Aspirates	108
(57)	§ 4.—Primitive Voiced Explosives	109
(58)	CHAPTER V.—SIBILANT CONSONANTS	111
(59)	Section I.—*Initial Sibilant*	111
(60)	Section II.—*Medial Sibilants*	113
(61)	§ 1.—Voiceless Sibilant	114
(62)	§ 2.—Voiced Sibilant	116
(63)	Section III.—*Final Sibilant*	117
(64)	CHAPTER VI.—ACCENT	118
(65)	Section I.—*Word-Accent*	119
(66)	Section II.—*Sentence-Accent*	123

(67)
SECOND PART.
WORDS.
127

(70)	CHAPTER I.—PRIMITIVE DERIVATION	133
(71)	Section I.—*Primary Suffixes*	133
(72)	§ 1.—Nominal Stems	134
(81)	§ 2.—Verbal Stems	145
(86)	Section II.—*Secondary Suffixes*	150
(87)	§ 1—Nominal Stems	150
(92)	§ 2.—Verbal Stems	156
(94)	CHAPTER II.—ENGLISH AND GERMAN DERIVATION	160
(95)	Section I.—*Prefixes*	160
(96)	§ 1.—Nominal Prefixes	161
(97)	§ 2.—Verbal Prefixes	161

		PAGE
(101)	Section II.—*Suffixes properly so-called*	170
	§ 1.—Nominal Suffixes	170
(102)	*A.*—Nouns	171
(105)	*B.*—Adjectives	176
(106)	§ 2.—Verbal Suffixes	177
(108)	Section III.—*Old Words changed to Suffixes*	182
(109)	§ 1.—Nouns	182
(110)	§ 2.—Adjectives	184
(111)	§ 3.—Adverbs	188
(112)	CHAPTER III.—COMPOSITION	190
(113)	Section I.—*Classification of Compounds*	190
(114)	§ 1.—Grammatical Classification	191
(115)	§ 2.—Functional Classification	193
(116)	Section II.—*Formation of Compounds*	195
(117)	§ 1.—Form of the First Term	196
(118)	§ 2.—Form of the Last Term	200
(119)	CHAPTER IV.—THE SYSTEM OF NUMERATION	203
(120)	Section I.—*Cardinal Numbers*	203
(121)	§ 1.—Units and Sums of Units	203
(122)	§ 2.—Tens	206
(123)	§ 3.—Hundreds and Thousands	208
(124)	Section II.—*Derivatives from Cardinal Numbers*	209

THIRD PART.

(125)

DECLENSION. 213

(126)	CHAPTER I.—ARTICLES	215
(127)	Section I.—*Definite Article*	216
(128)	§ 1.—Origin and Primitive Declension	216
(129)	§ 2.—Modern State	218
(134)	Section II.—*Indefinite Article*	222
(135)	CHAPTER II.—NOUNS	223
(136)	Section I.—*Gender*	223
(137)	Section II.—*Number*	226
(138)	§ 1.—General Remarks	228
(139)	§ 2.—Plurals in *-s*	230
(140)	§ 3.—Plurals in *-en*	234
(143)	§ 4.—Plurals in *-e* without Metaphony	240
(144)	§ 5.—Metaphonical plurals with or without an *-e*	243
(145)	*A.*—English metaphony	244
(146)	*B.*—German metaphony	245
(147)	§ 6.—Metaphonical plurals in *-er*	248

c

xiv TABLE OF CONTENTS.

		PAGE
(148)	Section III.—*Cases*	249
(149)	§ 1.—Accusative	249
(150)	§ 2.—Genitive	252
(152)	§ 3.—Dative	255
(153)	CHAPTER III.—ADJECTIVES	259
(154)	Section I.—*Declined Adjective*	260
(155)	§ 1.—Strong Declension	260
(156)	§ 2.—Weak Declension	261
(157)	Section II.—*Invariable Adjective*	263
	§ 1.—In German	263
	§ 2.—In English	264
(158)	CHAPTER IV.—PRONOUNS	266
(159)	Section I.—*Demonstratives*	266
(160)	§ 1.—Demonstratives properly so called	268
(161)	§ 2.—Interrogative and Indefinite Pronouns	268
(162)	§ 3.—Relative Pronouns	270
(163)	Section II.—*Personal Pronouns*	271
(164)	§ 1.—First Person	271
(165)	§ 2.—Second Person	273
(166)	§ 3.—Third Person	274
(167)	§ 4.—Reflexive Pronoun	276
(618)	§ 5.—Possessives	278

FOURTH PART.

(170)

CONJUGATION. 282

(171)	CHAPTER I.—TENSES	284
(173)	Section I.—*Perfect : General Survey*	285
(175)	Section II.—*Strong Perfect and Participle*	289
(176)	§ 1.—Perfects with vowel-gradation	290
(179)	A.—Type *drive=treiben*	292
(180)	B.—Type *choose=kiesen*	295
(181)	C.—Type *drink=trinken* and *swell=schwellen*	297
(182)	D.—Type *steal=stehlen*	300
(183)	E.—Type *see=sehen*	303
(184)	F.—Type *slay=schlagen*	304
(185)	§ 2.—Reduplicated Perfects	306
	G.—The only Type being *fall=fallen*	306
(186)	Section III.—*Weak Perfect and Participle*	310
(187)	§ 1.—Apparent Anomalies	310
(188)	§ 2.—Principle of Formation	315
(189)	§ 3.—Applications	319

TABLE OF CONTENTS. XV

		PAGE
(190)	CHAPTER II.—MOODS	321
(191)	Section I.—*Subjunctive*	321
(192)	§ 1.—Present Subjunctive	321
(193)	§ 2.—Perfect Subjunctive	323
(196)	Section II.—*Imperative*	327
(198)	CHAPTER III.—PERSON-ENDINGS	330
(199)	Section I.—*Ordinary Conjugation*	330
(200)	§ 1.—Present-Endings	330
(204)	§ 2.—Present-Metaphony	335
(208)	§ 3.—Perfect-Endings	341
(211)	§ 4.—Subjunctive-Endings	343
(213)	§ 5.—Imperative-Endings	345
(214)	§ 6.—The English Verbal Plural	346
(215)	Section II.—*Anomalous Conjugations*	349
(216)	§ 1.—The Verb "to be"	349
(218)	§ 2.—Other Root-Verbs	352
(222)	§ 3.—Preterito-Presents	355
(223)	Type *A*.	357
(224)	Type *C*.	358
(225)	Type *D*.	359
(226)	Type *E*.	360
(227)	Type *F*.	360
(228)	Unclassed	361
(229)	CHAPTER IV.—VERBAL PERIPHRASES	362
(230)	Section I.—*Periphrastic Tenses*	365
	§ 1.—Present	365
(231)	§ 2.—Past	365
(232)	§ 3.—Future	367
(233)	Section II.—*Periphrastic Moods*	369
	§ 1.—Indicative	369
(234)	§ 2.—Subjunctive	370
(235)	§ 3.—Conditional	370
(236)	§ 4.—Imperative	371
(237)	Section III.—*Periphrastic Aspects*	372
(238)	§ 1.—Reflexive Aspect	372
(239)	§ 2.—Passive Aspect	373
(240)	CONCLUSION	375
	INDEX OF WORDS.—I. English	377
	II. German	384
	INDEX OF TERMINATIONS.—I. English	392
	II. German	393

TRANSLITERATION.

In the transliteration of words and forms quoted either from the Indo-European or Pregermanic mother-tongue, or in general from any language, which, having no literature, naturally lacks a conventional orthography,—such as rural dialects,—as also whenever it is necessary to emphasize the true pronunciation of any form even of a literary language, the spelling is strictly phonetic, so that every symbol must be given its specific and precise value, as defined at the beginning of this work (no. 10–14): thus, the vowels, *a, e, i, o, u*, are the so-called Latin, never the English vowels, and ought to be sounded everywhere, for instance, a = E. *a* in *father*, $\bar{\imath}$ = E. *ee* in *see*, u = E. *oo* in *soon* (German *u*), and so forth; ȝ, þ, ð and ƀ are the spirants which respectively represent the German *g* of *ewige*, E. hard and soft *th*, and E. *v*[1]; š is E. *sh*, and ž is French *j* (*z* in *glazier*); *w* and *y*, semivowels, E. *w* and *y* in *young*, etc. The latter sound, however, is denoted by a *j* in Pregermanic and Gothic, as it was in Old High German and is still in all the continental Germanic languages.[2]

In regard to accent and prosody, the reader must always distinguish very accurately such symbols as: ă or simply *a*, unaccented short vowel; á, accented short vowel; ā, unaccented long vowel; ā́, accented long vowel; occasionally, à, short vowel with a secondary accent; and the like.[3]

[1] Though not quite exactly, the ƀ being a bilabial sound, whereas E. *v* is rather denti-labial.
[2] The reason, here, for infringing the law of uniformity in transliteration, is merely a practical one, namely, because all Germanists agree in using this spelling: wherefore also the diphthongs *ay* and *aw* will be written *ai* and *au* in Pregermanic.
[3] In such languages as no longer exhibit any written evidence of accentu-

The theoretical transliteration adopted for the mother-tongues, as a rule, holds good for their offspring, apart from the additions and modifications which are forced upon it by usage or conventional orthography, and may be briefly summed up as follows.

Sanskrit.—The *c*, in any position, like E. *ch* (in *church*); the *j*, like E. *j*. Non-italic t, d, and n, in italic words, are cacuminal consonants; but, of course, we may be allowed to blend them with the corresponding dentals. The *s* is never soft and is sounded in every position like initial E. *s* or French *ç*.

Greek.—The so-called Erasmian pronunciation[1] is not quite correct; but it may be deemed sufficient for our purpose, provided the long vowel be always carefully distinguished from the short one. The F, a merely dialectic sound, is E. *w*.

Latin.—The rules for correct Latin pronunciation are both plain and short, viz.:—each vowel has its phonetic value;—*c*, in any position, like *k*, and *g*, in any position, as in E. *give*;—*j* = German *j* (E. *y*), and *v* = E. *w*;—*s* hard (never like *z*), even when medial;—the accent, always on the penult, or on the antepenult if the penult is a short syllable.

Gothic.—The *ei* is not a diphthong, but a simple *i* (E. *ee*). The *ai* is a short open *e* (E. *set*), and the *aú* a short open *o* (E. *not*), whereas *ái* and *áu* are true diphthongs, sounded as they would be in Modern German (E. approximately *I* and *how*). If the symbol exceptionally lacks the distinctive accentuation, then it must be inferred that its real value is as yet unknown. In the diphthong *iu*, the stress is on the *i*, and the glide on the *u*.

The sound of *b*, *d* and *g* is a double one,—a fact, however, which it will be sufficient to bear in mind, without troubling to reproduce it,—namely: medial between vowels, they are changed to spirants and become respectively ƀ, ð and ʒ. The

---

ation (Gothic, Old English, Old High German, etc.), accent should be neglected, and there remains but the distinction between short and long vowels. The Latin accent, though well known, is never marked, because it is of no importance for Indo-European comparison: see my *Gramm. of Gr. and Lat.*, no. 80-82.

[1] Each vowel with its phonetic value, and $\theta = t + h$ (not E. *th*): cf. my *Gramm. of Gr. and Lat.*, no. 23, 24 and 54.

þ, of course, is E. hard *th*. The *s* is always hard, and the *z*, as in English, is the corresponding soft sibilant.[1] The *v*, which is written *w* by many Germanists, is equivalent to the E. *w*, and the *q* is to be pronounced like *kw*. Lastly, the *g*, before a *k* or a *g*, represents the guttural nasal ṅ (*briggan* like E. *bring* and G. *bringen*).

Old Norse.—The æ, the œ and the *y*, whether short or long, respectively, like German *ä*, *ö* and *ü* (French *u*). Spelling keeps the voiced dental spirant (ð), apart from the voiceless (þ); but the labial spirant, whether voiceless or voiced (*f* or *v*), is always written *f*. Other symbols present no difficulty. The quotations, moreover, are very few.

Old English.—The exact pronunciation of the vowels and diphthongs is lost altogether; but there is little chance of error in pronouncing the words as they are written, that is, each letter with its phonetic value.[2] We should only observe that the *æ* is a simple vowel, not a diphthong; for it arises from a primitive *a* and has returned to E. *a*: it is the sound of *a* in *bag, cab*, with but this difference, that it may be either short or long. The *y* is French *u* (G. *ü*), likewise either short or long. The groups *ea, ēa, eo, ēo, ie, īe* do not form two syllables: they are mere diphthongs, the stress being laid on the first component, and the second uttered very swiftly as a kind of semivowel.

Old English indifferently spells ð (later þ) the dental spirant, whether voiced or voiceless: hence we are unable to distinguish them from each other with absolute certainty, and the best course will be, always to pronounce the ð as a hard E. *th*. The *f*, likewise, is sometimes an *f*, and sometimes a *v*. The *c* is sounded *k* before any vowel, though it may have assumed, quite early, in certain positions, the slightly palatal shade which later on resulted in the present sound of E. *ch*[3] The *g* was a spirant

---

[1] Beware of pronouncing it as Modern German *z*.
[2] Beware, above all, of sounding the Old English, and even the Middle English vowels and diphthongs, with the strange value they have now acquired in contemporary speech (cf. *infra* no. 17-20): *gōs* (a goose), not *gūs*, and *gēs* (geese), not *gīs*, and so forth; of course, Old English *u* is German *u*.
[3] Thus, in *ic* (I), pr. *ich*: some E. dialects have the form *chill* for *I will*, where the apparent initial of the verb is really only the final of the pronoun.

in all the numerous cases in which it has now become E. *y*: the symbol for it was ʒ; indeed, it is from the Old English alphabet itself, that our contemporary phonetics have borrowed this peculiar letter to denote the voiced palatal spirant.[1] But ordinary pronunciation need not dwell upon these minute details. The semi-vowel *w* is E. *w*, and the *i*, when representing the Germanic semi-vowel *j*,—as, for instance, in the ending of verbs in *-ian*,—is also confined to the value of a simple glide or semi-vowel.

Middle English.—Take each letter almost for its phonetic value, obscuring however such unaccented sounds as later have become mute. The *th*, either hard or soft, according as it is pronounced in the corresponding Modern English words.

High German (Old and Middle).—The vowels and diphthongs are to be sounded as they are spelled, that is, very nearly as in Modern German, but with a clear distinction between short and long vowels: thus, the student should beware of lengthening the first syllable in *gëban* (=*geben*), or shortening the final in *habēn* (=*haben*). It is superfluous to make any difference between *ë* and *e*, the former being written for primitive Germanic *ĕ*, and the latter for posterior *e* arising from the metaphony of *a*. In the diphthongs *ea*, *ia*, *eo*, *io*, *uo*, the stress is on the first component.

The consonants, in general, are those of Modern German, except in the case of four: medial *h* before a consonant, and final *h*, like G. *ch* (*naht*=*nacht*); ʒ and ʒʒ, approximately a hard *s*[2]; *s*, hard in any position; *w*, as in English.[3]

Slavonic.—Immaterial, owing to the rareness of quotations. Follow the spelling: *ŭ* is an obscure vowel; *š*=E. *sh*; *č*=Sanskrit *c* or E. *ch*.

Modern Languages.—The reader is supposed to be acquainted with their pronunciation, or else must be referred to

---

[1] In this *Grammar*, however, the O.E. palatal has been written *g*, simply to avoid an unfamiliar symbol, and to emphasize the perfect correspondence of both the English and the German sound.

[2] But *z* or *zz*, just as at present (*ts*).

[3] In Middle German, *w* verges on its present sound, namely, English *v*. Old and Middle German *v* has the sound of *f*, with only a slight difference which is now quite lost.

pronouncing dictionaries. The traditional orthography of Modern German has been retained in this work, because it is still the best known and most current out of Germany, and differs too little from the new one, to involve here any inconvenience; though, indeed, the recent reform ought to be encouraged; for, inconsistent as it may be, England and France have a great deal to do for themselves, before they can be allowed to find fault with the modest improvement in spelling attained in Germany.

CONVENTIONAL SIGNS.

acc.	accusative.		*nomin.*	nominative.
adv.	adverb.		*nt.*	neuter.
advb.	adverbial.		*O.E.*	Old English.
cf.	compare.		*O.F.*	Old French.
dat.	dative.		*O.H.G.*	Old High German.
defl.	deflected.		*O.N.*	Old Norse.[2]
E.	English.		*part.*	participle.
e.g.	for instance.		*pf.*	perfect.
F.	French.		*pl.*	plural.
fm.	feminine.		*pl.* 1, 2, 3.	1st, 2nd, 3rd person of the plural.
G.	German.[1]			
gen.	genitive.		*pr.*	pronounce.
Go.	Gothic.		*pref.*	prefix.
Gr.	Greek.		*Preg.*	Pregermanic.
i.e.	that is.		*pres.*	present.
I.-E.	Indo-European.		*red.*	reduced.
impf.	imperfect.		*sg.*	singular.
ind.	indicative.		*sg.* 1, 2, 3.	1st, 2nd, 3rd person of the singular.
inf.	infinitive.			
L.	Latin.		*Sk.*	Sanskrit.
Lith.	Lithuanian.		*Sl.*	Old Slavonic.
M.E.	Middle English.		*sq.*	and following.
metaph.	metaphonical.		*subj.*	subjunctive.
M.F.	Middle French.		*suff.*	suffix.
M.H.G.	Middle High German.		*vb.*	verb.
Mod.	Modern.		*voc.*	vocative.
msc.	masculine.		*Zd.*	Zend (Avestic).

All other abbreviations will be self-explanatory.

The sign of equality (=) between two forms implies their complete iden-

---

[1] That is, what is called "German" in English, namely *Hochdeutsch*. The word "Germanic" is never abbreviated.

[2] That is, especially, Old Icelandic.

tity, whether the one proceeds from the other, as in E. *book* = O.E. *bōc*,[1] or both are to be traced back to a common ancestor, as in E. *book* = G. *buch*. A formula $a:b=c:d$ denotes a proportion, to be read as in arithmetic.

An asterisk before a form denotes that it does not rest on any historical evidence and is merely restored by conjecture.[2] Of course, this is the case with all the so-called Indo-European or Pregermanic forms.

A hyphen, placed before or after a form, denotes an element of language which never appears by itself and cannot be used but by becoming united with some other element, namely:—the form followed by the hyphen is either a prefix detached from the compound it belongs to (E. *be*-, G. *ver*-), or a bare stem curtailed of its grammatical endings (G. *seh*- "to see");—and the form preceded by the hyphen, is either a stem which does not occur without a prefix (G. *-kunft*[3]), or (more often) a derivative suffix or a grammatical ending (E. *-y* = G. *-ig* as in *holy* = *heilig*, E. sg. 2 *-st* = G. sg. 2 *-st*, etc.).

The work has been divided into 240 sections, numbered uninterruptedly from the beginning to the end, each of which forms as homogeneous a whole as possible. All the references introduced by the words *supra* and *infra* refer to these divisions.

The Indexes will be found at the end of the volume.[4]

---

[1] The signs > and <, which respectively should mean "resulting in" and "derived from," are not used here: 1. because the exposition could do without them; 2. because they are equivocal, scholars having not yet come to a full agreement as to their value.

[2] Quite exceptionally, as on p. 1, it precedes a form which neither is nor ever was extant. On the contrary, it cannot be too strongly insisted upon, that *the restored forms are not at all fictitious*, but based on a strictly scientific induction and, therefore, as sure in most cases as if they were actually found in some book. Thus no word *varm-s*, which would mean "warm," is to be read in any Gothic text; but both E. and G. have *warm*, to which a Go. *varm-s* is the strictly phonetical correspondent; and, on the other hand, Gothic has a derivative vb. *varm-jan* "to warm," which necessarily presupposes a nominal basis *varm-*: hence, we may affirm with absolute certainty that Gothic once possessed an adjective *varm-s*, and the asterisk here is an almost superfluous symbol.

[3] In the compounds *aus-kunft, zu-kunft, ein-künft-e*, no word *kunft* being now extant; but the adjective to *zu-kunft* is *künft-ig*, which irresistibly points to the nominal basis *kunft*.

[4] The reader will be pleased to remember that a given word may occur more than once under the same number, and to peruse the notes as well as the text.

BIBLIOGRAPHICAL NOTE.[1]

BEHAGHEL (O.). Die Deutsche Sprache. *Leipzig und Prag*, Freytag, 1886. Engl. Transl. by Emil Teichmann *sub tit.* Short History of the German Language. *London* and *New York*, Macmillan, 1891.

Beiträge zur Geschichte der Deutschen Sprache und Literatur, herausgegeben von H. PAUL and W. BRAUNE (E. SIEVERS). I.-XVIII. *Halle*, Niemeyer, 1874-94 (*in progress*).

Beiträge zur Kunde der Indogermanischen Sprachen, herausgeben von Dr. Ad. BEZZENBERGER. I.-XX. *Göttingen*, Peppmüller, 1877-94 (*in progress*).

BRAUNE (W.). Gotische Grammatik, mit einigen Lesestücken und Wortverzeichniss [1880]. 3te auflage. *Halle*, Niemeyer, 1887. Eng. transl. by G. H. Balg, *sub tit.* Gothic Grammar, with selections and glossary, *New York*, Westermann (London, S. Low & Co.) 1883.

BRAUNE (W.). Althochdeutsche Grammatik [1886]. 2te auflage. *Halle*, Niemeyer, 1891.

BRAUNE (W.). Abriss der Althochdeutschen Grammatik. *Halle*, Niemeyer, 1886.

BRAUNE (W.; ed.). Althochdeutsches Lesebuch, zusammengestellt und mit Glossar versehen [1875]. 3te auflage. *Halle*, Niemeyer, 1888.

BRUGMANN (K.). Grundriss der vergleichenden Grammatik der Indogermanischen Sprachen. *Strassburg*, Trübner, 1886-93. Eng. transl. *sub tit.* Elements of the Comparative Gram-

---

[1] This list has been purposely confined to the narrowest limits. Readers who desire to prosecute their studies further, will find in the books quoted here new references to guide them.

mar of the Indo-germanic Languages, vol I. [Introduction and Phonology], by Dr. Joseph Wright. *London*, Trübner, 1888; vols. II.–III. [Morphology] by R. Seymour Conway and W. H. D. Rouse. *London*, Paul, 1891-2.

CHAMPNEYS (A. C.). History of English, a sketch of the origin and development of the English language. *London*, Percival, 1893.

DELBRÜCK (B.). Vergleichende Syntax der Indogermanischen Sprachen. I. [=vol. III. of Brugmann's Grundriss, *ut supra*]. *Strassburg*, Trübner, 1893.

EARLE (J.). The Philology of the English Tongue. *Oxford*, Clarendon Press (*New York*, Macmillan), 1892.

HENRY (V.). A Short Comparative Grammar of Greek and Latin. Authorized translation by R. T. ELLIOTT [1890]. 2nd edition. *London*, Swan Sonnenschein & Co. (*New York*, Macmillan & Co.) 1892.

Indogermanische Forschungen, Zeitschrift für Indogermanische Sprach- und Alterthumskunde, herausgegeben von K. BRUGMANN und W. STREITBERG. I.–III. *Strassburg*, Trübner, 1892-94 (*in progress*).

KLUGE (Fr.). Nominale Stammbildungslehre der Altgermanischen Dialecte. *Halle*, Niemeyer, 1886.

KLUGE (Fr.). Etymologisches Wörterbuch der Deutschen Sprache [1882-83]. 5ᵗᵉ auflage. *Strassburg*, Trübner, 1894. Engl. transl. by J. F. Davis. *London*, Bell, 1891 [made from the edition of 1889].

MAYHEW (A. L.). Synopsis of Old English Phonology, being a systematic account of Old English Vowels and Consonants and their correspondences in the cognate languages. *Oxford*, Clarendon Press (*New York*, Macmillan), 1891.

NOREEN (A.). Altnordische Grammatik, I. Altisländische und Altnorwegische Grammatik, unter Berücksichtigung des Urnordischen [1884]. 2ᵗᵉ auflage. *Halle*, Niemeyer, 1892.

OLIPHANT (T. L. Kington). The Old and Middle English [1873]. 2nd edition. *London* and *New York*, Macmillan, 1891 [Based on his *The Sources of Middle English*.]

PASSY (P.). Étude sur les changements phonétiques et leurs caractères généraux. *Paris*, Didot, 1890.

PAUL (H.). Principien der Sprachgeschichte. 2ᵗᵉ auflage. *Halle*, Niemeyer, 1889. English translation by Prof. H. A. Strong [1888]. 2nd edition. *London* and *New York*, Longman, 1891.

PAUL (H.). Mittelhochdeutsche Grammatik [1881]. 3ᵗᵉ auflage. *Halle*, Niemeyer, 1889.

PAUL (H.). Grundriss der Germanischen Philologie. I. *Strassburg*, Trübner, 1891.

SCHERER (W.). Zur Geschichte der Deutschen Sprache [1868]. 2ᵗᵉ ausgabe (Neuer Abdruck). *Berlin*, Weidmann, 1890.

SCHLEICHER (A.). Die Deutsche Sprache [1860]. 5ᵗᵉ auflage, hrsg. J. Schmidt. *Stuttgart*, Cotta, 1888.

SIEVERS (E.). Grundzüge der Phonetik [1876]. 4ᵗᵉ auflage. *Leipzig*, Breitkopf und Härtel, 1893.

SIEVERS (E.). Angelsächsische Grammatik [1882]. 2ᵗᵉ auflage. *Halle*, Niemeyer, 1886. Engl. tr. by A. S. Cook, *sub tit.* Old English Grammar [1886]. 2nd edition. *Boston, U.S.*, Ginn (*London*, Arnold), 1888.

SKEAT (W.). An Etymological Dictionary of the English Language. *Oxford*, Clarendon Press (*New York*, Macmillan), 1884. Abridged Edition [1881] 1891.

SKEAT (W.). Principles of English Etymology. Part I. *Oxford*, Clarendon Press (*New York*, Macmillan [1887], 1892. Part II. 1891.

SOAMES (L.) Introduction to Phonetics : English, French, and German. *London*, Swan Sonnenschein & Co. (*New York*, Macmillan), 1891.

Société de Linguistique de Paris (Bulletin et Mémoires de la). I.-VII. *Paris*, Vieweg (Bouillon), 1869-92 (*in progress*).

STREITBERG (W.). Zur Germanischen Sprachgeschichte. *Strassburg*, Trübner, 1892.

SWEET (H.). A Primer of Phonetics. *Oxford*, Clarendon Press (*New York*, Macmillan), 1890. [First pubd. *sub tit.* Handbook of Phonetics, 1877].

SWEET (H.). A History of English Sounds, from the earliest period, with full word-lists. *Oxford*, Clarendon Press (*New York*, Macmillan), 1888.

SWEET (H.). An Anglo-Saxon Primer, with Grammar, Notes and Glossary. 6th edition. *Oxford*, Clarendon Press (*New York*, Macmillan), 1890.

SWEET (H.). An Anglo-Saxon Reader, in Prose and Verse, with Grammatical Introduction, Notes and Glossary [1876]. 6th edition. *Oxford*, Clarendon Press (*New York*, Macmillan), 1892.

SWEET (H.). A New English Grammar, logical and historical. I. Introduction, Phonology and Accidence. *Oxford*, Clarendon Press (*New York*, Macmillan), 1892.

VIETOR (W.). Elemente der Phonetik des Deutschen, Englischen und Französischen [1884]. 3te auflage. *Leipzig*, Reisland, 1894.

WILMANNS (W.). Deutsche Grammatik (Gotisch, Alt-, Mittel- und Neuhochdeutsch). I. Lautlehre. *Strassburg*, Trübner, 1893.

WRIGHT (J.). A Primer of the Gothic Language, with Grammar, Notes and Glossary. *Oxford*, Clarendon Press (*New York*, Macmillan), 1892.[1]

Zeitschrift für vergleichende Sprachforschung, herausgegeben von (Th. Aufrecht), A. KUHN (E. Kuhn und J. Schmidt). I.-XXXIV. *Berlin*, Dümmler (*Gütersloh*, Bertelsmann), 1852-94 (*in progress*).[2]

---

[1] From the same scholar we have a recent and detailed, most interesting, dialectical monograph, namely: a Grammar of the Dialect of Windhill, in the West Riding of Yorkshire (London, 1892).

[2] Readers who are desirous of an easy and agreeable introduction to the dialects of Southern Germany,—as those of Central Germany differ but slightly from standard German,—are referred to Hebel's *Alemannische Gedichte* and to Arnold's *Pfingstmontag*.

A SHORT COMPARATIVE GRAMMAR OF ENGLISH AND GERMAN.

INTRODUCTION.

(1) WHEN parents or masters are teaching a child a spoken or a literary language, they usually frame it on some dogmatic, arbitrary, and often contradictory rules, the reasons for which he is unable to make out for himself, the more so as his elders would be quite at a loss to make them out for him. Why, for instance, is the plural of *ox*, *oxen*, and not *boxen the plural of *box*? Why, again, the plural of *ship*, *ships*, but not *sheeps the plural of *sheep*? Why should it be a vulgar blunder to say *he *knowed*, though it is quite correct to say *he bowed*? Because we *ought to* speak so and so. No further answer is ever given. Learnt in that way, a language must appear a mere chaos. The pupil may master it perfectly well: that is merely a matter of practice and memory; but his knowledge of it lacks any basis of reason, no trace of scientific spirit is ever allowed to pervade it, and thus it is he obtains a grossly misleading view of the whole of a large domain of human thought. While the other works of man are stamped with the seal of his genius, language, the first and noblest of all, and the chief characteristic which differentiates him from other living beings, seems some strange and monstrous building, swarming with traps and blind-alleys, planned at random and founded on caprice.

The fact is that a language, taken by itself, is as unable to account for its own existence as would be any other human fact. Let us glance at the map of Europe, and inquire why the countries in it, and even the provinces in these countries, are cut up into such irregular patterns. Why should they not have been so many squares carefully drawn across the ground?

Well, their history answers the question. In the same way we may trace back the history of a language, and the higher we trace it back, the better we become aware of the causes of such discords as offended us at the outset, seeing them gradually, as it were, blended into some superior harmony. This is the task of **Historical Grammar,** which does for languages what History does for nations.

Yet however far it may be carried back, the investigation must come to an end before most of the problems have received a solution. If he lacks witnesses, the historian becomes silent; so, where written documents are wanting, language escapes the attempts of the grammarian. Now a language, before it is ever written down, has already lived for centuries as vulgar speech, unknown to learned people, or despised by them. Even the most cultivated tongues are descended from popular dialects. How easily, too, might the meagre documents of a language when first written be either disfigured or lost! The earliest French text, short as it is and corrupted by generations of scribes, goes back to the ninth century. The spoken French which superseded Latin in Gaul was certainly very much older.

What are we then to do, if the authorities fail? A political historian is at a loss; not so he who deals with the history of languages. When he lacks the language he is studying, he may refer to that from which it has arisen. So, as French down to the ninth century stands beyond his reach, but is well known to be descended from Latin, he will require Latin itself to account for French. This must often answer his purpose, since with the aid of Latin he can go back to the third century B.C., whence the field of his researches is more than doubled. Even supposing that Latin also were lacking, that is to say, the whole Latin literature, epigraphy and civilization had perished without leaving any relics but its mere name, he would nevertheless find a way to it. The Latin parent had other children besides French: Italian, Spanish, Portuguese, Roumanian, descend from the same stem. Let the linguist therefore put together and compare with one another all these languages, each of which is sure to have preserved more or less pure some feature of the original type; let him unify what they have in common, eliminate or conciliate their discords, and then he may be able to restore the deficient Latin, not of course in its minutest details, much less in the delicacies of its style, but sufficiently in the general outlines of its grammatical structure to bring back into unity its diverging offspring and thus mend up the tie accidentally loosened. This at any rate he would be compelled to do, if he wished to go back beyond Latin, since the unknown Prelatin whence it has come can never be avouched by any written document. It is irretrievably lost, and yet, through the comparison of Sanskrit and Greek, the grammarian has succeeded in restoring it.

Hence, as sooner or later evidence is wanting, and literary or monumental tradition vanishes in the mists of the past, **grammar** cannot be truly and consistently **historical** without being at the same time **comparative**.[1]

(2) Such is in particular the case with English and German. They are well known to be near relations; and yet they are not descended from one another, nor both from any language historically known. English is not derived from German, as might be inferred from the large number of erroneous statements still current, which teachers and learners cannot too carefully avoid.[2] The two languages sprang, before the fifth century A.D., from a common stem, and thereafter flourished apart, diverging more and more down to the present time. Let us now inquire what this common stem was. Certainly not

[1] One point should be carefully insisted upon, namely, that the comparison of two linguistic types, as of two natural species, does not pretend to restore an *intermediate* type, exhibiting the characteristics of both, but a type *prior* to both, wherein the divergent characteristics find a common origin. Such a mistake would not be made by any one conversant with scientific methods. Thus Darwin teaches us (*Origin of Species*, London, 1872, p. 265): "I have found it difficult, when looking at any two species, to avoid picturing to myself forms *directly intermediate between them*. But this is a wholly false view; we should always look for forms *intermediate between each species and a common but unknown progenitor*; and the progenitor will generally have differed in some respects from all its modified descendants. To give a simple illustration: the fantail and pouter pigeons are both descended from the rock-pigeon; if we possessed all the intermediate varieties which have ever existed, we should have an extremely close series *between both and the rock-pigeon*; but we should have no varieties *directly intermediate between the fantail and pouter*; none, for instance, combining a tail somewhat expanded with a crop somewhat enlarged, the characteristic features of these two breeds."

[2] Cf. Skeat, *Principles*, i. p. 73.

Gothic,[1] as perhaps is still wrongly believed by some students. Gothic is not the ancestor, but at most an elder brother. The documents inherited from it are four centuries earlier than the most ancient texts written in Old English or Old German, so that it reflects a more archaic if not altogether purer form of the primitive Germanic type; for it will be seen that in many respects English and German stand nearer to the original standard.[2]

Now, to proceed to an exact account of their relationship, **Continental German** (*Deutsch*) admits of two main divisions: **High German** or High Teutonic (*Hochdeutsch*), and **Low German** (Netherlandish,[3] Flemish, *Plattdeutsch* along the Baltic shore). What we properly call German, whether literary or conversational, is genuine High German, with here and there scanty borrowings from Low German. On the other hand, a long time before the division of Continental German had taken place, a dialect called Anglic or Saxonic or, in one word, **Anglo-Saxonic**, had emigrated from its native land, and, for ever insulated by the sea, though subject to many foreign influences which did not affect Continental German, has now become **Modern English**[4] (*Englisch*). The common language, historically unknown, but capable of restoration through linguistic comparison, from which both English and German are descended, is now known by the conventional term of **West Germanic**.

[1] In the French edition of this work the word is spelt without an *h*; but we cannot venture to introduce this spelling into English, as there the *th* is not only written, but even pronounced. For the sake of correctness, however, it would seem advisable to drop this *h* altogether—allowing Gothic writing and architecture to preserve it if they choose—as it lacks any support in Germanic orthography.

[2] Thus the so-called West Germanic branch has preserved, and English and German still sometimes preserve, the primitive Indo-European *ĕ*, which Gothic almost everywhere changed to *ĭ*.

[3] To these alone we now apply the name (*Dutch*) that properly belongs to all Teutons. Curiously enough the sense has become restricted. The French language, on the contrary, has extended to the whole Teutonic race the name of a southern tribe (L. *Alamanni*) which was first known to the Franks after their conquest of Gaul.

[4] English has modified its vowels, while its consonants are still even purer than they are in Low German; High German, on the contrary, has shifted all its explosives: thus, High German and Low German stand nearer to each other in their vocalism, whilst in their consonantal system English and Low German are more closely related.

INTRODUCTION.

West Germanic, again, had two sisters, through which we are able to trace back one degree more. **Gothic** (*Gotisch*) is indeed nearly akin to English and German, though far less so than these are to one another. The same is the case with **Old Norse** (*Altnordisch*), which still survives in the so-called Scandinavian languages: Icelandic, Norwegian, Danish, and Swedish.[1] Now, Gothic and Old Norse show more traces of relationship with one another than with West Germanic, though a serious amount of specific differences hold them apart, forming two groups called respectively **East Germanic** (*Ostgermanisch*) and **North Germanic** (*Nordgermanisch*). A step farther we come back to the great parent, lost of course though also restorable. Its existence is necessarily presupposed by the fact of Germanic having spread out in three branches, Eastern, Northern, and Western. This is the primitive or common **Germanic language**, in short the **Pregermanic** (*Urgermanisch*), a language never written, but spoken, at the time when Hellenic civilization began to flourish, among the barbarous tribes that were wandering about through the woods and moors of Central Europe.

The historical and prehistorical series thus described will, if now traced downwards, assume the form of a pedigree, as given below, in which the asterisk denotes the dead languages from which no written document survives.

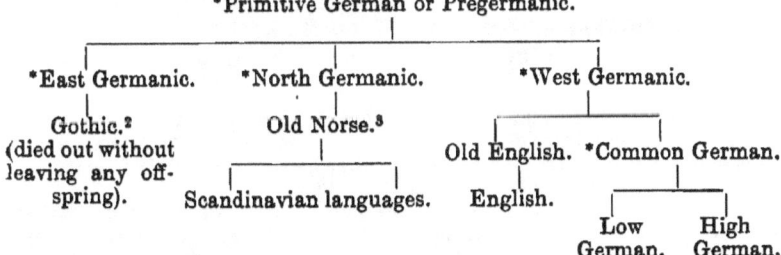

[1] Modern Icelandic has preserved the original features of Old Norse better than any other modern language.

[2] Gothic is the language of the civilized and Christianized Goths (L. *Goti*) of Moesia, a Roman province between the Danube and Balkans. It is preserved in the text of the Four Gospels, St. Paul's Epistles, and a few fragments of other books of the Bible, the remains of a complete translation of the Old and New Testament, composed for the use of his diocese by Bishop Ulfilas (Vulfila, that is, "little wolf") in the fourth century.

[3] The earliest remains of Old Norse are quite as old as those of Gothic,

(3) Thus, as surely as the Romance languages carry us back to Latin, the Germanic languages point to a primitive German, save that Latin was both spoken and written, whereas Pregermanic never was more than spoken. But are Latin and Pregermanic two isolated tongues, without a tie between them? Have we now come to the limit of our knowledge, and to the end of prehistorical induction? No, the way remains still open A science already mature though scarcely a hundred years old, has led us by infallible methods to the power of uniting into one family a considerable number of languages, still represented at the present day by numerous offspring which cover more than half the habitable world. In Asia, **Sanskrit**, Zend, Persian, and their modern posterity; in Europe, **Greek**, **Latin**, and the Romance languages transplanted in our days into America; **Celtic** with its now dying offshoots; **Germanic**, spread in every direction mainly through the expansion of English; **Lithuanian**, spoken eastwards to the Baltic Sea; and **Slavonic**,[1] occupying the whole of the East and part of the Centre of Europe (Old Slavonic, Bulgarian, Croatian-Serbian, Ruthenian, Russian, Polish, and Czech). Some of the hymns of the Rig-Veda, the earliest documents of Indian literature, may be as old as the tenth century B.C., and the primitive stock of the Homeric poems carries us back almost to the same date. Hence Sanskrit and Greek are justly deemed the best witnesses of an original speech,[2] optionally termed Aryan, Prearyan, Indo-Germanic (*Indogermanische Ursprache*), or still better the **common Indo-European language**.[3]

perhaps even earlier (third to fourth century); but they merely consist of short Scandinavian inscriptions written in so-called Runic characters. Only as late as the twelfth century appear the first literary texts of Old Icelandic, and a little later the rich literature of the Eddas.

[1] The last two are akin to one another, and can be referred to an earlier Letto-Slavonic or Balto-Slavonic. We can also restore Celto-Latin. Less certain, though still possible, would be the so-called Greco-Italic and Germano-Letto-Slavonic groups.

[2] Sanskrit has better preserved its consonants; Greek has kept the vowels purer. As far as vowels only are concerned, Greek is the standard Indo-European speech, except that it has often changed their genuine accent; in this respect Sanskrit is far superior.

[3] To this term I adhere, cumbrous as it is, for the sake of greater accuracy. Terminology, of course, is of secondary importance. Whatever its name, it

INTRODUCTION. 7

But all these tongues, even the latest, must be brought into the discussion, as the scattered pieces of a broken mirror should be framed together to reflect the likeness of yore, and thus every one, or at least some one, among the Indo-European languages must be consulted whenever we are attempting to trace back the history of any given word or form of English and German.

A further pedigree will show the above stated division of the Indo-European family into six main groups:

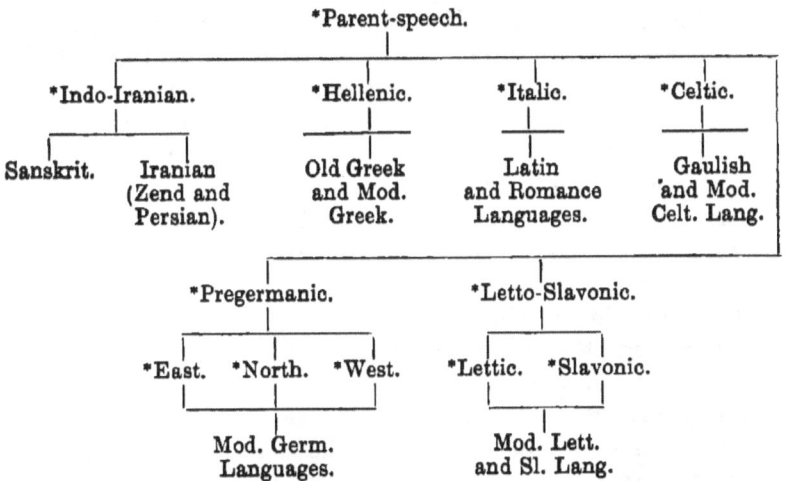

Having thus stated the place occupied by Modern English and German in the great family to which they belong, we must return to these, the special objects of our study.

(4) English is the official language of the British Empire; the current tongue of both islands—excluding the few rural

must be understood from our previous statements that Indo-European is a prehistoric language, *restored but in no way fictitious*. It is also clear that this language is the limit of our present knowledge: beyond it lies an unlimited past, but this past we are unable to reach. We can go back beyond English and German by means of Gothic and Old Norse; even beyond Pregermanic, by means of Greek and Sanskrit; but we cannot pass beyond Indo-European since there is no other left besides it. The case would be different if we could find out any relationship between it and another family of languages, *e.g.* the Semitic group (Assyrian, Hebrew, Syro-Arabian). This, however, can scarcely be expected.

districts in which Celtic dialects still survive (Welsh, Scotch, and Irish Gaëlic)—of the United States of North America, of nearly the whole Dominion of Canada, Australia, and several other colonial centres scattered through the world; lastly, the common speech of trade and intercourse in all the great havens and marketplaces of Eastern Asia, inasmuch as they are thriving either under the actual protection or at least the prevailing influence of the United Kingdom. To this marvellous growth of a language that has now become universal, let us oppose its humble and obscure beginnings.

In the course of the fifth century some tribes, originating from the north of Germany (the isthmus of Sleswig and the estuary of the Elbe), severed themselves from the nations then called Angles, Saxons, and Jutes, whose idioms were nearly related though not identical, and repaired by successive emigrations to the great island of Britain, then occupied by a Celtic population. Here they founded seven kingdoms generally known by the name of the Heptarchy. The settlements of the Jutes lay in the south-eastern corner of the land (Kent) and in the Isle of Wight; those of the Saxons, on the river Thames and the Channel (Essex, Middlesex, Sussex, and Wessex); the Angles conquered the eastern protuberance (East Anglia), viz. Suffolk and Norfolk, the great central square (Mercia)—the corners of which in the main coincide with the mouths of the Severn, the Mersey, and the Humber, and the present seat of the Metropolis,—lastly, Northumberland up to the boundary of Scotland. It is chiefly from the dialect of the Angles, or more accurately speaking from **Mercian that our Modern English is derived**: hence it is quite appropriately named. But it must be well understood that a great many Saxonic elements have intruded into it, the more so because the Metropolis lies on the boundary of the two domains. Unfortunately enough, moreover, no important document has come down to us from Old Mercian; for it entered rather late into its literary period and was fairly overrun by the neighbouring Saxonic,[1] the Wessex dialect. In this, the very numerous

---

[1] Northumbrian had preceded even Saxonic; but the brilliant Northum-

literary texts[1] go back to the ninth century, and the little Latin-Saxon glossaries to the eighth at least. It is therefore this language, usually termed Anglo-Saxon or Old English, that represents to us the most ancient form of our present tongue that we can reach. Yet we must never forget that, when tracing back the latter to the former, we are contrasting it not with a real ancestor, but, as it were, with a twin brother of this ancestor.[2]

The historical and still surviving dialects of English are three in number: the Northern (Northumbrian and Lowland Scotch), and the Central (Midland) dialect (this again divided into Eastern and Western), are descended from Anglic; the Southern is Saxonic. The Jutic tongue has left but insignificant traces.[3]

Chronologically the language may be divided into three periods: **Old English,** conventionally limited to the end of the twelfth century; **Middle English,** till about the beginning of the sixteenth century, chiefly represented by Chaucer (1328-1400), and **Modern English,** from the year 1500 down to the present day.

(5) Since Old English is a fortuitous though unequal mixture of Anglic, Saxonic, and Jutic, English, of course, cannot be expected to be a language altogether pure. Many other causes, however, occurred in the course of these fourteen centuries to alter its character. Firstly, a few words were borrowed from the Celtic idioms still living beside and beneath it. In the ninth century, the struggle against the Danes brought into the island a considerable number of **Scandinavian elements,**

brian civilization perished under the Danish invaders, who did not reach the southern part of Britain.

[1] Works of Alfred the Great (died 901), viz. translation of Gregory the Great's *Cura pastoralis*, of Orosius' Chronicles, etc.; Saxon Chronicles; a Northumbrian version of the New Testament, called *The Lindisfarne Gospels*, etc. The poetical works (*Beowulf* = "the bees' wolf,") is the most often quoted) appear only in the following centuries.

[2] Thus the vocalic phenomena called "Anglo-Saxonic breakings" (*infra* 21) do not occur in Mercian, wherefore pure English is free from them.

[3] Neither Irish nor American-English are true dialects, but mere varieties of classical and official English, as introduced by relatively recent conquest or immigration.

strengthened afterwards by the political supremacy of the invaders under the reign of Knut the Great (1006). Much greater still were the results of the battle of Hastings (1066), when the Norman yoke was laid upon England. French became the official language, the more so because noblemen could and would speak no other, and even at the time of the Great War against France, the English court was nearly as French as the French court itself. When the national tongue prevailed, there yet remained a considerable stock of **French words** pronounced with an English accent.[1] Lastly, from that time, and uninterruptedly up to the present, but especially under the influence of the literary revival in the sixteenth century, English as well as French adopted a great many **learned terms**, borrowed either from French itself, or from Latin, or more lately from Greek. These new words became every day more necessary, thanks to the daily increase of new ideas, so that the present English vocabulary is, to the extent of more than a half, of Romance origin.[2]

In spite of this mixture, **English** remains a truly, purely, and **exclusively Germanic** tongue. For the vocabulary of any language whatever, and, up to a certain point, even its syntax, are mere accidents, complacently yielding to every process of admixture. Grammar alone is able to resist external influence. Now English grammar, excluding a few derivative types borrowed from Romance,[3] does not show one feature that is not Germanic, inasmuch as all the foreign words we now use as native ones have been forced into all the laws of Ger-

---

[1] Hence, in English, so many doublets, *hue* and *colour*, *kindred* and *relations*, *husband* and *spouse*, etc., sometimes with a slightly varying sense, as *sheep* and *mutton*, *shape* and *form*, *fulness* and *plenty* (= O.F. *plenté* = L. *plenitátem*). The whole question must be left here, and the reader referred to Skeat's *Principles* (II., pp. 3-248), and Behrens, *Französ. Elem. im Engl.*, in Paul's *Grundriss*, I., p. 799 sq.

[2] Scientific language, in particular, admits many Romance and Latin elements; but literature, and even poetry, by no means exclude them, much less so the common speech. In a recent letter from London I counted 13 Germanic and 12 Latin words, that is, among the nouns, adjectives, and verbs, since, of course, the prepositions, conjunctions, and pronouns are all Germanic. Counted without this distinction, the words of the Lord's Prayer are but four French to forty-four Germanic words.

[3] As, for instance, the feminine suffix *-ess*, *infra* 69 and 87.

manic accidence.¹ Whilst the latter has been kept unchanged in its general outlines, the former elements are but moving and fortuitous atoms, which should never be taken into account in a scientific comparison of English and German.²

(6) German is geographically far less extensive than English. It comprises hardly more than the greater part of the German Empire, apart from the French, Danish, and Polish districts,³ three-fourths of Switzerland, the German provinces of Austria, and in part the Baltic provinces of Russia. In the New World, however, especially in the United States and Brazil, prosperous centres of immigration have given rise to conspicuous groups of German-speaking population.

In regard to dialects, Northern Germany being occupied by those of Low German, High German proper, with which alone we are dealing, is divided into two groups: Central or **Frankish-Saxonic**, and Southern or **Alamanno-Bavarian**. The Central group, again, comprises Saxonic, Thuringian, High and Middle Frankish.⁴ The Southern dialects are Alamanno-Swabian (Württemberg, Baden, Alsace, Switzerland), and Bavarian, including Austrian German. Among all these **Saxonic** is well known to have exerted a prevalent influence upon **literary German,** since the time of Luther and the diffusion of his Bible. But the earliest documents bequeathed to us from mediæval High German belong for the most part to the Alamannic group.⁵

---

¹ Thus we say *the barber's shop* like *the father's house, he save-d* like *he live-d*, declining and conjugating the borrowed term as though it were a thoroughly English one.

² One instance will suffice. Considering the identity of the two words for *butter* (G. *butter*), who would doubt them to be related through the parent speech? Yet it would be an egregious error; for, if they were, they would be less alike: E. *butter* requires a G. **butzer* or **busser* (cf. E. *water* = G. *wasser*); to G. *butter* would correspond E. **bodder* (cf. E. *fodder* = G. *futter*). So, as a matter of fact, the two words have been formed and separately borrowed, in each language, from the L. *butyrum*.

³ German, indeed, is the official tongue of all these countries, as it is likewise of the Northern provinces of Germany, in which the current speech is Plattdeutsch.

⁴ *Niederfränkisch* belongs to Low German.

⁵ Of *Schwäbisch* we have but scanty remains, but a fair number of *Alamannisch*, namely, several collections of glossaries (eighth century), the Dominicans' Rule, the Hymns (ninth century), and the works of Notker, a

In its historical evolution, German, like English, is successively assigned to three periods. **Old High German** (*Althochdeutsch*) begins with the most ancient texts, dating from the eighth century, and ends with the end of the eleventh. These consist, firstly, of glossaries of Latin words with brief comments, and little charters, such as the famous oath taken at Strassburg by the sons of Louis le Débonnaire (842);[1] later, of short fragments, such as the mutilated epic called *Hildebrandslied*,[2] and, lastly, of long formal works, viz. Tatian's Evangelical Harmony, Otfrid von Weissenburg's Evangelical Poem (High Frankish), considerable extracts from the Bible, and the Alamannic documents mentioned above. According as final syllables are weakened,[3] and the process of metaphony [4] gradually gains ground, **Middle High German** (*Mittelhochdeutsch*) appears with features more and more distinct, and then lasts, like our Middle English, down to the year 1500. In this language were written the famous poem of the Nibelungen (twelfth century), and the songs of such Minnesinger or troubadours as assembled at the poetical and perhaps legendary meeting of Wartburg in Thuringia (1206?) The Saxonic translation of the Bible opens the era of **Modern German**, which, however, in forms or constructions, differs very slightly from its immediate predecessor. Of course, the words have become a little shorter; some final syllables, already half-mute, have been entirely dropped; and the grammar is simplified, while, on the other hand, the syntax displays new means for the expression of new ideas; but, on the whole, the language is still one and the same, so that, at least, in this primer, it will seldom be neces-

---

monk of St. Gall, who died in the year 1022. This dialect, through an erroneous extension of Grimm's second law (*infra* 47), was once taken for High German proper (*Strengalthochdeutsch*), and termed by this name. This view has now been abandoned.

[1] But the manuscript of the historian Nithard, who has preserved it for us, is not earlier than the eleventh century, or the tenth at most. The dialect is the Frankish spoken along the Rhine (*Rheinfränkisch*).

[2] A curious but corrupt text, because High and Low German have been interwoven in its transliteration. The poem of the Saviour (*Heliand*), a short time later, is written in old Saxonic, that is, in pure Low German.

[3] O.H.G. *dĕmu* = M.H.G. *dĕme dĕm* = G. *dem* is a good illustration of this gradual change. But see below, the examples in 19.

[4] For German metaphony (*Umlaut*) the reader is referred to 22 *infra*.

sary to quote the Middle German form as an intermediate link in the clear and obvious genealogy traced from High to Modern German.

German, as may be understood from what we have stated, is also a mixed tongue, but not nearly so much so as English; for it has grown on its own soil, and thus it neither borrows words from a conquered race, nor receives any from the foreign influence of a conqueror. Its vocabulary, it is true, contains some Low German terms, always easily distinguishable; Roman civilization has poured a great many into it; the Southern dialects infused into the softness of the Central pronunciation a shade of their own rudeness and energy, and contributed on a large scale to enrich the general tongue;[1] but the main stock remains, nevertheless, Central German, or rather Saxonic, such as is spoken, more or less purely, by all educated people, from Göttingen to Königsberg, from Berlin to Bern or to Vienna. Further, in regard to literary or scientific words, drawn from Greek and Latin, it could not help following the fashion of all civilized nations; and yet it has adopted fewer of them than English and French, preferring—whether rightly or wrongly—such as its native genius could afford.[2] More recently, as the French literature and fashions of the seventeenth and eighteenth centuries gained in Germany an almost overwhelming vogue, the language of the higher classes was turned into a macaronic cant of French words supplied with Germanic endings, of which many have survived to the present time.[3] But these have been lately

---

[1] Thus, the diminutives in *-chen* (L.G. *-ken* = E. *-kin*), belong to Central German; those in *-lein* (O.H.G. *-lin*, Swiss *-li*), are taken from the Southern dialects. Literary German now admits of both. Cf. *infra* 103 (IV).

[2] A German would say, for instance, *eindruck, ausdruck, gleichung, wasserstoff*, and even *fernsprecher*, whereas we use the words *impression, expression, equation, hydrogen*, and *telephone*. Scientific terms thus manufactured are clear enough to a German child, but perplex foreigners, and do nothing to advance that desideratum of the future, an international scientific language!

[3] Hence have come such words as *genie, mode, marsch, marschieren, parlieren, räsonnieren* (the latter two somewhat contemptuous), altered sometimes by fanciful and popular etymology. Thus, *abenteuer* (M.H.G. *āventiure*, "a tale," an old borrowing from F. *aventure*), sounds to the illiterate ear like *abend-theuer*, "dear to eventide" (because evening companies are fond of story-telling), and F. *trottoir* (footway), has become Berlin. *tretoir* or *trittoir*, as though from the verb *treten* (to tread), *er tritt* (he treads), etc.

proscribed, and are disappearing, under a perfectly justifiable sense of national independence, which, however, is not altogether free from a certain ridiculous exaggeration.

(7) Our comparative examination of English and German must comprise four parts; the first devoted to **Phonetics** or the **Science of Sounds**; the other three, to **Morphology** or the **Comparison of Forms**. In other words, after we have compared the vowels and consonants of the two languages, we have to contrast in both the **Formation of words**, then the accidence of declinable words (nouns and pronouns) or **Declension**, and lastly, the accidence of conjugable words (verbs) or **Conjugation**. Syntax, as already hinted above, is only an accessory part of Grammar properly so-called.

FIRST PART.

SOUNDS.

(8) **The sounds of every human language are in a state of perpetual change.** The son's speech is never quite the same as the father's; but the difference is so slight that they can scarcely be aware of it, else the father would try to correct the son. It grows greater between grandfather and grandson; but these still understand each other pretty well, and are conscious of uttering the same sounds. This, however, is not at all the case between more widely-separated generations, as sooner or later the gap must appear, and, after five or ten generations, the ancestor and his offspring would no longer understand one another. But, let the changes be ever so slow or so fast, it is clear, to any one who has ever considered a language at two distinct stages of its evolution, that they all obey or follow some natural and consequently constant laws. This is as much as to say that, if a given sound or group of sounds, in a given position, has undergone such or such mutation, it must needs have undergone the same change in every word (of the same language) wherein it happened to occupy the same position.

Common sense itself forces this conclusion upon us. Thus, supposing an English group, *e.g.* initial *fl*, and an individual physically incapable of pronouncing it correctly, and compelled to replace it by something like *fy*,[1] he will, of course, not be able to pronounce it in any one word more than in any other, and, if he says *a fyower*, he ought to also say *the fyoor*. Briefly, this man's tongue will never admit of an initial *fl*, at least before

---

[1] Compare Italian *fiore* and F. *fleur* = L. *flōrem*.

a vowel *o*. In his children's speech this peculiarity might be neutralized by some external influence; otherwise, an English dialect will arise from him, in which every initial *fl* is replaced by *fy*. This necessary consequence we express by saying that, in a language absolutely pure, **the laws of sounds are constant**. In other words, a given sound, in one and the same position, cannot give rise to two different sounds.

But, as we have been taught by the history of English and German, no language in the world can claim absolute purity, and none is free from some foreign admixture. Side by side with the individual who pronounces *fyower* and *fyoor*, lives another who says correctly *flower* and *floor*. If the latter's pronunciation also spreads, there will appear side by side two parallel dialects, in one of which initial *fl* is changed to *fy*, whereas it is kept in the other. Supposing them to be for ever severed, they would in time become distinct dialects; but as soon as conquest, trade, or mere proximity brings them into contact, it may easily happen either that the *fyower*-dialect will borrow the word *floor* from the other, or that the *floor*-dialect will borrow the word *fyower* from the former; and thus there may strangely appear, in one and the same dialect, the two contradictory forms *fyower* and *floor*. In either case, the phonetic law, "*fl* becomes *fy*," or "*fl* is kept unchanged," will seem to be at fault. Now, nothing is more common, in any language whatever, than a similar process of borrowing. Each one of us is subject to it daily, inasmuch as we talk with others, and our language must needs become a kind of compromise with the others that surround us. Hence we see that the constancy of phonetic laws, though theoretically necessary, can never be directly observed in any dead or living language, since a collective language is but a fortuitous aggregate of a great many individual speeches.

The **principle of constancy**, therefore, must be deemed, above all, a **methodic** one. It tells us to beware of hasty guessings, specious and arbitrary identifications or fanciful analogies. Soundly interpreted it amounts to this; we must collect and classify all' the phenomena which agree together,— these, at any rate, will be seen to far outnumber the exceptions,

—and, when this is done, we must try our best to explain the apparent irregularities.

But we cannot understand how the sounds are transformed, unless we have some knowledge of the means through which they are formed. This is the province of physiological phonetics, a difficult and delicate science, though its elementary and unquestioned principles may be summarized in a very short chapter.

CHAPTER I.

THE ELEMENTS OF PHYSIOLOGICAL PHONETICS.[1]

(9) Like every wind-instrument, the vocal apparatus may be said to consist of a pair of **bellows**, emitting a current of air; a **sonorous tube,** in which the current of air, more or less impeded, causes vibration, and of a **sounding-board,** by contact with which the volume of the sound is increased.

The bellows are the lungs. As they can only supply air during the process of expiration, the moments of inspiration are intervals of rest, such as are denoted by punctuation. There are, at any rate in the European languages, scarcely any inspiratory sounds, with the exception of a few instinctive exclamations.[2]

The air expired, escaping through the windpipe, reaches the **larynx,** which forms a gristly protuberance that can be easily seen at the upper end of the windpipe. The larynx, in its turn, opens into the pharynx by a round aperture called the **glottis.** The upper margins of the glottis, called **vocal chords,** are hard and elastic, and, by contracting, are able to oppose an obstacle to the current of air, and consequently vibrate while it is passing through.

The sounding-board consists of the **double cavity of the mouth and nostrils.** The shape and size of this cavity may vary, in such a way as to modify the sound emitted through the glottis, under the influence of three chief factors.

1. The **elasticity** of the inner and outer walls of the

---

[1] The following pages are taken from my *Grammar of Greek and Latin*, with, however, such slight alterations as were advisable in a Grammar of English and German.

[2] The most obvious example would be the sound of a kiss uttered as an admiratory exclamation.

mouth, which can be made longer by being narrowed and shorter by being widened.

2. The action of the **soft palate** (*velum palati*). In front, that is, for two-thirds of their extent, the nose and mouth are completely separated by the bony arch of the palate; but from the pharynx to the nasal cavities there is a communicating passage, which can however be closed by means of a fleshy and movable prolongation of the palate, called very appropriately the "veil of the palate." When, the mouth being at rest, the veil falls like a loose curtain, the two cavities are in free communication with one another; but when the veil rises and rests on the back part of the pharynx, it isolates the nasal cavities and so renders the whole of the upper half of the sounding-board ineffective. The soft palate has a small continuation, of the shape of a grape, called the **uvula**, which can be perceived in a mirror by opening the mouth wide. The share it has in modifying sounds will be seen below.

3. The extreme **mobility of the tongue**, which by resting successively against the soft palate, the back, middle, or front part of the palatal arch, the gums, the teeth, etc., is capable of producing an infinite variety of modifications in the shape of the mouth and its mode of opening.

Whilst the sounding-board reflects, increases and varies the musical sounds emitted through the glottis, the movements of the tongue and lips, at the same time, produce noises, which may be either momentary and explosive, when the mouth opens or shuts suddenly, or continuous and fricative, when the mouth being almost closed allows the air to escape at any point through a very narrow passage. **The musical sounds are the vowels; the noises**, whether accompanied or not by glottal sound, **are the consonants.**

SECTION I.

THE PRODUCTION OF SOUNDS.

(10) 1. Before coming into action, the vocal apparatus may be said to rest in an **indifferent position**, the mouth being

very slightly open, the soft palate lowered, the tongue resting flat on the bottom of the mouth, and the glottis permitting the air to pass freely through it: in short, the position assumed during deep thought or tranquil sleep. Neither sound nor noise is then produced, although during expiration there passes a gentle current of air, which contains in itself the potential utterance of a vowel.[1] This is the **inaudible sound** which in certain modes of writing is represented by a particular symbol, *e.g.* the Greek soft breathing or the French and Spanish *h*. If the air is expired with more energy and a certain amount of effort, we have the English or German *h*, what is quite improperly called the aspirated *h*.

2. The organs being in the first position, the soft palate is raised and cuts off all communication with the nasal cavities; at the same time the vocal chords contract and vibrate. In this way a pure or **oral vowel** is produced, *a, i, u,* etc.

3. If the vibration takes place without the soft palate being raised, the vowel is sounded in both cavities at the same time,[2] and so we obtain a **nasalized vowel**, written in French *an, in, un,* etc.

4. If the mouth, when in the third position, is closed by means of the lips or the tongue at any point, then the air expired being only able to escape by the nostrils, no oral sound can be produced. The result is a **nasal sound**, *m, n,* etc.

5.[3] The open mouth lets the current of air pass through; but its passage is impeded by an elastic obstacle, which is displaced, and afterwards returns to its original position with a rapid alternate quivering or trilling sound, viz. the **trilling *r*** (*infra* 13, 1 A).

---

[1] That is, supposing the position to remain unchanged, a vowel is heard as soon as the vocal chords vibrate.

[2] This can easily be proved by experiment. A looking-glass placed in front of the mouth and nostrils, and protected by a screen from the breath of the mouth, remains clear after the pronunciation of *o*, but not after the pronunciation of the nasalized vowel *on*.

[3] In this and all the following positions, the soft palate is raised, and consequently the nasal cavity plays no part in the production of sound, except in the case of persons who, from some fault in the structure of the organs, or from idleness in using them, are unable to raise the soft palate, whence they "speak through the nose."

6. The mouth is open, but the tongue completely obstructs the middle part of it, leaving only the two sides free; the current of air, being thus impeded, is obliged to split itself up into two portions in order to find an outlet, and vibrates with forcing a passage for itself in the narrow space between the cheeks and teeth. This is the **lateral trill** *l*.

According as the nasal and trilled or **liquid** sounds are accompanied or not by a slight vibration of the vocal chords, they are said, like all other consonants (*infra* 7), to be sonorous (voiced) or surd (voiceless). The former case is by far more frequent; but a nasal or a liquid may become voiceless, when it is either preceded or followed by a voiceless consonant, to the character of which it becomes adapted.

It is now time to ask whether the various sounds corresponding to positions 4, 5, and 6, are consonants or vowels. Of course, a nasal or liquid is a consonant, when preceded or followed by a vowel that combines with it to form a syllable,[1] as in E. *note, undo, mare, rare, lame, elbow*, etc., and in G. *nein, mein, baum, rad, fern, lahm, salz*, etc. But let us now consider such very common English and German final syllables as E. *even, buxom, sister, middle*, etc., and G. *rasen, gutem, mutter, mittel*, etc.; and, **putting the spelling quite out of account**, for in phonetics spelling is but a conventional and deceptive element, let us allow only our mouth and our ears to bear testimony of what the end of these words contains. It is not a vowel followed by a consonant; for we do not pronounce them as *ĭvĕn, bŏksĕm, sistĕr, mĭdĕl,* nor as *răzĕn, gūtĕm, mŭtĕr, mĭtĕl,* but simply as *ĭvṇ, bŏksṃ, sistṛ, mĭdḷ,* and *rāzṇ, gūtṃ, mŭtṛ, mĭtḷ*; that is to say, the nasal or liquid itself fills the whole syllable and supports the preceding consonant. Hence, in this position, it is a true vowel, and we are led to the conclusion, that the **nasals** and **liquids** are **alternately consonants and vowels**: consonants when they are supported by a vowel; vowels generally whenever they support a consonant, and particularly when they occur between two consonants (E. *fatherless,*

---

[1] Apart from the well-known (13, 1 A) and peculiar pronunciation of E. *r*.

G. *vergehen*);[1] for which reason they are termed here **consonant-vowels.**

7. Further, if the mouth, when closed at any point, is opened suddenly in order to let the current of air escape, or if, when already opened in order to pronounce a vowel, it then is closed completely at any point and suddenly arrests the current of air, the result is not a sound, but a noise, a **momentary consonant**, called **explosive** in the former case, and **implosive or occlusive** in the latter.[2] If this noise is not accompanied by voice in the glottis, the consonant is called surd or **voiceless**, *k, t, p*; if however, while the current of air is passing through, there is a slight contraction of the glottis, together with vibration of the vocal chords, then we have a sonorous or **voiced momentary** consonant, *g, d, b.*[3]

8. Lastly, if the mouth, instead of being completely closed and then opened wide, is obstructed at any point, in such a

---

[1] It must be again understood, once for all, that the spelling should always be neglected. Conventional orthography is one thing, and pronunciation quite another.

[2] Thus, in the group *pa*, the *p* is purely explosive, as the closed lips are suddenly opened in order to utter it. In such a group as *appa*, if the two *p*'s are pronounced, the first is implosive (uttered by closing the mouth after it has been opened for the emission of the *a*), and the second is explosive (uttered by opening the mouth again in order to pronounce the following *a*). In the similar group *abba*, the occlusion and explosion, though less energetic, are likewise quite perceptible. Hence we may infer that, in a group *apa* or *aba*, the single *p* or *b* is both implosive and explosive. In *abma*, the *b* is implosive; for the lips do not open until the *m* is sounded. And, lastly, in *amba*, the *b* is explosive; for the lips have been closed, immediately after the *a*, in order to utter the *m*. All these distinctions ought to be taken into account by those who wish to obtain a correct view of the reciprocal influences of contiguous sounds in any vocalic or consonantal group.

[3] The reader may prove by experiment the existence of this unconscious vibration of the glottis. First practise the pronunciation of *p* or *b* by mere explosion, without letting any vowel follow. This result obtained, if you pronounce *p*, and at the same time tightly close the ears, no sound is heard; whereas, if you pronounce *b*, you will be conscious of a deep rumbling sound. This is the "glottal buzz" or vibration of the vocal chords, which penetrates into the ear through the internal auditory meatus. It can often be perceived even more simply by touching with the finger the protuberance of the throat (Adam's apple). Certain ethnic groups however pronounce the voiced consonants almost without voice: this is the case with South German and Alsatian *d* and *b*, which to a French or English ear sound like *t* and *p*; and, as a matter of fact, apart from a certain weakness in the utterance, there is scarcely any difference between a voiceless and a thus unvoiced consonant.

way as to allow the expiratory current to escape only through a narrow opening in the centre, the air passes through this opening with a noise of friction, which constitutes a **continuous, spirant** or **fricative consonant**. According as it is or is not accompanied by glottal vibration, this consonant also is called **voiced**, *e.g. z* or *v*, or **voiceless**, *e.g. s* or *f*.

SECTION II.

CLASSIFICATION OF SOUNDS.

(11) A brief analysis of the action of the vocal apparatus, reduced to eight main positions, has allowed us to divide all human sounds into four distinct classes: mere expiration (case 1); **vowels** (cases 2, 3); **consonant-vowels** (cases 4-6), and simple **consonants** (cases 7, 8). We must now go a little further into particulars.

§ 1. *Vowels, Semi-vowels and Diphthongs.*

(12) 1. Oral **vowels**.—The two opposite poles of vocalism are *i* (E. *ee*), the high-toned vowel, and *u* (E. *oo*), the low-toned vowel. In pronouncing *i*, the larynx rises and the corners of the mouth are widened in such a way as to give to the sonorous tube the least possible length; whereas, in pronouncing *u*, the larynx is lowered[1] and the lips are thrust forward, so that the length becomes as great as possible. Between these two lies the vowel of equilibrium, *a* (E. *father*), the sound which is produced when, the organs being in the indifferent position (*supra* 10, 1), the soft palate is raised and the glottis begins to vibrate.

Between these three chief notes of the vocalic scale there is naturally room for a large number of intermediate sounds. Thus we ascend from *a* to *i* through open *e* (E. *net*, G. *netz*) and close *e* (E. *ere*, G. *ehre*); and again we descend from *a* to *u*

[1] These movements may be verified by placing the finger on the protuberance of the throat whilst uttering alternately *i* and *u* with some energy. Everybody moreover has experienced the extreme difficulty of singing an *ee* syllable on a low tone, or inversely the word *wood* on a high one.

through open *o* (E. *hot*, G. *soll*) and close *o* (E. *home*, G. *lohn*). The *o* sounds and the *e* sounds, in their turn, are connected together through the intermediate sounds of G. *ö*, E. *u* in a close syllable (*but*), and English, German or French so-called *e* mute. Lastly, if the larynx takes the position required for *i*, while the lips are placed in the position required for *u*, we shall hear the mixed sound represented by G. *ü* or F. *u*, which does not appear in the English pronunciation.[1]

2. Nasalized vowels.—From the description given above (10, 3) it will have been understood that to each oral vowel there may correspond a nasalized vowel. Such, however, is rarely the case in practice. French, for instance, has but four nasalized vowels. As they do not occur at all in the correct pronunciation either of English or German, we need not dwell further upon them.

3. **Diphthongs.**—Let us consider such a group as G. *ai*, and inquire of what it consists. Not of two vowels, certainly; for it is not sounded *a-i* in two distinct expirations, but simply *ai* in one syllable. In other words, the *a* in it is a vowel, but the *i* is not a vowel, since we miss in its utterance the expiratory effort described above (10, 1) as the necessary condition for the emission of a true vowel. The same is to be observed of the *u* in the G. group *au*. This attenuated *i* or *u*, which forms only one syllable with the preceding or following vowel, is what we call a semi-vowel. **Semi-vowels,** in a consistent phonetic spelling, are written respectively *y* and *w*, thus *ay, aw,* and *ya, wa.* The real combination of a vowel and a semi-vowel into one syllable constitutes a diphthong.[2] English has a great many **Diphthongs**; German, perhaps even more.

4. **Long and Short** vowels.—Every vowel, whether oral,

---

[1] Here in particular the student must not be deceived by appearances and spelling: each language uses no more than five or six vocalic symbols, more or less diversified by accessory signs; but there is not a language in the world which has not, at the very least, ten vowels; and English, German, and French have many more, both short and long.

[2] *Real*, because it may be only apparent and due to conventional spelling: thus, E. *ai* and G. *ie* are not diphthongs, since they are merely sounded as *ē* and *i*; whereas the single *i* is a true diphthong in our word *fine*, which is pronounced *fayn*.

nasalized, or in a diphthong, may either be uttered very quickly or prolonged through the whole of a single expiration: hence an indefinite number of degrees of quantity, which may be easily observed in language. For the sake of simplicity, grammarians have reduced these varieties to two, short and long, thus ă and ā, and have also agreed to regard the duration of a long vowel as about twice that of a short one.[1]

§ 2. *Consonant-Vowels.*

(13) I. **Liquids.**—A. We have seen the medial liquid *r* to be caused by a vibrating obstacle interposed to the passage of the expiratory current. This obstacle may be either the margins of the glottis, or the uvula, or the tip of the tongue. **Glottal** *r*, however, is very rare in European languages.[2] But **uvular** and **lingual** *r* occur very often in all of them. The latter is the English *r* as it is sounded when correctly trilled at the beginning of a word or between vowels (*raven, caring*); but, when final (*fair, sister*), or before a consonant (*earth, careless*), it is untrilled, and becomes a vague vocalic sound, easier to reproduce than to describe. Uvular *r* is produced by the uvula vibrating against the back of the tongue, as in the Northumbrian burred *r*. German *r* generally appears, with many local and individual exceptions, lingual in the Northern provinces and uvular in the Southern. If, when final, it happens to be untrilled, it may become an uncertain vocalic sound approaching to ă.[3]

B. In order to form the **lateral trill** *l*, the tongue usually

---

[1] French sometimes denotes the long vowel by a circumflex accent. English has no particular sign, but often doubles a medial consonant in order to indicate that the preceding vowel is short. German occasionally uses the doubled vowel (*saat*=E. *seed*), or writes an *e* after an *i* (*viel, vieh*), or introduces an *h* (*zahm, sohn*). But none of these conventional and irregular spellings have any etymological value. (O.H.G. *sāt, filu, fihu, zam, sunu*).

[2] But frequent in the Semitic languages, as in Modern Arabian. In some dialects of German Switzerland the pronunciation of the deeply guttural *ch* produces a rasping of the throat which much resembles glottal *r*.

[3] Thus I have seen quoted the curious word *fyamenna*, heard at a railway station as the train stopped. Though it could be easily mistaken for an Italian word, it is merely the G. *für männer* pronounced in that affected way.

rests against the sockets (*alveoli*) of the upper teeth. This is the dental or, better still, alveolar *l*. Now, the tongue may also rest against some inner part of the mouth. This is mainly the case when the *l* is followed by another consonant, whence it is modified to a deeper sound rather akin to that of a *w* : thus, in the English words *false* = L. *fálsum*, *falcon* = L. *falcónem*, etc., the *l* has caused the preceding vowel to change to an *o* sound. So also in their French equivalents *faux*, *faucon*, whereas in G. *falsch* and *falke* the *a* and the *l* are sounded separately and distinctly heard.

2. **Nasals.** — The complete closure which determines the utterance of a nasal may take place at any point whatever of the cavity of the mouth. If in front, and through the lips joining together, we have the **labial** nasal, *m* ; if through the tip of the tongue resting against the upper teeth or the upper sockets, we get the **dental** or alveolar nasal, *n*; if again, further back, through the root of the tongue resting against either the hard or soft palate, the nasal becomes either **palatal** or **velar**, both of which are often included under the common and inaccurate, but convenient name of **guttural** nasal, *ñ*, which is simply written *n* in English and German (E. *pink*, *ink*, *ringing*, *tongue* ; G. *schlank*, *henker*, *schwingung*, *zunge*, etc.).

§ 3. *Consonants.*

(14) 1. **Explosives.**[1]—The closing of the mouth, necessary for the production of a voiceless or voiced explosive, may also take place at various points. With the lips closed, and then opened, we get the **labial** explosive, *p*, *b*; with the tongue exploding against the teeth or sockets, the **dental** or alveolar, *t*, *d*[2]; against the hard palate, the **palatal**, *k*, *g*, sounded as in *king*, *gift*; against the soft palate, the **velar**, *q*, *g*, sounded as

---

[1] According to the general custom of English grammarians, this term is henceforth applied to all momentary consonants whatever, whether explosive or implosive.

[2] The tongue may also be slightly rounded, in such a way as to touch the dome of the palate : then the consonant becomes cacuminal. Thus, *t* and *d* are rather cacuminal in the standard English pronunciation, whereas they are strictly alveolar in German and French.

in the G. words *kuh*, *gunst*; the latter two classes being likewise included under the less precise appellation of **gutturals** with a more or less deep utterance.[1]

2. **Spirants.**—Imperfect closure of the mouth may naturally vary in position as much as complete closure. If the lips are half closed, we hear the **labial** spirant (either bi-labial, or denti-labial), voiceless *f*, voiced *v*. Between the teeth is uttered the **interdental** spirant, voiceless *þ*, voiced ð (E. *th*, respectively in *thin* and *this*). Against the sockets, the **dental** or alveolar, voiceless *s*, voiced *z*. Against the upper part of the palatal arch, the **cacuminal** spirant, voiceless *š* (E. *sh* = G. *sch*), voiced *ž* (E. *z* in *glazier*). In the back part of the hard palate we have the **palatal** spirant, either voiceless (G. *ch* in *ich*, *blech*), or voiced (G. *g* in *wiegen*, *lüge*); and, against the soft palate, the **velar** spirant, either voiceless (G. *ch* in *doch* = E. *though*, *nacht*, *hoch*), or voiced (G. *g* in *tage*, *gelogen*).[2] We may conveniently unite the two latter under the common term of **gutturals**, and denote them by the same symbol, *h* for the voiceless,[3] and χ for the voiced, whether palatal or velar.

3. **Modifications of the Consonants.**—The two chief possible modifications of the consonants are aspiration and palatalization (French *mouillement*).

A. **Aspiration** affects scarcely any but the explosive consonants. It consists in the explosion being more energetic, and accompanied by the forcible expiration[4] which we have designed by *h*. Hence the consonants thus modified are denoted in phonetic spelling by *ph*, *th*, *kh*, *qh* (voiceless), and *bh*, *dh*, *gh*, *ġh* (voiced). These aspirates can hardly be said to occur in

[1] It has already been observed that the Southern Germans show a general propensity to confuse, in all these classes, the voiced consonants with the voiceless.

[2] This difference of pronunciation in the *ch* and the *g* depends, as is well known, on the nature of the preceding vowel. In standard German, however, the *g* is never sounded as a spirant, save in the final syllable of words ending in -*ig*.

[3] The reader must not confuse the expiratory *h*, which only occurs as initial (O.H.G. *hūs* = G. *haus*), with the medial *h* written for the guttural spirant (O.H.G. *naht* = G. *nacht*).

[4] Thus for these consonants also (see above, 10, 1) the term "aspirate" is very inappropriate; but this terminology being consecrated by usage will be retained.

Modern English. German has no voiced aspirates, but its voiceless explosives almost always, and chiefly when initial, receive some more or less energetic aspiration: thus *pabst* (pope), nearly as *phăpst*. Sometimes it appears even in writing: *thun*=E. (*to*) *do*, *that*=E. *deed*, *thal*=E. *dale*, etc. *Kh*, not a mere *k*, is heard in *kind* (child), and the initial of *kuh*=E. *cow* is a real *qh*.

When the explosion of the consonant gradually coalesces with the expiratory breath which follows it, the two sounds end by uniting into one, that is to say, into the corresponding spirant. Thus the transition is easy from *ph* to *pf* and *f*, from *th*, either to *tþ* and *þ* (E. *th*), or to *ts* (G. *z*) or *s* (G. *sz*, *ss*)[1]; and the initial aspirate guttural of G. *kind* and *kuh* has become a decided spirant in the Alamannic dialects of Switzerland.

B. **Palatalization** consists in a consonant (chiefly *l* and *n*) coalescing into one sound with a following *y*. This phenomenon is well known in the Romance languages; but, apart from its influence in causing metaphony,[2] it may be said to have very little importance in the Germanic family, and none at all in modern English or German.

---

[1] This observation is of the utmost importance in the history of Germanic languages, inasmuch as nearly the whole system of Grimm's laws (*infra* 47 sq.) is based upon it.

[2] Or vowel-mutation, *infra* 22.

CHAPTER II.

VOWELS AND DIPHTHONGS.

(15) A chapter devoted to the study of English and German vowels and diphthongs must naturally also include the semi-vowels so far as they form a diphthong with the preceding vowel. As for the semi-vowels by themselves, it will be more convenient to take them with the consonant-vowels, with which they will be seen [1] to exhibit some remarkable analogies.

If the object of our inquiry has been made sufficiently clear in the Introduction, the reader will understand that our present task is to examine in detail the vocalic systems of English and German, to contrast and compare them, in their historical and prehistorical stages, either with one another or with the vocalism of other Germanic languages, and so to trace them back to that Pregermanic system from which they are descended; and then, this Germanic unity being restored, to carry our inquiry, through it and the other Indo-European groups (Sanskrit, Greek, Latin, Slavonic), up still further to the original vocalism of the Indo-European family. Thus, we begin with the latest phenomena.

SECTION I.

VOCALIC LAWS IN ENGLISH AND GERMAN.

(16) Under this name we comprise all the causes which are known to have altered the vowel systems of the two languages, either recently and within the historical period, or earlier in

---

[1] In the section of Vowel-Gradation, *infra* 43–45.

West Germanic, and even up to the Pregermanic stage in which they are brought to agreement with Gothic and Old Norse.

§ 1. *Recent Vowel Change.*

(17) I. All who have any acquaintance with the two languages must have observed at the first glance that their near likeness, though obvious when they are written, vanishes strangely enough as soon as they are spoken. If we put a page of English, with a German translation, under the eye of a student ignorant of both languages, he would immediately point out several pairs of similar words. But, if we were to read a few English lines to a German hearer, he would not understand a single word. We need only contrast together such forms as are almost identically spelled: E, *fare*, G. *fahren*; E. *bare*, G. *baar*; E. *even*, G. *eben*; E. *slide*, G. *schlitten*; E. *dumb*, G. *dumm*; E. *maid*, G. *maid*; E. (*he*) *was*, G. (*er*) *war*, etc. Thus, even when the written symbol betrays clearly enough the original vocalic identity, the pronunciation actually disguises it in such a way as scarcely to let it appear at all.

Continuing the examination we soon perceive that English is especially responsible for this discord. For the German vowels are still pronounced with nearly the same sound they once represented in the Latin alphabet, from which they are borrowed as in English and French. The *a* is a Latin *a*, whether short or long; the *e* is a Latin *e*, either open or close; and the *u*, as in many Romance languages, has preserved the primitive value which corresponds to our double symbol *oo*. Now, to the same letters English assigns quite different values: our phonetic *a* is called $\bar{e}$; our *e*, $\bar{i}$; our *u*, $y\bar{u}$; and so forth. The conclusion lies near at hand: **English has shifted its vowels at a time when its spelling was already fixed.**[1] These alterations are so various, so delicate,

---

[1] This would be plain enough from the contrast with German, even if the history of both were quite unknown. But history throws a new light on the results of comparison. We can ascertain from indubitable evidence, and particularly from the study of rhyme and assonance, that Old English and even Chaucer's English were very nearly pronounced as they were spelled. Cf. Skeat, *Principles*, I., pp. 24 sq., 51 sq.

and sometimes so capricious, through the infusion of so many dialects into the literary language,[1] that we are compelled to refer the reader to special grammars or, better still, to common use, the only true guide in details. The general outlines, however, may be here briefly and conveniently sketched.

1. A.—Long *a* in a close syllable[2] usually remains *ā* (*far, hard*), whereas, in the same position, *ă* whether primitively short or lately shortened,[3] verges on the sound of open *ĕ* (*bag, cab, bath, to have*).[4] But long *a* in an open syllable is almost everywhere—excluding *father, rather*, etc.—changed to a close long *e*, so long and so close indeed that it is now followed by a slight *i* sound, which forms with it a kind of diphthong: thus *cave* is pronounced nearly as *kéyv*[5]; so also E. *knave* = G. *knabe*; E. *to lade* = G. *laden*, etc.; occasionally even in some close syllables, as in E. *haste* = G. *hast* (both borrowed from M.F.).

Before or after *w*, or before a consonantal group which begins with *l*,[6] *a*, whether short or long, is influenced of the consonant, and, being shifted one degree lower in the vocalic scale, assumes a duller sound almost identical with open *o*; while the following *w* or *l* becomes more or less blended with the vowel: E. *draw* = G. *tragen*, E. (*he*) *saw* = G. (*er*) *sah*, E. *wash* = G. *waschen*, E. *water* (long open *o*) = G. *wasser* (short and pure *a*), E. *all* = G. *all*, E. *fall* = G. *fallen*, E. *false* = G. *falsch* (cf. L. *falsus*), E. *balk* (the *l* is quite mute) = G. *balken*, etc. In a few

---

[1] Cf. *supra* 4, 5, 8, and *infra* 21.
[2] A syllable is said to be open when it ends in a vowel, and close when ending in a consonant. In other words, a syllable is close when final and ending in a consonant (*far*), or when medial, if its vowel is followed by two consonants (*farther*). The only exception is when the two consonants are an explosive followed by a liquid, as in *table*, the *l* being then really a vowel.
[3] Cf. *infra* 20. The reader is advised to note such references and eventually to multiply them himself. Phonetics suppose the knowledge of a great many laws, which complete or contradict each other: they cannot be well understood if learned by fragments. Here, for instance, the *a* of *hard* (cf. G. *hărt*) is long only because it is followed by *rd*; and, on the contrary, the *a* of *bath* (cf. G. *bad*, and E. *to bathe*) has been kept short only because it stood in a close syllable.
[4] The final *e* is quite mute; hence the syllable is actually a close one.
[5] Here the *e* is also mute. But it was sounded in Middle English, at least in the plural *caves* (pr. *kāvĕs*, now *kéyvz*): thus the syllable *ca* was open.
[6] Cf. *supra* 13, 1 B, and add F. *chevaux* (horses) = O.F. *chevals* = L. *cabállos*.

cases before *l*, the vowel was even shifted further to a pure *o*, and so spelled: E. *old* = O.E. *ăld eald* = G. *alt*; E. *cold* = O.E. *cald ceald* = G. *kalt*; E. (*to*) *hold* = O.E. *haldan* = G. *halten*.[1]

2. E.—Accented *e* in an open syllable becomes *i*, which, when long, is diphthongized almost to *iy*: E. *mere* = G. *meer* (sea); compare the unshifted pronunciation of the same *e* in the close syllable of the compound word *mer-maid*. Still more so, of course, with *ē*, whether long or lengthened, usually spelled *ee* or *ea*: E. *see* = G. *sehen*[2]; E. *to breed* = G. *brüten* (cf. the corresponding nouns *brood* and *brut*); E. *to speak* = O.E. *specan* = G. *sprechen*; E. *queer* = G. *quer* (oblique, transverse, awry). Short *e*, even when unaccented, assumes the *i* sound in monosyllables (*he, me, we*), and a sound akin to *i* in the prefixes in an open syllable (*be-fore, be-cause*, cf. G. *be-*).[3] In a close syllable short E. and G. *e* (open) have been kept quite alike (*net* = *netz*, *to set* = *setzen*), apart from the peculiar sound imparted to an *e* or *ea*, as likewise to an *i* in English, by a following consonantal group beginning with *r* (*her, serve, person, heard, earth* = G. *erde*, etc.).

3. I.—E. and G. *i* correspond pretty well to one another; for short *i* in a close syllable remains *i* in both languages (*he will* = *er will, bit* = *bisz, to swim* = *schwimmen, wind* = G. *wind*); and long *i* in an open syllable, which is now sounded *ay* in English, is likewise pronounced as *ay*, though spelled *ei*, in German: *wine* = *wein* (borrowed from L. *vīnum*), *by* = *bei, while* = *weile* (a space of time), *mile* = *meile* (borrowed from L. *mīlle* "thousand").[4] Yet not seldom the quantity of the vowel differs in a close syllable before *l* and *n*: E. *wild* (pr. *wayld*) = G. *wild* (pr. *vĭld*); E. *to wind* = G. *winden*; E. *blind* = G. *blind*, etc., because English has lengthened the *i*. The gap is also large between the two cor-

---

[1] Cf. Dutch *oud* (old), *houden* (to hold), *stadhouder* = G. *statt-halter*; and for the Old English vocalic variations, see below, 21.

[2] The two apparent *e*'s in the English form are not to be mistaken as representing the two real *e*'s in the German one; for, in reality, the word *see* contains but one *e*, namely the long *e* of the stem *seh-*, here transliterated by *ee*; whereas the final *-en* has been dropped in English, like all other infinitive endings, *infra* 19, 2.

[3] But here the *i* is primitive, *infra* 19, 1 and 4, and 66, II., 2.

[4] The pronunciation *vīn, bī (pī), ĕ vīl* (a while), etc., still persists in South Germany (Alamannic), but it is proscribed in classical and official (Central) German.

responding *i*'s when followed by a consonantal group beginning with *r*. Under the influence of this consonant, E. *i* has become a duller sound, which cannot better be compared than with the sound of E. *ŭ* in a close syllable, or of G. open *ö*: E. *birch*=G. *birke*; E. *birth*=O.E. *(ge-)byrð*, cf. G. *(ge-)burt*; E. *first*=O.E. *fyrst*=G. *fürst* (prince), the E. vowel being the same that is heard in *burst*=O.E. *berstan*=G. *bersten* (to burst); *circle*=L. *círculum*; *virgin*=L. *vírginem*, etc. Lastly, final unaccented *i*, usually spelled *y*, as in *lusty*, *manly*, is well known to stand at an equal distance between *ĭ* and *ĕ* (cf. G. *lustig*, *männlich*).[1]

4. O.—Open *o* is the same in both languages: *ox*=*ochse*, *horse*=*rosz*, *bishop*=*bischof*=L. *episcopum*. But, as ancient E. *ā*, now pr. *ē*, becomes a diphthong with semi-vowel *y*, so also long *ō* is now followed by a sound of the semi-vowel nearer akin to it, that is, *w* the semi-vowel of *u*, and thus such a word as *bone* is sounded with a diphthong that could almost be spelled *bōwn*. This accessory sound sometimes prevailed in such a way as to change the original *o* to a decided *u*: *who*, *move*, and even E. *gold* (=G. *gold*) is vulgarly pronounced *guld*. The same is almost always the case with *o*, long by nature, its length being now denoted by the spelling *oo*: E. *loose* (borrowed from Scandian), cf. G. *los*=O.H.G. *lōs*; E. *hoof*=O.E. *hōf*=G. *huf*;[2] though the original sound is retained in E. *floor*=G. *flur*, and E. *door*=G. *thor*. The contrast between *ō* (sounded *ū*) and *ŏ* (spelled *u*, but sounded *ö*) can be nowhere better seen than in *room* and the derived verb *to rummage*.

5. U.—O.E. *u* was undoubtedly pronounced like G. *u*, and even E. *u* has still this value in several words, especially after a labial consonant, after an *r*, and before an *l*: E. *put*, *bull*=G. *bulle*; *bush*=G. *busch*, *butcher*=F. *boucher*; *rule*=O.F. *reule*=L. *régulam*; *full*=G. *voll*, etc. Everywhere else, in an open syllable, *ū* is diphthongized to *yu*; but this law concerns

---

[1] In German also, the *ĭ* in every position has a mixed sound, more akin to close *e* than the sound of pure *i*; we need but compare the pronunciation of *spielen* and *spinnen*.
[2] As for the latter type, both tongues agree in the sound, and vary in the spelling: cf. *infra* 18, 2. In *bolt*=*bolz*, E. has close *o*.

scarcely any other but borrowed words [1] (*tune, music, suit*); [2] and, in a close syllable, *ŭ* becomes that indistinct sound (*tub*) which resembles open *ö*: E. *dung* = G. *dung*; E. *funk* = G. *funke*; E. *hut*, borrowed from F. *hutte*, the latter itself borrowed from G. *hütte*; negative prefix E. *un-* = G. *un-*, thus *uneven* = *un-eben*, etc.

Besides the *u*, O.E. had an *ü*, short or long, then written *y*, and now entirely lost in English,[3] where it is changed to *i* and always pronounced *i*, even where it happens to be still written *u*: thus, *busy* = O.E. *bysig*, and *dizzy* = O.E. *dysig*, have the same vowel in their first syllable, though differently spelled; further, E. *to fill* = O.E. *fyllan* = G. *füllen*; E. *sin* = O.E. *synn* = G. *sünde*; E. *pillow* = O.E. *pyle* (*pylwe*), borrowed from L. *pulvinum*,[4] etc. Of course this *i* comes to be sounded either *ay* or *ö*, under the conditions which thus modify an original *i*: E. *a lie* = O.E. *lygen* = G. *lüge*; E. *first*, see above 3.

6. Many observations of this kind might be suggested here about English diphthongs, whether true or false, now more or less sounded as long and even short vowels, but still spelled as diphthongs. Thus, the development of *ea* is quite parallel to that of *e*, becoming *ī* in an open syllable, and open *ĕ* in a close one: E. *to read* = O.E. *rǣdan*, cf. G. *reden* (to speak), but *he read* = O.E. *rǣdde*, cf. G. *beredt* (eloquent); E. *clean* = O.E.

---

[1] Because primitive E. *ū* had already become *ow*, infra 18, 1.

[2] Hence the pronunciation of *u* has been confused with that of the group *ew* (*dew* = G. *thau*, sounded like *due* = F. *dû*, and *screw* = G. *schraube*, like *accrue* = F. *accru*), and consequently some few words have been written with a *u*, whereas the spelling *ew* would have been etymologically correct: E. *hue* = O.E. *hīw*; E. *Tuesday* = O.E. *Tīwesdæg* (the day of the god *Tiu*, which is the the same as Gr. Ζεύς and L. *Jū-piter*; G. *Dienstag* is corrupted by popular etymology, as if it were *dinges-tag*, "the day for law business," instead of the regular M.H.G. *ziestac*, which survives in the Southern dialects, *e.g.* in High Alsatian *tsištik*). On the contrary, the *ew* has occasionally prevailed in some cases when we should rather expect a *u* or *oo*: E. *view* = F. *vue*; E. *he slew* = G. *er schlug*.

[3] Englishmen are well aware of the difficulty in pronouncing correctly a F. *u*, especially when followed by *i*, as in *pluie* (rain).

[4] G. *ü* also is much nearer to *i* than F. *u*, and in certain dialects it does not differ at all from a pure *i*. Thus, sometimes even an etymological *i* is spelled *ü*: G. *fünf* = O.H.G. *finf* = Go. *fimf* = O.E. *fīf* = E. *five*; here, however, the word is corrupted, cf. *infra* 121, 5. But compare M.H.G. *wiste*, now become *wüszte*, *infra* 223, 3, 4.

$cl\bar{æ}ne$ = G. *klein* (little),[1] but E. *weather* = O.E. *weder*[2] = G. *wetter*, etc. Further, *oa* is a false diphthong, since its sound does not differ from close $\bar{o}$, and it therefore alternates with simple *o* in the transliteration of the long vowel derived from O.E. $\bar{a}$: E. *bone* = O.E. *bān*, but E. *loaf* = O.E. *hlāf* = Go. *hláif-s*[3] = G. *laib*; E. *road* = O.E. *rād*, and, with the same vowel, O.E. *rād*, now spelled (*he*) *rode*, pf. to the verb *ride* = O.E. *rīdan* = G. *reiten*, etc. But it will be better to let the student multiply these instances for himself,[4] and to conclude with the almost superfluous statement that in the whole world there is no language, including French, and excepting only Tibetan, wherein symbol and sound have so much diverged from one another as they have done in English.

(18) II. With the numerous cases in which English and German show the same spelling and varying pronunciation, we ought to contrast the equally important cases in which they are spelled differently and sounded alike. In such a case, and provided that the two words compared may be traced back to an earlier common form, both languages, separately undergoing an evolution either parallel or divergent, have come to a similar result, whereupon either or each of them has altered its spelling according to its own conventional use of written symbols.

1. The **evolution** has run **parallel** in the two languages. We have seen that every primitive $\bar{\imath}$ has been shifted to *ay* in German as in English: German spells it *ei*,[5] whereas English retains the symbol *i*. Primitive $\bar{u}$ has undergone a quite similar process, with this difference only, that the spelling has been altered in both languages; it is now a diphthong with semi-

---

[1] The original meaning is "pretty" (cf. G. *klein-od*, "jewel"), and then the transition is, in English, "pretty—neat—clean," and in German, "pretty—fine—little." In the preceding example, the G. *reden* is only quoted for the sake of the analogy in pronunciation; for it does not correspond to E. *read*, which is equivalent to *rathen* (to guess).

[2] Here, of course, there is no reason for spelling the word with *ea*.

[3] Go. final *s* is the ending of the nominative singular, which has been lost in English and German.

[4] The reader may be here referred to the very complete and suggestive statistics in Mayhew's *Synopsis of Old English Phonology*, and especially to the Appendices, pp. 257-259.

[5] Because, at a certain time, it was actually pronounced *ey*.

vowel *w* and vowel intermediate between *o* and *a*, the whole spelled E. *ow* or *ou*, G. *au*:[1] E. *brown* = O.E. *brūn*, and G. *braun* = O.H.G. *brūn*; E. *house*, borrowed from Scandinavian *hūs*, and G. *haus* = O.H.G. *hūs*, cf. the same *u* shortened in E. *husband* = Scand. *hūs-bōndi* "he who dwells (G. *bauend*) in a house"; E. *town* = O.E. *tūn*,[2] and G. *zaun* (an enclosure) = M.H.G. *zūn*, etc. As, however, vowel lengthening and vowel shortening did not obey precisely the same laws in the two languages,[3] it is but natural that we should occasionally find a *ū* answered by a mere *ŭ*, as in E. *found* = *fūnd, instead of G. (*ge-*)*funden*, and E. *pound* = G. *pfund* = L. *pondō*; but inversely E. *thumb* = G. *daumen* = O.H.G. *dūmo*, etc.

2. **The evolution, though it has been divergent, has led to a similar result.**—The vowel is nearly the same in *foot* and *fusz*, *brood* and *brut*, and many others. But the two languages have not reached the same point by the same road. The *ō* in O.E. *fōt* (Go. *fōt-u-s*, O.N. *fōt-r* [4]), now written *oo*, has been merely shifted to *ū*, as we have seen above. But in German it was at first diphthongized to *uo*, M.H.G. *vuoʒ*, O.H.G. *fuoʒ*,[5] whereupon the semi-vowel *o*, gradually uniting with the *u*, finally lengthened it. If, on the other hand, this *ō* has since been shortened in English, we then get the new correspondence : E. *ŏ* = G. *ū* (the latter itself eventually shortened to *ŭ*); E. *brother* = O.E. *brōðor*, for G. *bruder* = O.H.G. *bruodar*; E. *mother* = O.E. *mōdor*, for G. *mutter* (*ŭ*) = O.H.G. *muotar*; E. *goose*, but shortened *gosling*. Inversely, the *ō* has been kept long, and consequently become *ū*, in E. *moon* = O.E. *mōna*, and

---

[1] The same dialects which do not diphthongize the *i* (*supra* 17, 3) have also kept the primitive *ū* : Swiss *pruun* = *braun*, *huus* = *haus*; High Alsatian *tr tūmĕ* (with a long *ū*) = *der daumen*.
[2] English exhibits in its own dialects exactly the same phenomena of preservation as have just been stated for Southern Germany, namely : in Western dialects (Cornwall) the verb *shine* = G. *scheinen* is *šīn*; whereas, in Northern dialects (thus John Browdie in Dickens' *Nicholas Nickleby*), *town* is sounded as *tūn* (spelled *toon*); and so also, respectively, *tšild* for *child*, *dūn* for *down*, even *kū* for *cow*.
[3] Cf. *supra* 17, 3, and *infra* 20.
[4] O.N. final *-r* is the ending corresponding to Go. *-s*, *supra* 17, 6.
[5] The process of diphthongization is still quite perceptible in Southern Germany, the pronunciation being *fuĕs*, *pruĕt*, *puĕp* = *bube*, *muĕtr* = *mutter*, etc.

VOWELS AND DIPHTHONGS.   37

the consonantal group has not made it short in G. *mond*=
M.H.G. *mānde*=O.H.G. *māno*; but compare the identical vowel
of *Monday* and *Montag*.

(19) III. All the above statements, with the one exception
of final E. *y*, concern only the vowels of more or less accented
syllables. The laws of unaccented vowels, though they sometimes may seem arbitrary owing to the numerous irregularities
in spelling, show a remarkable conformity in both languages,
and may be reduced to five main principles.

1. The unaccented vowel, whether in prefixes or in finals,
assumes a dull and vague sound, usually represented by an *e*:
pref. *bi-*, in Go. *bi-gitan* (to find), *bi-satjan* (to beset), *bi-saihvan*
(to look at), *bi-hlahjan* (to laugh at); E. *beget, beset*; G. *besehen,
belachen*, etc.; pref. *ga-* in Go. *ga-baúrþ-s* (birth), *ga-juk* (pair);
G. *geburt, gejoch*, etc.; Go. *haban* (to have), *haba* (I have), E.
have, G. *haben, habe*; Go. *fiskōn* (to fish), *fiskō* (I fish), *fiskōda* (I
fished); E. *fish, fished*; G. *fischen, fische, fisch(e)te*, etc.

2. In the unaccented final *-en*, chiefly of infinitives and participles, the *n* was dropped early in M.E. (*have*, cf. O.E. *habban*
and G. *haben*); the *ě* then became absolutely mute, and was
either written or omitted, according to the conventional peculiarities of English orthography (*fish*=G. *fischen*). Thus, compare E. *to find*=O.E. *findan* with G. *finden*, and E. *found*=O.E.
(ge-)funden with G. *gefunden*.[1]

3. In German as well as in English, if this *ě* has come in
contact with a consonant-vowel, *m, n, r, l*, it has simply disappeared, and the consonant has become a vowel, $m̥, n̥, r̥, l̥$,[2] so as
to support the syllable: E. *oxen*, G. *ochsen*, pr. *óksn̥*; pref.
fra-, in Go. *fra-liusan-s* (lost), E. *for-lorn*, G. *ver-loren* (pr. *fr̥.-*);

---

[1] Final *n*, however, is often kept, as in E. *heathen*=G. *heide*, E. *maiden*
(but also *maid*)=G. *magd*, in the plural forms *children, oxen*=G. *ochsen*,
and in a great number of strong participles (*bidden* and *bid, hidden* and *hid,
fallen, known*, as opposed to the infinitives *fall, know*, etc., *infra* 179–185).
Without going into particulars, we may here observe: (1) that final *n*
was sounded when the following word began with a vowel (cf. in Mod. E. *an*
and *a*); (2) that certain dialects (Saxonic) lost the final *n* sooner than some
others (Anglic); (3) that, in consequence, the common tongue formed from
all these dialects kept, or even restored, the *n*, wherever it appeared to have
a decided grammatical value.

[2] Cf. *supra* 10, 6.

E. *mother* (pr. *móðr̩*) = O.E. *mōdor*, like G. *mutter* (pr. *mútr̩*) = O.H.G. *muotar*, etc.

4. Before any other consonant, *ĕ* has likewise been dropped in most cases, so that the word has lost one of its syllables: G. *bleiben* = O.H.G. *bilīban* = Go. *bi-leiban* (to remain); G. *glauben* = O.H.G. *gilouben* = Go. *ga-láubjan* (to believe); G. *begleiten* (to accompany) = *be-ge-leiten*, cf. G. *geleiten* and *leiten* = E. *to lead*; E. gen. *son's*, G. *sohns* = *sohnes*; E. *slept* = O.E. *(ge)slǣped*; G. *gehabt*¹ = O.H.G. *gihabēt*, etc. And even when it is marked in writing, it is well known to be almost always eliminated in pronunciation, as in E. *walked* (pr. *wôkt*, just like *slept*), chiefly in rapid and vulgar speech, thus *b'lieve* = *believe*. In fact, it cannot be said to persist necessarily, except when it stands between two consonants of the same order, which could not be sounded at all without some intermediate vowel: E. pl. *sons, rats*, but *kisses, houses*; E. *slept, walked*, but *blotted, mended*; G. *geliebt, angeregt*, but *geleuchtet, geredet*. Even in this position it is liable to disappear: E. pl. *oaths, paths, months*, etc.; G. *geredet* (spoken), but *beredt* (eloquent).² When, the *ĕ* being dropped, two incompatible consonants become contiguous, an assimilation takes place, as already seen, or the first consonant is entirely dropped; E. *hast* = **havest*, and G. *hast* = **habest*, etc.; E. *had* = **havde* and **haved*, like E. *head* = O.E. *hēafod* = Go. *háubiþ* = O.H.G. *houbit* = G. *haupt*, instead of **haubĕt*.

5. Lastly, even where writing does not denote the neutral character of the unaccented vowel by the use of the symbol *ĕ*, its dulness and vagueness are quite perceptible in actual pronunciation. Thus, though we spell with an *o* the second syllable of the word *buxom* = O.E. *būhsum* (flexible, cf. G. *biegsam*), we really pronounce it *bôksm̩*, with a consonant-vowel, as in G. *allem* actually sounded *álm̩*; and, in spite of orthography, the same vowels are heard in E. *thousand* and G. *tausend*.

---

¹ Actually pr. *gĕhapt*, the *b* being assimilated to the *t*.
² Thus also *geredet* becomes *kret*, for instance, in Alsatian. Here the syncope is very early: cf. *infra* 187.

VOWELS AND DIPHTHONGS. 39

§ 2. *Shortening and Lengthening.*

(20) We have just seen English and German vowels to suffer various changes of value, according as they were short or long. But which of them were short, and which long? Were these the same in both languages? In other words, is the quantity of each vowel in both now exactly such as it was in their Pregermanic unity? No, indeed, since we have seen the same vowel treated as long in English and short in German, and *vice versâ.* Thus, before the period of sound-shifting,[1] there must have been a previous period, during which the Pregermanic vowels were either shortened or lengthened, in English and in German, apart from one another, and according to the different laws which prevailed in each. To this period we are now going back.

At the outset a great principle pervades the whole evolution of vowel-quantity: whether in English or in German, an **accented vowel has a decided tendency to lengthen in an open syllable, and shorten in a close one.** Thus, the reader may compare: E. *to keep* = O.E. *cēpan,* and E. *he kept* = O.E. *cepte*; *sleep* and *slept, leave* and *left, read* and *read* (respectively O.E. *rēdan* and *rædde*), *lose* and *lost,* etc.; G. *ich sage, er sagt*; *ich lege, ich legte* (I lay, I laid); *tragen* (to bear), *tracht* (dress); *möge* (may) and *macht* (the might), etc.; G. *stube* (a room; F. *étuve,* "a warmed room") = O.H.G. *stŭba* = O.E. *stofa* = E. *stove,* etc., etc.

But, if the law be the same in the two languages, we should

---

[1] The chronological succession of phonetic facts is always to be taken into account, as being, at least, as important as the facts by themselves. This is a consideration of which the student cannot be too earnestly reminded. In the study of language, as of geology, every fact bears its own date, if properly observed. Supposing a geological stratum, and a sinking of the ground in the same place, has the former taken place before the latter, or the latter before the former? We know that if the stratum is older than the sinking, it will be broken up like the strata below; if not, it will have remained level. So also, has the E. *u* of **fund* (cf. G. *gefunden*) been lengthened to *ū* before or after the *ū* of *hūs* had been shifted to *ou*? The answer is: before, since this *u* also has become *ou,* inasmuch as we pronounce *found* like *house.* If the *u* of **fund* had become long after the shifting of *ū* to *ou,* we should now have the dissimilar forms *house* and **fūnd.*

expect to find in both the same long and the same short vowels. Such, however, is far from the case, as may be inferred from the last example quoted. Whence arises the difference? The principle, of course, is identical; but its effects have been carried on separately, in various dialects and various periods of English and of German, and consequently have resulted in the most violent and striking contrasts.

1. The fact is, that our principle, as given above, does not indicate any precise and positive phenomenon, but a mere general tendency, which was not equally observed by all dialects. In German, for instance, the law of shortening in a close syllable does not belong as such to the common language, but mainly to the dialects of Low German, the peculiarities of their pronunciation having sometimes intruded into the literary language. Hence many words hesitate between the two quantities: G. *genüg* and *genüg*, compared with E. *enough* (the final always short). German shortening appears nowhere earlier, and therefore more consistent, than before the medial group *ht*: G. (*er*) *brächte* = M.H.G. *brāhte* = O.E. *brōhte* = E. (*he*) *brought*; and yet even here it is seen not to have taken place before the modern period. English shortening began far earlier.[1]

2. Such later changes in the pronunciation as took place in the two languages may have caused a given vowel to stand in a close syllable in the one, and in an open syllable in the other. Thus, the *ĕ* in an unaccented syllable being only slightly sounded or entirely dropped, the preceding syllable varies accordingly. We have the short vowel in *he read, he led*; whereas German has the long one in the corresponding forms *er redete, er leitete,* in which the *ĕ* mute has been retained or rather restored in contrast to O.E. *rǣdde*, etc.[2] So also, in the genitive, E. *son's*, but G. *sohnes,* hence *sohns*, etc.

3. In the course of declension or conjugation, the radical vowel might occur alternately in a close or open syllable, and

---

[1] Though in this case the corresponding vowel seems to have remained long, it is only long because the sound of the *h* (*gh*) has coalesced with the preceding vowel and lengthened it.

[2] The dialects in which *geredet* is pronounced *kret* sound the *e* short (as in E. *met*).

consequently it was, according to rule, in turn short and long. Now **grammatical analogy** naturally levelled most of these differences,[1] and thus either the long vowel or the short one was carried throughout the whole flexion. German, for instance, has everywhere the short one in *gemacht, er macht, ich machte, ich mache, machen,* whereas English shows everywhere the long one in *made* (O.E. *macode*), *he maketh, I made, I make, to make,* etc. G. *glas* has the gen. *glases,* pr. *gläses,* whence the long vowel also pervades the nomin., pr. *glās* = E. *glăss*. Similarly the gen. *sohnes* caused the nomin. to become *sohn*[2] instead of O.H.G. *sunu* = Go. *sunu-s* = O.E. *sunu* = E. *sŏn*. Thus, in German, the long vowel of the pl. form *waren* = M.H.G. *wāren* has been transported to the sg. *war* = M.H.G. *was,* whereas, in English, the long vowel in the pl. *were* = O.E. *wǣron* had no influence upon the short one in the sg. *was,* because the sound of the latter was different.[3] More instances of the kind the reader may easily discover by himself.

4. Lastly, some subsidiary laws, especially in English, have modified the original quantity of the vowels.

A. Before a group *nð, ns, nf,* in Old English, any vowel is lengthened while the nasal disappears:[4] E. *us,* shortened in a close and unaccented syllable,[5] from O.E. *ūs* = Go. *uns* = G. *uns*; E. *five* (shortened in the close syllable of *fifth* and *fifty*) = O.E. *fīf* = Go. *fimf* = G. *fünf*.

B. From the earliest period an accented English vowel is lengthened before a group consisting of a nasal or liquid and a voiced explosive. Thus disappear the differences in quantity which have been partly stated above, between E. *find, mild, gold, old* (O.E. *āld*), *word, sound* (in health), *hound,* and G. *finden, mild, gold, alt, wort, (ge)sund, hund,* etc. Moreover, in

---

[1] On the effects of analogy and the part it plays in language, see Henry, *Grammar of Gr. and Lat.,* 83 and 183, and below 22, 55, 177, etc.
[2] Pr. *zōn*. The *h* only denotes that the vowel is long, *supra* 12, 4.
[3] Thus is explained the double discord in sound and quantity mentioned on the second page of this chapter, For *r* = *s,* see *infra* 61, I. 2.
[4] This is the Old English compensatory lengthening; cf. *infra* 24. The phenomenon is the same in Greek (τοὺς ἵππους = τὸνς ἵππονς) and in Latin (*equōs* = *equŏ-ns*). See Henry, *Gramm. of Gr. and Lat.,* 189, 2, and 206, 3.
[5] Cf. *supra* 19, and *infra,* 65, 5, and 66, II. 4.

Mod. English, an *r* before any consonant whatever lengthens the preceding vowel by coalescing with it:[1] thus, for instance, compare *hard* with *hart*, *heart* with *herz*, *learn* with *lernen*, *hark* with imper. *horche*, *sharp* with *scharf*, etc. Even in German, however, we find *bärt* (beard), *zärt* (tender), *ērde* = *earth*, and a few others.

§ 3. *Old English Vowel-Breaking.*

(21) The English process of lengthening lastly mentioned is but one effect of a more ancient and more general cause, which also produced the curious process of the diphthongization of the vowels, called **Vowel-breaking** (G. *brechung*, F. *fracture*). Though this phenomenon does not properly belong to English, since it seems not to have taken place in Mercian, yet, as it was immensely developed in the Southern dialects (Wessex), it could not fail to find its way somehow into the common language.[2] Omitting many details, we may briefly summarize the effects of this law as follows: before a consonantal group beginning with *r*, *l* or *h* (including the *x* = *hs*), the two vowels *a* and *e* became respectively "broken" to *ea* and *eo*. Thus, Old English opposes *wearm*, *feallan* (Merc. *fallan*), *heord*, *seolfor* (Merc. *sylfur*), *seox*, *cneoht*, *neaht*, *healf* (Merc. *half*), etc., to E. *warm* = G. *warm*, E. *to fall* = G. *fallen*, E. *herd* = G. *herde*, E. *silver* = G. *silber*, E. *six* = G. *sechs*, E. *knight* = G. *knecht*, E. *night*[3] = G. *nacht*, E. *half* = G. *halb*, etc., etc.

In all these cases English appears quite free of any breaking. The process is exclusively Saxonic,[4] and the only counterpart of it in classical English is a mere lengthening. A lengthening it is also, most likely, when the *a* is shifted to *ō* in the words quoted above, *old*, *cold*, *hold*, *sold*, etc., in which Saxonic has the broken vowel (*eald*, *ceald*, *healdan*, *seald*) instead of

---

[1] Cf. *supra* 13, 1 A.
[2] A point already alluded to, *supra* 4.
[3] In these three words, the vowel *i* is due to a kind of metaphony (*infra* 22), which is regularly produced by the following palatal consonant.
[4] Hence it follows, as a matter of course, that the Southern dialects must contain a very large number of broken forms. It is mainly for this reason that they so widely differ from classical English.

the pure Mercian vowel (*āld, cald, sald*).[1] But the change appears already much greater in *worth* = O.E. *weorð* = G. *werth* = Go. *vaírþ-s*, E. *sword* = G. *schwert*, E. *work* = G. *werk*, E. *world*[2] = O.E. *weorold*, cf. G. *welt* = M.H.G. *wëralt*[3]; hence, in these words and some other, we may perhaps recognise a process akin to breaking, if not the breaking itself. The more so with the E. *a* corresponding to Germanic *e* in such words as: E. *far* = O.E. *feor*, as opposed to Go. *faírra* and G. *fer-n* = O.H.G. *vërr-ana*; E. *star* = O.E. *steorre*, compared with M.H.G. *stërre*, now replaced by *stern* = M.H.G. *stërne* = O.H.G. *stërno* = Go. *staírnō*, etc. Lastly, the breaking is still clearly visible in the spelling, and partly preserved in the pronunciation of such words as E. *beard, earth, learn* (O.E. *leornian*), *heart* (O.E. *heorte*), *hearth*, as opposed to G. *bart, erde, lernen, herz, herd*, and some others.

§ 4. *Metaphony (Vowel Mutation or Modification)*.[4]

(22) Our search has now brought us back very near to the Pregermanic period; but we have not yet reached it. The remarkable process we call **Metaphony** (G. *umlaut*) took place in English and in German separately; yet it is in both so early and general, that it seems impossible not to attribute it to a tendency inherited from West Germanic. Gothic alone is free from it. It is found everywhere else, though at various dates: in English metaphony appears fixed before the earliest written documents of Old English; in German, we can still trace its slow

---

[1] G. *alt, kalt, halten*, and M.H.G. *sal* (delivery) = E. *sale*, still surviving in *sal-buch* (a register of lands); for the vb. *sell(en)*, now used in English in the sense of L. "vendere," has reached it through the sense of "assigning." [a piece of land].

[2] Here the effect of a preceding *w*, as described, *supra* 17, 1, may perhaps have combined with a kind of breaking.

[3] The word would be Go. **vair-ald-u-*, and mean "a man's age." For the first part, compare L. *vir*, and G. *wer-geld* (compensation for a man, that is to say, for a man's slaughter), G. and E. *wer-wolf*, etc. The original meaning of the word was L. "sæculum," whence it became "world," just as *sæculum* has done in Ecclesiastical Latin, and F. *seule* in *Eulalia's Song* (line 24).

[4] Since the usual term "Mutation" is altogether vague, designating any kind of vowel-shifting whatever, I have ventured to introduce into the English terminology the word "Metaphony" for German "Umlaut," as already in my French edition. It seems indeed convenient to adopt a separate term for such "mutations" as are described under this head.

progress, step by step, from the Old High German, wherein it begins, down to the year 1150, when it is entirely accomplished; and it may, therefore, be deemed a very convenient distinction between Old and Middle High German.[1] Under this name are comprised the mutations undergone by **a vowel,** *a, e, o, u,* **when immediately followed by a syllable which contains an** *i* (or its semi-vowel, written *j* in Germanic), under the influence of which it acquired a **slight** *i-* **sound,** and altered accordingly.[2]

Let us, for an instant, consider only German metaphony, as it is more recent, and, in consequence, clearer; and, further, let us consider it only in such pairs of words as *mann männlich, erde irdisch, gott göttlich, (zu)kunft künftig,* etc., where its cause is quite obvious. Here we may very well understand how the palatal vowel of the second syllable at first palatalized the preceding consonant (*supra* 14, 3 B), which in its turn modified the sound of the preceding vowel, so as to shift it one degree nearer to *i* (*supra* 12, 1). The effect, indeed, is wholly adequate to the cause.[3]

But, at the very outset, an objection must be faced: in contrast with the numerous cases which actually exhibit metaphony, a great many words might be quoted, wherein a following *i* has no such effect; thus *gelb* (yellow) *gelblich, gold goldig, ruhe* (rest) *ruhig,* etc. How can this be? We must never forget that a language constantly and daily creates new words, whereas a particular phonetic law cannot outlast in any language a given

---

[1] More accurately speaking, the mutation of *ă* is certainly Teutonic (West Germanic), and perhaps even partly Pregermanic (*infra* 26, I. 3); the mutation of *a* begins in O.H.G. about 750; that of *u* is scarcely at all visible in it; that of *o*, as will be seen, is late and due to analogy. Germanists, however, generally agree in thinking that the mutation took place in the usual pronunciation long before it was marked in writing: Wilmanns, *Deutsche Grammatik,* I. p. 192.

[2] We have also in English a metaphony caused by a following palatal consonant (*supra* 20), and in German, another caused by a following *u* (*infra* 26, I. in fine); but they need only be mentioned here for the sake of completeness. On the other hand, there are some groups of consonants which impede or seem to impede metaphony. For these particulars, the reader must here be referred to more detailed works.

[3] In some cases, the spelling itself may illustrate the process of metaphony: thus, metaphonized *u* is spelled *ui* or *iu* in O.H.G., and G. *ü* is well known to be called *ui*.

period. If, for instance, *ruhig* has been derived from *ruhe* at a late date, when the law of metaphony had long exhausted its effect, and if, as is the case, a regularly metaphonical form *gülden*, still mentioned in every German vocabulary as archaic and poetical, has been currently replaced by a word *golden* on the analogy of the primitive *gold*, it is clear that the cause and effect of the phenomenon remain invariable and unquestionable, in spite of exceptions due, in particular cases, to some accessory and accidental causes which have nothing to do with the principle. Nay, the contrary would appear far more wonderful; for supposing, for instance, that the language had ever created such a regularly metaphonical compound as **häls-binde* (a neckcloth); since both terms of it, namely, *hals* and *binde*, must always remain present to the linguistic consciousness of any speaking subject, he cannot fail, sooner or later, to alter the compound accordingly, and restore the non-metaphonical form instead of the seemingly corrupt one.

On the other hand, we meet with a great number of similar cases of metaphony, although no *i* appears in the second syllable: G. *lamm* (lamb), pl. *lämmer*; G. *geben* (to give), pres. sg. 2 *du gibst*; G. *hoch* (high), *höher* (higher); G. *buch* (book), pl. *bücher*, etc.; and compare E. *man men, brother brethren, goose geese, foot feet*. But if, instead of confining our attention to the modern form of these metaphonical words, we proceed to examine them in O.H.G., or, even beyond O.E., in that Gothic speech, through which we are able to trace them back to Pregermanic, then we shall, almost invariably, find the second syllable to have contained a primitive *i* or *j*, more lately dropped or changed to *ĕ* in consequence of the laws of final and unaccented syllables.[1] Thus we shall find, for instance, O.H.G. *lamb lembir, gëban gibis, hōh hōhir*, etc. The vowel which has vanished still betrays itself through the mutation it has effected, and the mutation, which seems arbitrary at first sight, is quite satisfactorily explained by the vowel as preserved in an earlier state of the same language.

Lastly, if we find metaphony taking place in cases where we

[1] See *supra* 19, and *infra* 34.

should not expect it, namely before a syllable that does not and never did contain either an *i* or a *j*, even then we need not fear for our theory. For, as non-metaphonical forms may have influenced metaphonical forms and abolished some regular mutations,—thus, *ruhig* and *goldig* modelled on *ruhe* and *gold*,—so also, of course, the latter may have altered the former, that is to say, Germans might as well have come to say **güld* for *gold*, from *gülden*, as they have come to say *goldig* and *golden*, from *gold*. Hence arise some false analogies in metaphony, as, for instance: G. *thräne* (a tear)=M.H.G. *trēne* (but O.H.G. *trahan trān*), altered under the influence of its pl. **trēni*=Old Saxonic *trahni*; E. *friend* for O.E. *frēond* (G. *freund*), and E. *fiend* for O.E. *fēond* (G. *feind*), both altered on account of the datives O.E. *friend*=**frēond-i*, and *fiend*=**fēond-i*.[1] The conclusion is thus forced upon us, that a metaphonical vowel in either language may very well correspond to a non-metaphonical vowel in the other, and the case will be seen to occur frequently.

All that has been said above about German applies, of course, as well, and even better, to English. English also has created new words since the end of its metaphonical period, and in much greater number than German could do, because in English this period ended far earlier; English also has lost, after metaphony had wrought its effects, the *i*'s and *j*'s that caused it, and, still for the same reason, on a much larger scale than German[2]; lastly, English has also levelled, during a longer period, the metaphonical and the non-metaphonical forms, in such a way as to cause either the former or the latter to extend throughout a whole system of derivation, declension, or conjugation; thus *gold golden, man manly, god godly*, contrasted with G. *gülden, männlich, göttlich*. Besides these considerations, English metaphony, less visible in spelling of older date, and partly disguised by the effects of Old English breaking, cannot be reduced to the exact parallelism exhibited by the almost algebraic formula of present German metaphony, viz:

[1] See declension, *infra* 139, 1, 5, and 152, 3.
[2] Most of them are already dropped in Old English.

VOWELS AND DIPHTHONGS.   47

Pure vowels:[1]   *a* | *e* | *o* | *u*
Metaphonical vowels: *e, ä*[2] | *i* | (*ü*) *ö*[3] | *ü*

Whereas English has the following correspondences:

Pure: *a ā* | *e* | *o ō* | *u*[4] | (broken or   *ea eo*
Metaph.: *e ǣ* | *i* | *y ē* | *y* | otherwise) *ie y*

(23) Some instances of metaphony have been quoted above; a great many others will occur in the study of forms, so that here it will prove sufficient to mention a few mutations selected among the most interesting derivations of words containing either an *i* or a *j*- suffix.

A.—G. *ameise* = O.H.G. *ameiʒʒa* = O.E. *ǣmette* (E. *ant*); but O.H.G. *emiʒʒig* (busy), M.H.G. *emʒic*, G. *emsig.*—G. *rettich* and O.E. *rētic*,[5] borrowed from L. *rādīcem.*—G. *pfanne* and E. *pan*, borrowed from L. *patina*; but, with a derivative suffix, G. *pfenning pfennig*, E. *penny* (on account of its being round like a pan?).—E. *Angle* (ethnic name), but *English*; so also, E. *France*, but *French* = **Frankish* (cf. G. *Fränkisch*), E. *Wales*, but *Welsh* (cf. G. *Wälsch*, opposed to *Deutsch*), etc.—E. *a tale*, but *to tell* = O.E. *tellan* for Germanic **tal-jan*; quite as G. *zahl* (number) and *zählen* (to count) = O.H.G. *zellen* = **zal-jan*.[6]

---

[1] With barely any distinction between short and long vowels, that is to say, *ă* is mutated to short *ä*, and *ā* to long *ä*, and so forth.

[2] The variation is merely one of writing. O.H.G. has been seen to write *e*. Mod. German has been influenced by an etymological scruple: the vowel is spelled *ä* when another form survives wherein the pure vowel *a* is preserved; but the spelling *e* is retained if such is not the case, or if the language has forgotten the metaphonical origin of the vowel: thus, *mann männer, kalb kälber* = O.H.G. *chalbir*, etc.; but *ende* = O.H.G. *enti* = Go. *andei-s* showing the *i* whence the metaphony arose (cf. E. *end* = O.E. *ende*, from a Preg. **andja-* which is akin to Sk. *ánta-*, "a limit"); thus also, *hand hände*, but in composition *behende* = O.H.G. *bi henti*, literally "by the hand" (*hent-i* is a dative case), whence the sense "convenient, easy, swift."

[3] When *o* is mutated to *ü*, as in *gülden*, the *o* stands for a primitive *u*, and the mutation has taken place in the early period when the vowel was still sounded as *u*. Cf. infra 28, I.

[4] Long or short, that is to say, *ŭ* becomes *y*, and *ū* becomes *ȳ*; and similarly, *ēa* and *ēo* are mutated, the one to *ie*, and the other to *ȳ*. What these again may become in the shifting from Old to Modern English, has been stated above.

[5] E. *radish* is borrowed from F. *radis*.

[6] For the sense, compare G. *er-zählen* (to relate).

E.—G. *gern* (willingly)=O.H.G. *gërno* (Go. *gairn-s*, "covetous"), vb. *begehren* (to wish for)=O.H.G. *gërōn*; but *gier* (avidity)=O.H.G. *giri, gierig* (covetous), *begierig, begierde*, etc.— G. *feder* = E. *feather*, but *fittich* (wing).—G. *pilgrim* and E. *pilgrim*, borrowed from L. *peregrinum*, cf. F. *pèlerin* and Ital. *pellegrino*.—E. *silly* = O.E. *syllic* = *seollic (broken vowel)=Go. *silda-leik-s* (strange, queer); cf. E. *seld-om* = G. *selt-en*, G. *seltsam* (strange), etc.

O.—G. *gold*, but *gülden*; O.E. *gold*, but *gylden*, the latter now altered to *golden*, though the metaphony survives in the vb. *to gild* = O.E. *gyldan* = *guld-jan.—E. *fore* = G. *vor*; but E. *first* = O.E. *fyrst* = *fur-ist; cf. G. *fürst* (prince).—E. *fox*, but *vixen*[1]; cf. G. *fuchs* and *füchsin*.—O.E. *dōm* (judgment) and E. *doom*; but E. *to deem* = O.E. *dēman* = *dōm-jan. So also, *food* and *to feed*, *brood* = G. *brut*, and *to breed* = G. *brüten* = O.H.G. *bruoten*, which latter would be Go. *brōd-jan, etc.

U.—O.E. and E. *full*, O.H.G. *fol* and G. *voll* = Go. *full-s*; but O.E. *fyllan* and E. *to fill*, G. *füllen* = O.H.G. *fullen* = Go. *full-jan*. —E. *dizzy* = O.E. *dysig*, contrasted with O.H.G. *tusig*, M.H.G. *dusel* (disorder), G. *dusel* (dizziness); cf. also E. *bustle* and the actual pronunciation of *busy*[2] = O.E. *bysig*.—O.E. *fūl* and E. *foul*, O.H.G. *fūl* and G. *faul* (Go. *fūl-s*, O.N. *fūll*); but M.E. *file* (to defile), E. *to defile* and *filth*; cf. G. *fäule fäulnisz*.—E. *mouse* = O.E. *mūs*, pl. *mice* = O.E. *mўs*; cf. G. *maus*, pl. *mäuse*.

It seems superfluous to dwell upon the English broken vowels, whereof *silly* has afforded an instance. But we may recall here, by way of general recapitulation, the chief grammatical classes in which German, remaining truer to its origins than English from the main reason that the origins are more recent, has preserved the regular process of metaphony, though occasionally it may be obscured by false analogies.

1. Feminine nouns in *-in*: *gott göttin*, etc.
2. Neuter collectives, with prefix *ge-*: *berg* (mountain) and *gebirg* = O.H.G. *gi-birg-i*; so also *stern* (star) and *gestirn* (constellation), *tosen* (noise) and *getöse*, etc.

[1] The word belongs to a Southern dialect, which changes initial *f* to *v*. Cf. E. *vat* = G. *fasz* (tub).
[2] *Supra* 17, 5, though often spelled O.E. *bisig*.

VOWELS AND DIPHTHONGS. 49

3. Abstract feminine nouns in -*e* (formerly -*ī*): *hoch* (high) and *höhe* (height) = O.H.G. *hōh-ī*.

4. Diminutive nouns in -*el*, -*chen*, -*lein*, and -*ling* (O.H.G. -*ila*, -*kīn* or -*chīn*, -*līn* and -*linc*): these types are common and well known (*infra* 103).

5. Adjectives, denoting material, in -*en* (formerly -*īn*): *gülden* (golden), *irden* (made of earth), etc.

6. Adjectival derivatives in -*icht*, -*ig*, -*lich*, etc.

7. Comparatives, *hoch* = Go. *háuh-s*, but *höh-er* = *háuh-iza*; and superlatives, *höch-(e)st* = Go. *háuh-ist-s*, etc.

8. So-called metaphonical plurals, as *füsze* (feet), *kälber* (calves), *väter*, etc.

9. Causative and denominative verbs, because there is a primitive suffix -*jan* hidden in their ending: to the previous instances, add *to set* = G. *setzen* = Go. *sat-jan* (to cause to *sit* down, to settle).

10. Formation of the imperfect subjunctive in the so-called strong verbs: *er nahm* (he took), *er nähme* (O.H.G. *nam* and *nāmi*); *trug*, *trüge*; *zog*, *zöge*, etc.

11. Conjugation of strong verbs in the 2nd and 3rd person sg. of present indicative, sometimes also in the 2nd person sg. imperative, thus: *sprechen* (to speak), *er spricht* (he speaks), *sprich* (speak); *schlagen* (to strike), *er schlägt*; *ich fahre* (I am travelling), *du fährst, er fährt, wir fahren* = O.H.G. *faru, ferist, ferit, farēn*.[1]

§ 5. *Pregermanic Compensatory Lengthening.*

(24) We are passing at length the boundary of the primitive Germanic language; and, on this very line there appears to

---

[1] Let us end with a well-known but curious derivation with a twofold metaphony, the G. compound *elend* = O.H.G. *eli-lenti*, "from another land" (*eli-* = Go. *alji-* = L. *alio-* appears likewise with metaphony in E. *el-se*), hence "foreign, outcast, wretched," and "exile, wretchedness."—It must be borne in mind that metaphony has been considered here only as a general phonetic phenomenon, abstracted from the enormous differences, either in chronology or in application, which may characterize it in the historical life of English and German. It will be met with in every province of both languages, and seen to exhibit itself in very various conditions. Cf., for instance, *infra* 26 (i., 1, 2, 3), 28 (i.), 80 (xvi.), 144–146, 147, 194, 197, 204–206, etc., etc.

E

us a phenomenon, which, though it is common to all Germanic dialects and must therefore be attributed to the parent-speech, can nevertheless be verified without any intervention of other Indo-European idioms. In a single word, as exhibited by the generality of Germanic vocabularies, we observe a regular vocalic and consonantal variation, namely: here, a short vowel, followed by a nasal and a guttural explosive; and there, the same vowel lengthened, while the nasal has disappeared and the guttural has become a spirant. Hence the law may be easily inferred: every Pregermanic short vowel, $ă$, $ĭ$, $ŭ$,[1] followed by a group of nasal and surd guttural spirant ($ñh$), is lengthened, whilst the nasal is dropped.

1. Group $ă + ñh$.—Go. *þagkjan* (to think), O.E. *ðœncean* and E. *to think*, O.H.G. *denchen* and G. *denken*,[2] everywhere with short vowel and nasal, from a Preg. **þañkjanam*. But, if the k becomes an h,[3] as in Preg. **þañhta* (he thought), the a becomes $ā$, and the $ñ$ is dropped: hence Preg. **þāhta*, and its offspring, Go. *þāhta*, O.E. *ðōhte* and E. *he thought*, O.H.G. *dāhta* and G. *er dachte*.[4] So also: Go. *briggan*=Preg. **breñʒanam*, and pf. *brāhta*=Preg. **brañhta*; E. *to bring, brought, brought*; G. *bringen, brachte, gebracht*, etc.

2. Group $ĭ + ñh$.—O.N. *þing* (lawsuit, business), O.E. *ðing* and E. *thing*, with a more general sense, as in O.H.G. *dinc* and G. *ding*, everywhere with nasal and short vowel, from a Preg. **þiñʒ-*. But, from a secondary verb **þiñhan*, changed to **þīhan*, the Go. *gadeihan*, G. *gedeihen* (to thrive, to succeed), and O.E. *geðēon*, which still shows the nasal and the short vowel in its participle *geðungen*.[5]

3. Group $ŭ + ñh$.—Go. *þugkjan* (to seem), the root being that of *þagkjan*, only with reduced vocalism.[6] O.E. *ðyncan* and E.

---

[1] The case cannot take place with $ĕ$ nor $ŏ$, because in this position they respectively become or remain $ĭ$ or $ŭ$: *infra* 26, i., 5, and 28, i.
[2] The vowel is metaphonical owing to the suffix -*jan*.
[3] On this change, see below 53 C, and note.
[4] Shortened in Modern German, *supra* 20, 1.
[5] G. *gediehen* is formed by analogy with *gedeihen*, and such verbs as contain a primitive $ī$ (*schreiben geschrieben, leihen geliehen*). But *gedungen* and *bedungen* still exist as participles of the verbs *dingen* and *bedingen*.
[6] See the Section on Vowel-Gradation, *infra* 45, 4.

think, the latter being confounded with earlier *ðœncean*, and having thus assumed its meaning. O.H.G. *dunchan*, M.H.G. *dunken*, G. *dünken* (to seem). Thus, everywhere the nasal and the short vowel suggesting a Preg. *þuñkjanam, pf. *þuñhta, whence *þūhta: Go. *þūhta* (it seemed); O.H.G. *dūhta* and G. (*mich*) *deuchte*[1] or *däuchte*, with metaphony (borrowed from the subjunctive) instead of *dauchte; and, an infinitive being formed on this new pattern, the analogous vb. *däuchten*.

Section II.

PRIMITIVE VOWELS AND DIPHTHONGS, AND THEIR EVOLUTION.

(25) We have examined the series of transformations undergone by the vowels of English and German during the historical and prehistorical life of both languages. Now, if Pregermanic were known to us through any direct tradition, it would only remain to show how its sounds are reproduced in each of them. But, since Pregermanic is lost, and can only be restored by the comparison of its offspring, and, subsidiarily, of the other Indo-European languages, we must now apply to them in order to discover that necessary link of the chain which we have so far followed upwards, but which we are now attempting to trace downwards. We shall thus, as it were, prove the operation, provided that Sanskrit, Greek and Latin agree with English and German in confirming what we have already learnt about Pregermanic vocalism; and then our Germanic phonetics will rest on a true scientific basis.

According to the evidence afforded by the Indo-European languages, the primitive vocalism of their parent consisted of: five short vowels, $\breve{a}, \breve{e}, \breve{\imath}, \breve{o}, \breve{u}$; the six corresponding diphthongs, *ay, ey, oy*, and *aw, ew, ow*; the five corresponding long vowels, $\bar{a}, \bar{e}, \bar{\imath}, \bar{o}, \bar{u}$;[2] and, lastly, an indeterminate vowel *ä*, which, at least in the European languages, has been entirely confounded

---

[1] This is the archaic and proper form. The usual one *mich dünkte* is due to the analogy of *dünken*.
[2] Occasionally also in a diphthong, thus *āy, ēw*, etc. But in this short grammar we are compelled to omit these rare sounds.

with ă, and therefore need not be distinguished at all from it in this work (I.-E. *pătér-, Gr. πατέρ-, L. pater, Go. fadar, E. father, G. vater).¹

The Indo-European a and o, whether short or long, have become blended together in the Germanic branch, ă and ŏ being Preg. ă, and ā and ō being Preg. ō. Apart from some partial mutations, the other vowels are quite distinctly kept. Thus, it will seem advisable to begin our study with e, i and u.

§ 1. *Short and long e.*

(26) The vowel e may be said to be the touchstone of the European languages; for the Asiatic (Indo-Iranian) group of our family² has changed it to a in every position. The Germanic group shows it still almost as clearly as any other European Language.

I. I.-E. ĕ = Gr. ĕ = L. ĕ = Preg. ĕ: I.-E. *bhérō (I carry, cf. Sk. bhárā-mi), Gr. φέρω, L. fĕrō, Preg. *bérō, whence Go. baír-an³ (to carry), O.E. bĕran and E. to bear, O.H.G. bĕran, M.H.G. bĕrn and G. (ge)bären (to bring forth a child), cf. the original meaning preserved in bahre (a hand-barrow); I.-E. *pĕll-a (skin), Gr. πέλλ-α, L. pell-i-s, Preg. *fĕll-a, whence E. and G. fell; I.-E. *éd-ō (I eat; cf. Sk. ád-mi), Gr. ἔδω, L. ĕdō, Preg. *étō, whence Go. it-an (to eat), O.E. etan and E. eat, O.H.G. ëʒʒan and G. essen, etc.

Preg. ĕ has been generally kept. In five main cases, however, it became ĭ at the very earliest period.

1. In the primitive diphthong ĕy, first changed to ĭy owing to the law stated under 3 below, and this again then contracted to ī: I.-E. *stéyghō (I go up), Gr. στείχω, but Preg. *stīʒō, whence Go. infinitive steigan, O.H.G. stīgan and G. steigen.⁴

[1] The Asiatic languages here have an ĭ, thus, Sk. pitár-.
[2] Cf. supra 3.
[3] As a matter of fact, Gothic, less pure in this respect than any other Germanic tongue, changes every Preg. ĕ to ĭ; the ĕ, however, is restored, though spelled aí, before an r or an h: hence arises the contrast between baíran = E. bear, and itan = E. eat.
[4] O.E. stigan and E. sty; the latter being obsolete and replaced by F. mount. On the later evolution of this i in both languages, cf. supra 17, 3, and infra 27, II.

2. In the same group before a vowel: the group first becomes *ĭy*, which then is reduced to a simple *y*. Such is the case with all causative verbs. These verbs will be seen to require in I.-E. the deflected root,[1] accompanied by a suffix -*ĕyŏ*-, which suffix takes the person-endings: thus, Sk. *bhár-ā-mi* (I carry) and *bhār-áyā-mi* (I cause to carry), Gr. φορέω; root *mĕn* (to think), L. *moneō* (I cause to think, I warn) = **mon-eyō*; root *nek* (to die, cf. L. *nex nec-is*), L. *noc-eō*, etc. Consequently, a root *sed* (to sit down, Sk. *sád-as*, "seat," Gr. ἕδος, L. *sed-eō sēd-ēs*, etc.), when assuming the causative meaning "I make to sit," will become I.-E. **sod-éyō*. Now, the Go. *sat-jan* (to place) refers us to a Preg. **sat-ja-*, which is quite identical with **sod-éyō*, the only difference being that the *ey* is changed to *y*; hence, with the necessary metaphony, O.E. *settan* and E. *to set*, O.H.G. *sezzen* and G. *setzen*, as opposed to *sit*, *sitz* and *sitzen*.

3. When the following syllable contains either a prehistorical *i* or *y*[2]: I.-E. **médh-yo-s* (placed in the middle, cf. Sk. *mádhyas*), Gr. μέσος = μέσσος = **μέθ-yo-*s, L. *medius*, but Preg. **mið-ja-z*, whence Go. *midjis*, O.E. *midd* and E. *mid*, O.H.G. *mitti* and G. *mitte*; I.-E. **és-ti* (he is, cf. Sk. *ásti*), Gr. ἐστί, L. *est*, but E. (*he*) *is*, G. (*er*) *ist*, etc.

4. As final, always, and sometimes in certain other unaccented positions less easy to define: I.-E. final **-ĕ* in the 2nd person sg. imperative, as **ném-ĕ* (take), Gr. νέμ-ε (divide), L. *ĕm-ĕ* (buy), but Preg. **nĭm-ĭ*, whence O.H.G. *nim*[3] and G. *nimm*; I.-E. final **-ĕs* in the nomin. pl., as **pód-ĕs* (feet), Sk. *pād-as*, Gr. πόδ-ες, but Preg. **fót-ĭz*, whence the metaphony in O.E. *fēt* (sg. *fōt*) and E. *feet*. Here the change of *ĕ* to *ĭ* seems attributable to the following *z*.

5. Before any group beginning with a nasal: I.-E. root

---

[1] See the Section on Vowel-Gradation, *infra* 44.

[2] This is the first appearance of Germanic metaphony, already alluded to, *supra* 22, note. The same influence which, in Pregermanic, had altered the *ĕ* before an *i*, more and more extended to other vowels in E. and G. This is the reason why we find such scanty instances of the mutation of *ĕ* (*supra* 23 E) separately in the two languages, and especially in English: *ĕ* was mutated before their separation.

[3] Final *ĭ* has vanished, but shows its existence through the metaphony it has caused.—Observe that L. *emere* preserves the meaning "to take" in the compounds *sūmere*, *eximere*, etc.

bhĕndh (to bind), Sk. bandh (to bind), bándh-u-s (a relation), Gr. πενθερός = *φενθ-ερό-ς (father-in-law), πειστήρ = *φενθ-τήρ (a cable), but Go. bind-an, O.E. bindan and E. to bind, O.H.G. bindan and G. binden; I.-E. root wē (to blow), cf. G. wehen, and L. ve-ntu-s, but E. and G. wind; I.-E. *péñqe (five), whence a probable derivation *peñq(e)-ró-s (fivefold), Go. figgr-s (finger), O.N. fingr, G. and E. finger.

The ĕ persists everywhere else. Only in O.H.G. it becomes ĭ, if the following syllable has a u: I.-E. *septm̥ (seven), Sk. saptá, Gr. ἑπτά, L. septem, Preg. *sebun, whence Go. sibun, O.E. seofon and E. seven, but O.H.G. sibun, M.H.G. siben, G. sieben.[1]

II. I.-E. ē has become, in Pregermanic as in Greek (η), a very open ē: from this have arisen, in Gothic and Old English, a very close ē, and, on the other hand, in Old High German, the still more open sound of ā. Examples are: I.-E. root ĕd (to eat), pf. *ēd-, Sk. ād-imá (we ate), Gr. (ἐδ-)ήδ-α-μεν, L. ēd-imus, Preg. *ēt-umé, whence Go. ētum, O.E. ǣton and E. (we) eat (pf.), O.H.G. āʒum and G. (wir) aszen; I.-E. root dhē (to place, to do), Gr. θή-σω from τί-θη-μι, L. fē-c-i, Preg. *ðē-ði-s (action), whence Go. dēþ-s, O.E. dǣd and E. deed, O.H.G. tāt and G. that; I.-E. root sē (to sow, to throw), Gr. ἵημι = *σί-ση-μι (I throw), ἧ-μα (a throw), L. sē-men (seed), Preg. *sē-ði-s (seed), whence Go. (mana-)sēþ-s (mankind), E. seed, G. saat; I.-E. root nē (to spin, to sew), Gr. νῆ-μα (tissue), L. nē-re (to spin), thus I.-E. *nē-tro- or *nē-tlo- (an engine for sp. or s.), Gr. νῆτρον (distaff), Go. nēþla (needle), E. needle, G. nadel.

§ 2. Short and long i.

(27) I. The ĭ is a very consistent vowel, as it remains unchanged in all the Indo-European languages, Pregermanic included: I.-E. root bhĭd (to split), Sk. bhĭd (id.) L. fĭdimus (pf.), Preg. *bĭt-umé (we bit), Go. bitum, O.H.G. biʒʒum and G. (wir) bissen, E. (we) bit; L. pisci-s, Go. fisk-s, O.N. fisk-r, E. fish, G. fisch; Sk. vidhavā (a widow), L. vidua, Go. viduvō, O.E. widewe and E. widow, O.H.G. wituwa and G. wittwe.

Before an r or an h, Preg. ĭ, in Gothic only, becomes ĕ (spelled

---

[1] The vowel lengthened in an open syllable, supra 20.

ai): I.-E. root *migh* (to be moist, to make water), Sk. *mih* (id.), Gr. ὀ-μῑχ-έω (id.), ὀ-μίχ-λη (a cloud), L. *ming-ere*, but Go. *maih-stu-s* (moisture, fog, mist)=E. *mist*=G. *mist* (dung),[1] the latter both preserving their *ĭ*.

In the five cases wherein *ĕ* becomes *ĭ*, *ĭ* of course remains unaltered. But, excluding these, Preg. *ĭ* is changed to *ĕ*, whenever the following syllable contains an *a* or an *o*: I.-E. *wĭr-o-s (man), L. *vir*, Preg. *wĭr-a-z, whence *wĕr-a-z, Go. *vair-s* (man), O.E. and O.H.G. *wër*, surviving in E. and G. *wer-wolf*, in E. *world* and G. *welt*[2]; I.-E. root *sed* (to sit), whence a compound *ni-zd-ó-s (home, nest), Sk. *nĭdá-s*, L. *nĭdus*, but Preg. *nistás becomes *nestás, G. and E. *nest*. This law, however, is not yet well defined and remains subject to some alternations, so that we are able to point to many such contrasts as: E. *to lick* and G. *lecken* (I.-E. root *ligh*, in Sk. *rih*, "to lick," Gr. λείχ-ω, L. *ling-ō*); E. *to live* and G. *leben*; E. *liver* and G. *leber*; E. *quick* (cf. L. *vīvus*=*gvīgv-o-s) and G. *queck* (cf. the vb. *er-quick-en*, "to vivify") in the compound *queck-silber*=E. *quick-silver*.

II. The *ī* is even more consistent than the *ĭ*: Pregermanic keeps it unchanged; Gothic pronounces it *ī*, though spelled *ei*[3]; in English and German, unless it has undergone later shortening, it is sounded *ay*, though written respectively *i* and *ei*.[4] I.-E. *sū-s (a hog), Sk. *sū-*, Gr. ὗ-ς σῦ-ς, L. *sū-s*, O.E. *sū* and E. *sow*, O.H.G. *sū* and G. *sau*; hence, a secondary I.-E. adjective *su-īno-s *sw-īno-s, used as a substantive in Germanic, Preg. *swīna-z, Go. *svein-s*, O.E. *swīn* and E. *swine*, O.H.G. *swīn* and G. *schwein*.

§ 3. *Short and long u.*

(28) I. I.-E. *ŭ*=Sk. *ŭ*=Gr. *υ*=L. *ŭ*=Preg. *ŭ*: I.-E. *kŭn-* (dog), Sk. *çun-*, Gr. κύων κυν-ός, Preg. *hunð-a-z,[5] whence Go.

---

[1] Because it steams. Thus, F. *fumier* (dung), which comes from L. *fimus*, is modified by analogy with the vb. *fumer* (to smoke).
[2] Supra 21, and the note on *wëralt*.
[3] Ulfilas borrowed this symbol from Byzantine Greek, where the old diphthong ει had contracted to *ī*.
[4] This spelling is due to the M.H.G. *i* having first passed through the sound of *ëy*, still preserved in some dialects, before it came to be pronounced *ăy*.
[5] The ð added in Germanic is of doubtful origin.

hund-s, O.N. *hund-r*, O.E. *hund* and E. *hound*,[1] O.H.G. *hunt* and G. *hund*; I.-E. root *dhŭbh*, with a vague meaning of infirmity or bodily defect, Gr. τυφλός (blind) = *θυφ-λό-s, Preg. *ðumb-a-z, whence Go. *dumb-s* (dumb), O.N. *dumb-r*, O.E. and E. *dumb*, O.H.G. *tump tum* and G. *dumm* (stupid); I.-E. *yúwen- (young), Sk. *yúvan-*, L. *juven-i-s*, whence a derivative I.-E. *yuwṇ-kó-s, Sk. *yuvaçás*, L. *juvencus*, Preg. *yuwuñzás contracted to *yuñzás, Go. *jugg-s*, O.E. *geong* and E. *young*, O.H.G. and Mod. G. *jung*, etc.

Under the same conditions under which Go. *ĭ* becomes *ĕ* (written *aí*),[2] Go. *ŭ* becomes *ŏ* (written *aú*): I.-E. *dhur-ó-m (door, cf. Sk. *dúr-* and Gr. θύρ-ā), whence Preg. *ðŭr-á-m, but Go. *daúr*.

We have seen that a following *a* or *o* changes *ĭ* to *ĕ*. Under the same restriction,—that is to say, everywhere but before a group of nasal and consonant,[3] and moreover with a serious number of exceptions,—Preg. *ŭ* becomes *ŏ*, if the following syllable has *a* or *o*: Preg. *ðŭr-á-m,[4] Go. *daúr*,[5] E. *door*, G. *thor*; I.-E. root *yug* (to join), *yug-ó-m (yoke), Sk. *yugám*, Gr. ζυγόν, L. *jugum*, Preg. *yukám (Go. *yuk*), whence *yŏkám, O.E. *geoc* and E. *yoke*, O.H.G. *joh* and G. *joch*; I.-E. root *ghu* ("to pour out," cf. Gr. χέ-ω χυ-τό-s, and "to offer a libation," cf. Sk. *hu-tá-s*, "offered in libation"), whence a participial form I.-E. *ghu-tó-s, "he who is worshipped through libation, a god," Preg. *ʒŭ-ðá-s, then *ʒŏ-ðá-s, Go. *guþ-s* (God), E. *God*, G. *Gott*, etc.[6]

II. I.-E. *ū* = Sk. *ū* = Gr. *ῡ* = L. *ū* = Preg. *ū*[7] : I.-E. root *pū*

---

[1] With regular lengthening before *nd*, supra 20, 4 B.

[2] Supra 27, I.—These phenomena are of no direct interest for E. or G., since they occur only in East Germanic; but they must nevertheless be briefly mentioned, or else the student would be unable to follow the phonetic correspondences.

[3] For the preservative effect of a nasal, compare the participles *swollen* and *geschwollen*, from *swell* and *schwellen*, with the participles *bound* and *gebunden*, *found* and *gefunden*, from *bind* and *binden*, *find* and *finden*.

[4] The quality of the vowel is proved by Preg. *ðŭr-i-*, whence O.H.G. *turi* and G. *thür* with metaphonical *ü*: supra 22.

[5] Thus, in Gothic, there are two reasons for the *ŭ* appearing as *ŏ*.

[6] It is obvious that, in spite of appearances, the regular metaphony of *o* must be *ü* (cf. supra 22 in fine): if *göttin* were an early word, it would be *güttin*; the *ö* shows it to have been a later derivation from *gott*.

[7] Whence, in English and German, a process of diphthongizing which runs parallel to that of *ī*: supra 18, 1.

(to be foul), Sk. *pūy* (id.), Gr. πῦ-θω (id.), L. *pū-s*, in a Preg. derivation **fū-lá-s*, whence Go. *fūl-s*, O.E. *fūl* and E. *foul*, O.H.G. *fūl* and G. *faul*; I.-E. root *rū* ("free space," cf. L. *rū-s*, "country"), in a Preg. derivation **rū-má-s*, whence Go. *rūm-s* (space), O.E. *rūm* and E. (exceptionally not diphthongized) *room*, O.H.G. *rūm* and G. *raum*. Further compare: E. *house* and G. *haus* = O.E. and O.H.G. *hūs* = O.N. *hūs* = Go. **hūs* (only in *gud-hūs*, "God's house, temple"); E. *thousand* and G. *tausend* = O.E. *ðūsend* and O.H.G. *dūsunt* = Go. *þūsundi*. We have already found *eu* for *au* in G. *deuchte*. It is less easy to explain in G. *euter* = O.H.G. *ūtar* (E. *udder* with shortening), cf. L. *über* = Gr. οὖθαρ = Sk. *údhar* (udder).

§ 4. Diphthongs of short e.

(29) To *ĕ* correspond the diphthongs *ĕy* and *ĕw*. Now, *ĕy* has been seen to become *ī* before a consonant and *y* before a vowel.[1] The treatment of *ĕw* is far more intricate. It might be said, in theory, to continue in the form *eu*, with the exception that Gothic, changing *ĕ* to *ĭ*, naturally changes *eu* to *iu*[2]: I.-E. root *gŭs* and *gĕws* (to examine, taste, choose, cf. L. *gus-tu-s*, G. *kos-t-en*), Gr. γεύω = **γεύσ-ω*, theoretically Preg. **keus-anam* (to appreciate, choose), then Go. *kius-an*. But, in fact, each of the elements which form the diphthong obeys exactly the same law that it would obey when isolated; in other words, as *ĕ* becomes *ĭ*, so also *eu* becomes *iu*, if the following syllable contains *i* or *j*; and, as *ŭ* is changed to *ŏ*, so *eu* is changed to *eo*, if the following syllable contains *a* or *o*; which is as much as to say that *eu* will hardly ever appear in its original form.

Afterwards, in English, *eu* and *eo* are sounded *ēo*, whereas *iu* becomes *ie* and *ȳ*[3]; in German, *eo* becomes *io*, and lastly *ie*, which ends by contracting to *ī*,[4] whereas *iu* contracts to long

---

[1] Cf. *supra* 26, I. 1, 2.

[2] It is seen here, and will still better be seen below, with what mathematical regularity the application of a phonetic law takes place throughout a language.

[3] Metaphonical vocalisms already mentioned, *supra* 22 in fine.

[4] Afterwards eventually shortened. The old diphthong is still very perceptible in South Germany: Alsatian *tiĕf*, *liĕp*, *liĕcht*, etc.; cf. G. *tief* (deep), *lieb* (dear), *licht* (light), pr. *tĭf*, *lĭp*, *lĭcht*, etc.

ü, which in Central Germany is diphthongized to *eu*.[1] Thus, an I.-E. root *dhub* (hollow, deep, cf. Lith. *dub-ŭ-s* "hollow") gives the I.-E. derivate **dhĕwbos*, Preg. **ðeupaz*, which becomes **ðeopaz*: hence, Go. *diup-s*, O.N. *djöp-r*, O.E. *dēop* and E. *deep*, O.H.G. *tiof* and G. *tief*. The same root before an *i* or a *j*, in Preg. **ðeup-janam* (to dive), becomes **ðiup-jan*, O.E. *dýfan* and E. *dive*, cf. also E. *to dip*.[2] These complex correspondences are still more complicated by the influence of analogy; for the two diphthongs *eo* and *iu* were too much alike not to be easily confused, so that the metaphonical form and the pure one largely usurped each other's legitimate place, though the pure one as a rule proved the stronger. The vb. **keusanam* quoted above, for instance, ought to be in the infinitive **keosanam* (O.E. *cēosan*, and O.H.G. *chiosan*), and in sg. 3 pres. indicative **kiusit* (O.E. *cīest* and O.H.G. *chiusit*); but Mod. E. actually knows no other stem but *choose* (the substantive *choice* being re-borrowed from French), and Mod. German, no other but *kies-en*. So again, a noun **leod-u-* had a pl. **liud-i*; but O.E. extends to the plural the non-metaphonical form, thus *lēode* (people); whilst O.H.G. carried into the sg. *liut* (a people) the metaphonical form which is regular only in the pl. *liuti*, G. *leute*; and there are many similar cases.

With this remarkable treatment of the Preg. diphthong *eu* may be classed numerous alternations; as, for instance, G. *licht* = O.H.G. *lioht* = O.E. *lēoht*,[3] and G. *leuchten* (to enlight); G. *ziehen* (to draw) = Go. *tiuhan* (cf. L. *dūcō* = **deucō*), and G. *zeugen* (to produce); G. *biegen* (to bend) = Go. *biugan*, and G. *beugen* (to inflect).[4] Lastly, the reader may compare: O.H.G.

---

[1] Just as *ū* is diphthongized to *au*; for long *ū* and *eu* are the metaphonical vowels corresponding to the pure ones *ū* and *au*. The old vowel is kept by the Southern dialects, which also preserve the *ī* and *ū* free from diphthongizing: Swiss *t'lüt* (long *ü*) and Alsatian *t'lit* = G. *die leute* (the people).

[2] G. *tuafen* = Go. *dáup-jan*, which has acquired the technical sense of "christening" (thus Gr. βαπτίζειν, "to dip, to christen"), shows, as a causative verb, the deflected grade of the same root. If G. had retained a neutral vb. "to dive" in this series of words, this would be Alamannic **tüfen* with long *ü*, and classical **teufen*. Cf. also O.E. *fýr* = E. *fire*, and O.H.G. *fiur* = M.H.G. *viur* = G. *feuer*, with Gr. πῦρ.

[3] On the E. *i* in *light*, see above 21, note.

[4] These verbs are causatives: thus, they had in I.-E. a diphthong *ŏw*, which has become Preg. *au* (*infra* 32); but the result is the same, since this

diota (people) and O.E. ðēod = Go. þiuda = I.-E. *tewtā, further O.H.G. diutisk (translated into L. theotiscus), now Teutsch and Deutsch (Alamannic tütsch and titsch), with the non-metaphonical forms still surviving in M.H.G. diet (people) and proper nouns as Dietrich (L. Theodoricus, F. Thierry). And above all should be mentioned the archaic conjugation of the vb. fliegen (to fly), viz. ich fliege, du fleugst, er fleugt, wir fliegen, which will be recalled at its proper place.[1]

§ 5. Short a and o, and their Diphthongs.

(30) I.—1. I.-E. ă = Sk. ă = Gr. ă = L. ă = Preg. ă: I.-E. *sáld (salt), Gr. ἅλ-ς = *σάλ-ς, L. sāl = *sǎld, Preg. *sǎlt, whence Go. salt, E. salt, G. salz; I.-E. *dákru (a tear), Gr. δάκρυ, L. dacru-ma (lacrima), Preg. *táhru *taȝrú, whence Go. tagr, O.E. *teahr and tēar (broken vowel), E. tear, O.H.G. zahar and G. zähre with metaphony; I.-E. *agró-s (field), Sk. ájra-s, Gr. ἀγρό-ς, L. ager, Preg. *akrá-s, whence Go. akr-s, O.E. œcer and E. acre, O.H.G. acchar and G. acker; L. scǎb-ere (to scratch), Go. skab-an (id.), E. to shave, G. schaben, etc.

2. I.-E. ŏ = Sk. ă ā = Gr. o = L. ŏ, but Preg. ă: I.-E. *ghortó-s (turf, enclosure), Gr. χόρτος, L. hortus, Preg. *ȝarǒá-s, whence Go. gard-s (enclosure), and cf. E. gard-en and G. gart-en, E. yard; I.-E. *yhŏsti-s "a foreigner," whence either "an enemy" or "a guest," L. hosti-s (enemy), Go. gast-s (guest), E. guest,[2] and G. gast; I.-E. *ŏktôw (eight), Sk. aštáu, Gr. ὀκτώ, L. octō, Go. ahtáu, O.E. eahtu broken, and E. eight, G. acht; I.-E. *ŏzdŏ-s (twig), Gr. ὄζος, Go. ast-s, G. ast, etc.

(31) II. Hence it must follow that the two primitive diphthongs ăy and ŏy unite in the Preg. ai. This is well kept in Gothic.[3] But in O.E. it has become ā, which in English is

au has again become eu through metaphony before the causative suffix -jan. Cf. supra 26, I. 2.

[1] Infra 206 B.—Of this development the reader may, if he choose, for the present, retain only the general conclusion in the following formulas which at first sight seem contradictory:
  Preg. eu changed to eo appears in Mod. G. as ie, i;
   „ eu „ iu „ „ eu.
[2] With the metaphony we also meet with in the G. pl. gäste.
[3] Here, as already observed, we always write it ái, in order to distinguish it from the false diphthong Go. ai, which is simply an open ě.

changed to ō. In Old German *ai* has only undergone the metaphony to *ei*, while M.H.G. *ei* has gradually returned to the sound of *ay*, so that it in no way differs,—excluding, of course, the Southern dialects,—from the *ay*, likewise spelled *ei*, which proceeds from O.H.G. $\bar{\imath}$.[1] As early however as O.H.G., the diphthong *ai* contracted to *ē*, when followed by *r*, *h* or *w*; see below *lehren* and *ewig*, and add here: Go. *sáivala* (soul), O.E. *sāwul* and E. *soul*, but O.H.G. *sē(w)la* and G. *seele*; Go. *sáir-s* (pain), O.E. *sār* and E. *sore*, but O.H.G., M.H.G. *sēr* (pain), the etymological sense of which is preserved in G. *ver-sehr-en* (to damage), and much weakened in G. *sehr* (very).[2]

1. I.-E. *ăy* = Sk. *ē* = Gr. αι = L. *ai œ* = Preg. *ai*: I.-E. **slaywó-s* (left, left-handed, awkward), Gr. λαιός = *σλαιϝό-ς, L. *lœvo-s*, O.E. *slāw* and E. *slow*, cf. O.H.G. *slēo*; I.-E. **ayw-* (time, age, century), Gr. αἰών = *αἰϝ-ών, L. *æv-o-m*, Go. *áiv-s* (time, eternity), whence the secondary G. *ewig* (eternal) = O.H.G. *ēw-ig*; O.N. *heit-r* (warm), O.E. *hāt* and E. *hot*, O.H.G. *heiʒ* and G. *heisz*; M.E. *bōthe* and E. *both* = G. *beide*; L. *cœd-ere* (to cut), Go. *skáid-an* and G. *scheiden* (to divide), etc.

2. I.-E. *ŏy* = Sk. *ē* = Gr. οι = L. *oi* (*ū* or *ī*), but Preg. *ai*: I.-E. root *wĭd* (to see), whence a pf. **wŏyd-ĕ* ("he has seen," so "he knows"), Gr. οἶδε = ϝοῖδ-ε, L. *vĭd-it*, Sk. *véd-a*, Preg. **wait-e*, Go. *váit*, O.E. *wāt* and E. *(he) wot*, O.H.G. *weiʒ* and G. *(er) weisz*; I.-E. **ŏy-nó-s* (one), Gr. οἰνό-ς, L. *ūnus* = *oino-s*, Preg. **ainá-s*, whence Go. *áin-s*, O.E. *ān* and E. *one*, O.H.G. *ein* and G. *ein*; compare the same *ā* mutated and shortened in O.E. *ǣnig* and E. *any*, cf. G. *einige*; Preg. root *lĭs* (Go. **leis-an*[3] "to learn"), forming a causative vb. which would be I.-E. **lŏys-éyō*, "I teach,"[4] whence Go. *láis-jan*, O.H.G. *lēren* and G. *lehren*, naturally the root we also find in O.E. *leornian* and E. *to learn*,

---

[1] In other words, classical G. pronounces *ein* like *scheinen*, whereas Alamannic says *ayn* for the one and *šinĕ* for the other, etc. Dutch (Low German) in the same way distinguishes *een* from *schijnen*. Cf. *supra* 17, 3, and 18, 1.

[2] The successive meanings would be: "with pain—with struggle—with intensity—very."

[3] Cf. the Go. pf. *láis* (he knows), which would be I.-E. **lŏys-e*, formed like **wŏyd-e*.

[4] Cf. *supra* 26, I. 2.

O.H.G. *lërnen* and G. *lernen*, which would be Go. **liz-n-jan* (to learn).

(32) III. A further consequence is, that the two I.-E. diphthongs *ăw* and *ŏw* unite in Preg. *au*. This is still retained in Gothic.[1] In Old English, strangely enough, it has become *ēa*, still mostly written *ea* in Modern English, but sounded either *ī* or open *ĕ*, as we have seen above, according as it stands in an open or in a close syllable. In German, *au* remains unchanged, apart from a slight *ou-* sound, and usually so spelled in O.H.G. writing; before a dental, however, as before *r, l, h,* and occasionally in other positions, O.H.G. *au* contracts to *ō*. These processes may be illustrated by the following instances.

1. I.-E. *ăw* = Sk. *ō* = Gr. *av* = L. *au* = Preg. *au* : I.-E. root *awg* (to increase), Gr. αὐξάνω, L. *aug-eō*, etc., Preg. advb. **auk* (besides, also), whence Go. *áuk*, O.E. *ēac* and E. *eke*, O.H.G. *auh* and G. *auch*;[2] I.-E. **kă(w)p-et-* (head, cf. L. *cap-ut*), Preg. **haub-iþ*, whence Go. *háubiþ*, O.N. *haufuþ*, O.E. *hēafod* and E. *head*, O.H.G. *houbit* and G. *haupt*, etc.

2. I.-E. *ŏw* = Sk. *ō* = Gr. *ov* = L. *ou ū*, but Preg. *au* : I.-E. root *rŭdh* (red, cf. Sk. *rudh-irá-s* = Gr. ἐ-ρυθ-ρό-ς = L. *rub-er*), whence a deflected derivative **rŏwdh-ó-s*, L. *rūf-u-s*, Preg. **rauð-á-s*, Go. *ráuþ-s*, O.E. *rēad* and E. *red*, O.H.G. *rōt* and G. *roth*; I.-E. root *dhŭbh* (bodily defect),[3] whence a similar derivation **dhŏwbh-ó-s*, Preg. **ðaub-á-s*, Go. *dáuf-s* (stupid), O.E. *dēaf* and E. *deaf*, O.H.G. *toup* and G. *taub*,[4] with contracted vowel *ō* in *toben* (to deafen).

We need not go back farther than Germanic itself in mentioning: O.E. *dēað* and E. *death*, G. *tod* = Go. *dáuþ-u-s*, and

---

[1] Written *áu*, as *ái* above, in order to distinguish it from the open *ŏ* which is spelled *aŭ*, *supra* 28, I.

[2] Thus, primitive *au* and primitive *ū* are no longer distinguishable from one another in classical German; but, like primitive *ai* and primitive *ī*, they are distinguished in the Southern dialects. Alamannic *au* (High Alsatian *ŏy*) = G. *auch*, but Al. *fūl* = G. *faul* (foul); and so also, *paue pŏye* = *bauen* (to build), *frau frŏy* = *frau*, *lauch lŏych* = *lauch* (leek), etc.; but *sūr* = G. *sauer* = E. *sour*, *hūs* = O.H.G. *hūs* (*haus*, house), *sufĕ* = G. *saufen* (to drink, from animals). The correspondence is constant, though High Alsatian has *sŏy* = G. *sau* (a sow).

[3] Already seen in τυφλός and *dumb* = *dumm*, *supra* 28, I.

[4] Compare the vocalism in High Alsatian *tŏyp* (deaf), and *tüp* (long *ü*) = G. *taube* = E. *dove*.

likewise *dead=todt, great=grosz*; O.E. *hlēapan* and E. *to leap*, O.H.G. *loufen* and G. *laufen* (to run)=Go. *hláupan*; O.E. *lēaf* and E. *leaf*, O.H.G. *loub* and G. *laub* (foliage); O.E. *lēak* and E. *leek*, G. *lauch*, the former shortened in the second term of the compound *gar-lic*, the latter shortened likewise in the dialectal *knobloch=knoblauch* (garlic); Go. *ga-láub-jan* (to believe), O.E. (metaph.) *gelȳfan* and E. *belief, to believe*, O.H.G. *gilouben* and G. *glauben*;[1] Go. *áusō* (ear, cf. Gr. οὖς, L. *auris*), O.E. *ēare* and E. *ear*, O.H.G. *ōra* and G. *ohr*; Go. *táuh* (he drew), pf. of *tiuh-an*, that is to say, I.-E. **dŏwk-ĕ* deflected from a root *dĕwk*, which is reproduced in L. *dūc-ere*, G. pf. (*er*) *zog* from the same vb. *zieh-en*, etc.

§ 6. *Long a and o.*

(33) The long *ō* which comes in Pregermanic from both I.-E. *ā* and *ō*, remains *ō* in O.E. and O.H.G., and then undergoes in Modern English and German a similar modification.[2]

1. I.-E. *ā*=Sk. *ā*=Gr. ā (Ionian-Attic η)=L. *ā*, but Preg. *ō*: I.-E. **bhāgó-s* (a certain tree), Gr. φᾱγός φηγός (oak), L. *fāgus* (beech), Preg. **bōká-s* (beech), whence Go. *bōk-s*, O.E. *bōc-trēow*, which would have become E. **book-tree*,[3] and E. *book*,[4] O.H.G. *buohha* and G. *buche* (beech), *buch* (book); I.-E. root *sthā* (to stand), derivative I.-E. **sthā-ló-s* (firm, anything that stands), Sk. *sthā-lá-m* (porringer), Gr. στή-λη (pillar), Preg. **stō-lá-s*, whence Go. *stōl-s* (throne), O.E. *stōl* and E. *stool*, O.H.G. *stuol* and G. *stuhl*; I.-E. **mātér-* (mother), Sk. *mātá*, Gr. μᾱτηρ μήτηρ, L. *māter*, O.E. *mōdor* and E. *mother*, O.H.G. *muotar* and G. *mutter*; so also, L. *fráter*=E. *brother*=G. *bruder*; Gr. ἡγ-έο-μαι (to lead), L. *sāg-īre* (to be acute), Preg. **sōk-jana-m* (to search), whence Go. *sōkjan*, pf. *sōkida*, O.E. pf. *sōhte* and E. *sought*,[5] O.H.G. *suohhan*, pf. *suohte*, G. *suchen suchte gesucht*, etc.

---

[1] Contrast High Alsatian *klŏyvĕ* (to believe) with *klüve* (long *ü*)=G. *klauhen* (to scratch)=O.H.G. *chlūbōn*.
[2] Cf. *supra* 18, 2.
[3] The extant form *beech* is metaphonical, O.E. sg. *bōc*, pl. *bēc*, cf. *feet* from *foot*, etc. But the pure form, shortened, appears in the compound *buck-mast* (actually "the food from a beech").
[4] Cf. the meaning of G. *buch-stabe* ("a letter," actually "a beech-stick"), because the first Runic writings were made of sticks.
[5] The infinitive *seek*=O.E. *sēcan* is metaphonical like *beech*. Cf. also the inf. *beseech*, with pf. *besought*.

VOWELS AND DIPHTHONGS.

2. I.-E. $\bar{o}$ = Sk. $\bar{a}$ = Gr. ω = L. $\bar{o}$ = Preg. $\bar{o}$: I.-E. *pôd-s (foot), Sk. pád, Gr. πούς πώς = *πώδ-ς, Preg. *fōt-s (Go. fōt-u-s, O.N. fōt-r), whence O.E. fōt and E. foot, O.H.G. fuoʒ and G. fusz; I.-E. root bhlō (to bloom, cf. L. flō-s), in derivation Preg. *blō-man-, whence Go. blōma (flower), O.E. blōma and E. bloom,[1] O.H.G. bluomo bluoma and G. blume; cf. the metaphony, in G. blühen (to bloom) = Preg. *blōjanam, and the shortening in E. blossom = O.E. blōstma; I.-E. root plō (fluid), Gr. πλω-τό-ς (swimming), Preg. *flō-ðú-s (flood), O.E. flōd, and E. flood shortened, O.H.G. flōt float fluat fluot, and G. flut, etc.

Without going beyond Germanic, we may quote: O.E. blōd and E. blood,[2] O.H.G. bluot and G. blut; E. stud and stud-book,[3] G. stute (mare); E. boy = *bōf-ig(?) diminutive to O.E. *bōf = M.H.G. buobe and G. bube.

SECTION III.

VOWELS IN FINAL SYLLABLES.

(34) By accurately observing the preceding laws, the student will find himself easily able to account for almost any vowel or diphthong of either language, and to identify it with the corresponding sound of the other language, or even of Greek and Latin. But the sounds which in primitive Indo-European stood in a final syllable underwent a peculiar treatment, which took place after Germanic had thrown back the word-accent to the first syllable.[4] The result is comparable to the process we may historically trace in the transition from Latin to French, as in pórtum (haven) becoming port, pórta or pórtam (door), or pórtat (he carries) becoming porte, and pórtās (doors, or thou carriest) becoming portes. We must distinguish the primitive vowels according as they were either themselves final or followed by a final consonant.

---

[1] Flower, of course, is borrowed from French.
[2] Also shortened. The metaphonical vowel appears in the vb. bleed = Preg. *blōð-janam; but the G. vb. bluten is taken from blut without metaphony.
[3] The metaphony in steed = O.E. stēda.
[4] On this recessive accent, see below 65, II.

§ 1. *Final vowels.*

I. Short.—**Every short final vowel** is kept in Pregermanic, and then **disappears** in all the dialects descended from it, without leaving any trace of its existence but the metaphony it may have caused.[1] Final *ŭ* survives only in Gothic and Old High German, but is dropped everywhere else: L. *pecŭ* (cattle) = Preg. **féhŭ*, whence Go. *faíhu*, O.E. *feoh*, O.H.G. *fëhu fihu* and G. *vieh*; Gr. πολύ (much), Go. *filu*, G. *viel*, etc.

II. Long.—**Every long final vowel** remains unchanged in Pregermanic, and then **becomes shortened** in Gothic and West Germanic;[2] whereupon, in the further evolution of the latter, it either gives place to a weaker sound, or is quite dropped;[3] lastly, the vowel, if preserved, has become even weaker or vanished altogether in Modern English and German.[4] Thus, the final *ā* in feminine nouns of the so-called 1st Greek declension (ἡμέρᾱ χώρᾱ) will be seen to have become Preg. *ō*, Go. *a = ŏ*, O.H.G. *a*, O.E. *u e* (a sound duller than *a*), Mod. G. *e*, and even completely dropped in Mod. English.

III. Diphthongs.—Primitive *ey* (as has been said) becomes *ī*. On the other hand, primitive *ay* and *aw*, if final, are sometimes retained in Gothic and spelled *ái* and *áu*, but elsewhere they contract to *ē* and *ō*. The consequence is, that in West Germanic every final diphthong is changed to a long vowel, and treated accordingly. The applications of this law will be met with on a large scale in the study of declension and conjugation.[5]

---

[1] Examples have been given above: 22, 26, I., 4, etc.—In point of fact, the law is more intricate than as here given, at least in West Germanic, and it depends on the position of the accent; but, as it was afterwards affected by many analogical influences, it will be better not to follow it in its arbitrary applications.

[2] This shows that the vowel was the same in Pregermanic; for, if it had been shortened there, the subsequent languages would have lost it altogether.

[3] A dull vowel, in a dissyllable with short first syllable; no vowel at all anywhere else: this is the rule, apart from analogical influences. Cf. *infra* 143, II., and 157, § 2.

[4] Cf. *supra* 19, 1.

[5] As, for instance, in the dat. sg. (152), in the nomin. pl. (143, II.), in the pres. subj. (192), in the pf. subj. (193, *sq.*), etc., etc.

VOWELS AND DIPHTHONGS. 65

§ 2. *Non-final vowels.*

I. Short.—Every short vowel in a Pregermanic final syllable is treated as if itself final, without distinction, whether the following consonant is itself dropped, or is preserved:[1] I.-E. *agró-s (field), acc. *agró-m, Sk. ájra-s ájra-m, Gr. ἀγρό-ς ἀγρό-ν, L. *ager agru-m*, Preg. *akrá-s *akrá, whence Go. akr-s akr, O.E. *æcer* and E. *acre*, O.H.G. *acchar* and G. *acker*; I.-E. *sūnú-s (son), acc. *sūnú-m, Sk. sūnú-s sūnú-m (cf. Gr. υ-ιό-), Preg. *sunú-s *sunú,[2] whence Go. sunu-s sunu, O.E. sunu and E. son, O.H.G. sunu and G. sohn, etc.

II. Long.—A non-final long vowel in a final syllable survives in Gothic and West Germanic and further undergoes in English and German the usual process of weakening: I.-E. *wl̥qos (wolf), pl. *wl̥qōs, Sk. vŕ̥kas vŕ̥kās, Preg. *wulfaz *wulfōz, Go. vulfs vulfōs, E. wolf wolves, etc.[3]

III. Diphthongs.—The law for a long vowel holds good for any diphthong.[4]

---

[1] On the treatment of final consonants, cf. *infra* 39, 1-2, 46 and 63.

[2] The short vowel, instead of the long one in Sk., is probably due to a different grade of root *sū* (to bring forth).

[3] In monosyllables, the long vowel or diphthong, whether final or non-final, always remains long: cf. the declension of the definite article, *infra* 129 sq.

[4] The investigation of Preg. finals is leading to new results. The reader to whom it is of interest may be referred to Hanssen's and Hirt's essays, in *Kuhn's Zeitschrift*, xxvii. p. 612, and *Indogermanische Forschungen*, i. pp. 1 and 195. But, as their leading principle, namely, the distinction between the acute and the circumflex accent on the final long syllable, cannot be said to find as yet any sure application except in Gothic, it need not be more than briefly mentioned here.

CHAPTER III.

SEMI-VOWELS AND CONSONANT-VOWELS.

(35) The correspondences of the semi-vowels and consonant-vowels being all of the utmost simplicity, it seems expedient to trace them at once from the Indo-European period down to our days. Having thus established the continuous descent of these mixed sounds, we shall further enquire into the conditions under which they alternately played, in the Indo-European speech, the part of consonants or vowels. This point will be discussed in the section on Vowel-Gradation.

SECTION I.

SEMI-VOWELS.

I.-E. had the two semi-vowels of i and u, viz. y and w, which, in certain positions, were able to form a syllable by themselves, inasmuch as they became changed to their respective vowels. Pregermanic, we have seen, represents the two vowels by i and u; we have also seen how it represents y and w, when following a vowel and forming a diphthong; the consonants y and w, so far as they survived, Pregermanic represented by $j=y$ (spelled Go. and G. j, E. y) and w (sounded v in Mod. German).

§ 1. *Semi-vowel y.*

(36) I. I.-E. initial $y=$Sk. $y=$Gr. ζ or rough breathing $=$ Lat. $j=$Preg. j: we have already quoted *yoke* and *joch*, *young* and *jung*, etc.; *you* and *euch* will appear among the pronouns; here we may add I.-E. root *yĕr yŏr* (a space of time), Zd. *yāre*

SEMI-VOWELS AND CONSONANT-VOWELS. 67

(year), Gr. ὧρος ὥρᾱ (time, season, year), Preg. *jēr-a-, whence Go. jēr, O.E. gēar¹ and E. year, O.H.G. jār and G. jahr.

II. **Medial.**—1. **Between vowels**, I.-E. *y* is kept in Gothic and O.H.G. (as also in Sk.), but dropped in O.E. and M.H.G. (as also in Greek and Latin), and thus vanishes, betraying itself only by the occasional metaphony: O.H.G. *bluo-jan*, G. *blühen* (to bloom); Go. **kiu-jan* (to chew), O.E. *cēow-an* and E. *chew*, O.H.G. *chiuw-an* and G. *kauen*, with the metaphony preserved in the compound *wieder-käuen*.

2. **After a consonant**, whether primitive, or arising from the primitive diphthong *ĕy*,² the *y* is preserved in Gothic; but, in the later dialects, it causes the preceding consonant to be doubled, and then unites with it and disappears.³ I.-E. **ten-yō* (I spread out), Gr. τείνω = *τέν-yω, O.E. ðen-ian (to spread out) and ðennan, O.H.G. dennen and G. dehnen (to extend).⁴ Go. hlah-jan (to laugh), O.H.G. hlahhen and G. lachen, O.E. (metaph.) hliehhan and E. laugh. I.-E. root stheg teg (to cover), Gr. στέγω στέγος τέγος (covering, thatch), L. teg-ō tog-a, etc.; hence, a derived noun, Preg. **þak-á-s* = I.-E. **tog-ó-s*, reproduced by Go. **þak* = E. thatch = G. dach; from this again is derived a denominative vb., Preg. **þak-jan-am*, Go. þakjan (to cover), O.E. ðeccan, O.H.G. decchan⁵ and G. decken (the latter three, of course, are metaphonical). The causative vb. of the E. to wake and G. wachen points to a Preg. **wak-jan-am*, whence Go. vakjan (to rouse from sleep), O.E. weccean, O.H.G. wecchan and G. wecken. To these may be added: O.E. settan (E. to set, G. setzen) = Go. sat-jan (to cause to sit); and Go. mid-ji-s (= L. med-iu-s), O.E. midd and E. mid, O.H.G. mitti and G. mitte.⁶

¹ For this *g*, see *infra* 50, II.
² See above, 26, I., 2.
³ As in Greek the λ in ἀγγέλλω = *ἀγγελ-y-ω.
⁴ The group *nn* shortened to *n*, whereupon the preceding vowel became long. Group *ll* in Go. vil-ja, E. will, G. wille.
⁵ More exactly *decchen*; for it is a law in O.H.G. that *j* changes a following *a* to *e*; but analogy has often made the law ineffective, that is to say, *decchan* was restored on the model of such infinitives as *sĕhan* (to see, now *sehen*) = Go. *saíhvan*, where the *a* had no *j* before it. See Braune, *Ahd. Gr.*, § 58.
⁶ It is not only before a *j*, but in several other positions, especially before a nasal or a liquid, that a preceding consonant is liable to be doubled in German words; further, as in the course of declension or conjugation

§ 2. *Semi-vowel w.*

(37) I. **Initial.**—1. **Before a vowel**, I.-E. w = Sk. v = Gr. Ϝ (dropped in Ionic and Attic) = L. v = Preg. w: we have already cited *wine* and *wein* (borrowed from Latin), *he wot* and *er weisz*, *wind* and *wind*, etc.; we may add *water* and *wasser* (Slav. *voda*), I.-E. *$w\underset{.}{l}qo$-s = Sk. *vŕka-s* = Go. *vulf-s* = E. *wolf* = G. *wolf*.

2. **Before a consonant**, the w, still sounded in Preg. and Gothic, is lost in German; in English it is nothing more than a written survival: Go. *vrit-s* (a scratch, an engraving), G. *ritz* (a scratch), O.H.G. *riʒan* and G. *reiszen* (to tear), *risz* (a rent), O.E. *writ-an* (to scratch), whence E. *to write*.

II. **Medial.**—1. Between vowels, w is retained, but unites afterwards with the preceding vowel, which thus assumes a slightly labialized sound. In such cases it may well happen that the w is no longer visible, even in spelling, as in *hue* instead of **hew, Tuesday*,[1] etc. Further instances are: E. *true* = O.E. *treowe*, and G. *treu* (faithful) = O.H.G. (*gi*)*triuwi*, contrasted with the deflected form of the same root in E. *to trow* = G. *trauen*; E. *snow* = O.E. *snāw*, and G. *schnee* = O.H.G. *snēo*, cf. Go. *snáiv-s*, pointing to a Preg. **snaiw-á-s* (L. *nix niv-em*); E. *tree* = Go. *triu*, related to Gr. δρῦς (gen. δρυός = *δρυϝ-ός) and to Russian *derevo* (tree).

2. **After a consonant**, primitive w is rather uncommon,[2] but generally survives: I.-E. **dwó-* (two) = Preg. **twá-*, whence Go. *tvái*, E. *two*,[3] G. *zwei*; I.-E. root *kwit* (to shine), derived I.-E. **kweyt-o-s*, Sk. *çvēt-á-s* (shining, white), Preg. **hwit-a-z*, whence Go. *hveit-s*, O.E. *hwīt* and E. *white*, O.H.G. *hwīʒ* and G. *weisz*. The group *nw*, however, is assimilated to *nn*: I.-E. **mánu-* (man), whence the secondary **manw-ó-s* (human, man),[4] Preg. **mann-á-s* (cf. Go. *manna*), E. *man* = **mann*, G. *mann*.[5]

adjacent sounds may vary (thus, nomin. *knabe*, gen. *knaben* with a nasal, etc.), the consonant is liable to appear alternately simple and double; whence arise such doublets as *knabe* (boy) and *knuppe, rabe* (raven) and *rappe* (black horse), etc.

[1] Cf. *supra* 17, 5.
[2] The common initial group *sw* will be referred to below, 59, II.
[3] Of course the *w* melts into the sound of the following *ū*.
[4] The *u*, before a vowel, must become a consonant (*w*). The prototype *manu-* is from Sk., where the progenitor of all men is called Manu.
[5] The treatment of *w* may sometimes appear very inconsistent; but it

SEMI-VOWELS AND CONSONANT-VOWELS.   69

SECTION II.

CONSONANT-VOWELS.

(38) The consonant-vowels, *i.e.* the nasals and liquids, as sounded in the Indo-European speech, were either consonants or vowels. In either case, their correspondences are very simple.

§ 1. *Nasals.*

(39) **The regular tendency of the nasals,** throughout the Indo-European family, **is to become** partly **assimilated to the following consonant,** that is to say: the nasal is labial if followed by a labial, dental if followed by a dental, etc. A language, therefore, must possess as many nasals as it has classes of explosives; for instance, four in I.-E., three in Preg., Gothic, English and German.[1] Moreover, if in the course of its evolution the articulation of any explosive happens to be changed, the preceding nasal is strictly compelled to vary in accordance with this change. Thus, the nasal was velar in I.-E. **péñqe* (five), and has remained guttural in L. *quīnque*; but it has become labial in Gr. (Æolic) πέμπε and Go. *fimf,* and dental in common Gr. πέντε and G. *fünf.*[2] This main point being settled, the nasals exhibit an exact correspondence in all languages.

I. **Consonants.**—1. Labial: I.-E. *m* = Preg. *m* everywhere retained, save in primitive finals. Such instances as *mid = mitte, room = raum,* etc., have already occurred. The reader may add: *comb* and *kamm* = Sk. *jámbha-s* (jaw) = Gr. γόμφο-ς

should be borne in mind, that its position was not constantly the same in the same word, because in declension or conjugation it was alternately medial and final. Thus, the *w* is final in the O.E. nomin. *geolo* = **geolw,* but medial in the gen. *geolw-es,* so that E. *yellow* appears as a compromise between the two forms. O.H.G. shows likewise a nomin. *gëlo* and a gen. *gëlw-es,* whence the doublet *gehl* (Alamann.) and *gelb*; cf. L. *helv-o-s* (yellow). And a similar change of *w* to *b* will be observed in such double words as *fahl* and *falb* (fallow), in *wittib* (widow), in *hieb* (a blow) and pf. *er hieb,* as opposed to *witwe* (L. *vidua*) and vb. *hauen* (to strike), etc.

[1] Cf. *infra* 52.
[2] The difference between Gothic and German arises from the *f,* as this letter is bi-labial in Gothic, but denti-labial in German.

(a peg), etc.; E. *mead* = O.E. *meodo*, and G. *meth* = O.H.G. *mëtu* = Gr. μέθυ (wine) = Sk. *mádhu* (a sweet and intoxicating drink); Go. *qiman*, E. *to come*, G. *kommen*; E. *to swim*, G. *schwimmen*; E. *lamb*, G. *lamm*, etc.

Primitive final *m* became Preg. *n* (Gr. *v*). The fact is seen only in the uncommon cases where this *n* has been preserved by the support of an affix: G. acc. *den* = Go. *þan-a* = Gr. τόν = Sk. *tám* = L. *(is-)tum*, and *tum* advb. accusative.

Apart from these exceptions, every final nasal is dropped in Pregermanic, and then the preceding vowel is treated as final:[1] Go. acc. *akr* (field) = Gr. ἀγρόν = L. *agrum*.

Again, medial *m*, when made final by the disappearance of the final vowel, becomes *n* in the O.H.G. period, whenever it existed as a grammatical ending:[2] dat. pl. O.H.G. *tag-um*, later *tag-un*, G. *tag-en*, from *tag* (day). A like change took place in the passage from O.E. to M.E.

2. Dental: I.-E. *n* = Preg. *n*, always preserved, except when originally final. We have already instanced *night* and *nacht*, *needle* and *nadel*, *snow* and *schnee*, *one* and *ein*, *son* and *sohn*, *man* and *mann*. To these we may add E. *can*, *ken*, *land*, *sand*, etc., and G. *kann*, *kennen*, *land*, *sand*, etc.

3. Guttural: I.-E. ñ = Preg. ñ, written *g* in Go.,[3] elsewhere *n*: I.-E. root *siñq* (cf. Sk. *siñc-ati* "he pours out"), Go. *sigq-an* (to dive), E. *to sink*, G. *sinken*; L. *long-u-s*, Go. *lagg-s*, E. *long*,[4] G. *lang*. Add E. *to drink* (Go. *drigk-an*), *to hang*, *finger*, *tongue*, and G. *trinken*, *hangen*, *finger*, *zunge*.[5]

---

[1] Cf. *supra* 34, § 2, I.
[2] In the other cases, the *m* is generally preserved for the sake of analogy, since it was not final everywhere: thus, *arm* (arm) has not become *arn, because there existed a gen. *arm-es*, and *nim* (take) could not be changed to *nin, because it belonged to the same series as the infinitive *nĕm-an*. We have, nevertheless, the contrasted forms: G. *boden* = E. *bottom*; G. *faden* (thread) = E. *fathom*; and the like.
[3] A spelling borrowed from Greek by Ulfilas.
[4] A nasal group changes a preceding O.E. *a* to *o*: thus, we have *man* and *mon* (now dialectal), *hand* and *hond*, *land* and *lond*. This pronunciation, however, was not Mercian, and therefore it has disappeared from classical English, leaving only such scanty survivals as *long*, *tong* = G. *zange*, *song* = G. *sang*, etc.
[5] The correspondences are very numerous. But E. *angel* and G. *engel* should not be included among them: the latter is Go. *aggilus*, borrowed

(40) II. **Vowels.**—An Indo-European nasal vowel becomes simply $\check{a}$ in Sk. and Gr. (a); Latin vocalizes the $m̥$ to *em* (*im*) and the $n̥$ to *en* (*in*); the Preg. vocalization results respectively in *um* and *un*,[1] whereupon the group thus obtained naturally follows all the laws which have been already stated as to *u*, *m* and *n*.

1. I.-E. $m̥$.—The I.-E. language had a root *sĕm*, signifying unity, which we recognize, for instance, in L. *sem-el* and Gr. εἷς = *σέμ-ς; now, when this root happened to lose the *ĕ*, there remained $sm̥$, as in the derived pronoun *$sm̥m$-ó-s* (a certain, whoever), which has become Sk. *sam-a-s*, Gr. ἁμ-ό-ς, Go. *sum-s*, O.E. *sum* and E. *some*. The same is the case with an I.-E. root *gĕm* (to go), Gr. βαίνω = *$gm̥$-yō, and L. *veniō* = *gvem-yō*: losing its *ĕ*, it gave rise to *$gm̥$-ti-s* (marching), Sk. *ga-tí-s*, Gr. βά-σι-ς, etc.; and this form again occurs in Go. (*ga-*)*qum-þ-s* (arrival, meeting), and G. (*aus-*) (*ein-*) (*zu-*)*kunft*, in contrast with G. *kommen* = Go. *qiman* = L. *veniō*. Gr. ἀμφί (around) shows that the related Sk. *abhí* (towards) must have contained a latent nasal, thus I.-E. *$m̥bhí$* faithfully reflected by O.H.G. *umbi* (around, towards), M.H.G. *umb*, G. *um*. Final *um* naturally becomes *un*: I.-E. *$dékm̥$* (ten), Sk. *dáça*, Gr. δέκα, L. *decem*, Preg. *téhum*, whence *téhun*, Go. *taíhun*, E. *ten*, G. *zehn*; and the same with Go. *sibun* = E. *seven* = G. *sieben*.[2]

2. I.-E. $n̥$.—The negative I.-E. particle was *nĕ*, Sk. *ná*: the *ĕ* being dropped, according to a general rule, when the word entered into a compound, the syllable was reduced to *$n̥$-, Sk. *a-*, Gr. ἀ- (both privative), L. *in-* (negative), lastly the well known negative Germanic prefix *un-*, as in E. *un-fair*, G. *un-rein*, etc., exact parallels to Gr. ἀ-σθενής (unforcible), L. *in-firmus*, etc. An I.-E. word *$sn̥tér$* (apart, without), mainly illustrated by Gr. ἄτερ (without), assumes in Germanic the form Go. *sundrō* itself from Gr. ἄγγελος (observe the metaphony produced in the *a* by the following *i*); whilst *angel* is O.F. *ángele* = L. *ángelum*, this also borrowed from Gr. If *angel* were a Germanic word, it would not be pronounced *ēnžl̥*, but *añgl*; cf. E. *angle* = G. *angel*.

[1] And, as a matter of course, *ṅ*, if vowel, becomes *uñ*: cf. E. *to drink* and *drunk*, G. *trinken* and *getrunken*, infra 181.
[2] The *n*, which should have been dropped as Preg. final, was preserved by the analogical influence of the ordinal numbers: Go. *sibun-da* (seventh).

(apart, but), O.E. *sundor* and E. (*a-*)*sunder*, O.H.G. *suntar*, G. *sonder* with its many derivates. Further instances are: I.-E. **ṇdhero-s* (inferior), Sk. *ádhara-s*, L. *inferu-s*, Go. *undar* (under), E. *under*, G. *unter*; I.-E. **mṇ-tó-*, L. *men-tu-m* (chin), Go. *mun-þ-s* (mouth), O.E. *mūð* = **mun-ð*,[1] and E. *mouth*, G. *mund*, etc.

§ 2. *Liquids.*

(41) The liquids, *r*, *l*, whether consonants or vowels, are reproduced with considerable exactness, both in Germanic and in the other members of the I.-E. family.

I. **Consonants.**—1. I.-E. *r* = Sk. *r* = Gr. ρ = L. *r* = Preg. *r*, preserved in the later languages.[2] We need but remind the reader of *red* and *roth*, *read* and *rathen*, *ride* and *reiten*, *brother* and *bruder*, etc. Let him further add: I.-E. **dér-ō*, Gr. δέρ-ω (I flay), Preg. **tér-ō*, whence Go. (*ga-*)*tair-an* (to tear), E. *to tear*, G. (*ver-*)*zehr-en* (to devour); L. *hester-nu-s* adjective, Go. *gistra-*(*dagis*) "yesterday," E. *yester-*(*day*), G. *gester-n*; I.-E. **priy-ó-s* (dear, cf. Sk. *priy-á-s*, id.), whence a derived Germanic vb. **frijōn* (to love), Go. *frijōn*, of which the pres. participle is *frijōnd-s* (friend), O.E. *frēond* and E. *friend*, O.H.G. *friunt* and G. *freund*[3]; Gr. καρπ-ό-ς (fruit), L. *carp-ere* (to gather fruit), E. *harv-est*, G. *herb-st* (vintage).

2. I.-E. *l* = Sk. *r* = Gr. λ = L. *l* = Preg. *l*, preserved in the later languages. I.-E. root *lŭk lĕwk* (to shine), Sk. root *ruc* (id.), cf. Gr. λευκ-ό-ς (white), L. *lūx lūc-em*, etc.: hence a derived noun, Go. *liuh-aþ*, O.E. *lēoht* and E. *light*, O.H.G. *lioht* and G. *licht*. I.-E. root *klŭ klĕw* (to hear), whence Sk. *çru-tá-s* (heard, famous) and *çráv-as* (glory), Gr. κλυ-τό-ς (famous) and κλέος = **κλέϝ-ος* (glory), L. (*in-*)*clu-tu-s*, etc.; the same word in the Germanic compound *Hlut-hari* (Merovingian proper name).[4] From the same root *klŭ*, after assuming the lengthened form *klū*, is derived a Preg. participle **hlū-ðá-s* (heard), whence:

---

[1] O.E. compensatory lengthening, *supra* 20, 4 A.
[2] Observe, however, that the *r*'s now extant are not all descended from a primitive *r*; for a great many of them are to be traced to a rhotacized *s* (*z*), *infra* 61, I.
[3] O.E. pure; the other forms show metaphony.
[4] Actually "he who has a *famous army*" (G. *heer* "army").

O.E. *hlūd* and E. *loud*, O.H.G. *lūt* and G. *laut* (loud), *laut* (sound); cf. the Swiss vb. *losen* (to listen). Gr. ἄλσος (forest) =*Fάλτfoς (?), G. *wald*, O.E. *weald* and E. *wold*, which latter became blended with *wood*=O.E. *wudu*=O H.G. *witu*.[1] This example, however, lacks certainty. But Go. *fugl-s* (bird), O.E. *fugol* and E. *fowl*, O.H.G. *fogal* and G. *vogel*, admits of no doubt.

(42) II. **Vowels.**—The I.-E. liquid vowels, $r̥, l̥$, only remain as such in Sanskrit ($r̥$). In the other languages they are accompanied by a slight indefinite vocalic sound, whence arise the various groups: Gr. αρ, ρα, and αλ, λα; L. *ŏr, ŭr*, and *ŏl, ŭl*; Preg. *ŭr, rŭ*, and *ŭl, lŭ*, respectively, according as the vocalic epenthesis is inserted before or after the liquid.[2] The *ŭ* afterwards undergoes the modifications required by the phonetic laws of each later language: thus, we have regularly Go. *aúr* and *ul*, E. and G. either *or* and *ol*, or *ur* and *ul*, as determined by the nature of the following syllable[3]; and eventually further lengthening.

1. I.-E. $r̥$.—I.-E. has a root *mĕr* (to die), Sk. *mar*, which is reduced to *m̥r* in such derivations as Sk. *m̥r-tá-s* (dead)=L. *mor-tuu-s*, and Sk. *m̥r-ti-s* (death)=L. *mors* (gen. *mor-ti-s*); another and no less correct formation would be *m̥r-tró-m*, with the meaning of "death-instrument,"[4] and this is reproduced by Go. *maúr-þr*, O.E. *morðor* and E. *murther murder*; cf. G. *mord*=*m̥r-tó-s*. Again, I.-E. has a root *kĕr*, with the sense of "head" and "horn," cf. Gr. κέρ-ας: the root is reduced to *k̥r* in Gr. κάρ-ᾱ (head) and κρά-νο-ς (helmet), L. *cŏr-nu* (horn), which latter (*k̥rnu*) is nearly related to Go. *haúrn*, E. and G. *horn*. I.-E. root *tĕrs t̥rs* (to be thirsty), Sk. *t̥r̥š-ti-s* (thirst), Go.

---

[1] Lost in Mod. German, though still visible in *wiedehopf* " whoop " (bird) =O.H.G. *witu-hopfo*, as we should say a " wood-hopper."

[2] The latter case is by far the rarer, and belongs to analogy rather than to phonetics. Let us consider an I.-E. root *bhrĕg* (to break), cf. the L. pf. *frēg-ī*: its reduced form *bhrg* has become Preg. *brŭk*, not *burk* (Go. *bruk-an-s* =E. *brok-en*=G. *(ge-)broch-en*); but the main cause of this difference is that the consonant and the vowel naturally tended to shift themselves to the same place they respectively occupied in the present and in the perfect (Go. *brik-a brak*, E. *break brake*, G. *brech-en brach*).

[3] Cf. *supra* 28, I.

[4] See Derivation, especially 79 (xiii). All these words have taken the sense of "violent death," while another stem assumed the more general meaning of " death."

paúrs-tei, O.E. (metaph.) *ðyrst* and E. *thirst*, G. *durst*, without metaphony; but compare the metaphony in G. *dürr* (dry)= O.H.G. *durr-i*=I.-E. **tṛs-i-*. L. *porca* (the ridge between the furrows)=I.-E. **pṛká*, O.E. *furh* and E. *furrow*, G. *furche*, etc. 2. I.-E. *ḷ*.—I.-E. **wḷq-o-s* (wolf), Sk. *vṛ́k-a-s*, L. *lup-u-s*, Preg. **wŭlf-a-z*, Go. *vulf-s*, E. *wolf*, G. *wolf*. I.-E. root *pĕl* (to fill), reduced to *pḷ*=Gr. πλα in πίμ-πλα-μεν (we fill), and likewise in the derivate **pḷ-nó-s* (full), Sk. *pūr-ná-s*, L. *plē-nu-s*[1]: hence we must infer a Preg. **fŭl-ná-s*, assimilated to **fullás*, Go. *full-s*, E. *full*, G. *voll*. I.-E. root *mĕl* (to grind), Sk. *mar* (to grind), reduced to *mṛ*: Gr. μύλ-η (millstone), L. *mola*, O.E. *myln* (metaph. instead of **mul-in*) and E. *mill*, O.H.G. *mulīn mulī* and G. *mülle*.[2]

Section III.

INDO-EUROPEAN VOWEL-GRADATION (APOPHONY).

(43) Whilst stating and exemplifying the forms of the I.-E. semi-vowels and consonant-vowels, we have been constantly led to suppose that they could appear, in the same word, either as consonants or as vowels, which is as much as to say that an **Indo-European root could alternately assume several aspects.** We have now to determine the laws of these variations. This will be the final effort of our inductive method, and the highest point we are able to reach in the prehistoric evolution of I.-E. vocalism: earlier, indeed, the terms of comparison are wanting; and later, the vocalic correspondences are obscured by the phonetic laws of each particular language. Hence it is only Indo-European which can give us the key to the vocalic change which is usually called **Vowel-Gradation** (F. *apophonie*, G. *ablaut*); a change which, simple as it is in principle, has produced many intricate consequences throughout all the languages of our family, inasmuch as almost every particular of their grammar is influenced by it, and especially the con-

---

[1] The long vowels in Sk. and in L. may be attributed to an I.-E. alternation between short and long *l*.

[2] These words, however, may as well have been directly borrowed from Late Latin *molīnum* (F. *moulin*).

jugation of the so-called strong verbs in the Germanic branch remains quite unintelligible unless we trace it back to this origin.

§ 1. *The Principle of Vowel-Gradation.*

(44) I. We must begin by examining the principle in the easier cases, which are likewise the more frequent, namely, when the primitive syllable contains an ĕ. Every such syllable, whether a root or a suffix, may successively exhibit three main **grades of vocalism**, which we denote by the terms "**normal**," "**reduced**" (weak), and "**deflected grade.**" In the first grade, the syllable keeps the ĕ; in the second, the ĕ vanishes entirely[1]; in the third, the ĕ is replaced by an ŏ. Supposing, for instance, a root *pĕt* (Sk. *pát-ati*, L. *pĕt-ere*) with the sense of "falling" and "flying": if normal, it is *pĕt*, Gr. πέτ-εσθαι (to fly), in the present; if reduced, it becomes *pt*, Gr. πτ-έσθαι (to fly), in the aorist of the same verb, and πί-πτ-ω (I fall); lastly, if deflected, it becomes *pŏt*, as in Gr. ποτ-άομαι (I flutter). So also, root *bhĕr* (to carry, Sk. *bhár-ati*, Gr. φέρ-ω, L. *fer-ō*), viz.: normal in φέρ-ω φέρ-ειν; reduced in (δί-)φρ-ο-ς (seat for two persons); deflected in φορ-ό-ς φόρ-ο-ς φορ-ά φορ-έω.

It is the province of morphology, whether derivative or grammatical, to determine the formations in which each of these three grades should regularly appear. Some few instances, however, of their occurrence will be stated below. As for the cause of the process, nothing could be more obvious; at any rate, as far as the normal and the reduced grade are concerned: a syllable is normal if accented, whereas it becomes reduced when the accent is shifted to another syllable, as may be inferred at once from the contrast in πέτεσθαι and πτέσθαι.[2]

---

[1] If the syllable forms a consonantal group which would be unpronounceable without an intermediate vowel, the ĕ is retained; in which case, of course, the reduced grade no longer differs from the normal.

[2] The Sk. language is by far the most instructive in this respect, because it has kept the original word-accent almost unchanged: for instance, the conjugation of *é-mi* (I go), *i-más* (we go), gives the reason for root *ĕy* being reduced to *i*, whereas Greek, having thrown back its accent throughout (εἶ-μι ἴ-μεν) merely preserves the mutation, the principle of which has disappeared. Some of these alterations, in accent and vocalism, occurred as far back as Indo-European, so that we find in it, here and there, reduced and accented

The change of ĕ to ŏ in the deflected syllable may perhaps also depend on accent, but this point has not yet been decided.

The instances quoted as yet assume that the variable syllable contained a single ĕ between consonants: if the ĕ is dropped, no other sound remaining that is able to support the syllable, the latter disappears as a syllable, and its consonants become supported by the adjacent vowels. But, if the ĕ was followed by any semi-vocalic sound, then, of course, as soon as it disappears, the following semi-vowel or consonant-vowel becomes changed to a pure vowel, in order to support the syllable which otherwise would be altogether unpronounceable; in other words,

to a normal grade ĕy, ĕw, there corresponds a reduced grade ĭ, ŭ,
„ „ ĕm, ĕn, „ „ m̥, n̥,
„ „ ĕr, ĕl, „ „ r̥, l̥,

the corresponding deflected grades still remaining, naturally, ŏy, ŏw, ŏm, ŏn, ŏr, ŏl, with ĕ changed to ŏ.

Thus, the I.-E. semi-vowels and consonant-vowels are consonants when they follow or precede a vowel, and vowels when they support a group of consonants.

It is in Greek and, though not so clearly, in Latin that these gradations can be best observed.[1] Let us then quote a single Greek example of each of the six types described above: pres. λείπ-ειν (to leave), aorist λιπ-εῖν, pf. λέ-λοιπ-α; fut. ἐλεύ(θ)-σο-μαι (I will go), aorist ἤλυθ-ο-ν, pf. εἰλ-ήλουθ-α; εἷς (one) = *σέμ-ς, ἁ- = *sm̥- in ἅ-παξ (once), and ὁμ-ό- (same) = *som-ó-; πένθ-ος (pain), aorist παθ-εῖν (to suffer) = *πn̥θ-εῖν, pf. πέ-πονθ-α; pres. δέρκ-ο-μαι (I see), aorist ἔ-δρακ-ο-ν (Sk. á-dr̥ç-a-m), pf. δέ-δορκ-α; pres. στέλ-λω (I send), passive aorist ἐ-στάλ-η (he was sent), στόλ-ο-ς (expedition). Similar instances occur in Latin: thus, tĕg-ō and tŏg-a; dīc-ō (I say) = deic-ō, and (causi-)dĭc-u-s (barrister); fug-iō and pf. fūg-i-t (he fled) = *foug-i-t; pĕndō (I weigh) and pŏnd-us (weight). Further, a few Latin roots appear even in all three syllables, or unaccented and normal syllables, just as Germanic has shown us metaphonical syllables which ought to be free from metaphony, and the reverse (supra 22).

[1] Sanskrit clearly illustrates the normal and the reduced grades; but, since it changes both the ĕ and the ŏ to ă, it has almost everywhere obscured the passage of the normal into the deflected grade.

grades, as they would in Greek: normal *fĭd-ō*=*feid-ō* ("I trust," cf. Gr. πείθ-ο-μαι "I believe"); reduced *fĭd-ēs* (faith), as in the Gr. aorist ἐ-πιθ-ό-μην (I believed); deflected *foed-us* (treaty)= *foid-os, as in the Gr. pf. πέ-ποιθ-α.

II. The second case where the normal syllable has no *ĕ*, but a long vowel, *ā, ē, ō*, is perhaps nothing more than a variation of the preceding.[1] However this may be, the vowel-gradation has assumed in it a different aspect. The three grades are as follows, the reduced and the deflected grade being respectively the same for the three classes, whilst in the third class the deflected cannot be distinguished at all from the normal grade:

normal *ā*, reduced *ä*,[2] deflected *ō*;
,, *ē*, ,, *ä*, ,, *ō*;
,, *ō*, ,, *ä*, ,, *ō*.

§ 2. *Germanic Vowel-gradation.*

(45) I. The syllable has an *ĕ*.—1. The *ĕ* is isolated, the type being *pĕt—pt—pŏt*: the Pregermanic correspondences would be *fĕþ—fþ—făþ*,[3] whereupon each of these syllables follows, in each later language, its own laws of evolution. Now Greek has shown us that the radical vowel in the sg. of the pf. regularly assumes the deflected state, in contrast with the present, which has usually the normal root; on the other hand, the past participle of strong verbs, when regularly derived, reduces the root: thus, these three forms, viz. present infinitive, past participle, and perfect in the singular, appear respectively the most convenient to exemplify the normal, reduced and deflected grade of any root.

Here, however, at the first step, we have to state an irregularity: roots of this kind are not capable of reduction in Germanic. In imitation of the few cases in which the reduced grade elsewhere kept the *ĕ*, Germanic has preserved it every-

---

[1] Inasmuch as the long vowel may proceed from some older contraction of the radical *ĕ* with another vowel.

[2] The sound which has become *ĭ* in Sk., and *ă* anywhere else, *supra* 25.

[3] Since I.-E. *ŏ* results in Preg. *ă*, and so forth. The reader will kindly refer to the vocalic correspondences stated above. Still more accurately the three grades would be *fĕþ—ft—fað* or *faþ*. But the text illustration is simpler for our present purpose.

where, so that its vowel-gradation, as far as regards isolated *ĕ*, only admits of two grades. Examples:

Normal: Go. *saíhv-an* (to see), E. (*to*) *see*, G. *seh-en*;
Reduced: „ *saihv-an-s* (seen), „ *seen*, „ (*ge-*)*seh-en*;
Deflected: „ *sahv* (he saw), „ (*he*) *saw*, „ (*er*) *sah*.
Normal: „ *gib-an* (to give), „ (*to*) *give*, „ *geb-en*;
Reduced: „ *gib-an-s* (given), „ *giv-en*, „ (*ge-*)*geb-en*;
Deflected: „ *gaf* (he gave), „ (*he*) *gave*, „ (*er*) *gab*.

2. Now to a root where the *ĕ* forms a diphthong with a *y*, I.-E. type *stĕygh—stĭgh—stŏygh* (to go up), the Preg. correspondences are *stīz̧—stĭz̧—staiz̧*, as may be easily verified:

Normal: Go. *dreib-an* (to drive), E. (*to*) *drive*, G. *treib-en*;
Reduced: „ *drib-an-s* (driven), „ *driv-en*, „ (*ge-*)*trieb-en*;
Deflected: „ *dráif* (he drove), „ (*he*) *drove*.[1]

The German deflected form would have become *treib, and would not have differed from the normal grade. The question how German came to lose this form must be reserved for further examination. But it still persists in some grammatical survivals, which were secured by their isolation from any analogical influence: G. *er weisz* = E. *he wot* = O.E. *wāt* = Go. *váit* = = Gr. Ϝοῖδ-ε (οἶδε). In this perfect the plural quite regularly passes to the reduced grade [2]: G. *wir wissen* = Go. *vit-um* = Gr. Ϝίδ-μεν (ἴδμεν).

3. If the *ĕ* forms a diphthong with a *w*, it gives us the I.-E. series *ĕw—ŭ—ŏw*, to which corresponds a Pregermanic series *eo* or *iu—ŭ* or *ŏ—au*, as follows:

Normal: Go. *lius-an (to lose), E. (*to*) *lose*, G. *lier-en; [3]
Reduced: „ *lus-an-s (lost), „ (*for-*)*lor-n* „ (*ver-*)*lor-en*;
Deflected: „ *láus (he lost) „ „ (*er*)(*ver-*)*lor*.

[1] O.E. *drāf*. Observe the difference in quantity between *drĭven*, and (*to*) *drive* = O.E. *drīfan*. In the G. *getrieben* the *ĭ* is lengthened in an open syllable.

[2] It will be seen that, in the plural of the perfect, the primitive accent was thrown forward to the ending, and the root consequently reduced; but in German and English, as in Greek, the vocalism of the plural became almost everywhere assimilated to that of the singular, or the reverse: *infra* 176, 3, and 177, 3.

[3] As conjugated in the well-known compound verb, Go. *fra-liusan*, O.E. *for-lēosan*, G. *ver-lieren*.

English has lost the deflected grade in conjugation, but shows it in the O.E. derivation *lēas*[1] (loose)=G. *los*. In German, owing to the later lengthening, the reduced has been blended with the deflected form; but they are still distinguishable in many other words, as in *ver-lus-t* (loss), and in *gieszen* (to melt, Go. *giut-an*, normal grade), reduced *gusz* (melting), deflected *er gosz* (he melted), etc.

4. The *ĕ* is followed by a nasal: I.-E. *ĕn—n̥—ŏn*; Preg. *ĕn* or *ĭn—ŭn* or *ŏn—ăn*; and these again further modified in West Germanic. As examples may be chosen the two I.-E. roots *bhĕndh* (to bind) and *nĕm* (to take, Gr. νέμ-ω).

Normal: Go. *bind-an* (to bind),   E. (*to*) *bind*,   G.   *bind-en*;
Reduced: „   *bund-an-s* (bound),   „   *bound*, „   (*ge-*)*bund-en*;
Deflected: „   *band* (he bound), O.E.   *bond*,[2] „   (*er*) *band*.
Normal: „   *nim-an* (to take),   „   *nehm-en*;
Reduced: „   *num-an-s* (taken),   „   (*ge-*)*nomm-en*;[3]
Deflected: „   *nam* (he took),   „   (*er*) *nahm*.

O.E. preserves the corresponding tenses *nim-an—num-en—nam*, whereas E. has lost the verb altogether. But let the student again compare, form with form, the three verbs:

Go.   *qim-an* (to come), *qum-an-s* (come),   *qam* (he came),
E.   (*to*) *come*,   *come*,   (*he*) *came*,
G.   *komm-en*,   (*ge-*)*komm-en*,   (*er*) *kam*,

wherein both G. and E.,—though they have obscured the normal grade by introducing into the infinitive the labial vowel of the participle, a process favoured moreover by the labial nature of the preceding consonant,—exhibit the deflected form as clearly as Gothic itself.

5. Lastly, the *ĕ* is followed by a liquid: I.-E. *ĕr—r̥—or*;

---

[1] Whence the E. suffix -*less*, *infra* 110, VIII.
[2] With *o* instead of *a* before a nasal, *supra* 39, 3, note. English has *bound*, through confusion with the past participle; but it has kept in the derivation the old word *bond* (a chain)=G. *band*, and the corresponding *band at least in the metaphonical form *bend*; E. *band* is borrowed from F. *bande*, which is itself taken from G. *band*.
[3] The double *m*, of course, as well as the *h* in *nehmen nahm*, is but a device to denote that the vowel in the one case is short, and in the other long.

whence Preg. ĕr—ŭr or ŏr—ăr, and the same series for l. Let us consider the two roots, I.-E. wĕrt (" to turn," Sk. várt-ati "he turns," L. vert-ere, the Germanic meaning being " to become "), and Preg. hĕlp " to help."

Normal: Go. vaírþ-an (to become), G. werd-en ;
Reduced: „ vaúrþ-an-s (become), „ (ge-)word-en ;
Deflected: „ varþ (he became), „ (er) ward.
Normal: „ hilp-an (to help), E. (to) help, „ helf-en ;
Reduced: „ hulp-an-s (helped), „ (ge-)holf-en ;
Deflected: „ halp (he helped), „ (er) half.

English has lost the former and the gradation in the latter; but O.E. has the corresponding forms: weorðan—worden—wearð, helpan—holpen—healp. In the plural perfect (reduced grade) Gothic has, also quite regularly, vaúrþ-um = O.E. wurd-on = G. (wir) wurd-en, which form, transported by analogy to the sg., occasions a German type ich wurde, existing side by side with the primitive ich ward.

II. If the syllable, instead of ĕ, has a long vowel ā, ē, ō, then the correspondences in vowel-gradation will theoretically be:

I.-E. ā ä ō | ē ä ō | ō ä ō
Preg. ō ă ō | ē ă ō | ō ă ō

Here, the second class is kept apart from the first and third classes, which latter become blended together, and further, do not distinguish the deflected from the normal grade. Thus the three are reduced to two, namely the sixth and seventh classes in our Germanic terminology.

6. The vowel is an I.-E. and Preg. ē, as in the I.-E. root dhē (to set, to do): normal Gr. θή-σω (I will set) and L. fē-c-it (he did); reduced θε-τό-s (placed); deflected θω-μό-s (heap). Preg. ē—ă—ō.

Normal: Go. lēt-an (to let), E. (to) let, G. lass-en ;
Reduced: „ lat-s (loose, idle), O.E. læt, „ lasz ;[1]
Deflected: „ (laí-)lōt (he let).

[1] The vowel-gradation is here much obscured by later processes in each language. We need only observe that the short æ in læt corresponds to a

Here G. and E. have no longer any trace of the deflected grade. But it may be seen in the offspring of the I.-E. root *dhē* quoted above, viz. E. (*to*) *do* = O.E. *dō-n*, and G. *thun* = O.H.G. *tuo-n*, in contrast with the normal grade we had already occasion to point out in the E. *deed* = G. *that*.

7. The normal vowel is an I.-E. *ā* or *ō*, Preg. *ō* in either case: normal Gr. στᾱ-σω στή-σω (I shall set), reduced στᾰ-τό-ς (placed); normal Gr. δώ-σω (I shall give), reduced δο-τό-ς (given). The Germanic correspondences are here irregular, inasmuch as the vowel in the normal grade has become the same as in the reduced forms, in order to maintain, as it were, with the utmost clearness the peculiar characteristic of the perfect tense, which otherwise would exhibit no difference in vocalism from the present. Thus, instead of *ō—ă—ō*, we have Preg. *ă—ă—ō*.

Normal: Go. *slah-an* (to smite), E. (*to*) *slay*, G. *schlag-en*;
Reduced: ,, *slah-an-s* (smitten), ,, *slai-n*, ,, (*ge-*)*schlag-en*;
Deflected: ,, *slōh* (he smote), ,, (*he*) *slew*, ,, (*er*) *schlug*.

German *schlug* = O.H.G. *schluog*, is quite regular, and English *slew* (pr. *slū*) is nothing but a conventional spelling for *oo* = *ō* (O.E. *slōg*).[1]

Germanic *ă*, whereas the long *ǣ* in *lǣtan* is a Preg. *ē* (*supra* 26, II.), now shortened in *let*, just as the *ā* in O.H.G. *lāʒʒan* appears now shortened in G. *lassen*. Thus the regular correspondences are quite obvious.

[1] This section, it must be remarked, belongs to the study of conjugation almost as much as to phonetics; wherefore, important as it is, it cannot be thoroughly understood, unless we subjoin to it the theory of strong perfects and past participles, as explained below 175-184.

CHAPTER IV.

EXPLOSIVE CONSONANTS AND THEIR SUBSTITUTES.

(46) The first view of the consonantal system in both English and German shows us the impossibility of studying the explosives and the spirants apart from one another; for we often find an English spirant corresponding to a German explosive, or the reverse. It is, therefore, convenient to compare together, in the same chapter, the **explosives of both languages**, and the **spirants of either** where these are merely **substitutes for explosives of the other**. Of course, such sounds as exhibit the character of spirants in both form a class by themselves.

Here, at the beginning, a general restriction is necessary: none of the laws that will be stated below can apply either to a final explosive or to its substitute, because **every Indo-European final consonant** (properly so-called), **with the single exception of** *s*, **is dropped in Pregermanic**, and leaves no trace of its former existence in the later languages [1]; whereupon the vowel preceding the lost consonant is treated in its turn as a final vowel.[2] As for such consonants as became final after the loss (in Germanic) of a final vowel, we scarce need observe that they were primitively medial, and consequently are comprised as such in the following exposition.

---

[1] The same is known to happen in Greek; cf. Henry, *Comp. Gr. of Gr. and Lat.*, no. 65. Occasionally the consonant is kept, in the very rare case when it was covered by an affixed vocalic particle: cf. G. *dasz* = E. *that* = Go. *þat-a* = Sk. *tád*, in the declension of the article, *infra* 130.

[2] Cf. *supra* 34, § 2.

Section I.

THE SECOND CONSONANTAL SHIFTING.

(47) In considering, in English and German, such instances as *to think* and *dünk-en*, *thumb* and *daum-en*, *thin* and *dünn*, *thorn* and *dorn*, which might be indefinitely multiplied, we see at once that German uniformly represents the English voiceless spirant[1] by a voiced explosive of the same order.

Now, if we glance at the other languages of the Germanic family, we find in them, with equal consistency, the same spirant as in English: Go. *þagk-jan* (to think); O.N. *þum-all* (thumb), which would be Go. **þum-al-s*; O.N. *þunn-r* (thin), which would be Go. **þunnu-s*; Go. *þaúrnu-s* and O.N. *þorn* (thorn), etc. Thus, at the outset, we are led to the supposition that English has preserved an old and Pregermanic consonantal state which became in some way modified in High German.

Looking for further contrasts, still in the same order of consonants (dentals), and at the beginning of a word, we find, for instance, *death* and *tod*, *deed* and *that*, *day* and *tag*, etc., that is to say, a German voiceless explosive corresponding to an English voiced explosive; and here, again, the related languages are at one with English, Go. *dáuþu-s* (death), *dēþ-s* (deed) and O.N. *dāð*, Go. *dag-s* and O.N. *dag-r* (day).[2] Further, we find *tongue* and *zunge*, *timber* and *zimmer* (room),[3] *ten* and *zehn*, namely a voiceless simple consonant in English corresponding to a voiceless double one in German; and again it is the English sound we find in Go. *tuggō* (tongue), *ga-timr-jan* (to build, to timber), *taíhun* (ten), O.N. *tunga*, *timbr*, Swede *tiv* (ten), etc.

If we pass from the dentals to the two other orders of consonants, gutturals and labials, a series of similar phenomena occur, though with less exactness and regularity, so that the whole process here described may be summed up in a brief and

---

[1] Occasionally voiced (*the* = *die*, *that* = *das*, *thou* = *du*), in consequence of an English process of softening which will be explained, *infra* 49, I. 2.

[2] In this and the following case, Low German agrees with English.

[3] The etymological meaning is still seen in *zimmer-mann* (carpenter) and similar words.

provisional phonetic law, which our further analysis will define with greater precision, as follows :

The Pregermanic consonantal state seems to have been preserved almost unaltered in East and North Germanic, and likewise in the English and Low German branches of West Germanic, whereas High German shows a general tendency to substitute, in each order, a voiced explosive for a voiceless spirant (*d* for *þ*), a voiceless explosive for a voiced explosive (*t* for *d*), and a voiceless spirant for a voiceless explosive (*z*=*ts* for *t*).

This principle was discovered by Grimm, though he assigned to it some effects which are now known to stand beyond its reach. It is the second Grimm's law or Second Consonantal Shifting (*zweite Lautverschiebung*), so called in opposition to the first consonantal shifting, which is common to all the Germanic dialects, and must, therefore, be deemed much earlier. We cannot go back to the latter, until we have traced, throughout each order of English and German consonants, al the consequences of the former.

§ 1. *Labials.*

(48) I. Since our formula has been said to be of a provisional and approximate character, we cannot illustrate it better than by particularizing a case in which it proves ineffective, German having kept without alteration the Germanic consonantal type. This is the case of the voiceless labial spirant *f*, which appears common to all the Germanic dialects, though it will be seen further on to proceed from an Indo-European explosive.

1. **Preg.** *f* = E. *f* = G. *f* (often written *v*).[1]

Examples are: Go. *fadar*, E. *father*, G. *vater*; Go. *fisk-s*, O.N. *fisk-r*, E. *fish*, G. *fisch*; O.N. *flesk*, E. *flesh*, G. *fleisch*; Go. *fugl-s*, E. *fowl*, G. *vogel*; Go. *fimf-taihun* and *fimf tigjus*, E. *fif-teen* and

---

[1] This is merely conventional spelling, the actual pronunciation being always *f*. As to the origin, however, of the double orthography, the reader may consult Wilmanns' *D. Gr.*, § 93, 94 : Preg. *f* primitively differed from German *f* = Preg. *p*, *infra* III.

fíf-ty, G. *fünf-zehn* and *fünf-zig*; O.N. *stıf-r*, E. *stiff* (= O.E. *stīf*), G. *steif*; Go. *vulf-s*, E. *wolf*, G. *wolf*; O.E. advb. *sōfte* = E. *soft*[1] = G. *sanft*, etc.

2. E. *f* between two vowels becomes voiced and softened to *v*: cf. the plural *wolv-es* = O.E. *wulf-as*, and G. *wölf-e*; E. *oven* = O.E. *ofen* = O.N. *ofn* = G. *ofen*; E. *shovel* = O.E. *sceofl* = G. *schaufel*.[2] This process of softening extends to all spirants.

II. From the voiceless spirant we now pass to the voiced spirant (b̌), written *v* in English. Here the German sound no longer appears the same: it is an explosive, the voiced *b* as in G. *geben* = E. *give*, G. *schaben* (to scrape) = E. *shave*. German, however, exhibits some remains of an earlier b̌, inasmuch as the spirant has been kept, though unvoiced, before a voiceless consonant, in such derivatives as G. *gif-t* (poison) = E. *gif-t*,[3] G. *schaf-t* = E. *shaf-t*,[4] etc. Thus, here as elsewhere, and according to the testimony of German itself, the English spirant is the original consonant, viz.:

1. Preg. b̌ = E. *v* = G. *b*.

Examples: Go. *gib-an*, O.N. *gef-a*, O.E. *gif-an*[5] and E. (*to*) *give*, O.H.G. *gëb-an* and G. *geb-en*: Go. *skab-an* (to scratch, to scrape), O.N. *skaf-a*, O.E. *sceaf-an* and E. (*to*) *shave*, O.H.G.

---

[1] The word *sănfte* has become O.E. *sŏnfte* under the influence of the nasal, and then *sōfte* through compensatory lengthening, lastly *soft* as shortened before a group of consonants. Here the *ŏ* could not return to *ă* (as it did in O.E. *mon* which is now E. *man*), because it had been lengthened in the meantime.

[2] Even in other positions, the student will find, in English as elsewhere, some irregular processes of softening or strengthening, which are very easy to explain. Such a word as O.E. *fíf*, if occurring before a voiced consonant, as for instance in the collocation *fíf dagas* (five days), could not but be sounded as *fiv*, which form extending throughout became E. *five*. These assimilating shiftings of a voiceless to a voiced consonant, or of a voiced to a voiceless consonant, are occasionally to be met with in any spoken language, especially in familiar speech, so that this observation will not need repetition.

[3] Strange as it is, the German euphemism becomes quite intelligible when compared with F. and E. *poison*, which means really nothing more than "drink" Lat. *pōtiōnem*.

[4] Literally "[a thing] scraped or planed."

[5] Go. *b* between vowels is a b̌, as noted above. O.N. and O.E. *f*, in the somewhat clumsy orthography of these languages, is an ambiguous symbol which may correspond either to the voiceless or the voiced spirant. Here no doubt it stands for a *v*.

scab-an and G. *schab-en*; Go. *ibn-s* (plane), O.E. *efn* and E. *even*, O.H.G. *ëban* and G. *eben*; Go. *liuf-s* (gen. *liub-is*), O.N. *ljūf-r*, O.E. *lēof* and E. *lief*, O.H.G. *liob* and G. *lieb* (dear); Go. *kalb-ō* (a female calf), whereof the msc. would be **kalf-s*, O.N. *kalf-r*, O.E. *cealf* and E. *calf*, O.H.G. *chalb* and G. *kalb*. From the last two instances we may infer that, in contrast with the change of intervocalic f to $v = b$, original b becomes shifted to f when final in English; compare the voiced consonant kept in E. *love* = G. *liebe*, E. pl. *wives*[1] of sg. *wife* = O.E. *wīf* = G. *weib*, E. *to live* = G. *leben*, but substantive *life*, etc.

2. If under the influence of an adjacent voiceless consonant, primitive b has been unvoiced (f), it then naturally obeys the same law as f, that is to say, it is preserved in German as well as English: compare the instances quoted above, and add G. *hälf-te* derived from **halb* = E. *half* = G. *halb*.

3. **Preg. b, when initial or medial after a nasal, was changed to b** in the Pregermanic period, wherefore it appears as such in all the later languages.[2] Hence in this respect again English and German are in full agreement. We have already given: *book* = *buch*, *beech* = *buche*, *bull* = *bulle*, *to bind* = *binden* etc. Here we may add: E. *to bite* = G. *beiszen* (Go. *beitan*), and E. *bit* = G. *bisz*; E. *buck* = G. *bock* (he-goat); E. *brother* = G. *bruder* (Alam. *pruader*); E. *bride* (with metaphony) = G. *braut*; E. *bone* (O.E. *bān*) = G. *bein* = Preg. **bain-*; E. *to blow* = G. metaph. *blähen* (cf. O.E. *blāwan*); E. *beard* = G. *bart*; and a great many others. After a nasal: E. *comb* = G. *kamm*; E. *womb* = G. *wamme*; because the group *mb*, though kept in English spelling, here becomes nearly assimilated to *mm*, and completely assimilated to it in German writing and pronunciation.

[1] German also has a general tendency to unvoice every voiced final consonant, a process which even influenced the orthography of M.H.G., such words being there preferably spelled *liep*, *kalp*, etc. (but *lieb-en*, *kelb-er*). The spelling has now been made uniform, and literary German spells *lieb*, *hand*, *tod*, though the actual sound is rather *līp*, *hant*, *tōt*, etc.

[2] But Alamannic, as we have often remarked, changes it to *p*. This is the reason why Grimm, considering that Alamannic here underwent a "shifting" (*verschiebung*) which he missed in High German, wrongly deemed that dialect to be the only true representative of the *Hochdeutsch*, and favoured it with the title of *Strengalthochdeutsch*. *Supra* 47 in fine.

III. We have now traversed the whole system of Pregermanic labials, with the exception of the voiceless explosive, English *p*.

1. E. *p* never corresponds to G. *p*, unless it stands in the group *sp*. Compare: E. *to spew* and G. *spei-en*; E. *to spin* and G. *spinn-en*; E. *spear* and G. *speer*.

2. Everywhere else we find the correspondence already mentioned in our general formula, namely, the G. voiceless spirant instead of the E. voiceless explosive, thus:

Preg. *p* = E. *p* = G. *pf* or *ff* or *f*.

The High German change is as follows: the *p*, first, developed after itself an aspirate, *ph*; then, the aspirate *ph* became *pf*,[1] which remained when initial. But, when medial, the explosive combined with the following spirant, the group thus resulting in *ff*:[2] Go. *vaírp-an* (to throw), E. *to warp*, O.H.G. *wërpf-an wërfan*, G. *werfen*; Go. (*ga-*)*skapjan*, O.E. *scyffan* and E. *to shape*, O.H.G. *scepfen* and *scaffan*, G. *schöpfen* and *schaffen*; E. *sleep*, G. *schlaf*, *schlafen*, and *schlaff* (lazy). Initial *p* is very rare in Pregermanic,[3] and can scarcely be found anywhere but in the early borrowings from Latin adopted by the West Germanic speech, but here at least it is quite common: L. *patina*, E. *pan*, G. *pfanne*; L. *pālus*, E. *pale*, G. *pfahl*; L. *pondō*, E. *pound*, G. *pfund*; L. *pāvō*, E. *pea*(*-cock*), G. *pfau*; L. *planta*, E. *plant*, G. *pflanze*; L. *Pentecosta* "fiftieth [day]," G. *Pfingst-en* (Whitsunday); Late L. *paraveredus* (cf. F. *palefroi* and E. *palfrey*), O.H.G. *pfarifrid*, G. *pferd* (horse), etc.

IV. Putting together the results of the last paragraph and those we had already obtained[4] in regard to the Pregermanic

---

[1] Cf. *supra* 14, 3 A.
[2] Reduced to simple *f* after a long syllable. In certain dialects initial *pf* likewise became *f*, whereas on the contrary, in certain others, medial *pf* survived; lastly, the Low German dialects, which keep the *p* unaltered, introduced a few words into High German: hence the existence of such double forms as *flaum* and *pflaum* (Lat. *plūma*), *schaffen* (to work) and *schöpfen* (to create, a false spelling for the regular metaphonical *schepfen*), *pabst* (pope) and *pfaffe* (priest) = Late Lat. *papa*. Further, for these insignificant variations, we must always take into account the process of spontaneous reduplication in Germanic explosives, as stated above, no. 36 note.
[3] The reason will be seen below (57, I.).
[4] Cf. *supra* 37.

labials, we may summarise the correspondences between these consonants as follows:—

explosives $\begin{cases} \text{voiced} & : \text{E. } b = \text{G. } b; \quad\quad\quad \text{G. } b \quad\quad = \text{E. } v, f, b. \\ \text{voiceless}: & \text{„ } p = \text{ „ } pf, f\!f, f, p; \text{ „ } p \quad\quad = \text{ „ } p \text{ (rare).} \end{cases}$

spirants $\begin{cases} \text{voiced} & : \text{„ } v = \text{ „ } b, f, w; \quad\quad \text{„ } w \quad\quad = \text{ „ } w. \\ \text{voiceless}: & \text{„ } f = \text{ „ } f, b; \quad\quad\quad\text{„ } f, f\!f, pf = \text{ „ } f, p. \end{cases}$

§ 2. *Dentals.*

(49) I. We have already stated the general correspondence :

1. Preg. þ = E. þ (written O.E. ð, E. *th*) = G. *d*.

In other words, the voiceless dental spirant, kept everywhere else, first became in German a voiced spirant (ð) in all positions, and then this spirant was changed to the corresponding explosive,[1] just as b was shifted to *b*. Further instances are: O.E. ðurh and E. *through*, O.H.G. *duruh* and G. *durch*; Go. þúsundi, O.E. ðúsend and E. *thousand*, O.H.G. *dúsunt túsunt* and G. *tausend*[2]; E. *path* = G. *pfad*; Go. *anþar* (other, second) = Sk. *ántara-s*, whence O.E. *anðer, *onðer, lastly öðer = E. *other*, O.H.G. *andar* and G. *ander*; Go. *brōþar* = L. *fräter*, O.E. *brōðor* and E. *brother*, O.H.G. *bruoder pruoder* and G. *bruder*; O.N. *fjoþr*, O.E. *feðer* and E. *feather*, O.H.G. *fëdara*, M.H.G. *vëdere* and G. *feder*, etc.

2. From the last three examples it follows that, in English and between two vowels, just as *f* becomes *v*, so þ is voiced and softened to ð, leaving, however, the spelling unchanged. Now, initial *th* also may occasionally become voiced, either owing to the weak accent of the little words in which this softening is seen,[3] or because,—since these words became one with the preceding word, in such collocations as *by thee, to them, do that*, etc.,—the *th* actually stood between two vowels. Analogy after-

---

[1] A similar shifting is to be observed in some dialectal or bad pronunciations of Modern English, *de = the, dey = they, dat = that*, etc., and in Low German throughout.

[2] An apparent irregularity in Modern German, owing to a later alternation between *d* and *t*, as shown by the hesitation in O.H.G. spelling. The irregularity E. *father* = G. *vater*, E. *mother* = G. *mutter*, etc., is more puzzling; but here English is answerable for the discord, *infra* II. 2.

[3] On the effect of atony, see below 66, II. 4.

wards extended the voiced pronunciation to other cases, such as *thou, they, their,* and so forth.

3. The Germanic group *lþ* had become *ld* in O.E., as later in German: whence the complete identity in E. *gold* = G. *gold* = Go. *gulþ* ; E. *wild* = G. *wild* = Go. *vilþei-s*, etc.

II. Preg. ð has undergone the same changes as Preg. ƀ, with the only difference that the former passed through a phonetic grade more. Initial, or medial after a nasal, it became Preg. *d*, but was kept as ordinary medial ð, and is still seen as such in the Gothic survivals; in West Germanic, this ð again was changed to *d* in all positions, a grade in which it continues throughout in English; lastly, High German shifts the *d* to *t*, in any position[1] except when following a nasal.[2] Hence the following simple correspondences :

1. Preg. ð = E. *d* = G. *t* when initial. Examples as above, and also: Go. *daúhtar*, O.E. *dohtor* and E. *daughter*, O.H.G. *tohter* and G. *tochter*; Go. *dius* (wild beast), O.E. *dēor* and E. *deer*, O.H.G. *tior* and G. *thier*[3]; Go. *dreiban*, O.E. *drīfan* and E. *to drive*, O.H.G. *trīban* and G. *treiben*; O.N. *draum-r*, E. *dream*, O.H.G. *troum* and G. *traum*, etc.

2. Preg. ð = E. *d* = G. *t* when medial : Go. *fadar*,[4] O.N. *faðer*, O.E. *fæder*, O.H.G. *fater* and G. *vater*; O.N. *mōðer*, O.E. *mōdor*,[5] O.H.G. *muotar* and G. *muiter*; Go. *nadr-s*, O.N. *naðr*,

---

[1] It must of course be understood that the whole process had taken place before—and perhaps a very long time before—the existence of the new voiced spirant ð, which has been seen to arise in German from a Preg. þ, and then not to have advanced beyond the grade of *d*; else, the latter would have become blended with the former, and both would have advanced to the grade of *t*. The consonantal shifting is unintelligible, if supposed to have taken place "at once," as it was described in Grimm's times: on the contrary, it should always be borne in mind that this shifting is only the main result of many little causes, which, though similar in their principle, wrought their effects successively and at long intervals. The importance of chronology in phonetics (*supra* 20, note) can be nowhere more deeply felt.

[2] As a matter of fact, the *d* became O.H.G. *t* even after a nasal (*bintan, blintēr*); but the group *nt* was generally softened to M.H.G. *nd* (*binden, blinder*) : so that the result is the same. Cf. however E. *under* = G. *unter*.

[3] The original meaning still seen in *thier-garten*. And so too, E. *deer* with the general sense of "game," down to the time of Shakespeare (once, *King Lear*, III. 4, 144).

[4] The reader must not forget that Go. intervocalic *d* is a ð.

[5] Here, Mod. E. has the Go. and O.N. consonant, *father, mother*; this, however, is not a survival, but a restoration, and a very late one, being hardly

O.E. *nœddre* and E. *adder*,[1] O.H.G. *natara* and G. *natter*, cf. also *middle* = *mittel*, *saddle* = *sattel*, etc. ; Go. *mōd-s* (anger, gen. *mōd-is*), O.E. *mōd* and E. *mood*, O.H.G. *muot* and G. *muth* (courage) ; cf. also E. *tide* = G. *zeit* (time), E. *seed* = G. *saat*, etc.

3. Preg. ð, then *d* = E. *d* = G. *d*, after a nasal : compare *hand* and *hand* (O.H.G. *hant*, M.H.G. *hant* owing to the unvoiced final), *land* and *land*, *bind* and *binden*, *blind* and *blind* (O.H.G. *blint*), etc.

III. The shifting of the voiceless dental explosive is identical with that of the voiceless labial : initial, in German, we have *ts* instead of *t* (as *pf* instead of *p*) ; medial it becomes *ss* (like *ff* in the former case).

1. Preg. *t* = E. *t* = G. *t*, only after *s*, *ch* (E. *gh*) and *f*, which consonants preserve the *t* in German : E. *stand* (position), G. *stand* ; E. *first*, G. *fürst* ; E. metaph. *fist*, G. *faust* ; E. *daughter*, G. *tochter* ; E. *flight*, G. *flucht* ; E. *oft* *oft-en*, G. *oft*, etc.

2. In any other position, **Preg. *t*, retained in E.**, first became aspirated to G. *th*, which further became a *t* accompanied by the corresponding spirant *s* : the group *ts*, spelled *z*, survived when initial and, occasionally, when medial in dialectal forms, but generally when medial it became a mere sibilant, written O.H.G. ȝȝ,[2] and now sounded like a voiceless *s* (spelled *ss* or *sz*, according to a well known distinction).— Examples :—When initial : no. 47 above, and Go. *ga-tam-jan* (to tame), O.N. *tam-r* (tame), E. *tame*, G. *zahm* and *zähmen* ; E.

---

found before the year 1500. Mr. Skeat (*Principles*, I. p. 147) seems to explain it solely by the analogy of the regular *brother* ; but, since we find it also in E. *weather* = O.E. *weder* = G. *wetter*, which is not a word of relationship, it is more likely to be attributable to some obscure influence of the following *r*, though both causes may have combined, and though no such has taken place in *adder* = *natter*, *fodder* = *futter*, *udder* = *euter* ; for, in the latter words, the explosive had been doubled, as following a short vowel. On two other and very momentous irregularities, *fifth* = *fünfte* and similar cases, and *he hath* (now *has*) = *er hat* and similar cases, cf. *infra* 124 and 202, 3. In *forth* = G. *fort* = Go. *faúrþ (the comparative being *faúrþ-is* = E. *furth-er*), the G. consonant is really a *d* (O.H.G. would be *ford), but unvoiced as final, *supra* 48, II. 1.

[1] The word-group *a* *nadder was separated as *an adder* (as in F. *ma mie* = m' *amie*), whence the irregular dropping of an initial *n*. Cf. also E. *apron* borrowed from M.F. *naperon* (napkin).

[2] The precise value is unknown, but it was no doubt a voiceless sibilant. After a long vowel, or final, it is spelled ȝ.

EXPLOSIVE CONSONANTS AND THEIR SUBSTITUTES. 91

tin, two, tale, to tell, and G. *zinn, zwei, zahl, zählen* ;—When medial : Go. *batiza* (better), O.E. metaph. *betera* and E. *better,* O.H.G. *beʒʒiro,* M.H.G. *beʒʒer* and G. *besser* ; Go. *vat-ō,* O.N. *vat-n,* O.E. *wœt-er* and E. *water,* O.H.G. *waʒʒar* and G. *wasser,* cf. *to bite=beiszen,* and *bit=bisz* ; Go. *sūt-s,* O.N. *soet-r,* O.E. *swēte* and E. *sweet,* O.H.G. *suoʒi* and G. *süsz* ; E. *sweat=*G. *schweisz,* and E. *to sweat=*G. *schwitzen,* showing the alternation between *ts* and *ss*. But, after a nasal or a liquid, the substitute for Preg. *t* regularly remains *ts*: Go. *haírt-ō,* E. *heart,* G. *herz* ; E. *salt,* G. *salz* ; L. *moneta,* borrowed in E. *mint,* and in G. *münze.*

IV. Recapitulation of dental correspondences :
explo- ⎧ voiced   : E. *d* = G. *t, d* ;   G. *d*   = E. *th, d.*
sives ⎩ voiceless: „ *t* = „ *z, sz, ss, t* ; „ *t*   = „ *d (th), t.*
spi-   ⎧ voiced   : „ *th*= „ *d (t)* ;   „ [1]   = „
rants ⎩ voiceless: „ *th*= „ *d* ;   „ *z, sz, ss*= „ *t.*

§ 3. *Gutturals.*

(50) I. The Preg. voiceless spirant (*h*) is in some cases a mere aspirate (written *h*) ; in other cases, it is a true spirant (written G. *ch*) ; while, in several positions, it has been dropped altogether.

1. **Preg. *h*=E. *h*=G. *h* when initial.**—If, however, it precedes *l, r* or *n,* both languages agree in ceasing to sound or even to write it. The same is the case in German before *w,* whilst English still spells the group (inverted) *wh,* but can hardly be said to preserve it always in pronunciation.[2]—Examples :—Go. *háuh-s,* O.E. *hēah* and E. *high,* O.H.G. *hōh* and G. *hoch* ; O.N. *hār,* O.E. *hǣr* and E. *hair,* O.H.G. *hār* and G. *haar* ; O.N. *hagl,* O.E. *hagel* and E. *hail,* O.H.G. *hagal* and G. *hagel* ; cf. further *to hate=hassen, hand=hand, to hold=halten, hard=hart, hundred=hundert,* etc. ;—Go. *hlapan,* O.E. *hladan* and E. *to lade,* O.H.G. *hladan laden* and G. *laden* ; cf. *to leap= laufen, to laugh=lachen, loud=laut,* etc. ;—O.N. *hring-r* (circle), O.E. *hring* and E. *ring,* O.H.G. *hring* and G. *ring* ; O.N. *hrafn,*

---

[1] Neither the G. voiced spirant (*s* pronounced E. *z*), nor the E. spirants *s* and *z* belong to this chapter.
[2] In fact E. *wh* is an unvoiced *w.*

O.E. *hræfn* and E. *raven*, O.H.G. *hraban* and G. *rabe*, etc.;— O.N. *hnot*, O.E. *hnutu* and E. *nut*, O.H.G. *nuʒ* and G. *nusz*, etc.; —Go. *hváitei-s*, O.N. *hveite*, O.E. *hwǣte* and G. *wheat*, O.H.G. *weiʒi* and G. *weizen*, cf. likewise *white* = *weisz*; O.N. *hvetja*, O.E. *hwettan* and E. *to whet*, O.H.G. *wezzen* and G. *wetzen*; initial of relative pronouns, *what* = *was*, etc.

2. **Medial Preg. *h* = E. *gh* = G. *ch* or simply *h*.**

The spirant *h* was retained in O.E. (*h*) and in E. (spelled *gh*), whereupon, at least when final, it was changed to the labial spirant (*f*), while in other positions it was dropped by the same process that affected the voiced spirant ʒ; but all these changes usually left the spelling unaltered. The *gh*, moreover, happened occasionally to be sounded in certain positions where it ought to have become mute. This was due to the analogy of words in which it was regularly sounded, as in *laughter* pronounced like *to laugh*.[1] Or it became mute where it should have been sounded, as in *through*, owing to the numerous cases where this word was followed by an initial consonant.[2] We need but compare, on the one side, *to laugh* and *lachen*, *rough* and **rauch*;[3] and, on the other, *might* and *macht* (power), *night* and *nacht*, *neighbour* and *nachbar*, *light* and *licht*, *light* and *leicht*, etc.

G. *h* is here seen to remain a spirant (spelled Mod. G. *ch*) before a consonant or when final; but, between two vowels, it was reduced to the simple aspirate (*h*), which moreover has now become a mere graphic symbol: compare, for instance, the varying sound in *hoch* and *höhe höher* (O.H.G. *hōh* "high," *hōhī* "height," *hōhir* "higher"), in *nach* (E. *nigh*) and *nähe näher* (E. *near*, where the spirant has vanished as in *toe* = G. *zehe*), in

---

[1] Cf. *slaughter*, which was not subject to a similar analogy, so that the *gh* in it has become mute, in contrast with the G. vb. *schlachten*. The dialects still distinguish sg. *enough* = M.E. *inōh*, and pl. *enow* = M.E. *inōw-e*; cf. *infra* II. 5.

[2] *gh* is always mute after a palatal vowel (cf. *infra* II. 4): *high*, *nigh*, *thigh*, *to neigh*, etc. In some words, as in E. *fee* = O.E. *feoh* = G. *vieh*, the mute *gh* even ceased to be spelled.

[3] This is the true and original form,—still preserved in Alamannic *rūch* (rough), and in class. G. *rauch-werk* (rough skins, peltry),—of the word which, when isolated, has become *rauh* through a confusion that will be explained below.

EXPLOSIVE CONSONANTS AND THEIR SUBSTITUTES. 93

sicht and *sehen* (Go. *saihvan*) = E. *sight* and (*to*) *see*, etc. Of course one of the two forms will occasionally be found to have exerted an analogical influence upon the other; thus some dialects have *höcher* as comparative of *hoch*, and classical German has an adjective *rauh* (rough) formed from the comparative *rauher*, etc.[1]

II. The voiced guttural spirant (ʒ) may be treated on the same lines as the other voiced spirants, though they differ in some particulars. Preg. ʒ was a true spirant in any position, even when initial, and had never become *g*, unless it followed a nasal; in the latter case this Preg. ʒ was changed to G. *g* and, usually, to E. *y*.

G. *g* is kept in the spelling, but dialectally assumed, between two vowels or after a liquid, a spirant sound which partly invaded even the classical speech.[2]

English has no *g*, except as initial, in which case it is sometimes spelled *gu* (*guest* = G. *gast*) or *gh* (*ghost* = G. *geist*), so as to insist upon its explosive value. Even when initial, if followed by *e* or *i*, the *g* had usually become a mere *y* as early as the Anglo-Saxon period.[3] When medial, it was gradually adapted to the character of the preceding vowel. It was written *y* if the vowel was *i*, *e* or *a*, and *w* if the preceding vowel was *u* or *o*, and combined with the vocalic sound in such a way as to disappear throughout, sometimes even in spelling (chiefly after an *i*). On the contrary, when it had become final, it underwent occasionally, and chiefly when preceded by *u* or *o*, a strengthening to *gh*, as illustrated by the typical instances: *borough* = G. *burg*[4]; *dough* = G. *teig*, and *enough* = G. *genug*.[5]

1. Preg. ʒ changed to *g* after a nasal = E. *g* = G. *g*: Go. vb.

[1] So also *schuh* = E. *shoe*, for *schuch*, from the pl. *schuhe*, and *er sah* (he saw), for *er *sach*, from the pl. *sie sahen*, etc.
[2] It is known to hesitate, for instance, between *lēgn* and *lēʒn* = *leg·n*, often with a preference for the latter. Some dialects go as far as the grade of *y*: Germans are well known to make fun of the Berlinese pronunciation of G. *g*.
[3] The fact is proved by the O.E. spelling *g* (ʒ) the initial of some words which in I.-E. began with a *y*, and in consequence certainly never had a true initial *g*. Cf. *supra* 36, I.
[4] Cf. O.E. *burg* and *burh*, dative *byrig* = *burg-i*.
[5] Cf. however *infra* 55.

huggr-jan, O.N. *hungr*, O.E. *hungor* and E. *hunger*, O.H.G. *hungar* and G. *hunger*; Go. *figgr-s*, E. *finger*, G. *finger*; E. *tongue*, G. *zunge*; E. *long*, G. *lang*. Observe moreover that the group *ñg*, when swiftly uttered in ordinary speech, is barely distinguishable from a simple *ñ*.

2. **Initial Preg.** ʒ=E. *g*=G. *g*: Go. *gast-s* (=*gasti-s*, L. *hosti-s*), E. *guest*, G. *gast*; Go. *gōd-s*, O.N. *gōd-r*, O.E. *gōd* and E. *good*, O.H.G. *guot* and G. *gut*; cf. likewise *God* and *Gott*. Even sometimes before *e* or *i*:[1] *to give*=*geben*; *gift*=*gift* (poison); *to gild*=O.E. *gyldan*, cf. G. *gold*.

3. **Initial Preg.** ʒ=E. *y*=G. *g*: Go. *gairn-jan* (to wish for), O.N. *gjarn* and O.E. *georn* (covetous), E. *to yearn*, O.H.G. *gërno* and G. *gern* (willingly); O.E. *geolo* and E. *yellow*, O.H.G. *gëlo* (gen. *gëlw-es*) and G. *gelb*; E. *yester(-day)*=G. *gester-n*; E. *to yield*=G. *gelten*, etc. The Go. prefix *ga-* (O.E. ʒe-=G. *ge-*) is still spelled *y-* in M.E.; then it disappears, without leaving any trace but, occasionally, an ill-defined vowel, which appears as *a* in *asunder*=G. *gesonder(t)* (severed), and *e* in *enough*=G. *genug*.

4. **Medial Preg.** ʒ=E. *y*=G. *g*.—Following *a* or *e*: Go. *dag-s*, O.N. *dag-r*, O.E. *dæg* and E. *day*, O.H.G. *tac* and G. *tag*; Go. *vig-s*, O.E. *weg* and E. *way*,[2] O.H.G. *wëc* and G. *weg*; Go. *áugō*, O.N. *auga*, O.E. *éage* and E. *eye*, O.H.G. *ouga* and G. *auge*; Go. *fagr-s* (convenient, able), O.E. *fæger* and E. *fair*, cf. G. *fegen* (to sweep)[3]; Go. *magaþ-s*, O.E. *mægd* and E. *maid*, O.H.G. *magad* and G. *magd* (dialectal *maid*). Compare also: E. *to lay*=G. *legen*; E. *lain*=G. *(ge-)legen*; E. *rain*, *nail*, *hail*, *sail*, *to say*, and G. *regen*, *nagel*, *hagel*, *segel*, *sagen*, etc.—Following *i*, the *g* seems to have been exceptionally retained in E. *twig*=G. *zweig*. But, everywhere else, it becomes *y*, which combines with

---

[1] It is easy to verify the fact that *g* appears only before *a, o, u*: *guest* is the metaphony of *gast*; *to gild* has by analogy the consonant of *guld gold*; *to get*, that of *got*; *to give*, that of *gave*, and so forth. The word *guilt guilty* comes from the root of the O.E. vb. *geldan* (to compensate, G. *gelten*, to be worth, and *vergelten*, to compensate), which formed a pf. *gald*, whereas the regular E. form is the vb. *to yield*.

[2] For *wey*, the sound being the same.

[3] Originally "to put in order," then "to cleanse, to purify"; cf. the latter meaning preserved in *fegefeuer*=M.H.G. *vëye-viur* (purgatory).

[4] E. *egg*=G. *ei* is borrowed from O.N.

EXPLOSIVE CONSONANTS AND THEIR SUBSTITUTES. 95

the *i* and disappears altogether : Go. *ligan*, O.E. *licgan* and E. *to lie*, O.H.G. *licken ligen* and G. *liegen*; Go. *liugan* (to tell a lie), O.E. *lēogan* and E. metaph. *to lie*, O.H.G. *lugin* (a lie) and G. *lüge lügen*; L. *tēgula*, whence the early borrowed word, O.E. *tigel* and E. *tile*, O.H.G. *ziagal* and G. *ziegel*; further compare *to fly* to *fliegen*, *a fly* to *fliege*, and add G. *hügel* (hill)[1]; in unaccented finals, E. *fifty* = O.E. *fīftig* = G. *fünfzig*, E. *holy* = O.E. *hālig* = G. *heilig*, etc., etc.

5. **Medial Preg.** ʒ = E. *w* = G. *g*.—Following *o* or *u* : Go. *biugan*, O.E. *būgan* and E. *to bow*, O.H.G. *biogan* and G. *biegen*, cf. also *a bow* and *bogen*; E. *fowl* = G. *vogel*; E. *low*, from the same root as the vb. *to lie* = G. *liegen*; E. *how* (hill), from the same root as G. *hüg-el*, etc.—Sometimes even after *a*[2] : Go. *dragan*, O.N. *draga*, O.E. *dragan* and E. *to draw*,[3] O.H.G. *tragan* and G. *tragen* (to carry); O.N. *eiginn*, O.E. *āgen* and E. *own*, O.H.G. *eigan* and G. *eigen*.

6. **Preg.** ʒ, when **followed by** *w*, is subject to a peculiar treatment. When initial, it was reduced to simple *w* in the Pregermanic period :[4] Go. *varm-jan* (to warm), O.E. *wearm* and E. *warm*, G. *warm*. Medial ʒw survived, and is occasionally still visible in Gothic; but, according to the nature of the preceding vowel, it became afterwards a single sound, either ʒ, or *w*, whereupon analogy arbitrarily confounded the one with the other series of forms.[5] Here we need but mention : Preg. *snaiʒwá-s ("snow," chiefly attested by L. *ningu-it*, "it snows," and Slav. *snég-ŭ*, "snow"), Go. *snáiv-s*, O.N. *snǣ-r*, O.E. *snāw* and E. *snow*, O.H.G. *sneo* and G. *schnee*; cf. *schneien* = O.H.G.

---

[1] The same root as in *high* and *hoch*, by Verner's law, *infra* 54, III. 1-2. But not E. *hill*, which is akin to L. *collis*.
[2] This may be due either to a dialectal mixture, or to a peculiar deepening of the *a*-sound, or else to the analogy of cases in which the *g* actually followed *o* or *u* : thus, O.E. *dragan* had a regular pf. *drōg* (G. *er trug*), whence E. *drew*, and analogically *to draw* in the present.
[3] The doublet *to drag* is reborrowed from the Scandinavian.
[4] Hence it is only the Indo-European speech that can betray it, *infra* 56, IV. B.
[5] The ʒw is very difficult to distinguish, the more so because under certain conditions, as noted above, simple ʒ may become E. *w* : Go. *maúrgin-s* (morning), G. *morgen* (morning, to-morrow), O.E. *morgen*, E. *morn* and derivative *morn-ing*, but O.E. dat. *tō morwe* and E. *to-morrow*; cf. likewise *to follow* = G. *folgen*, *tallow* = G. *talg*, and *supra* 37 in fine.

snīwan. Further compare the treatment of the Preg. group *hw* in: Go. *saíhvan,* G. *sehen* and E. *to see,* and Go. *sahv,* G. (*er*) *sah,* E. (*he*) *saw;* O.E. *māwan,* E. *to mow* and G. *mähen.*

7. The group *gg,* which proceeds from assimilated *gj,* is changed to E. *dž* (spelled *dg*), but hardened to G. *kk*: O.N. *egg,* from a Preg. *aȝjō (cf. L. *ac-iēs*), O.E. *ecg* and E. *edge,* but O.H.G. *ekka,* G. *ecke eck* (corner); E. *hedge* = G. *hecke.* E. *g* never assumes the sound of *dž* but in this one position, or else in the many words borrowed from Norman French, classical French or Latin.

III. The correspondences of the voiceless explosive (*k*) are quite clear: English keeps the *k* (written *k* or *c*), except when it is changed to *tš* (written *ch*) in certain well-defined positions; German likewise keeps the *k* (*ck*) when initial or following a consonant, but shifts it to the voiceless spirant (written *ch*) after a vowel.[1] The group *sk* and the group *kw* should be considered apart from the general cases.

1. **Initial Preg.** *k* = E. *k* (*c*) = G. *k*: Go. *kald-s,* O.N. *kald-r,* O.E. *ceald cald* and E. *cold,* G. *kalt;* Go. *kaúrn,* O.N. *korn,* O.E. E. *corn,* O.H.G. *chorn* and G. *korn;* O.N. *kȳ-r,* O.E. *cū* and E. *cow,* O.H.G. *chuo kuo* and G. *kuh;* O.N. *konung-r,* O.E. *cyning* with metaphony, syncopated to *cyng,* and E. *king,* O.H.G. *chuning* and G. metaph. *könig;* Go. *kniu,* E. *knee,* G. *knie.* The latter example shows that initial E. *k* before an *n* has become merely a graphic symbol.

2. **Preg.** *k* = E. *k* = G. *k* **after a consonant:** Go. *þagk-jan,* E. *to think,* O.H.G. *denchen* and G. *denken,* cf. the O.E. noun *ðanc* (gratitude) and the E. *thank-s,* O.H.G. *danc* and G. *dank*: Go. *vaúrk-jan,* with the reduced grade of the root which appears normal in G. *werk,* cf. E. *work* = O.E. *weorc,* and E. *to work.*

3. **Preg.** *k* = E. *k* = G. *ch* **after a vowel:** Go. *wakan* (to sit up), O.E. *wacian waeccan,* E. *to wake, a-wake,* O.H.G. *wahhēn* and G. *wachen;* cf. *to make* = *machen, book* = *buch, strike* = *streich,* etc. The group *chs* has reverted to the sound of *ks*: G. *wachs* = E. *wax.* The law moreover admits a number of apparent exceptions, owing to some Low German words, which had

---

[1] In O.H.G. also often when initial or after a consonant. As to the actual sound, cf. *supra* 14, 3 A.

kept the *k* unchanged, having been introduced very early into High German.[1] Thus we find side by side: class. G. *backen*, but Alamannic regularly *bachen* = O.H.G. *bahhan* = E. *to bake*; O.H.G. *acchar* and G. *acker* = E. *acre*; G. *dach* (thatch), but *decken* (to cover) = O.H.G. *decchan*; O.H.G. *lëcchōn* and G. *lecken* (cf. the G. derivate *lechzen*) = E. *to lick*, etc

4. Preg. *k* (G. either *k* or *ch*) = E. *ch*, owing to a palatal assimilation, when preceding or following a palatal vowel (*e, i*), even before the *e* which proceeds from O.E. breaking, and before the *e* of verbal endings in *-an* when changed to the duller sound *-en*.[2] Initial: Go. *kiusan*, O.E. *cēosan* and E. *to choose*, G. *kiesen*; Go. *kinnu-s* (cheek), E. *chin*, G. *kinn* (chin); O.E. *ciele* and E. *chill*,[3] the root being the same as in *cold*, cf. G. *kühl* (cool); L. *calcem*, whence O.E. *cealc* and E. *chalk*, G. *kalk* (lime). Medial: Go. *svaleik-s*, O.E. *swilc* and E. *such*, O.H.G. *sulih* and G. *solch*; E. *rich* = G. *reich*; O.E. *stearc* (strong) = G. *stark*, but E. noun *starch*, together with the adjective *stark*; and the doublets *to wake* and *watch*, *book* and *beech*, *to bake* and *batch*, *to seek* and *to beseech*,[4] etc.

Probably on the analogy of such endings as *-age* in words borrowed from French (*courage*), this *tš* has become voiced (*dž*) in the suffix *-ledge*, as in *knowledge* = M.E. *know-leche*, borrowed from the Scandian *-leiki*.

The *k*, like the *g*, is mute in unaccented finals, as in *earth-ly* = O.E. *eorð-lic*, cf. the G. suffix *-lich*.

5. The group *sk* was kept free from any shifting either in English or German,[5] and underwent in both a separate though parallel treatment, whereby it gave place to the simple cacuminal spirant *š* (written E. *sh*, G. *sch*): Go. and O.N. *skip*, E. *ship*, G. *schiff*; Go. (*af-*)*skiuban* (to remove), O.E. *scūfan* and E. *to shove*, O.H.G. *sciuban* and G. *schieben*, cf. *shovel* = *schaufel*,

---

[1] Frankish, though a dialect of High German, keeps it unshifted when doubled (*ck* = *kk* = *kj*, supra 36, II. 2).
[2] It is thus that L. *k* has become F. *ch* = *š* in *cheval* = *caballum*, *chien* = *cánem*.—It seems scarcely necessary to observe that E. *ch* survived even after the vowel from which it proceeded had been regularly dropped.
[3] In *king* explained above, *kin* = Go. *kun-i*, *kiss* metaph. = O.E. *coss* = G. *kusz*, the *k*, in fact, did not stand before an *i*.
[4] Cf. the identity of the participles *sought* and *besought*.
[5] Just like *sp* and *st*, supra 48, III. 1, and 49, III. 1.

H

to shape=*schaffen*, sheep=*schaf*; Go. *fisk-s*, O.N. *fisk-r*, E. *fish*, G. *fisch*; L. *discus*, borrowed in O.E. *disc* and E. *dish*, in G. *tisch* (table), cf. *rash*=*rasch*, *flesh* (O.N. *flesk*)=*fleisch*, *fresh*=*frisch* (O.H.G. *frisc*). In the rare cases which show the group *sk* preserved in English (O.E. *āscian* and E. *to ask*=O.H.G. *eiscōn* and G. *heischen*), the word is probably borrowed from Old Norse.

6. The group *kw* is retained in English, but it may lose its *w* in German: Go. *qiva*-[1] (alive, cf. L. *vīvu-s*), E. *quick*, G. *queck* (in *quecksilber* and *erquicken*), but also *keck* (bold). When preceding the vowels *u* or *o=u*, *w* is dropped even in English: E. *come*=G. (*ge-*)*kommen*=Go. *quman-s*, and, analogically, also in the other tenses, *to come*=*kommen*, instead of Go. *qiman*, and (*he*) *came*=(*er*) *kam*=Go. *qam*.

IV. Recapitulatory scheme for guttural correspondences:

explo-	{ voiced :	E. g = G. g, k;	G. g = E. g, y.
sives	{ voiceless :	„ $k\,(c)$ = „ $k\,(ck), ch$;	„ k = „ k, ch, g.
spirants	{ voiced :	„ y = „ g;	„ g = „ y.
	{ voiceless :	„ gh = „ ch, h, g	„ ch = „ gh, k, ch.
palatal (voiceless) :		„ ch = „ k, ch;	„ „
cacuminal (voiceless):[2]	{	„ sh = „ sch;	„ sch = „ sh.
aspirate	:	„ h = „ h;	„ h = „ h, gh.

Section II.

THE FIRST CONSONANTAL SHIFTING.

(51) Having thus stated the correspondences of the English and German consonants with the Pregermanic system from which they have arisen, we now proceed to trace back the latter to the consonantal system of the Indo-European language, as exhibited to us by the comparison of the classical languages.

---

[1] Remember that Go. *q* is a symbol for *kv*.

[2] The voiced palatal does not exist in English, apart from the type *edge*. German has neither the voiceless nor the voiced palatal. German also lacks the voiced cacuminal ž (F. *j*), which occurs in English only as a peculiar modification (palatalization) of the *z* in such words as *glazier*, *pleasure*, *occasion*.

Let us, for an instant, confine our attention to Latin: considering, for example, the initial consonants in *brother = bruder*, *father = vater*, *guest = gast*, and comparing them respectively with the initials in L. *fräter, pater, hostis*, we become immediately aware of some symmetrical contrasts which resemble more or less closely those we have met with in the direct comparison of English and German; in other words, we are irresistibly led to think that we shall find in the passage from Indo-European to Pregermanic, a coherent system of consonantal mutations, a system prior indeed, but obviously similar to the shifting which characterizes the passage from Pregermanic to West Germanic, or from West Germanic to English and to German. This Pregermanic series of phenomena was discovered by Grimm, and was called by him *erste Lautverschiebung*. Its principle may be very shortly explained and easily understood.

In point of fact the **First Consonant Shifting** differs essentially from the second, in that it extends in the same manner over the whole series of Indo-European explosives, and is therefore capable of being comprised in a single formula or law. It does not follow that all the changes occurred at the same time, or were due to the same cause, as it were, to a single turn of the wheel.[1] Far from this: many circumstances agree to prove that these changes were made at different dates and at long intervals, occasioned perhaps by various and quite dissimilar causes. But the law for p holds good for t and k, the law for b holds good also for d and g, so that, as far as the mere final result is concerned, it is as if the whole series of Indo-European explosives had changed places under a common and simultaneous impulse.

With one exception, however; for, if we no longer confine our comparison to initials, but take into account the contrast between L. *fräter* and *pater*, in which the medial is the same, and G. *bruder* and *vater*, in which the medial differs, we again become aware of a gap in the parallelism, the cause of which is to be sought for in some secondary law crossing, as it were, and

---

[1] It is almost superfluous to observe how obsolete and unnatural such a view of phonetic phenomena would be.

modifying the normal effects of Grimm's law. This was discovered and formulated only fifteen years ago by Dr. K. Verner.[1]

§ 1. *Grimm's and Verner's Laws.*

(52) In order to understand these two laws it is necessary to be familiar with the whole Indo-European consonantal system, consisting of sixteen explosives, which the comparison of Sanskrit, Greek, and Latin has enabled us to restore, namely: the four orders of explosives, labials, dentals, palatals, and velars; and, in each order, the voiceless and the voiced explosive, either simple or aspirated.[2]

	Labials.				Dentals.			
	I.-E.	Sk.	Gr.	L.	I.-E.	Sk.	Gr.	L.
Voiceless ..	p	p	π	p	t	t	τ	t
Voiceless asp.	ph	ph	ϕ	f	th	th	θ	t
Voiced ...	b	b	β	b	d	d	δ	d
Voiced asp. .	bh	bh	ϕ	f, b	dh	dh	θ	f, d, b

	Palatals.				Velars.			
	I.-E.	Sk.	Gr.	L.	I.-E.	Sk.	Gr.	L.
Voiceless .	k	$ç$	κ	k, c	q	k, c	π, τ, κ	qu, c
Voicel. asp.	kh	kh	χ	h, c	qh	kh, ch	χ	gu
Voiced ..	g	j	γ	g	g	g, j	β, δ, γ	gu, v, g
Voiced asp.	gh	h	χ	h	gh	gh, h	ϕ, θ, χ	f, v

Sanskrit alone, it is seen, has preserved the whole system. Generally speaking, the voiced and the voiceless aspirates in each order have been confused: Greek, especially, represents both by voiceless aspirates. Latin is even more corrupted: here, most aspirates have become spirants. No consonant, however, has passed from one order to another, apart from the velars, which in Greek are often represented by labials or dentals.

This is also just what happened in Pregermanic: the first

---

[1] See his admirable article, in *Kuhn's Zeitschrift*, XXIII. p. 97.
[2] Cf. *supra* 14, 1 and 3 A, and, as to the particulars in Græco-Latin correspondences, my *Gramm. of Gr. and Lat.*, no. 57–60.

three orders in our present scheme strictly correspond to the three orders we have distinguished in primitive Germanic, so that we may write the formulas:

I.-E. labial = Preg. labial;
" dental = " dental;
" palatal = " guttural.

In regard to the velars, it must be first observed that, as early as the I.-E. period, they were liable to a peculiar influence (which, however, did not modify them in every case any more than it followed them throughout every branch of the I.-E. family). They often became accompanied by a labial semi-vowel, so that q, qh, g, and gh were respectively sounded almost like kw, khw, gw, and ghw. This phenomenon is commonly termed **labialization**, and consequently we give the term labializing languages to those which have kept some traces of it, viz. Greek, Latin and Germanic, as opposed to Slavonic and Sanskrit.[1]

In Germanic, the non-labialized velar cannot be distinguished from the ordinary guttural, and therefore it is included in the last of the three orders given above. The labialized velar, on the contrary, falls under a double law: in some cases the I.-E. group is simply transferred into Pregermanic, which in consequence exhibits the ordinary guttural followed by a w, respectively hw, kw, and $\jmath w$; or else, similarly to the Greek process, the sound of the parasitic consonant partly absorbs the sound of the original one, and the whole group then results in an ordinary labial consonant, respectively f, p, and b.[2]

Thus it is that in every way **the four orders of Indo-European explosives** resulted in **the three orders of Germanic consonants** preserved in English and German.

(53) The unerring and strictly parallel course of this pro-

---

[1] These labialized velars are changed to Gr. π or τ, β or δ, ϕ or θ, whereas pure velars remain κ, γ, χ. The same is the case in Latin with the contrast between qu and c, gu (v) and g.

[2] The latter case is by far the rarer, but this is all that may be stated about it, its determining circumstances remaining as yet obscure. See however Brugmann, *Grundriss*, I., § 444.

cess will be illustrated by the following four main formulas, wherein the whole of it is contained:

A. **The voiceless aspirates** became completely confounded **with the voiceless explosives,** whereupon both were naturally shifted in the same way. Since, moreover, voiceless aspirates are very rare in I.-E., and sometimes doubtful, this single mention will suffice for them. We need but compare: I.-E. *wóyd-e (he knows), Sk. véd-a, Gr. οἶδε = ϝοῖδ-ε, Go. váit, and G. (er) weisz; with I.-E. *wóyt-tha (thou knowst), Sk. vét-tha, Gr. οἶσθα = ϝοῖσ-θα, Go. váis-t,[1] and G. (du) weisz-t.

B. **The voiceless explosive,** when immediately **preceded by** s, escapes the effect of Grimm's Law, that is to say, it **remains in Germanic just what it was in Indo-European**: L. spu-ere (to spew), Go. speiv-an, E. to spew, G. spei-en; Sk. spaç paç (to look out), L. *spec-iō, G. späh-en (to spy); Sk. sthā (to stand), Gr. ἵστημι = *σί-στᾱ-μι (to place), στα-τό-ς (set), L. stā-re si-st-ere stă-tu-s, E. to stand and he stood, G. steh-en and er stand, etc.; Gr. στείχ-ω, Go. steig-an, E. to sty, G. steig-en; Gr. σκι-ά (shadow, reflect), Go. skei-nan, E. to shine, G. scheinen. The same is the case with t following any other I.-E. voiceless explosive: Sk. napti (daughter, granddaughter), L. neptis (granddaughter, niece), O.E. nift, O.H.G. nift[2]; Gr. ὀκτώ, L. octō, Go. ahtáu, O.E. eahta and E. eight, O.H.G. ahto and G. acht; L. rēctu-s, Go. raíht-s, O.E. reoht and E. right, O.H.G. rëht and G. recht; Gr. πέμπτο-ς, L. quīnctu-s, Go. fimfta, M.E. fift, G. fünfte, etc.

C. **Grimm's Law.**—In each order of I.-E. explosives, **the voiceless explosive becomes shifted to the Preg. voiceless spirant, and the voiced aspirate becomes shifted to the voiced spirant,** whereas **the voiced non-aspirate** remains an explosive, but **becomes shifted to the voiceless explosive,** thus:

---

[1] From this example the reader might infer that the primitive group tt, assimilated from dt, has become st in Pregermanic as well as in Greek. This however would be a false view: assimilation changed tt to ss; but, here as in many other cases, analogy restored the group st (cf. the impf. O.H.G. wissa, M.H.G. wisse and wiste, G. wuszte, on the pattern of konnte mochte), so that the law, inexact as it is, may suffice for practical purposes.

[2] E. niece is borrowed from F., and G. nichte is taken from Low German, where ft is changed to cht.

I.-E. p (ph) = Preg. f; I.-E. bh = Preg. ƀ; I.-E. b = Preg. p;
„ t (th) = „ þ; „ dh = „ đ; „ d = „ t;
„ k (kh) = „ h; „ gh = „ ʒ; „ g = „ k.¹

D. **Verner's Law.**—The above shifting having taken place in a medial syllable, and further supposing the immediately preceding syllable not to be marked with the I.-E. accent,² then the voiceless spirant which followed the unaccented syllable (f, þ, h) is softened to a Pregermanic voiced spirant (ƀ, đ, ʒ), and therefore, in the whole course of its further evolution, it is no longer distinguishable from such voiced spirants as have regularly sprung from I.-E. voiced aspirates.³

This may be illustrated from the example already mentioned: I.-E. *bhrā́ter- (L. frāter) quite regularly became Preg. *brṓþer-, whereupon no further change could take place, since the first syllable of the word was accented; but I.-E. *pətḗr- (L. pater), after it had become Preg. *faþér-, according to Grimm's law, could not help becoming Preg. *fađér-, through further softening, according to Verner's law, because the preceding syllable was unaccented in Pregermanic; and thus it is that the word assumes in the Germanic speeches (Gothic, English, German, etc.) the same aspect it would exhibit if it had arisen from a non-existing I.-E. form *pədher-.

It follows from Verner's law, that each I.-E. voiceless explosive—but, of course, these only—has in Germanic two representatives, according as it was or was not immediately preceded by the I.-E. and Preg. accent.

---

¹ It must, of course, be understood, that, if in the I.-E. period a primitive voiced explosive had already become voiceless by being adapted to a following voiceless consonant, then its Pregermanic treatment would not differ at all from that of a primitive voiceless explosive: thus, the I.-E. groups gt ght and bt bht become respectively Preg. ht and ft, and cannot become anything else, since in I.-E. they were already changed respectively to kt and pt. Gr. Ϝέργ-ο-ν = E. work; but the E. pf. of the vb. to work is wrought = O.E. worh-te = I.-E. *u̯ě-wr̥k-tay, wherein the radical g is assimilated to the following t. See some other Germanic instances, supra 24.
² On this primitive accent, which is altogether lost in later languages, but survived in Pregermanic, cf. infra 65, I.
³ The groups sp, st, sk, ft, ht, and subsidiarily ss, fs, hs, which are not subject to Grimm's law, also escape the effects of Verner's law.

A further consequence is, that, if the movable accent happened to be displaced in a given word, in the ordinary course of accidence, whether in derivation, declension, or conjugation, the medial consonant of this word changed accordingly and gave rise to such alternations as are illustrated by the three German types: *hof* (court) = Preg. **húfa-z*, but *hübsch* ("beautiful, select," now, as it were, *höfisch* "courtlike") = O.H.G. *hübesch* = Preg. **hubiská-s*; *ich siede* (I seethe) = Preg. **séuþ-ō*, but *gesotten* (sodden) = Preg. **suðaná-s*; *ich ziehe* (I draw) = Preg. **téuh-ō*, but *gezogen* (drawn) = Preg. **tuʒaná-s*,[1] etc.

It remains to point out the application of Grimm's and Verner's laws in detail throughout the Germanic consonantal system.

§ 2. *Primitive Voiceless Explosives.*

(54) I. **Labial.**—1. Initial, or following an accented syllable (Grimm's law): L. *pisci-s*, Go. *fisk-s*, etc.[2]; Sk. *pitá*, Gr. πατήρ, L. *pater*, Go. *fadar*; Sk. *prī* (to love), *priyá-s* (dear), Go. *frij-ōnd-s*, E. *friend*, G. *freund*; Sk. *pīy* (to blaspheme, to hate), Go. *fij-and-s* (enemy), E. *fiend*, G. *feind*; Sk. *nápāt-* (son, grandson), Gr. νέποδες (offsprings),[3] L. *nepōs* (grandson, nephew), O.E. *nefa* and E. *nephew*,[4] O.H.G. *nefo* and G. *neffe*; Gr. κώπ-η (handle), L. *cap-ere* (to seize), G. *haf-t* msc. (a tie), *haf-t* fm. (capture), *hef-t* (handle), O.E. *hæf-t* (prisoner) = L. *cap-tu-s*, E. *haft* (handle), etc.

2. Medial and following an unaccented syllable (Grimm's law, and then Verner's law, *p* shifted to *f*, and *f* softened to ƀ): the same root *kăp* in Go. *haf-jan* (to lift), O.N. *hef-ia*, O.H.G. *heffen*, but E. *to heave* and G. *heben*, where the ƀ extended

---

[1] This is what Germanists call *grammatische wechsel*. Compare the E. contrast in *seethe* and *sodden*. Of course the alternation was afterwards liable to disappear under the influence of analogy: cf. *infra* 55, 179, 184, etc.

[2] As for the English and German evolution of words already mentioned, the reader must trust to his memory, or refer to the preceding section. The English and German words have been repeated in the Indexes even when they are not quoted as such under the following numbers (54–57).

[3] Always observe the Sk. and Gr. accent.

[4] Pr. *nĕƀyū* (medial *f* softened to *v*), but the ending is borrowed from F. *neveu*.

throughout the conjugation, after the analogy of such cases as would require it regularly, e.g., Preg. *hab-aná-s (taken) [1]; Gr. ἀπὸ, L. ab=*ap, Preg. *aba (but Go. af with the final unvoiced), E. of (pr. ov, but off when actually final), G. ab; Sk. upári (over), Gr. ὑπὲρ, hence a Preg. *ubéri, cf. E. over and a-b-ove, G. über and oben; L. aper=*ap-ró-s, G. eber (boar),[2] etc.

II. **Dental.**—1. Initial, or following an accented syllable: Sk.tṛ́-na-m (a blade of grass), Go. þaúr-nu-s (thorn), etc.; Sk. root tan (to extend), Gr. ταν-ύω, L. ten-ui-s (expanded, thin), O.N. þunn-r (thin), etc.; Sk. tum-rá- (thick, strong), zd. tūm-a- (strong), L. tum-ēre (to swell), O.N. þum-al-(fingr) "the thick finger, thumb," etc.; Sk. bhrátar- (brother) and Preg. *bróþer-, etc.; I.-E. root pĕt (to fly), Gr. πέτ-ο-μαι, Sk. pátram (wing)= *pát-tra-m, Preg. *féþram, etc.

2. Medial, when following an unaccented syllable (t shifted to þ, and then þ softened to ð): Sk. pitár- (father), and Preg. *faþér-, afterwards *faðér-, etc.; Sk. mātár- (mother), and Preg. *móþér-, afterwards *móðér-, etc.; Sk. damitá-s (tamed),[3] Preg. *tamiþás, whence *tamiðás, Go. (ga-)tamida, E. tamed, O.H.G. (gi-)zemit and G. gezähmt, and so also with every ending of the past participle in so-called weak verbs.

III. **Palatal.**—1. Initial, or following an accented syllable: Gr. κάχλ-ηξ (little stone) and Preg. *házl-a-z (hail), etc.; Lith. kaúk-a-s (knob) and Preg. *háuh-a-z (high), etc.; Gr. κάρτ-α (vehemently), καρτ-ερό-ς and κράτ-υ-ς (strong), Preg. *harð-ú-s (hard), etc.[4]; Gr. κόρ-αξ, L. cor-vu-s (raven), Preg. *hra-bná-s, etc.; Sk. çvětá-s (white) and Preg. *hwītá-s, etc.; Sk. páçu nt. (cattle), L. pecu, Preg. *féhu nt., etc.; Lith. raúka-s (rough) and Preg. *ráuha-z, etc.

2. Medial, when following an unaccented syllable (k shifted to h, and then h softened to ʒ): the same root I.-E. kewk (high) in Preg. *huʒilá-s (hill), etc.; I.-E. *dékm̥ (ten), Gr. δέκα, L. decem, Go. taíhun; but, the accent being moved, as in Gr. δεκάς (tithing), Preg. *teʒún-, whence Go. *tigu- in fimf tigjus

---

[1] Go. haf-an-s is due to the same though inverted analogy.
[2] E. York=O.E. Eofor-wic "borough of the boar."
[3] Remember the constant accent of Greek verbal nouns in -τό-s.
[4] Hence we see that E. to call has nothing to do with Gr. καλεῖν.

(five tithings, fifty), etc.; Sk. *akśi-* (eye) and Lith. *aki-s* (cf. Sl. *ok-o*, Gr. ὄσσε "both eyes"=ὀκ-yε, L. *oc-ulu-s*), Preg. **auhí-*, whence **auʒi-*, etc.; I.-E. root *īk* (to be master), Sk. *īç-ānā́-s* (sovereign, master), Preg. **aihaná-s*, whence **aiʒaná-s* (own), etc.

IV. **Velar.**—A. Non-labialized (confounded with the palatal).—1. Initial, or following an accented syllable: I.-E. root *qĕl* (to act, to deal with, to manage), Sk. *car* (to move, to act), Gr. πέλ-ο-μαι (to exist), likewise labialized in *aἰ-πόλο-ς* (goatherd), but without labialization in βου-κόλο-ς (cow-herd), again labialized in L. *(in-)quil-īnu-s* (inhabitant, planter) and *cŏl-ō=*quĕl-ō* (to cultivate), but without labialization in Go. *hal-dan* (to keep), E. *to hold*, G. *halten*; I.-E. **nóq-t-s* (night), Sk. *nák-ti-s*, Gr. νύξ νύκ-τ-a, L. *nox noc-t-em*, Go. *nah-t-s*, etc.—2. Medial, when following an unaccented syllable: L. *vinc-ō=*vinqu-ō* (to vanquish) and Go. *veih-an* (to fight)=I.-E. **wéyq-ō*, but O.H.G. *wīgant* (warrior) and G. *weigand*, G. *weigern* (to resist), O.E. *wīgend* (warrior) lost in Mod. English.

B. Labialized, Preg. either *hw* or *ʒw*.—1. Initial, or following an accented syllable: Sk. *cud* (to whet), from an I.-E. root *qĕd qŏd=kwĕd kwŏd*, Preg. **hwat-ja-*, E. *to whet*, G. *wetzen*; I.-E. pronoun **qó-*, Gr. πό-, L. *quo-*, Preg. **hwá-*, etc.; I.-E. root *sĕq* (to follow), Gr. ἕπ-ο-μαι, L. *sequ-o-r*, Preg. **séhw-ō*, whence Go. *saíhv-an* (to see), etc.—2. Medial, when following an unaccented syllable: perhaps I.-E. root *merq mr̥q* (dull), Sl. *mrak-ŭ* (dark), *mrŭk-na-tĭ* (it is dark), whence a Preg. derivate **murʒwena-*, O.N. *morgunn* (morning), etc., though Go. *maúrgin-s* shows no apparent labialization.

C. Labialized, Preg. either *f* or *ƀ*.—1. Initial, or following an accented syllable: I.-E. **pénqĕ* (five), Sk. *páñca*, Gr. πέντε πέμπε, L. *quīnque*, Preg. **fémfĕ*, etc.; I.-E. *wl̥qo-s* (wolf), Sk. *vŕ̥ka-s*, Gr. λύκο-ς, L. *lupu-s*, Preg. **wúlfa-z*, etc.—2. Medial, when following an unaccented syllable: I.-E. **wl̥qí* (she-wolf), Sk. *vr̥kí*, Preg. **wulfí*, whence **wulƀí*, preserved exclusively in O.H.G. *wulpa* and M.H.G. *wülpe*.[1]

---

[1] We should expect **wülbe*; but the *b* has been doubled (*supra* 36, II. 2), and the group *bb* becomes G. *pp*, just as *gg* becomes *ck* (*supra* 50, II. 7). Mod. G. *wölfin* has analogically restored the medial consonant of *wolf*.

(55) V. We have already stated the **grammatical alternations** which proceed from the application of Verner's law: they are easily seen in the earlier Germanic languages, and, though analogy has levelled them in the later languages, they again become obvious through the comparison of one tongue with another. Thus, the contrast of *enough* with G. *genug* may be due to an alternation of this kind: a G. *genuch, the only form which would regularly answer E. *enough*, is to be restored from Go. *ganōh-s* (sufficient), *ganaúh-a* (sufficiency), in O.H.G. *ginah* (it was sufficient), *ginuht* (sufficiency), in M.H.G. *genuhtsam* (sufficient), etc., so that we may suppose the form with *h* and the form with ȝ to have been normally interchangeable according to the accent, whereas analogy preserved the latter in German and the former in English; hence the divergence in the two related languages.

It will be seen, in fact, that the I.-E. accent often changed its place, especially in conjugation. For instance, an I.-E. vb. *déwk-ō (I lead, I draw, L. *dūc-ō*), in the present indicative, had the root in the normal grade, with accented radical syllable, thus: Preg. *téuh-ō, Go. *tiuh-a*, G. *ich ziehe*. In the pf. sg. the root was deflected, but it kept the accent: I.-E. *de-dówk-ă, Go. *táuh*, O.H.G. *zōh*, M.H.G. *ich zōch* (I drew). But in the pf. pl. the accent was transferred to the ending and the root was reduced: I.-E. *de-dŭk-ṃmé, whence a Preg. *tuȝ-umé and G. *wir zogen*; and so also in the past participle, Preg. *tuȝaná-s (drawn) and G. *gezogen*. The analogical change in Mod. G. is quite plain: owing to *wir zogen* and *gezogen*, the sg. has become *ich zog*, instead of *zoch. German, however, has preserved the curious alternation seen in *ziehen* and *gezogen*, which cannot be understood unless it is traced back to Pregermanic. Gothic, though older, is much more corrupt: here the *h* extended throughout. On the pattern of such regular forms as *tiuhan* and *táuh*, Gothic irregularly has *taúhum* (we drew), instead of *tugum, and *taúhan-s*[1] (drawn), instead of *tugan-s, which forms, if reproduced in a Mod. German conjugation, would give us the paradigm *ziehen*, *ich* *zoch, *wir* *zohen,

---

[1] Naturally, with *aú*, instead of *u*, before *h*, *supra* 28, I.

gezohen. Observe, moreover, the contrast of G. *zucht* with G. *zug*, all these words being derived from the very same root.

Such analogical processes could not but take place sooner or later, and in time give the regular variability of the Germanic consonantal system a fictitious and seemingly satisfactory unity. No Germanic tongue is free from them, Gothic least of all, old as it is. We have just seen Mod. German to be purer even than Gothic, and the same is the case with Old English, as the conjugation of this very verb shows, *tēon* (to draw), *togen* (drawn), etc. Gothic also shows the medial consonant unchanged throughout the whole conjugation of the vb. *hafja* (I take) = L. *capiō*, and pf. *hōfum* (we took), whereas O.H.G. keeps the alternation in *heffu* and *huobum*, which latter gave rise in M.H.G. to the vb. *heben* (to heave, to lift). Sometimes, however, Gothic has preserved an alternation which has been lost everywhere else: thus, the Go. conjugation of the pf. *þarf* (I need) is in the pl. *þaúrbum* = Preg. *þurb-umé*,[1] a remarkably pure survival, whilst O.E. ðurfan, pf. sg. 1 ðearf, pl. 1 ðurfon, and G. (metaph.) *dürfen*,[2] pf. sg. 1 *darf*, pl. 1 *dürfen*, both placed the voiceless consonant where only the voiced would be regular.

§ 3. *Primitive voiced aspirates.*[3]

(56) I. **Labial.**—I.-E. root *bheyd*, Sk. *bhinád-mi* (I split) and *bhid-yá-tē* (it is split), L. *find-ō*, Preg. *bīt-ō (I bite), Go. *beit-a*, etc.; Gr. φηγός, L. *fāgus*, G. *buche*, etc.; I.-E. root *bhlā* (to blow), L. *flā-re*, E. *to blow*, G. *blähen*; I.-E. root *bhĕndh* (to bind), Go. *bind-an*, etc.; I.-E. root *lĕwbh* (to delight in), Sk. *lúbh-ya-ti*, L. *lub-et lib-et*, Preg. *leub-a-z (dear), whence Go. *liuf-s*, etc.; L. *scab-ō* (I scrape), E. *to shave*, G. *schaben*; Sk. *garbhá-s* (an embryo, a young one), and Preg. *kalb-á-s (calf), etc.

II. **Dental.**—I.-E. *dhughäter- (daughter), Gr. θυγάτηρ, Sk. *duhitár-*, Go. *daúhtar* = Preg. *ðuhter-, etc.; I.-E. root *dhē* (to

---

[1] I.-E. *te-tórp-a and *te-tṛp-mmé respectively.
[2] For the meaning, compare *bedürfen*.
[3] From this point to the end of the chapter, we have of course no longer to deal with Verner's law.

set, to do), Sk. *dhā*, Gr. θη (τίθημι), E. *do*, G. *thun*; I.-E. root *bhĕndh* and Preg. *bind, above; I.-E. *médh-yo-s (placed in the middle), Sk. *mádh-ya-s*, Gr. μέσος = μέσσος = *μέθ-yo-s, L. *med-iu-s*, Go. *mid-ji-s*, etc.; I.-E. root *dhegh* (to burn, to shine), Sk. *dáh-a-ti* (it burns), whence a nominal derivation *dhogh-ó-s, Preg. *ðaʒá-s, Go. *dag-s* (day), etc.

III. **Palatal.**—I.-E. *ghósti-s (foreigner, enemy, guest), L. *hosti-s*, Preg. *ʒásti-z, Go. *gast-s*, etc.; I.-E. *ghans-* (swan, goose), Sk. *hans-á-s* (swan), Gr. χήν (goose), L. *anser* = *hans-er, Preg. **ʒans-*, whence G. *gans*, O.E. *gons gōs, and E. *goose*; I.-E. root *dhigh* (to mould), Sk. *dih* (to besmear), Gr. θιγ-εῖν (to touch), τεῖχ-ος (wall), L. *fing-ere*, Preg. root *ðiʒ*, whence Go. *deig-an* (to mould), E. *dough* and G. *teig*, etc.; I.-E. **ghyes-* (yesterday), Sk. *hyás*, Gr. χθές, L. *her-ī hes-ternu-s*, Go. *gis-tra-(dag-is)*, etc.

IV. **Velar.**—A. Non-labialized, confounded with the palatal: I.-E. *dhoghó-s (day), as above II.; L. *helvu-s* (yellow), E. *yellow*, G. *gelb*.

B. Labialized, Preg. ʒw : I.-E. root *snigh snĕygh* (to be moist), Sk. *snih*, Gr. acc. νίφ-α (snow), νείφ-ει (it snows), L. acc. *nivem* = *nihv-em, Go. *snáiv-s*, etc.; Sk. *gharmá-s* (warm), Gr. θερμό-s, L. *formu-s*, Preg. *ʒwarmá-s, afterwards *warmá-s, etc.

C. Labialized, Preg. ƀ : no certain examples.

§ 4. *Primitive voiced explosives.*

(57) I. **Labial.**—No certain examples, apart from I.-E. root *dhub dhĕwb*, Lith. *dub-ù-s* (deep), perhaps Preg. *ðéup-a-z, Go. *diup-s*, E. *deep*, G. *tief*.[1]

II. **Dental.**—Sk. *jihvá* (tongue) = *dihvá, L. *lingua = dingua* = I.-E. *dṇghwá, whence a Preg. **tuñʒō-*, etc.; I. E. **dékm̥* (ten) and Preg. *téhun; I.-E. *dém-ō (I build), Sk. *dám-a-s*

---

[1] I.-E. *b* is an extremely rare sound, and the very few Greek or Latin words which might bear testimony of it happen not to have any corresponding forms in Germanic, and reciprocally we do not find elsewhere but in Germanic such Preg. roots as *sláp* (E. *to slerp*, G. *schlafen*, cf. however Sl. *slab-ŭ* = G. *schlaff*, "lazy"), *skăp* (E. *to shape*, G. *schaffen*), etc., which would presuppose an I.-E. *b*. The latter, perhaps, might be identified with L. *scab-ō* (to scrape); but, according to the resemblance in meaning to E. *shave* and G. *schaben*, the primitive form *skabh* seems more probable for the L. vb. In Preg. *wĕrp* (to throw) the *p* has arisen from a velar, *infra* IV., C.

(house), Gr. δέμ-ω δόμ-ο-ς, L. dom-u-s, Go. (ga-)tim-r-jan (to build), cf. E. *timber* and G. *zimmer*; I.-E. root *bhĕyd*, as above, 56, I.; I.-E. *swādú-s (sweet), Sk. svādú-s, Gr. ἡδύς = *σFαδύ-ς, L. suāvis = *suād-ui-s (cf. the vb. suād-ēre),[1] E. *sweet*, G. *süsz*; Sk. *svid* (to sweat), Gr. ἰδίω = *σFιδ-ίω, L. *sūdor* (sweat) = *svoid-os, E. *sweat* and *to sweat*, G. *schwitzen* and *schweisz*, etc.

III. **Palatal.**—Sk. *jánu* (knee), Gr. γόνυ, L. *genu*, Go. *kniu*, etc.; L. *grānum* = *gr-nó-m, Go. *kaúrn*, etc.; Gr. φώγ-ω (to roast), E. *to bake*, G. *back-en bach-en*; Gr. ἀγρό-ς, L. *ager*, Go. *akr-s*, etc.; Sk. *juš* (to choose, to accept), Gr. γεύομαι = *γεύσ-ο-μαι (to taste), L. *gus-tu-s* (taste), Go. *kius-an* (to prove, to choose), etc.

IV. **Velar.**—A. Non-labialized, confounded with the palatal: I.-E. root *gĕl* (cold, frost), L. *gel-u*, Go. *kal-d-s* (cold); I.-E. *sthĕg tĕg* (to cover), Sk. *sthag-a-ti* (he covers), Gr. στέγ-ω (I cover), στέγ-η (shelter), τέγ-ος (thatch), L. *teg-ō tog-a*, Lith. *stóg-a-s* (thatch), O.E. *ðæc* and E. *thatch*, G. *dach* and *decken*, etc.

B. Labialized, Preg. *kw*: I.-E. *gôw-s (cow), Sk. *gáu-s*, Gr. βοῦ-ς, L. *bō-s*, E. *cow* and G. *kuh*; I.-E. root *gem* (to go), Sk. *gam* (to go), Gr. βαίνω, L. *ven-iō*, Go. *qim-an*, etc.

C. Labialized, Preg. *p*: I.-E. root *wĕrg* (to throw), cf. Sl. *vrŭg* (id.), whence a Preg. root *wĕrp*, Go. *vairp-an*, O.E. *weorp-an* and E. *to warp*, O.H.G. *wĕrf-an* and G. *werf-en*.

[1] "To make [something] sweet [to somebody]," is as much as "to persuade him of it."

CHAPTER V.

SIBILANT CONSONANTS.

(58) The Indo-European speech had two sibilants, voiceless *s*, voiced *z*; but, the voiced sibilant having only arisen from the process of adapting the voiceless sibilant to a following voiced consonant,—as, for instance, in a group *sd* changed to I.-E. *zd*,—the two were originally but one, and it will be better to keep them together.

The I.-E. sibilant may be either **initial**, or **medial**, or **final**. In all these positions it has been remarkably well preserved in Pregermanic, and the slight modifications it has undergone are to be assigned to the later languages, so that its evolution may be traced at once from the beginning down to the present time.

SECTION I.

INITIAL SIBILANT.[1]

(59) I. Before a vowel.—All the I.-E. languages, including Germanic, have faithfully preserved the primitive initial *s*, with the single exception of Greek,[2] where it is changed to *h* (rough breathing): I.-E. root *sū* (to bring forth), whence Sk. *sū-nú-s* (son), Gr. υἱός = *συ-ιό-ς, Lith. *sūnŭ-s*, Sl. *synŭ*, Go. *sunu-s*, O.N. *sun-r*, O.E. *sunu* and E. *son*, O.H.G. *sunu* and G. *sohn*;[3] L. *sat sat-is* (enough) *sat-ur* (fed), Go. *saþ-s* (fed), O.N. *sað-r*,

---

[1] The *z* seldom occurs as initial, and is never final.
[2] More exactly, the same remark applies to Avestic (Zend), and in part to Celtic.
[3] We need scarcely remark that this *s*, as well as the medial intervocalic *s*, has become voiced in the correct pronunciation of classical German (*sohn*, pr. *zōn*).

O.E. *sœd* (fed) and E. *sad* ("made to loath"), O.H.G. *sat* and G. *satt*; I.-E. root *sē* (to throw, to sow), Gr. ἧ-μα (a throw), L. *sē-men* (seed),[1] Go. *sai-an* (to sow), O.E. *sāw-an* and E. *to sow*, O.H.G. *sā-en* and G. *säen*, further E. *seed* = G. *saat*; Gr. ἅλ-ς, L. *sāl* = *săld, E. *salt*, G. *salz*; Sk. *sád-as* (seat), Gr. ἕδ-ος, L. *sĕd-ēs* and *sĕd-ēre* (to sit), E. *to sit*, G. *sitz-en*; Gr. ἔθος = *ἔθ-ος, Go. *sid-u-s*, O.E. *sidu*, lost in E., O.H.G. *situ* and G. *sitte* (custom, behaviour); Sl. *s'rebro* (silver), E. *silver*, G. *silber*, etc.

II. Before a semi-vowel.—The initial group *sy* is rare and of no importance, since the *y* is dropped: E. *to sew* and G. *säu-le* (awl), cf. Go. *siu-jan* = Gr. (κα-)σσύ-ω = L. *su-ō*. The initial group *sw*, on the contrary, is extremely common and generally survives, though High German now changes the *s* to *š*, as it does before any other consonant. Thus, E. *swine* = G. *schwein*, E. *swim* = G. *schwimmen*, E. *sword* = G. *schwert*, E. *sweat* = G. *schweisz*, etc., have been already mentioned. Here we may add: L. *suāsum* (a dark colour), Go. *svart-s* (black), O.N. *svart-r*, O.E. *sweart* and E. *swart*, O.H.G. *swarz* and G. *schwarz*; Gr. σῑγή (silence) = *σϝῑγ-ά, O.E. *swīg-ian* and G. *schweig-en* (to be silent); Sk. *svásar-* (sister), L. *soror* = *svĕsor, Go. *svistar* (O.N. *syster*), O.E. *sweostor*, O.H.G. *swëster* and G. *schwester*, etc. The exceptions to this law are only apparent: E. *sister* is borrowed from the Scandinavian; the two words E. *swamp* and G. *sumpf* probably contain two different grades of the same root; as for G. *süsz* = E. *sweet*, we need but go back to the O.H.G. form *suoʒi swuoʒʒi*, where the *w* and the *u* are seen to have combined, owing to an absolute identity in sound.

III. Before a nasal or a liquid, Greek and Latin usually drop the *s*, but Germanic keeps it intact.

1. Before *m*, *n*, *l* (E. *s*, G. *s* changed to *š*): Sk. root *smi* (to laugh, to wonder), L. *mī-ru-s* (wonderful), *mī-ro-r* (I admire), E. *smi-le*, cf. G. *schmei-cheln* (to caress); E. *small* = G. *schmal* (thin); Sk. root *snih*, Gr. νίφ-α, L. *niv-em*, E. *snow*, G. *schnee*; L. *lub-ricu-s*, E. *to slip*, G. *schlüpf-en*; L. *lac-er* (rent, put to pieces), E. *to slay*, G. *schlag-en*, etc.

2. Before *r*, Germanic and Slavonic insert a *t*: I.-E. root *srŭ srĕw* (to flow), Sk. *sráv-a-ti* (it flows), Gr. ῥέει = *σρέϝ-ει;

[1] Cf. Gr. ἵημι = *σί-ση-μι, and L. *seı ō* = *si-sō*.

from this root, a derived noun with deflected root would be
*srow-mó·s (current), which has become Preg. *strau-má-s, O.E.
strēam and E. stream, O.H.G. stroum and G. strom.¹ Cf. Russian
o-strov-ŭ (island), similar in meaning to a G. word um-ge-ström-t
(surrounded by a current).²

IV. Before an explosive, we have seen that the s is remaining,
and the explosive is not affected by Grimm's law.³ The group
sk becomes š; for instances, see above (50, III. 5), and add:
G. schreiben (to write), O.E. scrīfan, borrowed from L. scrīb-ere;
E. shrine = G. schrein,⁴ etc. In the case of sp and st, Mod.
German is well known to admit of both pronunciations, sp st,
and šp št.

The greater part of such roots as began with the group
in question exhibited already in the I.-E. period a peculiar
alternation: in some conditions, which are not yet precisely
defined,⁵ they were liable to lose their initial s, a process fully
illustrated by the Sk. doublet spaç and paç (to see).⁶ The
same alternations are to be observed between the Germanic
and the related languages: thus we have already mentioned
Gr. στέγω and G. dach decken; reciprocally, we have Gr. κοέω
(to remark) = *κοϝ-έω, and L. cav-ēre (to take care), without
initial s, whereas the s reappears in the whole Germanic branch,
especially in O.E. scēaw-ian (to consider) and E. to show, O.H.G.
scouw-ōn (to spy) and G. schau-en (to look at).

Section II.

Medial Sibilants.

(6o) **Verner's Law** governs the voiceless dental Preg.
spirant (s), since it is a general law for all Germanic voiceless

---

[1] We should expect *straum, but cf. supra 32.

[2] This insertion is constant. In stride and schreiten, either we have two different roots, or, in any case, G. has kept unaltered an initial group skr, whilst E. has accidentally changed the k to a t, the more so since O.E. has a vb. scridan (to stride).

[3] Cf. supra 53 B.

[4] Both borrowed from L. scrinium (a box).

[5] Cf. my Gramm. of Gr. and Lat., 68, 4.

[6] Then, of course, in Germanic, the explosive being thus uncovered again falls under Grimm's law.

spirants. The voiced spirant (*z*), on the other hand, falls indirectly under the application of **Grimm's Law**.

§ 1. *Voiceless Sibilant.*

(61) I. Between vowels.—General formulas of Verner's law.

A. **Medial** *s*, if preceded by the I.-E. and Preg. accent, **is kept unchanged throughout the whole Germanic branch**, with this difference only that Mod. E. and G. now sound it mostly as *z*, though the spelling *s* is usually retained (always spelled *s* in German, occasionally *z* in English).[1]

B. But medial *s*, when **following an unaccented syllable, is changed to a** voiced spirant, Preg. *z*, which is kept in Gothic; **West Germanic again changes this** *z* **to the** liquid *r*, thus displaying a process of **rhotacism** which is similar to the Latin mutation in *arbōs* (tree), acc. *arbŏr-em*, and *gen-us* (birth), gen. *gen-er-is* = *gen-es-is = Sk. *ján-as-as* = Gr. *γέν-εσ-ος, then γένεος and γένους.[2]

This new and constant application of Verner's law cannot be better illustrated than by certain alternations between *s* and *z*, which are distinctly preserved in some archaic conjugations, though more or less obliterated by analogy in the later languages.[3] Thus, for instance, the Preg. vb. *kéus-ō (Go *kius-a*, Gr. γεύ(σ)-ω) shows the *s* in the O.E. infinitive *cēos-an* (E. *to choose*), where the accent is known to have rested on the first syllable or normal root, while its participle is O.E. *cor-en* (chosen) = Preg. *kŭsaná-s, regularly changed to *kŭzaná-s, because here the accent is thrown on to the suffix; and, in the same way, archaic and literary German has an infinitive *er-kies-en*, the past participle being *er-kor-en*; but Mod. English created *chosen* after the analogy of the infinitive *choose*. The E. vb. *to lose* = Go. *lius-an* had likewise an O.E. participle *lor-en*, still preserved in Mod. E. *for-lor-n*, an old word which became

---

[1] Cf. G. *glas*, pl. *gläs-er*, but E. *glass*, derivative *glaz-ier*, wherein the group *z+y* takes the sound of *ž*.

[2] The position of the vocal apparatus is the same for lingual *r* as it is for *z*. If we arrange it to utter a *z*, a very slight quivering of the tongue will give us a trilled *r*. Cf. the F. doublet *chaise* (chair) and *chaire* (cathedra), though here, contrariwise, the *r* has been changed to *s* (*z*).

[3] Cf. *supra* 55. The parallelism is absolute.

severed from its original stock, and therefore escaped the analogical influence of the other conjugated forms, whereas a new participle *los-t* was created on the pattern of *lose*. Now, in German, we have exactly the reverse of the English process: *ver-lor-en* was kept, and the infinitive, which should be *ver-lies-en = O.H.G. *vir-lios-an*, adopted the participial *r* and became *ver-lier-en*, so that the regular *s* is only seen in the derivative *ver-lus-t* (loss). The same is the case with E. *frost* = G. *frost*, contrasted with E. *to freeze* = G. *frieren*, etc.

1. After an accented syllable: I.-E. *s* = Preg. *s* = E. and G. *s.* — Sk. *mūš-* (mouse), Gr. μῦς, L. *mūs* and acc. *mūr-em*,[1] O.N. *mūs*, O.E. *mūs* and E. *mouse*, O.H.G. *mūs* and G. *maus*; Sk. *nāsā* (nose), L. *nāsus nārēs*, O.E. *nasu nosu* and E. *nose*, O.H.G. *nasa* and G. *nase*; Preg. *lés-ō (I gather), Go. *lis-an*, O.N. *les-a*, O.E. *les-an* and E. *to lease*, O.H.G. *lës-an* and G. *les-en*, etc. The I.-E. word *kaso-s (hare) probably varied in accentuation, inasmuch as O.H.G. *haso* = G. *hase* supposes a derivation from a Preg. *hása-z, whereas O.N. *here*, O.E. *hara* and E. *hare* do not admit of any other primitive but a Preg. *hazá-s, which is moreover confirmed by the Sk. *çaçá-s*.

2. After an unaccented syllable: I.-E. *s* = Preg. *z* = Go. *z* = E. and G. *r.* — E. *hare* has just been mentioned. To Sk. *máhīyas-* (greater), L. *mājus mājor mājōr-em*, must correspond a Preg. **máẓis-*, changed in consequence to **máẓiz-*, whence: Go. *máiza*[2] (more), O.E. *māra* and E. *more*, O.H.G. *mēro* and G. *mehr*; and so also with every comparative, Go. *bat-iza*, E. *better*, G. *besser*. The I.-E. root *wes* (to dwell, Sk. *vas*) has a pres. sg. 1 Preg. *wés-ō, which is regularly reproduced, with the *s* unaltered, in Go. *vis-an* (to remain, to be), O.E. *wes-an*, G. *wes-en* (an infinitive used as a substantive); but, in the pl. of the pf., the accent is known to have passed from the root to the ending, whence a Preg. **wēs-m̥mé* and **wēz-m̥mé*, E. *we were*, G. *wir waren*.[3] The I.-E. word **óws-* (ear) shifted the accent in

---

[1] The I.-E. *s* is medial everywhere but in the nominative sg.
[2] Putting out of question the puzzling loss of the medial *z*. The comparison, of course, is confined to the sibilant.
[3] Cf. the E. sg. *I was*. In German the *r* has intruded into the sg., *ich war*. In Gothic, on the contrary, which theoretically should have sg. *vas*,

declension to some of its endings, as shown by the Gr. alternation οὖς ὠτός : hence, as opposed to L. *aur-i-s* = **aus-i-s* (cf. *aus-cultō*, "I listen"), we may conceive a Preg. doublet **áus-a-* and **auz-á-*, the former of which is reproduced only by Go. *áus-ō*, all the remaining members of the stock showing the rhotacized *z*, viz. O.N. *eyr-a*, O.E. *ēar-e* and E. *ear*, O.H.G. *ōr-a* and G. *ohr*.

II. Before or after a semi-vowel. This case seldom occurs, and is of no importance.

III. Before or after a nasal or liquid.—Verner's law holds good, unless the *s* has been assimilated to the neighbouring sound: thus, *sn* is changed to *zn*, and, subsequently, to *rn*, cf. G. *lern-en* (to learn) and *lehr-en* (to teach); but *rs* and *rz* give *rr*; *ls, lz, sl* and *zl* become *ll*; and lastly, *sm* and *zm* give *mm*. In the group *sr*, we have the same inserted *t* as when initial, whence *str*, in E. *sister* = G. *schwester*, cf. the Sk. dat. *svásr-ē* (to the sister).

IV. Before or after an explosive: the treatment is the same as when initial.[1]

§ 2. *Voiced Sibilant.*

(62) In the I.-E. groups *zb, zd, zg, zg*, the explosive becomes respectively Preg. *p, t, k*, according to Grimm's law; whereupon assimilation unvoices the *z*, and the final result is *sp, st, sk*. We need but quote one typical instance: the I.-E. root *sĕd* (to sit, to dwell), losing its accent and being reduced in a derivative, formed an I.-E. word **nĭ-zd-ó-s*[2] (dwelling, nest), Sk. *nīdá-s*, L. *nīdu-s*; this word in Pregermanic became **nistá-s* **nestá-s*, E. and G. *nest*, cf. G. *nist-en* (to nestle). The same is the case with Sk. *hĕd-as* (anger), compared with E. *ghost* and G. *geist* (mind).

pl. **vĕzum*, the *s* has been carried on throughout the whole tense, and we have *vas vĕsum*.

[1] Nothing indeed can be clearer than that Verner's law is unable to govern such groups as *sp, st, sk*, or even such as *ps, ks*, changed respectively to *fs, hs*; for, the *s* being here accompanied by a voiceless consonant, even supposing that it could have become *z*, this *z* would again have reverted to the sound *s* by assimilation, *infra* 62.

[2] For the meaning, compare G. *ein-sitz-en*.

SIBILANT CONSONANTS. 117

In the I.-E. groups *zbh, zdh, zgh, zgh*, the Preg. explosive became respectively ƀ, ɖ, ʒ, and therefore the *z* was kept unchanged; then West Germanic regularly altered it to *r*: I.-E. *mizdhó-s (salary), Sk. *mīdhá-s*, Gr. μισθό-ς, Go. *mizdō*, O.E. *meord*, cf. E. *meed* and G. *miethe* (rent). So also *zn* has become *rn*. Everywhere else, the *z* is assimilated (*supra* 61, III.).

SECTION III.

FINAL SIBILANT.

(63) I.-E. has no final sibilant but *s*. It is obvious that in Pregermanic this *s* must either remain *s*, or become *z*, according as it is or is not preceded by the Preg. accent, so that *kasós becomes *hazás, while *kásos gives *hásaz, supra 61, I. 1. Unfortunately, clear as it is, the fact cannot be verified in Gothic, where the final sibilant is always spelled *s*. In O.N. we find exactly the reverse: final *z*, though regular only at the end of an unaccented syllable, was extended throughout, and analogically replaced the final *s*; it was then rhotacized, and thus we find the *-r* to be the regular ending of the nomin. sg. in a great many words quoted from this language. West Germanic is no less corrupted, but, as it were, without a decided preference for either sound; for, in some cases, the *s*, and, in some other cases, the *z* was kept and extended throughout. Further, **final *s* remained** (G. gen. *vater-s, sohn-es*), occasionally however becoming voiced to *z* (E. gen. *father's, son's*, E. pl. *fathers, sons*); whilst **final *z* was dropped** altogether, though kept and, of course, changed to *r* in those little words which became united in pronunciation with the following word, so as to form a single group of sounds. Thus, we have G. *wir* (we) = Go. *veis*, because, in such a locution as Go. *veis bindam* = G. *wir binden* (we bind), the two words were blended into one, and the final *z* was treated as medial.[1]

---

[1] E. *we* has lost the *z* even in this case. Further applications of these laws will occur frequently in the accidence, *infra* 137, 139, 143, 150, 212, etc.

CHAPTER VI.

ACCENT.

(64) Rhythm is as natural and essential an element of human speech as the words themselves. It is only by an artificial method of abstraction that we can sever these two essential factors of any spoken language. Even in the most commonplace sentence the tune, as it were, accompanies the words. Though, of course, these tunes are less marked, less modulated, and, therefore, less artificial, in language, than they are in music, the ear, nevertheless, easily recognises them in respect of both measure and melody. The principal time in each measure is what we call a **stress-accent** (expiratory accent, emphasis, intensity), whereas the high note in the spoken melopœa is said to bear a **pitch-accent** (musical, chromatic, tonic accent).

Stress and pitch are combined, though in very unequal proportions, in every human language, and the character of the speech varies according as the one or the other prevails. Thus, for instance, our European tongues admit very little of a singing tune, at least, in the accurate and conventional pronunciation of educated people [1]; Swedish, however, has developed a pitch-accent, which is the more noticeable because it is often separated from the stress-accent, some syllables being sung on a high note without stress, and others being emphatically uttered though in a lower tone. The languages of Oriental Asia are well known to have developed this musical power of spoken language, so that in Chinese and, above all, in Annamite,

---

[1] For rural dialects and even provincial languages are not at all free from musical intonations, which often sound strange and unpleasant to an unaccustomed hearer.

a given monosyllable may assume the most various meanings, according to the note to which it is sung. But, even in the tongues of Europe, the sentence-accent, if not the word-accent, allows an attentive ear to perceive some musical intervals.

In this province, however, and especially in English and German, the stress-accent decidedly prevails. Thus, an Englishman can scarcely conceive the extreme difficulties under which young people in France long labour before they have mastered the energetic stress of the German accent, which usually rests on the first syllable of the word: *scharf, schärfe, scharfsinnig, scharfsinnigkeit.* The English, in fact, differs from the German accent only in degree: though the syllables are uttered less emphatically, their respective value is very nearly the same in both languages, whereas in French the stress-accent, as resting regularly on the ending of each word, is much duller to the ear, and, moreover, seems to have been of late in process of transformation.

From this **word-accent**, which lays stress on one syllable, and—in the languages we are studying—always on the same syllable of a given word, we must carefully distinguish the **sentence-accent**, which, in a given phrase, according to its meaning and to the respective place of the word-accents contained in it, lends a cadence to the whole speech, as the speaker lays stress upon one syllable, slowly drawls out another, and swiftly gets rid of the remainder, thus indefinitely varying his tones according to his special purpose.

SECTION I.

WORD-ACCENT.

(65) I. In contrast with the fixed and expiratory accent in our modern languages, the Indo-European accent was essentially musical and moveable: a pitch-accent, for it consisted of an alternation of grave and acute tones, which had been preserved even in Greek, as we learn from the testimony of ancient grammarians; a moveable accent, for it was shifted from place to place, throughout the whole system of derivation, declension,

and conjugation, resting at one time on the root, and at another passing to the suffix or to the ending; and these alternations of the accent have already been seen to provoke such strengthenings and weakenings of syllables as are comprised under the general name of I.-E. vowel-gradation, a process still surviving after the death of the living accent which gave rise to it.[1]

It remained musical in Sanskrit and Greek; musical also in Latin, but here it became fixed. Then, at the outset of the Middle Ages, it changed its character and became a stress-accent both in Modern Greek and the Romance languages.

The same change had been accomplished, even in the prehistorical period, throughout the Germanic family: here, the primitive accent survived in the place it had occupied in the Indo-European words; it was still moveable, as shown by the numerous and delicate effects of Verner's law[2]; but it had become a stress-accent. For these effects are inexplicable, unless we suppose the accented syllable to have been pronounced with a greater intensity and a strengthened expiratory breath, so that the following spirant was maintained with its full value, whereas the same spirant, when following an unaccented syllable uttered with less energy, became weakened, and assumed a voiced sound.

II. This Pregermanic accent, however, is no longer to be recognised except in its effects; for it has disappeared in the historical languages. As early as the Pregermanic period another accent had been developed, namely, a stress-accent, invariably resting on the first syllable of each word; the same, perhaps, as the stress which may be observed in Latin, where it produces such well-known processes of vocalic degradation as are best illustrated by the L. types *făctus confĕctus, lĕgo ēlĭgō, cædo occīdō*, and *claudō sēclūdō*. This new initial accent gradually prevailed over the old one, and finally destroyed it. It has now long been the governing accent. Let us briefly state the general principles of this Germanic stress.

1. As a rule, every word, unless it is either enclitic or proclitic,[3] has one, and only one accented syllable.

[1] Cf. *supra* 44.
[3] Cf. *infra* 66, II.
[2] Cf. *supra* 53 D, 55 and 61.

2. From this we are not to infer that all unaccented syllables should be uttered in the same way: what they have in common is, that all are less marked than the accented syllable; but some are more marked than others. This may be easily verified by experiment with such words as E. *opportúnity* and G. *unstérblichkeit*.

3. Especially in compound nouns, the chief accent always rests on the first syllable of the first term, but the first syllable of the second term also retains its accent, though there it has only a secondary stress: E. *bláck-bìrd*, contrasted with the sentence, *the ráven is a bláck bírd*; E. *yéllow-hàmmer*, corrupted from *ammer = O.E. *amore* = O.H.G. *amero* and G. *ammer*, cf. G. *góld-àmmer*; G. *sónnen-fìnsternisz* (eclipse of the sun); E. *brídegroòm* = O.E. *brȳd-guma*, and G. *bräuti-gam* = O.H.G. *brúti-gòmo*,[1] etc.

4. The same is the case with compounds formed of prefix and verb, so far at least as prefix and verb remain present to the speaker's mind as two distinct words, each keeping its own and original meaning, nay, even still separable from one another in German: E. *to óver-loòk*, G. *eín-sètzen*, etc. If, however, the prefix has become blended with the verb into one compound inseparable in meaning, then, of course, the prefix loses its accent, and the accent of the verb is alone retained: we need but compare G. *über-sétzen* (to get over) and *übersétzen* (to translate). Under these conditions the prefix is reduced to a dull syllable (Go. *fra-lúsan-s*, E. *for-lórn*, G. *ver-lóren*; Go. *bi-gítan*, E. *to be-gét*, G. *be-kómmen*, "to receive," *be-quém*, "handy"; Go. *ga-vaúrpan-s*, G. *ge-wórden*, "become," etc.); occasionally in current speech, and even in the written language, to a mere consonant (G. *b-leíben*, *g-laúben*; G. *zwar* = O.H.G. *zi-wā́re*, "forsooth," which in Mod. G. would be *zu wahr, cf. G. *für-wáhr* and E. *for-sóoth*).

5. The peculiar energy of this initial stress, which causes every syllable but one to be more or less slurred over, explains quite satisfactorily, in the Germanic as well as in the Romance languages, the well-known and forcible syncopes, which often

---

[1] Literally "the bride's man," cf. Go. *guma* = L. *homō*. The *r* inserted in English proceeds from the false analogy of *groom* (a youngster).

shortened, so as to scarcely allow of their recognition, both original Germanic words, and those which were early introduced into English and German from Latin or other tongues. Some examples have already occurred: E. *world* and G. *welt*; G. *pferd*, *Pfingsten*, etc.; G. *pfalz* = L. *palatium*; E. *minster* and G. *münster* = L. *monasterium*. Here may be added a few more, selected from the oldest compounds: E. *neighbour* and G. *nachbar*, whereof the second term is *bũr* (planter, peasant), still visible in the G. doublet *Nachbaur* (proper name) [1]; G. *armbrust*, corrupted by a popular etymology from *arm* (arm) and *brust* (chest), really the L. word *arcu-balista*, cf. E. *arbalist* = F. *arbalète*, Italian *balestra*; E. *marshal* and G. *marschall* = O.H.G. *marah-scalc* (horse-groom),[2] also latinized to *mariscalcus*, F. *maréchal*; G. *Samstag* (Saturday) = O.H.G. *sambaʒ-tac* = *sambata-*, cf. Go. *sabbatō dags*; E. *hussy* = *house-wife*; E. *lady* = O E. *hlāf-dige*, literally "she who kneads the bread,"[3] and E. *lord* = O.E. *hlāford* = *hlāf-weard* "loaf-ward"; E. *sheriff* = O.E. *scīr-gerēfa* "officer of the shire," cf. E. *reeve*, etc. Lastly, in English, compare the word *borough* with the final in *Canter-bury* = G. *burg*, and the word *home* with the final in *Notting-ham* = G. *heim* (abode).[4]

6. The tendency to regressive accent is so strong and so universal in the Germanic languages, that it has survived down to the present day. Not only such French words as were brought into English through the Norman conquest, *mútton*, *cóward*, *dánger*, *réason*, etc., underwent this general influence; but, even in Mod. English and German, it often modifies the

---

[1] Alamannic *nōchpr̥*, with the second term completely reduced.
[2] Cf. the modern words E. *mare*, G. *mähre* (mare), Low Breton *marc'h* (horse).
[3] This being deemed the essential function of a landlady. For the terms of the compound, see the words *loaf* and *dough*.
[4] Still more exactly, *-bury* = O.E. *byrig* is the dative of *borough* = *burg*. The most extreme reduction is no doubt to be observed in G. *messer* (knife) = M.H.G. *meʒʒer*, corrupted from *meʒʒeres*, which was mistaken for a genitive, and this again representing an O.H.G. *meʒʒiras* = *meʒʒirahs*, with regular rhotacism, for *meʒʒi-sahs*, literally "a blade for eating." For the first term, compare Go. *mat-s*, O.H.G. *maʒ*, O.E. *mete* (meal), the latter surviving with a restricted sense in E. *meat* (cf. Fr. *viande* "meat" = L. *vivenda* "victuals"); for the second term, L. *sax-u-m* (stone), O.H.G. *sahs* and O.E. *seax* (blade, sword, knife), which trace back the birth of this curious expression to the stone-age.

ACCENT. 123

learned words introduced, not excepting some nearly contemporary borrowings: E. nátion, coúntry-dance = F. contredánse; G. ócean, léutnant = F. lieutenánt.[1] But these processes, curious as they are, it is the province of the dictionary, not of the grammar, to describe.

Section II.

SENTENCE-ACCENT.

(66) The various and almost infinite shades of expression comprised under the general name of sentence-accent would, even were they capable of classification, naturally stand far beyond the reach of the present work. We have here to deal with two cases only: the pitch-accent, illustrated by the well-known contrast between question and answer; and the stress-accent, as affecting the relative atonic character of certain little words, called either **proclitics** or **enclitics**.

I. The difference between an interrogative or exclamatory sentence and a mere affirmation never escaped the most inaccurate ear, the less so because it is often from the tone only that we are able to learn the purpose of the speaker. The characteristic pitch in the former was remarked by Greek grammarians, and was expressed by an invariable acute accent on the interrogative pronoun τίς, whereas the indefinite pronoun τις always remains unaccented. In English, we need but repeat in the usual key such short phrases as "*they are here,*" and "*are they here?*" the concluding syllable in each being sung respectively on the lowest and on the highest note of the spoken melopœa. The intervals, descending or ascending, may in this instance be estimated at the average value of a fifth at most, though increasing whenever the speaker is labouring under strong emotion; and the same may be observed, though with even more vigour, in similar German phrases.[2] A further combination of word-accent and sentence-accent will even reproduce

---

[1] If, however, the word is a long one, the accent is hardly ever thrown back beyond the antepenult: E. *opportúnity,* etc.
[2] Cf. the triple notation of the phrase "*er geht fort*" (he goes off), in Behaghel, *die Deutsche Sprache,* p. 145.

the four musical tones of the peculiar Chinese accentuation in a single English question and answer, as: "You wish *to* stay *two* days, *do* you?—I *do.*"[1]

II. In current speech, such auxiliary words as articles, prepositions, conjunctions, etc., are unaccented and closely united to the words by which they stand. In the English sentence, "*he was thére as I cáme,*" the hearer actually perceives but two words, each of three syllables, whilst grammar finds in it six monosyllables. This case is termed **proclisis**, *i.e.*, the unaccented words are leaning forward upon one following. In the contrary case, **enclisis** takes place, that is, the unaccented words are leaning backwards upon a preceding word as in the sentences, E. *gó on, yés Sir, téll it me,* G. *er schlägt ihn,*[2] *schäme dich, was máchst du?, gieb es mir,* etc.

It follows from the definition that the so-called category of enclitics and proclitics is at once large and indefinite; for it depends entirely on the speaker, who may glide over a word upon which in any other sentence stress would be laid,—as in *don't play the fool,* where the verb *to play* is almost lost in the command given,—or, on the other hand, he may dwell upon some monosyllable which otherwise would appear insignificant, as in "*you* shall *do it,* this *won't do, that's* too *bad,*" and so forth. Here we must confine ourselves to certain main general principles.

1. The so-called demonstrative, especially when weakened to the vague meaning of the definite article, is proclitic and leans upon the following noun: E. *the man,* G. *der sohn.* To this unaccented article are to be referred many syncopes in

---

[1] Viz. *to,* short and brusque; *two,* raised and monotonous; 1. *do,* raised and ascending; 2. *do,* raised and descending. In other words, an affirmative sentence is a completed tune, which concludes on the tonic, or, at least, on the dominant note (authoritative tone), whereas an interrogative sentence is an uncompleted tune, which lacks a conclusion (the answer), and is waiting for it.

[2] Of course, *er* is proclitic, and the three monosyllables make one word.— In these alternations of accented and unaccented syllables, M.H.G. possesses some very delicate laws of secondary accentuation, which might be illustrated by a thorough study of the metrical sources displayed in the *Nibelungenlied*; but here we are unable to enter into such minute details. Cf. Paul, *Mhd. Gramm.,* p. 8.

both languages: G. am=an dem, zur=zu der, even (Alamannic) s puĕch=das buch; vulgar E. tother=*thĕt other, where the article has lost everything but the final t, the same that still appears in the demonstrative that.[1] As to the indefinite article, we have the contrast between G. éin mánn " one man " and G. ein mánn " a man," and this becomes more marked in popular speech, as in Swiss ĕ mā. The same difference has caused the spelling of the word to diverge in English, the O.E. ān (one) having become one in the former case, and an a in the latter.[2] Any other determinative word with slight signification may undergo a similar degradation: we need but compare the swift and short utterance of the possessive, in mylord, mylady, with its emphatic and diphthongized pronunciation in O my Lord and Father!

2. A preposition is proclitic upon the following noun. The two G. words zu (too) and zu (to) are both from O.H.G. zuo= Preg. *tō: the sole difference lies in the accentuation, which, although well marked in German, appears even more clearly in the English spelling, too and to.[3] The same is the case with the contrast between the E. and G. preposition in and the G. prefix ein-: the former was always unaccented; the latter occasionally had the stress laid upon it. Thus every preposition appeared under a double form, which some of them still retain in current speech, though in the literary language one of the two usually prevailed and made the other disappear: E. by=G. bei, both strong, as opposed to the same word reduced to an inseparable prefix, E. be-, G. be-; E. out=G. aus, invariably strong[4]; but E. up, invariably weak, may be contrasted with G. auf, which is no less constantly strong; and there are many such.

[1] Cf. infra 130, 1.—Usually but wrongly spelled t'other, as if the word actually proceeded from an elision of the other.

[2] An before a vowel, a before a consonant (cf. supra 19, 2, note), and consequently also before initial u, since u is sounded yu, and y is a consonant. But, of course, an urn, etc.

[3] Even zu (too) and too may become proclitic if we do not lay stress upon their meaning. The contrast is well marked in Alamannic, proclitic tsĕ, accented tsuĕ.

[4] The weakened vocalism would be E. *ut, G. *us. Cf. E. b-ut (apart from, however), where b- is be-, E. utt-er comparative, and ut-most superlative to out, further to utter (to bring out), etc.

3. The pronoun, when subject, is almost always proclitic upon the verb, unless the speaker means to lay some stress upon the pronoun, a process which is familiar in popular elocution, as in Alamannic *tĕ vayš s võl* "you are aware of it," but *yō tū vayš s* " of course *you* are fit for it" (ironically).

4. Under the same reservation, the pronoun, when object, is generally enclitic—or proclitic if placed before—upon the verb upon which it depends. It is owing to this loose and unaccented pronunciation, that in E. *him* and *her* the initial *h* is no longer heard, nor even written in *it*=O.E. *hit*.[1] From this also many syncopes arise, more or less violent : E. *I told 'em = I told them*,[2] G. *i kenn's=ich kenne es*.

5. The auxiliary verb is rather proclitic—or enclitic if following—upon the principal verb. The process is quite regular in English pronunciation: *I've, I'm, he'd*, etc.,[3] and here, at any rate, much more constant than in German, because G. syntax often severs the auxiliary from the principal verb, so that they cannot lean on one another. But in both languages, at least in the great majority of cases, the verb "to be," even when it does not play the part of auxiliary, is either unaccented, or at most has a secondary accent.

6. Little conjunctions, E. *and, if, when*, G. *und, wenn, wann*, etc., are mostly proclitic. Hence the reduction of O.H.G. *al-sō* "quite so" to G. *als* and (dialectal) *às*, and of the same word O.E. *eal-swā* to E. *as*, whereas the non-proclitic type still survives in E. *also* and G. *also*.

These summary remarks must suffice for the theory of English and German accentuation. A more particular view may be derived from the study of special grammars, or, better still, from the practice of the two languages.

[1] Hence also the weakening of a voiceless to a voiced spirant in *thee, them*, where, owing to enclisis, the *th* was really medial; it then followed by analogy in the nominatives, *thou, they*, and also in *this, that, the*, and the like proclitic monosyllables. The same is the case with *of* and *off*: the former is proclitic, and never final, thus *of him, of the*, pr. ĕvĭm, ĕɩðĕ; the latter is always final and has the secondary accent, as in *he goes off*, pr. hĭyōwzŏf. Cf. *supra*, 49, I., 2, and 54, I., 2.

[2] Strictly speaking, however, *'em* is not syncopated from *them*, but from the old regular plural of *him, infra* 166, II.

[3] Compare the pronunciation of *it 's done* and *'t is done*, according as the enclisis obliterates either the auxiliary or the pronoun.

SECOND PART.

WORDS.

(67) It is a trite and common-place remark, that, however rich a language may be, the whole bulk of its words, if submitted to analysis, amounts to very few. Let us, for example, take such a series as *to respect, respectable, respectful, respectfulness*, all depending on the same word, *respect*. It will only require a slight power of reflexion, even without any knowledge of Latin, to add *aspect, to suspect*, and many others, including their derivatives. Further, any one who is but slightly acquainted with the history of language, may find, as it were, from every part of the dictionary, such distant words as *species, spice, bishop, respite*, etc., all coming to rank under the same head. Shortly, designating by the conventional term "**root**" the **irreducible syllable** which either appears or is concealed in each one of these words and yields it its general meaning, we might enumerate more than a hundred English words which more or less directly have arisen from the Latin root *spec* (to look).

Yet, at the outset, there is a fundamental difference to be noted between these offsprings of a common ancestor. Some of them are formed according to a process of which every speaking person still remains vaguely conscious, and which may at any time be used anew to enrich the tongue with new words at command. In this century, indeed, in this very decade, *steamer* and *boycotter* have sprung from *steam* and *to boycott*, just in the same way as *spice* and *to respect* had formerly produced *spicer* and *respecter*. Others, on the contrary, are old and fixed forms, which are no longer capable of reproduction, inasmuch as historical or prehistorical research would be required in order to discern their primitive elements : thus, the word *respect*, through L. *re-spec-tu-s*, goes back to L. *re-spic-ere*, and claims a place in the numerous family of such Latin nouns as were created by adding to the root a syllable *-tu-*; but it can no longer serve as a pattern for new English formations, since, as a matter of course, people who now-a-days are speaking English know nothing of the word *respectus*, or of the way in which it once arose from *respicere*. If, then, we designate by "**suffix**" the formative **element subjoined** in each of these words, we may say that the suffix *-er* in *boycott-er*, etc., is a **living suffix**, still recognised and used as such by all English speakers, whereas the final *t* in *respect*, though representing a Latin suffix *-tu-*, is a **dead suffix**, a fossil, as it were, dug out of the ground by linguistic exploration.

This distinction likewise holds good for the **prefix, or element added** before a root. It is true that *re-* in *re-spect* is no longer recognised as a prefix to root *spec*; but it is still recognised as such in *re-turn*, *re-place*, *re-flow*, and many others, so as to render possible the creation of such verbs as *re-bellow*, *re-borrow*, *re-photograph*, the meaning of which would be plain to any hearer. On the other hand, though the collective prefix *co-* may be recognised in a great many English words, and though it is still living in the learned derivation of some technical terms, viz. *to co-habit*, *co-heir*, *co-partner*, etc., to be sure no member of a group would think of saying: "We were **co-photographed*." And, if he did, he would scarcely be understood.

All spoken languages, perhaps English and German more than any others, suggest these and similar observations.

First, they exhibit, quite visible and still endowed with a great amount of vitality, the process of **composition**, which is well nigh lost in French. Naturally the two terms in a compound, unless it is very old and has undergone in the course of time considerable phonetic reduction,[1] remain almost always clear to the mind's eye, so that new compounds may be formed

---

[1] See the instances, *supra* 65, 5, and *infra* 114 sq.

just as they are needed, the old ones serving as models for further imitation.

Next, **some** relatively recent **derivations are really compositions**, with but this difference, that their second term is no longer used as a single word: thus we have E. *child-hood* and G. *kind-heit*, whereas E. *hood and G. *heit have now no meaning by themselves. They are dead words, but living suffixes, so intensely living indeed, that the speaker is fully sensible of the specific function he attaches to them, inasmuch as no other derivative from E. *child* and G. *kind* would represent exactly the same shade of meaning.[1]

The case is somewhat different, if we consider, for instance, E. *child-ish* and G. *kind-isch*. Although the suffix *-ish* and *-isch* is a living one and used in forming new words, its meaning is no longer so distinct as in the former case: in other words, a little reflection will show that some other word,—let us say *child-ly, had usage sanctioned it, or *kind-lich* (cf. *männ-lich*), had it not assumed a different shade of signification,—would suit as well. Here we have a **suffix properly so-called**: perhaps, long ago, this suffix also was a word in itself, like *hood and *heit, or like *ly and *lich, which it resembles in force.[2] But it no longer bears any trace of the fact, and the meaning which is now attached to it,—though still accessible to the speaker's mind, and, therefore, still capable of reproduction in some new formation,—is so vague and yielding as to allow half a dozen periphrases to be equally fit for replacing it.

Further, the same suffix *-ish* or *-isch* is to be found in E. *Wel-sh*, from *Wales*, or in G. *men-sch*, from *mann*. Here we may say, if we choose, that it is still perceived, though less

---

[1] And therefore the creation of such new terms as *fenian-ship* (cf. *gypsy-dom*, G. Eliot, *Mill on the Floss*, XI.) or *brahmanen-thum* is always possible, though they are now becoming uncommon. It is because the illiterate have rarely occasion to exert their skill in this way, whereas cultured people are accustomed all their lives to the use of Greek and Latin suffixes (*fenian-ism*, *brahman-ismus*, etc.).

[2] Common sense indeed would suggest that there was a time,—however far back,—when every suffix had a real and distinct meaning; thus every suffix was once a word, and every derivation, strictly speaking, is a composition. However, such deductions are of little practical value to the philologist.

K

clearly. But it is dead and buried, no reproduction of it being at all conceivable. A German would never forge such a word as *gött-sch* "a being of a divine nature," nor an Englishman, such a word as *Burm-sh* " an inhabitant of Burma." And, if this is the case with an element still visible though phonetically weakened, how much more with a great many prehistorical suffixes, which are often reduced to a single consonant, or have even disappeared altogether, leaving but an accidental change, a metaphony to bear witness of their presence, or even vanishing without a vestige to betray them!

(68) The distinction of dead and living suffixes is important not only in respect of their actual use in a given language: it ought also to be considered in the light of such accidental alterations as current speech might impose upon these unstable elements. A word is an organism: while living, it is struggling for life; when dead, it becomes inert and is readily corrupted. Supposing, for instance, that, after the Norman conquest, our word *tree* had been replaced by *arbre*, though the old compounds *apple-tree*, *plum(e)-tree*, *nut-tree*, etc., had been preserved, what would fain have become of these survivals? Since the word *tree* was dead, it would no longer be recognised in such compounds, except as an arbitrary element added to the name of the fruit. Thus, the two *t*'s in *nut-tree* being easily blended in rapid utterance, the word would be likely to become **nutree*. Now, as the speaker would be aware that the difference between *nut* and **nutree* consisted only in an affixed syllable *-ree*, he might well be induced to affix the same syllable to *apple, cherry*, etc., and thus to form such tree-names as **appleree*, **cherryree*, etc. Further, as the final would be unaccented and no longer defended by any outer protection, the dictionary might now exhibit something like **nutry*, **applery*, etc., wherein the primitive *tree* would be completely lost.[1] Now, such blunders as these,

[1] This is just what historically happened to O.N. *þriðjung-r* (a third, a division by three), which was pronounced *riding* in *North-thriding*, whence the names of the two other thirds, *East-* and *West-Riding*, so that now the territorial divisions of Yorkshire appear to have something to do with equestrian exercise. A reversed accretion to a primitive element is likewise possible and even more frequent: thus, from the same cause, Go. *-assu-* became E. *-ness* and G. *-nisz*, G. *-heit* produced *-keit*, etc., as stated below.

more or less extended or restricted as to their effects, are quite common throughout the history of every language, so that even the most complete etymological repertories cannot pretend to register them all in every particular.

Since derivation is liable to such irregularities, it follows that we cannot study it methodically except by tracing it back to its origins; for there, and there only, must it appear as free as possible from perturbing influences. But there is a further reason: living suffixes, however recent they may be, however degraded by successive sound-reductions, however increased by subsequent accretion, differ from the earliest derivative syllables only in form, and not in substance; the processes in language may become more and more intricate, but their nature remains unaltered. A creation out of nothing would be as inconceivable for a suffix as for a word: there is not a derivative element in English or German which may not claim descent from the whole Indo-European past, and the structure of such a modern verb as *veröffentlichen* is based on the same principle as that of a radical verb like *heb-en* = Go. *haf-jan* = L. *cap-iō*. It is a slow and uninterrupted process of **analogical breeding**, that enriches a tongue whether in the case of primitive monosyllables or modern polysyllables; and thus we are compelled to begin with the root, as being the foundation of the building, in order to distinguish and classify such materials as have been brought together and added to it in successive accretions.

(69) We must, therefore, study briefly **Primitive Derivation**, which gave West Germanic, as well as Gothic or any other Indo-European language, its first stock of pattern-words. From this first stock, English and German formerly drew, and are still drawing new words, by applying to them the same processes which served to form the old ones: this is what we call **English and German Derivation**. To these derivative resources, which had become inadequate owing to the phonetic reduction undergone by many suffixes, English and German subjoined some others, such as **accumulation of several suffixes**, or borrowing from a foreign derivation,[1] or

---

[1] As a matter of course, the following pages deal only with Germanic

wide extension of a so-called **false suffix**. This last-named had been first a word in itself, had then become the second term in a compound, and finally losing its meaning, had but the value of a nought at the end of a number. And the last of these processes establishes an easy transition from derivation by suffixes to **Composition** properly so-called, a process transmitted likewise, without noticeable change, from the early Indo-European to the contemporary English and German languages.

suffixes, while those which were borrowed from French, Latin, and Greek require at most very brief mention. Here we may quote: (1) E. *-ess* (F. *-esse* = L. *-issa*), which serves to form the feminine (*mistr-ess*), even for nouns of Germanic origin (*quak-er-ess*); (2) E. *-able*, with the same meaning as F. *-able*, borrowed from L. *-abilis*, and similarly extended (*eat-able*, *read-able*), as well as its derivative *-ability* ; (3) E. *-y*, G. *-ei*, which is simply the O.F. *-ie*, widely extended, E. *butcher-y*, *grocer-y*, then amplified, as in *yeoman-ry*, G. *arzen-ei*, *reiter-ei*, then further amplified, as in *sklave-rei*, etc.; (4) Gr. suffix -ιστής, L. *-ista*, F. *-iste*, E. and G. *-ist*, in common use, in spite of its learned origin, E. *novel-ist*, G. *artiller-ist*, *hobo-ist*, *horn-ist*, etc. Further add, in English, the Latin or Romance suffixes, all of them more or less naturalized, of such words as *fulfil-ment*, *slumber-ous* (F. *-eux*), *hindr-ance*, *starv-ation*, *Siam-ese* (F. *-ois*), etc. As far as derivation is concerned, English might be deemed almost as much a Romance as a Germanic tongue.

CHAPTER I.

PRIMITIVE DERIVATION.

(70) The **combination of a root with a single suffix**,[1] being the simplest element in spoken language after the pure root, is called a **stem**, or, more accurately, a **primary stem**. To the primary suffix may be added a **secondary** one; to this, a third, and so on indefinitely.[2] Since, however, the derivative process remains uninterrupted and invariable, we need but distinguish two degrees in the scale of derivation, namely primary and secondary suffixes, the latter including any degree whatever beyond the primary, observing, moreover, that the so-called secondary suffixes are for the most part either primary suffixes, or accumulations of primary suffixes, which have been analogically extended from primary to secondary formation.

SECTION I.

PRIMARY SUFFIXES.

(71) The primary **stem** derived from a root may be either **nominal** or **verbal**, that is to say, adapted for playing in any proposition the part either of a noun or a verb, according as it is capable of receiving, by accretion to its characteristic suffix, the peculiar endings of declension or conjugation. This funda-

---

[1] The I.-E. language knew nothing of derivation by prefix. The element which has become, for instance, G. *ge-* or *ver-*, was originally a word in itself, and indeed quite as independent a word as may now be G. *auf* or *durch*; which is as much as to say that in Germanic the prefixation is primitively a true composition.

[2] We may instance, starting from an I.-E. root $p\bar{u}$ (to be foul):—primary stem, I.-E. *$p\bar{u}$-ló-* = O.E. *fū-l* = E. *fou-l*; — secondary stem, O.E. *fȳ-l-ð* (= *$f\bar{u}$-l-ið*), E. *fi-l-th*;—tertiary stem, E. *fi-l-th-y*;—quaternary stems, E. *fi-l-th-i-ly*, *fi-l-th-i-ness*,—and so forth; for, if a vb. *to* *filthify* ever happened to be formed, the quinary *filthification* would ensue without difficulty.

mental distinction governs the whole of grammar,[1] and no other could here better suit our purpose.

§ 1. *Nominal Stems.*

(72) I. Root-Stems.—In some rare cases, the bare I.-E. root, without any suffix, may be declined and therefore plays the part of a noun. Thus, an I.-E. root, normal *pĕd*, deflected *pŏd*, was declined with the nominal meaning "foot," whence, after a vocalic lengthening which often appears in the nomin. sg., I.-E. **pēd-s* or **pōd-s*, Sk. *pâd*, Gr. πούς = πώς = *πώδ-ς, L. *pēs* = **pēd-s*, etc.; these forms, in Germanic, become O.N. *fōt-r*, O.E. *fōt* and E. *foot*, O.H.G. *fuoʒ* and G. *fusz*. As, however, the stems belonging to the classes given below, after they had regularly dropped the final vowel, were no longer distinguishable from stems formed without any suffix-vowel at all, analogy could not fail to group together these apparently similar words, so that the root-stems were as a rule not distinguished from further derivations.[2]

II. Stems ending with a short vowel: -ŏ- (-ĕ-),[3] -ĭ-, -ŭ-.—It is of course impossible to recognise, in the nomin. sg., either in West Germanic or Gothic, a stem formed by addition of a bare suffix -ŏ- or -ĭ-.[4] But the vowels reappear, in Gothic, in the other cases; and, even in English and German, they may be sometimes inferred from the declension, especially from a metaphony which the ĭ had produced before it was dropped. In these formations, the root generally assumes either the normal or deflected grade.

1. Stems in -*o*-, masculine or neuter, never feminine: I.-E.

---

[1] *Speech consists of no other words than nouns and verbs*: the adjective and the pronoun are but varieties of the noun; invariable words, as far as they admit of an etymology, ought to be traced back to ancient cases of nouns, adjectives, and pronouns, which survived from a forgotten declension.

[2] Thus, G. *fusz* (pl. *füsz-e*) is declined as if it were derived from a Preg. **fōt-i-*, and, even in Gothic, the regular **fōt-s* has become nomin. *fōt-u-s*, through the analogy of acc. *fōt-u* = **fōt-u-m* (cf. L. *ped-em*) = I.-E. **pŏd-m*.

[3] It should always be borne in mind that any syllable containing I.-E. ŏ, may change this ŏ to ĕ, and *vice versa*, *supra* 44: Gr. nomin. sg. ἴππ-ο-ς, voc. sg. ἴππ-ε. As a matter of fact, however, the grade ŏ (Preg. ă), favoured by analogy, was the only one retained in suffixes ending with a vowel; the alternation between ŏ and ĕ, when followed by a consonant, will occur below, 74 and 80.

[4] Cf. *supra* 34, § 2.

root *dhegh* (Sk. *dah*, " to burn, to shine "), whence a msc. stem **dhogh-ó-s* (day), Preg. **ðaʒ-á-s*, Go. *dag-s*, O.N. *dag-r*, O.E. *dæg* and E. *day*, O.H.G. *tac* and G. *tag*; I.-E. root *yĕwg* (Sk. *yuj*, " to join, to team "), whence a nt. stem **yŭg-ó-m* (yoke), Sk. *yugám*, Gr. ζυγόν, L. *jugum*, Preg. **yŭk-á-m*, Go. *juk*, O.E. *geoc* and E. *yoke*, O.H.G. *joh* and G. *joch*.

2. Stems in -*i*-, in the three genders: I.-E. root *bhĭd* (to split, cf. L. *find-ere*), whence msc. **bhid-i-s* (the act of splitting or biting), Preg. **bĭt-i-z*, Old Saxonic *bit-i* and E. *bit*, G. *bisz*; so also, Go. *slah-s* (a blow), O. Sax. *sleg-i*, G. *schlag*[1] msc.; Sk. fm. **jān-i-s* (woman), Go. *qēn-s*, E. *queen*; L. nt. *mare* (sea) = **mar-ĭ*, Go. *mari-* only in composition, E. *mere*, and G. *meer* (sea), where the *i* has caused metaphony.

3. Stems in -*u*- (the *u* is kept in Gothic, but is dropped everywhere else, so that the class has become obscured): Gr. κράτ-υ-ς (strong), Go. *hard-u-s*, E. *hard*, G. *hart*; Go. *hand-u-s* (hand), E. and G. *hand*, the G. pl. being *händ-e*, as if the declensional stem were **hand-i-*.

(73) III. Stems ending with a long vowel -*ā*, essentially feminine.—This class, which corresponds to the so-called first declension in Greek and Latin, is of considerable importance in Indo-European, and yet of little significance in modern Germanic languages, final -*ā* (Preg. -*ō*) having become Go. -*a*, and then being changed to the dull vowel, or even completely dropped in later languages (Go. *airþa*, O.N. *jorð*, O.E. *eorðe* and E. *earth*, O.H.G. *ërda*, M.H.G. *ërde* and G. *erde erd*); whereupon the declension, which had lost its characteristic feature, became the sport of analogy.[2] But we must here lay stress upon the old and constant **parallelism between the fm.** *ā*, **and the msc.-nt.** *ŏ* which has been illustrated above. From this it follows, that any suffix, viz. -*ŏ*-, -*mŏ*-, -*nŏ*-, -*tŏ*-, etc., ending

---

[1] Thus, in the sg., G. *tag* and *schlag* are alike; but in the pl. we have *tag-e* = Go. *dagōs* = I.-E. **dhoghôs* contracted from **dhogh-ó-ĕs*, and metaph. *schläg-e* which would be Go. **slageis* = **slag-iy-ĕs*, so that the suffix-vowel becomes visible.—Observe moreover that it is not at all necessary that a given derivation should always exhibit the same suffix throughout the I.-E. family: the word which, for instance, is L. *pisc-i-s* (fish), is Germanic **fisk-a-z* (Go. sg. *fisk-s*, pl. *fiskōs*), whence we may infer two distinct I.-E. forms, viz. **pisk-i-s* and **pisk-o-s*.

[2] *Infra* 142, 4, and 150, 1.

with ŏ and forming a masculine or neuter stem, may likewise end with ā, thus -ă, -mā, -nā, -tā, etc., and represent under this shape a correlative feminine. In particular the nouns of three genders, that is to say the adjectives, exhibit the three well-known endings: Sk. msc. *priy-á-s* (dear), fm. *priy-â*, nt. *priy-á-m*; Gr. δίκα-ιο-ς δικα-ία δίκα-ιο-ν, καλ-ό-ς καλ-ή καλ-ό-ν; L. *bon-u-s bon-a bon-u-m*, etc. This process still appears very clearly in Gothic: *lagg-s lagg-a lagg, liuf-s liub-a liuf*, etc. And though, of course, the German alternation, *lang lang-e, lieb lieb-e*, can no longer be said to reproduce it,[1] yet there is still some resemblance between the two processes; indeed, the latter proceeds indirectly from the former, inasmuch as the final in *lang-e* is borrowed from a primitive demonstrative stem which originally formed its feminine in that way.

IV. Stems with suffixes -*yo*- (-*yā*) and -*wo*- (-*wā*).—The laws of Germanic sounds have completely altered these once important classes: I.-E. **médh-yo-s* **médh-yā*, Sk. *mádh-ya-s*, Gr. μέσος = μέσσος = **μέθ-yo-ς*, L. *med-iu-s med-ia*, Go. *mid-ji-s*, whereof the metaphony survives in E. *mid*, G. *mit* (by means of, with), and G. fm. *mitte* (middle); I.-E. root *rō rǎ* (to rest), Gr. ἐρωή (rest) = **ρω-Fā*, Preg. **rō-wō*, whence O.H.G. *ruowa* and G. *ruhe*.[2]

(74) V. Stems with suffixes -*ĕn*- (reduced -*n*-, deflected -*ŏn*-) and -*yĕn*- (red. -*īn*-, defl. -*yŏn*-).—Here at length we have come to an end of the suffixes which could not escape being completely defaced in Germanic phonology. Every one of those which follow contained at least one element capable of resisting this perverting influence; and, in the case of the present nasal suffix, the *n* not only subsisted, as it regularly ought to do except when final, but even spread out on a large scale, a process which in grammar constitutes what we may call the encroachment of the **weak declension**.[3] In order to account for it, we must observe first, that the vowel in this suffix is lengthened in the nominative, and further that it passes in

---

[1] Cf. *infra* 155 and 157.
[2] It is the same root which, with another suffix and in a different (reduced) grade, became Go. *ra-sta* (staple), E. *rest*, G. *rast*.
[3] Cf. *infra* 140–142, 149, 150, 156, etc.

declension through the three vocalic grades: Gr. κύ-ων (dog), but gen. κυ-ν-ός; L. hom-ō (man), but gen. hom-in-is. Now the I.-E. n in this suffix, when final, that is to say only in the nomin. sg., might either be kept or disappear.[1] All these alternations, variously distributed, are to be found again in Germanic stems: thus, Gothic answers the L. hom-ō, quite regularly, with nomin. sg. gum-a; it answers the L. gen. hom-in-is with its gen. gum-in-s, wherein the vowel is altered, and the n likewise reappears; and lastly, like Gr. κύ-ων, Go. has the nomin. sg. tuggō, with a long final vowel irresistibly pointing to a Preg. *tuñʒōn (tongue), inasmuch as the ō, if uncovered, would have been shortened.

1. Stems in -ŏn-.—A. Nomin. sg. in -ō changed to -ă, msc. nouns: Sk. ukš-án- ("bull," nomin. ukš-á, gen. ukš-n-ás), Go. nomin. aúhs-a and gen. aúhs-in-s, O.E. ox-a and E. ox (pl. ox-en), O.H.G. ohs-o and G. ochs-e ochs (gen. ochs-en); so also, Go. han-a ("cock," gen. han-in-s) and G. hahn, to which the L. correlative would be *can-ō (singer) with gen. *can-ōn-is; Go. gard-a (enclosure), gen. gard-in-s, cf. E. yard and G. gart-en, which would be L. *hort-ō *hort-in-is (cf. hort-u-s), etc.

B. Nomin. sg. in -ōn changed to -ō.—(a) With further extension of the long vowel to the oblique cases, feminine nouns:[2] Go. tugg-ō (gen. tugg-ōn-s),[3] O.E. tung-e and E. tongue, O.H.G. zung-a and G. zung-e (pl. zung-en); Go. azg-ō (gen. azg-ōn-s), O.E. æsc-e and E. ash, O.H.G. asc-a and G. asch-e, etc.—(b) Without this extension, neuter nouns (very few, but important): Go. áug-ō (gen. áug-in-s), O.E. ēag-e (gen. ēag-an) and E. eye, O.H.G. oug-a and G. aug-e (pl. aug-en); likewise, Go. haírt-ō, E. heart and G. herz, Go. áus-ō, E. ear and G. ohr.

2. Stems in -yŏn-.—A. Nomin. sg. in -yō changed to -ja,

[1] Greek keeps it throughout, Latin never.
[2] Thus, Germanic is seen to have made the most of the old distinction between short and long vowel, by employing it subsidiarily to distinguish its masculine from its feminine stems.
[3] Sk. jihv-â and L. lingu-a = *dingu-a appear without any nasal suffix; but, owing to the fact that both suffixes Preg. -ō (=I.-E. -ā) and -ōn (=I.-E. -ōn) had assumed a feminine function, the latter, as being better preserved and, in consequence, more characteristic, showed an early tendency to replace the former. This may be deemed the first step in the expansion of the weak declension.

masculine nouns: Go. *arb-ja* ("heir," gen. *arb-jin-s*), O.E. *yrf-e*, replaced in E. by *heir*=O.F. *hoir* from L. *hērēs*, G. *erb-e* (pl. *erb-en*); Go. *fráu-ja* (lord), cf. O.H.G. *frō*, the derivative base of an adjective *frohn*, preserved, for instance, in *frohn-dienst* (husbandry service).

B. Nomin. sg. in *-yōn* changed to *-jō*, feminine nouns: Go. *arb-jō* ("heiress," gen. *arb-jōn-s*); likewise, G. *frau* ("lady," pl. *frau-en*) = O.H.G. *frouw-a*, which presupposes a Go. **fráu-jō* fm. of the msc. *fráu-ja* above.

C. Nomin. sg. in *-īn* (changed to *-ī*), due to a transfer by analogy, to the nominative, of the suffix-form which originally belonged to the oblique cases: thus, a fm. abstract noun Preg. **hauh-jōn* (height) had a regular gen. **hauh-īn-az*; analogy gave a nomin. **hauh-īn*, whence **hauh-ī*, Go. *háuh-ei* (gen. *háuh-ein-s*), O.H.G. *hōh-ī* and G. *höh-e*[1] (pl. *höh-en*); similarly, Go. *manag-ei* (multitude), O.E. *menig-o*, O.H.G. *menig-ī* and G. *meng-e*, cf. G. *manch*=O.H.G. *manag*=E. *many*. The whole German derivation of abstract nouns, as *tief-e, läng-e, kürz-e*, as opposed to *tief, lang, kurz*, is based on the addition of this suffix,[2] which is further to be found in such Latin types as *leg-iō* (gen. *leg-iōn-is*), *ob-sid-iō* (siege), etc.

(75) VI. Stems with suffix *-mo-* (*-mă*), quite common: I.-E. root *gher* (heat), whence an adj. **ghor-mó-s* (warm), Sk. *ghar-má-s* (Gr. θερ-μό-ς), L. *for-mu-s*, Preg. **ʒwar-má-s*, Go. **var-m-s*, E. and G. *war-m*; I.-E. root *dhē* (to place, to do), whence a noun **dhō-mó-s*, Gr. θω-μό-ς (heap), Preg. **ðō-má-s* (business, judgment, jurisdiction), Go. *dō-m-s*, O.E. *dōm* and E. *doom -dom*, O.H.G. *tuom* and G. (suffix) *-thum*;[3] I.-E. **bhudh-mó-s* (bottom, cf. Gr. πυθ-μήν), O.E. *botm* and E. *bottom*, O.H.G. *bodam* and G. *boden*; similarly, E. *strea-m* and G. *stro-m*=I.-E. **srow-mó-s*, from a root *srŭ srĕw* (to flow); E. *roo-m* and G. *rau-m*=I.-E. **rū-mó-s*; L. *cul-mu-s* (stubble), O.E. *heal-m*, O.H.G., G. and E. *hal-m*, etc.

VII. Stems with suff. *-men-* (*-mn-, -mŏn-*), reproducing exactly

---

[1] Observe the constant and regular metaphony.
[2] English replaced it by another derivation, *infra* 90 (V. 2), but still preserves it in such alternations as *proud pride*=O.E. *prūt prȳte*.
[3] Cf. *infra* 109, II.

PRIMITIVE DERIVATION.

the alternations of suff. -ĕn-: compare Gr. πυθ-μήν πυθ-μέν-ος, δαί-μων δαί-μον-ος, and (nt.) ὄνο-μα (=*ὄνο-mṇ), Sk. ná-ma (=*nŏ-mṇ, gen. ná-mn-as), L. nō-men nō-min-is, etc.—Msc. Go. blō-ma=Preg. *blŏ-mō (flower) =I.-E. nomin. sg. *bhlō-mō, from a stem *bhlō-men- and a root bhlō (to bloom), O.E. blō-ma and E. bloom, O.H.G. bluo-mo msc., and G. blu-me now fm.[1] Further compare: O.H.G. msc. sā-mo and G. sa-me, to L. sē-men (seed), from root sē (to sow, G. sä-en); Go. nt. na-mō, O.H.G. msc. na-mo and G. na-me (gen. na-men-s), E. na-me, to L. nt. nō-men, etc. The double suff. -mṇ-to- in the L. nt. type co-gnō-men-tu-m, etc., is represented by G. leu-mund (renown) =*hliu-mun-d= I.-E. *klĕw-mṇ-to-, from root klŭ (to hear), cf. Gr. κλυ-τό-ς and L. in-clu-tu-s (famous).

(76) VIII. Stems with suff. -ro- (-rā) and -lo- (-lā), -ri- and -li-, -ru- and -lu-.—Of these six liquid-classes, which have been more or less confused with one another and have lost a great number of their examples, only three can be recognised in Germanic.

1. Stems in -ro-: we need only recall the words already quoted, E. acre=G. acker (Gr. ἀγ-ρό-ς), E. year=G. jahr (Gr. ὤ-ρᾱ, ὥ-ρο-ς), E. timber=G. zimmer=Preg. *tem-rá- (Gr. δέμ-ω, "to build"), and add such adjectives[2] as E. sour and G. sauer= O.N. sū-r-r=I.-E. *sū-ró-s, Go. fag-r-s (apt, convenient), O.E. fœg-r and E. fair, cf. G. feg-en ("to sweep," originally "to purify, to adapt"), etc.

2. Stems in -lo-: I.-E. root pū (to be foul, cf. Gr. πῦ-θω, L. pū-s, etc.), whence adj. *pū-ló-s, Preg. *fū-lá-s, Go. fū-l-s, O.N. fū-l-l, O.E. fū-l and E. foul, O.H.G. fū-l and G. faul; I.-E. root syu (to sew, Gr. κα-σσύω, L. suō, etc.), whence a noun of instrument I.-E. *syu-lá (awl), O.H.G. siu-la and G. säule. In some cases the suffix is preceded by an s of doubtful origin: L. āla (wing, arm-pit) =*áxla =*ak-slá (cf. L. axilla "arm-pit"), O.H.G. ah-sala and G. ach-sel (shoulder), O.E. eaxl lost in E. Further, an accessory i, which was developed by the resonance of the liquid, gave birth to a Germanic suffix -ila, which plays

---

[1] With the n re-appearing in the Go. gen. blō-min-s, and in the G. pl. blu-men.

[2] Remember the numerous Gr. adjectives in -ρό-ς.

an important part in the diminutive derivation, as will be seen below (no. 88 and 103).

3. Stems in -*ru*-: O.E. *flō-r* and E. *floor*, M.H.G. *vluo-r* and G. *flur*, from a msc.-fm. Preg. **flō-ru-s*=I.-E. **plā-ru-s*, root *plā* (even, plane, cf. L. *plā-nu-s*); I.-E. nt. **dák-ru* (tear), Gr. δάκ-ρυ, L. *lac-ru-ma*, Go. *tag-r*, O.N. *tār*=**tah-r*, O.E. *tēar*=**teah-r*, and E. *tear*, O.H.G. *zahar* and G. *zähre*.

(77) IX. Stems with suff. -*no*- (-*nă*), -*ni*- and -*nu*-.—1. The I.-E. suff. -*no*- is a common one, as also in Germanic: I.-E. root *pel* (to fill), whence Sk. *pūr-ná-s* and L. *plē-nu-s*, Preg. **ful-ná-s*, Go. *fulls*=**ful-n-s*, E. *full*, G. *voll*; I.-E. root *dĕyk* (to show, cf. Gr. δείκ-νῡ-μι and L. *dīc-ere*), whence a derivation **doyk-no-s* (sign), Preg. **taik-na-z*, Go. *táik-n-s*, O.E. *tāc-n* and E. *tok-en*, O.H.G. *zeihh-an* and G. *zeich-en* (cf. the G. vb. *zeig-en*, "to show"); but these scanty nominal survivals give but little idea of the extent to which in one particular form this suffix has become used.

As early as the I.-E. period, there existed a suff. -*eno*- or -*onó*-, which, inasmuch as it could be declined in the three genders (-*onó-s* -*onâ* -*onó-m*), was directly added to the root by way of forming certain stems of middle and **passive participles**. Let us consider a root *wĕrt* (to turn), Sk. *várt-ati* (he turns), L. *vert-ere*: the pf. middle participle was **we-wr̥t-onó-s* (Sk. *vā-vr̥t-āná-s*), with the threefold meaning "turning, turning himself, turned." Now, the literal transliteration of this **we-wr̥t-onó-s*, omitting the reduplication, is the Go. participle *vaúrþ-an-s* (become), G. (*ge-*)*word-en*. Thus, nothing could be clearer than the whole formation, both in English and German, of the so-called past participles (in -*en*) of strong verbs.[1] The same suffix, again, inasmuch as it was invariable in a neuter form -*ono-m*, was a characteristic ending for neuter nouns of action: thus, from an I.-E. root *bher* (to carry, φέρ-ω, *fer-ō*), an I.-E. word **bhér-ono-m* (the act of carrying), Sk. *bhár-ana-m*, Preg. **bér-ana-m*, whence Go. *baír-an*. Now, this *baír-an*, having lost its whole declension, merely serves as an **infinitive** to the verb *baír-a* (I carry)=L.

---

[1] It should be noticed that the suffix is accented and, in consequence, duces the root. As to this process, the reader is referred to the study of owel-gradation, as stated above and illustrated by this derivative, *supra* 45.

fer-ō; and so also with any Go. infinitive: *steig-a* (I go up), *steig-an* (to go up), G. (*ich*) *steig-e* and *steig-en*, etc., etc. In short, the ending -*an*, O.E. -*an*, dropped in M.E.,[1] O.H.G. -*an*, G. -*en*, is a survival from the formative suffix of an ancient neuter noun, which signified "the act of doing" what was meant by the verbal root. Hence, this single suffix -*ono*- gives us the key to two grammatical categories of great importance, and, at the same time, we are taught that in Germanic, as also in every other representative of the I.-E. family,[2] neither **the infinitive** nor **the past participle** is a mood of the verb, both being in reality **nominal formations**, respectively, a noun denoting an action and a noun denoting a state.

2. Stems in -*ni*- : a few adjectives. I.-E. had a root *skaw* (to look at, to spy), Lat. *cav-ēre*, G. *schau-en*: hence proceeded a word **skăw-ni-s* (conspicuous, beautiful), O.H.G. *scō-ni*, reproduced without metaphony in G. *schon*,[3] with metaphony in O.E. *scȳ-ne* and E. *sheen*, M.H.G. *schœ-ne* and G. *schön*. Compare also : root *kri* (to discern, to purify), L. *cri-bru-m* (sieve), whence a word **kroy-ni-s* (pure), Preg. **hrai-ni-z*, Go. *hrái-n-s*, G. *rein*.[4]

3. Stems in -*nu*- : I.-E. root *sū su* (to bring forth), Sk. *sū-nú-s* (son, cf. Gr. υἱός = **συ-ιο-ς*), Go. *su-nu-s*, E. *son*, G. *sohn*; Sk. nt. *tṛ-na-m* (blade of grass), Go. *þaúr-nu-s*, E. *thorn*, G. *dorn* msc.; L. nt. *cor-nu*, Go. *haúr-n*, E. and G. *horn* nt. In the last two instances, suff. -*nu*- is seen to alternate with suff. -*no*-.

(78) X. Stems with suff. -*to*- (-*tā*), -*ti*- and -*tu*-.—Any suffix with initial *t* will usually present itself in three Germanic forms, according to a distinction stated above,[5] namely : *t* (after *s*, etc.) ; *þ* (Grimm's law), and *ð* (Verner's law). Recalling this once for all, and leaving it henceforth to the reader, we need only observe that suff. -*tó*- of past participles is regularly accented in Greek and Sanskrit (-*tá*-), and so also, in Sanskrit, with the suff. -*ti*- of nouns denoting an action.

[1] Cf. *supra* 19, 2.
[2] Henry, *Gramm. of Gr. and Lat.*, 115 (5), 117 and 125.
[3] The meaning is "fairly," whence "already."
[4] E. *clean* (= G. *klein*, supra 17, 6) is similar in meaning and formation, but the root is unknown.
[5] Cf. *supra* 53.

1. **Stems in -to-.**—This very extensive formation essentially consists of words of three genders, derived from a verbal root and having the sense of **passive participles**[1] : Sk. root *ric* (to leave), *rik-tá-s* (left); Gr. λείπ-ω, λειπ-τό-ς; L. *linqu-ō*, *līc-tu-s*, etc. In Germanic primary derivation, it is chiefly represented by certain adjectives no longer connected with any verb: thus, L. *rēc-tu-s* (right) may still be recognised as the participle of the vb. *reg-ere* (to guide), whereas Go. *raíh-t-s*, E. *righ-t* and G. *rech-t* now appear quite isolated. In the same way a great many similar English and German adjectives were originally participles of an obsolete verb, as: Go. *kal-d-s* (cf. L. *gel-u*), E. *col-d*, G. *kal-t*; Go. *vun-d-s* (hurt) and G. *wund*, Preg. fm. **wun-ðá* (wound), E. *wound*, G. *wun-de*; Go. *dáu-þ-s*, E. *dead*, G. *todt*; E. *tigh-t* = G. *dich-t*; E. *sligh-t* = G. *schlech-t* (bad), the primitive sense being "flattened"; E. *lou-d* = G. *lau-t*, already contrasted with Gr. κλυ-τό-ς (heard of); E. *un-couth*, the negative to O.E. *cū-ð* = G. *kun-d* (known), cf. Gr. γνω-τό-ς, etc.

As a participial suffix, the primary element *-tó-* occurs with equal frequency: here we may recall *though-t* and *ge-dach-t*, *brough-t* and *ge-brach-t*,[2] E. *weep wep-t*, *sleep slep-t*, *lose los-t*, etc. But these are analogical formations: cf. G. *ge-schlaf-en*, *ver-lor-en*. Originally primary *-tó-* could scarcely resist the almost overwhelming influence of suff. *-onó-* = Germanic *-en*, which had assumed the same meaning. It will be seen, on the other hand, to have prevailed in weak verbs, that is to say, in secondary derivation.

2. **Stems in -ti-.**—This suffix, also very common, formed many **nouns of action** or of object, in gender almost constantly feminine: Sk. *ga-tí-s* (march), Gr. φά-τι-ς (speaking, word), L. *ves-ti-s* (garment), etc. Both meaning and gender are well preserved in Germanic: compare G. *komm-en* and *-kunf-t* (with an *f* phonetically inserted, cf. Go. *ga-qum-þ-s* "meeting"), G. *kenn-en* and *kun-st* (art), the suff. here receiving

---

[1] On the ordinal function of this suffix, cf. *infra* 124.
[2] On the phonetic relation between *think* and *thought*, etc., cf. *supra* 24 and 53 C.

PRIMITIVE DERIVATION. 143

an initial accretion, E. *to do* and *dee-d*, G. *thu-n* and *tha-t*, E. *to give* and *gif-t*, G. *geb-en* and *gif-t* (poison, now msc.), E. *to see* and *sigh-t*, G. *seh-en* and *sich-t*, E. *he may* and *migh-t*, G. *mög-en* and *mach-t*, G. *denk-en* (to think) and *an-dach-t* (piety), E. *flight* = G. *fluch-t*, etc.

3. Stems in *-tu-*.—Rare in Greek, though very common in Sk. and Latin (*sta-tu-s*, *gus-tu-s*, *flūc-tu-s*, and all the so-called supines in *-tu-m* and *-tū*), these are likewise nouns denoting an action, nearly synonymous with the former class, but strictly masculine. They are still seen in Gothic: thus, from an I.-E. root *plō* (Gr. πλω-τό-ς "navigable"), an I.-E. stem *plō-tú-s*, Preg. *flō-ðú-s*, Go. *flō-du-s* (flood). But, after the *u* had been dropped in the later languages, these stems no longer remained distinguishable from those in *-ti-*, so that both classes were blended together: O.E. *flōd* and E. *flood*, O.H.G. *fluot* and G. *flut* fm.; similarly, Go. *luf-tu-s* (air), but O.E. *lyft*, which is shown by its metaphony to be **luf-ti-*, and G. fm. *luft* with metaph. pl. *lüf-te*.

(79) XI. Stems with suff. *-t-* and *-nt-*.—The former is rare, though well marked in I.-E. **noq-t-* (night), Gr. νύξ (gen. νυκ-τ-ός), L. *nox* (gen. *noc-t-is*), Preg. **nah-t-*, Go. *nah-t-s*, O.E. *neaht* and E. *night*, O.H.G. *naht* and G. *nacht*. The latter is the regular suffix for active participles, in which function it will be illustrated by the secondary derivation. It seems to have been kept as primary only in I.-E. **do-nt-* red. **d-ṇt-* (tooth), Sk. *dá-nt- d-at-*, Gr. ὀδούς (gen. ὀδό-ντ-ος), L. *dēns* (gen. *d-ent-is*), Preg. **ta-nþ- *t-unþ-*, whence Go. *tunþu-s*,[1] O.E. **tŏnð tōð* and E. *tooth*, O.H.G. *zand zan* and G. *zahn*.

XII. Stems with suff. *-tér-* (*-tr-*, *-tor-*).—This formation is common in Sanskrit, Greek and Latin, and comprises a considerable number of so-called nouns of agent, either primary or secondary: Sk. *dā-tár-* "giver," Gr. δο-τήρ δώ-τωρ, L. *da-tor*. In Germanic it has been supplanted by another derivation of secondary origin,[2] the only survivals being the nouns of re-

---

[1] The second *u* proceeds from the analogy of the acc. *tunþu* = L. *dentem* = I.-E. **dṇt-m̥*. But this corruption is an exclusively Gothic one, the O.E. plural being (metaph.) *tēð* = **tŏþ-ĭz* = **tŏnþ-ĭz* = **dṇt-ĕs*.
[2] Cf. *infra* 102.

lationship "father, mother, brother, daughter," which have often occurred in our exposition.

XIII. Stems with suff. -trŏ- (-trā) and -tlŏ- (-tlā), homologous to the preceding stems, but essentially **nouns of instrument**, very common: I.-E. root *pă* (to feed, L. *pă-scō, pă-bulu-m* "food"), whence I.-E. **pă-tró-m*, Preg. **fŏ-ŏrá-m*, O.N. *fō-dr*, O.E. *fōdor* and E. *fodder*,[1] O.H.G. *fuotar* and G. *futter*; noun of action, E. *laugh-ter* and O.H.G. *hlah-tar*, whence G. collective *ge-läch-ter*; E. *slaugh-ter*, etc.; I.-E. root *nē* (to spin, to sew, cf. L. *nē-re*, Gr. *νῆ-μα*, G. *näh-en* = O.H.G. *nā-en* = Go. **nē-jan*), whence Preg. stem **nē-þlō*, Go. *nē-þla*, O.E. *nǣdl* and E. *needle*, O.H.G. *nādal* and G. *nadel*; G. *beil* (hatchet) = O.H.G. *bī-hal*,[2] from the I.-E. root *bhid* (to split), etc.

XIV. Stems with suff. -tero- (-terā).—This element originally indicated an alternation between *two* things: Sk. *ka-tará-s* "which of both?" Gr. *πό-τερο-s*, L. *u-ter, al-ter*, etc. It is dead, but still visible in: E. *ei-ther* and G. *je-der*; E. *nei-ther* and G. *we-der* = O.H.G. *ni-wë-dar*; O.E. *wi-ðer* (against), whence E. *with*, G. *wi-der* (against) and *wie-der* (again); perhaps E. *fur-ther* and G. *vor-der*, etc.

(80) XV. Stems with suff. -ĕs- (-ŏs): neuter nouns.—This is a most important class of words in Sanskrit, Greek and Latin: thus, from an I.-E. root *gen* (to beget), we have Sk. *ján-as* (birth, race), gen. *ján-as-as*, Gr. *γέν-ος*, gen. *γένεος* = **γένεσ-ος*, L. *gen-us* gen. *generis* = **gen-es-is*; and the like. Considering then a Sk. stem *ráj-as* (dark space) = Gr. *ἔρεβ-ος*, its exact correspondent is Go. *riq-is* (darkness), gen. *riq-iz-is*, pl. *riq-iz-a*, etc. Now, in every other Germanic dialect, the final *-is* in the nomin. sg. is dropped, so that this case is no longer distinguished by any sign; but, in the other cases, and especially in the plural, the medial syllable *-iz-* reappears in its rhotacized form (*-ir-*), and the reason becomes obvious why such G. neuter nouns as *chalb* (calf), *lamb* (lamb), etc., are in the plural number *chalb-ir-(u)* = Go. **kalb-iz-a, lemb-ir-(u)*, Mod. G. *kälb-er, lämm-er*, etc. An old **formative suffix**, being lost

---

[1] The same suffix in the form *-stro-*, in O.E. *fō-ster* (food), E. *to foster*.
[2] Still in Bavarian *beichl*.

everywhere but in the plural, has been changed to a plural ending.

XVI. Stems with suff. -yĕs- (-is-, -yŏs-): comparatives, cf. L. mel-ius mel-ior (better) ; further, by adding the suff. -to- to the reduced syllable, a suff. -ĭstŏ-, characteristic of superlatives, Gr. μέγ-ιστο-ς (the greatest), etc.—This derivation is of constant use for the formation of Germanic comparatives and superlatives: Go. háuh-is-, in declension háuh-iz-a, O.H.G. hōh-ir-o, E. high-er, and G.'höh-er, with the regular metaphony, which survives in E. old eld-er eld-est [1] ; further, Go. háuh-ist-s, E. high-est, G. höh-est höch-st; Go. bat-iz-a bat-ist-s (from a positive which became obsolete in Preg., cf. Sk. bhad-rá-s "happy"), E. better best (metaph.), G. besser beste ; E. last, cf. the positive late, and G. letzt ; E. nigh and next = G. nächst ; Go. má-iz-a (cf. L. mag-is), O.H.G. mĕro and G. mehr, E. more, and superlative E. most = G. meist. The reader will easily supply further examples.

§ 2.—Verbal Stems.

(81) I. Root-Stems.—Primitive verbal derivation, like nominal derivation, had its root-stems; that is to say, many bare roots could be conjugated as such, without any suffix, and by mere addition of the person-endings to the radical syllable. The well-known Greek verbs in -μι clearly illustrate this simple conjugational system, which has been quite lost in Germanic, apart from the conjugation of the vb. "to be," and from the formation of the perfects of strong verbs, both of which will be found in their proper places.[2] The root was often preceded by a reduplication, Gr. δί-δω-μι, τί-θη-μι, and this element is still visible in G. beb-en (to tremble) = Sk. bi-bhê-mi (I am afraid), from a root bhī (to fear); but this verb, no less than any other, is now conjugated like the following classes. Hence Germanic may be said no longer to possess any primitive verbs, but the so-called verbs in -ω, which correspond to the third Latin conjugation.

[1] In a special sense, whereas "I am older than you," after the analogy of old.
[2] Infra 216–217, 175–184, and 208–209.

L

(82) II. Stems with suff. -ŏ- (-ĕ-).—In every verbal suffix which ends with this characteristic short vowel, the normal and the deflected grade are substituted for one another according to a regular alternation which has become slightly altered in Latin, but was faithfully kept throughout Greek and Germanic: in the first person sg. and pl., and in the third pl., the vowel is ŏ; it is ĕ in the three other persons, without exception in either case. One instance will suffice, namely, the present indicative of the vb. Gr. νέμ-ω (I divide) = Go. nim-a (I take):

νέμ-ω νέμ-ει-ς νέμ-ει νέμ-ο-μεν[1] νέμ-ε-τε νέμ-ο-ντι
nim-a nim-i-s nim-i-þ nim-a-m nim-i-þ nim-a-nd.[2]

This point being understood, the stems with suff. -ŏ- assume three distinct aspects.

1. The radical syllable is in the normal grade (by far the most common case): I.-E. root ĕd (to eat), Gr. ἔδ-ω, L. ed-ō, Go. it-an, E. to eat, G. ess-en; I.-E. root bhĕr (to carry), stem *bhér-ō (I carry), Gr. φέρ-ω, L. fer-ō, Go. baír-an (to carry) and ga-baír-an (to bring forth), O.E. ber-an, ge-ber-an, and E. to bear, O.H.G. gi-bër-an and G. ge-bär-en; I.-E. root bhĭd (to split), stem *bhéyd-ō (I split), Go. beit-an (to bite), E. to bite and G. beisz-en; I.-E. root dĕr (to tear), Gr. δέρ-ω, Go. ga-taír-an, E. to tear, G. zerr-en and ver-zehr-en; I.-E. root bhĕndh (to bind), Go. bind-an, E. to bind, G. bind-en; I.-E. root stĕygh stĭgh (to go up), Gr. στείχ-ω, Go. steig-an, E. to sty, G. steigen; I.-E. root lĕyq (to leave), Gr. λείπ-ω, L. linqu-ō, Go. leihv-an (to lend), O.E. lēon (cf. E. loan and to lend), G. leih-en; I.-E. root dŭk dĕwk (to lead), L. dūc-ō = *deuc-ō, Go. tiuh-an (to draw), G. zieh-en; I.-E. root gŭs gĕws (to taste, to appreciate, to select), Gr. γεύω = *γεύσ-ω, Go. kius-an, E. to choose, G. kies-en, etc.

2. The radical syllable is in the reduced grade, because the original accent was shifted to the suffix:[3] I.-E. root skăbh (to

---

[1] Here Latin has the e: lĕg-ĭ-mus = *lĕg-ĕ-mus, instead of *lĕg-ŏ-mus = Gr. λέγ-ο-μεν.

[2] The identity of these stems with the Greek and Latin verbs being thus put beyond question, it will be convenient to quote them hereafter in the shape of the infinitive (supra 77, 1), viz. Go. nim-an, G. nehm-en, etc.

[3] Observe the contrast, in Greek accentuation and vocalism, between the types φεύγειν and φυγεῖν, λείπειν and λιπεῖν, etc.

scratch, to scrape), L. *scab-ō*, Go. *skab-an*, E. *to shave*, G. *schaben*; I.-E. root *bhăg bhōg* (to cook), Gr. φώγ-ω, but O.E. *bac-an* and E. *to bake*, O.H.G. *bahh-an* and G. *back-en* (pf. *buck*); similarly E. *to take*, pf. *took*, borrowed from Scandinavian; I.-E. root *wĭd wĕyd* (to know), Go. *vit-an*, G. *wiss-en*; the radical grade is doubtful in Go. *faran*, E. *to fare*, G. *fahren*, contrasted with the Gr. root περ πορ (to pass over).

3. The radical syllable becomes nasalized (compare Gr. λαμβ-άνειν and λαβ-εῖν, L. *find-ō linqu-ō* above from roots *bhĭd lĭq*, etc.) : I.-E. root *păg păk*, Gr. πάγ-η (machinery, trap), L. *pang-ō* (to drive in), G. *fang-en* (to catch), cf. the root without nasal in *fach* (compartment); I.-E. root *siq siñq* (to pour), Sk. *siñc-ā-mi* (I pour out), *sik-tá-s* (shed), Go. *sigk-an*, E. *to sink*, G. *sink-en*; Gr. σπέρχ-ο-μαι (I run), E. *to spring*, G. *spring-en*; E. *to cleave* (to cling) and G. *kleb-en*, but, with an inner nasal, E. *to climb* and G. *klimm-en*, etc.

(83) III. **Stems with suff. -yŏ- (-yĕ-).**—This class is no less considerable than the preceding,[1] and admits of a similar division.

1. The root is in the reduced grade (the more frequent case): I.-E. root *stĭg* (to sting), Gr. στίζω=*στίγ-yω (cf. fut. στίξω= *στίγ-σω), E. *to stitch* and G. *stick-en*; I.-E. root *swĭd* (to sweat), Sk. *svid-yā-mi*, Gr. ἰδ-ίω, O.H.G. *swizz-en* and G. *schwitz-en*; I.-E. root *kăp* (to seize), L. *cap-iō*, Go. *haf-jan*, O.E. *hebban*= *heb-jan*, and E. *to heave*, O.H.G. *heffan* and G. *heben*; I.-E. root *bhĭdh bhĕydh* (to persuade), Gr. πείθ-ω=*φείθ-ω, but Go. *bid-jan* (to pray), E. *to bid*, G. *bitt-en*; Go. þ*ugkjan* (to seem), E. *to think*, G. *dünken*; Go. *bug-jan*, E. *to buy*, etc.

2. The root is in the normal grade: I.-E. root *sĕd* (to sit), Gr. ἔζομαι=*σεδ-yo-μαι (cf. L. *sed-ēre*), O.N. *sit-ja*, E. *to sit*, G. *sitzen*; I.-E. root *lĕgh* (to lie, cf. Gr. λέχ-ος, L. *lec-tu-s* " bed "), O.N. *ligg-ja*, O.E. *licg-an* and E. *to lie*, G. *liegen*. There are probably two different grades of root *wĕrg* (to act, to work, cf. Gr. Ϝέργ-ο-ν " work ") to be recognised in E. *to work*=Go. *vaúrkjan*=I.-E. **wr̥g-yō*, and G. *wirken*=Preg. *wérk-yō.

IV. Stems with suff. -ĕyŏ- (-ĕyĕ-): **causative verbs**.—It

---

[1] Even still more, if we take into account the important part it plays in secondary derivation, *infra* 92–93 and 106–107.

seems advisable to place this class immediately after the -yŏ-class, for the sake of the contrast between them in such notable pairs as *to lay* and *legen, to set* and *setzen*, as opposed to *to lie* and *liegen, to sit* and *sitzen*. As early as the I.-E. period, a suffix -*ĕyŏ*-, added to the deflected root, formed a great many causative verbs: thus, from root *bhĕr*, a verb **bhŏr-éyō* (I cause to carry), Sk. *bhār-áyā-mi*, Gr. φορ-έω (I carry).¹ Similarly, from root *lĕgh* above, an I.-E. vb. **lŏgh-éyō*, which would be Gr. **λοχ-έω, meant "I cause to lie down." Now, I.-E. **lŏgh-éyō*, becomes Go. *lag-ja* (I lay), the suffix here being no longer distinguishable from an original suffix -*yo*-, whereas the radical grade remains clear and characteristic. Further, *lag-jan*, with the regular metaphony, results in O.E. *lecgan* and E. *to lay*, O.H.G. *lecken legen* and G. *legen*. In the same way, *to set* and *setzen* should be traced back to Go. *satjan* = I.-E. **sŏd-éyō* (I cause to sit down); and the process may be further illustrated by E. *to fell* and G. *fällen*, O.E. *fēran* and G. *führen* (to lead) = **fōr-jan*, O.E. *hangian*² and G. *hängen*, E. *to raise* = Go. (*ur-*)*ráis-jan*, G. *lehren* (to teach) = Go. *láis-jan*, etc., in contrast with E. *to fall* and G. *fallen*, E. *to fare* and G. *fahren*, E. *to hang* and G. *hangen*, E. *to rise* = Go. (*ur-*)*reis-an*, G. *ler-n-en*, etc.³

(84) V. Stems with suff. -*nŏ*- (-*nĕ*-): Gr. πι-εῖν (to drink) and pres. πί-νω, L. *lĭ-nō* (I besmear), supine *lĭ-tu-m*; I.-E. root *skĭ* (to shine, to appear, cf. Gr. σκι-ά "shadow, image"), Go. *skeinan*, E. *to shi-ne*, G. *schei-nen*; I.-E. root *gnō gn̥* (to know, cf. Gr. γι-γνώ-σκω, L. (*g*)*nō-scō*, etc.), Go. *kun-nan*, O.H.G. *chun-nan* and G. (metaph.) *kön-nen*⁴; Gr. σφάλ-λω (I throw) and σφάλ-

¹ Compare: root *mĕn* (to think) and L. *mŏn-eō* (I cause to think, I warn, G. *mahn-en*); root *nĕk* (to perish), L. *nex* "death," and L. *nŏc-eō* (I harm).
² We should expect E. *to *heng*, cf. G. *henk-er* (hangman); but the intransitive *to hang* acquired the active meaning.
³ Since, moreover, it is natural that a causative verb should govern both the accusative of its direct object and the accusative of the person caused to act, we may understand at once why G. *lehr-en* and the like, as well as L. *dŏc-eō*, require a double accusative. This rule was far better observed in M.H.G. than it is now, such regular expressions as *ich verhehle ihn die sache* having been replaced by *ich verhehle ihm*, etc., after the analogy of verbs governing the person in the dative case (*sagen, geben*).
⁴ E. *can* has the vocalism of the pf. *can* = G. *kann*, infra 224. E. *ken* = G. *kennen* is the causative, Go. *kannjan*; several German provinces are known to confuse *kennen* and *können*. E. *to know* = O.E. *cnāw-an* is the verb formed by suffix from the radical form *gnō*.

λο-μαι (I fall), L. *fal-lō* (I betray)=**fal-nō*, Go. **fal-lan*=**fal-nan*, O.N. *falla*, E. *to fall*, G. *fallen*, etc.

VI. Stems with suff. -tŏ-, -dhŏ- and -dŏ- : Gr. νέ-ω and νή-θω (I spin), L. *ten-dō*, etc.; I.-E. root *qĕl* (to behave, to manage, Gr. πέλ-ο-μαι " I find myself," L. *col-ō*=**quĕl-ō* " I cultivate," etc.), whence a vb. **ql̥-tô*, Go. *hal-dan* (to hold), E. *to hold*, G. *halten*[1]; I.-E. root *plŭ plĕw* (to flow, cf. Gr. πλέF-ω πλεύ-σω " to ship "), whence a vb. **plĕw-dō*, which would be Go. **fliu-tan*, O.E. *flēotan* and E. *to fleet*, O.H.G. *flioʒʒan* and G. *flieszen* ; similarly, Gr. χέF-ω (to pour), L. *fu-ndō*, Go. *giu-tan*, G. *gieszen*, etc.

VII. Stems with suff. -skŏ- : Gr. βά-σκω, L. *crē-scō*, etc.; I.-E. root *wăd ŭd* (water), Preg. **wat-skō* (I wash), E. *to wash*, G. *waschen*; I.-E. root *prĕk* (to ask, to pray, cf. L. *prec-o-r*), whence a vb. **pr̥k-skō*, L. *poscō* (I ask)=**porc-scō*, Germanic **forh-skan*, but O.H.G. *forscōn* and G. *forschen*, this verb having afterwards assumed a form of secondary derivation,[2] as is the case with many others of the same class, viz. E. *to wish*=O.E. *wȳscean*, and G. *wünschen*=O.H.G. *wunsken*, E. *to ask*=O.E. *āscian*, and G. *heischen* (with inorganic *h*)=O.H.G. *eiscōn*, the latter perhaps related to L. *æruscō* (to beg), etc.

(85) VIII. Stems with suff. -ē-.—The primitive I.-E. language probably possessed a number of verbal stems with reduced root-form and invariable suffix -ē-, with a general intransitive meaning as opposed to some transitive verbs belonging to the preceding classes: thus, Gr. ἐ-τύπ-η-ς (thou wast struck), but τύπ-τει-ς (thou strikest) ; L. *jac-ē-s* (thou liest),[3] but *jac-i-s* (thou throwst), etc. Similarly, we find in Germanic : O.H.G. *leb-ē-n*, G. *leben*, E. *to live*, contrasted with a root *līp* shown by Gr. λῑπ-αρής (clinging to), cf. the compound *bleiben* (to remain) =Go. *bi-leib-an*; O.H.G. *hab-ē-n*, G. *haben*, E. *to have*, which would have been I.-E. **kăp-ē-*, from the root that produced L. *cap-iō* and G. *heben*,[4] etc. Very early, however, stems with

---

[1] Of course the suffix might equally well be -*dho*-, with the accent optionally on the radical or the suffix-syllable.
[2] Cf. *infra* 92, 93 and 174.
[3] The original meaning must have been " thou art cast down."
[4] An etymology which would sever E. *to have* ⇒ G. *haben* from L. *habēre*.

final long vowel were conjugated in Germanic, by adding, at least in some of their personal forms, the suff. -*ja*- = I.-E. -*yo*-, to the vowel : just in the same way as we have in Latin a first person *jaceō* from *jacēs*, formed after the analogy of *moneō monēs*, though the two words originally belong to quite different verb-classes, so Gothic corrupted the conjugation of the type **hab-ē-, to such a degree as no longer to exhibit its characteristic *ē*; and, though this *ē* is still extant in O.H.G., later languages blend these primitive formations with the much more recent verbs which have arisen from secondary derivation. This point here need only be hinted at, as it will appear more clearly in the further development of the system of verbal derivation built on the foundations thus briefly laid.

SECTION II.

SECONDARY SUFFIXES.

(86) We must not expect to meet, in the secondary derivation, with every one of the suffixes we have studied in the primary formation; on the other hand, we may meet with some new suffixes. Some of these appear to be of a later origin, having spread out at a time when the language had already created nearly all its primary stems. Further, the suffix-accumulations, being longer and more cumbrous than mere syllables, were in less danger from the action of phonetic laws, and therefore had a far greater power of duration and multiplication. Lastly, a lawless and capricious analogy encumbered the language with a swarm of neologisms and useless synonyms, which a clearer and more sober speech was fain, in some way or other, to get rid of. It is thus, that Germanic derivation, though extremely rich, may be reduced, upon analysis, to a very small number of primitive elements.

§ 1. *Nominal Stems.*

(87) Owing to the reason just given, suffixes consisting of a simple vowel, including also the suff. -*yo*-, which plays such a momentous part in the derivative system of Sanskrit, Greek and Latin (type *pitr-ya-s* πάτρ-ιο-ς *patr-iu-s*), barely occur in

PRIMITIVE DERIVATION. 151

Germanic secondary stems.[1] A feminine suffix, however, characterized by a long vowel, -ī, and so rare in primary derivation that it has not yet required our attention, here occupies a prominent place.

I. The I.-E. suff. -ī has the special function of forming the feminine of such stems as do not end with the suffix-vowel -o-[2]: Sk. svād-ú-s (sweet), fm. svād-v-î, Gr. ἡδ-ύ-ς ἡδ-ε-ῖα; Sk. bhár-a-nt- (carrying), fm. bhár-a-nt-ī, Gr. φέρων φέρουσα,[3] etc. But this simple process, though extant in Gothic,[4] has not been retained by its sister-tongues, being in these illustrated by a single survival, which moreover is lost in English and corrupted in German: G. nicht-e (niece) = I.-E. *nept-î, derived from *nepōt- (nephew). A suffix-accumulation, however, has preserved down to the present time the old I.-E. feminine formation.

The -ī, being occasionally added to a stem in -en-,[5] produced a combination -ĕn-ī, which Germanic changed to -in-i. Thus a derivative in -ĕn- (-ŏn-), from a root dŭk (to lead), was I.-E. *dŭk-ĕn- (leader), which in Latin would be nomin. sg. *ducō and appears strictly reproduced in O.H.G. heri-zog-o (chief of an army, duke). Now, to this, the regular fm. (I.-E. *dŭk-ĕn-ī) is naturally heri-zog-in-i, wherein the syllable -in- belongs to the msc. stem. But, since this syllable no longer survives in the nomin. msc. heri-zog-o, the speaker was led in thought to separate from heri-zog-in-i the ending -ini, mistaking it for the characteristic symbol of the feminine gender, and henceforth to transfer it as such to new formations, as göttin from gott, füchs-in (O.E. fyx-en and E. vix-en) from fuchs, etc.

At the end of the O.H.G. period, a further addition changed this ending to -inna, M.H.G. -inne, to which corresponds the modern spelling -inn, now obsolete in the singular.[6]

[1] Though we have E. shep-herd (*shep=sheep) and G. hirt-e = O.H.G. hirt-i = Go. hairˈd-eɩ-s, from, as it were, a Preg. *herð-ja-z "which belongs to the herd." The same suffix will occur below in a neuter collective G. formation (96, I.).
[2] And even of these concurrently with -ā, supra 73.
[3] On Gr. -ιᾰ = -ī, see my Grammar of Gr. and Lat., no. 112.
[4] Go. mag-u-s (boy), ma-v-i (lass), frij-ōnd-i (female friend), etc.
[5] Cf. supra 74, and never forget that all parts of the derivative system are intimately connected with one another.
[6] English has lost this ending and replaced it by -ess borrowed from

II. The same suffix -*ĕn*-, which, by combining with the ending -*ī*, endowed German with such a remarkable element of feminine derivation, also underwent, even when isolated, a peculiar process of analogical extension: for it will be seen that a great many nouns, which did not originally belong to the so-called weak declension, passed to it by later analogy, either in the plural, or in both numbers, and that the whole of the weak declension of adjectives is also due to a blundering use of this element -*en*-, which, though a derivative suffix, was mistaken for a grammatical ending.[1]

(88) III. The suff. -*ro*- was not productive; but the corresponding -*lo*- multiplied, especially as a **diminutive**. When added to primary stems in -*ĕ*-/-*ŏ*-, it gives -*ĕlŏ*-, -*ŏlŏ*-, which in Greek characterises some derived adjectives (εὐ-τράπ-ε-λο-ς "buxom," εἴκ-ε-λο-ς "alike"), whereas in Latin it has a decidedly diminutive meaning (*parv-o-lu-s* "tiny," *agellus* = **ag-ro-los* "little field"). These forms would be represented in Germanic by -*ila*- and -*ala*-, which are actually exhibited by a great many derivatives, viz.: ordinary adjectives, E. *cripp-le* and G. *krüpp-el*, cf. Gr. γρυπ-ό-ς (crump); names of animals, E. *weas-el* and G. *wies-el*, cf. G. *wies-e* (meadow); nouns denoting instruments, E. *shov-el* = G. *schauf-el* = O.H.G. *scūv-ala*, E. *spind-le* (with inserted *d*) = G. *spind-el* = O.H.G. *spinn-ila*, G. *meiszel* (chisel) = O.H.G. *meiʒ-il*; lastly and chiefly, diminutives, with a regular metaphony pointing to the suffix-form -*ila*, E. *litt-le* = O.E. *lȳt-el*, and G. *lütz-el*[2] = O.H.G. *luzz-il*, O.H.G. *tur-ila* (little door) and G. *thür-el* (valve), O.E. *cyrn-el* and E. *kern-el*.[3]

(89) IV. The suff. -*no*- has spread widely.

1. Form -*onó-s*, Germanic -*an-s*: after the analogy of radical verbs, those with suff. -*to*- and -*no*- form their past participle

---

French. In German, on the contrary, it is so common a feminine derivative form as to have been even added to feminine nouns which were borrowed ready made from foreign languages: F. *princ-esse*, but G. *prinz-ess-in*; M.H.G. *ebbet-isse* (abbess) = L. *abbatissa*, but G. *äbt-iss-in*.

[1] Cf. *infra* 140 sq., 149, 150 and 156.
[2] Preserved in proper names: *Lützel-burg*, *Lützel-stein* "Littlestone."
[3] Further: E. *thimb-le*, "little finger," from *thumb*; G. *ärm-el* (sleeve), "little arm." E. *hill* and G. *hügel* have already occurred.

according to the strong conjugation, namely: Go. -*an-s*, etc.; E. *held*, G. *ge-halt-en*; E. *fall-en*, G. *ge-fall-en*; even G. *ge-wasch-en*, though the other verbs in -*sko*- belong to the weak conjugation; a few verbs in -*yo*- followed the same method, E. *sat*, G. *ge-sess-en*; the other verbal derivatives, chiefly those in -*éyo*- and -*ē̆*- (-*ēyo*-), as well as those of secondary derivation, admit only of the dental suffix, E. -*d* or -*t* = G. -*et* or -*t*.[1]

2. Form -*ono-m*, Germanic -*an*: verbs of every class have been seen above to form the infinitive by adding the nasal suffix, Go. -*an*, etc., to the present stem.

3. Form -*ī-no*-, due to the combination of certain stems in -*ī*- with the adjectival suffix -*no*-, Germanic -*īna-z*, then -*īn-s*.— This derivation is to be traced back to I.-E., in L. *su-īnu-s* (belonging to swine), Go. *sv-ein-s* (swine), E. *swine*, G. *schwein*. It will also be found below in the possessive adjectives.[2] It is common in Gothic in the formation of **adjectives denoting material**: *gulþ-ein-s* (golden), *aírþ-ein-s* (made of earth), *stáin-ein-s* (of stone), etc. Phonetic reduction changed -*īn*- to -*ĭn*-, whence the regular metaphony in the preceding syllable, and further to -*en*: O.E. *gyld-en*, which has again become E. *golden*, and G. *gülden*, now obsolete and replaced by *gold-en*; G. *ird-en* (made of earth), etc., etc. This -*īn*-, when added to a stem in -*es*-, as in I.-E. *reg-es-īno-s = Go. *riq-iz-ein-s* (dark),[3] resulted in West Germanic in an ending -*eren*, which is seen in such German words as *stein-ern* (of stone), *hölz-ern* (wooden), etc.

(90) V. The suffixes consisting of a *t* and a vowel are kept in one of the two languages, and occasionally in both.

1. Suff. -*to*- and -*e-to*-, whence in Germanic a dental consonant, either alone, or preceded by an *ĭ* which very early assumed the duller sound of *ĕ*.

(*a*) In the formation of the past participles of derived verbs: Gr. νεμ-ε-τό-ς (divided), L. *gen-i-tu-s* (born), *dom-i-tu-s* (tamed); likewise, Go. *ga-tam-i-da*, from vb. *tam-jan*, E. *tam-e-d*, G. *gi-zem-i-t ge-zähm-t*, etc., etc.

(*b*) In the formation of adjectives proceeding from nouns,

---

[1] *Infra* 90, 173 sq. and 186 sq. [2] *Infra* 168.
[3] From *riq-is* (obscurity), *supra* 80.

as L. *cord-ā-tu-s* (noble-hearted), *crīn-ī-tu-s* (hairy): Go. *un-qĕn-i-þ-s* (having no wife), O.N. *hǣr-ð-r* (hairy), O.H.G. *gi-stirn-ō-t* (full of stars), M.H.G. *ge-jār-e-t* (aged), G. *be-jahr-t*, especially in E. compounds, such as *fair-hair-ed*, *red-nos-ed*, *hump-back-ed*, etc.

(c) In the derivation of ordinal from cardinal numbers.

2. The fm. suff. *-tā*, usually *-i-tā*, serves to form **abstract nouns from adjectives**: L. *juven-ta* (youth), Go. *jun-da*, O.E. *geogvð* and E. *youth*, O.H.G. *jugun-d* and G. *jugen-d*; Go. *háuh-s*, whence *háuh-i-þa* (height), O.H.G. *hōh-i-da*; G. *heil* (whole, sound), whence *heil-i-da* (health), etc. This mode of derivation has become extinct in German, but still exists and has been much developed in English, where it accounts for the metaphonical contrast in such types as *high heigh-t*, *whole heal-th*, *broad bread-th*, *long leng-th*, *strong streng-th*, *foul fil-th*, *merry mir-th*, as well as for the shortening in *wide wid-th*, *deep dep-th*, and, in short, for a considerable number of abstract nouns.

3. The two suffixes *-ti-* and *-tu-*, after a long vowel, like the Latin type *sen-ā-tu-s*, may be recognised in such secondary derivatives as: G. *arm-ut* (poverty) = O.H.G. *aram-uoti*; G. *heim-at* (fatherland) = O.H.G. *heim-uoti*; G. *ein-öde* (solitude) = O.H.G. *ein-ōti*[1]; O.E. *mōn-að* and E. *mon-th*, O.H.G. *mān-ōd* and G. *mon-at*, from stem *mōn-* (moon).

VI. The suffix *-nt-*, which characterizes the words *friend* = *freund* and *fiend* = *feind*, when added to the stem-vowel of an ordinary verb, forms with it a combination, I.-E. *-o-nt-*, Go. *-a-nd-*, G. *-e-nd-*, lost in E., the constant and regular ending of **present participles** in all verbs, whether primitive or derivative: Go. *nim-and-s bair-and-s*, G. *nehm-end ge-bär-end*; O.E. *Hǣlend* and G. *Heiland* "the Saviour," cf. G. *heil-en* = E. *to heal*, the causative derived from G. *heil* = E. *whole*.

VII. The suffixes *-tro-* and *-tero-* find scarcely any application in secondary derivation,[2] though we are probably right in

---

[1] Primitively unconnected with *öde* (desert) = O.H.G. *ōt-i* = Go. *áuþ-s* = O.N. *auð-r* (void), though corrupted under this influence.

[2] The nouns of instrument now adopt the suffix of nouns of agent, *infra* 102: E. *a bore-r*, *a decant-er*; G. *läuf-er* "the runner" (mill-stone).

tracing back to one of them, at least indirectly, the O.E. ending -*stre*, which formed a great many feminine nouns, and still survives in E. *youngster* and *spinster*.[1]

VIII. The suffix -*es*- of neuter nouns has been seen not to survive, except as a grammatical ending for the plural of these nouns, in the form -*er*, which belongs to the study of declension.

IX. The comparative (-*yos*-) and superlative (-*isto*-) suffixes, in their modern form respectively -*er* and -*est* (-*st*), and with the regular metaphony which almost always accompanies them in German,[2] remain in both languages the specific and constant form of comparison for all adjectives, primitive or derivative. English, however, in modern and, especially, in learned adjectival formations, preferred the periphrastic locution by *more* and *most*, borrowed, no doubt, from French syntax, whereas German adheres to the traditional formation, thus: *merkwürdig-er*, *wissenschaftlich-er*, *dynamisch-er*.

(91) X. The I.-E. suff. -*kó*- is extremely rare in the primary derivation of any I.-E. language, whilst, in all (Gr. φυ-σι-κό-ς ἱππ-ι-κό-ς, L. *cīvi-cu-s Hispān-i-cu-s*, etc.), it attains a prominent place in secondary formations: a remark which holds good for Germanic as for any other member of the family.

1. When added to a stem in -*i*-, the suffix becomes either -*i-kó*- or -*ī-kó*-. It is chiefly the latter, changed to Preg. -*īʒá*-, that has survived and extended in adjectival derivation: Go. *gab-eig-s* (open-handed) and G. (*frei-*)*geb-ig*; Go. *maht-eig-s*, O.E. *meaht-ig* and E. *might-y* (*hand-y*, *filth-y*, *swarth-y*, etc.), O.H.G. *maht-īg* and G. *mächt-ig*; O.H.G. *rëht*, whence a derivative *riht-īg*, now *richt-ig* (right, exact), etc.

2. The same suffix, when added to a stem in -*en*-, formed with the stem-syllable a combination -*eṅkó*- or -*ṅkó*-, Preg. either -*iṅʒá*- or -*uṅʒá*- (O.H.G. *arm-ing* "poor man," *edil-ing*

---

[1] Literally "a spinning person," whence "an unmarried damsel."
[2] More accurately, Gothic has two comparative suffixes, rather arbitrarily distributed, namely, -*iz*- the reduced grade of I.-E. -*yŏs*-, and -*ōz*- of doubtful origin. Thus, the German metaphonical and unmetaphonised types are likely to correspond respectively to the former and the latter form. Further particulars must be looked for in ordinary grammars.

"noble man," *werd-unga* " dignity," from *werd* " worth "), the various forms and uses of which will appear below in the modern languages.¹

3. In the form -*isko*-, the guttural suffix occurs in a number of, mainly diminutive, Greek secondary derivatives, such as παιδ-ίσκο-ς, νεᾱν-ίσκο-ς, ἀσπιδ-ίσκιο-ν, and in one of the most widely extended forms of adjectival derivation in Germanic: Go. *þiud-isk-s* (popular), representing L. *gentilis*, O.H.G. *diut-isc* and G. *Deut-sch*, etc.; O.H.G. *ird-isc* and G. *ird-isch* (earthly) ; O.E. *engl-isc*, *wīel-isc*, and E. *English, Welsh, French*, etc.

§ 2. *Verbal Stems.*

(92) The chief factor in I.-E. secondary verbal derivation is the suffix -*yó*-, by means of which, from almost any nominal stem, may be formed a corresponding verbal stem, a process clearly illustrated by Sanskrit grammar, *e.g.* *dēvá-s* (god), *dēv-a-yá-ti* (he adores); *gŏ-pá-s* (cowherd), *gŏ-pā-yá-ti* (he guards), etc. This suffix becomes rather more obscure in Greek: ἱππ-εύ-ς (rider), ἱππ-εύ-ω (I ride) = *ἱππ-εύ-γω; τῑ-μή (honour) = τῑ-μᾱ, and τῑ-μά-ω (I honour); φίλ-ο-ς (dear), and φιλ-έ-ω (I love); δῆ-λο-ς (clear), and δη-λό-ω (I show), etc. It is still less clear in Latin, owing to the regular contraction: *for-ma* (shape), and *formō* (I shape) = *for-ma-yō*. In Germanic we must expect to find it equally obscured: in fact, it could no longer be discerned without the help of linguistic comparison; by this light, however, we are able to perceive that a Go. vb. *salbō* (I salve, G. [*ich*] *salbe*) must have been formed from a fm. noun *salba* (salve),² just in the same way as τῑμάω and *formō* were respectively derived from τῑμᾱ and *forma*, or, in other words, that an I.-E. fm. noun **solp-ā*, changed to Preg. **salb-ō*, produced the verb by adding the formative suffix -*yó*-, changed to Preg. -*ja*-, to which the person-endings were added in conjugation.

But here a previous observation is necessary. We have

---

¹ *Infra* 103.
² Not Gothic, but found everywhere else : G. *salb-e* (salve).

already seen that Germanic often added this suffix -*ja*- to verbal stems originally ending in a long vowel, where there was no reason at all for this accretion.[1] On the other hand, the reverse also happened: even as early as I.-E., verbs with suff. -*yó*- might be, at least in some forms, conjugated without this element. Thus, side by side with the common Gr. form φιλ-έ-ω = *φιλ-έ-yω, we have Æolic φίλ-η-μι, wherein the person-ending is added directly to the nominal stem; and, even in ordinary Greek, no form but that of present-stems (φιλ-ή-σω ἐ-φίλ-η-σ-α πε-φίλ-η-κ-α) exhibits any trace of a formative suffix. So, too, in Latin, though the first person *albeō* (I become white) is certainly **alb-e-yō*, with the suff. -*yo*-, the second person *albēs* may as well—and perhaps better—be explained by *alb-ē-s*, with the person-ending immediately attached to the derivative base, as it would be by a contraction of **alb-ĕ-yĕ-s*; and so also for every other person, and further for the conjugation of *formō formās*.

The same alternation occurred in Germanic. Here, moreover, the distinction of the forms which did or did not possess the formative suffix, is often impossible and, at all events, hardly more than theoretical guess-work, since the forms which possessed it became, by dropping the intervocalic *j* and contracting the remainder, exactly the same as the forms in which the endings were immediately added to the nominal base. Thus, it does not matter whether we resolve Go. *salb-ō-þ* (he salves) into *salb-ō-þ* = I.-E. **solp-ā-ti*, or into **salb-ō-ji-þ* = I.-E. **solp-ā-yé-ti*, since either equally well explains both the historical form and the actual E. (*he*) *salv-e-th* and G. (*er*) *salb-t*.

(93) This point being settled, we must distinguish the

---

[1] Cf. *supra* 85. This circumstance occasioned a confusion between the conjugation of the ē-class and that of the derived or denominative verbs here referred to, a curious process in the older languages, though of no importance for modern speeches, where all conjugational classes are now blended together. Thus, O.H.G., purer in this respect even than Gothic, still preserves *hab-ē-m* (I have, Go. *hab-a*), and also, analogically, *salb-ō-m* (I salve, Go. *salb-ō*). But Mod. G. conjugates *hab-e*, *salb-e*, like *nehm-e*, *fahr-e*; and it is only from the lack of metaphony in the 2nd and 3rd persons of the two former verbs, that we are able to see that they are not all of the same origin. In English, the metaphony in the present of strong verbs being lost altogether, the confusion is past remedy.

denominative formation according to the nature of the nominal stems to which it is applied.

1. The nominal stem ends in -ā, Preg. -ō.—The formation is plain and regular, as shown above: *salb-a* (a salve), Go. *salb-ō-n*, E. *to salve*, G. *salb-en*; O.H.G. *āht-a* (care), *āht-ō-n* (to take care), G. *acht-en*, etc. Then, the derivative verbs in *-ō-* being partly confused with the primary verbs in *-ē-*, the class also admitted of a secondary formation in *-ē-*, which, of course, is now no longer to be distinguished from the former: Go. *saúrg-a* (care, anxiety), vb. *saúrg-a-n* like *hab-a-n*, O.H.G. *sorg-ē-n* and G. *sorgen*, but O.E. (with suff. *-ja-*) *sorg-ia-n* and E. *to sorrow*.

2. The nominal stem ends in a short vowel, type φιλ-έ-ω.— In this case, since both *-ĕ-yŏ-* and *-ĭ-yŏ-* become Preg. *-ja-*, while *-ŭ-yŏ-* seems to have done the same through analogy, the form of the verb is necessarily the same as if the nominal stem had ended with a consonant, e.g. I.-E. **koy-ló-s* (whole, safe), cf. Sk. *kêva-la-s* (whole), Preg. **hai-lá-s* (Go. *háil-s*, O.E. *hāl*, E. *whole*, G. *heil* "health"), whence Go. *háil-ja-n*, E. *to heal*, G. *heilen*.

3. The nominal stem ends in a consonant.

A. Normal formation.—The suff. *-ja-*, which still remains visible in Gothic, is adapted to the final consonant of the nominal base, whatever it may be; next, the *j* vanishes in the later languages, and nothing is left, but the obscure and uniform ending, *-e* in sg. 1 pres. indicative, *-en* in the infinitive, and so forth. Thus, supposing the base to end with *t*, it will form with the suffix a Go. complex *-t-ja-n*, which in German becomes *-zen*. After a final *s*, we should expect a Preg. *-z-ja-n*; but, analogy restoring the *s*, we find O.E. *-sian* and E. *-se*. Lastly, these derivative syllables will be seen below to extend their influence beyond their proper place, and to become in their turn productive of new word-classes.[1]

B. Analogical formation.—From a similar cause, the vowel *ō*, borrowed from verbs derived from stems in *-ā*, was transferred, even in the Pregermanic period, to such as were derived from consonantal stems. Just as Latin constructed on the base

[1] *Infra*, 106-107.

honor a vb. *honōr-ā-re*, as if there were a fm. noun **honōr-a*,[1] so, Germanic has formed a great many weak verbs, simply by adding its derivative *ō* to the final consonant of a stem ending in *-es-* or *-en-*: Go. *hat-is* (hate), *hat-iz-ō-n* (to hate); Go. *fráu-ja* (lord, gen. *fráu-jin-s*), *fráu-jin-ō-n* (to be lord). Further, these final compounds, *-izōn*, *-inōn*, becoming independent, at once made their way as general forms for secondary derivation: the former, no less than *-sian* above, might have resulted in E. *-se*; the latter was blended with the E. ending *-en*,[2] as must be inferred from E. *to fast-en*, which is the equivalent of O.H.G. *fest-inōn*, derived from O.H.G. *fest-i*, now G. *fest* (fast). Thus, the elements of English and German verbal derivation have been confused and reduced to a very slight number; but these again, as will be further seen, have been extensively used.

These brief remarks will prove sufficient to summarize the principles of Germanic verbal formation, the more so as our modern endings have been made uniform by analogy and have degenerated under the action of phonetic laws, to such a degree that no stress should be laid upon the particular form of their original components.

[1] On the pattern of *oper-ā rī* (and the like), which was traced back to *opus* (gen. *oper-is*), whilst it really proceeded from the fm. noun *oper-a*.
[2] Cf. *infra*, 106, I.

CHAPTER II.

ENGLISH AND GERMAN DERIVATION.

(94) In the preceding pages the reader has met with a large number of **English and German Suffixes**, which, altered and shortened as they may be, yet clearly reproduce a primitive suffix-type. The following pages are intended to show, that, among all the suffixes as yet used and recognised as such by a speaker in both languages, there is not one that cannot claim the same origin. To such derivative resources, however, as were afforded by its original stock of words, Germanic added two new processes, which both arose from the primitive process of composition or, at least, juxtaposition of independent words, namely: the so-called **Inseparable Prefixation**,[1] and the **Suffixation of** some **nominal elements**, now void of any independent meaning. Thus, the present chapter must be divided into three sections.

SECTION I.

PREFIXES.

(95) **Prefixes**, like suffixes, may be either **nominal or verbal**. But it must be understood, at the outset, that any

---

[1] We need scarcely recall the reason why separable prefixes are to be excluded: in point of fact, they are still independent words; inseparable prefixes are the only ones that can be said to have descended to the grade of a mere derivative element. Thus, in *ein-treten*, *aus-treten*, etc., even in *ein-tritt*, *nach-druck*, indeed, even in *ein-kunft*, *zu-kunft*,—though *kunft no longer exists as a separate word,—the speaker distinctly perceives two words, and a kind of compound; whereas, in *be-treten*, contrasted with *treten*, he simply perceives a word modified by a mere exponent of meaning, since *be-*, by itself, means nothing at all.

verbal prefix is also a nominal prefix, inasmuch as every verb derived by prefixation may again serve as a basis for further substantival or adjectival derivation: thus, after the analogy of the relation he perceives between *werf-en* and *wurf*, a speaker naturally forms *ent-wurf* from *ent-werf-en*; and, as soon as a vb. *be-weg-en* (to move) has been formed, such derivatives as *be-weg-ung*, *be-weg-lich* and *be-weg-lich-keit* easily follow. We must, therefore, confine the name of nominal prefix to such as characterize either nominal or adjectival formations which appear to be independent of any verbal formation. There are very few of them, and still fewer in English.

§ 1. *Nominal Prefixes.*

(96) I. By far the most common of nominal prefixes is the syllable which appears as *ga-* in Gothic. Its meaning, still clearly copulative and collective in a great many nominal formations, points to an original connection with the L. preposition *cum* (with) = *cŏm*, as, for instance, L. *pār* (equal) and *com-pār* (pairing), cf. G. *ge-paar-t*: Go. *sinþ-s* (walking), whence Go. *ga-sinþ-a* (fellow-walker, companion), O.E. *ge-sīð*, O.H.G. neuter collective *gi-sind-i* (attendance) and G. *ge-sind-e*. But it is the common fate of such derivative elements to have their value gradually obscured and defaced[1]: no wonder, therefore, if we often find the prefix *ga-* in words which have almost or altogether dropped their old collective meaning.

In form, this unaccented *ga-*[2] is weakened to O.E. *ge-*, O.H.G. *gi-*, M.H.G. and Mod. G. *ge-*. O.E. *ge-* was still spelled *y-* in M.E.; but it afterwards disappeared, except when it was changed to an obscure vowel, as in E. *e-nough* = G. *ge-nug*, and E. *a-ware* = O.E. *ge-wær* = G. *ge-wahr*, so that a modern English speaker no longer recognises this formative syllable.

[1] Cf. L. *co-gnoscere* nearly synonymous with the simple *noscere*.
[2] The phonetic correspondence is irregular, as we should expect Preg. *hă-* = L. *cŏ-*, according to Grimm's law. But the reader will observe that, in the middle of a sentence, the initial might appear either as *hă-* or *ʒă-*, according as the last syllable of the preceding word was or was not accented: so, supposing the form *ʒă-* to have extended through analogy, the case would fall under the head of Verner's law.

M

As to the function, the **copulative** value is quite obvious in: G. *g-leich* = Go. *ga-leik-s*, and E. *a-like*, cf. E. *like*; G. *ge-mein* = Go. *ga-máin-s*, cf. L. *commūnis* = *com-moin-i-s, and E. *mean* (vulgar) = O.E. *ge-mǣne*; G. *ge-mahl* (husband) = O.H.G. *gi-mahal-a*, from *mahal* (assembly, contract); G. *ge-fährt-e* (fellow-traveller), from *fahr-t* (journey); G. *ge-vatter* (godfather), *ge-sell-e* (fellow), etc. The **collective** function is likewise well marked in the numerous G. neuter nouns, like: *ge-birg-e* = O.H.G. *gi-birg-i*, from *berg* (mountain),[1] *ge-fild-e* (fields), *ge-fieder* (plumage), *ge-stirn* (constellation), etc.; in O.E. *hand-ge-weorc* and *hand-ge-cræft*, now become E. *handiwork* and *handicraft*, the collective prefix, reduced to a mere vowel, is scarcely visible except to an etymologist.

II. An isolated prefix, which cannot be recognised in any other I.-E. language, though common to the whole Germanic domain, appears as Go. *us-*, with the meaning "out."[2] In nominal prefixation, this syllable keeps its accent and its vowel unshifted, O.E. and E. *or-*, G. *ur-*, as in O.E. *or-dāl* (judgment)[3] and E. *or-deal*, O.H.G. *ur-tel* and G. *ur-theil*, cf. E. *deal* = G. *theil*. The function did not survive in English. But, in German, either owing to the sense of "extraction" which was contained in it,—*e.g.* in *ur-sache* (cause), *ur-sprung* (origin),—or merely after the analogy of the word *ur-alt*, wherein the meaning "of yore," though originally inherent in the adjective, has become attached to the prefix, this particle assumed a specific value as denoting **origin** and still survives as such, giving to any noun or adjective to which it is affixed the force of an epithet like "ancestral": *ur-ahn* (ancestor), *ur-heimat*, *ur-sprache* (mother-tongue), *Ur-germanisch*, etc.

---

[1] The suffix in these words is I.-E. *-yŏ-*, cf. L. *con-jug-iu-m* (marriage). It is sometimes added to primary stems in *-eto-*, whence in Germanic a derivative complex *-ĭp-ja*. G. *-de* with metaphony: G. *ge-mähl-de* (marriage) = O.H.G. *gi-mahal-idi*; G. *ge-bäu-de* (building) = O.H.G. *gi-bū-idi*.

[2] It may, however, be identified with Russian *voz-* (Meillet). But, at any rate, it must be carefully distinguished from the G. preposition *aus* = E. *out* = Go. *ut* = Sk. *úd*, which is phonetically different and, moreover, has retained an independent meaning and use.

[3] Properly "distribution," then "judgment," and especially "God's judgment." Low L. *ordalium* and F. *ordalie* are borrowed words.—On the unaccented form of the same prefix (verbal), see below, 98 (II.).

III. The old preposition which is Gr. ἀντί (against, in exchange), L. antĕ (opposite, before), was not kept as such in Germanic, but still survives as a prefix, which, if accented, is O.E. and- and G. ant-, if unaccented, G. ent-: O.E. and-swaru and E. an-swer, cf. Sk. svár-a-s (sound) and G. schwören (to take an oath) = O.H.G. swer-ien; G. ant-wort (answer) = O.H.G. ant-wurti, cf. G. wort = E. word; O.E. and-wlita and G. ant-litz (face), cf. Go. vlit-s (face); for the meaning, compare Gr. ἀντί-δωρον (mutual gift), etc. The particle is reduced to a single a in E. a-long = O.E. and-long = G. ent-lang, and in E. a-gain (a-gain-st) = O.E. on-gēan = G. ent-gegen (opposite), cf. G. gegen.[1]

IV. The **negative** prefix, E. and G. un-,[2] has already been explained as the reduced grade of the I.-E. negative particle *nĕ, that is *n-. If this consonant happened to lean on a following vowel, it remained a consonant, as in L. nōn (not) = *n-oino-m (literally "not one"), e.g.: E. n-one (not one), and G. n-ein, now a mere negation; E. n-ought (cf. aught), likewise weakened to a mere negation in the unaccented form not, and so also G. n-icht = O.H.G. n-eo-wiht, cf. Go. ni vaíht-s (not a thing); E. n-ever, n-either, n-or, etc.; G. n-ie ("never," cf. je "ever"), n-immer = n-ie mehr, noch = L. ne-que, nur (only) = O.H.G. ne wāri (literally "were [it] not"), etc. This negative n is now a dead element. But its counterpart un-, arising from the cases in which it had become ṇ by meeting with an initial consonant, was retained and multiplied to such an extent as to be considered the general and exclusive prefix denoting negation, both before a vowel or consonant: thus, E. un-even, as un-like, and G. un-eben, as un-gleich; cf. L. in-ermis, as in-firmus, etc. Moreover, chiefly in German, it is currently associated even with Romance words: E. un-just, G. un-sicher, etc.

V. The **pejorative** prefix mis-, in E. mis-take, and G. misz-fall (accident), etc., had originally nothing to do with the Romance pejorative prefix mes- (F. mé-fait "misdeed," mé-dire

---

[1] M.E. again is commonly used for against. Its present meaning "anew," presents no difficulty: cf. G. wider (against) and wieder (again).
[2] This is not to be confounded with the inversive E. prefix un-, which is an exclusively verbal prefix, infra, 98 (III.).

"to speak evil") = L. *minus*, though, being similar in form and meaning, they naturally became blended in English as soon as French had crossed the Channel (E. *mis-chief* = O.F. *mes-chief*). In Germanic, the prefix is really a past participle, that is to say, a nominal stem with suff. *-tó-*, seen in Gothic as *missa-* = *miþ-tá-*, in *missa-déþ-s* = E. *mis-deed* = G. *mis-that*, literally "a missed deed," the root of the past participle being the same as that of the L. vb. *mitt-ere* (cf. *ā-mitt-ere* "to lose"), the G. vb. *meid-en* (to avoid), and the secondary derivative E. *to miss* = G. *missen*. In consequence of this etymology, *mis-*, as well as the preceding, ought to be an exclusively nominal prefix, but analogy has extended it to verbal formation.[1]

VI. Lastly, for want of a better place, we may mention here the E. prefix *a-*, an unaccented form which represents a number of prepositions, retained in English in their accented form, *at*, *of*, *on*, viz.: E. *a-do* = *at do* (to do), *at* being the sign of the M.E. gerund, as *to* is now of the infinitive; E. *out a-doors* = *out at doors* or *out of doors*, cf. L. *forīs forās* (out) and *forēs* (door); E. *a-down* = O.E. *of dūne*; E. *a-way* = O.E. *on-weg* (on the way), cf. G. *weg* (away) = M.H.G. *en-wëc*; E. *a-foot* = *on foot*; E. *a-kin*, most probably *of kin*, and many others.[2]

§ 2. *Verbal Prefixes.*

(97) I. The Go. pref. *ga-* is as widely diffused throughout verbal derivation as *cŏn-* in Latin, and its primitive value frequently remains obvious; for, just as the L. vb. *con-struere* (to build) involves an idea of "assembling materials," so there

---

[1] Thus, G. *misz-griff* (for the sense, compare *fehl-griff*) produced a vb. *misz-greifen*; then followed *misz-deuten*, *misz-fallen* (to displease), after the analogy of *ge-fallen* (to please) and *misz-fall* (accident), etc. Still more so in E., owing to the influence of F. *mes-* : *to mistake, to mislead*, etc.

[2] The preposition *at* (= L. *ad*) is O.H.G. *aʒ*, now lost in Mod. German, though still visible in *bis* (till) = *bi aʒ* (the first term being now *bei* = E. *by*). —E. *on*, with O.E. *o* = *a* before a nasal, is G. *an*.—Of course, prefixes of Romance origin have been here omitted. An instance of them is O.E. *œrce-* and E. *arch-* = O.H.G. *erzi-* and G. *erz-* = L. *archi-* = Gr. ἀρχι- (chief-): E. *arch-bishop*, G. *erz-bischof*; prefixed even to German words, *erz-herzog* (archduke). In English we have also the negative Romance prefix *in-*, which is used concurrently with the native *un-*, and associated as a rule with borrowed words, *in-defatigable, in-expedient, in-definite*, but *un-defined*, etc.

can be hardly any doubt that a Go. vb. *ga-timr-jan* denotes the act of "adjusting timber"; and similarly with many others, *ga-háit-an* "to con-vocate," *ga-nim-an* "to con-ceive," *ga-lis-an* "to col-lect," etc. Even in Gothic, however, a number of verbs with pref. *ga-* in no way differ in meaning from simple verbs: *ga-bau-an* (to dwell), like *bau-an*; *ga-sat-jan* (to place), like *sat-jan*, etc. The same is the case with G. *ge-währ-en*, *ge-winn-en*, contrasted with O.H.G. *wër-ēn* and E. *to warr-ant*, O.H.G. *winn-an* (to win); and, in English, among the scanty relics of this prefix *ge-*, we have *to afford* = M.E. *a-forth-en* = O.E. *ge-forð-ian* (to put forward), as opposed to G. *forder-n* (to exact), the former derived from *forth*, and the latter from its comparative *vorder*.

Thus, at the outset, this prefix is seen to be wholly unconcerned with the formation of the past participle: in other words, a Go. vb. *lis-an* had a participle *lis-an-s*, whereas *ga-lis-an-s* (G. *ge-les-en*) was the participle of vb. *ga-lis-an*; and so also with *bau-an bau-ida*, and *ga-bau-an ga-bau-ida* (G. *ge-bau-t*), etc. But it happened that West Germanic speakers took to using, instead of the past participle of the simple verb, the past participle of the prefixal verb, so that this syllable *ge-* seemed and actually became the **grammatical exponent of the past participle**. Such is its specific value in O.E. as well as in German. In M.E. the initial syllable is reduced to *y-* (*y-clept* "named," *y-covered*, etc.),[1] and then disappears, so that *found* and *had* no longer differ from *to find* and *to have*. On the contrary, in German, the rule is that every native verb, unless already provided with an inseparable prefix, assumes in the past participle, whether in *-en* or *-et*, the inseparable prefix *ge-*.

A further consequence, paradoxical enough at first sight, of the extended use of the prefix in German is, that, apart from its grammatical function, it is now as dead in German as in English where it has been phonetically suppressed; for, as soon as, for instance, *ge-les-en*, *ge-zimmer-t* were considered to be the

---

[1] Still very common in Chaucer and contemporary writers: *yclad* (clad), *yborn*, *ytold*, etc., though, probably owing to Danish influence, Mercian had lost the participial prefix quite early.

regular participles of the verbs *les-en, zimmer-n*, etc., the existence of such verbs as **ge-les-en = ga-lis-an, *ge-zimmer-n = ga-timr-jan* naturally appeared to be somewhat strange and contradictory, and thus they soon became obsolete; and, in consequence, the prefix *ge-* now characterizes but a very few G. verbs: either those of which the unprefixal form had become obsolete in early times, as *ge-nes-en* (to be healed), from a primitive vb. **nës-an* (cf. the Go. causative *nas-jan* "to heal"), which is no longer to be met with; or those in which the compound had acquired a new meaning, apparently unrelated to that of the simple verb, as *ge-fall-en* (to please),[1] as opposed to *fall-en*; or else, especially, such compounds as had assumed a decidedly transitive or causative sense, viz. *ge-steh-en* (to maintain, to own), *ge-schweig-en* (to silence),[2] contrasted with *steh-en* (to stand), *schweig-en* (to be silent), etc.

(98) II. The pref. *ur-*, losing its accent when added to a verb, is G. *er-*; for there is no difference, except in the accent of the prefix, between *ur-theil* (judgment) and *er-theil-en* (to divide), *ur-laub* (permission) and *er-laub-en* (to allow), *ur-kun-de* (document) and *er-kenn-en* (to acknowledge),[3] etc.; and the same unaccented prefix is concealed in the E. vb. *to a-rise* (cf. *to rise*) = O.E. *a-rīs-an* = Go. *ur-reis-an* (to arise).[4]

III. The pref. *and- ant-*, when verbal and therefore unaccented, is changed to E. *un-*, G. *ent-*, assimilated to *emp-* before an initial *f*: *emp-fang-en = *ent-fang-en, emp-find-en*, etc.[5] The primitive sense of reciprocity or contrariety inherent in the

---

[1] Literally "to fall in with."

[2] The intransitive meaning still preserved in *ge-schweige* (the more so), literally "should we [even] forbear to mention."—Of course, the type *ge-sell-en* (to accompany), though often met with, is here beside the question, as not being formed by adding a prefix *ge-* to a verb, but derived from a noun which already had this prefix, *supra* 96, I.

[3] Though, as a matter of course, *urtheil* produced a vb. *urtheilen*, whereas, on the other hand, *erkennen* produced *erkenntnisz*, supra 95.

[4] Hence initial E. *a-* is seen to be the etymological representative of six distinct particles at the very least.

[5] Literally: "to take in exchange," whence "to receive"; "to find or acquire in exchange, to answer any outer fact with a corresponding and adequate impression," whence "to feel," etc.—No modern verb, however, but these two and *emp-fehlen*, preserves the form *emp-*: everywhere else, *ent-falten, ent-führen, ent-färben*, the form *ent-* has been restored after the analogy of the other members of this class.

I.-E. particle (Gr. ἀντί) does not always appear with clearness, or even seems to have vanished in such German formations as *ent-schlafen* (to fall asleep), *ent-laufen* (to run away), *ent-flieszen* (to flow off), etc. But this meaning is quite plain in the common use of the prefix, which may be termed **inversive**, as involving the contrary action to that which is expressed by the simple verb, in other words, the reverse of the function of the G. prefix *be-* or *ver-*, and synonymous with L. *dis-*, F. *dé-* (in *dé-faire, dé-planter*): G. *ent-decken* (to discover), *ent-binden, ent-ehren* (to dishonour); and similarly in English, *to un-do, to un-bind, to un-fold* = G. *ent-falten*,[1] etc.

(99) IV. It has been already stated that the E. and G. pref. *be-* is merely the unaccented form of the preposition, E. *by*, G. *bei*, which may again be discovered in the final element of the preposition, Sk. *abhi* (towards), Gr. ἀμφί (around, about). Though unaccented, it is still a preposition in such adverbial locutions as E. *be-fore, be-neath*, G. *be-hende* (close at hand, swiftly), etc., and, in the same form, it was very early adapted to a large number of simple verbs, with a greater or less signification of tendency or accession: Go. *bi-git-an*, E. *to be-get*, cf. *to get*; O.E. *be-cum-an* (to suit), E. *to be-come*, G. *be-kommen* (to receive); O.H.G. *bi-ginn-an* (cf. Go. *du-ginn-an*) and G. *be-ginn-en* = E. *to be-gin*, etc. English rarely uses the prefix in other senses, though it possesses some derived verbs, with causative meaning, like *be-dim, be-spread, be-set*, even developed from a French basis, as *be-siege*, etc.; but, in German, the prefix is a living one, and has undergone a considerable extension in a special direction.

As shown by the contrast in meaning between E. *become* and G. *bekommen*, the prefix contains nothing to assign a transitive value to any verb it modifies. But, though of course "to come to" may merely result in "to become" ("to suit" or "to grow"), it is no less capable of meaning "to reach, to get," and of governing, as such, a complement in the accusative; and this is just the case with the G. verb.[2] Thus also, since *sitzen*

---

[1] The development of the inversive meaning was carried very far in G. *ent-setzen* "to unsettle—to overturn—to terrify."
[2] And partly down to M.E., since *to be-siege* is derived from a noun which

means "to sit," *be-sitzen*, "to sit by" or "round," gains the meaning "to occupy, to possess," *be-fallen*, "to fall upon," becomes "to attack," [1] and so forth. Hence the first stage in the evolution of prefixed *be-*, namely, the **possibility of converting** nearly every **verb from intransitive to transitive value**, *folgen be-folgen, schwören be-schwören, streiten be-streiten, siegen be-siegen*, etc.

Secondly, no sooner had such verbs as *bestreiten, bekämpfen, besiegen* become current, than the speaker's mind took to associating them, no longer with the simple verbs whence they had arisen, but directly with the nouns, *streit, kampf, sieg*, which were respectively visible in each. Then, in consequence, it seemed but natural to **construct from any noun, or even any adjective**, by means of the prefixed *be-*, **a transitive or causative verb**, which should involve an idea of "providing, endowing with" the object or quality denoted by the noun or adjective, viz.: *bau* (building), *be-bau-en* "to build upon [a ground]"; *frucht, be-frucht-en* (to fertilise); *frei, be-frei-en* (to free); *fähig, be-fähig-en* (to habilitate); lastly, there arose a fresh set of analogical creations, *be-günst-ig-en* (to befriend) on the basis *gunst* (favour, kindness), *be-vollmächt-ig-en* (to authorize) on *voll-macht* (full power), etc.[2]

V. The G. pref. *ver-*, no less widely diffused, and retained also in a few E. compounds (*for-lorn = ver-loren, to for-give = ver-geben*), represents not only the Go. *fra*,—which again might correspond both to Gr. πρό (before) and L. *prō* (for),—but also reproduces the Go. particles *faír faúr*, which represent L. *per* (by, for, cf. E. *for* and G. *für*), and probably, also, go back to another I.-E. pref. **pĕr-* inasmuch as the latter is suggested by Gr. παρά (sideways, awry), and by the pejorative meaning of such L. verbs as *per-dere, per-īre*, etc. In short, several words

is certainly borrowed from French.—By the way, observe the arbitrary substitution of these exponents with obliterated meaning: E. *to be-seech* is equivalent to G. *er-suchen*.—Observe also the peculiar sense in E. *to be-head*.

[1] Cf. again the intransitive sense in E. *to befall*.

[2] The same may be said of the following (*ver-breiten, ver-einigen, ver-nachlässigen*), and also, to a certain extent, of the preceding prefix: *er-leichter-n, er-mannen, er-ledigen* (there being no such verbs as **mannen, *ledigen*).

have been blended together in this unaccented syllable, which is successively O.H.G. *for-*, *fur-*, then *far-*, lastly *fir-* and *fer-*. Thence proceed the manifold and various functions assigned in G. to this prefix, which in one place appears decidedly significant, and in another expresses but a slight shade of meaning, perhaps **intensive** at the outset, but afterwards more or less weakened: G. *fr-essen* = Go. *fra-it-an*[1]; G. *ver-lieren*, E. synonym *to lose*; G. *ver-ändern*, synonymous with *ändern* (to change), etc. Under the **pejorative** head may be said to fall, more or less directly: the idea of excess, in *ver-brauchen* (to wear out), *ver-blühen* (to shed its blossoms); the idea of error, oblivion, in *ver-gessen* (cf. E. *to get* and *to for-get*), *ver-führen* (to seduce), *ver-legen* (to lose); the idea of ruin, destruction, in *ver-gehen*,[2] which corresponds to L. *per-ire*, *ver-geben-s* (vainly); that of a deed taken in ill part, *ver-leumden* (to defame, cf. *leumund* "fame"); and even a completely negative meaning, in *ver-bieten* (cf. E. *to for-bid*), *ver-achten* (to despise), etc. Lastly, as used at present, the pref. *ver-*, like the preceding one, may change an intransitive into an **active verb**, thus *dienen ver-dienen*,[3] or from a nominal basis may form a corresponding **causative verb**, with slight differences of meaning, however, which must be learnt from a special study of German, or rather from use and practice.[4]

(100) VI. The **dissociative** prefix, O.E. *to-*, O.H.G. *za-*, *zi-*, *ze-*, then subsidiarily *zur-*, *zar-*, *zer-*, the latter being the only one preserved in Mod. G., has certainly nothing to do with the

---

[1] Intensive "to devour," and, therefore, confined to the feeding of animals, or else used humorously. E. *to fret*, by passing through the meanings "to devour—to bite—to gnash the teeth," has become used for strong and outward emotion.

[2] It must not be confounded with E. *to fore-go*, which contains an accented form, G. *vor* = Go. *faúra* (before): Go. *faúra-gaggan*, "to go forward, to precede," whence "to outreach" and (E.) "to give up."

[3] "To serve (*dienen*) on account of," whence "to earn" and "to deserve." —On the contrary, from the active *recken* (to stretch, cf. L. *por-rig-ere*), we have the pejorative participle *ver-reck-t* (stiffened, dead), whence the intransitive verb *ver-reck-en* "to die" (animals).

[4] Observe both the transitive and the pejorative function cumulated in such locutions as *seine zeit vergeigen* "to waste one's time by playing upon the violin," and the contrasted meaning in *kaufen* (to buy) and *verkaufen* (to sell), Go. *káupōn* meaning only "to trade."

E. preposition *to* = G. *zu*, and seems, like the preceding, to be of manifold and rather intricate origin, inasmuch as it corresponds to two Go. particles: one, visible in Go. *tvis-standan* (to stand apart), which at once recalls Gr. δίς = *δϝίς (twice), and the well-known dissociative prefix, L. *dis-*[1]; the other, of pejorative force, Go. *tuz-* = Gr. δυσ- = Sk. *dus-* (ill-). The prefix no longer occurs in English except in the old verb (pf.) *to-brake* = G. *zer-brach* (he broke to pieces); but it remains in common, specific and extended use in German, either as modifying the sense of a simple verb (*zer-reiszen, zer-stampfen, zer-flieszen, zer-bröckeln*, etc.), or even, occasionally, as forming a verb from a nominal stem (*zer-fetzen, zer-fleischen, zer-nichten, zer-lump-t* "ragged," no vb. *lumpen* existing, at least with this meaning).

From this contrasted study of E. and G. verbal prefixes, it follows that both languages, though starting from the same point and still preserving many identical formations, have now reached quite a different stage in the evolution of their verbal prefixes: all of them are still living in German, apart from *ge-*,[2] whilst all are dead in English, with the single exception of *un-*.[3]

Section II.

SUFFIXES PROPERLY SO-CALLED.

(101) **English and German Suffixes**, like those in I.-E. and Preg., are either **nominal** or **verbal**.

§ 1. *Nominal Suffixes.*

Nominal stems formed by suffixes fall under a double head, according as they respectively play the part either of **nouns** or of **adjectives**.

---

[1] It is almost superfluous to state that whenever the prefix occurs in this shape in English (*to dis-honour, to dis-qualify*), it is simply borrowed from Latin.
[2] Dead as a derivative element, though living as a grammatical exponent.
[3] Thus, such a sentence as "we must *un-boycott* Ireland" would be consistent with the genius of our language.

A. Nouns.

(102) I. E. *-er*, G. *-er*: **nouns of agent.**—The interesting history of this extremely common and still wonderfully active suffix, may be given in a few characteristic processes, by starting from an original form, *-ar-ja-*, or *-ār-ja-*, that is to say, I.-E. suff. *-yo-*, added to a stem of secondary derivation with suff. *-ro-*, e.g.: Sk. *rátha-s* (chariot), whence a vb. *ratha-r-yá-ti* (he drives a chariot).

1. Latin is rich in adjectives in *-āriu-s*, all of which are derived from nouns: *ferr-āriu-s* (of iron), *pisc-āriu-s* (of fish), etc. Now, these adjectives, when qualifying a person, acquire a substantival meaning, viz.: (*faber*) *ferrārius*, literally "ironsmith"; *piscārius* (fisher), etc. The same is the case with the Go.: *vull-arei-s* (woollen-draper), *bōk-arei-s* (transcriber); and the Go. suff. *-arei-* is to be recognised, though with an initial long vowel, in the metaphonical forms, O.E. *-ēre*, M.H.G. *-œre* (=O.H.G. *-āri*), then *-er*, E. and G. *-er*, the function of which is identical in the types *fish-er* (O.E. *fisc-ēre*) and *fisch-er*, and many similar, all derived from nouns, which will at once occur to the reader's mind.

2. This element, of course, could be added to a nominal stem in *-en-* as well as to any other: E. *gard-en-er*, and G. *gärtn-er* = M.H.G. *gart-en-œre* = O.H.G. *gart-in-āri*, cf. the E. name *Gardiner*; O.H.G. *ohs-an-āri* (cowherd), G. *öchs-n-er*, etc. Further, the peculiar property of these stems in *-en-*, as stated above, is to drop the *n* in the nomin. sg., so that, when compared with a nomin. O.H.G. *gart-o* and M.H.G. *gart-e*, O.H.G. *ohs-o* and G. *ochs*, etc., the *n* inserted in the derivative seems a part of the second suffix: whence a fictitious suffix *-ner*, which appears in G. *bild-ner* (statuary),[1] *pfort-ner* (porter), *harf-ner* (harper), and several others.

3. It will be understood from these considerations that suff. *-er*, like L. *-ārius*, cannot, in theory, be added to a verbal stem, and that its function, as clearly verified by the earliest

---

[1] In the fourteenth century, *bild-en-œre*, but before that the regular *bild-œre*.—The E. forms in *-ar* (*li-ar*) and *-or* (*sail-or* = *sail-er*, *warr-ior*, cf. *law-yer*) are mere varieties of spelling.

known formations, is merely the derivation of nouns from nouns, *e.g.*: O.E. *bōc* (book), whence O.E. *bōc-ēre* (scribe), cf. L. *libr-ārius*; O.H.G. *fano (flag),¹ whence *fan-eri* (ensign-bearer), M.H.G. *venre*, Mod. G. corrupt *fähnrich*, cf. L. *vexill-ārius*, etc. But it often happened that, side by side with such a noun, there existed a verb, either identical in form, or at least closely akin, and it was easier for the speaker to refer, *e.g.*, the words *fisher* and *fischer*, to the verbs *to fish* and *fischen*, than to the substantives *fish* and *fisch*, whence they really proceeded.² The analogical and necessary consequence of this confusion led to the derivation of a noun of agent from any verb by the mere addition of suffix *-er*, a process still widely used in both tongues: E. *shave-r*, *hate-r*, *make-r*; G. *käuf-er* (purchaser), *säuf-er* (drunkard), *schneid-er* (tailor), etc. This occasioned moreover, in German, a number of doublets, which were afterwards partly eliminated, either by one of them becoming obsolete, or else by each assuming a slightly different meaning: O.H.G. *sang-ari*, a normal derivative from *sang* = E. *song*, now *säng-er*, and G. *sing-er*, an abnormal derivative from *sing-en*; G. *schnitt-er* and *schneid-er*; G. *ritt-er* (knight), cf. *ritt* (ride), and *reit-er* (rider), from *reit-en* (to ride), etc.

4. The further use of the same element in the derivation of nouns denoting inhabitants (E. *London-er*, G. *Berlin-er*) is consistent with its adjectival origin, though, of course, L. *-ārius* never assumed such a function.

5. This suff. *-er* ought not to be confounded with another, identical in form, but quite different in meaning, and of very rare use, which characterizes the names of some male animals: E. *cat* and G. *katze* as generic name, but E. *cat-er preserved in *cater-waul*, and G. *kater* = O.H.G. *chat-aro*; E. *goose* = *gons = *gans, and G. *gans*, but O.E. *gand-ra* and E. *gand-er*, M.H.G. *ganʒ-er* and G. *gänserich*.³

¹ In the compound *gund-fano* (battle-ensign), borrowed in F. and thence in E. *gonfanon*.
² Cf. *supra* 99, the reversed process as to *bestreiten*, which was referred to *streit*, while it really came from *streiten*, and *infra* IX. (105). "Blunders" of this kind are very common in all languages, and greatly increase their derivative power.—All these words form their feminine in E. *-ess* (if at all needful), and G. *-in*, supra 69, note, and 87, I.
³ Corrupt like *fähnrich* above; cf. *enterich*, *täuberich*.

(103) II. E. -*ing*, G. -*ung* : **nouns of action.**—These two suffix-forms are not identical, but the difference between them is almost immaterial, as they are Germanic substitutes respectively for I.-E. -*eñ-ko-* and -*ņ-ko-*,[1] especially as German will be seen to show the form -*ing* in some cognate derivations, whereas O.E., even in this very class, has the form -*ung*, now lost in English: O.E. *leorn-ung* = G. *lern-ung*, but E. *learn-ing* (as noun), etc. In both languages, in fact, it is the specific function of this suffix to form either a noun denoting an action or an abstract noun constructed on a verbal basis.

1. This is the only function it assumes in German, where it has been developed on a considerable scale, but has remained strictly derivative: O.H.G. *hantal-ōn* (to deal with), fm. *hantal-unga*; *man-ōn* (to warn), fm. *man-unga*; G. *handel-n handl-ung*, *mahn-en mahn-ung*; further *führ-ung*, *rüst-ung*, *fest-ung*, *brech-ung*, etc.

2. In English, although it remains derivative (*a yearn-ing*, *a liv-ing*, *a hunt-ing party*, *a danc-ing master*,[2] etc.), it has also become an important grammatical element. Final -*end* in the present participle, at least in some parts of England, had come to be sounded nearly like -*ing*,[3] so that a confusion of the two was possible. On the other hand, O.E. had many such sentences as *ic wæs on huntunge*, where *huntunge* is the dative of a noun denoting an action, and this sentence, becoming E. *I was a-hunting*, could very easily be understood as *I was hunting* (pres. part.), especially as *a-waiting* (and the like), in the sentence *I am a-waiting*, might be mistaken for the pres. part. of the vb. *await*, whereas it is really a noun of action preceded by a preposition. From this arose in English a curious confusion between the forms of the noun denoting an action, of the gerund and of the **present participle**, so that, in a great

---

[1] Cf. *supra* 91, 2.
[2] Thus, and not by the present participle,—as in F. *une matinée dansante*, etc.,—are to be explained similar E. locutions, which are really compound words in which the first term is no less clearly a noun than in the G. type *erlernungs-mittel*, etc. The same is the case with the form in -*ing* when governed by a preposition: *on asking*, i.e. " upon interrogation," *of doing*, *for playing*, etc., etc.
[3] Cf. *supra* 90, VI. The pronunciation -*ing* is attested by spelling as early as 1200.

many cases the ending -*ing* has completely lost its nominal character, the word thus formed being mistaken for a verb and treated as such in syntax : *for having done ; nature's chief masterpiece is writing well* (Pope), etc.

III. E. -*ing*, -*ling*, G. -*ing*, -*ling* : **diminutives.**—1. The suff. -*ing* has no diminutive value in itself (cf. E. *king*=*cyn-ing*, and G. *könig*=*kon-ing*, the primary stem being a word which means "race, people"), though it is not to be denied that it often occurs in the designation of little objects : E. *shill-ing*, *farth-ing* ("one-fourth"), G. *schill-ing*, etc. It was uncommon and is now dead.

2. Secondly, by combining with -*ing* the diminutive suffix -*ila*, Germanic secured a diminutive suffix -*iling*, -*ling*, which, though still tolerably well represented, hardly enters into any new formations : O.E. *gōs-ling* and E. *gos-ling* ; E. *darling*= *dear-ling, caressing diminutive ; E. *young-ling* and G. *jüng-ling* =O.E. *geong-ling* and O.H.G. *junga-ling* ; E. *lord-ling*, and even *lord-ing*, contemptuous diminutive ; O.E. *œdeling* and G. *edeling* (nobleman), without any precise diminutive value, etc.[1]

IV. G. -*lein* and -*chen* (E. -*kin*) : **diminutives.**—1. The suff. -*īn*, added likewise to the diminutive suff. -*ila*, formed a complex -*ilīn*, -*līn*, which no longer appears either in English or Low German, but is in very common use in High German : O.H.G. *fugil-īn* (little bird), *chezz-ilīn*, *chind-ilīn* ; G. *vöglein*, *kätzlein*, *kindlein*, *männlein*, etc.

2. The same -*īn*, adapted to a stem with final guttural, formed a complex -*kin*, unknown in pure High German, though current in Low German : Dutch *skipe-kīn* (little ship). English borrowed this ending (*manni-kin*), without however further developing it.[2] In Central German it became -*chen* and spread widely : *männ-chen*, *schäf-chen* (little sheep), *häus-chen*. As far as popular speech is concerned, suff. -*chen* is exclusively used in the Northern, and suff. -*lein* exclusively in the Southern countries of Germany ; but the literary language is well known

---

[1] Quite common as such in E. : *weakling, fondling, changeling, hireling*, etc. Cf. also G. *zög-ling* (pupil), *häupt-ling* (chieftain), *flücht-ling* (runaway).

[2] Though we have *lamb-kin*, *nap-kin* (literally "little table-cloth," F. *nappe*), and a few proper names (*Jenkin*).

to admit of both concurrently, and no Germanic formation is in more constant use.

(104) V. E. *-sel, *-sle; G. -sal, -sel: **abstract nouns.**— The origin of this element is doubtful, owing to the many phonetic alterations which it underwent from I.-E. down to Pregermanic. It may be explained in several ways, all fairly plausible, though none can be deemed beyond doubt. The simplest, however, would be to start from the I.-E. suff. -tlo-,[1] and to suppose it to be added to a root ending with a dental consonant, so that the primitive group became I.-E. -t-tlo-, Preg. -ssla-, which was afterwards used as a whole in other derivations.[2]

1. The suffix is still clearly visible in German, having partly escaped the effects of the law which causes unaccented finals to become obscured. Thus, it often keeps the vowel a: trüb-sal (affliction) = O.H.G. truob-i-sal, lab-sal, schick-sal,[3] etc. But its power of extension is nearly extinct. Still more so, of course, with its duller form -sel: wech-sel (exchange) = O.H.G. wëh-sal, from an I.-E. root wĭk meaning alternation, cf. L. vic-ēs, vic-issim; räth-sel (riddle) = O.H.G. rāt-isal, from G. rath-en = O.H.G. rāt-an (to guess); über-bleib-sel (remainder), etc. Most of these nouns are true to their instrumental origin in keeping the neuter gender.

2. In English, the suffix is hidden under a double veil. Firstly, the word which is G. räthsel is O.E. rǣdels, the two consonants having changed places.[4] So we should expect to find E. a *riddles; but the final s was mistaken for the sign of the plural number, and dropped in consequence to form the seemingly correct singular riddle. In the same way we have E. burial = M.E. burials = O.E. byrg-els, derived from byrg-en (to

---

[1] Of nouns denoting instrument, supra 79 (XIII.).

[2] The s was not changed to z, because it was double. Besides, a euphonic vowel was inserted between the s and the l (O.H.G. -isal), which prevented the former from becoming š.

[3] In some words the syllable was probably mistaken for the second term of a compound, such as -sam or -bar, and was therefore sounded with a secondary accent, which preserved the vowel.

[4] No process is more common, in any language, than the metathesis of liquid sounds: cf. P. Passy, Changements phonétiques, no. 542 sq.

bury), cf. G. *berg-en* (to bury, to hide). We need scarcely observe that this method of formation has long been dead.

VI. E. *-ness*, G. *-nisz*: **abstract nouns**, also mostly neuter. —This suffix, though far more important than the preceding, and still living in both languages, has no less doubtful and intricate an origin. The earliest form known to us is a msc. Go. suff. *-assu-s*, wherein the final element is probably the I.-E. msc. suff. *-tu-*. If so, the E. and G. initial *n* cannot belong to the suffix: it must have arisen from cases in which *-assu-* was added to a stem in *-en-*, *e.g.* Go. *þiud-a* (people, gen. *þiud-in-s*, cf. L. *Teut-ō* pl. *Teut-ōn-ēs*), whence a derivative *þiud-in-assu-s* (kingdom, in the Lord's Prayer), and several others. So also with derivatives from participles ending in *n*, as O.H.G. *for-loran-issa*, which should be E. **forlorn-ess* (altered to *forlorn-ness*) and G. **verlorn-isz*. These words gave rise to a false suffix, E. *-ness*, G. *-nisz*, which took the place of the true form:[1] E. *holy-ness* = O.E. *hālig-ness*, *high-ness*, *sour-ness*, *forgive-ness*; O.H.G. *hart-nissa* (hardness), *got-nissa* (divinity); G. *zeug-nisz* (testimony), *bild-nisz* (image), *bünd-nisz* (alliance, league), etc.[2]

B. *Adjectives.*

(105) VII. E. *-en*, G. *-en*, further *-ern*: **adjectives of material.**—From a Preg. suff. *-ina-* = I.-E. *-īno-*, supra 89, 3.

VIII. E. *-ish*, G. *-isch*: **adjectives of extraction and attribution.**—This element is alive in English, though it has generally given place to the suff. *-ly*[3] or the borrowed French formation (*Americ-an*, *Pruss-ian*). It is largely used in German (*Französ-isch*), where it forms even learned terms (*psycholog-isch*) or is added to words of Romance origin (*Latein-isch*, *Amerik-an-isch*, *Chin-es-isch*, *Annam-it-isch*). For its earlier form, Preg. **-iska-* = I.-E. **-isko-*, see above, 91, 3.

IX. E. *-y* (= O.E. *-ig*), G. *-ig*: **adjectives of qualifica-**

---

[1] It is more active in English than in German; for it is used not only with native words, but indifferently, with words borrowed from French (*coy-ness*, F. *coi* "quiet") and learned adjectives imported from Latin (*acid-ness*).

[2] In *gefängnisz* (gaol), if analysed *ge-fäng-n-isz* (cf. the part. *ge-fang-en* "prisoner"), we might perhaps find the original form of the suffix.

[3] Contrast, for instance, *heaven-ly* with *himml-isch*, *earthly* with *ird-isch*, etc.

tion.—Still living and quite common : E. *heart-y, mood-y, health-y, fil-th-y, silver-y*; added to borrowed words, *greas-y, juic-y*, etc. ; G. *herz-ig, muth-ig, zorn-ig, zott-ig, woll-ig, gold-ig*, etc. ; in compounds, *vier-füsz-ig, weit-schweif-ig*.¹ Its origin is discussed above, 91, 1.

X. O.E. *-iht* (lost in E.), G. *-icht*: with the same meaning, though not at all common.—It looks like a compound formed by an exclusively Germanic combination of the I.-E. suffixes *-ko-* (*-iko-*) and *-to-* : O.E. *stǣn-iht* (stony), G. *stein-icht, woll-icht, thör-icht* (foolish), etc. The adjective has become a substantive in *kehr-icht* (dirt), derived from O.H.G. *chara, which is the nominal basis of the vb. *cher-ian*, G. *kehr-en* (to sweep).

§ 2. *Verbal Suffixes.*

(106) We have already stated that the whole E. and G. verbal derivation now rests on the ancient Germanic suffix *-jan*, which moreover has been blended with the whole verbal endings *-ēn* and *-ōn*: that is to say, it rests on the ending *-en* for the German infinitive, and on no ending at all for the English infinitive. But this general derivation will appear clearer, if we first get rid of some less productive formations, which depend on the addition of the same final *-jan* to a prior nominal suffix, or on some similar combination.

I. E. *-n, -en* (rather common), G. *-n-en* (much rarer) = Germanic *-n-jan* and *-n-an*: **mostly causative verbs.**—In principle, in English as well as in German, the simple addition of suff. **-jan* to a stem is sufficient to give the derivative compound the meaning of causality which is originally involved in this verbal suffix ² : thus, from *warm*, we have the vb. *to warm*, as in G. *wärm-en* = Go. *varm-jan* ; from *better*, the vb. *to better* = G. *besser-n*, etc., etc. But in consequence of English having

---

¹ Such adjectives as *gläub-ig, streit-ig, irr-ig*, etc., which really proceed from nouns, *glaube, streit, irre*, etc., being afterwards referred to the verbs *glaub-en, streit-en, irr-en*, etc., analogy subsequently produced *er-biet-ig* (the normal form is *er-böt-ig* from the noun *er-bot*), *aus-find-ig, zu-läss-ig, ab-häng-ig*, etc., from *er-biet-en, aus-find-en, zu-lass-en, ab-hang-en*, and many more. Cf. *supra* 99, 102 (3), and *infra* 110 (I. 2, II., III.), etc. All these processes fall under the same head.

² See the so-called causative and denominative verbs in Sk., Gr. and L., *supra* 83 (IV.) and 92.

dropped the final *n*, the causative verb was occasionally no longer clearly distinguishable, either from the word whence it proceeded, or, in particular, from an intransitive verb derived from the latter, so that the speaker naturally preferred a more characteristic derivative process. Now, Germanic had formed from its past participles in *-an-*, as well as from other adjectives, either causative or intransitive verbs, the former with an infinitive in *-n-jan*, the latter with an infinitive in *-n-an*. These afterwards, by the loss of the *j*, became more or less blended together, assuming however as a rule the causative meaning. Let us consider therefore a root *wak*, Go. vb. *wak-an* (to be awake): from this root came a part. Preg. *wak-aná-s (awake), and, from this again, an intransitive vb. *ʒa-wak-an-an (to become awake) and a causative vb. *ʒa-wak-an-jan (to make awake); the O.E. correspondent *a-wœc-n-an* still means "to become awake"; but the E. offspring *to a-wak-en* hardly means anything else but "to make awake," in opposition to the purely intransitive *to a-wake*, which would be Germanic *ʒa-wak-an (to become awake).[1]

After this final *-en* had been thus obtained, it was deemed the specific exponent for causative verbs, and was used to modify any adjective (*deep-en, sharp-en, soft-en, rough-en, straight-en*), and even some substantives (*height-en, length-en, strength-en*), always with the same causative value, which however concurrently admits of the intransitive use (*to ripen* is "to become" and "to make ripe," *to sick-en*, "to fall" and "to render sick," etc.). In German, since the formative element **-jan* still remained perceptible enough, it was felt to be sufficiently clear, so that the verbal derivation by *-n-en* seemed useless, and was not developed, though we find here, as in English, such old and legitimate types as *ler-n-en* (E. *to learn*), *leug-n-en* (to deny, O.E. *lȳg-n-an* "to call [a thing] a lie"), *war-n-en* (E. *to war-n*), as opposed to *lehr-en, lüg-en, wahr-en*.

[1] The argument seems somewhat far-fetched, owing to the fact that the E. final syllable is dropped. The reader need only be reminded, that an E. infinitive ending without an *n* ought to have one, and that therefore an E. infinitive ending with an *n* ought to have two *n*'s: hence, for instance, E. *sharp-en* and G. *schärf-en*, though outwardly alike, are etymologically different; the G. verb corresponding to E. *to sharp-en* would be *scharf-n-en.

II. E. -se=-is-an and -s-ian (supra 93): causative verbs.—From an adjective *hreinn* (pure) O.N. has a verb *hrein-sa* (to wash), whence E. (borrowed) *to rinse*. From *clǣne* (clean) O.E. likewise derives *clǣn-s-ian*, cf. E. *clean* and *to cleanse*. The types *to clasp*=M.E. *clap-s-en*, and *to grasp*=*grap-s-en* (cf. *to grapp-le*) fall under the same head, having undergone a metathesis.

III. E. -le, -l, -er; G. -eln, -ern: frequentative verbs.—This simple suffix consists of a nominal stem in -*ila* or -*ira*, to which is added the ordinary verbal element. The diminutive meaning of the nominal suffix -*ila* satisfactorily explains the frequentative force of the verbal ending thus obtained.[1] Instances are extremely numerous: E. *to hurt-le, to snuff-le, to draw-l*, etc., compare *to hurt, snuff, to draw*[2]; G. *läch-eln* (to smile), *schütt-eln* (to shake), *klüg-eln* (to affect wisdom), *näs-eln* (to speak through the nose), as opposed to *lach-en, schütt-en*,[3] *klug, nase*; E. *to glimm-er, to glitter*=G. *glitz-ern, to flutter*, contrasted with *gleam*, *glit* (Go. *glit-mun-jan* "to shine"), *to float*, etc.; G. *er-schütt-ern* (to shake), *folg-ern* (to draw a consequence), *zög-ern* (to balance, to protract, cf. *ziehen* "to draw," pf. *zog*), and so forth.[4]

IV. G. -zen=-t-jan (supra 93): frequentative verbs.—A well known and common formation: *schluch-zen* (to sob, cf. *schluck-en* "to swallow"), *kräch-zen, grun-zen, jauch-zen, äch-zen*, etc. In *seuf-zen* (to sigh)=O.H.G. *sûft-ôn* (cf. E. *to sob*), the *z* has intruded (M.H.G. *siuft-en* and *siuf-zen*) after the analogy of other verbs with a similar regular ending. In *du-tzen* (to thou) the exponent was also originally frequentative, but has become reduced to the ordinary verbal value.[5]

[1] Thus, "to drink small draughts" may be "to drink often," and so forth.
[2] From *spark*, a frequentative *to spark-le*, the only derivation. The meaning is merely intransitive in *to kneel*.
[3] Still in the sixteenth century, *er-schütt-en*, "to throw down, to stagger."
[4] The type *ver-stein-ern* must not be confused with the frequentative formation; it contains simply the suffix of adjectives denoting material, supra 105. So also, E. *to girdle* is the verb formed on *girdle*, not the frequentative of the simple *to gird*. The G. ending -*eln* occasionally claims a descent from some other suffix: *handeln* (to deal with) is O.H.G. *hant-alôn*.
[5] By combination of suffixes III. and IV., we have G. *bren-z-eln* "to have a burnt smell."

(107) **V. No exponent** at all in E.; in G. the simple ending *-en*: ordinary verbal derivation.—This important formation is the modern form of the Germanic suffix *-jan* and its equivalents, and may therefore form indifferently intransitive, transitive and causative verbs. It is impossible here to go into details, but the general features of the formation may be shortly summarised.

1. Firstly, in form, it admits naturally of the regular metaphony (G. *scharf schärf-en*, *queck* (*keck*) *er-quicken* "to vivify," *los lös-en* "to unbind," *voll füll-en*, *brut brüt-en*), but this again may be defaced by analogy[1]: from *gold*, we have E. *to gild*, whereas G. *ver-güld-en* is replaced by *ver-gold-en*; and vice versa, G. *wärm-en*, but E. *to warm*. In fact, the O.E. metaphony has become quite extinct: English now derives all its verbs without any metaphony, whilst in German the process, being later, still survives.

2. The G. derivation, as a matter of course, admits of every verbal prefix which has been described above: *be-fremd-en er-höh-en*, *ent-blösz-en*, *ver-dunkel-n*, etc. On the contrary, in E., where the use of prefixes has been lost[2] and the verbal final dropped, the derivative verb became identical with its derivative base, whatever the latter might be. After the analogy of such cases was developed an extremely simple derivation of verbs, which is peculiar to English, namely, the power of forming a verb from any word by merely conjugating it as it stood: *to ink a pen*, *to pen a word*, *to word a thing*, *to boycott a man*; and so forth. English may be said to have thus regained the simplicity of structure of the so-called

---

[1] No mutation being possible from *still* to *still-en* (to quiet), from *süsz* (sweet) to *ver-süsz-en*, etc., the language was led to create, also without mutation, *trockn-en* (to dry), *er-starr-en* (to stiffen), *er-blass-en* (to turn pale), *ver-dumpf-en*, *ver-faul-en*, etc. Even German dialects are at variance in this respect: thus *nütz-en* (to use) is Alamannic *nutz-en*. It has been stated besides that the derivation by *-jan* was confounded with the derivation by *-ēn* and *-ōn*, and the latter naturally do not require any mutation (*supra* 92–93). For English metaphony, compare *full* and *to fill*, *doom* and *to deem*, *brood* and *to breed*, *food* and *to feed*, etc.

[2] Apart from the inversive *un-* (*supra* 98, III.), and a number of Romance prefixes, *to en-able*, *to dis-own*, etc.

primitive languages, where nearly every word may play the part either of a noun or a verb.

3. The function, as we have said, varies widely. Passive intransitives: E. *to ache*, G. *fieber-n* (to be in a fever). Active intransitives: E. *to ship* = G. *schiff-en*. Simple transitives: E. *to love* = G. *lieb-en*. Causative transitives: G. *schwäch-en, schwärz-en, kränk-en*. Sometimes the meanings are cumulated: E. *to ripe* = G. *reif-en* (to become ripe and to cause to ripen). If more precision is wanted in marking the causative sense, German uses its prefixes *be-, ver-*, and *ent-* (inversive), whilst English uses its suffix *-en*. It is chiefly a matter of usage.

4. G. *-ig-en.*—A most important development of the causative derivation remains peculiar to German. Such verbs as M.H.G. *eineg-en, nōteg-en, schedeg-en, schuldeg-en,* G. *einig-en, nöthig-en, schädig-en, schuldig-en, kräftig-en, be-mächtig-en,* — which are quite regularly derived from the adjectives *einec, nōtec, schadec, schuldec,* respectively *kräftig, mächtig*, etc.,—having been erroneously traced back to the simple words *ein, noth, schade, schuld, kraft, macht*, etc., the speaker formed, in the same way, from *ende* and *theil*, for instance, the verbs *end-ig-en* and *be-theil-ig-en*, though no adjectives *end-ig and *theil-ig actually exist. From this false analogy has sprung the **causative suffix** *-igen*, which is widely diffused: *be-fehl-igen, be-schäft-igen, ver-ein-igen, ge-nehm-igen, be-schön-igen*, etc.

VI. G. *-ieren, -iren.*—It is only on account of the wide use of this element, that it may be held to deserve a place in our list; for it is of Romance origin, though modified by the general G. infinitive ending: G. *spazier-en* = L. *spatiārī* (to walk). It characterizes chiefly borrowed verbs (*räsonn-iren*), or such as are derived from borrowed words (*stud-iren*). But, at the time when it became general under the influence of the French language (XVIIth–XVIIIth century), it was even attached to some Germanic stems, as in *stolz-iren* (to strut), *schatt-iren* (to shadow), *buchstab-iren* (to spell).

Section III.

OLD WORDS CHANGED TO SUFFIXES.

(108) This subject has been seen above to belong properly to the study of composition, inasmuch as, for instance, *child-hood* and *kind-heit*, if referred to their origin, are no less truly compound nouns than *child-birth* and *kind-bett*. The only difference lies in the fact that *birth* and *bett* are still extant in their respective languages, while **hood* and **heit* have long been obsolete. Now, this difference, though theoretically quite insignificant, is important in practice; for, since these final syllables have no longer any meaning by themselves and are merely used as a vague derivative exponent, they have gradually acquired various significations, and have moreover undergone slight alterations which would have been prevented if the isolated word had survived.[1] Therefore this peculiar Anglo-German derivation, which might be termed **derivative composition**, is well fitted to mark a transition from the matters previously dealt with to the following subject.

The old words changed to derivative suffixes were either nouns or adjectives, so that the result of derivative composition is either a **noun** or an **adjective**. Some adjectives, moreover, here and there became **adverbial locutions**.

§ 1. *Nouns.*

(109) I. E. *-hood* and (if unaccented) *-head* = O.E. *-hād*; G. *-heit* = **hait* = Go. *hai-du-s* (manner) : **abstract nouns.**—From an I.-E. root *qi* (to see, to remark, to discern, Sk. *ci*) proceeded an I.-E. stem **qoy-tú-*, Sk. *kē-tú-s* (sign), Preg. **hai-ðú-s* (sign, quality, manner): thus O.H.G. *chint-heit* means simply "the quality, the state of a child," and so with any similar words, English or German.

1. The E. form *-hood* is common, whereas the form *-head* is rare: *maiden-hood* and *maiden-head* = O.E. *mægden-hād*. It is added to borrowed as well as native words: O.E. *biscop-hād*, E.

[1] Cf. *supra* 68.

priest-hood. But it forms scarcely any derivatives except from substantives : *brother-hood, neighbour-hood, man-hood,* etc., though we have *false-hood*. In German, on the contrary, *-heit* may be added to adjectives as well as to substantives, forming abstract nouns from both classes, indeed, the derivation from adjectives is now far commoner: O.H.G. *magat-heit, man-heit,* etc.; Mod. G. *schön-heit, frei-heit, bos-heit* (wickedness) = *bōsi-hait*,[1] etc.

2. Whenever the syllable *-heit* was attached to an adjective ending in *-ec* (Mod. G. *-ig*), which was a very common case in M.H.G., the whole became a complex *-cheit*: thus, from *milt-ec* (piteous), the abstract noun *milt-ec-heit*. Now, beside the derivative *milt-ec*, there existed a simpler adjective *milte* (Mod. G. *mild* = E. *mild*), and this, contrasted with *miltecheit*, naturally created the false suffix *-cheit*, which was then used in other cases: *eitel-keit, lust-ig-keit, dank-bar-keit, freund-lich-keit,* etc. Both suffixes *-heit* and *-keit* have the same meaning as well as the same origin, and their employment is merely a matter of usage.[2]

II. E. *-dom* = O.E. *-dōm*; G. *-thum* (*-tum*) = O.H.G. *-tuom*: abstract nouns (occasionally concrete nouns, as E. *king-dom*, G. *herzog-thum*).—The word is the same as E. *doom*, which has been seen to come from a root meaning "to do," cf. E. *do*, G. *thu-n*. It forms in both languages several derivatives either from nouns or adjectives: O.E. *biscop-dōm, hālig-dōm*; E. *earl-dom, free-dom, wis-dom*; O.H.G. *meistar-tuom, frī-tuom*; G. *bis-thum* (syncopated), *heilig-thum*, etc. It is a living suffix, especially in German, where such formations as *junkertum, brahmanentum* are still current.

---

[1] The vowel was syncopated early enough not to have occasioned metaphony, cf. *böse* = O.H.G. *bōsi*.—In derivation from nouns, G. gave the preference to suff. *-schaft* (compare *bruder-schaft* with *brother-hood*), while, in derivation from adjectives, E. usually used suff. *-dom* (compare *freedom* with *freiheit*, *wisdom* with *weisheit*).—Observe the variety of resources displayed: for the abstract noun from "high," E. and G. together have four different derivatives (E. *height* and *highness*, G. *höhe* and *hoheit*), of course with various shades of meaning.

[2] Again, from a further combination of *-ig* and *-keit*, arose a suff. *-igkeit* (*neu-igkeit, klein-igkeit, genau-igkeit*), which spread in the same way as verbal *-igen*, supra 107 (V. 4).

III. E. -*ship* = O.E. -*scipe*; G. -*schaft* = O.H.G. -*skaft* : **abstract nouns.**—The two words, though not identical, both mean "shape, form," inasmuch as they have sprung, by different suffixes, from the root which produced *to shape* and *schaffen*. Besides, O.H.G. still possesses a simpler suff. -*skaf* = Preg. *skap-i-, which is even nearer to the E. form : O.H.G. *lant-skaf* = E. *land-scape*, the latter borrowed from Dutch, but M.E. *land-skip*. The formation is common in both languages : E. *friend-ship, town-ship, worship* = **worth-ship, court-ship*; G. *freund-schaft, diener-schaft*,[1] *gesell-schaft, herr-schaft, bürger-schaft*, etc. Exceptionally a few derivatives from adjectives : *gemein-schaft, eigen-schaft* ("peculiar quality," contrast the meaning with that of *eigen-tum*, "property, estate").

IV. E. -*red* in *kind-red* (cf. *kin*) and *hat-red* (cf. *to hate*) comes from the same root as E. *read-y* and G. *be-reit*. It occurs rather often in O.E., but is nearly extinct in later times, and seems never to have existed in German. As to E. *hund-red* = G. *hund-ert*, see the chapter on Numeration.

V. E. -*lock*, in *wed-lock*, and -*ledge*, in *know-ledge*, are two forms (the latter being Scandinavian) of the same suffix of obscure origin (O.E. -*lāc*, M.E. -*lŏc*), which was once more widely used and has now become obsolete.

VI. E. -*ric*, in *bishop-ric*, is O.E. *rīc-e* = Go. *reik-i*, still existing as a separate word in G. *reich* (kingdom), cf. the compound *kaiser-reich* (empire).

§ 2. *Adjectives.*

(110) I. E. -*ly* = O.E. -*lic*, shortened (as unaccented) from *līc* = E. *like*[2] ; G. -*lich*, shortened (as unaccented) from O.H.G. -*līh* = Go. -*leik-s* ; cf. the derivative *g-leich* (alike) = Go. *ga-leik-s* : **adjectives denoting resemblance, manner or attribute.** —This class is extremely important.

1. It is easy to see, at once, the formation of such adjectival compounds as E. *man-ly* = G. *männ-lich*, namely "man-like";

---

[1] Acquired a concrete sense, and so also the following words: cf. E. *her ladyship*, F. *la domesticité* (the servants), etc.
[2] The full form is to be seen in modern compounds such as *court-like*. The original sense is "body, substance," cf. G. *leiche* (corpse).

so also, *woman-ly* and *weib-lich*, *father-ly* and *väter-lich*, *king-ly* and *könig-lich*; again, when added to names of things or to abstract nouns, *world-ly* = *weltlich*, *night-ly* = *nächt-lich*, *höf-lich*, *häss-lich*, *lieb-lich*, *anfäng-lich*, the latter type greatly developed in German.

2. Secondly, these adjectives happening in German to be referred to verbs instead of nouns (thus, to *hass-en*, *lieb-en*, *anfang-en*, etc.), it was only natural that new ones should be formed directly by derivation from other verbs, whence *begreifen*, *empfind-en*, *beschreib-en*, according to a process which must now have become familiar to the student, produced such adjectives as *begreif-lich*, *empfind-lich*, *un-beschreib-lich*.

3. It is clear, from its original meaning, that suff. *-lich* might as well modify an adjective as a noun, either by lessening in some degree the adjectival sense (*röth-lich*, "red-like, reddish"), or even without any definite value (*reich-lich*, "rich, plentiful"). This is the case with E. *silly* = O.E. *syl-lic*, supra 23 E.

4. In order to understand the further evolution of the suffix, it must be borne in mind that the West Germanic adverb is merely a certain case—probably the instrumental case—of the adjective, its ending being an *-e*, which had a tendency to disappear: e.g. Go. *hlūt-r-s* (pure, cf. L. *lau-tu-s* "washed") and O.E. *hlūtor*, whence O.E. *hlūtr-e*, O.H.G. *lūttar* and G. *lauter* (purely, merely),[1] etc. To the M.H.G. adjectives *frō-līch* (gay), *grōʒ-līch* (great), etc., naturally corresponded the adverbs *frō-līch-e* (gaily), *grōʒ-līch-e* (greatly), etc. Now, these forms, if directly opposed to the simple adjectives *froh*, *grosz*, etc., contained an ending *-līche* *-lich*, which was mistaken for the characteristic of the adverbial function and transferred elsewhere with this value by an obvious analogy. This process was carried on with great energy in M.H.G., and, though now extinct, has left some traces in the contemporary speech, several formations with suffix *-lich* being even now exclusively used with an adverbial meaning: *frei-lich* (to be sure), *kürz-lich* (in short), *schwer-lich*, *hoffent-lich*.

---

[1] Final *-e* kept in G. *lang-e* (a long time), contrasted with the adjective *lang*.

5. English has gone the same way, but farther, and quite consistently: E. -*ly* is no longer an adjectival suffix, except when added to a noun; if added to an adjective, it forms an **adverb**. Thus, the type *reich-lich* is essentially an adjective in G., while its E. representative *rich-ly* can be nothing but an adverb. This transformation gave English a specific adverbial exponent, whereas German usually employs as such the old instrumental case, now represented by the undeclined adjective, as final -*e* has dropped long ago. The E. suff. -*ly* modifies indifferently any adjective, whether primitive or derivative (*wise-ly*, *idly* = *id-le-ly = G. *eit-el-lich, *form-er-ly*, *sorrow-ful-ly*), native or borrowed (*veri-ly*,[1] *vacant-ly*, *glorious-ly*), and even some nouns (*night-ly*, *name-ly*, *purpose-ly*).[2]

II. E. -*som*- -*some* = O.E. -*sum*, the unaccented form of E. *same*; G. -*sam*: **adjectives denoting qualification or aptitude.**—The word is lost in German, but may be found in O.N. *sœm-r* (able) and traced back to Sk. *sam-á-s* = Gr. ὁμ-ό-ς (alike, same, cf. L. *sim-ili-s*). Its meaning being very nearly that of the preceding word, both were equally used in deriving an adjective from a noun or an adjective: Go. *lustu-sam-s* (lustful); O.E. *hȳr-sum* (obedient), *long-sum* (tiresome); O.H.G. *gihōr-sam* (from a noun *gihōr*, "hearing, obedience"), *ein-sam* (united), *heil-sam* (wholesome); E. *hand-some* (actually "clever"), *win-some*, *trouble-some*, *weari-some*; G. *müh-sam*, *arbeit-sam*, *duld-sam*, etc. Further, analogically, some adjectives were immediately derived from verbs: *folg-sam*, *erfind-sam*, *bieg-sam*,[3] etc.

III. G. -*bar* = *-*bār-i*, from the same root as the vb. *bër-an* (to carry), and with the same meaning as Sk. *bhār-á-s*, Gr. φορ-ό-ς, L. -*fer* at the end of a compound: **adjectives denoting**

---

[1] E. *very* = O.F. *verai*, now *vrai* (true). The native adverb is *sooth-ly* = O.E. *sōð-lice*, wherein *sōð = *sōnð is the present participle of the vb. *I am* (cf. Gr. ὤν ὄντ-ος, L. *sons sont-is* "culprit").—Moreover, E. still exhibits some adjectives used adverbially: *he works hard, he speaks loud, pretty nigh*, and *very* itself.

[2] So, to conclude, *like-ly* contains the same word twice over.

[3] In *buxom* = O.E. *būxum* = *būh-sum, the vocalism shows a derivation from a noun (cf. *bough* = O.E. *bōg*), whereas *bieg-sam* is formed from *bieg-en* (to bend).

production and consequently **aptitude.**—The etymological sense is still clear in such types as O.E. *lēoht-bǣre* (L. *lūci-fer* "carrying light") and G. *frucht-bar* "bearing fruit," and it is but slightly distorted in *furcht-bar, wunder-bar, gang-bar, dank-bar*, etc. The suffix is lost in English, but has reached in German a high degree of development, thanks to the analogical process by which it was directly added to many verbal stems: thus, *streit-bar*, really a derivative from *streit*, but erroneously referred to *streit-en*, led to the creation of *esz-bar, les-bar, nenn-bar, annehm-bar, erreich-bar*, and many others, the power of creation being as yet by no means exhausted.

IV. G. *-haft* = Preg. **haf-tá-s* = L. *cap-tu-s* (taken), literally "seized by," whence "endowed with," the exact force of the Mod. G. derivative *be-haft-et* (no trace of it either in E. or O.E.): **adjectives of qualification.**—As required by its etymology, this class is rich in derivatives from nouns (*herz-haft, tugend-haft, fehler-haft*), but poor in derivatives from adjectives (*wahr-haft* "sincere,"[1] *bos-haft*), and much poorer still in derivatives from verbs (*schwatz-haft* "prattler").

V. E. *-fast* = O.E. *-fæst* (the same as G. *fest* = O.H.G. *fest-i*, "fast, firm"), a suffix resembling the preceding in function, in O.E. *hūs-fæst*, "having a house," kept only in *stead-fast*, literally "having a stead, a foundation."[2]

VI. E. *-fold* = O.E. *-feald*; G. *-falt* = Go. *falþ-s*: **adjectives of multiplication.**—For the etymology, compare E. *fold* and G. *falte* with L. *sim-plec-s* "having but one fold," *duplex* (two-fold), etc. E. *two-fold, twenti-fold*, etc.; Go. *áin-falþ-s* (simple, good, stupid), M.H.G. *ein-falt* (id.), whence the derivatives, Go. fm. *áin-falþ-ei*, O.H.G. *ein-falt-ī* and G. *ein-falt* (stupidity), O.H.G. *ein-falt-īg*, M.H.G. *ein-velt-ec* and G. *ein-fält-ig*, etc.

VII. E. *-ful*: **adjectives of qualification.**—Well-known to be the E. *full* = G. *voll*. But whilst, in such a G. compound as *bewunderungs-voll* (full of astonishment), the meaning of the word *voll* still remains present to the speaker's mind, the case

---

[1] Might be translated etymologically "endowed with truth," the adjective *wahr* (true) being used as a substantive.

[2] O.E. *sceam-fæst*, M.E. *sham-fast* is thus derived, but has been changed by popular etymology to *shame-faced*.

is quite different with the element *-ful* in *thank-ful, aw-ful, wonder-ful, sorrow-ful, merci-ful, fanci-ful,* etc. Even the spelling emphasizes the difference: the syllable is unaccented, and, being now added to any noun whatever, simply plays the part of a convenient but vague and commonplace formative ending.

VIII. E. *-less*, unaccented form of O.E. *lēas* (loose, void, false); G. *-los* = O.H.G. *lōs* = Go. *láus* (void): **negative** of the preceding suffix.—G. *los* still exists as a single word.[1] Its value as a suffix is quite clear: *father-less* = *vater-los, life-less* = *leb-los, god-less* = *gott-los,* forming a negative adjective from almost any noun.

§ 3. *Adverbs.*

(111) **Adverbs**, which fall under this head of derivation, are simply **ancient cases** of the original declension **of nouns or adjectives.** The case, if it happened to be accusative or instrumental, is no longer to be discerned at first sight, since its ending has been dropped [2]; but, if a genitive, it shows the characteristic *-s*. Now West Germanic was very rich in adverbial locutions in which the genitive was used, and the later languages, especially German, still preserve a considerable number of such expressions. We need but mention: O.E. *dæg-es* "by day," *niht-es* "by night," lost in E.; E. *el-se* (cf. L. *al-iu-s* "other"), *need-s, after-ward-s, al-way-s,*[3] *sin-ce* = M.E. *sīth-en-s* (cf. O.H.G. *sīd,* G. *seit*), *on-ce, twi-ce,*[4] etc.; G. *tag-s, nacht-s, fall-s* and *jeden-fall-s, ring-s, recht-s, unter-weg-s* (by the way), *augen-blick-s* (suddenly), and more complex constructions like *gerad-es weg-es, recht-er hand, all-es ernst-es, mein-es eracht-en-s, rein-es herz-ens, hunger-s sterben* (to starve), etc., etc. Thus the adverbial use of nouns or adjectives in this way is easily explained.

I. E. *-ly* (= G. *-lich*): the ordinary adverbial suffix, *supra* 110, still adjectival in German.

---

[1] And so also E. *loose,* but that is borrowed from Scandinavian.
[2] See Declension, *infra* 149.
[3] For this word, as historically traced, does not mean "by all ways," but "the whole way."
[4] Cf. Numeration, *infra* 124, II.

II. E. *-wise*: a few adverbs, *like-wise, no-wise.*—It is the noun *wise* = O.E. *wīse* = G. *weise* (manner), afterwards in French written *guise*. German has the genitival locution, *e.g. merkwürdig-er-weise* (remarkably), and a few modern compounds, as *theil-weise* (partly), *kreuz-weise, paar-weise.*

III. E. *-ling*, G. *-ling-s* (gen.): a few adverbs.—This suffix seems to come from the gen. pl. of nouns in *-ing* [1] used adverbially: M.E. *hed-l-ing*, corrupted to *head-long*; E. *dark-ling, side-ling* and *side-long*, etc.; G. *blind-ling-s, seit-lings, rück-ling-s* (backwards), *schritt-ling-s* (step by step), etc.

IV. E. *-ward* (also adjectival) and *-ward-s* (advb. gen.); G. *-wärt-s* (id.): adverbs of direction.—The O.H.G. form is *-wërt-es*, the genitive of an adjective which is Go. nomin. sg. *vairþ-s*, from the same root that may be seen in the Go. vb. *vairþ-an* (G. *werden* "to become") = L. *vert-ere* (to turn): E. *to-ward* and *to-ward-s, back-ward, after-ward-s, sea-ward, lee-ward, wind-ward, awk-ward* (literally "turned awry"), etc.; G. *vor-wärt-s, rück-wärt-s, auf-wärt-s*; and, in further derivation, E. *in-ward-ly*, G. *wider-wärt-ig* (contrary), etc.

The remaining E. and G. derivations are exceptional and may be neglected here, especially as the reader will find an easy explanation for each of them in some one of the processes described above.

[1] Cf. the formation of nouns in *-ung, -ing, -ling*, supra 103. Of course in G. the gen. is in the sg.

CHAPTER III.

COMPOSITION.

(112) The process of **compounding words with one another** is Indo-European: remarkably well preserved, and even developed, in Sk. and Gr., less familiar in Latin, and almost lost in the Romance languages, it was bequeathed to Pregermanic, where it remained in full vigour, and is still extremely active in English and German. This may be said to be one of the most important points in which the Germanic languages differ from the neighbouring Romance tongues, and especially from French: such relations as the latter expresses by a periphrasis (*nuit d'été*) or a derivation (*pomm-ier*) are as a rule, and clearly enough, given in English and German by the mere juxtaposition of two stems, the first usually limiting or qualifying the second: *summer-night, sommer-nacht; apple-tree, apfel-baum.*

The details of English and German composition belong to ordinary grammar, or else must be sought in an etymological dictionary. Here we have only to sketch the general outlines of the classification and formation of those compound words, which are found in the two languages as well as in the other members of the I.-E. family.[1]

SECTION I.

CLASSIFICATION OF COMPOUNDS.

(113) Compound words must be regarded in a double light, according as we consider their **form**, or their **meaning**, the

[1] Cf. Henry, *Grammar of Gr. and Lat.*, 175–181.

COMPOSITION. 191

former being usually quite independent of the latter, and *vice versa*: thus, G. *hund-fliege* and *hund-s-fliege* (horse-fly) are exactly synonymous, though their principle of formation is quite different; whereas E. *red-lead* and *red-breast*, though identical in formation, widely differ in sense, the former merely meaning " a red lead," and the latter, "*having* a red breast," a distinction explained below.

§ 1. *Grammatical Classification.*

(114) As to their grammatical formation, compounds, whether I.-E., or English, or German, must be divided into two classes, namely: **syntactical** and **non-syntactical** compounds.

I. Syntactical composition occurs when two words assume in respect to each other the form required by the ordinary rules of grammar and syntax, *e.g.* the type, E. *king's wife*, G. *könig-s-sohn*, where the first term appears in the genitive as governed by the second. Such a locution, indeed, cannot be termed a true composition, and strict logic would even banish from this chapter the study of all syntactical compounds. They only claim our notice from the fact that they influenced, chiefly in German, non-syntactical composition, in such a way as to render the study of the latter impossible to one who had not considered the essential types of syntactical construction from which these analogies arose.

1. The first term stands in the genitive and is governed by the second term.[1]

A. Genitive singular.—(*a*) Of so-called strong nouns (gen. in -*s*). E. *Tue-s-day* and G. *Diens-tag* = *zio-s-tac* have already occurred. Further instances are: E. *Thur-s-day* = O. N. *þōr-s-dag-r* (cf. the name of the god *Thōr*), and G. *Donner-s-tag*, cf. *donner* = *thunder*; E. *kin*, and *kin-s-man*; E. *daisy* = **day's eye*, *i.e.* "[little] sun," the ending shortened because unaccented; O.H.G. *gotes-hūs* and G. *Gottes-haus*, but Go. *gud-hūs* (temple) non-syntactical; O.H.G. *hundes-fliuga* and G. *hunds-fliege*

[1] We need scarcely observe that a compound may contain more than two terms; theoretically, however, the number of terms is wholly indifferent, the rules being always the same for the relation of one to another.

(horse-fly), but also *hunt-fliuga* and *hund-fliege* non-syntactical; G. *land-s-mann* (compatriot), but non-syntactical *land-mann* (peasant),[1] etc. English possesses and still may create many juxtapositions of this kind, though they are usually spelled in two separate words, as (*mid-summer*) *night's dream, new year's day, love's labour,* etc.,[2] having, in fact, kept here, and almost nowhere else, the use of the genitival *s* for nouns which do not denote living beings.

(*b*) Of so-called weak nouns (gen. in *-en, -n*).—This is the type: O.H.G. *ohs-in-zunga* (the name of a plant), G. *ochs-en-zunge*; O.E. *el-n-boga,* literally " arm's bow," also *el-boga,* E. *el-bow,* which might represent either form, but G. *elle-n-bogen* syntactical. English, having dropped its finals, has generally lost this formation: thus, it answers *ochs-en-zunge* with the seemingly non-syntactical *Ox-ford*; cf. however the compound *maid-en speech.* But in German, the process has been favoured by the analogy of the composition with the genitive plural and partly confounded with it.[3]

B. Genitive plural.—(*a*) Of so-called strong neuter nouns and strong adjectives (in *-er*): G. *all-er-erst, all-er-höchst,* and the like; G. *rind-er-schaar* (a flock of oxen), *rind-er-hirte,* etc.; no further development.

(*b*) Of so-called weak nouns (in *-en, -n*): O.H.G. *Franch-ōno-lant* and G. *Frank-en-land,* etc.; M.H.G. *vrouw-en-zimmer* and G. *frau-en-zimmer,* literally " women's hall," whence " female attendance," and lastly, with concrete meaning (the only one surviving), " waiting gentlewoman, young lady."

2. The first term governs the second term, usually in the accusative, very seldom in any other case, occasionally with a preposition between the two: an exceptional type.—G. *störe-n-fried* (trouble-feast), wherein the *n* is the syncopated form of

---

[1] Compare likewise *wasser-noth* (scarcity of water) with *wassers-noth* (over-flowing).

[2] Spelled in one word, *coxcomb* = *cock's comb.*

[3] *Infra* B *b.*—Confounded in form, not in meaning; for it would be a gross mistake, in most cases, to explain it by a plural instead of a singular in the first term. The supposition is true for *Frank-en-land,* and may be true for *mensch-en-freund, biene-n-korb,* etc.; but it is obviously false for the type *todt-en-kopf, lind-en-baum, tinte-n-fasz,* which has been indefinitely multiplied.

the accusative *den*, literally "trouble the peace," the noun, however, showing no case ending; G. *vergisz-mein-nicht* "forget me not" (mouse-ear), which is a sentence rather than a word[1]; G. *spring-ins-feld* (light-headed youngster), etc. In English, the general loss of unaccented endings does not allow us to determine whether the similar type *Shake-speare*[2] ever possessed an accusative ending.

II. The composition is said to be non-syntactical, when the relation of meaning which unites the terms, whatever this relation may be,—namely, appositional (E. *to ful-fil*, G. *still-schweigen*), possessive (E. *hus-band*, G. *haus-herr*), adnominal (E. *church-yard*, G. *hof-thor*), locative or temporal (E. *nightingale* =O.E. *nihte-gale*, G. *nachti-gall*, "sounding by night"), instrumental (E. *steam-boat* and *god-father*, G. *dampf-schiff* and *hand-haben*), etc., etc.,—lacks any peculiar exponent, and is denoted by **mere juxtaposition of the two terms**, without the help of a grammatical ending between them. This is true primitive composition and would still be, as noted above, the only true English and German composition, had it not undergone a number of alterations caused by the intrusion of syntactical types. Sometimes, however, though rarely, a composition is only apparently non-syntactical, having sprung from some old syntactical construction which has been misunderstood and consequently transferred to places where it had no business to be: thus, an O.H.G. sentence *sie sind ein anderen ungelīh*,[3] which taken by itself is grammatically clear and correct, gave rise to a false compound *ein-ander*, which was afterwards invariably used, in any sentence or position, with a meaning of reciprocal action.[4]

§ 2. *Functional Classification.*

(115) When the function is considered, compounds may be divided into three great classes, namely: **copulative, determinative** and **possessive** compounds.

[1] The vb. *vergessen* formerly governed the genitive. Cf. *infra* 164, I. 3.
[2] "He who shakes his spear," cf. the proper name *Make-peace*, etc., *infra* 117, III. 2.
[3] Literally "they are, one to other, unlike."
[4] Cf. the simple juxtaposition in E. *one another*.

I. The copulative is a compound, the meaning of which would require between its two terms, if separated and grammatically construed, an inserted particle "and." The type is rather rare: it appears in numerals (E. *four-teen*, G. *fünf-zehn*), in some proper names (E. *Griqua-namaqua-land*, G. *Oestreich-Ungarn*) and in a few double adjectives (G. *taub-stumm*, but E. *deaf and dumb*). In Sk., of course, it has multiplied, but may be neglected elsewhere.[1]

II. The determinative compound is equivalent to a locution wherein either of the terms, and usually the second, would govern the other and require it to take some case-ending. According as the governed term would be put in the same case as the governing one, or in a different case, we have to distinguish respectively attributive or appositive, and dependent compounds.

1. Appositive compounds: Gr. type μεγαλό-πολι-ς (great city).—E. *wo-man* = M.E. *wim-man* (compare the pronunciation of the pl. *women*) = O.E. *wīf-man*, as it were "human being of female sex." E. *gospel* = O.E. *god-spel* (*god-* shortened instead of *gōd*), originally "good spell, good news," a literal translation of Gr. εὐ-αγγέλιο-ν. E. *wer-wolf, wal-nut* "nut from Welsh (non-German) land," *New-haven, pea-cock, she-wolf, hen-canary-bird*, etc.—G. *grosz-vater*, and, curiously enough, an analogical formation *grosz-sohn*; so also, E. *grand-son* from *grand-father*. G. *all-od*, a word borrowed from Low L. *allodium*, but this again borrowed from O.H.G. *al-ōd*, "whole or full property." G. *süsz-holz* (liquorice), *wer-wolf, fürst-bischof, Herr-gott, Christ-kind, Neu-stadt*, etc.

2. Dependent compounds: Gr. type ἄνδρ-άδελφο-ς (husband's brother, brother-in-law), L. *lūci-fer*, E. *bride-groom*, G. *pelz-waaren-händler*, etc.—Instances will occur to the reader in such considerable number, that it would be superfluous to quote any more; indeed, the student may even form any new compounds

---

[1] Compounds made of two adjectives are almost always determinative compounds: so *roth-gelb* does not mean "red and yellow," but "yellow with a tinge of red," and so forth. In *bitter-süsz* and a few more, we may hesitate between the two shades of meaning.—A true O.H.G. copulative compound may be found in the fourth line of the *Hildebrandslied*: *sunufatarungo* "the son and the father."

he chooses, for the process is still alive in both languages, and the bulk of their compound words are of very recent formation.[1]

III. The **possessive** compound is only a form of the determinative, inasmuch as here too one of the terms determines the other; but the whole adds an additional idea to the meaning of the two words separately: thus, Gr. ῥοδο-δάκτυλο-ς and E. *red-breast* do not mean simply, "rose-finger" or "red breast," but "endowed with rose-fingers," "(a bird) showing a red breast," and so forth. In short, the possessive compound is always an epithet, which involves the existence of a subject possessing the character or realizing the idea expressed by the union of the two terms: E. *light-foot, heart's ease, wag-tail*, etc.; G. *Roth-käppchen, drei-fusz, lügen-zunge, plage-geist*, etc. This composition is of essentially popular origin and goes hand in hand with the preceding.

SECTION II.

FORMATION OF COMPOUNDS.

(116) The power of composition in either language is theoretically unlimited.[2] But since, however numerous they may be, the successive terms qualify one another in turn, any compound may theoretically be reduced to two terms, as it were, the first and the second, each again being either the qualifying or the qualified term.

[1] Further, the reader may be referred to *supra* 65, 5, and *infra* 117, I., II. and III. 1.
[2] Three terms: E. *pine-apple-juice*; G. *haupt-zoll-amt, dudel-sack-pfeifer.* Four terms: E. *midsummer night's dream*; G. *eisen-bahn-hof-strasse, kupferschmied-werk-zeug* (here, instead of determining one another, the four terms are divided into two groups, and the first group determines the second, as, in each group, the first term determines the other; that is to say, *kupferschmied* and *werkzeug* bear exactly the same relation as if each of them were a simple word; the case is very common). Five terms: *alt-milch-ferkel-markt-platz* (where *milchferkel* is one word in relation to *markt*, and *milchferkelmarkt* one word in relation to *alt*), etc. Humorous accumulations: *the United Metropolitan Improved Hot Muffin and Crumpet Baking and Punctual Delivery Company* (Dickens, *Nickleby*).

§ 1. Form of the First Term.

(117) **The first term** of a compound **may be a nominal stem** (noun, adjective or pronoun), **or a particle** (invariable word), **or a verbal stem.** Each of these cases will be separately examined.

I. **The first term is a nominal stem.**—The general principle of I.-E. composition is, that any nominal stem, occurring as the first term of a compound, must appear **in the shape of a bare stem**, without any ending whatever. Let us consider, for instance, the I.-E. stems in *-o-* : the term taken from words like Sk. *áçva-s*, Gr. θεό-ς, L. *auru-m*, is neither the nominative, nor any other case in compounds like Sk. *áçva-yōga-s* (whereto a horse is put), Gr. θεο-φιλής (dear to the gods), L. *auru-fex* (goldsmith), etc.; it is neither the dual nor the plural, though there may be two horses to the chariot, and the gods actually are many in number; it is simply the bare stem, *áçva-*, θεό-, *auru-*, which, owing to the place it occupies, becomes able to express either the instrumental, dative, or accusative case, or indeed the singular, dual or plural number, together with many other grammatical relations. Such is also the general rule for English and German composition, the applications of, or exceptions to, which we shall now pursue throughout the various classes of primitive stems.

1. If the first term ends with a vowel, the formation usually conforms to the rule given above, save that the characteristic vowel, being unaccented and consequently more or less altered, is no longer seen as it is in Gr. or L.: E. and G. *wer-wolf*, representing an I.-E. word *wiro-wḷqo-s, which would be L. *viri-lupu-s = *viro-lupo-s (man-wolf); O.H.G. *tago-stërno* and *taga-stërn* (morning-star); O.H.G. *wëgo-wīso* and *wëga-wīso*, cf. G. *weg-weiser*, E. *way-mark*; O.H.G. *junc-frouwa* (damsel)[1] and G. *jung-frau*; O.H.G. *turi-sûl* and G. *thür-säule* (door-post), cf. Gr. κασί-γνητο-ς (brother); G. *viel-blatt*, cf. Go. *filu-* (in composi-

---

[1] Adj. *junc-* = **yuṅgo-*, not *yuṅgâ, that is to say, the epithet does not agree with the noun: cf. Gr. 'Ακρό-πολις instead of ἄκρᾱ πόλις. When the noun is declined, the adjective undergoes no change.—With the second (unaccented) term reduced, we have *jungfer*.

tion) = Gr. πολυ- (much); Go. *faíhu-gaírn-s* (covetous), cf. L. *pecu-* (cattle) and the G. type *vieh-zucht*, etc. After such patterns were created the invariable and common compounds by mere juxtaposition (G. *tag-lohn, früh-stück, hand-habe,* E. *daybreak, way-farer, hand-mill*), from which English hardly ever deviates, apart however from the occasional insertion of the genitival *s* if justified by the meaning.[1] In German, the same insertion is often possible, or even necessary (*tages-stern*), and is now always found in certain classes of words, especially those in *-heit* (*freiheits-liebe*), whence it has even extended to those in *-ung* (*rettungs-ufer, wässerungs-graben*), though the latter never really had or could have any genitive ending in *-s*. German further admits of the insertion of the *n* which belongs to the weak declension, especially for such words as end in *-e* in the nominative singular, when involving in their compounded state an idea of plurality[2]: *gaben-reich, bienen-korb, enten-teich, stunden-glas* (but *sohl-leder, rede-kunst,* since the first term may be referred to the verbs *sohlen* and *reden*),[3] etc.

2. Stems originally ending with any other consonant but *n* and *s* follow the general rule without exception: E. *foot-step, mother-less, night-mare*; G. *fusz-boden, vater-land, nacht-mahl*. Very often in English, and rather arbitrarily in German, the *s* is inserted, when required by usage or euphony.[4]

3. Stems in *n* have been seen to assume a double form. The simple form, without final *n*, is here the regular one, and constantly appears in the earliest examples of Germanic composition: Go. *guma-kund-s* "of male sex," cf. the same shortened stem in L. *homi-cīda* (from *homin-*); O.H.G. *hano-crāt* (cock's comb), *namo-haft* (having a name) and G. *nam-haft* (famous); Go. *áuga-daúrō* "eye-door" (window), O.H.G. *oug-brāwa* (eyebrow), M.H.G. *ouge-lit* (eye-lid), etc. But, besides this ancient type, Germanic also formed the compound with the first term in the genitive sg. or pl., viz. *ochsen-zunge* and *Franken-land*;

[1] *Supra* 114, I. 1 A.
[2] *Supra* 114, I. 1, and cf. the note.
[3] Cf. the verbal compounds, *infra* III. 1.
[4] Examples: *sommernachts-traum, vaters-bruder* and *vaters-bruders-sohn*, but *vaters-bruder-frau*; and so also with other compounds, *jahr-gang* and *jahres-bericht, monat-schrift* and *monats-heft*.

and this, in German, quite overwhelmed the type *nam-haft* and *fried-los*, which is now exceptional. The usual form is as follows: *hahnen-kamm*,[1] *ochsen-hirte*, *sonnen-schein*, *namen-buch*, *augen-brauen*, *augen-lid*, *hasen-pfote*, etc.; secondly, analogically, *christen-thum*, *studenten-blume*, etc.; lastly, even with a double genitival exponent, *namens-tag*, *friedens-richter*, *herzens-wunsch*.[2] Nothing similar occurs in English: *eye-brow*, *eye-lid*, *sunshine* (cf. *Sun-day* = *Sonn-tag*), *ox-lip* = O.E. *oxan-slyppe*, etc.

4. Stems ending in *s* show a similar peculiarity. West Germanic is known to drop the final *s* of the nomin. sg.: G. *sieg* = Go. *sigis* = Sk. *sáhas* (strength, victory) = I.-E. **séghos*[3]; so also, *ei* (egg), *kalb* (calf), since the plurals *eier* and *kälber* reveal the presence of a hidden *s* in the sg. stem. Now, this *s* naturally also belonged to the compounded stem, cf. Gr. σακεσ-παλος (shaking his shield, nt. nomin. σάκος, gen. σάκεος = *σάκεσ-ος), ἀνθεσ-φόρος (carrying flowers, ἄνθος ἄνθεος); and, no less naturally, being here medial, it was fain to survive. It was kept therefore, according to a well-known distinction, either as *s* or *r*: G. *sieges-lohn* = Go. *sigis-láun*, and compare the proper names which begin with *Sigis-*; M.H.G. *eier-vël* (the thin skin in an egg) and G. *eier-gelb* (yolk), etc. Of course, these forms *sieges-*, *eier-* are the bare stems, and nothing more; but, if contrasted with the nomin. sg. *sieg*, *ei*, they now look as if they were declensional forms, namely either a gen. sg. or pl.; and thus it is they have contributed to the expansion of the syntactical composition-type containing an apparent genitive either in *-s* or in *-er*, according as the first term was understood to be either singular or plural, c.g. *kalbs-fleisch*, *rinds-fleisch*, and *rinder-stelze* (wag-tail), *wörter-buch* (dictionary).[4] Here, as elsewhere, English has only *s*: *calf's leg*.

---

[1] Notwithstanding that the usual genitive to *hahn* is no longer *hahn-en*, but *hahn-s*.
[2] Generally, however, the simple form *herz-*. Cf. *infra* 150, 1 b.
[3] Originally neuter, cf. *supra* 80 (XV.). For the form of such words in composition, cf. the L. type *veneri-vagus*, where the *s* of *Venus* also became *r*.
[4] The latter is not widely diffused, though, in the case where it survives, it remains true to its origin, inasmuch as it does not involve any necessary idea of plurality: a plural would be absurd in *eier-gelb*, and *kälber-magen* is strictly synonymous with *kalbs-magen*.

II. **The first term is a** preposition or invariable **particle :** types, E. *out-law,* G. *ab-fall,* etc.—This very simple case requires no explanation, but it may be of some interest to observe that the particle thus used sometimes no longer survives as a separate word in the present language, or has sometimes lost its original meaning which is retained only in the compound: E. *mid-wife,* where the first term is the same as G. *mit* (now replaced as a preposition by *with*)=Gr. μετὰ, literally "a woman that helps"; G. *after-wort* (abuse), the first term being identical with E. *after*,[1] which is no longer a G. word; E. *alone* = **all-one*, where *all* would now be replaced by *quite*,[2] cf. G. *all-ein*; G. *aber-glaube* (superstition), the particle being the same as Sk. *apara-m* (after) and consequently expressing a pejorative meaning akin to the sense of *after-*, while isolated *aber* is now merely an adversative conjunction.

III. **The first term is a verbal stem.**—This formation is unknown in Indo-European etymology proper: in Sanskrit, Latin, and even Gothic, no compounds are found except with a noun or a particle as first term; English and German, however, separately developed in their historical period many compounds in which the first term has a verbal form and meaning. These must be divided into two classes, according to the different causes from which they arose.[3]

1. **The first is the determining term.**—We have already seen how such a compound as *schiff-bar*, which may be translated literally "bearing a ship," was wrongly supposed to contain the vb. *schiffen* " to ship," and how this error led to the formation of such erratic compounds (now called derivatives) as *esz-bar, trink-bar, les-bar*, from the verbs *essen, trinken, lesen*.[4] Now, since derivative composition is but a particular case of composition, the same, as a matter of course, happened with

---

[1] The change of meaning is " late—coming too late—improper—bad."
[2] Afterwards pleonastically, *quite alone*; and, by syncopating the initial vowel, which seemed an insignificant element (cf. *supra* 96, VI., and 103, II. 2), the words *lone, lonely, loneliness*.
[3] Greek has likewise created such compounds, but only of one kind, the second, namely δακέ-θῡμος " biting the heart," τερπι-κέραυνος " shaking the thunder," φαεσί-μβροτος " enlightening the mortals."
[4] *Supra* 110, III., and cf. *supra* 99, 102 (3), etc.

compounds properly so-called: thus, G. *bet-haus* = O.H.G. *bete-hūs* (prayer-house) being referred to vb. *beten* (to pray), on this and the like were and still may be created, if needed, the G. types *wohn-haus, schiesz-pulver, mieth-kutsche*, etc. In English the same process would have been possible; but here it is no longer to be recognised, because there scarcely exist any verbs without homonymous nouns.[1] It must be observed, however, that English verbs, when they occur in the first term of a compound, are always used in the present participle, which is as much as to say that the first term is etymologically a nominal form[2]: *eating-house, frying-pan, racing-club*, etc.

2. **The first is the determined term.** — Locutions in which the first term is a verb governing the second term are very common, chiefly as popular nicknames, which have often become proper names, or are still used as epithets in familiar speech. We have already noted E. *Make-peace*, and *Shakespeare*, which was sometimes parodied as *shake-scene*; here we may add *turn-back, wag-tail, break-fast, spend-thrift, run-away, would-be, pin-afore, round-about*, and such possible nicknames as *Kill 'em all, Go-to-bed*, etc. In German we have proper names, as *Bleib-treu* (remain true), *Lebe-recht*, and familiar epithets, *tauge-nichts* (good-for-nothing), *sauf-aus* (drunkard), *wage-hals* (rash), *stell-dich-ein* (appointment), *spring-ins-feld*, etc. As, in such compounds, the verb always shows the bare stem-form, they probably proceed, at least to a large extent, from familiar exclamations which required the verb to stand in the imperative mood: a few nicknames of this kind, being once created, might easily serve as models for further imitation.

§ 2. *Form of the Last Term.*

(118) The last term of any English or German compound is always a nominal stem; in other words, every compound properly so-called, in either language, is a noun or an adjective; there are no compound verbs. Such verbs as are com-

---

[1] As *to ink* was drawn from *ink*, so also, reversely, a noun *drink* was formed from *to drink*, so that, in English, the originally nominal and verbal stems are now scarcely distinguishable.

[2] Like the G. type *rettungs-ufer*. Cf. *supra* 103 (II.).

monly termed by this name, will be seen to belong to one of these three classes:—(a) verbs with an inseparable prefix, already analysed under derivation;—(b) verbs with a separable prefix (G. *aus-gehen*, E. *to go out*), well-known types of simple juxtaposition, so loose indeed that they form two distinct words in English and are often separated in German[1];—(c) verbs derived from compound nouns or adjectives, an important class treated below.

This point being settled, the rules for the last term of an English or German compound are extremely simple.

1. As a general rule, the last term of a compound undergoes no change, and does not differ from the isolated word, apart from such mechanical alterations as may be caused by its being unaccented and swiftly sounded.[2]

2. This rule, of course, does not prevent a compound, when formed, receiving, like any other word of the language, a derivative suffix, and developing in this way new derivatives, which might prove more generally used than the word from which they sprang: thus, E. *light-footed* and G. *vier-füszler* cannot be deemed true compounds, since there are no words E. *footed and G. *füszler; they are derivatives from the compounds *light-foot* and *vier-fusz*. Now, this process having once become familiar, a language could easily construct such derivatives on the basis of two simple words, without any intermediate compound ever existing, e.g. E. *gray-headed* on *gray* and *head*,[3] G. *ein-äugig* on *ein* and *auge*, and so forth: this in fact still constantly happens.

3. For the same reason it will be understood that a verb may be derived from a compound as from any other word, and that the process of derivation is the same in this case as for ordinary verbal derivation: thus, from E. *lord*, we have the intransitive *to lord*, and the transitive *to unlord*, and further such verbs as *to husband, to elbow, to mildew, to worship, to horse-*

---

[1] The inseparable type, E. *to over-eat* [o. s.], G. *über-setzen* (to translate), is a peculiar and rarer variety of the same class.

[2] See the numerous instances mentioned in their proper places: 65, 5; 114, I. 1; 115, II. etc.

[3] There exists no word *headed*, in this acceptation at least, and the existence of a word *gray-head is only a possibility.

whip, etc.; G. *arg-wohn* (distrust) has produced *argwöhnen*,—for there is no G. vb. **wöhnen*,—and, in spite of appearances, *handhaben* (to handle) is not a mere compound of *hand* and *haben*, but a derivative from the nominal compound *hand-habe* (a handle). The same is the case with the types *rechtfertigen*, *wetteifern*, *lustwandeln*, etc.; similarly, with still more complex derivatives, *nothzüchtigen* from *noth-zucht*, *bevollmächtigen* from *voll-macht*[1]; and thus there will be no difficulty in understanding how, by imitating such patterns, German even sometimes united into one verb two words which ought to remain syntactically separated, and formed such faulty verbal compounds as *lobsingen* and *wahrsagen*.[2]

---

[1] Cf. *supra* 107 (V. 4).
[2] As a counterpart, E. has *to vouchsafe*, wherein the verb is *to vouch*, *safe* being a mere apposition; but a strange confusion caused the verb to be conjugated as a whole, so that the person-endings are now adapted to *safe* instead of to *vouch*.

CHAPTER IV.

THE SYSTEM OF NUMERATION.

(119) Germanic Numeration is an Indo-European decimal system, depending on the general principles of derivation and syntactical as well as non-syntactical composition previously described. It therefore forms a suitable vehicle for a recapitulation of the Second Part and, as it were, an exercise on the rules we have stated. We must first distinguish the so-called cardinal numbers, and the various numeral expressions which have been derived from them.

Section I.

CARDINAL NUMBERS.

(120) The I.-E. units are conventional expressions, of unknown origin, and without any visible etymological connection with one another. The tens are either derivatives from, or combinations of units. The numbers 100 and 1000 are isolated expressions, which however show a prehistorical derivative relationship with the tens.

§ 1. *Units and Sums of Units.*

(121) 1. The primitive root of "one" is i, probably the same that occurs in the L. demonstrative *i-s i-d*. Its numeral value may be seen in the Homeric *ἴ-α* (one fm.).[1] But it appears but seldom in such a bare state: usually it is deflected

[1] Not to be confounded with εἷς μία ἕν, since this proceeds from a different root, namely *sem*, also in Latin *sem-el* (once).

and followed by a derivative suffix, Sk. *ê-ka-s* (one), Zd. *ae-va-*, Persian *ai-va-*. In Latin, Germanic and Slavonic, the accompanying suffix is *-no-*: I.-E. **ŏy-no-s*, L. *ŭ-nu-s=oi-no-s*,[1] Preg. **ai-na-z*, whence Go. *ái-n-s*, O.N. *einn*, O.E. *ān* and E. *one* (*an* or *a* when unaccented), O.H.G. *ein* and G. *ein*.

2. The primitive stem was **duó-* and **dwó-*, furnished with the ordinary dual endings: nomin. msc. **duôw*, fm. **duáy*, nt. **duóy*; Sk. msc. *dváu*, fm. nt. *dvê*; Gr. δύω δύο invariable; L. *duo, duæ, duo*. Gothic had partly adopted the plural-endings: msc. *tvái*, fm. *tvōs*, but nt. *tva=*dwóy*. West Germanic likewise altered the primitive endings: O.E. msc. *twēgen*, fm. *twō*, nt. *tū*; O.H.G. msc. *zwēne*, fm. *zwō*, nt. *zwei*.[2] Whereupon the declension was reduced to one form, the neuter serving for all genders: E. *two* (which however keeps the old spelling of the fm. *twō*)=O.E. *tū*; G. *zwei*.—In composition, the stem of number 2 assumed a form **dwi-*, Sk. *dvi-*, Gr. δι-, L. *bi-*, Preg. **twi-* eventually lengthened to **twī-*, which latter are respectively to be recognised in: E. *twi-n, to twi-ne*, and *twi-light*, *i.e.* "a double, doubtful light"; G. *zwie-fach* (two-fold, double), *zwi-r-nen* (to double, to twist), and *zwei-fel* (doubt)=O.H.G. *zwī-fal*.[3]

3. I.-E. root *tri*, in the normal grade and with the pl. msc.-fm. ending **tréy-ĕs*, Sk. *tráy-as*, Gr. and L. (the *y* being dropped and the vowels contracted) τρεῖς *trēs*, nt. τρί-α *tri-a*. Similarly in Germanic: Go. msc.-fm. *þreis* (contracted from **þrij-is*), nt. *þrij-a*; O.E. *đrī* and *đrēo*, the latter being now E. *three*, the former extinct; O.H.G. *drī drīo drīu*, whence G. *drei*.[4]

4. I.-E. stem **qetwor- *qetwṛ-*, Sk. msc. *catvár-as*, Gr. τέτταρες

---

[1] Thus we read OINO(M) in early Latin inscriptions.
[2] The msc. *twēgen* and *zwēne* are as yet unexplained. The fm. *twō* and *zwō* reproduce Go. *tvōs*. The nt. *tū* is Go. *tva*. As to the nt. *zwei*, it probably contains the diphthong seen in the stem of the Gr. derivative δοι-ot.—All these forms survived very late: down to the seventeenth century, classical German still distinguished *zween männer, zwo frauen, zwei kinder*, and some traces of the distinction persist even now in Alamannic, and in class. E. and G. in the number *twen-ty* and *zwan-zig*, infra 122, 20.
[3] Literally "double case."—The diphthong is not the same in *zwei* and *zweifel*, since, in Alamannic, we find *tsvay*, but *tsvifl*.
[4] Numbers 2 and 3 had a strong tendency to become invariable, because numbers 5 and the following very early became, or even had always been, invariable words. For number 4, cf. L. *quatuor* invariable.

THE SYSTEM OF NUMERATION. 205

τέσσαρες = *τέτfαρ-ες, L. *quattuor*, Go. *fidvōr*, O.N. *fjōr-*, O.E. *fēower* and E. *four*, O.H.G. *fior* and G. *vier*, though the loss of the medial dental is a riddle as yet unsolved.

5. I.-E. *péṅqe, Sk. *páñca*, Gr. πέμπε πέντε, L. *quīnque*, Go. *fimf*, O.N. *fimm*, O.E. *fīf* and E. *five*, O.H.G. *finf*, then *funf* from the intrusion of the vocalism of the ordinal number, M.H.G. *vünf* with metaphonical vocalism imitated from *vünf-zic* (fifty), and G. *fünf*.[1]

6. I.-E. *swéks *séks, Sk. šáš, Gr. ἕξ = *σfέξ, L. *sex*, Go. *saihs*, O.N. *sehs*, O.E. *seox = seohs*, and E. *six* (metaphony caused by the *h*), O.H.G. *sëhs* and G. *sechs*.

7. I.-E. *septm̥, Sk. *saptá*, Gr. ἑπτά, L. *septem*, Go. *sibun* (the final from *sibun-da* " 7th "),[2] O.E. *seofon* and E. *seven*, O.H.G. *sibun* (*u-* metaphony) and G. *sieben*.

8. I.-E. *oktôw, Sk. *aštáu*, Gr. ὀκτώ, L. *octō*, Go. *ahtáu*, O.E. *eahta* and E. *eight*, O.H.G. *ahto* and G. *acht*.

9. I.-E. *néwṇ, Sk. *náva*, Gr. ἐννέα = *ἐ-ννεfα, L. *novem* = *nevem* (cf. *novus* "new " = Gr. νέος), Go. *niun* = *niwun, O.E. *nigon* and E. *nine*, O.H.G. *niun* and G. *neun*.

10. I.-E. *dék-m̥, Sk. *dáça*, Gr. δέκα, L. *decem*, Go. *taíhun*, O.E. *tīen tēn* and E. *ten*, O.H.G. *zëhan*, M.H.G. *zëhen* and G. *zehn*, the last three being traceable to an I.-E. form *dékom(t) with deflected last syllable.

11-12. These two numbers assume a peculiar shape only in Germanic: they are formed by non-syntactical composition, the last term being *-lĭbi-, a stem abstracted from the root which produced Go. *bi-leib-an* = G. *b-leib-en* (to remain), thus *aina-lĭbi-* " 1 left [above 10] ": Go. *áin-lif*, O.N. *ellifu*, O.E. *ándleo-fan*[3] *endleofan* and E. *eleven*, O.H.G. *einlif*, M.H.G. *eilif eilf* and G. *eilf elf*; Go. *tva-lif*, O.N. *tolf*, O.E. *twelf* (metaph.) and E. *twelve*, O.H.G. *zwelif* (metaph.), M.H.G. *zwelf*, and G. *zwölf* for *zwelf*.[4]

[1] E. and G. *fing-er* seems to be a cognate word.
[2] Cf. *supra* 39, 1, and 40, 1. Of course the group *pt* is here reduced to simple *p*.
[3] A euphonic *d* is inserted between *n* and *l*. Final *un* is here probably a superadded plural exponent, from which *twelf* has remained free.
[4] Compare the spellings *schöpfen, schwören*, instead of *schepfen, schweren*, and a few others.

13-19. As in every other I.-E. language (cf. Gr. ἕν-δεκα, L. *un-decim*), these numbers are compounds, the last term being 10: O.H.G. *drī-zëhan*, etc., and G. *drei-zehn*; O.E. *ŏrī-tēn-e*, with a subjoined ending, owing to which the preceding vowel, since it no longer stood in a close syllable, was not shortened as it was in *ten*, whence E. *-teen*.[1] The initial unit undergoes no change; in English, however, the shortening in a close syllable changed *fīftēne* to *fifteen*, whereas *ŏrītēne*, sounded M.E. *thritteen*, became by metathesis *thirteen*.

§ 2. *Tens.*

(122) The names for the I.-E. tens are compound words: Sk. *vin-çatí*, Gr. τριᾱ-κοντα,[2] L. *quadrā-gintā*, etc. The Germanic corresponding terms are only apparent compounds. In origin they are locutions, consisting of two words, the name for the unit governing in the plural number the name for the ten, thus "two tens"=20. But this archaic formation is hidden from the eye, both in German and English.

In order to understand it, we must consider some equivalent Gr. form, e.g. τρεῖς δεκάδες=30. The word δεκάς (stem δεκάδ-, observe the accent) represents an I.-E. noun **dekm̥t-* which is derived from **dekm̥* (ten) and has become Preg. **teʒun*, then **teʒu*, whereupon, as it appeared to be a stem in *-u-*, it was declined as such: Go. sg. **tigu-s*, pl. *tigjus*, acc. *tigu-ns*, etc. From this arose such juxtapositions as nomin. *tvái tigjus* and acc. *tvans tiguns*=20, which, by dropping their endings, reduced the last term to O.E. *-tig* and E. *-ty*, O.H.G. *-zug*,[3] M.H.G. *-zic* and G. *-zig*, which are invariable.

Hence grammatical exactness would require the noun governed by a ten to stand in the gen. pl., and this rule in fact often holds good in early O.H.G., e.g. *feorzuc wëhhōnō*, literally

---

[1] This was afterwards abstracted from such compounds, and became an independent word.

[2] The last term is a shortened derivative from number 10: cf. *infra* 123, I.

[3] This strange and as yet unexplained vocalism is probably due to a reduced grade of the radical syllable in **dékm̥*.—As to G. *z* for Preg. *t*, observe that the *t* here is really an initial consonant, *supra* 49, III. 2.

THE SYSTEM OF NUMERATION. 207

"four tens of weeks," as in L. *tria milia hominum*. But, as the unit-numbers governed the nominative, the same case was used throughout.

When a unit is added to the ten, they form together a merely syntactical compound : E. *three and twenty*, G. *drei und zwanzig*. English, however, probably influenced by French, also admits of the simple juxtaposition : *twenty-three*.

20. Go. *tvái tigjus*, O.E. *twēn-tig* and E. *twenty*, O.H.G. *zweinzug* and G. *zwanzig*, cf. the nomin. msc. *twēgen zwēne*.

30. Go. acc. *þrins tiguns*, O.E. *ðrī-tig ðrittig* and E. *thirty* (like *thirteen*), O.H.G. *drī-ʒʒug* (the *t* treated as it usually is when medial, but also *drī-zug*) and G. *dreiszig*.

40. Go. *fidvōr tigjus*, O.E. *fēower-tig* and E. *forty*, O.H.G. *fiorzug* and G. *vierzig*.

50. Go. *fimf tigjus*, O.E. *fīf-tig* and E. *fifty*, O.H.G. *finf-zug funf-zug*, M.H.G. *vünf-zic* and G. *fünfzig*.

60. Go. *saíhs tigjus*, O.E. *siex-tig* and E. *sixty*, O.H.G. *sëhs-zug sëhzug* (by reducing the group) and G. *sechzig*.

70–90. The three following tens are now formed after the pattern of the first five; but such was not always the case, for Go. has no type *sibun tigjus, etc. Indeed, the process formerly used was exactly the reverse : the term is *sibuntē-hund*, wherein *sibuntē-* is a gen. pl. governed by *-hund* (this shortened from *taíhund), the whole meaning " the tithing of sevens "; and so also, *ahtáutē-hund*, *niuntē-hund*, and even *taíhuntē-hund* "tithing of tens"= 100. In O.E. the two terms changed places, whilst analogy substituted the syllable *-tig* for the syllable *-tē*: *hundseofontig*, *hundeahtig*, *hundnigontig*; then, the syllable *hund*, which seemed meaningless, was dropped. In O.H.G., however far we go back, this *hund* has already disappeared : *sibun-zo* (instead of *-ʒo*, owing to the analogy of the *z* in *-zug*), *ahto-zo*, even *zëhan-zo* (100); whereupon, analogy working its way throughout, we have *sibun-zug*, now *siebenzig*, etc.[1]

---

[1] Except that *zëhanzug* is replaced by *hundert*. The process, though it has quite disappeared, is interesting inasmuch as it throws light upon the pre-historical formation of number 100.—As to *-zug* and *-zo*, observe moreover that the sibilant often followed a nasal, and cf. *supra* 49, III. 2 in fine.

§ 3. *Hundreds and Thousands.*

(123) I. The word for 100 was I.-E. **km̥-tó-m*, neuter noun : Sk. *ça-tá-m* nt., Gr. ἑ-κα-τό-ν (one hundred), L. *cen-tu-m,* Lith. *szim-ta-s*, Go. *tva hunda* "two hundreds," which literally translated would be L. *duo *centa*. If we traced farther back the origin of this form, an easy explanation could be suggested, namely, a derivation from **dékm̥* by addition of the suff. *-tó-*; this syllable, being accented, suppressed the accent of the first syllable, which then appeared in the reduced grade: an I.-E. **dkm̥-tó-* or **tkm̥-tó-*, being barely pronounceable, might have lost its initial consonant, and, finally, **km̥-tó-m* would very well mean "the tithing to ten."

This is, without doubt, the meaning of Go. *taíhuntē-hund,* O.E. *hund-tēontig*, O.H.G. *zëhanzo*, which are the only ancient Germanic terms for 100. But the simple **hund*=L. *centum* nevertheless also existed, since we find it in Gothic forming every multiple of 100 : *þrija hunda, fimf hunda*, etc. Now, this word very early entered into composition with a noun **raþ-*, akin to Go. *raþ-jan* (to count)=G. *reden* (to speak), whence the modern forms, E. *hund-red*, G. *hund-ert*, are obviously substantives literally signifying "a count of hundred."

II. The old multiples are O.E. *tū hund*, etc., O.H.G. *zwei hunt,* etc.=Go. *tva hunda*, etc. The substitution of *hundred* and *hundert* took place as a matter of course. But, although the latter were originally and, in fact, still are substantives in both languages, being as such capable of receiving the sign of the plural (E. *hundreds*, G. *hunderte*), yet they never assume this sign in numeration (*two hundred, zwei-hundert*),[1] and moreover have ceased to govern the following noun in the genitive. The tens and units, if needed, are added by juxtaposition.

III. The word for 1000 is only found in Germanic and Letto-Slavonic[2] : it is Go. *þūsundi*, a fm. noun (once nt.), which has

---

[1] This is not at all an irregularity, but very likely a survival from a time when a great many nouns kept the singular form in the plural without alteration : cf. G. *vier-mal, zehn mann, sechs fuss*, and popular E. *three year,* infra 139, III. 1; 143, II., and 147, 4.

[2] In Sk. and Gr. (χίλιοι) we have quite a different term, and another still in L. (*mille*, pl. *milia*).

THE SYSTEM OF NUMERATION. 209

become nt. in O.E. ðūsend and E. thousand, O.H.G. dūsunt tū-sunt and G. tausend. As the word occurs, in Salic Frankish and elsewhere, with an inward aspirate (thūs-chunde, cf. O.N. þūs-hundrað " 1200 "), we are led to explain it as an old compound meaning "the large hundred."[1]

IV. Though this term is a substantive, it does not vary in the multiples (two thousand = zwei-tausend) and governs the multiplied noun in the nominative.

V. Numbers beyond 999999 are, as elsewhere, learned terms constructed on the basis of Latin stems.

Section II.

DERIVATIVES FROM CARDINAL NUMBERS.

(124) I. Ordinal numbers.—Among the derivatives, the ordinals are the simplest and most regular: several suffixes were used, but Germanic preserved but one, I.-E. suff. -to-, cf. Gr. πέμπ-το-ς (fifth), L. quinc-tu-s quintus, etc. The accent of such words, being variable in Sk. and even in Gr. (δέκα-το-ς, but εἰκοσ-τό-ς), probably also varied in the primitive speech. Now, in Germanic, after an unaccented syllable, as in Sk. catur-thá-s (fourth), we should expect regularly E. *four-d and G. vier-te; after an accented syllable, as in Sk. saptá-tha-s (seventh), we should expect, on the contrary, E. seven-th and G. sieben-de; lastly, after an f or an s, the I.-E. t here remaining unaltered, the result would be E. six-t and G. sechs-te.[2] All these distinctions hold good for the earliest state of both languages, but we see at once what has become of them in later times: excepting only number 3, analogy in E. extended the exponent -th throughout, and the exponent -te in G., so that E. and G. now disagree in the consonant of their ordinal suffix.

1. The ordinal is nowhere cognate with the cardinal: Go. fru-ma (cf. Gr. πρό "before" and L. prī-mu-s), superlative frum-ist-s = O.E. fyrm-est (cf. the E. comparative form-er),

[1] For Preg. *þūs, cf. Sk. távas (strength) and tavás (strong, mighty, great).
[2] Of course the final G. e is a declensional ending, cf. infra 156.

which a popular etymology finally corrupted to E. *fore-most*; another superlative is Go. *faúr-ist-s, O.N. *fyr-st-r*, O.E. *fyr-st* and E. *first*, O.H.G. *fur-isto*, M.H.G. *vür-ste* (first), and G. *fürst*, now confined to the sense of "prince" (cf. L. *princeps* "first"); another still, from the same root that produced Gr. ἦρ-ι (early), E. *ere* and *ear-ly*, etc., is O.E. *ǽr-est* (lost in E.), O.H.G. *ēr-ist* and G. *er-st*, cf. Go. *áir-is* (sooner).

2. No relation with the cardinal: Go. *an-þar*, the comparative of the root occurring in Sk. *an-yá-s* (other)[1]; O.E. *on-ðer, whence *ōðer*, but E. *second* borrowed; O.H.G. *an-der*,[2] but G. *zwei-te*, a late derivation from *zwei*.

3. Go. *þri-dja* = Sk. *tṛ-tíya-s* (for **tri-*) = L. *ter-tiu-s*; O.E. *ðri-dda* (and *ðir-da*), E. *thir-d*; O.H.G. *dri-tto* and G. *dri-tte*.

4. O.E. *féower-ða*[3] and E. *four-th*, after the analogy of *seven-th* and the like (cf. L. *quar-tu-s*); O.H.G. *feor-do* and G. *vier-te*.

5. O.E. *fīf-ta*, M.E. *fif-t*,[4] altered to E. *fif-th*; O.H.G. *finf-to funf-to* regular (the latter probably reproducing a form with reduced radical syllable, I.-E. *pṇq-tó-s) and G. *fünf-te* (the metaphony as in *fünf*).

6. Go. *saíhs-ta*; O.E. *siex-ta*, M.E. *six-t*,[4] altered to E. *six-th*; O.H.G. *sëhs-to* and G. *sechs-te*, regular forms.

7-10. E. *seven-th*, *eighth* (syncopated from *eight-th), *nin-th*, *ten-th* (the noun *ti-the* being an older form with O.E. compensatory lengthening). G. *sieben-te* (corrupted from M.H.G. *siebende*), *achte* (syncopated from O.H.G. *ahto-do*), *neun-te*, *zehn-te*.

11-19. The formation is the same throughout.

20-90. The same formation in English; but O.E. *g* developed before the suffixal *ð* a euphonic vowel, which is kept in E. *twentieth*, etc. German here changes its system: to the cardinal is now added a superlative-suffix (O.H.G. *zweinzug-ōsto*), whence the modern type *zwanzig-ste*.

---

[1] It must be borne in mind that suff. *-tero-* involves an idea of choice or alternation between *two* things only; cf. Gr. δεύ-τερο-ς "second" and δεύ-τατο-ς "last."

[2] A meaning preserved in G. *ander-t-halb* (*infra* III.) and in the current E. locution *every other day*.

[3] Where the *ð* might very well be still voiced.

[4] Still used in some provincial dialects.

THE SYSTEM OF NUMERATION. 211

100–1000. E. *hundred-th, thousand-th*; but G. *hundert-ste, tausend-ste*: as above.

Ordinal adverbs are derived: in E., by means of suff. *-ly*; in G., by adding an old genitive-ending, *erst-ens*.

II. **Multiplicatives.**—1. The formation of multiplicative adjectives, namely, E. *-fold* and G. *-falt -fältig*, has been given above. But Mod. G. uses by preference a composition with the word *fach* (compartment, class), viz. *zwie-fach* or *zwei-fach* (double), etc.

2. The E. multiplicative adverbs, *once* (O.E. *ān-es*), *twice* (M.E. *twi-es*) and *thrice* are old genitives used adverbially; next comes a syntactical locution, *four times*. G. *einst* (once) = O.H.G. *ein-ēst* seems to have been influenced by the ordinals; for it looks very like an old genitive *ein-es*, the more so because the corresponding *ander-s* (otherwise) has also become *ander-st* dialectally. Apart from these two, all are syntactical (*ein-mal, zwei-mal*, etc.), the invariable nt. noun *mal* being perhaps akin to the L. final in *semel* (once) and *simul* (at once) = *semol*. The very late adverbs in *-lei* are likewise syntactical forms, but in the genitive case, thus *einer leie* "of one sort,"[1] now *einer-lei*, and analogically *zweier-lei*, etc.

III. **Partitives.**—The partitive **halba-*, though common to all the Germanic dialects, is not found in the rest of the I.-E. family. Its original meaning was probably "side," so far as we can judge from such curious compounds as G. *meiner-halb-(en)* = M.H.G. *mīn-halp*, as it were "on my side" (in my concern, upon my account)[2]. Preg. **halba-* is O.E. *healf*, E. *half*, G. *halb*, and its derivative *hälf-te*. The compounded type **þriðja-halba-*, literally "the half of a third," that is "two and a half," is likewise Pregermanic: O.E. *ðridda-healf, féorða-healf*, etc.; G. *dritt-halb, viert-halb*: but it is quite lost in Mod. English.[3]

Further partitives are: in E. (as in F.), the ordinals, *a third, a fourth*, etc.; in G., non-syntactical compounds, the last term

---

[1] M.H.G. *leie* (manner) is borrowed from O.F. *ley*, now *loi* (law).
[2] Sk. *árdha-* likewise means "side" and "half."
[3] Analogy transferred the medial *t* of *dritt-halb, viert-halb*, etc., into *ander-t-halb* = O.E. *ōðer-healf* "one and a half."

of which, as unaccented, is reduced to a dull syllable, *drittel* = **dritt-theil* (M.H.G. *drit-teil*), *viertel*, etc.

IV. Distributives. — The old distributive derivation by means of the I.-E. suff. -*no*- (L. *bĭ-nĭ trĭ-nĭ*, Go. *tvei-h-nái* and O.N. *tven-ner* "two by two") is no longer represented except by a few survivals : E. *twi-n* = I.-E. **dwi-no-s*, and *to twi-ne* ; G. *zwir-n* (twist) = I.-E. **dwis-no-s*,[1] and vb. *zwir-n-en*. The distributive locutions now used are E. *two by two* and G. *je zwei*.

[1] For the medial *s*, compare E. *twist* and G. *zwist* (discord).

THIRD PART.

DECLENSION.

(125) Under the name of **Declension** are comprised the various **modifications**, either in stem or termination, **undergone by nominal and pronominal stems, and corresponding to** the various **relations of meaning** of which they are capable.

These relations are **three** in number, namely: **gender, number,** and **case.**

Indo-European had three genders, **masculine, feminine,** and **neuter.** All these are kept in the Germanic languages.

Indo-European had likewise three numbers, **singular,** dual, and **plural.** But the dual, which is preserved in Sk. remarkably, and in Gr. tolerably well, has left in Latin but two isolated representatives ($ambō$ and $duo=*duō$), and is completely lost in the Germanic group,[1] being replaced everywhere by the plural.

Lastly, the relation between an I.-E. noun or pronoun and the other members of any given sentence comprised eight cases, which are still exhibited by the Sk. and partly even by the Mod. Russian declension. But this number is well known to have been already reduced to six in Latin, and in Greek to five. A further simplification took place in Germanic: the vocative or calling-case was everywhere blended with the nominative; the locative (situation in) and the ablative (coming from) were expressed by means of prepositions[2]; the

---

[1] The few cases in which it survives have been just mentioned above (121, 2).

[2] Respectively:—E. *in* or *at*, G. *in* or *zu* (with the dative), cf. Gr. ἐν, L. *in*;—E. *from* or *out*, G. *von* or *aus* (with the dative).

instrumental (means or accompaniment) survived a little longer, though Gothic has already lost it; O.E. and O.H.G. still show it in use,[1] but it died out later and was also replaced by a periphrastic locution.[2] In short, M.H.G., like Go., is confined to four cases, still surviving in Mod. German, viz.: **nominative**, or **subject-case**; **accusative**, or **object-case** (direct complement); **genitive**, or case of **possession** and adnominal **determination**; and **dative**, or case of **attribution** to a given subject; with this restriction, however, that the accusative in nouns very seldom differs from the nominative. In English, the same confusion is constant, and the dative is denoted by a preposition[3]: so that the English declension is reduced to two cases, nominative and genitive, the latter, moreover, being often replaced by the concurrent use of the particle *of*.

The words which admit of these three relations of gender, number and case, are distinguished under four grammatical categories, respectively called **article, noun, adjective**, and **pronoun**.[4]

---

[1] The adverbial formation (*supra* 110, I. 4) still exhibits a number of (at least probable) instrumentals.

[2] E. *with, by*, or *through*; G. *mit* (dative) or *durch* (accusative).

[3] Usually *to* = G. *zu*. The possibility, however, of construing occasionally a so-called indirect complement without any preposition (*the land yields* the *owner two hundred a year*, cf. G. *es gilt* dem *besitzer* . . .) is an important survival from the old dative, which will further be found in the pronominal declension (*infra* 161 and 166). Hence, the dative may be said still to be a living case, as far as function is concerned, though, in form, it is one with the nominative-accusative.

[4] The participle, of course, inasmuch as it is a declinable word, is a mere adjective; the adverb has been seen to be a case-form of the noun or adjective: so that six among the ten parts of speech fall under the above divisions. The verb (with the participle as a form of it) is the subject of our Fourth Part. The remaining three classes of invariable particles require but little etymological explanation; the reader should refer for these to the alphabetical indexes where very many will be found. Hence the work comprises the whole of Anglo-German comparative Grammar.

CHAPTER I.

ARTICLES.

(126)   Properly speaking, **the article is** simply **a demonstrative pronoun**, a part it often plays in German. As such, it ought to fall under the head of chapter IV., and it might appear to be an error in method to separate it. In a strictly historical sense, it *is* an error, no doubt; for Indo-European, and even Pregermanic never had an article; Slavonic still does without it; and this essential part of English and German speech is but a late product of the improper and somewhat blundering use of an old demonstrative stem in a weakened and vague meaning. From a practical point of view, however, which is the one here chiefly requiring consideration, it seems advisable to isolate the article: being of frequent and often obligatory use, it occupies a distinct place among the demonstratives; having strongly influenced the other parts of speech, it is well fitted to afford us a general paradigm of declension, which it allows us to analyse once for all; and lastly, at least in German, where it has preserved its endings unaltered while the noun has mostly dropped them, the article is the chief exponent of gender, number, and case, so that the declension of the noun necessarily supposes a knowledge of this prefixed and declined particle.

Yet more accurately, the article is either an old demonstrative or an old numeral; for it seems, in every language, the unavoidable destiny of the little word meaning "this," to become, sooner or later, an insignificant aid to speech, as of the numeral "one" to degenerate into the indefinite article. L. *caballus* means equally "the horse" and "a horse": so, whenever a speaker wanted to express more precisely one of the two meanings, he naturally said either *ille caballus* or *unus caballus*, whence O.F. *li chevals* and *uns chevals*; the same thing exactly happened in passing from Pregermanic to English and German.

Section I.

DEFINITE ARTICLE.

(127) The greater part of the declension of the definite article proceeds from an I.-E. demonstrative *só *tó, which, though more or less altered, may be found in any member of the I.-E. family. A few forms, however, are borrowed from another demonstrative, nearly akin indeed, viz. *syó *tyó, which scarcely appears anywhere but in Sk., though there with perfect clearness.

§ 1. *Origin and Primitive Declension.*

(128) I. The demonstrative, I.-E. nomin. msc. sg. *só, fm. sg. *sấ,[1] never showed an initial *s* except in these two forms only : Sk. msc. *sá*, fm. *sấ*; Gr. ὁ ἡ (article). Everywhere else, that is to say, in the nomin. nt., in every other case of the three genders, and in any case of the plural, the stem-form became *tó- : I.-E. nomin. nt. sg. *tó-d, Sk. *tá-d*, Gr. τό,[2] L. (*is-*)*tu-d*; I.-E. acc. msc. sg. *tó-m, Sk. *tá-m*, Gr. τό-ν, L. (*is-*)*tu-m*; I.-E. nomin. msc. pl. *tóy, Sk. *tê*, Gr. τοί,[3] L. (*is-*)*tī*, etc. Now, in Sk., Homeric Gr. and even in the L. compound, the word has kept its full demonstrative value ; but, in classical Gr., it has already become an article, merely meaning " the "[4] and accompanying the noun throughout. In the history of the Germanic languages we find a similar evolution : the same stem, which is essentially a demonstrative pronoun, only with somewhat weakened stress, in Go., O.E. and O.H.G., is an article, that is to say, a kind of nominal prefix, almost constant and obligatory in German speech, and likewise obligatory, in the great majority of cases at least, in English.[5] How this

[1] Cf. *supra* 73 (III.).
[2] For *τό-δ, since any final explosive disappears in Greek.
[3] A Doric form. Ordinary Gr. *οἱ* after the analogy of ὁ.
[4] The meaning " this " was then confined to the juxtaposition ὁ-δε
[5] Except when the noun is conceived in a general and undefined meaning (*man delights me not*), an exception which confirms the rule, as strictly agreeing with the original demonstrative value of the article.

change came to pass, is also easily seen: when we read, for instance in Ulfilas [1] "*mannē sums áihta tvans sununs, jah qaþ sa jūhiza izē du attin*, of-men some-one had two sons, and quoth *this* younger of-them to father," or in Old English [2] "*sóðlice út éode se sǽdere his sǽd tó sáwenne*, soothly out went *this* sower his seed to sow," we translate at once without any difficulty "*the* younger told . . . ," "*the* sower got out . . . "; and, in fact, the demonstrative here is already a mere article.

The Gr. declension of this demonstrative nearly reproduces the I.-E. accidence; again, the Gothic declension is truly reflected by the German: nothing, therefore, would appear better fitted to smooth the way from one to the other, than a Go. paradigm with the similar Gr. cases. The agreement will at once strike the eye.

Singular.

	msc.	fm.	nt.
N.	$sa = \acute{o}$	$s\bar{o} = \acute{\eta}$ [4]	$þa\text{-}t\text{-}a^3 = \tau\acute{o}$
A.	$þa\text{-}n\text{-}a$ [3] $= \tau \acute{o}\text{-}\nu$	$þ\bar{o} = \tau \acute{\eta}\text{-}\nu$	$þa\text{-}t\text{-}a = \tau\acute{o}$
G.	$þi\text{-}s$	$þi\text{-}z\bar{o}s$	$þi\text{-}s$
D.	$þa\text{-}mma$	$þi\text{-}z\acute{a}i$	$þa\text{-}mma$

Plural.

	msc.	fm.	nt.
N.	$þ\acute{a}i = \tau o\acute{\iota}$	$þ\bar{o}s$	$þ\bar{o} = \tau\acute{a}$ [6]
A.	$þa\text{-}ns = \tau \acute{o}\text{-}\nu\varsigma$ [5]	$þ\bar{o}s$	$þ\bar{o} = \tau\acute{a}$
G.	$þi\text{-}z\bar{e}$	$þi\text{-}z\bar{o}$	$þi\text{-}z\bar{e}$
D.	$þ\acute{a}im$	$þ\acute{a}im$	$þ\acute{a}im$

In comparing, however, this old declension with that of Mod. German, the reader must remember that the demonstrative, after it had become confined to the function of an article, was apt to become proclitic and, therefore, to undergo several phonetic alterations.[7]

---

[1] Parable of the Prodigal Son, Luke xv. 11–12.
[2] Parable of the Sower, Matt. xiii. 3.
[3] The *a* is a subjoined particle (as in F. *ce-ci*), which maintained the consonantal ending by covering it, *supra* 39 and 46.
[4] Remember that I.-E. *ā* is always shifted to common Gr. η.
[5] Cretan. Lengthened to Gr. τούς.
[6] Originally *τά (Sk. *tā́*), but shortened in Greek, as also in Latin.
[7] Cf. *supra* 34 and 66, II.

II. The I.-E. demonstrative *syó likewise assumes this stem-form in the nomin. sg. msc. and fm. only, Sk. syá syâ. Everywhere else, the stem is *tyó- : Sk. nt. tyá-d, etc. The declension was the same as the preceding; but, since Germanic borrowed from it only two forms, we need not lay any further stress upon it.

§ 2. *Modern State.*

(129) Of this elaborate declension English is well known not to exhibit even a trace: it is all reduced to a single monosyllable. Hence German, as having to a large extent retained it, claims here the foremost place. But, at the outset, a general observation is indispensable: even German no longer knows anything of a stem either *só or *syó in the nomin. sg. msc. fm.[1]; in other words, the analogy of the other cases, in which the stem began with a t, transferred the t to the nominative and extended to the whole declension a stem *tó-[2] or *tyó-, the Preg. form of which is naturally *þa- or *þja-. This being understood, we have to consider successively, in the order of the above paradigm:—the sg. forms which proceed from the stem *þa-;—the pl. forms from the same stem;—the few sg. or pl. forms which proceed from the stem *þja-;—and the indifferent English form.

(130) I. Singular.—1. Nominative.—In the masculine, Sk., Gr. and Go. agree in showing the bare stem without any ending; but the demonstrative, nevertheless, could always take the ordinary ending -s of the nomin. msc. sg., thus Sk. also sá-s[3]; and this is just what has happened in German. Now, an I.-E. nomin. *tó-s, next *té-s[4] would become in turn Preg. *þé-s, then *þe-s proclitic, whence *þe-z, West Germ. *þe-r, O.H.G. dër and G. der.—The fm. is taken from *tyó-, infra III.—The I.-E. nt. exponent is -d: Sk. tá-d, Gr. τό, L.

---

[1] Both of them were kept in O.E., and we shall find the fm. *syâ among the personal pronouns, *infra* 166.
[2] The same is the case with Latin: nomin. sg. msc. (is-)te, fm. (is-)ta.
[3] Cf. L. (is-)tu-s, (ip-)su-s, and *infra* 137.
[4] The vocalism of the oblique cases (*infra* 3) intruding into the nominative (?). Or else, simply dër = *þar = I.-E. *tós, owing to lack of accent (?).

(is-)tu-d. An I.-E. *tó-d was changed to Preg. *þa-t, which should have become *þa; but the added -a prevented final t from dropping, Go. þa-t-a, so that, after this -a was again lost, there remained O.E. ðœ-t and O.H.G. da-ʒ. E. tha-t is still living, but only as a demonstrative or relative pronoun and a conjunction.[1] As to O.H.G. da-ʒ, no change is found in the modern article das, the relative das and the conjunction dasz[2] being, of course, only particular varieties of it, the latter distinguished by a somewhat stronger accent which is rather awkwardly represented by the usual spelling.

2. Accusative.—The ending of acc. msc. is -m: Sk. tá-m, Gr. τό-v, L. (is-)tu-m. I.-E. *tó-m gives Preg. *þa-n, which should have become *þa; but, final n being covered by the particle -a, we have Go. þa-n-a, O.E. ðo-n-e, O.H.G. dë-n and G. den.—The fm. belongs to class III.—The nt., even in the I.-E. period, was always identical with the nt. nominative.

3. Genitive.—In order to obtain a correct view of this and some further formations, we must recall the fact that every I.-E. stem in -o- is at the same time a stem in -e- [3]: hence, a stem *tó- may, under certain conditions, assume a form *té-, which becomes Preg. *þe- and Go. þi-; and such is the case here. Now the I.-E. exponent for the gen. sg. msc.-nt. in the demonstratives was a double ending: either *-syŏ, Sk. tá-sya, Gr. *τó-σιο changed to τοῖο and further contracted to τοῦ; or *sŏ, cf. Slav. ce-so gen. of the relative pronoun. The latter type, let us say I.-E. *té-sŏ, would give Preg. *þé-s, whence Go. þi-s, O.E. ðe-s, O.H.G. dë-s and G. des.—The fm. ending corresponding to msc.-nt. *-syŏ was *-syās: Sk. tá-syās. But Germanic, following the analogy of msc.-nt. *-so, likewise suppressed the j in the fm. exponent, whence Preg. *-sōs, gen. fm. *þe-zōz, Go. þi-zōs, where the final as well as the medial s is a z, owing to the syllable being unaccented, as shown by O.N. þei-rar. Final z was lost in West Germanic, and there remained O.E. ðǣ-re, O.H.G. dë-ra dë-ru and G. der.

---

[1] Though we have some traces of it in the article, supra 66, II. 1.
[2] Cf. the use of quod as a conjunction both in Latin and the Romance languages.
[3] Supra 72, II., and cf. the L. nomin. msc. (is-)te.

4. Dative.—The Gr. form τῷ is not primitive, but imitated from the similar form in the dative of nouns.[1] The I.-E. msc.-nt. dative inserted, between the stem *tó- and the specific ending *-ōy, a group -sm- of uncertain origin, Sk. *tá-sm-āi*; a formation well preserved in Go. *þa-mm-a*,[2] O.E. *ðǣ-m*, O.H.G. *dë-mu* and G. *dem*.—The fm. dative (Sk. *tá-syāi*, Go. *þi-zái*) was like the fm. genitive, except in its final diphthong, which is still visible in Go., but could not help being lost in the uniformity of the West Germanic unaccented syllables: O.E. *ðǣ-re*, O.H.G. *dë-ru* and G. *der*.

(131) II. Plural.—1. Nominative: msc. I.-E. *tóy, Sk. *tê*, Gr. τοί οἱ, L. (is-)tī, Preg. *þai, whence Go. *þái*, O.E. *ðā* and G. *dē*, the latter afterwards diphthongized to *dea*, *dia*, *die*, under which shape it became blended with the nomin. pl. fm. and nt. belonging with their accusative to class III.

2. Accusative.—As the acc. pl. nt. was identical with the nomin. even in I.-E. times, and the acc. pl. fm. had become so at least as early as the Pregermanic period, it was only natural that the acc. pl. msc. should also reproduce the corresponding nomin., O.E. *ðā*, G. *dē*, *die*.[3]

3. Genitive.—The Preg. stem is *þe-, as in the gen. sg. The ending, in the demonstratives, was I.-E. *-sōm, as shown by Sk. fm. *tá-sām*, Homer. Gr. fm. τάων=*τα-σων and L. fm. (is-)tā-rum =*tā-som. Now, the Preg. msc. and nt. being of course identical, the fm. could not differ very much from them, apart from the vocalic force of the Go. ending (viz. *þi-zē þi-zō*) which is not yet satisfactorily explained, but may well be neglected here, since it disappeared in the later languages: hence, in the three genders, O.E. *ðǣ-ra*, O.H.G. *dë-ro* and G. *der*.

4. Dative.—This case has nothing to do with the Gr. and L. so-called dative, τοῖς, (is-)tīs, which corresponds to a Sk. instrumental *táis*. Here the ending is *-mĭ(s),[4] and this, as also in the corresponding Sk. instrumental *tê-bhis*, is not attached directly to the stem *tó-, but to its pl. msc. nomin. form, thus

---

[1] Dat. ἵππῳ from nomin. ἵππος (horse), etc., cf. *infra* 152.
[2] *Supra* 61 (III.) and 34, § 1, III.
[3] Neither O.E. nor O.H.G. show even a trace of Go. *þa-ns*=Gr. τό-νς.
[4] Which will appear again in the nominal declension, *infra* 152, II.

I.-E. *tóy-mĭ(s), O. Slav. té-mĭ (with them), Preg. *þai-mi, whence, in the three genders, Go. þái-m, O.E. ð͞æ-m,[1] O.H.G. dē-m, next dē-n,[2] and G. den quite regularly.

(132) III. From the I.-E. declension of the stem *tó-, we have been able to deduce the whole G. accidence, with the exception of three forms, viz.: nomin.-acc. sg. fm., nomin.-acc. pl. fm., and nomin.-acc. pl. nt.

1. The stems in -o- form their fm. in -ā: to msc. *tyó the corresponding fm. is *tyá, Preg. *þjō, whence O.H.G. diu and G. die. The acc. is naturally *þjō-m, which also became G. die.[3]

2. The nomin.-acc. pl. fm. had the exponent -s, Sk. tyâ-s, whence Preg. *þjō-z, O.H.G. deo dio, G. die.

3. The nomin.-acc. pl. nt. is always identical with the nomin. sg. fm., cf. L. (is-)ta bona in both cases: I.-E. *tyâ, Preg. *þjō, whence O.H.G. diu and G. die.

Hence, nothing could prevent the various forms which proceeded from stem *tyó- being blended with the nomin. pl. msc. belonging to stem *tó-, so that the four-and-twenty theoretical forms of the G. article become finally reduced to six.[4]

(133) IV. This process of assimilation was carried on much farther in English, where the stem *tyó- plays no part at all. O.E. possessed a regular nomin. msc. sg. se sē = Go. sa, and a corresponding fm. sēo, which has become E. she. In later O.E., under the influence of the nt. nomin. ð͞æ-t and the oblique cases, there arose ðē and ðēo, and these new forms again became blended together, owing to their being unaccented; later still, the neuter was confounded with the msc.-fm., and all three resulted in the uniform unaccented M.E. the. On the other hand, the nomin. pl. ðā, from the same cause, assumed a duller

---

[1] Cf. the E. pronominal dative the-m, infra 160, 3, and 166, II.

[2] Here the m was final. It was not final in the dat. sg., cf. supra 130, 4. —In order to simplify the reader's task, I have reminded him, throughout the section, of every phonetic law that found an application in it; but henceforth I shall suppose him to be familiar with them.

[3] The O.H.G. acc., however, is not *diu, as theory would require, but dia, a somewhat puzzling form in its vocalism. But we may leave the point unsettled: for, as dia would also become die, which was favoured moreover by the analogy of the nomin., the confusion between the two forms was unavoidable.

[4] Namely: 8 die, 6 der, 4 den, 2 dem, 2 des, and 2 das.

vowel; the identity of the nomin. and acc., in the nt. and in the pl., induced the speaker to confuse the cases everywhere else; the increasing use of prepositions, influenced by the imitation of French syntax, gradually turned the other cases into useless and obsolete forms: in short, ultimately, English was confined to the single form *the*, a few others, however, being retained in the pronominal declension.

SECTION II.

INDEFINITE ARTICLE.

(134) In the sg. E. uses *an* and *a*, the unaccented and now invariable forms of *one* = O.E. *ān*. G. spells *ein* the word for the indefinite article, as well as for the number, but the stress in pronouncing the former is much weaker. The G. negative *kein* is O.H.G. *dihh-ein*, M.H.G. *dech-ein*, where, the *e* no longer being sounded, the initial *t* has become unpronounceable[1]; but the element *dihh-* is quite unexplained.[2] The declension of both is the ordinary declension for all determinatives.[3]

G. has no indefinite article for the plural number: *mensch-en* (some men), *wort-e* (some words). E. either uses *an-y* = G. *ein-ige* (several, some), or *some* = Go. *sum-s* (a certain)[4] = Gr. ἀμό-ς = Sk. *sama-* (whoever), both undeclined.

---

[1] Cf. I.-E. *$k\d{m}tóm$ = *$tk\d{m}tóm$, supra 123.
[2] The O.H.G. doublet *nihh-ein* is much plainer. The E. negative is the pronoun *none* = *n-one*, shortened to *no* (adjective and negative particle) = O.E. *nā*, cf. G. *n-ein*.
[3] Cf. *infra* 159 and 169.
[4] See the sentence quoted above (128) from Ulfilas. Likewise sg. in E. *some-body*, *some-thing*, etc., cf. *any-body*, etc. The inserted -*sm*- in Go. *þa-mm-a* = I.-E. *tó-sm-ōy (supra 130, 4) is probably a reduced grade of this stem.

CHAPTER II.

NOUNS.

(135) In the declension of E. and G. nouns, we have to deal with three grammatical categories: gender, number, and case.

SECTION I.

GENDER.

(136) As a general rule,—excepting the class of stems in -ā, which are all feminine nouns, and the specific ending of the nomin.-acc. in neuter stems in -o-,[1]—I.-E. gender had no influence on the accidence of nouns: thus, in Latin, *soror* is declined like *dolor*, and *frūctus*, like *manus*. On the contrary, in the Germanic declension, the genders have become of much importance, and are now heading the G. paradigms. The reason for this change is obvious: when the final syllables had been dropped, and the stem-class to which a noun originally belonged was no longer known, several nouns of various genders left the declension that suited their etymology, and were forced into agreement with other nouns of the same gender, but of different formation. Of this process, many instances will occur below. Here, one will suffice: G. *flut* (flood), which ought to be masculine, since it is an I.-E. stem in -*tu*- (Go. *flō-du-s*, O.H.G. *fluot* msc.), became feminine, together with many like it, in imitation of words which came from stems in -*ti*-, thus fm. *bucht* (bent, gulf)[2]: whereupon both *bucht* and *flut*, and a large number of other feminines, were declined after the pattern of *frau* (lady), which is a stem in -*en*-.

[1] L. *bonu-s bona bonu-m*, supra 72-73.
[2] *Supra* 78, 2-3. Cf. L. msc. *frūctus* borrowed and changed to G. fm. *frucht*.

English and German, although they kept the three I.-E. genders, distributed them in quite a different way.

It must be owned that the I.-E. distribution was very arbitrary and corresponded as little as possible to the meaning of the nouns to which it applied. Generally speaking, a noun denoting a male being or agent was masculine; the names of female beings or agents, feminine. But there was hardly any further attempt made to lend any system or order to the chaos of grammatical gender. We are not even able to assert that the names of male or female animals were all, respectively, masculine or feminine.[1] As for the names of inanimate beings and the abstract nouns, there is no rule whatever: some are masculine, some feminine, and some neuter; thus, among the nouns denoting instrument, though many end in -*tro-m*, there are also several stems in -*tro-s* or in -*trā*.[2]

In German this state of chaos still continues. This, however, must not be misunderstood as meaning that German has retained unaltered the primitive distribution. Since the distinction of genders is arbitrary, it is apt to become unsteady, inasmuch as a word may easily change its gender if the mind does not perceive any reason for assigning it to one class rather than to another. Such changes even took place in the short interval between Latin and French[3]; and they would be much greater in the course of forty centuries. Much more surprising, in fact, than this occasional gender-shifting, is the marvellous agreement with I.-E. gender, shown in a great number of cases: thus, in a single word, I.-E. **yugó-m*, Sk. *yugá-m*, Gr. ζυγό-ν, L. *jugu-m*, Go. *juk*, G. *joch*, Slav. *igo*, all neuter; in the whole class of feminines in -*īn-* = L. *iōn-* (L. fm. *leg-iō*, G. fm. *höh-e* = *höh-ī*); in the whole class of feminines in -*ti-*, G. -*t*; in the neuter formation of plurals in -*er*, etc., etc.[4]

---

[1] Indeed, most European languages, however logical they claim to be, have not passed this rudimentary stage: thus, in G. and F., *maus* and *souris* (mouse) are exclusively feminine, *schmetterling* and *papillon* (butterfly) exclusively masculine, so that the notion of their being male mice and female butterflies actually requires a slight effort of thought.

[2] L. *arā-tru-m* (plough), *cul-ter* (knife), *mulc-tra* (milking-pail).

[3] L. *arbor* fm., F. *arbre* msc.; L. *mōrēs* msc., F. *mœurs* (customs) fm.

[4] See the formation of words, and especially 74 (2 C), 78, 80.

NOUNS.   225

But the changes, none the less, embraced whole classes of words. So it happened that the masculines in -*tu*-, after the *u* had vanished, were classed with the feminines in -*ti*- whereof the *i* had been lost, and thus became feminine; a further consequence was, that the suffix -*heit* and -*keit*, which was a masculine noun (Sk. msc. *kē-tú-s*), became an essentially feminine exponent. So also, the Go. suff. -*n-assu*-, regularly masculine, became the G. suff. -*nisz*, which forms only neuter nouns and a very few feminines. From its origin, suff. -*sal* ought to have been applied indifferently to masculine or neuter nouns, whereas it is now exclusively neuter, with the exception of three feminine words. Lastly, the diminutives, probably as forming logically a class in themselves, were all made neuter.[1]

The triumph of logic is seen in the English distribution, where, apart from a few immaterial exceptions, the three genders rigorously correspond to the male, female and neuter sex (the last-named including animals in which the sex is neglected, inanimate beings, and abstract nouns). Of course, the language only arrived by degrees at this artificial levelling, another example of which could hardly be found throughout the whole of linguistic science: the O.E. genders still admit the anomalies that now survive in Mod. German; in M.E., the remnants of such old finals as would still allow the recognition of the original gender were dropped altogether, whereupon the gender itself became slowly modified, mainly under the influence of Anglo-French, and without exhibiting as yet any decidedly logical tendency; this, however, may be seen to prevail from the beginning of the fourteenth century, and, at the end of the sixteenth, arrived at the universal agreement which is now found to exist.

Further details with regard to gender should be sought in the ordinary grammars.

[1] The typical diminutive, viz. the word *kind* (child), is neuter, though it involves the idea of a sex: still more so such as do not involve it.

Q

Section II.

NUMBER.

(137) **The nominative singular,** whether in English or German, **has no ending,** and resembles a bare stem. But this is already known to be the combined effect of phonetic reduction and analogy. In fact, Pregermanic possessed, for the nominative singular, as for all other cases, even more than one ending, bequeathed to it by I.-E.; but from their very nature these endings were doomed to disappear.

From the Greek declension, which is extremely well preserved, we are able to restore five primitive types of nomin. sg. The ordinary masculine and feminine stems formed this case: either by a mere lengthening of the vowel in the final syllable, Gr. stems ἄκμον- (anvil, acc. ἄκμον-α), φέροντ- (carrying, acc. φέροντ-α), πατέρ- (father, acc. πατέρ-α), nominative sg. ἄκμων (cf. L. *homĭn-em* and *homō*), φέρων, πατήρ, etc.; or by adding a final -*s*, Gr. ἵππο- (horse, acc. ἵππο-ν), νύκτ- (night, acc. νύκτ-α), nomin. sg. ἵππο-ς (cf. L. *equŏ-s*), νύξ=*νύκτ-ς (cf. L. *nŏx*), etc. But feminine stems in -*ā*, -*ī*, -*ū*, even in the earliest period, lacked any nominative-ending: Sk. *áçvā* (mare), Gr. χώρᾱ (land), L. *terra* (earth), etc. Neuter stems in -*o*- added a final -*m* in the nominative as well as in the accusative: Sk. *yugá-m* (yoke), Gr. ζυγό-ν, L. *jugu-m*. Every other neuter stem remained unchanged: Sk. nt. *svādú* (sweet), Gr. nt. ἡδύ, cf. msc. ἡδύ-ς; Sk. *páçu* (cattle), L. *pecu*, Go. *faíhu*, etc.

Hence, West Germanic inherited a large number of neuter nominatives which lacked any case-sign. With these were already confounded neuter nominatives ending in -*m*, since final *m* was dropped in Pregermanic. Feminines ending in a long vowel first shortened, and then occasionally lost the vowel, which besides was not exclusively found in the nominative. The lengthened nominatives, type ἄκμων or *homō*, likewise shortened the vowel: thus, I.-E. *kanō (=L. *canō "the singer") became Go. *hana* (cock), O.E. *hona*, O.H.G. *hano*; and this short vowel again vanished later on, G. *hahn*. In short, four of the five I.-E. types could not help becoming nominatives without a case-sign in West Germanic.

There yet remained one type, and that the most important, the nominative in -*s*. This -*s* ought to have survived, at least after an accented vowel. Gothic, indeed, kept it, and even shows it by analogy[1] after an unaccented syllable. On the contrary, in Old Norse and West Germanic, after the -*s* of nomin. sg. had become -*z* when following an unaccented vowel, this -*z* analogically intruded everywhere else: whence the regular O.N. -*r*, and the total loss of the termination in West Germanic. A further consequence in the latter group is that the plural-exponents and case-endings henceforth seem to be adapted,—not to a declensional stem, as theory would require, and Go. and O.N. grammar still show them to be,—but to the nominative singular: which is as much as to say that this case is no longer a case; in the eyes of an English or German speaker, **it is the word itself.**

The singular having attained this simplicity of form, the plural necessarily followed: the various stems being no longer distinguishable from one another by the presence or absence of a nominative-ending, or by the character of their stem-vowels which had vanished long before, their declensional varieties, based on hidden differences in etymological structure, naturally tended to become levelled under the influence of analogy, so that a merely outward likeness, or occasionally, as noted above, a logical association would substitute, here and there, some new classification for the grammatical categories inherited from the past. In what measure the German plural,[2] after being thus shifted, either reproduces or alters the primitive formation, is a point easily settled by glancing at the curious and, in the main, regular forms exhibited by the Gothic declension.

1. Stems in -*o*- and -*yo*- :
msc. sg. *dag-s*,   pl. *dagōs*,   cf. G. *tag tag-e*;
    nt. „ *vaúrd*, „ *vaúrd-a*, „ „ *wort wort-e* (but also *wört-er*);
    msc. „ *harji-s*, „ *harjōs*, „ „ *heer heer-e* (nt.).

[1] Cf. *supra* 63 and the instances below.
[2] English, with its almost universal plural in -*s*, does not here concern us: in it the analogical levelling is complete.

2. Stems in -*ā* and -*yā*:
fm. sg. *aírþa,* pl. *aírþōs,* but G. *erde erden*;
„ „ *háiþi,* „ *háiþjōs,* „ „ *heide heiden* (heaths).

3. Stems in -*i* and -*u*-:
msc. sg. *gast-s,* pl. *gasteis,* cf. G. *gast gäste*;
fm. „ *dēþ-s,* „ *dēþeis,* but „ *that that-en*;
msc. „ *sunu-s,* „ *sunjus,* cf. „ *sohn söhne*;
fm. „ *handu-s,* „ *handjus,* „ „ *hand hände.*

4. Stems in -*en*- and -*yen*- (so-called weak declension):
msc. sg. *blōma,* pl. *blōman-s,* cf. G. *blume blumen* (fm.);
„ „ *arbja,* „ *arbjan-s,* „ „ *erbe erben*;
„ „ *garda,* „ *gardan-s,* but „ *garten gärten*;
„ „ *hana,* „ *hanan-s,* „ „ *hahn hähne* [1];
fm. „ *tuggō,* „ *tuggōn-s,* cf. „ *zunge zungen*;
„ „ *háuhei,* „ *háuhein-s,* „ „ *höhe höhen*;
nt. „ *haírtō,* „ *haírtōn-a,* „ „ *herz herzen.*

5. Stems in -*es*- (Gr. ἔρεβος, gen. ἐρέβε(σ)-ος):
nt. sg. *riqis,* pl. *riqiz-a,* cf. G. *kalb kälber.*[2]

6. Stems in any other consonant:
msc. sg. *frijōnd-s,* pl. *frijōnd-s,* but G. *freund freund-e*;
fm. „ *daúhtar,* „ *daúhtr-jus,* cf. „ *tochter töchter.*

Now, let the reader reflect that O.E. and O.H.G. had exactly the same declensional classes as Go. itself, and he will understand how far the modern languages have since gone astray. Our further task is to show the roads they took.

§ 1. *General Remarks.*

(138) Nowhere do English and German more widely disagree, than in the part of their grammar which deals with plural-formation: the characteristic English type is unknown to German; to the manifold German types, English opposes scarcely a dozen survivals. And yet nothing is more certain

---

[1] Also regular *hahnen,* but less used.
[2] In this and the preceding class, the outward agreement of Gothic and German is striking at first sight; but, if we scrutinize it closely, we perceive an intrinsic difference, namely, that an integral element of the Go. noun has become a G. plural-exponent.

than that both languages once started from a common declension, as illustrated by the Go. examples given above, and traced by linguistic comparison up to I.-E. Hence, our best course will be to define the starting-point and the present state of these endings.

I. The I.-E. nouns formed their plural with great simplicity, namely: the masculine and feminine, by adding a syllable -*ĕs*; the neuter nouns, by adding a vowel -*ā*.

1. When the stem ends in a consonant, the ending remains pure: Sk. *pắd-as* (feet), Gr. πόδ-ες, L. *ped-ēs*; Sk. pl. *bhắrant-as* (carrying), Gr. φέροντ-ες, L. *ferent-ēs*.[1]

2. When the stem ends in -*ŏ*- or -*ā* (Gr. and L. so-called second and first declension), the *ĕ* is contracted with the preceding vowel to a long vowel: I.-E. *ékwo-s (horse), pl. *ékwŏ-ĕs, whence *ékwōs, Sk. áçvās, Preg. *éhwōz; I.-E. *ékwā (mare), pl. *ékwā-ĕs, whence *ékwās, Sk. áçvās, Preg. *éhwōz, etc.[2]

3. When the stem ends in -*ĭ*- or -*ŭ*-, this vowel passes to the normal grade -*ĕy*- or -*ĕw*- before the plural-ending -*ĕs*: I.-E. root *trĭ (three), declined *trĕy-ĕs, Sk. tráy-as, Gr. *τρέy-ες *τρέες τρεῖς, L. *trĕy-ĕs *trĕĕs trēs; so also, Sk. gatí-s (march), pl. gatáy-as, Gr. μάντι-ς (prophet) pl. μάντεις, L. hosti-s (enemy), pl. hostēs; I.-E. *swādú-s (sweet) pl. *swādéw-ĕs, Sk. svādáv-as, Gr. *ἡδέϝ-ες ἡδέες ἡδεῖς, cf. L. manu-s (hand) pl. manūs, etc.[3]

4. If the neuter stem ends in -*ŏ*-, the plural sign -*ā* simply replaces the *ŏ*: I.-E. *yugó-m (yoke) pl. *yugá, Sk. yugá-m yugā́, Gr. ζυγό-ν ζυγά, L. jugu-m juga,[4] Go. juk juka, etc.

5. In any other case, the -*ā* is added to the stem-form: I.-E. nt. *gén-os, stem *gén-es-, pl. *gén-es-ā; Gr. γέν-ος, pl. *γέν-εσ-α γένεα γένη; L. gen-us, pl. *gen-es-a genera; Go. riq-is (darkness)

[1] The L. lengthening is later and secondary, being borrowed from the following class of words: see Henry, *Gramm. of Gr. and Lat.*, no. 206.

[2] The Gr. and L. forms are quite different: respectively ἵπποι and *equī*= *equoi*, *ἵππαι* and *equae*=*equāi*. But, that is because here the plural of these stems has followed the analogy of the similar demonstratives, cf. Gr. οἱ αἱ (article) and L. (*is-*)*tī* (*is-*)*tae*, supra 131.

[3] In other words, here as in the preceding case, final *s* follows a long vowel, which is the product of contraction between the final vowel of the stem and the *ĕ* of the termination.

[4] Shortened in Gr. and L., but still kept long in Preg., since it occurs as a short vowel in Gothic: if it had been short in Preg., it must have vanished in Gothic, supra 34.

= Gr. ἐρεβεσ-, pl. *riq-iz-a*; O.H.G. *chalb* (calf) = Preg. *kálb-iz, pl. *chelb-ir(-u)* = Preg. *kálb-iz-ō.

II. On the other hand, the English and German plurals may be divided into five main classes.

1. **Plurals in** -s: **exclusively English**; without any distinction of gender; no equivalent in German.

2. **Plurals in** -en or -n: **no metaphony ever occurring**; masculines (*bote boten, christ christen*), feminines (*zunge zungen, frau frauen*) and a few neuters (*auge augen, herz herzen*); so-called weak declension.

3. **Plurals in** -e **without metaphony**: German masculines and neuters (*tag tage, arm arme, wort worte*).

4. **Metaphonical plurals in** -e **or without any ending**: masculines (*sohn söhne, vater väter*) and feminines (*hand hände, mutter mütter*); cf. E. *goose geese*.

5. **Metaphonical plurals in** -er: neuters (*kalb kälber, lamm lämmer, haus häuser*) and a few masculines.

Let us now inquire how it could happen that the latter system proceeded from the former.

§ 2. *Plurals in* -s.

(139) It has been seen that every I.-E. masculine or feminine noun formed a plural which ended with *s*. Now this *s*, according as it was or was not immediately preceded by the accent, ought either to survive, or to be shifted to *z* and then disappear. History confirms this theory: O.E. has a minority of plurals in -*s*, and a large majority of plurals without -*s*, that is to say, in -*z*[1]; but in German, however far we go back, the latter had eliminated the former and are found throughout. O.H.G. in consequence as completely lacks the -*s* in the nominative plural, as West Germanic lacks it in the nomin. sg.: a new way has been found for plural-formation, and thus, **English having taken to propagating by analogy**[2] **the**

[1] As to these being in a majority, the reader is referred to § 1, where it appears that the ĕ in the termination -ĕs never had the I.-E. accent, so that the *s* could never be immediately preceded by the accent, except when the stem itself ended with an accented vowel which had coalesced with the initial ĕ of the ending. Now this case, of course, is by far the rarer.

[2] Analogy here is not the only responsible factor: after the Norman

very exponent that had become lost by analogy in German, it happened that the two sister-tongues diverged from each other as widely as possible.

The main processes of the English evolution may be easily and shortly retraced as follows.

I. Masculines.[1]—1. The plural-exponent *s* could nowhere be better preserved and nowhere more widely diffused, than in the class of primitive masculine stems in -*o*-, because there the words accented on their final syllable are rather common, so that the final *s* very often followed an accented vowel. We need but quote such Gr. words as στραβό-ς, φορό-ς, δεινό-ς, λυτό-ς, λαμπρό-ς, ἱππικό-ς, etc., etc. Thus, if we consider an I.-E. stem *dhoghó-s (day),[2] pl. *dhoghôs = *dhoghó-ĕs, the corresponding Preg. forms are sg. *ðaʒá-s, pl. *ðaʒôs, Go. *dag-s dagōs*, and nothing could be more regular than that the *s* should be retained in the O.E. pl. *dagas* of sg. *dæg*, whence E. *day day-s*. From this the O.E. plural-ending -*as*, which became E. -*es* or -*s*, was extended to all similar nouns, whatever might have been their original accent: O.E. *wulf* (L. *lupus*) *wulf-as*, *weal* (L. *vallus*) *weall-as*, *pæð* (Gr. πάτος) *pað-as*, *ende* (Sk. *ántyas*) *end-as*, *earm* (L. *armus*) *earm-as*, etc.; E. *wolf wolv-es*, *wall wall-s*, *path path-s*, *end end-s*, *arm arm-s*, and so indefinitely.

2. The same analogy, also as early as the O.E. period, largely contaminated the old stems in -*i*-, since, their -*i*- having been dropped, they were no longer distinguishable from stems in -*o*-. O.E. *lyge*, for instance, is Preg. *luʒi-z, as shown by the early metaphony which did not take place in G. *lug*: now, the old plural is *lyge* = *luʒiz (G. *lüge*); but another analogical plural is *lyg-as*, whence E. *lie lie-s*. Words in which the *i* had left no

---

conquest, French doubtless played a great part in this expansion of E. *s*; for, since words borrowed from F. used to form their plural in this way, native words could easily adopt the same exponent, the more so as some of them already admitted of it. At any rate, it is a remarkable fact, that the *s*-plural should have reached such a high degree of development in the two Germanic languages which were brought into nearest contact with French, that is, in English and Dutch, whereas it is lost everywhere else. A few instances occur also in Low German (*mädchens* " lasses," *fräuleins* " misses "), but these are generally acknowledged to be due to a modern French influence.

[1] Starting, as a matter of course, from the historical gender.
[2] Cf. *supra* 72, II.

trace were naturally even more liable to be altered in this way: thus O.E. *giest*=*$\gamma asti$-z* (=G. *gast*) has no other plural but *giest-as*, E. *guest guest-s*, and *wyrm*=*$wurmi$-z* (cf. Sk. *kŕmi-s*, G. *wurm*) has only *wyrm-as*, E. *worm worm-s*, and so forth. But the stems in -*u*-, as long as they keep the *u*, remain unaltered (O.E. *sunu*, pl. *suna*); this having vanished, their plural also gives way to the influence of analogy (E. *son son-s*).

3. Again, and as early as O.E., the same *s* became attached to one masculine noun denoting relationship: *fœder*, pl. *fœdr-as*; E. *father father-s*. But of *brōðor* the pl. is still *brōðor* or *brōðru*; later we have *brother brother-s*.

4. No less intelligible is the analogical process which modified the plural of the stems in primitive -*en*- and nearly effaced in English the so-called O.E. weak declension. We have seen and are yet to see further on[1] how it happened that the *n*, though lost in the nomin. sg., re-appeared in the other cases. Hence, a Preg. *$\gamma uman$-* (man), sg. *$\gamma umō$*=L. *homō*, pl. *$\gamma uman$-iz*=L. *homin-ēs*, becomes O.E. sg. *guma*, pl. *guman*; and, in the same way, we have *mōna mōnan, flēa* (=G. *floh*) *flēan, crēda crēdan*, etc. As long as this characteristic *a* was retained in common pronunciation, the weak declension remained free from any external corruption; but, the *a* being lost in M.E., nothing was left which could prevent such words as *moon, flea, creed*, etc., from forming such plurals as *moon-s, flea-s, creed-s*, etc. The pl. *oxen* from *ox* (O.E. *oxa oxan*) alone survived from this class.

5. The same is the case with the old metaphonical plurals. A Preg. *frijōnd-s *frijōnd-iz* had become O.E. sg. *frēond* and pl. *friend* (cf. Mod. E. *foot* and *feet*); but, the plural -*s* being added by analogy to the latter form, it gave way to a pleonastic plural *friend-s*, from which analogy again easily transferred the metaphony to the sg. *friend*[2]; and so also with O.E. *fēond fiend*, now *fiend fiends*.[3]

[1] *Supra* 74, 87, 114, 117, and *infra* 140.
[2] The more so, because there already existed in the sg. a metaphonical form, namely the O.E. dat. *friend*=*frēond-i* (cf. L. dat. *ferent-i*).
[3] Many other analogical blunders might have taken place: from sg. *foot* might have come a pl. *foot-s* (O.E. *fōt-as* is occasionally met with), or a pl. *feet-s*, whence there might have proceeded a sg. *feet*, or, in another form

II. Feminines.—1. O.E. *brōðor* has been seen to keep its plural unaltered. It stands to reason that the names of female relationship should keep it even better: *mōdor, dohtor, sweostor*; pl. *mōdru, dohtor*, etc. But, in imitation of *father* and *brother*, these nouns also took the ending -*s* in M.E., *mother-s, daughter-s, sister-s*.

2. The path being thus opened, no feminine could escape, especially as the stem-vowels in all had become dull and inaudible, while in a great many the gender had a tendency to shift. Thus, the long specific *ā* of the fm. sg., which had become a dull short vowel in O.E., being no longer sounded in M.E., we find such contrasts as: O.E. *cearu*, pl. *ceara*, but E. *care care-s*; O.E. *ondswaru*, pl. *ondswara*, E. *answer answer-s*, etc.

3. The same is the case with fm. stems in -*i*- and in -*u*-: O.E. *tīd* (= G. *zeit*), pl. *tīd-e*, E. *tide tide-s*; O.E. *hond*, pl. *hond-a*, E. *hand hand-s*; O.E. *flōr*, pl. *flōr-a*, E. *floor floor-s*, etc.

4. Further with stems in -*en*- (weak declension): O.E. *tunge*, pl. *tungan* (cf. Go. *tuggō tuggōn-s*), E. *tongue tongue-s*; O.E. *eorðe*, pl. *eorðan* (passed to the weak declension like G. *erde erden*), but E. *earth earth-s*, etc.

5. Lastly, with the metaphonical stems: O.E. *bōc*, pl. *bēc*, E. *book book-s*[1]; O.E. *burg*, pl. *byrg*, now *borough borough-s*, etc.

III. Neuters.—1. Neuter nouns could never have an *s*-plural, and therefore O.E. knows nothing of this formation. But the analogy of masculine stems first introduced it into neuter stems in -*o*-, a natural process; for a great many masculine nouns had become neuter through logical gender-shifting, and, these of course keeping their old *s*-plural, there appeared no reason why such a plural might not as well be added to any other neuters; on the other hand, the old neuter plural-ending -*ā* (-*ō*) being now phonetically dropped, the plural in this class did not differ from the singular,[2] although in most cases the speaker

---

of declension, the pl. *child-s *ox-es from *child ox*, etc. The few plurals which are known to be formed without -*s* and which will occur below, are interesting archaisms which succeeded in resisting the assaults of progressive analogy.

[1] The metaphony survives in *beech*, which was transferred to the sg., like *friend* above. Cf. supra 33, 1.

[2] Still *sheep*, pl. *sheep*, infra 143, II.

would wish to distinguish them. Hence: O.E. *wīf, word, geoc, dēor*; pl. *wīf, word, geoc* (= Go. *juka*), *dēor*; but E. *wife wive-s*,[1] *word word-s, yoke yoke-s* (*deer* still remaining *deer* in the pl.), etc., etc.

2. Stems in *-i-*: O.E. *spere*, pl. *speru*, E. *spear spear-s*; O.E. *gewile*, pl. *gewilu*, E. *will will-s*, etc.

3. Stems in *-en-* (weak declension): O.E. *ēage* = Go. *áugō*, pl. *ēagan* = Go. *áugōn-a*, E. *eye eye-s*; O.E. *ēare ēaran*, E. *ear ear-s*, etc.

4. Stems in *-es-*: here analogy was long kept at bay. Several representatives of the G. type *kalb kälber* occur in O.E., viz. *cild*, pl. *cild-ru, cealf cealf-ru, lomb lomb-ru*, etc. This ending not only survived, but even spread by analogy at the beginning of the M.E. period. It disappears in later times, slowly giving way to *calv-es, lamb-s, folk-s* (cf. G. *völk-er*), which are directly derived from the sg. *calf, lamb, folk*, so that *child-r-en*[2] remains the only instance of the former formation.

§ 3. *Plurals in -en.*

(140) The plural type which belongs to the **Weak Declension** is extremely simple, if we only bear in mind that I.-E. stems in *-ŏn-* and the like[3] lost the *n* in the nomin. sg. and kept it everywhere else. So, an I.-E. stem **uks-ón-* (ox) was sg. *uks-ō, pl. *uks-ón-ĕs, whence Sk. sg. *ukš-á*, pl. *ukš-án-as*, consequently Go. *aúhs-a aúhs-an-s*, E. *ox ox-en*, G. *ochs ochs-en*. So also, I.-E. stem **kan-ón-* (singer), sg. *kan-ō, pl. *kan-ón-ĕs, which would be L. *can-ō *can-ōn-ĕs: Go. has regularly *han-a* (cock) *han-an-s*, O.H.G. *han-o han-on*, and G. *hahn hahn-en*.

It is easy to restore the historical process: when the final *s* in the plural, retained in Gothic, had ceased to be sounded in West Germanic, **the preceding nasal syllable,** the only remnant of the ending, **was mistaken for the plural-**

---

[1] This, moreover, was shifted to the fm. gender at an early date.
[2] This again corrupted from another cause, *infra* 140 and 147, 2. But popular speech sometimes keeps it pure: thus we read *childer* in *Jane Eyre*, as used by an old servant-maid.
[3] Cf. *supra* 74 and 137.

exponent, for the sole reason that it was missing in the singular. This gave birth to a class of plurals formed by an exponent which Pregermanic knew nothing of. The observation, of course, applies not only to masculines as exemplified above, but also to similar feminines, which had lost the final *n* of the nomin. sg. only in the Preg. period (Go. *tugg-ō tugg-ōn-s*, O.E. *tung-e tung-an*, O.H.G. *zung-a zung-ŭn*), and even more to neuter nouns, which lacked the plural *-s* and never had it (Go. *haírt-ō haírt-ōn-a*, O.E. *heort-e heort-an* fm., G. *herz herz-en*). This formation, nearly forgotten in English, is a living and active one in Mod. German.

The further point, why here it proscribes metaphony altogether, is likewise easily settled by referring to its origin. The word-classes to which it can apply are but five in number: —(1) masculines in *-on-*, Go. *hana hanans, blōma blōmans*, G. *hahn hahnen, blume* (now fm.) *blumen*; —(2) masculines in *-yon-*, Go. *arbja arbjans*, G. *erbe erben*; —(3) feminines in *-on-*, Go. *tuggō tuggōns*, G. *zunge zungen*; —(4) feminines in *-yon-* and *-īn-*, Go. *managei manageins, háuhei háuheins*, G. *menge mengen, höhe höhen*; —(5) neuters in *-on-*, Go. *áugo áugōna*, G. *auge augen*.—
Now, in these five classes, we see plainly that the first, third and fifth can never have any metaphony in the plural, whereas the second and fourth must have it already in the singular; which is as much as to say that the plural of this declension can never differ from the singular as to the vowel of the stem-syllable.

Such being the case, it may well seem somewhat strange that, English having preserved three plurals of this kind, viz. *oxen, brethren* and *children*, one of them at least should be a metaphonical form. But *brethren* is not an English word (O.E. pl. *brōðor*): O.N. had for this noun a metaphonical plural, like the G. pl. *brüder*; thus, M.E. *brethre* was borrowed from O.N. and afterwards received an added *n* on the analogy of *children*.[1] Besides the pl. *oxan*, O.E. had also a metaphonical plural *exen*, which probably proceeded from the other vocalic form of suff.

---

[1] Because both denoted relationship. We need scarcely observe that *brethren* now belongs exclusively to ecclesiastical language.

-on- (*-en-*), found in L. *hom-in-ēs*. Lastly, *child-r-en* obviously contains a pleonastically double plural-ending. Every other weak plural has been replaced by the *s*-plural.

In German, the weak plural was also exposed to the influence, though far less active, of other formations; and, though it gave way here and there, yet on the whole it has rather gained than lost ground. The facts may be stated briefly, as follows.

(141) I. **Masculines.**—1. The *n*-plural requires no explanation in the masculines which still end in *-e*; for this *-e* represents, as a matter of course, a prehistorical long vowel,— otherwise it would have been dropped,—and this again is as a rule the representative of the final vowel of L. *hom-ō* = Go. *gum-a*, pl. *gum-an-s* = archaic L. *hom-ōn-ēs*. Thus, we have regularly: *knabe knabe-n*, *rabe rabe-n*, *löwe löwe-n* (cf. L. *leō leōnēs*), etc.; a class which naturally comprises the names of nations, *Sachse Sachse-n* (cf. L. *Saxō Saxōnēs*), and further the adjectives used with the same meaning, *Deutsche Deutsche-n*, and, generally speaking, every adjective used substantivally.[1]

2. But this sg. *-e* was not likely to be kept everywhere; for, though the old law of Germanic finals would protect it, the gradual weakening of modern finals, or even analogy alone might easily prevail against it: thus, the sg. for "ox" is *ochse*, but also *ochs*, so that, in *ochsen* when contrasted with *ochs*, the plural-sign seems to be *-en*. The same is the case in many words: *bauer* (peasant) = O.H.G. (*gi*)*būro*; *graf* (earl) = M.H.G. *grāve* = O.H.G. *grāvo grāvio*; O.H.G. *heri-zogo* "leader of an army," wherein the element *-zogo* bears the same relation to the vb. *ziehen* = Go. *tiuhan* (to lead, to draw) that a substantive *dŭcō would bear to the L. vb. *dūcere*; the pl. of *dŭcō would be *ducōnēs, hence O.H.G. pl. *herizogon*, M.H.G. *herzoge herzogen*, G. *herzog* (duke) and pl. *herzog-e* (now corrupt, see below); G. *herr* = O.H.G. *hĕrro* (lord), pl. *herr-en*; G. *mensch* = O.H.G. *mennisco*, an adjective used substantivally, or a noun derived from an adjective *mann-iská-s, the latter being formed in the same way as *Deutsch* = Go. *þiud-isk-s*, cf. Go. adjective *mann-isk-s* (human) and observe the regular German metaphony, etc.

---

[1] Cf. *infra* 156.

3. This plural formation in -*en* being now steadily fixed in the words which had a legitimate claim to it, analogy caused it to spread:—either, through a merely material association, to nouns ending with an -*e* in the nomin. sg., though this -*e* had actually no relation at all to that of the weak declension, as, for instance, to primitive stems in -*yo*-, namely *hirte* (also *hirt*) = O.H.G. *hirt-ī* = Go. *haird-ei-s*,[1] cf. E. *shepherd* = O.E. *scēap-hyrde*, etc. ;—or, above all, through logical association, and because the nouns mentioned above chiefly denoted male beings or agents (*knabe, bote, herr, graf, narr,* etc.), to other nouns of similar meaning as they were imported from foreign languages into German (*christ, soldat, philosoph,* etc.). Hence it happened that this plural was deemed the specific one for borrowed words, which still for the most part follow the weak declension, including even names of animals (*elephant*) and inanimate things (*planet*).

4. As opposed to this increase, a small apparent decrease may be observed, owing to the fact that the ending -*en* occasionally intruded into the singular. This process[2] is marked, in its gradual development, by three main types, as follows.— Gothic has a nt. *namō*, pl. *namn-a*, which is exactly reproduced, except in gender, by G. msc. *name*, pl. *name-n*. But, as some nouns are seen to have regularly the pl. like the sg. (*ofen, boden*),[3] the pl. *namen* gives birth to the sg. *namen*, whereupon both *name* and *namen* survive side by side. So also, *friede* and *frieden*,[4] *funke* and *funken*, *wille* and *willen* (Go. *vilja*, pl. *viljans*); further, the -*e* being dropped in the nomin. sg., *fleck* and *flecken*, *fels* and *felsen*, *daum* and *daumen*, etc.—Gothic has *brunna*, pl. *brunnans*. In German, the pl. *brunnen* produces a sg. *brunnen*, which replaces and supersedes the regular *brunn* = M.H.G. *brunne* (source).—Gothic has *garda* (enclosure), pl. *gardans*. The G. pl. *garten, produces a sg. *garten*, and this

---

[1] As it were Preg. **herð́-ja-z* " belonging to the herd."
[2] Similar to the extension, referred to above, of metaph. pl. *friend* to the sg., *supra* 139, I. 5.
[3] O.H.G. *ovan, bodam*. The metaphony in the plural is later, *infra* 146, I. 3.
[4] For this word, the process is still more intricate, for the stem did not legitimately belong to the weak declension, the nomin. sg. being Preg. *friþu-z. It became first shifted to the weak declension and then corrupted.

again, after the analogy of *väter*, *äpfel*, etc., introduces a new metaphonical plural *gärten*. So also : *laden* (shop), pl. *laden* and *läden*; *magen* (stomach), pl. *magen* and *mägen*, etc.

5. Lastly, though seldom, a noun may be shifted from the weak to the strong declension and assume in consequence a new ready-made plural formation. Thus, the often quoted *hahn* still keeps the old pl. *hahnen* = Go. *hanans*; but *hähne* is far commoner, and the whole case-declension agrees with the latter (gen. sg. *hahn-s*, no longer *hahn-en). The case-forms of *herzog* likewise exclusively correspond to the strong declension; indeed, the plural is now *herzoge*.

(142) II. **Feminines.**—1. Most weak fm. nouns still exhibit, in the shape of final -*e*, the ending -*ō* which characterized their Preg. and Go. nomin. sg. : G. *zunge*, pl. *zunge-n*, cf. O.H.G. *zunga zungūn* and Go. *tuggō tuggōn-s*; so also, G. *taube*, *sonne*, *wittwe* (O.H.G. *tūba*, *sunna*, *wituwa*); G. *blume*, pl. *blumen*, shifted to the fm. gender (Go. msc. *blōma blōmans*), etc.

2. The fm. nouns ending in -*ī* in their Preg. and Go. nomin. sg. belong to the same class in Gothic (*managei manageins*). Not so, however, in O.H.G., where the plural does not differ from the sg. : *hōhī*, pl. *hōhī*; though the type *hōhīn* is found occasionally. Later on, the *ī* being shortened, the words *menge*, *höhe*, *länge*, etc., become blended with the words *zunge*, *taube*, *sonne*, etc., in the nomin sg., and consequently also in the nomin. pl., viz. *mengen*, *höhen*, *längen*, etc.

3. The weak plural-formation is no less regular in nouns which no longer show an -*e* in the nomin. sg., but are known to have formerly ended with that representative of the Preg. fm. -*ō* of stems in -*on*-: G. *frau* = M.H.G *vrouwe* = O.H.G. *frouwa*, which would be Go. *fráujō, fm. of *fráuja* (lord), pl. *fráujans*; hence, G. pl. *frau-en* = Go. *fráu-jōn-s; G. *au* (meadow) = *aue* = M.H.G. *ouwe*; G. *ader* (vein) = O.H.G. *ādara*, etc.

4. After this termination, -*en* or -*n*, had become the apparent plural-exponent of a large number of feminine nouns, it gradually invaded the whole feminine accidence, either owing to the similar ending in the nomin sg., or merely from the influence of the gender itself. A brief enumeration must suffice.—(*a*) Stems in I.-E. -*ā*: Go. *airþa*, pl. *airþōs*; O.H.G. *ërda*, pl. *ërdā*;

but G. *erde erden*.¹—(*b*) Stems in I.-E. -*ī*, which in O.H.G. had yielded to the analogy of the preceding class: Go. *bandi* (tie), pl. *bandjōs*; but O.H.G. *sunta* (sin), pl. *suntā*, and G. *sünde sünden*; O.H.G. *kuningin*² *kuninginnā*, but G. *königin königinnen*, etc.—(*c*) Stems in -*ti*-, for the most part: Go. *náuþ-s* (need), pl. *náudeis*, O.H.G. *nōt nōti*, G. *noth nöthe* regular; but, on the contrary, G. *that that-en, schlacht schlacht-en*, etc.; so also, *tugend, arbeit*, and all nouns ending in -*schaft*.—(*d*) Stems in -*tu*-, wholly assimilated to the preceding class, viz. *flut flut-en, kost* (= L. *gus-tu-s*) *kost-en*, and further every substantive ending in -*heit* or -*keit*.³—(*e*) All abstract nouns in -*ung*, which, however far we go back, appear to have been distinguished from masculines of similar formation by being shifted to the weak declension (O.H.G. nomin. sg. -*unga*).—(*f*) One noun of female relationship: Go. *svistar*, pl. *svistrjus*; O.H.G. *swëster*, pl. *swëster*; but G. *schwester schwester-n*.—(*g*) Lastly, at any period, any feminine noun borrowed from a foreign language, from O.H.G. *phlanza phlanzūn, līra līrūn, kirihha kirihhūn* (G. *pflanze-n, leier-n, kirche-n*), down to the latest and contemporary words, as *universität-en, photographie-n*, etc., etc.—In short, this termination was used for every feminine, unless it originally possessed and kept, or subsequently adopted a metaphonical plural⁴; and, since these two exceptional cases hardly apply to more than forty nouns, the weak plural having spread here as elsewhere, the termination -*en* or -*n* may be deemed the specific and characteristic exponent for the plural of feminine German nouns.

III. **Neuters.**—Neuter stems in I.-E. -*on*-, which naturally could never have an ending -*s* in the plural, regularly dropped their plural-exponent -*a* in West Germanic, and, like the masculines and feminines, kept the bare nasal as a plural-sign. They are few in number and did not increase. We need but mention the three Germanic words: Go. *áugō áugōn-a*, O.H.G. *ouga*

---

¹ M.H.G. already *ërden*, though many nouns of this class are kept unaltered in M.H.G.: *gābe* (gift), pl. *gābe*, not *gäben*.
² *Supra* 87. Beware of confounding such nouns with stems in -*ī* = -*in*-.
³ Cf. *supra* 109, I. and 136.
⁴ Indeed, it has even often replaced the metaph. pl., since every stem in -*ī*- ought to have a metaph. plural, *infra* 146, II.

ougun, G. *auge auge-n*; Go. *áusō áusōn-a*, O.H.G. *ōra ōrun*, G. *ohr ohr-en*; Go. *haírt-ō haírt-ōn-a*, O.H.G. *hërza hërzun*, G. *herz herzen*.[1]

Summing up the results, we find that the plural in *-en* gained no ground in the neuter, though it influenced the masculine to a large extent, and was quite overwhelming in the feminine gender.

§ 4. *Plurals in -e without metaphony.*

(143) This class was originally large, but became reduced to scanty dimensions by the gradual influence of analogy: it may be said to exclude all feminine nouns,[2] with the exception of a few words in *-sal* and *-nisz*, which moreover were shifted to the feminine gender and did not originally belong to it; all original feminines adopted the weak plural, whereas masculines and neuters generally gave way to the analogy of the metaphonical plural.

I. **Masculines.**—Final *-e* in the G. pl. is the exact equivalent of the E. *-s* (*-es*)-plural,[3] with but this difference, that English extended the *s* after the analogy of the cases in which it had been kept, whereas German suppressed it everywhere after the analogy of the cases in which it had become voiced and been dropped: in other words, the E. pl. *days* being I.-E. **dhoghôs* and Preg. **δαӡόs*, the G. pl. *tage* no less clearly suggests I.-E. **dhoghōs* unaccented, changed to Preg. **δαӡōz*, whilst Go. *dagos* of course may represent either the one or the other form. O.H.G. in consequence has sg. *tag* = Go. *dag-s*, and pl. *tagā* = Go. *dagōs*; but, as early as O.H.G., the final vowel was shortened, thus *taga*, later on changed to the duller sound of *tag-e*, where the *-e* was mistaken for the actual plural-ending. So also: L. *armus* (flank), of which the regular pl. is **armōs*, G. *arm arm-e*; Gr. πάτος (path), regular pl. **πάτως*, G. *pfad pfad-e*; L. *calamus*, G. *halm halm-e*; Sk. *çaphás*

---

[1] Go. *namō* has been shifted to the msc., and O.H.G. *wanga* (G. *wange*), to the fm. On the other hand, *ende end* is an old msc. in *-yo-* (Sk. *ántya-s*).

[2] The regular plurals of *erde*, *königin*, etc., have been seen to be **erde*, **königinne*, etc., like *tage* to *tag*. But they have disappeared.

[3] And, therefore, of the so-called Gr. and L. second declension, *supra* 139, I.

(hoof), pl. çaphás, G. huf¹ huf-e; Sk. çrutás (heard), pl. çrutás, G. laut (sound) laut-e, etc.²

Had this class retained all the nouns which would regularly have been comprised in it, that is to say, all the German substantives which etymologically belong to the same suffix-formations as Gr. and L. nouns of the so-called second declension, it would have been an extremely rich one. But it was quite overwhelmed by the influence of the metaphonical class ³ and is now reduced to about sixty nouns, whereof:—a half, roughly speaking, may be traced back, with certainty or at least great probability, to I.-E. stems in -ŏ- (pl. -ōs), in which therefore this formation must be deemed primitive;—a few others are of undefined structure, as *hund* (dog), which may be a secondary derivative, with suff. -tó-, from the I.-E. stem *kun- (I.-E. *kun-tó-s, Preg. *hun-ða-z), or perhaps a mere corruption from the originally consonantal stem *kun- (Sk. çván- çun-, Gr. κύων κυν-ός), in which latter case the pl. in -e is analogical ⁴;—and, lastly, words borrowed from L. (*grad, punkt*), to which the plural in -e was applied by analogy.

English has nothing resembling this formation: *people* is not a plural, but a collective singular; and, besides, the word is not a Germanic one.

II. **Neuters.**—In this class the neuters correspond like the masculines to the second Gr. and L. declension, the more so since here there was no possibility of an *s*-plural. The type is I.-E. *yugó-m, pl. *yugá, Sk. *yugá-m yugá*, Gr. ζυγό-v ζυγά, L. *jugu-m juga*, Preg. *juká-m *jukō, whence Go. *juk juka*: final Preg. -ō ought to have become O.H.G. -ŭ, or to have been dropped, according to a well-known distinction⁵; but, in point of fact, it was dropped everywhere, after the analogy of cases where it disappeared regularly, and we find O.H.G. *joh*, pl. *joh*, *wort*, pl. *wort* (cf. Go. *vaúrd vaúrd-a*=L. *verbum verba*), *jār*, pl.

---

[1] O.H.G. *huof*, which presupposes a Preg. *hófaz*=Sk. *çâphas*.
[2] It is clear that such a formation cannot, any more than the plural in -*en*, admit of metaphony.
[3] *Infra* 146, I. The Southern dialects have gone so far as to create the plurals *täg(e)*, *ärm(e)*, and the like almost throughout.
[4] Such it is certainly in *herzog-e* for *herzog-en*, supra 141, 2 and 5.
[5] *Supra* 34, § 1, II.

jār, fuir, pl. *fuir* (G. *feuer*, pl. *feuer*), and a great many similar plurals.[1]

This equivocal plural type subsisted during the whole O.H.G. and nearly the whole M.H.G. period: a circumstance which must have strongly favoured the analogical shifting of neuter nouns to the metaphonical plural-formation in *-er*.[2] But, though this shifting was carried out on a large scale, M.H.G. in its later period also exhibits a tendency to add a final *-e* to these plurals, under the obvious influence, either of the preceding masculine nouns, or of the demonstratives and adjectives which occasionally accompany the neuter plural[3]; thus, the formation gives Mod. G. *joch joch-e, wort wort-e, jahr jahr-e, bein bein-e*,[4] etc. Besides the greater part of neuter collectives with pref. *ge-*, nouns in *-nisz* (formerly masculine), and nouns in *-sal* = I.-E. *-tlo-*, contemporary German comprises under this head about fifty neuter nouns, which according to their etymology may be divided as follows:—a few which immediately correspond to neuter nouns of second Gr. and Latin declension, as *schwein* = L. *suīnum* (adjective), *werk* = Gr. ἔργον, *recht* = L. *rectum*;—a great many nouns of possibly the same origin, as *thor* (door), which would be Gr. *θύρον*, cf. the fm. θύρᾱ, or *rosz*, which can scarcely be anything but Preg. **hrossam* (cf. E. *horse*), pl. *thor-e ross-e*;—some words which doubtless underwent an analogical shifting, as nt. *heer* = O.H.G. *heri* = Go. msc. *harji-s, knie* = Go. *kniu* = L. *genu, salz* = L. msc. *sāl* = **sald*;— lastly, a few borrowed nouns, *pferd* (horse), *pfund*, nt. *kreuz* (cross) = L. fm. *crux, fest* (feast), etc.

---

[1] Metaphony, of course, cannot occur here, and,- in fact, appears nowhere, but in words which already show it in the singular, that is to say, in words of other classes which were analogically transferred into this; namely stems in *-i-*: *meer* = L. *mare* = **mari*, pl. *meer-e* = L. *mari-a*; and the neuter collectives, *gestirn* = *g, stirn-e*, cf. *supra* 96, I.

[2] *Supra* 80, 137, and *infra* 147: thus *wort* had a pl. *wort-e*, but also a pl. *wört-er*, both exactly synonymous, though now a slight difference in meaning is observed between them.

[3] In such a combination as *diese wort* (these words), the final *-e* of *diese* naturally intruded into *wort-e*.

[4] The old plural, like the singular, survives in numeral locutions (*vier pfund, zehntausend pferd*), because here there is no ambiguity. So also in popular English (*thirty year*): cf. Wright, *Dialect of Windhill*, 337. And even currently, *ten pounds*, but *a ten-pound note*.

This very important class in German is represented in English by only three plurals formed without -s: deer, pl. deer, O.E. dēor dēor, O.H.G. tior tior, G. thier thier-e; sheep, pl. sheep, O.E. scēap scēap, G. schaf-e; swine, pl. swine, O.E. swīn swīn, O.H.G. swīn swīn,[1] G. schwein-e; though the double (sg. and pl.) sense of E. hair might well be due to its having been a primitive neuter invariable in the plural number, cf. Mod. G. haar haar-e.

§ 5. *Metaphonical plurals with or without an -e.*

(144) Here, an apparent likeness, at first sight, between the English and German plurals may be said to further emphasize the curious and constant contrast which keeps the two languages apart. German has a great many **metaphonical plurals**, Old English had some, and English has preserved six, which correspond exactly to six German metaphonical plurals: *man men, foot feet, goose geese, tooth teeth, mouse mice, louse lice*; cf. G. *männ-er*,[2] *füsz-e, gäns-e, zähn-e, mäus-e, läus-e*. And, notwithstanding all these coincidences, the English and German metaphonical plurals must be traced back, respectively, to quite a different origin, as having nothing in common but the form, and corresponding only by accident. This statement, strange and paradoxical as it appears, will prove clear and natural to any reader who bears in mind the chronological relation of the two metaphonies, namely, that the English metaphony is much older than the German, and therefore must have been occasioned, in primitive O.E., by some suffix-syllables which in this remote period could *not yet* produce it in O.H.G., whereas later, that is, when German metaphony took place, these same syllables, being then completely dropped, could *no longer* produce it.

Hence, the E. metaphony is the proper characteristic of the plurals of consonantal stems, while the German metaphony takes its origin from the declension of stems in *-i-*. Both points are easily verified.—A consonantal stem Preg. **fôt-* (foot) is nomin. sg. **fôt-s*, pl. **fôt-iz* = I.-E. **pôd-ĕs*. Now, in primitive

---

[1] Also, though late and rare, *swin-ir, tior-ir*, cf. *infra* 147.
[2] Only in this word the G. ending differs, cf. *infra* 147, 4.

O.E., the *i* in the termination causes metaphony in the stem, and we have pl. *fēti*, whence historical *fēt*. Nothing of the sort can happen in O.H.G.: the *ō* remains unaltered in its O.H.G. form *uo* (dat. pl. *fuoʒ-um*), so that, after the plural-ending had vanished, the nomin. pl. must have been **fuoʒ*, exactly like the nomin. sg. (cf. the pl. *man* of O.H.G. *man*). Afterwards, the word analogically passes to the declension of stems in *-i-*, and we have O.H.G. pl. *fuoʒ-i*. Finally, after many more centuries, that is, in M.H.G., the new ending produces metaphony in the stem, whence Mod. G. *füsz-e*.—Let us now take a primitive stem in *-i-*. Why should it not exhibit metaphony in the E. plural? Plainly because it has it already in the singular, so that the stem-vowel in the plural cannot differ from the stem-vowel in the singular. A Preg. sg. **ʒastiz* is **ʒastiz* in the plural: then, O.E. *ĭ* in **ʒastiz* occasions the metaphony in the stem, and disappears, whence O.E. sg. *giest*, E. *guest*; now, whatever else may become of the plural, whether O.E. regular **giest-e*, or analogical *giest-as*, E. *guest-s*, the stem-vowel appears the same in both numbers. But, on the contrary, in O.H.G., the final *ĭ*-syllable had vanished long before it could cause metaphony in the stem, the word thus being sg. *gast*, pl. **gastī*; in the latter, final *ī* is shortened, **gasti*, whereupon it produces metaphony, *gesti*; and thus comes the contrast which is still seen in *gast gäst-e*.

(145) A. English metaphony: consonantal stems.

I. Masculines.—The I.-E. stem **pód-* (foot) is declined Gr. sg. πούς πώς = **πώδ-ς, pl. πόδ-ες; on the other hand, we learn from Sk. sg. *pád* and pl. *pád-as* that the long vowel in the nomin. sg. may extend to the other cases, as, for instance, to the nomin. pl., which might equally well be Gr. **πῶδ-ες: this is what happened in Preg., where we have sg. **fôt-s*, pl. **fôt-iz*.

In consequence, such languages as admit of an early metaphony, viz. O.N. and O.E., agree in showing here a metaphony of the plural stem: *fōt-r, fœt-r* (long œ); *fōt, fēt*, whence E. *foot, feet*. So also, we have an I.-E. stem **dónt- *dént- *dṇt-*, meaning "tooth," Sk. *dánt-*, Gr. ὀδούς = **ὀδοντ-ς, L. *dēn-s* = **dent-s*, etc.: the form **dónt-s* produced Preg. **tánþ-s*, pl. **tánþ-iz*, whence O.E. *tōð tēð*, E. *tooth teeth*. The third plural

of this class is due to analogy; for it is primitively a stem in
-o-, a secondary derivative from I.-E. *man-u- (man, Sk. mán-
u-s), thus I.-E. *man-u-o-s *manwos (human, man), whence
Preg. *mannaz, O.E. man, mon, of which the plural is men =
*manniz, just as if the sg. were consonantal, E. man men. The
compound woman = wīf-man, pl. women = M.E. wim-men = wīf-
men, afterwards follows without difficulty.

II. Feminines.[1]—I.-E. had a stem *mūs- (mouse), nomin. sg.
*mûs = *mús-s, nomin. pl. *mûs-ĕs, Gr. μῦς μύ-ες, L. mūs mūr-ēs,
consequently Preg. *mûs *mûs-iz, exactly represented by O.E.
mūs mȳs, whence E. mouse mice. The same formation holds
for louse lice, though the word has no acknowledged kin.[2] Gr.
sg. χήν, pl. χῆν-ες = *χάνσ-ες, similarly points to a consonantal
stem *gháns- (goose), sg. *gháns, pl. *gháns-ĕs,[3] Preg. *ȝáns
*ȝáns-iz, O.E. gōs (= *gŏns) gēs, whence E. goose geese. And so
we have done with the English metaphonical plurals.

(146) B. German metaphony: stems in -i-.
I. Masculines.—1. The I.-E. stems in -ĭ- assume the normal
form -ĕy- before the plural-ending -ĕs: I.-E. *ghos-ti-s *ghos-
tĕy-ĕs, Sk. agní-s (fire) agnáy-as, Gr. μάντι-s (prophet) μάντεις =
*μάντεες = *μάντεy-ες, L. hosti-s hostēs = *hostĕĕs = *hostĕy-ĕs, con-
sequently Preg. *ȝasti-z *ȝastīz, Go. gast-s gasteis, O.H.G. gast
gesti, G. gast gäste. To this class, in which the etymology
strictly requires the metaphonical process, belong such words
as balg (E. bellow-s) bälg-e, sang säng-e (Go. balg-s balgeis,
saggv-s saggveis), most probably also schlag schläg-e, wurf würf-e,
and a few others.

2. As early however as O.H.G. this plural begins to spread:
first, to stems in -u-, Go. sunus sunjus, but O.H.G. sunu suni,

---

[1] Neuter nouns, since they never could have had an ending -iz, do not
enter into the question.
[2] The c in mice and lice is an artificial spelling, intended to indicate a
voiceless sibilant sound. The two remaining plurals in -ce have nothing to
do with metaphony: dice is a mere graphic variety for *dies (cf. twice =
twies, supra 124, II., and the spelling ice = O.E. is = O.H.G. is = G. eis), the
ordinary pl. of the word die borrowed from French; and pence is merely the
regular *penn(i)s, which lost its vowel when rapidly uttered. From this
again a new plural, some sixpence-s.
[3] Which likewise occurs, but accompanied by a derivative suffix, in Sk.
háns-a-s (swan, goose), and L. anser (goose) = *hans-er.

now *sohn söhn-e*; next, to some stems which formerly ended in -o-, Go. *ast-s* (= Gr. ὄζος = *ὄσδο-ς) *astōs*, but O.H.G. *ast esti*, G. *ast äste*; to consonantal stems, O.H.G. *zand zendi*, *fuoʒ fuoʒʒi*, G. *zahn zähne*, *fusz füsze*, etc. As the language grows older, the tendency grows stronger: O.H.G. still keeps *stuol stuola*, *hals halsa*, *scalk scalka*, *slāf slāfa*, whereas Mod. G. has *stuhl stühle*, *hals hälse*, *schalk schälke*, *schlaf schläfe*, *wolf wölfe*, etc. In short, the metaphonical plural has become the prevailing formation for masculine monosyllables.[1]

3. No less early it is occasionally found in some dissyllabic nouns ending with a liquid: O.H.G. *zahar* (tear), pl. *zahari*, now fm., with the metaphony transferred to the sg., and a new weak plural, *zähre zähre-n*; O.H.G. *aphul* (E. *apple*), pl. *ephili*, now *apfel äpfel*. Here the plural-ending is dropped altogether, and there remains no other plural-sign but the metaphony: in consequence of which, metaphony was mistaken for a plural-sign and assumed this function in many other words. Thus, the pl. to *nagel* (nail) is still M.H.G. *nagel-e* = Preg. *naʒlōz*, but now *nägel*; so also Preg. *fuʒlaz* (bird), pl. *fuʒlōz*, has become G. *vogel vögel*. Further, in nouns of male relationship: O.H.G. *bruoder bruoder*, *fater fater-a* [2]; but G. *bruder brüder*, *vater väter*. Further, *hammer hämmer*, *acker äcker*, etc.; then, for *ofen* (Gr. ἱπνό-ς), *boden* (E. *bottom*), *hafen* (a late borrowing), were formed the metaphonical plurals *öfen*, *böden*, *häfen*, etc., whence, for many words ending with a liquid or a nasal, metaphony alone is now considered to be the proper plural-sign.

4. On the other hand, it may be seen from *nagele* above that M.H.G. possessed a great many nouns with unaccented final syllable, which formed their plural without metaphony, so that, the plural-ending -*e* being once dropped, the pl. became exactly like the sg. Several nouns afterwards swelled this class: either such as were already metaphonical in the sg. (*gärtner*); or such as contained a vowel which was no longer capable of

---

[1] It must be understood that, if the vowel is not capable of metaphony in M.H.G. and Mod. G. (*berg*, *weg*), or if it never was (*fisch*), then, of course, both formations are outwardly identical, though historically distinguishable.

[2] It need scarcely be observed that this again is an irregular plural borrowed from stems in I.-E. -*o*-.

metaphony in M.H.G. or Mod. G. (*degen*)[1]; or, lastly, such as deserted a class in which no metaphony could primitively take place (*laden*).[2] Now, this type likewise, though partly influenced by the metaphonical class, held its own and even increased: whence the pl. always like the sg. in *adler* = O.H.G. *adel-ar* "noble eagle," *sommer* (cf. *winter*, where metaphony is quite impossible), and generally in the nouns, denoting agent, in *-er*, *bohr-er*, etc.[3]

II. Feminines.—1. The I.-E. plural, in stems ending in *-i-*, is the same for feminine or masculine nouns: cf. Gr. pl. πόλεις like μάντεις, L. pl. *vestēs* like *hostēs*, etc. G. *haut* (skin) *häute* may be said therefore to reproduce the L. *cutis cutēs*. It is chiefly in abstract nouns with suff. *-ti-*, that the process is seen: O.H.G. *maht mahti*, G. *macht mächte*, and so also *kraft kräfte, kunst künste*, etc. A great many of them, however, have been seen to have passed to the weak declension.[4]

2. An early confusion, as often noted, took place between the stems in *-ti-* and the stems in (primitive) *-tu-* : whence G. *luft* (air) *lüfte, lust lüste*, etc.

3. Moreover, in O.H.G., the feminines, as well as the masculines, in *-u-* had adopted the *-i*-declension: O.H.G. *hant* (= Go. *hand-u-s*) *henti*,[5] G. *hand hände*.

4. This formation was extended to some fm. monosyllables ending either with a consonant or a long vowel: *gans gänse, magd mägde, maus mäuse, laus läuse, nacht nächte, kuh kühe, sau säue*. In a quite different class, the analogy of *väter* and *brüder* gave rise to *mütter* and *töchter*, the only feminines which show no other plural-sign but metaphony.

5. In spite of this slight expansion, the weak plural, as stated above, got the upper hand, so that the feminine metaphonical plural is now reduced to about forty representatives.[6]

[1] F. *dague* imported into late M.H.G.
[2] *Supra* 141, 4: pl. *laden*, but also the analogical *läden*.
[3] In the neuters with similar endings, *feuer, fenster*, and the diminutives in *-chen* and *-lein*, the result is naturally the same, the cause being slightly different, though indeed of the same kind, *supra* 143, II.
[4] *Supra* 142, II. 4.
[5] M.H.G. has also the weak declension, which still survives in the locution *vor-hand-en* (ready, to be disposed of), literally "before the hands."
[6] For the sake of completeness may be mentioned a few irregular though

§ 6. *Metaphonical plurals in -er.*

(147) Unless a neuter noun forms its plural in *-e* or *-en* without metaphony, its regular plural-sign must be metaphony and an ending *-er*. Such is the case for the great majority of neuter nouns. After all that has been said of this curious word-class,[1] very few further details are here required.

1. Let us consider the Gr. nt. βρέφ-ος (child, young animal), gen. βρέφους = βρέφεος = *βρέφ-εσ-ος, pl. βρέφη = βρέφεα = *βρέφ-εσ-α. From a nearly identical root[2] might have been derived an I.-E. nt. *gólbh-os, pl. *gólbh-es-ā, which would become Preg. *kálbaz, pl. *kálb-iz-ō, O.H.G. *chalb*, pl. *chelb-ir(-u) chelb-ir*, G. *kalb kälber*. So also, most likely, in *lamb lembir, hrind hrindir, huon huonir*, G. *lamm lämmer, rind rinder, huhn hühner, ei eier*, etc., the metaphonical plural is attributable to an I.-E. -es-suffix.

2. O.E. has been seen to possess the equivalent forms, *cealfru, lombru*. The pl. of *cild*, however, is *cild*, and *cildru* is exceptional. The latter type, being, as it were, pluralized anew by the addition of the weak plural-ending, is now *child-r-en*, the only survival from this nt. class.

3. While English lost this characteristic formation, it became largely diffused even in the earliest period of O.H.G.: thus, from sg. *grab, rad, holz, krūt*, etc., the pl. *grebir, redir, holzir, krūtir*, etc., now *gräb-er, räd-er, hölz-er, kräut-er*, etc. This ending gradually gained ground and was considered the regular one, whence Mod. G. *bänd-er, wört-er, büch-er, häus-er*,[3] etc., etc.

---

easily explained forms: (1) the fm., with un-metaphonical pl., *drang-sal* and *trüb-sal* (formerly either nt. or msc.), and the fm. in *-nisz* (as *kennt-nisz*), formerly either msc. or nt.; (2) on the contrary, four metaphonical neuters, two of which, at least, are old masculines (*chor chöre, flosz flösze*), whereas the two others may well proceed from analogy (*rohr röhre, kloster klöster* borrowed from L.). Further details belong to ordinary grammar.

[1] *Supra* 80, 90 (VIII.) and 117 (I. 4).

[2] It is only an approximation, the vocalic grade being different, and Germanic showing an *l* instead of the Gr. *r*; but it must be understood that Gr. βρέφος is quoted here only as a representative of an I.-E. neuter class which is known to have comprised a great many primary stems.

[3] O.H.G. still possesses side by side the plurals *hūs* and *hūsir, bant* and *bantir*. In German, if preserved at all (*bande* and *bänder*), the doublets always assume different shades of meaning.

4. The few masculines which follow this declension are only slightly irregular: *irr-thum* and *reich-thum*, the only nouns in *-thum* which have kept the msc. gender, borrowed their plurals from the other nouns in *-thum* which had been shifted to the nt. gender (*supra* 109, II.); msc. *wald* is probably an old neuter, Gr. nt. ἄλσος (forest); msc. *Gott* is certainly a primitive neuter, for Go. *guþ* is nt. in the meaning "false god," and O.H.G. *abgot* has already the pl. *abgotir*; msc. *mann*, the regular pl. being *mann*,[1] adopted an analogical plural to that of *Gott*, on account of "God" and "men" being frequently opposed to each other; and the same is probably the case with msc. *geist* (mind) = Sk. nt. *hêdas* (anger), to which msc. *leib* (body) was very often opposed; the other words of this class (msc. *rand, ort, wurm, dorn, bösewicht*) are quite insignificant.

Section III.

CASES.

(148) Though German preserves twice as many cases as English, it has only four, and these moreover are often represented by the same external form. The **nominative** was the subject of our preceding section. Here we have to examine the **accusative, genitive,** and **dative,** in both numbers.

§ 1. *Accusative.*

(149) Either primitively, or more commonly owing to phonetic decay, the Preg. accusative was, almost everywhere, either like, or at least scarcely different from, the nominative: hence it afterwards was quite blended with this case, in English everywhere, and almost everywhere in German.

I. Singular.—1. Even in I.-E., the accusative of neuter nouns is always and everywhere like the nominative.[2]

2. In msc. and fm. nouns, the accusative-exponent is an ending *-m*, which remains *-m* if preceded by a vowel,[3] and becomes

---

[1] Kept in numeral locutions: *vierzehn mann*.
[2] Gr. τὸ ζυγ*ὸ*ν, γένος, κρέας, etc.; L. *jugum, genus, caput*.
[3] Gr. ἵππο-ν, χώρᾱ-ν, πόλι-ν; L. *equo-m, terra-m, manu-m*.

-m̭ if following a consonant.[1] Since, in either case, the Germanic laws require the final nasal to be dropped, the accusative, in most Gothic declensions, will be seen not to differ from the nominative except by suppressing the nominative-sign -s[2]; and, since this -s again has been lost in later languages, no English declension, and scarcely any German one, keeps a distinct form for the two cases.

3. In one class, however, the two cases are to be distinguished, not of course by the accusative-ending, which is completely lost everywhere, but by the form of the declensional stem: namely, in the L. type *hom-ō hom-in-em, leg-iŏ leg-iŏn-em*, where the *n* has been seen to disappear in the nomin. sg. and to persist in every other case; in other words, in the Germanic so-called **weak declension**. Gothic answers the L. forms with nomin. *gum-a*, acc. *gum-an, han-a* (cock) *han-an*; and, in fm. nouns, *tugg-ō tugg-ōn, háuh-ei háuh-ein,* etc. O.E. has likewise: *gum-a gum-an, ox-a ox-an* (Sk. *ukš-á ukš-án-am*); fm. *tung-e tung-an, eorð-a eorð-an.* Lastly O.H.G.: *han-o han-un, has-o has-un, bot-o bot-un, herizog-o herizog-un,* etc.; *zung-a zung-ūn, bluom-a bluom-ūn, sunna sunnūn, diorna* (now *dirne* "lass") *diornūn,* etc. But this regular formation of the weak accusative suffered from several encroachments.

(*a*) As the accusatives everywhere else were like the nominatives, M.E. effaced the distinction in this class also: E. *ox, tongue, earth,* etc.

(*b*) In the feminines in -*ī* = -*īn*, O.H.G. has already suppressed it, that is to say, the form is optionally either *hōhī* or *hōhīn* in the nomin. and the acc., whereas Mod. G. has but *höhe* in either case, *höhen* being confined to the plural. In other feminines M.H.G. still preserves the distinction: acc. sg. *die zungen,* etc. But, either from the analogy of feminines belonging to a different class (*erde, gabe*), where the two cases could not differ, or because such a form in the sg. was liable to an

---

[1] Gr. πόδ-α, ποιμέν-α; L. *pĕd-em, homin-em.*—For the first case, compare Go. *vulf* = L. *lupu-m* (nomin. *vulf-s* = L. *lupu-s*); for the second, Go. *fōt-u* = *fōt-um* = L. *pĕd-em* = *pĕd-m*.

[2] And not to differ from it at all, when the nomin. has no case-sign (*supra* 137), as in Go. *aírþa* (earth), acc. *aírþa* (L. *terra terra-m*).

NOUNS. 251

undesirable confusion with the plural (acc. pl. likewise *die zungen*), Mod. G. confined the ending -*n* to the latter number, and the sg. is *die zunge, frau, sonne, taube, dirne*, nominative and accusative alike, in all feminine nouns.

(c) A similar confusion being impossible in masculine nouns,[1] their declension remained by far the purer: most of them have kept their regular accusative sg. (*ochs-en, bote-n, hase-n, bauer-n*), indeed, it has even extended to some new words (*christ-en, philosoph-en, planet-en*).[2] Yet a few are already known to have been shifted to another declension, whence *den hahn, den herzog*, etc. It happened even more frequently that a masculine noun kept the weak declension in the plural, but assimilated its accusative singular to the nominative; then, of course, the weak forms are as completely lost in the whole sg., as they are in feminine nouns: thus we have pl. *die pfauen* = L. *pāvōnes*, but no longer acc. sg. *den *pfauen* = L. *pāvōnem*, the identity, as it were, in (*der*) *vogel* = (*den*) *vogel* having here produced a similar identity in (*der*) *pfau* = (*den*) *pfau*, etc.; and further, though a German correctly says *die bauern* and *den bauern*, and also *die nachbaren*, he will say *den nachbar* like *den mann*. The tendency to assimilation proved here stronger than the historical system of accidence, as shown even by the plural-formation.[3]

II. Plural.—1. The accusative of neuter nouns is even in I.-E., and everywhere, exactly like the nominative.

2. In the msc. and fm. gender, the exponent for the acc. pl. was everywhere an ending -*ns* (Sk. *áçvān* = **áçva-ns*, Gr. ἵππους = **ἵππον-s*, L. *lupōs* = **lupŏ-ns*), which is still visible in the Gothic forms, viz. nomin. *vulfōs*, acc. *vulfa-ns*.[4] But, either after the analogy of the neuter nouns, or because the nomin. and acc. of several declensions had become alike, owing to a peculiar phonetic treatment of the nasal when following a long

---

[1] Because acc. sg. *den boten* was clearly distinct from acc. pl. *die boten*.
[2] Cf. *supra* 141, 3.
[3] The masculines of this class, that is to say, weak in the plural, but without nasal ending in the singular, are about thirty: for a list, the reader may refer to any grammar.
[4] Cf. *supra* 128, I.: Go. þái = τοί (οἱ), and þans = τούς.

vowel,[1] Germanic speakers at an early period took to using the former case for the latter,[2] so that they were blended together as early as O.E. and O.H.G., and still more so of course ten centuries later.

§ 2. *Genitive*.

(150) I. Singular.—The formation of the gen. sg. was rather complicated in I.-E., and probably even in Pregermanic; but it became analogically simplified in German and especially in English. In order to understand it thoroughly, it will suffice here to distinguish three main I.-E. terminations:—an exponent -*sŏ*, borrowed from the demonstratives, and used exclusively with stems ending in -*ŏ*- (second Gr. and L. declension), as I.-E. *wḷqŏ-s (wolf), gen. *wḷqĕ-sŏ (cf. Gr. λύκοιο = *λυκο-σιο), whence Preg. nomin. *wulfa-z, gen. *wulfi-za;—an ending -*ŏs* or -*ĕs*, which appears very clearly in consonantal stems, Gr. ποδ-ός κυν-ός, L. *ped-is nec-is*;—lastly, a simple ending -*s*, which results from the contraction of the preceding exponent with the final I.-E. -*ā* of feminine stems, Gr. ἡμέρᾱ ἡμέρᾱ-ς, archaic L. *escā-s* for classical *escæ*, etc.—Observing at the outset that every one of these exponents contained an *s*, let us enquire what has become of them in Germanic.

1. German.—(*a*) In the last class, the *s* was but seldom preceded by the accent[3]: hence, West Germanic dropped it and the genitive here differed but slightly from the nominative: thus Go. *áirþa*, gen. *áirþōs*; but O.H.G. *ërda*, gen. *ërda ërdu ërdo*. Since, on the other hand, feminines in -*ā* formed a majority of feminine nouns, analogy favoured this assimilation, so that the genitive of fm. nouns, though still distinct from the nominative in a great many O.H.G. words,[4] finally became identical with it and the accusative. Weak feminines offered a stronger and longer resistance, but gave way in their turn:

---

[1] Go. nomin.-acc. pl. *áirþōs* (earths), *tuggōns* (tongues).
[2] Cf. the Gr. acc. τὰς πόλεις, the L. nomin.-acc. *manūs*, *ovēs*, etc.
[3] The first Gr. declension, for instance, chiefly consists of nouns accented on the penult; nouns accented on the last syllable are here in a minority.
[4] Namely, for instance, in stems in -*ti*-, the *i* here being kept in the gen. and causing metaphony: Go. *anst-s* (favour), gen. *ansteis* (cf. Sk. *agni-s* "fire," gen. *agnêṣ*); O.H.G. *anst*, gen. *ensti*.

NOUNS. 253

O.H.G. *dëro zungūn*, M.H.G. *dëre zungen*, but Mod. G. *der zunge, der frau*, etc.[1]

(b) Whilst the weak feminines thus everywhere lost the *n* of the oblique cases, the weak masculines preserved and even propagated it. In fact, here, the genitival *s* was likewise preceded by an unaccented vowel; and, in consequence, from the whole genitival ending, Gr. ποιμέν-ος, L. *homin-is*, Go. *hanin-s*, the *n* alone survived, the genitive being henceforth exactly like the accusative, G. *des ochsen, des boten, des herrn*,[2] etc. Now, we have seen that this class occasionally underwent a slight decay: in the same way as acc. *den hahn, den herzog, den pfau, den nachbar*, etc., there were created the genitives *hahn-s, herzog-s, pfau-es, nachbar-s*, etc., with a genitival -*s* imported from the following class; an analogy which likewise reached and completely swept away the weak declension of neuter stems, *auge-s, ohr-(e)s*, instead of O.H.G. *oug-en, ōr-en*. As to the rare genitives in -*en-s, name-n-s, herz-en-s*, we must beware of classing them with the Go. genitives *nam-in-s, hairt-in-s*; for O.H.G. and even M.H.G. drop the final -*s* here as everywhere else. Gen. *namen-s* proceeds from the nomin. *namen*, which is known to be an analogical type[3]; whereas *herzens* is an hybrid product of two cumulative genitive-exponents (regular O.H.G. and M.H.G. *hërz-en*, and irregular Mod. G. *herz-es*), and *schmerzens*, a later imitation of the hybrid *herzens*.

(c) In the ending -*ĕ-sŏ*, the *s* often followed an accented vowel: I.-E. msc. *dhogh-é-sŏ, nt. *yug-é-sŏ, whence Go. *dag-i-s, juk-i-s*, G. *tag-s, joch-s*. The same was the case, very often, with the ending in consonantal stems: Sk. *pad-ás*, Gr. ποδ-ός,

---

[1] A gen sg. *frauen* is still found as late as Goethe, *Herm. und Doroth.*, IX. 123.
[2] *Supra* 149, 3. More precisely, the O.H.G. gen.-dat. is *hanin hanen*, while the acc. is *hanon hanun*; but this difference has become lost in the uniformity of unaccented syllables.—The reason must now have become obvious, why weak masculines have all cases alike both in the sg. and pl.: it is because, properly speaking, they have nowhere kept any case-sign or number-exponent whatever.
[3] *Supra* 141, 4. The spoken language even went farther: then were once created the genitives *knabens, rabens*, etc.; but they could hardly survive, since there was no nominative *knaben, *raben (cf. E. *raven*) to support them.

O.E. *fōt-es*. Hence, particularly in all the masculine and neuter nouns which correspond to the 2nd Gr. and L. declension,—a remarkably rich class,—West Germanic may be expected to have, and actually has, an ending *-es*, O.E. *dæg-es*, *word-es*, O.H.G. *tag-es*, *wort-es*; and this case-sign, which appeared to be a most convenient one, easily became diffused. Thus, O.H.G. has already *lamb-es*, *chalb-es*,[1] *gast-es*, *sun-es*, and even *fater-es* side by side with gen. *fater*. Next, this syllable *-es*, often reduced to a mere *-s*, was gradually considered to be the specific exponent of the gen. sg. for all neuter nouns without distinction, and for all masculine nouns, except those which either adopted or regularly retained the weak declension.

2. English.—The latter process proved still far more widely energetic in English. As early as O.E., every msc. and nt. noun, unless of the weak declension, has a gen. sg. in *-es* (*dæg-es*, *word-es*, *giest-es*, *wyrm-es*, *sun-es*,[2] *fōt-es*, *fædr-es* side by side with gen. *fæder*, *frēond-es*, *lomb-es*, etc.)[3]; whereas the feminine nouns are free from contamination, and preserve the old genitive, which differs but slightly from the nominative (*cearu* "care," *sorg* "sorrow," *lyft* "air," gen. *ceare*, *sorge*, *lyfte*), and the weak declension, in the three genders, retains its nasal exponent (gen. *oxan*, *tungan*, *ēagan* = O.H.G. *ougen*): to sum up, O.E. is still much purer than Mod. German. But all these varieties soon disappeared: even Chaucer knows but little of a genitive formed without *-es*, which element, now spelled *'s*, is added to the nomin. sg. of any noun, including even feminine nouns (*mother's* after the analogy of *father's*, *queen's*, *wife's*, etc.), which theoretically ought not to have taken it, and never have taken it in German.[4] The syntax and use of this genitive belong to English grammar.

---

[1] It need scarcely be observed that the only regular form would be *chelbir (a dat. sg. *chelbir-e* occurs once) = Preg. *kalb̄-iz-az*, wherein final *s*, changed to *z*, was regularly dropped, and medial *s*, likewise changed to *z*, had become *r*; and so also, *lembir*, etc. But *lamb-es* (now *lamm-s*) was derived immediately from the nomin. *lamb*.

[2] Rarer however than the regular *suna*, and much later.

[3] E. *day's*, *word's*, *guest's*, *worm's*, *son's*, *father's*, *friend's*, *lamb's*, with this restriction however, that the genitive is now obsolete for nouns denoting anything but a man or woman.

[4] It must be noted, however, that in German also some feminine nouns

(151) II. Plural.—1. Even without investigating the formation of the I.-E. genitive plural, we are aware of the simple fact, that it always substitutes, for the ending of the nomin. pl., another ending with final nasal, either -ŏm or -ōm: Gr. ἵπποι (horses) ἵππων, ζυγά (yokes) ζυγῶν, πόδ-ες ποδ-ῶν, L. *ped-ēs ped-ŭm*, etc. This nasal having vanished, there remained a vocalic ending, not quite the same, to be sure, as that sounded in the final syllable of the nominative,[1] but not sufficiently dissimilar to prevent the two being blended together when the vowels were weakened ; and, since on the other hand the O.H.G. nomin. pl. in -*es* had everywhere lost its consonant, the two cases could no longer be distinguished from each other. Hence arose the constant likeness of nominative, accusative and genitive plural throughout the whole German declension.

2. It is a curious and singular exception, that English, poor as it is in declensional forms, should appear in this single case even richer than German ; for it has secured a distinct genitive plural, merely by transferring to the plural the case-sign of the genitive singular. German could do without it, because the article was a sufficient case-exponent; but English, having ceased to decline the article, would have been confined to the use of a preposition. Hence, the genitive of *child* being *child's*, it seemed a matter of course that that of *children* should similarly be *children's*.[2] Further, since in time almost every E. plural became provided with an *s*, this ending was deemed to represent at once both the number-exponent and the genitival *s*, the actual form being *fathers'*, *mothers'*, *sons'*, the only distinction from the nomin. pl. being in the spelling.

§ 3. *Dative*.

(152) I. Singular.—The Germanic so-called dative is in reality an old locative, which was formed by adding to the

adopted it, but only proper names, *Clara-s*, *Maria-s*, concurrently with *Mariä* (Lat.), *Marien* and *Mariens*.

[1] Go. *dagōs dagē, vaúrda vaúrdē, gasteis gastē*, etc. ; O.E. *dagas daga*, *word worda, giestas giesta*, etc. ; O.H.G. *tagā tago, wort worto, gesti gestio*, etc. (now, in both cases, *tage, worte, gäste*).

[2] We find the same process in Swedish, viz. nomin. sg. *fisk*, gen. *fisk-s*, nomin. pl. *fisk-ar*, gen. *fisk-ar-s*.

stem the I.-E. ending -*ĭ*. When the stem ends in a consonant, the case-sign is isolated and visible: Sk. *pád-i* (at the foot), Gr. ποδ-ί, L. *ped-e*[1] = **ped-ĭ*, etc. If the stem ends with a vowel, either -*ŏ*- or -*ā*, contraction gives a final diphthong: Sk. *áçvē* (to the horse) = **áçva-ĭ*, Gr. οἴκοι (at home), L. *humī* (on the ground) = *humoi*, Go. *vulfa* (to the wolf) = Preg. **wulfai*, etc. The whole of the modern formation may be said to proceed from these simple premises.

1. In feminines in -*ā*, the primitive diphthong still kept in Gothic (*airþa*, dat. *airþái*), became a simple vowel in O.E. (*cearu*, dat. *ceare*) and in O.H.G. (*ërda*, dat. *ërdu ërdo*), whereupon the final vowels, both in the nominative and the dative, were weakened to the same form: G. *erde*. Analogy completed the assimilation: the dative, as well as the genitive,[2] of feminine nouns, was everywhere blended with the nominative, even in stems in I.-E. -*ti*-, which formerly had a characteristic metaphonical dative,[3] and in the feminine weak declension, which, in consequence, no longer shows any trace of its old nasal element in any case of the singular.[4]

2. On the contrary, masculine nouns, inasmuch as they retained[5] or adopted the weak system, quite regularly exhibit the nasal as the sole remaining case-sign (Go. *han-in* "to the cock" = **han-in-ĭ*, cf. L. *hom-in-e*): whence we may say, that the dative, in the German weak masculine declension, differs from the nominative, and is identical with the accusative and genitive, thus *dem ochsen, dem herrn, dem bauern*, etc.

3. In the case of the other masculine and all neuter nouns, the influence of the dat. sg. in -*o-i* (2nd Gr. and L. declension) prevailed and formed a new termination. To the Preg. type **wulfai*, Go. *vulf-a* (nomin. *vulf-s*) corresponded in O.E. and

---

[1] Termed ablative; but really locative in such locutions as *in pede*, etc.
[2] Supra 150, 1 a.—The identity was regular in nouns denoting relationship: nomin. *muoter* = I.-E. **mātĕr*, dat. *muoter* = I.-E. **mātĕr-ĭ*.
[3] O.H.G. *anst* (favour), dat. *ensti* = Go. *anstái*.
[4] O.H.G. *dëru zungūn*, M.H.G. *dëre zungen*, G. *der zunge*. The last survivals of a fm. or nt. dat. in -*en* are found in such locutions as *auf erden* and *von herzen*.
[5] Cf. *supra* 150, 1 b. Of course, we have nt. *dem auge, dem herze*, msc. *dem hahn*, etc. for the reason explained above.

NOUNS. 257

O.H.G. a duller ending, respectively *wulf-e wolf-e*, which was dropped in English, but spread in German. Now, after the pattern of the regular datives, msc. *tag-e* = I.-E. **dhoghó-i, fisk-e* (also *fisk-a*), *stuol-e, stein-e*, nt. *johhe* = I.-E. **yugó-ĭ, wort-e* (also *wort-a*), *jār-e, lamb-e*,[1] etc., O.H.G. has the same types:— in masculine stems in *-i-*, *gast-e*, for **gesti* ;—in those in *-u-*, *sun-e* ;—in those ending with a consonant, *fater-e*, etc.[2] So this *-e* was added everywhere; but, being almost mute, it is now suppressed in dissyllables in which the accent rests on the first syllable (*dem vater, dem adler*), and may also be dropped in any other noun (*dem sohn, dem joch, dem lamm*). The main result is a dative which scarcely differs from the nominative in all classes except the weak declension.

II. Plural. — Several I.-E. cases in the plural number (instrumental, dative, ablative) are formed by adding to the stem a peculiar element, in which, though the vowel and final may vary, the initial is always a labial consonant: Sk. *-bhis, -bhyas*; Gr. (Homeric) *-φι, -φιν*; L. *-bos, -bus*. In Germanic, as well as in Balto-Slavonic, the initial labial is an *m*, and the form of the endings seems to have been *-mĭ* or *-mĭs, -mŭ* or *-mŭs*.[3] The initial *m* is the only sound we need lay stress upon, since the rest of the syllable naturally disappeared in the Germanic languages; and we find that, however far we go back, the case-sign for the dat. pl. is invariably an ending *-m*: Go. *daga-m, vaúrda-m, aírþō-m, gasti-m, sunu-m, brōþr-um*, etc.; O.E. *dagum, wordum, cearum, giestum, sunum, fœdrum*, etc.; O.H.G. *tagum* (*tagom*, whence also *tagon, tagun*), *wortum, ërdōm, gestim* (also *gestin* and *gesten*), *sunim* (instead of *sunum*, analogically assimilated to the preceding), *faterum, muoterum*, etc. English has altogether lost this form. M.H.G. completed the assimilation, by transferring to this case the plural-metaphony exhibited by the other cases, and, final *-m* being further regu-

---

[1] With the restriction mentioned in 150, 1 c; for, if the declension were quite pure, the dative ought to be **lembir* = **lamb-iz-i*.
[2] By the way, observe the remarkable purity of the O.E. datives *fēt, friend*, where the final *-ĭ* has caused metaphony (**fōt-ĭ, *frëund-ĭ*).
[3] Still in Mod. Russian: *slóv-o* (word), pl. *slov-á*, dat. pl. *slov-á-m(ŭ)*, instrum. pl. *slov-á-mi*, etc.

larly changed to -*n*,[1] the whole process may be summed up in the simple rule:

The dative plural is formed by adding an ending -*n* to the ordinary plural-form, unless this already ends in -*n*.[2]

---

[1] *Supra* 89, I. 1, in fine.

[2] It must be observed that a great many proper names, of feasts or places, are historically traced back to old dative cases, which have become invariable in this shape, because they were more frequently used than the corresponding nominatives; for it stands to reason that we should have more occasion for saying "about Easter-tide," or "he is in London," than for saying "Easter is a great feast," or "London lies on the Thames," etc.: whence, such German words as *Ostern* (E. merely *Easter* = O.E. *ēastre*), *Pfingsten*, *Weihnachten*, etc., geographical names as *Meyringen* (a very common type), etc. (In *Unterwalden*, the second term is a dat. pl. governed by the first term.) A parallel English type to *Meyringen* is *Canterbury*, the second term being the dat. sg. of *borough*, supra 65, 5.

CHAPTER III.

ADJECTIVES.

(153) Every **German adjective** is capable of **two declensions**, which, as is well known, are used in distinct syntactical combinations. Further, the **adjective**, when used as a **predicate**, is **invariable**, or incapable of receiving any exponent, either of gender, or number, or case : msc. sg. *der mann ist blind*; fm. *die frau ist blind*; nt. *das kind ist blind*; acc. *er machte ihn blind*; pl. *die männer sind blind*, etc.

The **English adjective is always invariable**: *a blind man, a blind girl, a blind dog, the blind men*, etc., like *the man is blind*, etc. Now, in order to understand how this twofold, or even threefold system could proceed from one and the same primitive declension, we must first distinguish the **declined** and **invariable adjective**.

Such a distinction, though already existing in Pregermanic, was quite unknown to the I.-E. language. The Sk., Gr. and L. adjective, for instance, agrees with the noun it qualifies, in whatever grammatical construction they may be found: L. *pater est bonus*, like *bonus pater*, etc. And, again, the declension of the adjective in these languages has no peculiar character, except that it is capable of the three genders; that is to say, an adjective is declined in the same way as a noun, provided they be of the same gender: Gr. καλός καλή καλόν, just like ἵππος κεφαλή ἔργον; L. *bonus bona bonum*, in the same way as *dominus terra jugum*, etc.[1]

---

[1] The adjectives we are here dealing with are only those which belong to the so-called (Gr. and L.) 2nd and 1st declension ; for this declension is the only one preserved for adjectives, in Germanic, and it has extended so far beyond its limits as to overwhelm any other : thus, the comparatives (G.

Hence we infer, at the outset, that Pregermanic has completely altered the primitive type, whereas English again shows not even the slightest trace of the Pregermanic declension. Let us now proceed to explain this simple evolution.

SECTION I.

DECLINED ADJECTIVE.

(154) The old I.-E. type *bonus bona bonum* is not dead in Germanic: it still survives in the invariable adjective. But, side by side with this ancient declension, analogy had created two other systems, which may be traced back to Pregermanic, and which survived into Mod. German, becoming in the latter the double, so-called **strong** and **weak**, **declension** of the adjective when used as an attribute to a following noun, viz. *blind-er mann*, and *der blind-e mann*.

The general rule for the use of either declension, in Go., O.E. and O.H.G., is nearly the same as in Mod. German, namely: if the adjective is not preceded by a demonstrative (article or the like), it supplies the place of the missing demonstrative, and assumes the demonstrative endings, or, in other words, the case-signs of the strong declension; but, if the demonstrative precedes, and sufficiently indicates the gender, number, and case, then the adjective assumes uniform and simplified endings which belong to the weak system.

§ 1. *Strong Declension.*

(155) The fact is, that the so-called strong adjectival declension merely proceeds from an analogical adaptation, to the adjectival stem, of the endings which were originally the property of the definite article and similar demonstrative words: an extension logically justified, since the adjective resembles the demonstrative so far as both are accessories to the noun. Hence, most of the Go. endings which have occurred

besser), though actually consonantal stems, are declined with the case-endings of their positives (G. *gut*), whereas in Greek and Latin they regularly retained their primitive (3rd) declension.

above in the declension of the article also became attached to the Go. adjective, whilst in O.H.G. the likeness is even more striking and almost complete. The reader need but compare with the earliest declension of the article that of the O.H.G. adjective, as given below:

	Singular.			Plural.		
	msc.	fm.	nt.	msc.	fm.	nt.
N.	blint-ēr	blint-iu	blint-aȝ	blint-e	blint-o	blint-iu
A.	,, -an	,, -a	,, -aȝ	,, -e	,, -o	,, -iu
G.	,, -es	,, -era	,, -es	,, -ero	,, -ero	,, -ero
D.	,, -emu	,, -eru	,, -emu	,, -ēm	,, -ēm	,, -ēm [1]

Further, remembering the duller sound of modern final syllables, the change of final *m* to *n*, and the analogical processes stated above for the article, we shall easily understand the contemporary type and may even dispense with transcribing it, since it exactly corresponds to the article.[2]

O.E. possessed a similar declension.[3] How it was lost in English, will be explained when we come to the invariable adjective.

§ 2. *Weak Declension.*

(156) In order to trace back to its origin the adjectival weak declension, we have but to note one historical fact, namely that, side by side with a great many adjectives in -*o-s* -*ā* -*o-m* (L. type *bonus bona bonum*), there existed other adjectives, with the same meanings, wherein the suffix-element was -*ĕn-* or -*ŏn-*, the common and familiar formative syllable which loses its *n* in the nomin. sg. and retains it everywhere else. Thus, in Greek, side by side with φάγος (glutton), we have φαγών (glutton), the plural of the latter being φαγῶν-ες, and of the former simply φαγοί. Thus also, in Latin, *catus* (wise, sensible), and the doublet **catō*, which may be assumed from the proper name (nickname) *Catō*, gen. *Catōnis*. Further instances are:

[1] Sg. also -*emo*, -*ero*; pl. also -*ēn*.
[2] Cf. *supra* 128-131. The only difference is nomin.-acc. sg. nt. -*es* instead of -*as* = O.H.G. -*aȝ*.
[3] And even as late as Shakespeare we find an adjectival genitive plural, *alder-liefest* " dearest of all," which corresponds to G. *aller-liebst*, and would be O.E. *ealra lēofesta*.

Gr. αἰθός (soot-colour) αἴθων, ἐθελημός (willing) ἐθελήμων, οὐράνιος (heavenly) Οὐρανίωνες (the gods), στραβός (squint-eyed) στράβων Στράβων (proper name), etc.; L. (*multi-*)*bibus bibō* (drunkard), *rebellis* (from *bellum* "war") *rebelliō, scelerus* (felon) *scelerō, susurrus* (murmuring) *susurrō*, etc. Now, supposing analogy to create other such doublets after these patterns, and that any adjective may assume a form either without or with a nasal suffix: Latin, for instance, along with *bonus, probus, prāvus, niger* (pl. *bonī, probī, prāvī, nigrī*), would exhibit the synonymous adjectives, *bonō, *probō, *prāvō, *nigrō (pl. *bonōn-ēs*, *probōn-ēs, *prāvōn-ēs, *nigrōn-ēs), and so forth, all interchangeable.

This is precisely what happened in Pregermanic. Besides the strong form, which is declined after the demonstrative, every Gothic adjective has a weak form, which is declined, if masculine, like *hana*, if feminine, like *tuggō*, if neuter, like *áugō*, which nouns are well-known to be the Germanic representatives of the I.-E. stem-formation with suffix *-on-* [1]; and the same correspondences are rigorously reproduced in O.E. and O.H.G.

English lost the weak declension in its adjectives as well as in its nouns. But, on the contrary, the German adjectives retained it even with more vigour and purity than the nouns themselves. For the latter have been seen to keep the regular ending *-en* only in the plural of the three genders and in the masculine singular declension, whereas, in the adjectives, this ending characterizes, quite regularly, any oblique case of any gender, whether plural or singular: thus, we find gen. *des auges* and dat. *dem auge*, for *des augen* and *dem augen*; but always gen. sg. nt. *des guten*, and dat. sg. nt. *dem guten*; so also, gen. dat. sg. *der zunge*, for *der zungen*; but gen. dat. sg. fm. *der guten*, etc. This strictly coherent system suffered encroachment in one point only, that is, the acc. fm. sg. was assimilated to the nominative,[2] owing to the preceding demonstrative having become the same in both cases: O.H.G. nomin. sg. *diu blinta*, acc. *dea blintūn*; M.H.G. nomin. *diu blinde*, acc. *die blinden*; but Mod. G. *die blinde* in either case.

[1] *Supra* 74, 140–142, 150 and 152.
[2] The acc. nt. sg., of course, can never differ from the nominative.

Section II.

INVARIABLE ADJECTIVE.

(157) The English **invariable** adjective and the adjectival form which is commonly called "*unflektiert*" in German grammar, were both originally declensional forms, and primitively no less variable than any that have occurred above. But this flexion no longer appears, because phonetic laws effaced most of their endings, and analogy afterwards disposed of the remainder.

§ 1. *In German.*

Let us return to the original type represented by L. *bonus bona* (=*bonā*) *bonum*. After the loss of final *s* or *m* together with the preceding vowel, both masculine and neuter assumed an indifferent form, the phonetic equivalent of which may be seen in F. *bon*, thus O.H.G. *guot, blint*, etc. The primitively long final vowel in the feminine, shortened in late Pregermanic (Go. *blind-a*), was destined to disappear in West Germanic, at least when the preceding syllable was long, as is the case with these two adjectives and with many others, thus fm. *guot, blint*, etc. Now O.H.G. analogically lost this termination even when the preceding syllable was short, so that the form of the adjective in the nominative singular became the same for the three genders.

Since this form is historically a declined one, no less than the so-called forms of strong or weak declension, it is but natural that it should appear fit for the same use and be construed in the same sentences, without any noticeable difference in the earliest documents. Hence O.H.G. has either: *blintēr man*, or *blint man*; *blintiu maʒad*, or *blint maʒad*; *blintaʒ kind*, or *blint kind*, etc. And, no less optionally, even: *dër man ist blintēr*, or *blint*; *diu magad ist blintiu*, or *blint*; *daʒ kind ist blintaʒ*, or *blint*, etc. As early, however, as this period, there may be observed a slight tendency to decline the qualificative adjective rather than the other, and to assign the invariable form to the predicative in particular.

Next, from this increasing tendency, arises a new consequence: the speaker being now accustomed to keep the adjective invariable in gender, began to make it invariable also in number. The plural, indeed, is still required in the construction *blinte man*,[1] but the agreement is optional in the sentence *die man sint blinte*, or *blint*; and similarly, in the three genders.

Lastly, that artificial regulation occurred, by which any language, sooner or later, aims at making the most of its resources. M.H.G., it is true, still often uses the invariable adjective as an attribute,[2] but rarely shows the variable form in a predicate.[3] And this adventitious distribution gradually became the modern German rule: the qualificative adjective agrees with its noun; the predicative adjective is always invariable.

§ 2. *In English.*

It is somewhat surprising to find that the so-called invariable adjective is less invariable in O.E. than in O.H.G.: of course, since the phonetic law applies equally to the whole West Germanic group, the type *gōd*, *blind*, etc., here also, is the same for the three genders in the singular; but, when the preceding syllable is short, O.E. regularly keeps the feminine ending, and declines, for instance, msc. *blæc*, fm. *blac-u*, nt. *blæc*, forms now replaced by E. *black*, and even in O.H.G. by msc. fm. nt. *flah* (flat).

The later process is quite plain: the same analogy that had corrupted the O.H.G. declension entered into action in M.E. and thus an invariable adjective *black* was formed on the pattern of the regularly invariable *good*. On the other hand, it must be observed that the analogy of the demonstratives, either in O.E. or in Go., had never affected the nominative of the declined adjective: in other words the O.E. strong declension had nothing like the G. nomin. *blind-er blind-e blind-es*, so that the adjective, either as predicate or attribute, had no other form but *gōd* in the three genders for the nomin. sg. The corre-

---

[1] It must not be forgotten that the pl. to *man* is regularly *man*.
[2] Rural dialects and popular speech still retain this use, which is likewise illustrated by many geographical names, as *Neuburg, Neukirch*, etc.
[3] A survival is found in the adj. *voll*, still declined, though a predicate, in such sentences as *der ort war voller leute*.

sponding plural forms were msc. *gōd-e*, fm. *gōd-a*, nt. *gōd*, the latter again like the singular; the primitive plural sign -*s*, which as a rule was omitted in the feminine, had been lost in the masculine, as it had also disappeared in the nominal G. type *tag-ā* (*tag-e*); and there was no reason for analogy to restore it in the adjectives as it had restored it in the nominal declension: in short, all circumstances conspired to a complete levelling of the adjective in the nominative of the three genders and the two numbers, whence the indifferent form *good*.

Now there remained the other cases and the forms of the weak declension. But in all these also the final syllables had become obscured; and, since the old distinction of cases had perished in demonstratives and nouns, it could not be expected to survive in adjectives, as there it was even less needed, the case being always indicated either by the noun itself[1] or else by a preposition. Hence the English adjective has kept no flexional forms but an analogical plural in -*s* which appears when the word is used substantivally (*the good-s*).[2] In any other position, whether qualificative or predicative, the English adjective is altogether invariable.[3]

[1] English, for instance, in *the good wife's*, expresses the case quite as clearly, as it would by *the *gooden wife's*, or as German by its threefold case-ending *des guten weibs*. Cf. however the archaic and still used locution *in the olden times.*

[2] So also *eatable-s*, etc , but *the wise* = *the wise men*; in M.E. *the other* is still plural, now *the others*; and the plural *the . . . ones* is even later.

[3] For comparatives and superlatives, adverbs, and other points which are usually dealt with in connection with the adjective, the reader must be referred to our Second Part, especially 80, 90, 111, etc.

CHAPTER IV.

PRONOUNS.

(158) The I.-E. **Pronouns** must be divided first into two great classes: **Demonstrative** and **Personal Pronouns**.

The declensional system of the two classes is quite different. But their main distinction lies in the following fact: the demonstratives, theoretically, agree in gender with the person or thing which they determine or represent, whereas the personal pronouns do not mark any difference in sex. Thus, in Latin, msc. *ille*, fm. *illa*, nt. *illud*, but *ego* "I," *tū* "thou," indifferently for the three genders.

The latter distinction holds good, in English[1] as well as in German, for the pronouns of the first and second person, and, in German alone, for the reflexive pronoun; while the third person is an exception in both languages, the so-called pronoun of the third person being really an old demonstrative used for this purpose.[2]

SECTION I.

DEMONSTRATIVES.

(159) The general paradigm for the declension of every I.-E. demonstrative is that of the stem **tó-*, which has become the Germanic article. Since this system has already been

[1] But here the contrast disappears, because the demonstrative has also become invariable in gender. It will be seen to have varied in O.E.

[2] Sanskrit, Greek, Latin, and even Mod. Russian agree in showing no other personal pronouns, except those of the 1st and 2nd person and the reflexive, which primitively represented all three persons, as it still does in Russian. Cf. *infra* 166.

studied and has not suffered change, either in German, or in the scanty relics of a demonstrative declension which English has retained, we need no longer dwell upon it. It will be sufficient to point out, as they occur, a few interesting peculiarities which present themselves in the different classes of demonstratives, namely :—demonstratives (either adjectives or pronouns) properly so-called;—interrogative and indefinite pronouns;—relative pronouns.

§ 1. *Demonstratives properly so-called.*

(160) I.-E. was well furnished with demonstratives of various forms and meanings; but most of them were lost in Pregermanic, and the whole of English and German demonstratives might be said, with one exception, to proceed from a single primitive pronoun, either shifted in its form, or altered in its meaning.

1. O.E. ðĕ-s ðēo-s ðĭ-s, and E. *this* in the three genders; O.H.G. *dëse dësiu diz*, and G. *dies-er dies-e dies-es*[1] : demonstrative for things close at hand.—This word was originally a mere juxtaposition of the ordinary demonstrative and an indeclinable particle -*se*,[2] as still clearly shown by the O.E. declension. In German, this inward declension is but partly visible, having been replaced by an outward declension imitated from the endings of the declined article; that is to say, the indeclinable particle adopted the case-signs, whilst the declinable stem lost them.[3] Lastly, in English, every trace of a declension was swept away, and nt. *this* serves for all genders. The O.E. pl. is ðā-s, and, with a slight vocalic shifting, ðǣ-s, which respectively became E. *those* and *these*: the latter is retained as the invariable plural of *this*, whereas the former now belongs to another system.

2. Go. *jáin-s*; O.E. *geon* and E. *yon*; O.H.G. *jen-ēr*, etc., and G. *jen-er jen-e jen-es*: demonstrative for distant objects.—This pronoun is of doubtful origin and belongs exclusively to the

---

[1] The regular form *dies* remains still in use as a neuter pronoun: *dies mag wohl sein=this may well be*. O.H.G. msc. sg. also *dësēr*, fm. sg. also *dïsiu*.
[2] As in F. *celui-ci, celle-ci, ce-ci*.
[3] Such confusions are not at all rare in pronominal declension: cf. F. pl. *quelconques*, which ought to be *quels-conque* = L. *quales-cunque*.

Germanic group. Besides it is nearly obsolete in English, though used in poetry; compare however *yon-der* and *be-yon-d*.

3. E. *that*: usual demonstrative for distant objects.—It is the neutral form of the ordinary demonstrative (article),[1] now stiffened in an invariable shape which serves for all cases and genders. The Mod. E. pl. is *those*, in reality a plural of *this* and a mere phonetic doublet of *these*. Popular English still shows a trace of the old dative: *in them days*.

4. G. *der-selb-e*, "this (pronoun), he," literally "the same," *die-selb-e*, *das-selb-e*, pl. *die-selb-en*, etc., obviously, a purely syntactical juxtaposition, wherein, as a matter of course, the demonstrative showing the strong forms, the adjective assumes the weak terminations. This adjective, Go. *silba*, O.N. *sjalf-r*, E. *self*, is a stem of uncertain etymology, which, in the Germanic family, plays the part of a pronoun denoting identity, and is further combined with personal pronouns.

5. G. *der-jenig-e*,[2] etc., the demonstrative which precedes a relative pronoun: a syntactical juxtaposition of the article with an adjective derived from the demonstrative *jen-*; whereas English in this construction merely uses *he* in the singular and *those* in the plural.

§ 2. *Interrogative and Indefinite Pronouns.*

(161) Both the interrogative and indefinite pronominal categories are expressed by the same I.-E. stem, either a stem in -*o*- or in -*i*-, characterized by an initial *q*, thus I.-E. *$q\acute{o}$-* and *$q\acute{i}$-*, whence further: Sk. *ká-s* (who?), fm. *ká*, nt. *kí-m*, and *ci-d* indefinite particle; Gr. stem πο-, with its many forms, ποῦ (where?), πόθεν (whence?), πότε (when?), πῶς (how?), and τί-ς (who?), fm. τί-ς, nt. τί = *τί-δ [3]; L. *quo-*, stem of the pronoun *quī quæ quo-d*, and *qui-*, stem of the pronoun *qui-s* (who?), *qui-d* (what?), etc. To these, the Preg. corresponding forms naturally were *$hw\acute{a}$-* and *$hw\acute{i}$-*, the former surviving as an

---

[1] Go. þa-t-a, supra 128 and 130, 1.
[2] Which replaced the simpler O.H.G. *dĕr jenĕr*.
[3] The unaccented forms, που, ποτε, πω, τις, τι, are indefinite adverbs or pronouns; and so also L. *quis quid*.

isolated pronoun, the latter as the first term of a compound, both interrogative and indefinite.

1. Go. msc. *hva-s*, fm. *hvō*, nt. *hva*, declined like the demonstrative, but without any plural-form; O.E. msc. *hwā*, nt. *hwœ-t*, and E. *who what*, no feminine or plural; O.H.G. msc. *hwë-r*, nt. *hwa-ʒ*, and G. *wer was*, no feminine or plural.—Here, exceptionally, English retains almost the whole declension, viz.: gen. sg. *whose* = O.E. *hwœ·s*; dat. sg. *whom* = O.E. *hwā-m* = Go. *hva-mma*, shifted moreover to the accusative-meaning instead of regular O.E. *hwo-n-e* = Go. *hva-n-a*. But the nt. is invariable, and admits of no other form but *what* (like *that* = Go. *þa-t-a*) for all cases.[1]—German has the four cases: *wer was*, *wen was*, *wessen*, *wem*. The regular gen. is O.H.G. *hwë-s*, M.H.G. *wës*, kept in the juxtapositions *wesz-wegen*, *wesz-halb*, etc., whereas *wess-en* is a recent and pleonastic form, created by subjoining to the old genitive a new genitive-ending of weak declension. The dat. *wem*, like the acc. *wen*, may only refer to a person.

2. Go. *hvi-leik-s*, a compound of the stem **hvi-* and the Preg. adjective **līka-* (like),[2] literally "to whom or what alike? of what sort? which?"; O.E. *hwylc* and E. *which* invariable; O.H.G. *wë-lich-*, and G. *welch-er welch-e welch-es*. The Mod. G. locution *was für*, which often replaces the interrogative adjective, must be interpreted thus: *was hast du für ein kleid?* "what hast thou for, instead of a garment?" whence "what garment do you wear?"

Further, the indefinite meaning may be emphasized by adding to these pronouns such adverbs or particles as E. *ever, so ever* (*whosoever*), G. *je, irgend*.[3] But these syntactical constructions have nothing to do with declension.

[1] The analogical process here is quite plain: *with whom* (dat.) *have you been?* being regular, and the dative being next used for the acc. in such a sentence as *whom have you seen?*, the regular construction *what have you seen?* naturally produced the fourth term *with what . . . ?* For acc. *whom*, see below 164, I. 4.

[2] Cf. *supra* 110, I., and compare Go. *sva-leik-s* (*sva* = E. *so* = G. *so*), E. *such*, G. *solch* (L. *tālis* "such," *quālis* "which").

[3] O.H.G. *io wer-gin*: *io*, the particle which has become G. *je*; *wer*, identical with E. *where*; and *-gin*, the same as Go. *-hun* and L. *-cum-* in *quī-cun-que* (whoever). So also, *immer* = O.H.G. *io mēr* (now *je mehr*), and *ever* = O.E. *æ-fre* = **æ-mre*.

§ 3. *Relative Pronouns.*

(162) The so-called relative pronouns, which introduce a subordinate sentence, cannot be properly said to have existed in I.-E. times; in origin, they appear to be in all the I.-E. branches either old demonstrative or old interrogative-indefinite pronouns, afterwards adapted to this new function. Thus, the Gr. article is also the relative pronoun in Homer and Herodotus, and even the ordinary relative, ὅς ἥ ὅ, shows some traces of its original demonstrative value. In Latin, on the other hand, it is the interrogative-indefinite stem that plays the part of the relative pronoun, *quī quæ quod*. The E. and G. relatives are taken from both sources concurrently.

1. G. *der die das*, identical with the article, demonstrative used as relative. In the latter function, however, and not earlier than Mod. German, the pleonastic process described above has developed some new case-forms with redundant endings: gen. msc. sg. *dess-en*, gen. fm. sg. and gen. pl. *der-en der-er*, dat. pl. *den-en*, as if the regular monosyllables seemed too short to express clearly what the speaker meant.[1]

2. E. *that*, identical with the demonstrative (neuter article), used as relative in all genders and numbers, though keeping its etymological value, inasmuch as it stands only for a nominative or accusative and is never governed by a preposition.[2]

3. E. *who* (gen. *whose*, dat.-acc. *whom*), primitively interrogative-indefinite, used as relative for both numbers and both the msc. and fm. gender, never neuter. Its neuter *what* never assumes the relative function.

---

[1] *Supra* 161, 1. Used also as a demonstrative pronoun (not adjective): *dessen*, "of him, his"; *es gibt derer zwei*, "there are two of them."—It is only use that gradually assigned to each of these forms a peculiar and distinct function: as late even as Goethe we find *der* for the gen. fm. of the relative pronoun, and on the other hand, as late as Klopstock, *derer* is used even for the gen. pl. of the simple article. There existed besides a common dat. sg. *deren*, which has become obsolete, *deren* being exclusively assigned to the genitival function, whereas *der* was used exclusively for expressing the dative. The same and very late distinction has been drawn between *deren* (now exclusively gen. fm. sg.) and *derer* (now exclusively gen. pl.), which once stood indifferently for each other.

[2] Further, *that* and *dasz* as conjunctions, *supra* 130, 1.

4. E. *which* invariable, and G. *welch-er welch-e welch-es*, usual relative pronoun, the same as the interrogative-indefinite.

We need not deal here with the ellipse of the relative pronoun, which is common in English.[1]

The various pronouns which have been purposely excluded from this summary require but little etymological explanation. Some have already appeared in the Study of Sounds[2]; at any rate, they belong rather to the province of the Dictionary than to that of Grammar properly so-called.

SECTION II.

PERSONAL PRONOUNS.

(163) In this class, we have to distinguish the **pronouns of the three persons in both numbers**, the **reflexive pronoun**, which theoretically knows no distinction in number, and lastly the **possessive pronouns and adjectives**, as being, in both languages, peculiar forms or derivatives from the corresponding personal pronouns.

Even in the earliest period, the primitive personal pronouns, that is to say, those of the first and the second person, are remarkable for the fact that **they are not declined on a single stem**, like most demonstratives, and thus they often assume different shapes, not only in passing from the sg. to the pl.,—as may be seen in L. *ego* and *nōs, tū* and *vōs,*—but from one case to another in the same number,—from nomin. sg., for instance, to acc. sg. in L. *ego* and *mē*.—Germanic and, in consequence, English and German reproduce all these peculiarities.

§ 1. *First Person.*

(164) I. Singular.—1. The probable I.-E. nominative was *egóm, Sk. *ahám*, Gr. ἐγώ, L. *ego*, Preg. **ik(a)*, whence: Go. *ik*,

---

[1] The relative was likewise often dropped in O.H.G.: *Fater unseer, thū pist in himile* (in the so-called "St. Galler Lord's Prayer"). It must be borne in mind that the relative is but a slightly modified demonstrative; and a demonstrative never need be used when the sentence can do without it.

[2] Refer to the Alphabetical Indexes of Words.

O.E. *ic*, M.E. *ich* and E. *I*, O.H.G. *ih* and G. *ich*. These present no difficulty.

2. Accusative. — Of the many accusative-forms of the primitive stem, the simplest (I.-E. **mé*) may be inferred from Gr. ἐμέ or μέ, which is often accompanied by a strengthening or emphatic particle, thus ἐμέ-γε, like nomin. ἔγω-γε, "as to me." The parallel form I.-E. **mé-ge* has become the Germanic accusative, Preg. **mi-k(i)*, Go. *mik*, O.E. *me-c mē me* and E. *me* (short because unaccented), O.H.G. *mi-h* and G. *mi-ch*.

3. The Go. genitive is *meina*, and really belongs, not to the personal pronoun, but to the possessive, as given below.[1] O.E. answers with *mīn*, lost in English. O.H.G. likewise has *mīn*, which as late as Mod. German[2] assumed a redundant case-sign and became pleonastically *mein-er*, by adding to *mein* the regular termination of the corresponding gen. pl. *uns-er*.

4. The puzzling Go. dat. *mis* cannot be traced back to any primitive type, and seems to have been formed after the analogy of a (lost) dat. pl. **nis* = Sk. *nas*. According as the final *s* (*z*) was merely dropped, or changed to *r*, we have now: O.E. *mē* and E. *me*, blended with the accusative[3]; O.H.G. *mir*, G. *mir*.

II. Plural.[4] — 1. The curious nomin. pl. with initial *w* is common to Sk. and Germanic (Sk. *vayám*, Go. *veis*), whereas it occurs nowhere else: it has become O.E. *wē* and E. *we*, O.H.G. *wir* and G. *wir*[5]; compare *me* = *mir*.

2. Accusative. — The initial syllable of the oblique cases clearly proceeds from an I.-E. nasal vowel, either *ṇ* or *ṃ*, which again is simply the reduced grade of the stem exhibited in its normal grade by Sk. *nas* "us" (cf. L. *nōs*), or by Gr. μέ

---

[1] It is a case-form of *it*, but which case? The question remains open; perhaps a weak msc. nominative, elsewhere obsolete, and surviving here in this shape. At any rate, the use of the possessive in the function of genitive to the personal pronoun ("my" instead of "of me") is everywhere common: thus, in L., *nōs* has the gen. *nostrum nostri*, and even *mei*, the gen. of *ego*, is probably identical with *mei* the gen. of *meus*.

[2] The pure form survives in the compound *vergisz-mein-nicht* (the flower).

[3] This confusion further caused the two cases to be confounded in the interrogative-indefinite declension, *supra* 161, 1.

[4] In all these declensions, Go. and O.E. had also retained some dual-forms; but O.H G. has lost the dual.

[5] Dialectal (Alam.) *mir* imitated from the singular-stem.

(cf. L. *mē*). The plural Sk. and Gr. forms moreover require a particle[1] to be inserted between the stem and the endings: I.-E. **n̥-smé-*; Sk. (ablative) *a-smá-d*; Homeric Gr. acc. ἄμμε= **á-σμέ-*; Attic ἡμεῖς for *ἀμές (long a)=*á-σμέ-s. But Pregermanic has merely *uns=**n̥s*, as attested by Go. *uns*. In O.E. and O.H.G., the analogy of the acc. sg. caused a new ending to be added to this simple form: O.E. *ūsic*=*uns-ic, and O.H.G. *uns-ih*. O.E. *ūs*, however, which survived concurrently, afterwards became the prevalent form: E. *us*; and so likewise G. *uns*.

3. Genitive.—Go. *unsara* is a case-form of the corresponding possessive, like *meina*: O.E. *ūser*, syncopated to *ūre*, lost in English; O.H.G. *unsēr* and G. *unser*.

4. Dative.—On the primitive basis *uns*, Gothic had constructed, after the analogy of sg. *mis* and of the pl. pronoun of 2nd person, a new dative *uns-is*. But E. and G. have only the pure form, *us, uns*, like the accusative. So in Sk. *nas* also serves for both cases.

§ 2. *Second Person.*

(165) I. Singular.—1. The nomin. was I.-E. *tŭ and *tū, Sk. *tvám*=*tu-ám, Gr. τύ (τύ) and σύ, L. *tū*, Preg. *þū, whence: Go. *þu*; O.E. ðū ðu, and E. *thou*=ðū; O.H.G. *dū du*, and G. *du*. These present no difficulty.

2. Accusative.—In the same way as in the 1st person, we get Preg. *þi-k. Go. has *þuk*, which has evidently been influenced by the vocalism of the nominative. But O.E. and O.H.G. retain the pure vowel: O.E. ðec ðē ðe, and E. *thee*=ðē (the emphatic form[2]); O.H.G. *dih* and G. *dich*.

3. Genitive.—Go. *þeina*, O.E. ðīn, O.H.G. *dīn* and G. *dein*, then *dein-er*, just as in the case of the 1st person.

4. Dative.—Go. *þus* instead of *þis, like *þuk*; but O.E. ðē ðe and E. *thee*, O.H.G. *dir* and G. *dir* (*supra* 164, I., 4).

---

[1] The same we have met with in Go. *þamma*, supra 130, 4, and 134.

[2] Hence it is obvious, that each personal pronoun ought to have two accusative-forms, respectively, emphatic *mee and *thee*, unaccented *me* and *the; but the first person kept only the unaccented type, whereas the emphatic type alone remained in the second person.

T

II. Plural.—1. The plural-stem of the 2nd person was I. E. *yu-, which occurs, for instance, in Sk. *yu-šmá-d* ablative, Gr. ὔμμε acc. Homeric, and ὑμεῖς = *yu-σμέ-ς. Gothic has the simple nomin. *jus*. But West Germanic has altered the vowel under the influence of the plural-stem of the 1st person: O.E. *gē* (like *wē*) and O.H.G. *ir* (like *wir*); E. *ye* and G. *ihr*. Usual Mod. E. *you* is an accusative, while literary and dialectal E. retains *ye*.

2. Accusative.—Go. *izvis* is not easy to explain and certainly corrupt, though the last syllable seems identical with Sk. *vas* = L. *vōs*. West Germanic has a monosyllabic form, O.E. *ēow* (cf. pl. 1 *ūs*), and a dissyllabic form, O.E. *ēow-ic*, O.H.G. *iuw-ih*, the ending of which is imitated from the corresponding sg. pronoun. Of these, *ēow* became E. *you*, whilst *iuwih* survives in G. *euch*. The difference in the initial diphthong is due to a different accentuation: in English, the first component is a semi-vowel, and the second a vowel; and the reverse in German. Further, *ye* and *you*, being nearly alike, were confused.

3. Genitive.—Go. *izvara*; O.E. *ēower* and O.H.G. *iuwēr* (like *ūser* and *unsēr*); lost in English; G. *euer*.

4. Dative.—Go. *izvis*, like acc.[1]; O.E. *ēow* and E. *you* (the same); O.H.G. *iu*, also without ending, but Mod. G. *euch*, assimilated to the acc. because in the 1st person *uns* is used for both cases (M.H.G. dat. *iu* and acc. *iuch*).

§ 3. *Third Person.*

(166) Indo-European, it has been seen, did not possess any personal pronoun for the third person. Such languages as secured one for their own use borrowed it from the demonstrative class: thus F. *il* proceeds from L. *ille*. This being the case, it is a remarkable fact that English and German, considering their strict correspondence to each other, should have chosen to adopt a different stem to supply the want. Not a single form, in the whole declension, is common to both languages, with the one exception of the nomin. fm. sg.: E. *she* =

---

[1] It is doubtless from this dative that the analogy arose which created pl. 1 *unsis* and further sg. *mis* *þis (G. *mir dir*).

O.E. *sēo*, and G. *sie* = O.H.G. *siu*, both identical with Sk. *syâ* = I.-E. **siâ*, which is the fm. of the well-known demonstrative **sió*.[1] Everywhere else the comparison must be confined to the mere endings.

I. Singular.—The E. pronoun proceeds from an I.-E. demonstrative stem **kyó-* and **ki-*, from which some scanty remains survive in other members of the family: Gr. σημέρον τημέρον (to-day) = **ky-ăμέρον*; L. demonstrative *hĭ-c hœ-c ho-c*[2]; Go. dat. *hi-mma dag-a* "in this day," and G. *heute* = **hiō taga* (to-day); E. *here*, and G. *hier, her, hin*, etc., locative adverbs.—The G. pronoun is the little demonstrative stem *i-*, which is chiefly illustrated by the L. pronominal declension, msc. *i-s*, nt. *i-d*, acc. msc. *i-m* (archaic), the latter identical with poetical Greek *ĭ-ν* (μίν νίν) "him."

1. Nominative.—O.E. msc. *hē* (cf. *thē* from the demonstrative **tó-*) and E. *he*; O.E. nt. *hi-t*, with the characteristic pronominal neuter-ending (cf. *tha-t* = I.-E. **tó-d*), and E. *it*, the initial aspirate being dropped.[3]—O.H.G. msc. *ër*, instead of **i-r* = L. *i-s*, owing to the vocalism of *dër*, and nt. *iȝ* = Preg.**i-t* = L. *i-d*; M.H.G. msc. *ër*, and nt. *ëȝ* owing to the vocalism of *ër*; G. *er* and *es*.—The fm. *she* and *sie* borrowed from another stem.

2. Accusative.—E. nt. *it*; in the two other genders the dative is used as an accusative (O.E. acc. msc. *hi-n-e*).—O.H.G. msc. *i-n* = L. *i-m*, also *in-an* with redundant termination, but G. merely *ihn* = *in* lately lengthened; fm. *siu*, next *sie*, and nt. *iȝ*, next *es*, like nominative.

3. Genitive.—O.E. msc. nt. *hi-s* and fm. *hi-re* (*hiere hyre*): compare, on one side, the ordinary genitive-endings of the demonstratives, and, on the other, the E. possessives.—O.H.G. fm. *i-ra*, without difficulty; but, in the msc. and (later) the nt.

---

[1] Cf. *supra* 127 and 128, II.—Even this slight agreement disappears in the oldest period of English and German, the latter always using *siu*, whereas O.E. declines the whole of the pronoun of the 3rd person on the stem of *he*: nomin. sg. fm. *hēo* (she), and even pl. *hēo* (they).—The initial E. consonant (*š* instead of *s*) is due to the influence of the following *i*, which was sounded as a semi-vowel (group *s+y*, as in *passion*), whilst in G. the *i* kept its vocalic value.

[2] The compared term is not the stem *ho-*, but the suffix *-c*, which represents a L. particle *-ce* = **kĕ* (cf. L. gen. *hujus-ce*).

[3] Cf. *supra* 66, II., 4, and further see the declension of the article.

gender, the analogy of *mīn* and *dīn* in the other persons led the language to adopt the correlative form of the reflexive possessive *sīn*,[1] which further became changed to a pleonastic genitive *sein-er* imitated from *mein-er* and *dein-er*.

4. Dative.—O.E. msc. nt. *hi-m* = Go. *hi-mma* (like *þa-mma*), and fm. *hi-re hiere hyre*; E. msc. *him*, fm. *her*, but nt. *it*, the accusative here serving for the dative.—O.H.G. msc. nt. *i-mu*, fm. *i-ru*; G. *ihm* and *ihr*.

II. Plural.—Here, deviating from the O.E. type, M.E. and Mod. E. use the case-forms of the Germanic demonstrative **þá-* = I.-E. **tó-*, the same from which O.E. had already derived its article: not the genuine O.E. case-forms however, but such as were borrowed from O.N. at the beginning of the M.E. period. German shows the same stem both in the singular and plural, save that its nominative-accusative belongs to the demonstrative I.-E. *sió.

1. Nominative.—E. *they* = O.N. *þei-r*.—O.H.G. msc. *sie*, fm. *sio*, nt. *siu*, whence G. *sie* in the three genders.

2. Accusative.—E. *them* (original dative).—G. *sie*.

3. Genitive.—M.E. *thei-r* = O.N. *þei-rra*, to be found again among the possessives.—O.H.G. *i-ro* regular, but Mod. G. *ihr-er*, with pleonastic genitive-ending.

4. Dative.—E. *the-m*, with the usual and well-known dative-ending.[2]—O.H.G. *i-m*, whence regularly *in*, and Mod. G. *ihn-en* with a redundant plural case-sign.

§ 4. *Reflexive Pronoun.*

(167) The reflexive pronoun is expressed in the two languages by a different process. The only primitive one is the German.

I. In the first and second persons, the reflexive G. pronoun is merely the personal pronoun: *ich denke mir*, "I am figuring to myself"; *du befindest dich*, "you find yourself," etc. But, in the third person, German still possesses the representative of

---

[1] *Infra* 168, I., 3, and *supra* 164–165 (I., 3).

[2] It is, of course, owing to a simple phonetic process (cf. *supra* 130, 4, and 131, 4), that the ending of this case has become identical in both numbers, so that even O.E. has *him* in the plural as well as in the singular.

the general I.-E. reflexive pronoun, which was characterized by an initial *sw* or *s*, and appears clearly in the whole I.-E. family, *e.g.* Sk. stem *svá-*, Gr. acc. ἒ=*σFέ, L. *sē*, etc. Of course, this stem could have no nominative. It was, moreover, **indifferently singular and plural**. All these characteristics had been faithfully kept by Pregermanic; but the Saxonic branch of West Germanic lost the pronoun altogether, as early as O.E.

1. Accusative.—Go. *si-k* = I.-E. **sé-ge*, cf. *mik* and *þuk*; O.H.G. *sih* and G. *sich*; all both singular and plural.

2. Genitive.—Go. *seina*, O.H.G. *sīn*, G. *sein-er*.

3. Dative.—Go. *sis*; but G. *sich*, the accusative here being used as dative (sg. and pl.).

In order to lay stress upon the reflexive meaning, the speaker may add to the pronoun of any person, an invariable word *selb-st*, which is apparently a superlative, but really a corrupt form of M.H.G. *sëlb-es*, nomin.-acc. nt. and gen. msc. nt. sg. of the adjective *sëlb* (self, same). This adjective formerly agreed in gender, number and case with the governing pronoun; but it has now become invariable.

II. This stem, by means of a somewhat different, though kindred construction, supplied English with a reflexive formation, which is now deemed obligatory.[1] Even in the O.E. period are to be found such juxtapositions as *sē seolfa*, literally "the self" (the same, himself nomin., cf. G. *der-selb-e*). From a similar juxtaposition with the pronoun *hē*, first proceeded the accusatives-datives *him-self*, *her-self*, *hit-self*, pl. *them-selv-es*. Next, since the form *her* could be equally referred to the possessive adjective, and since, therefore, *her-self* might easily be mistaken for a substantival use of the word *self*, thus "the self of her, her very person," the language at an early date also created *mīn-self* "my person," whence *my-self*, *thy-self*, *our-selv-es*, *your-selv-es*, and (sg.) *your-self*. The equivocal sense is the reason why the E. pronoun denoting identity, strangely enough, in one case appears to be formed with the possessive (1st-2nd person), and in another (3rd) with the pronoun itself;

---

[1] Authorised Version of the Bible, still *ye clothe you* (Haggai i. 6), now *you clothe yourselves*, etc.

but rural dialects still show many traces of the old regular types *me-self, thee-self, ye-self*,[1] etc. We now pass to the possessive element.

§ 5. *Possessives.*

(168) As a rule, the declension of the possessive adjectives or pronouns comprises,—beside the gender, number, and case of the possessed object, which is expressed in German by means of the declensional endings, but not at all in English,—the **number and**, only in the 3rd person, the **gender of the possessor**, which must be inferred from the stem-form.

I. Singular of the possessor.—In every I.-E. language the possessive adjectives and pronouns have been formed by some method of derivation from the corresponding personal pronouns. Now the derivative element adopted in Germanic in the singular number seems to be the same we have already met with· in E. *swine* = G. *schwein* = L. *su-īnu-m*, literally "that which belongs to hog." Thus, probably, Preg. *m-īna-z "which belongs to me," etc. Go. *mein-s, þein-s* and (nt.) *sein*, O.E. *mīn ðīn sīn*, and O.H.G. *mīn dīn sīn*.

In these words, when somewhat swiftly sounded and unaccented, either in English or in many German dialects,[2] the final *n* often happened to be dropped, whence there arose such doublets as E. *mine* and *my*. Further, in such monosyllables the accent necessarily becomes weaker, when they are used as adjectives, and consequently followed by an accented noun, than it is when stress is laid upon them as pronouns and representing the noun itself; and thus it is that English later made the most of this accidental distinction by assigning its two forms, respectively, to the adjectival and pronominal function, *my house is higher than thine*. German, in either case, has but the form with final *n*. Here, however, a process of secondary derivation by means of suff. *-ig* gave rise to a periphrastic and emphatic locution, concurrently used in the pronominal meaning: *der mein-ig-e, der dein-ig-e*, further pl. *der uns-r-ig-e*, etc.

---

[1] Cf. Wright, *Dialect of Windhill*, no. 353.—After the pattern of *my-self* was afterwards formed the late *one's self*, literally "somebody's person."

[2] Alsatian and Swiss *mi pfifti* = *mein pfeiflein* (my little pipe).

1. O.E. *mīn*, E. *mine* and *my*; O.H.G. *mīn* (nomin. msc. sg. *mīn-ēr* like *blint-ēr*, etc.) and G. *mein*.
2. O.E. *ðīn*, E. *thine* and *thy*; O.H.G. *dīn* and G. *dein*.
3. The two languages are here at variance.—English, having lost the reflexive, lacks the corresponding possessive, and replaces it by the genitive of the pronoun of the 3rd person: O.E. *hi-s* "of him," if the possessor be of msc. or nt. gender; *hy-re* "of her"; E. *his*,[1] *her*; whereupon, after the analogy of the relation observed between *he* and *his*, a neuter possessive was created, *it-s*. Again, the analogy of the relation observed between dat. *it* and possessive *it-s* induced the speaker to derive in the same way from dat. *her* a possessive *her-s*, which however, for the sake of distinctness, was confined to the pronominal function. Hence: adjective *his her its*; pronoun *his hers its.*—O.H.G. *sīn* and G. *sein*, which etymologically ought to serve for the three genders of the possessor, since the reflexive, like any other personal pronoun, knows no distinction of gender.[2] But, for a possessor of feminine gender, German, like English, took to using the genitive of the personal pronoun (G. stem *i-*), whence O.H.G. *i-ra* "of her," G. *ihr* (her).

II. Plural of the possessor.—In the same way, and in both languages, the plural of the possessor is denoted by the genitive of the corresponding pronoun, as it were "of us, of you, of them," but here the exponent of the gen. pl. is a syllable ending in *r*, of rather obscure origin, which cannot be certainly identified with any I.-E. element.[3]

[1] E. *his* with a possessor of neuter gender is quite common as late as Shakespeare, as also in the Authorized Version of the Bible: *And* it (*the rock*) *shall give forth* his *water* (Exod. xvii. 6).
[2] *Supra* 158 and 167: G. *sie sehnt sich* exactly like *es versteht sich.*—Observe that G. *sein* is still clearly reflexive, though not so rigorously as L. *suus*, since it is not allowed to stand in a sentence where it might be mistaken as referring to the subject. It would there be replaced by the genitive of the demonstrative pronoun: *er griff an sein schwert*; but *Rolland ritt hinterm vater her, mit dessen* (his father's) *schwert und schilde* (Uhland).
[3] Perhaps it is the same *r* that appears in locative derivations, Go. *hē-r* = G. *her hier* = E. *here*, Go. *þa-r* = G. *dar* (also *da*) = E. *there*, Go. *hva-r* (= G. *wo*) = E. *where*, etc., so that Go. *unsar* and O.H.G. *unsēr* would have meant originally "among us," as in the Russian sentence *estĭ li u vasŭ chlebŭ?* "is there with you bread?" that is "have you any bread?"—On the other hand, Go. *uns-ar* might very well be a true possessive, a derivative with a suffixal comparative element, like the Gr. possessive ἡμέ-τερο-ς.

1. Go. *uns-ar*; O.E. *ūser*, and (syncopated) *ūr*, whence E. *our*, and (pronoun) *our-s*, formed like *her-s*; O.H.G. *uns-ēr* (nomin. sg. *unser-ēr* like *mīn-ēr*, etc.) and G. *unser*.

2. Go. *izvar*; O.E. *ēow-er* and E. *you-r*, pronoun *your-s*; O.H.G. *iuw-ēr* and G. *eu-er*.

3. E. *thei-r* = O.N. *þei-rra* (gen. pl.), pronoun *their-s*. O.H.G. *i-ro* (gen. pl.) "of them," and G. *ihr*.

The use of the pronoun and possessive of pl. 2 (English and German), and of sg. 3 or, chiefly, pl. 3 (exclusively German), instead of sg. 2, is merely a matter of conventional usage.

(169) III. Declension.—English is well known to have dropped every exponent of gender, number and case in its possessives, even more constantly than in its demonstratives. German has no less naturally transferred to its singular possessives, inasmuch as they are genuine adjectives in the nominative case (*mein dein sein*), the usual endings of its demonstratives. In contemporary German, however, the nomin. msc. sg. and the nomin.-acc. nt. sg. always assume the invariable form, and the terminations appear in the following adjective; *mein vater, mein gut-er vater*; *dein haus, dein schön-es haus*.[1] The possessive pronoun has the endings even in these two cases: msc. *mein-er* and nt. *mein-s* (mine) = O.H.G. *mīn-ēr* and *mīn-aʒ*.

The possessives which are really genitival forms (*ihr* fm., *unser, euer, ihr* pl.), ought, of course, to be invariable: since *ihr nase* means "of-her the-nose," the word *ihr* is theoretically incapable of any further agreement with the word *nase*, and, in fact, fm. and pl. *ir*, even as late as M.H.G., never appear with any sign of gender, number or case.[2] But the reverse is the case with the genitives *unsēr* and *iuwēr*, which, even in O.H.G., were declined like *mīn* and *dīn*, as if they were genuine nominatives. Their declension was somewhat arbitrary: thus, the ending *-ēr* being mistaken for an ending of nomin. msc., the

---

[1] In other words, the declension of *mein dein sein* has been completely overruled by that of *ein*, a very plain and natural analogy.

[2] Such is also the case with F. *leur* (their), which ought to be invariable, as representing L. *illorum* (cf. Italian *loro* with either a singular or a plural noun), but is now analogically sg. *leur* and pl. *leur-s*.

endings of the other genders, numbers and cases naturally suppressed and replaced it with apparent regularity, msc. *uns-ēr*, fm. *uns-u*, nt. *uns-aʒ*, etc. (Frankish); on the other hand, *unsēr* being again mistaken for the invariable adjectival form, the other terminations became added to it in the ordinary way, msc. *unser-ēr*, fm. *unser-iu*, nt. *unser-aʒ*, etc. It is the latter type that prevailed in classical German and was moreover extended to the gen. *ihr*, msc. *ihr-er*, fm. *ihr-e*, nt. *ihr-es*, though under the restriction stated above. The derivatives in *-ig* require no further explanation.

FOURTH PART.

CONJUGATION.

(170) Under the name of **Conjugation** are comprised the various **modifications, either in stem or termination, undergone by the verbal stems, and corresponding to** the various **relations of meaning** of which they are capable.

These relations are five in number, namely: **Tense, Mood, Aspect** (or **Voice**), **Number,** and **Person.**

The category of tense corresponds to the notion of time, either present, past, or future. Indo-European possessed a great many tenses, as we may gather from the extraordinary richness of Sk. and Gr. conjugation. But Pregermanic kept only two of them, **Present** and **Historical Past.** All the other tenses are now supplied by various periphrastic locutions.

The category of mood states the manner in which the verbal idea is thought of: either as simply **affirmed or denied (Indicative)**; or as eventually **possible (Subjunctive), desired (Optative),** or **subordinate** to some uncertain event **(Conditional)**; lastly, as the object of **command** or prohibition **(Imperative).** The English and German conjugation admits of but three moods: indicative, subjunctive, and imperative.[1] All other shades of meaning, and occasionally even these three, are expressed by means of a periphrasis.

The aspect of the verb—what is termed **Voice** in Greek Grammar—is either **Active,** or **Reflexive** (middle), or

---

[1] The reader must not forget that neither the infinitive nor the participle is a verbal mood. Both are mere nouns (*supra* 77-78), which however, for the sake of completeness in the conjugational system, will be reviewed below (229) at the head of the Chapter on Verbal Periphrases.

Passive, according as the agent (subject) performs the action, or performs and at the same time suffers it, or simply suffers it. Latin and, in particular, Greek denote the last two aspects by various changes in the endings, which English and German do not possess. A periphrasis must here again supply the loss.

The categories of number and person are the same for verbs as for personal pronouns [1]; indeed, as stated above in the pronominal declension, they cannot be resolved into distinct exponents, as it were, a number-sign and a person-sign. A single element expresses both relations at once : whence a total of **six person-endings**, three for the singular and three for the plural.

In short, the **Tenses**, the **Moods**, the **Person-Endings**, and lastly, the various **Verbal Periphrases**, which fill up the gaps in English and German conjugation, are the four main objects of study which fall under the head of Conjugation.

[1] *Supra* 163 sq. The Gothic conjugation still keeps two persons (1 and 2) in the dual number; but nothing similar appears in the later languages.

CHAPTER I.

TENSES.

(171) Logic, as well as grammar, distinguishes three essential classes of tenses, viz. **Past, Present,** and **Future.** In grammar, however, the present-form is simply the form of the verb itself, as analysed above in the study of word-formation.[1] Further, the I.-E. future was completely lost as early as the the Preg. period, no Germanic tongue ever exhibiting the least trace of it; for all agree in replacing it by the present, or else, when more precision is required, by using one of the periphrastic constructions considered below. Hence, of the whole tense-system of English and German, there is nothing left for our present study but the expression of the past, so far as it does not itself consist of a periphrasis, but depends on some modification of the verbal form.

(172) The latter mode of expressing the past tense is, again, in Germanic, confined to one primitive grammatical form: of the various original past tenses, namely imperfects, aorists, perfects and pluperfects, best illustrated by the Sanskrit and Greek conjugations, Germanic has preserved but one, **the perfect,** which **plays the double part of an imperfect and an historical past,** E. *he was* and G. *er war,* both in stating a fact and in relating it. This somewhat awkward and ambiguous confusion took place very early; and, very early also, in order to remedy the inconvenience, English and German were compelled to look for a supply of periphrases. Indeed, it is a very remarkable fact, that the form which in Germanic, as well as in Latin and French, essentially assumes the function of an historical or

---

[1] *Supra* 81 sq., 92-93 and 106-107.

narrative past, has no such value at all in Greek, nor had it, most likely, in I.-E.: a Greek narrator regularly uses the aorists, whereas the Greek perfect involves the statement of an achieved action, and therefore very often acquires the force of a durative present[1]; on the contrary, in Germanic, the historical tense is the perfect, while the deficiency of a tense for achieved action is made up, as in French, by the introduction of auxiliary verbs. We need but contrast *I did* with *I've done*, and *er starb* with *er ist gestorben*, to become aware of the rigorous connection between the narrative meaning and the simpler and primitive verb-form.[2]

SECTION I.

PERFECT: GENERAL SURVEY.

(173) Thus we see that the study of the primitive English and German tenses is confined to the **Theory of the Perfect**. But this is worth a whole conjugation in itself, as the minutest phonetic processes and the most various analogical resources are here displayed, crossing and interacting upon one other in every way. It is, in particular, impossible to study it apart from the formation of the past participle, the first principles of which have been already explained,[3] though many more particu-

---

[1] Compare ἔθανε (he died) with τέθνηκε (he is dead), etc., and observe that this durative function is retained in a few Germanic perfects (termed preterito-presents, *infra* 222).

[2] An almost constant exponent in the I.-E. perfect is an initial reduplication (Sk. *bi-bhêd-a* "he split," Gr. λέ-λοιπ-ε "he has left," L. *ce-cid-it* "he fell"), which scarcely ever occurs in the aorist, and is likewise wanting in most Germanic perfects. On the other hand, it is the I.-E. aorist that performs the function of historical past, assigned to the perfect in the Germanic family. From this double contrast, a very probable, and even certain inference may be drawn, namely, that the Germanic preterite—many scholars preferably use this term in order to lay more stress upon the actual value of the historical past—really consists of a nearly equal number of primitive perfect-forms and aorist-forms, which were mixed together and blended into one tense. This, moreover, is found in Latin. But the suggestion here hinted at will not be repeated, since it would only cause needless complication; for, whether, for instance, Go. *bit-um* = E. (*we*) *bit* = G. (*wir*) *bissen* was originally a perfect-form (Sk. *bi-bhid-*), or an aorist-form (Sk. *bhid-*), the vocalism of the root, of course, must always become the same, so that the distinction is of no interest, except as explaining the meaning of the tense or the loss of the I.-E. reduplication.

[3] *Supra* 77-78 and 89-90.

lars will naturally be required here. There exists a close relation between these two grammatical categories: generally speaking, if an English or German verb shows a so-called **Strong Perfect**,—that is to say, with interior vocalic change and no other tense-exponent,—it will also exhibit a so-called **Strong past Participle**,—namely, a participle ending in *-en*, often with either a similar or different change in the root-vowel,— and reciprocally; if a verb has a so-called **Weak Perfect**,— without vocalic change, but formed by adding a suffix containing a dental consonant,—the past **Participle** is likewise a **Weak** one,—without vocalic change and with dental suffix,—and reciprocally. Indeed, the vocalic shade in the strong perfect must have often determined the vocalic shade in the strong participle, or reciprocally: we have but to compare E. *shine shone shone* and G. *scheinen schien geschienen*, wherein the radical vowel, though the same in the present, differs in the two languages in the other forms, but, in each, remains alike in perfect and past participle. Hence we ought to group the two forms side by side, as they are grouped in ordinary grammars, and examine them together in every class of strong verbs in which they were exposed to mutual contamination.

(174) But, at the outset, a question must be solved: whence arose, in the Germanic verbs, this fundamental and important difference in conjugation? or, in other words, **why are there Strong Verbs and Weak Verbs?** Language never produces any arbitrary creations: there can be no doubt that the distinction goes back to some ever-increasing difference in one primitive and characteristic feature; but this feature, neither English nor German, nor their immediate ancestors, nor even Gothic itself, would be able to reveal. In order to discover it we must trace the verb back to its earliest origin.

Such being the case, the rules of verbal derivation, as stated above, are the necessary premises of our present search: conjugation, without them, is mere chaos; with them, it becomes perfectly regular. For the answer to the previous question is found in a simple formula: there are strong and weak verbs, **because there are primary verbal stems**,—that is to say, verbs derived from the root merely by adding to it a single suffix,—and secondary (further tertiary, quaternary, etc.) verbs,—that is to say, later verbal derivatives from a nominal stem, the perfect of which must be a secondary and somewhat complicated construction, since even their present is already an aggregate of various elements added to the pure root-form.[1]

Let us emphasize the contrast: E. (*to*) *bear*, for instance (Go. *baír-an*), or G. *nehm-en* (Go. *nim-an*) has a pf. *bare* (Go. *bar*) or *nahm* (Go. *nam*), and further a part. *bor-n* (Go. *baúr-an-s*) or *ge-nomm-en* (Go. *num-an-s*), because it corresponds to an I.-E. verb derived directly from a root *bhĕr* or *nĕm*, a simple verb like Gr. $\varphi\acute{\epsilon}\rho\text{-}\omega$ or $\nu\acute{\epsilon}\mu\text{-}\omega$, the perfect of which, if it existed in that language, would be *$\pi\acute{\epsilon}\text{-}\varphi o\rho\text{-}a$ or *$\nu\acute{\epsilon}\text{-}\nu o\mu\text{-}a$, a form likewise constructed on the basis of the pure root by mere vocalic gradation. But, still keeping the same examples, we find that a Gr. causative like $\varphi o\rho\text{-}\acute{\epsilon}\text{-}\omega$, or a Gr. secondary derivative like $\nu o\mu\text{-}\epsilon\acute{\upsilon}\text{-}\omega$, can no longer draw its perfect from the pure root, since its present already contains other elements, or form it by vocalic change, since the root-vowel has already undergone such a change in the present: wherefore it forms a pf. $\pi\epsilon\text{-}\varphi\acute{o}\rho\text{-}\eta\text{-}\kappa\text{-}a$ or $\nu\epsilon\text{-}\nu\acute{o}\mu\text{-}\epsilon\upsilon\text{-}\kappa\text{-}a$, the perfect-exponent here no longer being an internal change in a stem which has now become invariable, but a new suffix -κ- added to the prior derivative complex. And this again is exactly the case with our weak perfect, except that the Germanic suffix has a dental for the Greek guttural: both elements, indeed, of equally obscure origin, but of equally clear and similar meaning: E. *ask* and *ask-ed*; G. *lieb-en* and *lieb-te*.

Hence,—putting aside the cases in which a derivative verb adopted a strong perfect and participle after the pattern of a radical verb, and the other and more frequent cases in which a primary stem has been analogically conjugated like the secondary verbs,[2]—we may formulate the general rule as follows:

[1] Cf. *supra* 70, 81 sq., 92-93, and 106-107. From this, however, it does not follow that every primary verb is a strong one: of course, analogy has interfered; but the formula is convenient and simple, true in a general sense, and quite satisfactory even for details, if restricted as shown below.

[2] Since the latter were in a majority and daily increased in number, they tended to ultimately prevail: a tendency, as will be seen, still far more energetic in E. than it is in G.

strong verbs correspond to primary verbal stems; weak verbs, either to secondary stems, or else to such as were at an early period assimilated to them. Still more accurately, **strong verbs are those which belong to classes II., III., V. and VI. of our primary verbal derivation**; for class I., being lost in Germanic, does not concern us; and the causatives (class IV.) even in Sanskrit have a periphrastic perfect[1]; classes VII.-VIII., though really primary, are well-known to have been treated as secondary in several parts of their conjugation, and particularly in regard to their perfect-formation.[2]

Of these so-called strong and often improperly termed irregular verbs, English has preserved only about a hundred, counting only simple verbs.[3] So great has been the power of analogy that even some of these strong verbs only betray their primitive character by forming a participle in -*en*, their perfect being weak and ending in -*ed*. German is much purer and retains twice as many, the complete enumeration of which belongs to

[1] In some cases it happened, from a merely phonetic and regular cause, that the present-vocalism of both the simple and the causative verb became identical: thus E. *sit* = G. *sitz-e* (= I.-E. *séd-yō) and E. *set* = G. *setz-e* (= I.-E. *sod-éy-ō), are still contrasted forms; but I.-E. *smeld-ō (Gr. μέλδ-ω "I become molten") and I.-E. *smold-éy-ō (Germanic *smalt-ja "I cause to melt") became respectively O.H.G. *smëlzen* and *smelzen*, which were further blended into G. *schmelzen*. The same is the case with E. *to melt*, which unites the two meanings. Next took place, analogically, either an extension of the strong forms which swept away the weak ones (G. now only recognises *schmolz* and *geschmolzen*), or a confusion which led to the two being indifferently used (E. *molt-en* and *melt-ed*): a process more or less illustrated by such G. verbs as *verderben* "to become corrupted" and "to corrupt," *löschen* "to become extinct" and "to extinguish," *quellen, schwellen*, etc., though the primitive distinction is not forgotten. A correct speaker will say *das licht erlosch*, but *er löschte das licht aus*. Likewise in E. *a swollen leg*, but *the rain has swelled the river*, though the pf. is *swelled* in either sense.

[2] Generally speaking, strong verbs correspond to the 3rd Latin conjugation, and weak verbs, to the three others, viz.: the type *suchen* (Go. *sōkjan* = L. *sāgīre*), to the fourth; the type *salben* (cf. Go. *fiskōn* = L. *piscāri*), to the 1st; and the type *haben* (O.H.G. *habēn* = L. *habēre*), to the second conjugation. Cf. the imperative-forms: *suochi* (seek) = *sāgī*; *salbo* (salve) like *amā*; *habe* (have) = L. *habē*; *infra* 196.

[3] It need scarcely be observed that a compound verb follows in general the conjugation of the simple verb: thus, *kommen* has *kam* and *gekommen*, in *an-kommen, zu-kommen*, etc. But, of course, we must not be deceived by the mere appearance of composition: the pf. and part. of *bewillkommen* are *bewillkommte* and *bewillkommt*, because the vb. is not a compound of vb. *kommen*, but a derivative from the adjective *willkommen* (cf. *supra* 118, 3). And the same is the case with E. *he overcame* and he *welcomed*.

ordinary grammar. Here our task will be to compare the strong verbs in the two languages by classifying them according to the regular vocalic changes which characterize their tenses, and to ascertain the occasional influences which either in English or German may have altered the original correspondences in their conjugation.

SECTION II.

STRONG PERFECT AND PARTICIPLE.

(175) The so-called strong perfects of Modern Germanic languages proceed from two distinct Pregermanic formations, which are still clearly illustrated by the Gothic and, sometimes, even by the later Germanic accidence, namely: **perfects with vowel-gradation** and **perfects with reduplication**. The former have been seen to change the root-vowel of the present-stem: Go. *bair-a* (I carry), *nim-a* (I take), pf. *bar* and *nam* with deflected root. The latter usually keep it unchanged, though some may also alter it, and the leading characteristic of this class, as of the Greek and Latin perfect, is a reduplication containing a vowel *ĕ* and prefixed to the root-syllable: Go. *háit-a* (I call), *lēt-a* (I leave), pf. *hai-háit* and *lai-lōt*; cf. Gr. λέ-λοιπ-α, L. *me-min-ī*, etc.

Of course, when taking these as two distinct classes, we are considering exclusively the Germanic family; for the fact is, that the deflected and the reduplicated perfects formed originally but one class, or, in other words, that any I.-E. primary perfect exhibited at the same time reduplication and vowel-gradation.[1] But the adventitious distinction which took place in Pregermanic may be easily accounted for: perfects in which, owing to the phonetic laws of the Germanic group, the root-vowel had become the same as in the present, kept their reduplication, as the only means of distinction from the other tenses; while, in the perfects which kept their vocalism plainly contrasted with that of the present, reduplication seemed a

[1] Thus, the reduplicated Gr. pf. λέ-λοιπ-α, from a root λειπ (to leave), shows exactly the same vowel-gradation that characterizes the primitive non-reduplicated pf. *olδ-a* = ϝοἶδ-a (I know) = Sk. *vêd-a*, from a root ϝειδ (to see).

needless and rather cumbrous element which might well be rejected.[1]

§ 1. *Perfects with Vowel-Gradation.*

(176) I. Let us recall the elements of I.-E. vowel-gradation[2]: it is a vocalic alternation between three main grades which have been termed respectively the normal, reduced and deflected grade. To each of these grades correspond some well-known I.-E. vowels. It remains to state the grade which ought regularly to correspond to each tense-form of the conjugated root. This point too is easily settled: Sanskrit, and, in particular, Greek, which are here in marvellous agreement with Gothic, allow us to summarize it under four short and invariable rules.

1. The present,—and consequently the Germanic **infinitive**, which always resembles the present,—generally has the **normal** grade (Gr. ἔδ-ω φέρ-ω λείπ-ω φεύγ-ω νέμ-ω), sometimes—though very seldom in Germanic—the reduced, never the deflected grade;—and this alone is sufficient to distinguish it from the perfect.

2. The **singular of the perfect** always has the **deflected** root: Gr. root Ϝειδ (to see), in εἶδ-ος (image), εἶδ-ο-ν (I saw), but pf. οἶδ-α (I wot) = Ϝοῖδ-α; Gr. λείπ-ω, pf. λέ-λοιπ-α; L. fūg-iō and pf. fūg-ī, vĭd-eō and pf. vīd-ī = *void-ei, etc.

3. In the **plural of the perfect**, the root is **reduced**[3]: Gr. οἶδ-α, but pl. ἴδ-μεν ἴσ-μεν (we know). The fact is nowhere better verified than in Sanskrit and Gothic: Sk. *bi-bhêd-a* (I split), pl. *bi-bhid-imá*; Go. *báit* (I bit), pl. *bit-um*.

4. The suffix *-onó-* of the **participle** (Sk. *-āná-*, Go. *-an-*) is accented and consequently always **reduces** the root: Go. *bit-an-s*, cf. E. *bitt-en* and G. *ge-biss-en*; Sk. root *vart* (to turn, L. *vert-ere*), pf. part. *vă-vrt-āná-s* = Go. *vaúrþ-an-s*, cf. G. *ge-word-en*, etc.

(177) II. Hence, if Pregermanic had kept the I.-E. tradi-

---

[1] The more so, because, as noted above (172), some aoristic non-reduplicated forms intruded into the perfect and strongly influenced it.

[2] *Supra* 43–45.

[3] Because here the primitive accent was shifted to the personal-ending: cf. the Sk. accentuation below, and *supra* 44, 45 (2), etc.

tion unaltered, the theory of the strong verb would correspond to the theory of vowel-gradation and would present a series of phonetic equations of the utmost simplicity. But no language of the European group is found in this state of archaic purity[1]: at various times and in various circumstances, the four forms stated above influenced one another, in such a way as to modify, confound, and even differentiate one another by adopting new characteristics, quite unlike their original features. Now these various processes may again be summed up in four corresponding formulas, the application of which will cross and limit the effect of the preceding rules.

1. In imitation of presents, which primitively had the reduced root,—that is to say, the vowel-grade of the participle,—it might well happen that other presents adopted,—chiefly as a means of distinction from the perfect, with which the effect of the Germanic phonetic laws tended to confound them,—the vowel-grade of the participle, and thus opposed the reduced root to the deflected root of the perfect.[2]

2. In some verb-classes, Germanic phonetics had blended both the reduced and the deflected grade to the same form; besides, in all of them, the vowel-grade was regularly the same in the participle and the plural of the perfect: from this to a closer assimilation and to the extension of the perfect-vocalism to the participle itself, was but one step, and this step the speaker often took.[3]

3. Even within the perfect itself, such forms as *báit bit-um* might easily seem to be strange: hence there was a natural tendency to adopt either one form or the other, and to conjugate the tense, either *báit* *báit-um, or *bit bit-um.[4] This

---

[1] Up to a certain point, Gothic may be said, together with Sanskrit, to abide by it most of all, since it still retains the curious alternation from the sg. to the pl., which is entirely lost, apart from some immaterial survivals, in Latin, and even in Greek.

[2] Such is especially the case with the type *slay* = *schlagen* (Go. *slah-a slah-an-s*), *supra* 45, 7, and *infra* 184.

[3] A fact already stated in regard to the E. part. *shone*, contrasted with the G. part. *geschienen*. Cf. *infra* 179 (2), 184 (2), 185 (III. 2), and observe moreover such popular blunders as *I have took*, etc.

[4] Thus too, in Greek, the regular conjugation λέ-λοιπ-α *λε-λιπ-μεν was soon forgotten, while a new pl. λελοίπαμεν was formed from λέλοιπα; or else,

analogy sooner or later worked its way throughout, and we are able to follow its progress from the mother-tongues, which are nearly free from it, down to the modern offspring, which passively obey its law.

4. Lastly, in imitation of the cases, in which the I.-E. reduced grade did not differ from the normal vocalism,—the participle and the present thus showing the same vowel,—it happened that the participle adopted the present-vocalism in other cases when it ought to have had the reduced syllable,—a corruption which is found in all the Germanic dialects and is, therefore, due to a vocalic peculiarity belonging to the common ancestor.[1]

(178) III. These general principles being well understood, we shall find that the English and German verbs with vowel-gradation or **deflected** perfects fall under **six** distinct heads; the verbs with **reduplicated** perfects constitute by themselves a **seventh** class. For the sake of brevity these seven types are distinguished by letters.[2]

(179)   A. Type *drive = treiben*.

The type *drive = treiben* corresponds to our 2nd class of vowel-gradation, that is to say, it comprises I.-E. verbs, the root of which contains, in its normal grade, a diphthong *ĕy* (Preg. *ĭ*), which, deflected, becomes *ŏy* (Preg. *ai*), and, reduced, merely *ĭ* (Preg. *ĭ*). Thus we shall have a triple alternation *ī ai ĭ*, which, when applied, for instance, to a Preg. vb. *ŏrĭb-ana-m (to drive), and retained in the further evolution of the later

---

when the plural-vocalism prevailed, a sg. ἐλήλυθα (for the regular Homeric εἰλ-ήλουθ-α) was created in imitation of the regular pl. *ἐλ-ηλυθ-μεν (we are come). Latin has many perfects with deflected root, like *fūg-i*, and many others with reduced root, like *tŭl-i*; but, whatever may be the actual vocalism, it always holds good for the whole tense, singular and plural. Apart from a few survivals, English and German have reached exactly the same point.— Cf. also F. *je treuve* and *nous trouvons* (*tróvo trovámus*), *j'aim* and *nous amons* (*ámo amámus*), now levelled to *trouve trouvons* and, inversely, *aime aimons*.

[1] The root kept without reduction in the participle is the leading characteristic of the type *see = sehen*, supra 45, 1, and infra 183.

[2] Hence our types A.-G. strictly correspond to the classes I.-VII. as distinguished in the historical grammars of the Germanic languages. The order in which they are enumerated is rather arbitrary; but it seemed convenient to abide by it, since grammatical usage has adopted the terminology.

languages, would produce the following historical, or theoretical, forms:

Preg. inf. *đrĭb̃-ana-m; pf. sg. *đráĭb̃-a; pf. pl. *đrĭb̃-umé; part. *đrĭb̃-aná-s;
Go.   ,,   dreib-an   ; ,,   dráif   ; ,,   drib-um   ; ,,   drib-an-s;
O.E.   ,,   drĭf-an   ; ,,   drāf   ; ,,   drif-on   ; ,, ge-drif-en;
E.   ,,   drive   ; ,,   I drove ; ,, we *drive[1] ; ,,   driv-en;
O.H.G.,, trĭb-an   ; ,,   treib   ; ,,   trib-um   ; ,, gi-trib-an;
G.   ,,   treib-en ; ,, ich *treib ; ,, wir trieb-en ; ,, ge-trieb-en.

We see at once the absolute purity of the Go., O.E. and O.H.G. conjugation. By contrasting, on the other hand, the historical and theoretical E. *we *drive* with the actual *we drove*, and the historical and theoretical G. *ich *treib* with the actual *ich trieb*, we easily become aware of the fact that, in the latter language, the sg. of the pf. was accommodated to the pl., whereas, in the former, the pl. borrowed its vocalism from the sg.

Dealing now, in the same way, with a Preg. vb. *bĭt-ana-m* " to bite" (I.-E. root *bhĕyd bhŏyd bhĭd*, cf. L. *find-ere* " to split," pf. *fĭd-ī*), we get the forms:

Preg. inf. *bĭt-ana-m; pf. sg. *báit-a; pf. pl. *bĭt-umé; part. *bĭt-aná-s;
Go.   ,,   beit-an   ; ,,   báit   ; ,,   bit-um   ; ,,   bit-an-s;
O.E.   ,,   bit-an   ; ,,   bāt   ; ,,   bit-on   ; ,, ge-bit-en;
E.   ,,   bite   ; ,,   I *bote ; ,, we bit   ; ,,   bitt-en;
O.H.G.,, biʒ-an   ; ,,   beiʒ   ; ,,   biʒʒ-um; ,, gi-biʒʒ-an;
G.   ,,   beisz-en ; ,, ich *beisz ; ,, wir biss-en ; ,, ge-biss-en.

Here, both in English and German, the asterisk stands in the same column, which is equivalent to saying that in both languages the analogical process was carried on in the same way, the sg. of the pf. being conjugated like the pl., thus E. *I bit* like *we bit*, and G. *ich bisz* like *wir bissen*.

These two verbs represent the whole of this class, which therefore requires but a few brief remarks.

1. English has about twenty and German about forty verbs of this type; though, excepting the constant alteration in the pl. of the perfect, English here is by far the purer, having often retained the vowel-gradation with three grades, *e.g.* in *rise rose*

---

[1] Pronounced like *give*, not like *drive* in the present.

risen, drive drove driven, shrive shrove shriven, smite smote smitten, write wrote written, ride rode ridden, etc.

2. The last verb, however, also admits of a participle *rode*, and, similarly, the vocalism of the pf. sg., after having invaded the pl., further corrupts the part. also in *abide abode abode, shine shone shone*, and *strike struck struck*,[1] which have only two vocalic grades; though, of course, *strick-en* survives as an isolated word.

3. The reversed process, as seen above, was no less possible; in that case the vowel-gradation was confined to the two grades $\bar{i}$ and $\breve{i}$, the vowel of the part. and pf. pl. being transferred to the pf. sg., *bite bit bitten* (and *bit*[2]), *chide chid chidden, hide hid hidden*, even *split*[3] *split split*.[4]

4. Now, in German, it is exclusively the latter process which has spread and affected the whole of this class. German has no more than two vocalic grades, namely, *ei* ($=\bar{i}$) for the present, and, for the whole of the perfect as well as for the participle, an *i* sounded either short or long[5] according as it stands in a close or an open syllable: *treiben trieb getrieben, reiben, leihen, schreiben*, etc.; *beiszen bisz gebissen, greifen griff gegriffen, schneiden schnitt geschnitten*,[6] *leiden, weichen, streiten,* etc. And consequently, as opposed to the regular E. *shone wrote rode*, we find the irregular G. *schien risz ritt*.

5. Having thus reduced its vowel-gradation, German applied it even to some obviously secondary verbs which never had anything to do with the primitive process: whence the strong

---

[1] With vowel-shifting, owing to the shortening in a close syllable, *supra* 17, 4. The verbs *stick stuck stuck* and *dig dug dug* belonged originally to type E (cf. G. *steck-en stack ge-steck-t*) and were transferred to type A by analogy.

[2] On the accidental loss of the syllable *-en*, cf. *supra* 19, 2.

[3] With shortening: cf. G. *spleisz-en splisz ge-splis-en*. The reader should supply for himself any comparison that may have been omitted for the sake of brevity.

[4] The verbs *rive* and *writhe* still preserve their strong parts. *riven* and *writhen*, but they have adopted a weak pf. *rived* and *writhed*. On the contrary, *strive* (cf. G. *streb-en*) is a weak verb analogically adapted to the strong conjugation.

[5] Further, this long *i* is already known to be spelled *ie*, *supra* 12, 4.

[6] In this verb and the following we have a remarkable instance of "grammatical alternation" (*supra* 53 D and 55), the Preg. being inf. **sniþ-ana-m* and part. **snið-aná-s*, with accent-shifting leading to consonantal change.

conjugation of *gleichen*, a derivative from the adjective *gleich* = Go. *ga-leik-s* (cf. E. weak vb. *like*); and, even to *preisen*, a derivative from *preis* (praise), which is a borrowed word (cf. M.F. *pris* and F. *prix*).

(180)   B. Type *choose = kiesen*.

This type corresponds to our 3rd class of vowel-gradation, namely to the roots which respectively exhibited the three vocalisms: normal *ĕw*, deflected *ŏw*, reduced *ŭ* ; Preg. *iu (eo) au ŭ*. Thus, a root *gĕws gŏws gŭs* (to taste, cf. Gr. γεύ-ω and L. *gŭs-tu-s*), treated according to our rule, assumes the following forms, rigorously reproduced in the earlier Germanic languages:

Preg. inf. *kéus-ana-m; pf. sg. *káus-a; pf. pl. *kŭz-umé; part. *kŭz-aná-s;
Go.   „   kius-an   ;   „   káus   ;   „   kus-um   ;   „   kus-an-s;
O.E.   „   céos-an   ;   „   céas   ;   „   cur-on   ;   „   ge-cor-en;
O.H.G.   „   kios-an   ;   „   kōs   ;   „   kur-um   ;   „   gi-kor-an.

Here, owing to the peculiar treatment of the I.-E. *ŭ* in the Germanic languages,[1] the threefold vowel-gradation has become a fourfold one in O.E. and O.H.G.[2] But analogy has greatly simplified this complicated conjugation.

I. English.—1. First of all, the O.E. grade *éa* in the pf. sg. vanished altogether: the O.E. type *fléog-an* (= G. *flieg-en*) *fléag flug-on ge-flog-en*, although the purest in the later language, is nevertheless confined to the three grades *fly*[3] *flew flow-n*; which is equivalent to saying, that, the infinitive and participle respectively keeping their primitive vowel, the vocalism of the pf. pl. was extended to the pf. sg., whence in the whole tense *flew* = *flug*, with the same change in spelling as in *slew* = *slōg*.[4]

2. No other verb has retained the three grades. The vowel of the participle corrupted the perfect everywhere else, as may be seen in: *shoot* (= G. *schiesz-en*) *shot shot*; *cleave* (= O.E. *cléof-an*) *clove cloven*; even *choose chose chosen*, where the double

---

[1] Cf. *supra* 28, I.
[2] Observe also the "grammatical alternation" between *s* and *z*, which, while entirely lost in Gothic, persists down to Mod. G. *kies-en er-kor-en*.
[3] On *y = eog*, cf. *supra* 21.
[4] *Supra* 45, 7, and *infra* 184.

vocalism is no longer betrayed except by the spelling, the *s* being moreover extended throughout.

3. Further, two E. verbs show the gradation *ee* [1] *o*, viz.: *freeze froze frozen* (instead of **fror-en*, cf. G. *frier-en fror ge-fror-en*, which, on the contrary, has extended the *r*), and *seethe sod sodd-en*, which in both languages (G. *sied-en sott ge-sott-en*) has kept the grammatical alternation.

4. These six verbs are the sole representatives of type B. All the rest were shifted to the weak conjugation, so that English, for instance, represents by verbs *lose lost lost* (formerly *loren*, cf. *for-lorn*), *lie lied lied, bow bowed bowed*, etc., the G. verbs *ver-lier-en -lor -lor-en, lügen log gelogen, biegen bog gebogen*, etc.

II. German.—1. Here, on the contrary, there are no less than thirty verbs of this class still existing; but all of them are confined to two vocalic grades. The old diphthong *io* in the present is now, of course, spelled *ie* and sounded *ī*. Now, the diphthong in the pf. sg. is either O.H.G. *ou* or O.H.G. *ō*, according to the neighbouring sounds [2]; but it has become levelled to *ō*, which again, in later times, was sounded either long or short, according as the syllable was open or close. This *ō*, in consequence, became blended with *ŏ* in the part., which was itself either short or long under the same conditions, and the *ŭ* in the pf. pl. proved unable to resist this double concurrence. In short, the modern paradigm is: *ziehen zog* (Go. *táuh*) *gezogen, fliegen, fliehen, wiegen* (analogical), etc.; *kriechen kroch gekrochen, gieszen, genieszen, triefen, sieden*, etc.

2. In some as yet undefined circumstances, an I.-E. root which had a *ŭ* in its reduced grade could assume a normal grade *ū* instead of the regular diphthong *ĕw*. The fact is verified as to two Germanic verbs, which, while exhibiting in the pf. and part. the vocalism of the preceding verbs, merely lengthen their root-vowel in the present: O.H.G. *sūf-an* and G. *sauf-en* (*soff gesoffen*); O.H.G. *sūg-an* and G. *saug-en* (*sog gesogen*). Their conjugation was afterwards applied to *schnauben* and *schrauben*.

3. The metaphonical verbs *er-kür-en* (cf. the primitive *kies-en*),

[1] For the different vowel in the presents *choose* and *freeze*, see below 204.
[2] *Supra* 32, the rule and the examples.

trüg-en (cf. the primitive (*be-*)*trieg-en*) and *lüg-en*, which are later derivatives from the nouns *kur* (choice),[1] *trug* and *lug*, analogically adopted the conjugation of the primitive verbs *kios-an*, *triog-an* and *liog-an*.

4. With the exception of these seven presents, the leading characteristic of type B is a vowel *ie* in the infinitive.

(181) **C. Type** *drink=trinken* **and** *swell=schwellen*.

Supposing the radical I.-E. $\breve{e}$ to be followed either by a nasal or liquid, we reach the fourth and fifth classes of vowel-gradation. But these two classes are not entirely comprised in type C: they only belong to it so far as the radical nasal or liquid is again followed by another consonant. When this is the case, the $\breve{e}$ before a liquid remains $\breve{e}$, but becomes $\breve{i}$ before a nasal in West Germanic: hence, in West Germanic, type C must be divided into two sub-classes, whereas in Gothic it is the same throughout.[2]

I. Let us consider an I.-E. root *dhreṅg* (to drink), deflected *dhroṅg*, reduced *dhrṇg*, and see what becomes of it in Pregermanic and the modern languages.

Preg. inf. *ð́riṅk-ana-m*; pf. sg. *ð́ráṅk-a*; pf. pl. *ð́ruṅk-umé*; part. *ð́ruṅk-aná-s*;
Go. „ drigk-an ; „ dragk ; „ drugk-um ; „ drugk-an-s ;
O.E. „ drinc-an ; „ dronc[3] ; „ drunc-on ; „ ge-drunc-en ;
E. „ drink ; „ I drank ; „ we *drunk ; „ drunk ;
O.H.G. „ trinch-an ; „ tranch ; „ trunch-um ; „ gi-trunch-an ;
G. „ trink-en ; „ ich trank ; „ wir *trunk-en[4] ; „ ge-trunk-en.

1. The similar process in English and German is at once obvious: the vowel of the pf. sg. was transferred to the plural, *we drank*, *wir tranken*, etc.; and consequently, even the purest verbs of this class, namely such as keep unaltered the threefold gradation *i a u*, never have any other grade but *a* in the perfect-stem.

[1] Also *chur* (election), whence *chur-fürst* (high elector), and cf. the compound *will-kür-lich* (arbitrary).
[2] Because Gothic changes every $\breve{e}$ to $\breve{i}$, supra 26.
[3] O.E. *o* for E. *a* before a nasal, *supra* 39, 3.
[4] Still M.H.G. (constantly) *ich trank* and *wir trunken*, *ich fand* and *wir funden*, *ich bran* (I burnt) and *wir brunnen*, etc.

2. Of the 25 E. verbs belonging to this type, eleven have preserved the regular alternation, e.g.: *begin began begun, sing sang sung, spring sprang sprung, sink sank sunk, swim swam swum,* etc.[1]; cf. G. *beginnen begann begonnen, singen sang gesungen, springen, sinken, schwimmen schwamm geschwommen,* etc.

3. But, even in the verbs which remain regular in English, the perfect is liable to be assimilated to the participle: thus, we may say either *sank* or *sunk, span* or *spun, stank* or *stunk* (G. always *sank spann stank*). Next, the regular grade was completely forgotten, and the gradation was confined to two sounds in *cling clung clung, fling flung flung, string strung strung, win won won* (G. regularly *gewinnen gewann gewonnen*), where the whole perfect is conjugated with the vowel of the plural-stem.

4. The latter has become the invariable rule for verbs in which the primitive $\breve{u}$ has been lengthened to $ou=\bar{u}$ before the group *nd*[2]: *bind bound bound, find found found, wind, grind,* contrasted with G. *binden band gebunden, finden, winden,* etc.

5. Though German, in this sub-class, is scarcely richer than English, it is seen at once, from a glance at the previous instances, to have preserved its original character far better. In fact, the threefold gradation *i a u* (*o*)[3] here survives nearly in every case. Occasionally, it is true, the vowel of the participle appears in the perfect (*ich begonn* archaic); but this can hardly be deemed an exception to the rule, as it is actually confined to an optional hesitation in the metaphonical vowel of the subjunctive of this tense (*ränne* or *rönne, gewänne* or *gewönne,* and always *begönne*). There are but four verbs in which this corruption is consistently found,—and out of these four there are two which once belonged to the weak conjugation,—viz. *glimmen* (cf. the E. derivative *glimm-er*) *glomm, klimmen* (=E. *climb*, likewise a weak vb.) *klomm* (also *klimm-te*), *schinden schund geschunden,* and *dingen dung* (*bedingen bedung*).

II. As the type of this sub-class we have chosen the verb

---

[1] In *run ran run* (G. *rinnen* "to flow," not to be confounded with its causative *rennen* "to run") the vowel of the part. has intruded into the present.

[2] *Supra* 20, 4 B.

[3] On the change of $\breve{u}$ to $\breve{o}$ (*gesungen gefunden,* but *gewonnen geschwommen*), cf. *supra* 28, I.

swell = *schwellen*, because it happens to be the only verb directly comparable in the two languages. In the theoretical paradigm, however, it will prove advisable to replace it by another verb, which has been preserved in Gothic, and to neglect the English type, which, with many more, has passed to the weak conjugation.

Preg. inf. *hélp-ana-m*; pf. sg. *hálp-a*; pf. pl. *hulp-umé*; part. *hulp-aná-s*;
Go.   „   *hilp-an* ; „   *halp* ; „   *hulp-um* ; „   *hulp-an-s* ;
O.E.   „   *help-an* ; „   *healp* ; „   *hulp-on* ; „   *ge-holp-en* ;
O.H.G. „   *hëlf-an* ; „   *half* ; „   *hulf-um* ; „   *gi-holf-an* ;
G.   „   *helf-en* ; „ *ich half* ; „ *wir half-en* ; „ *ge-holf-en*.

1. Here, as above in type B, and owing to the same circumstances in Germanic phonetics, we find a fourfold gradation, *e a u o*, which however in Mod. German has been reduced to three grades, *e a o*, on account of the vocalism of the pf. sg. having been extended throughout the whole tense.[1]

2. But English scarcely shows a single representative of this class, with the exception of a few participles: *molt-en* (cf. G. *ge-schmolz-en*), as opposed to pf. *melt-ed*; *holp-en*, now replaced by *help-ed*, etc. The whole set has been transferred to the weak conjugation, and in particular the curious vb. *starve* (cf. G. *sterb-en* " to die "), which, having adopted in the present the vowel of the perfect (G. *starb*),[2] developed on this new stem a new pf. *starv-ed*. Making these deductions, we find that only three verbs fall under this head: *swell swell-ed swoll-en*, where the pf. has become weak[3]; *burst burst burst* (G. *bersten barst geborsten*), where the vocalism is the same throughout; and, lastly, *fight fought fought*.

3. German is much purer in every respect. Here, the type *schwellen* comprises 22 verbs, namely:—10 with consonant *l* (*helfen, melken, schmelzen, schwellen, quellen, bellen*, etc.), including also *befehlen* = O.H.G. *bi-fëlh-an*, and *erschallen* (for *erschellen*) influenced by the vocalism of the substantive *schall* (sound) ;—8

---

[1] Still M.H.G. *half hulfen, warf wurfen*, etc., as above *fand funden*.
[2] Possibly this is only an effect akin to the O.E. breaking, supra 21.—Observe the restricted meaning, and compare F. *noyer* (to drown) = L. *necāre* (to kill).
[3] The regular M.E. *swal* in Chaucer, *e.g. Prioresses Tale*, 72.

with consonant *r* (*werden, werfen, werben, sterben, bergen, verderben,* etc.), including *wirren* (*verwirren*) = O.H.G. *wërran,* influenced by the metaphonical vocalism of the adjective *wirr* (intricate); —2 in which the liquid precedes the vowel, the phonetic result being naturally the same as far as the reduced grade is concerned,[1] *flecht-en* = L. *plect-ō* (cf. L. *plicō* "I fold" and Gr. πλέκ-ω), and *dresch-en* = E. *thrash* (weak verb)[2]; —2 analogically conjugated after the two preceding, *fechten* = E. *fight,* and *erlöschen* = O.H.G. *ir-lĕsk-an* (*ö* in spelling instead of *e*).

(*a*) The fourfold gradation persists but in one, namely *werden* = Go. *vairþ-an* = L. *vert-ī* (to be turned, to be changed, to become), which retains *ich ward, wir wurden* and *geworden,* together with subj. pf. *ich würde*; though, even here, the primitive conjugation is somewhat altered, inasmuch as the pl. *wir wurden* gave birth to a sg. *ich wurde,* which is now oftener used than *ward*. But there at least the grade *u* survives.

(*b*) Such is no longer the case anywhere else, but the metaphonical form *ü* appears occasionally in the subjunctive of the perfect: *stürbe, hülfe, verdürbe, würbe, würfe*; but also *stärbe, wärfe.*

(*c*) Among the ten verbs that still retain the triple gradation, several are already seen to admit concurrently either of the perfect-vowel or the participle-vowel in the perfect-stem: thus, side by side with *barst, drasch, schalt, galt, befahl,* we have *borst, drosch, scholt, golt, befohl,*[3] with the vowel borrowed from *geborsten, gedroschen,* etc.

(*d*) This anomaly becomes the rule in the remainder, whence the merely double gradation *e o* in: *schwellen schwoll geschwollen,* cf. E. *swell*; and so also, *quellen, melken, erschallen, erlöschen,* etc.

(182)　　　　　D. Type *steal* = *stehlen.*

This type comprises all the verbs of our fourth and fifth

---

[1] An I.-E. root *plĕk,* for instance, and an I.-E. root *pĕlk,* if reduced, must equally give *pļk.*

[2] The present *thrash* = **thresh,* like *starve* = **sterve* and *warp* = **werp* (G. *werfen*). Besides, *thresh* as a rural form, is used in G. Eliot (*Scenes of Clerical Life*) by a country-woman.

[3] The last two are archaic, but subj. *beföhle.*

classes of vowel-gradation, which do not belong to type C, or—theoretically at least—those in which the radical $ĕ$ is followed by a single nasal or liquid that is not followed by any other consonant; the nasal verbs, however, here are very few; and, on the other hand, analogy at an early date introduced into this class some verbs which contained neither a nasal nor a liquid, but were formerly, and still ought to be, conjugated after the type E.

In fact, type D well marks a transition from the preceding to the following verbs. It resembles the preceding, in that it depends on the presence of a nasal or liquid in the verbal stem: Preg. *ném-ana-m (to take), *bér-ana-m (to carry), Go. nim-an, baír-an. And, therefore, like the preceding, it strictly requires the gradation $e\ a\ u$[1]: Go. nim-an nam num-an-s (G. nehm-en nahm ge-nomm-en), qim-an qam qum-an-s, baír-an bar baúr-an-s (G. ge-bär-en ge-bar ge-bor-en), etc. But, like the following verbs, it assumes in the pf. pl. a peculiar vocalism, namely a grade $ē$ (Go. nam nēm-um, qam qēm-um, bar bēr-um), which, being unknown in I.-E. vowel-gradation, has excited the curiosity of many enquirers, without as yet betraying the secret of its origin.[2]

At any rate, the Go. alternation bar bēr-um necessarily gives O.E. bær bǣr-on and O.H.G. bar bār-um, that is to say, in each language, a very similar sound for both numbers. Hence there arose a tendency to unification, which took place everywhere, so that English, which ought to answer O.E. with *I bare* and *we *bere* (cf. *we were*), has merely *we bare*. In German, the case is still easier: for, as soon as the a was lengthened in an open syllable, and shortened in a close one, there no longer remained any reason why,—analogy moreover furthering the confusion,—the vowels in *ich gebar* and *wir gebaren*, *ich stahl* and *wir stahlen*, *ich kam* and *wir kamen*, *ich nahm* and *wir nahmen*, etc., should be dis-

---

[1] Indeed, apart of course from Gothic, the *e* here is never changed to *i*. The *u*, naturally, is changed to *o* under the usual conditions.

[2] To this $ē$, have been compared the L. $ē$ in *sēdi*, *vēni*, etc., contrasted with *sĕdeō*, *vĕniō*, etc., and a Sk. $ē$, which likewise occurs in the plural of certain perfects; but the connection between those various processes is quite doubtful. We would rather adhere to the supposition of a so-called "lengthened grade" of the root-syllable.

tinguished from each other. Thus, the gradation admits of but three grades at most: *e a o*.

German has 18 verbs of this type, namely:—2 with consonant *m*, *nehmen* = O.H.G. *nëm-an*, and *kommen* (E. *come*) = O.H.G. *quëm-an*, where the present has adopted the vowel of the participle;—2 with consonant *l*, *stehlen* (E. *steal*) = O.H.G. *stël-an*, and *verhehlen*;—4 with consonant *r*, *gebären* = O.H.G. *bër-an*,[1] *scheren gä(h)ren* and *schwären*;—5 with a guttural, though 4 of them have also an *r* in the root, *erschrecken, brechen*,[2] *sprechen, rächen* and *stechen*;—1 assimilated to the last type, *treffen*;—and, lastly, 4 verbs which in O.H.G. belonged to the type E and have passed to this, owing to the likeness of the stem-vowel in the present, viz. *pflegen, weben, bewegen* and *erwägen*. On the contrary, the vb. *verzehren* (= E. *tear*) has passed to the weak conjugation; but its old gradation still survives in *zorn* (anger), a participle used substantivally.

English has respectively:—*come*;—*steal*;—*bear, shear, tear*;—*break, speak*;—*weave, get, tread*, three verbs from class E [3];—*heave, swear*, from class F;—*wear*, formerly a weak verb, now assimilated to *bear*;—whereas *play* = O.E. *pleg-ian* = G. *pflegen* has now become a weak verb, as the latter may also be in German.

Of these 13 E. verbs, two only have kept the threefold gradation: *bear* (in the meaning "to produce") *bare born*, and *come came come*. Two others still keep it in M.E., *break brake* (G. *brach*) *broken*, and *speak spake*[4] *spoken*; but the analogical *broke* and *spoke* have decidedly prevailed. The vb. *beget*, in scriptural style, has the pf. *begat*, whilst the only pf. of *get* is *got*, and so with the rest: *steal stole* (cf. G. *stahl*) *stolen, weave wove* (cf. G. *wob*) *woven, bear* (to carry) *bore borne, shear*, etc.

German is purer. Ten of its verbs preserve the three grades: *nehmen, kommen, stehlen, gebären, erschrecken, brechen*,

---

[1] The *ä*, here as in some other cases, is only a different spelling for etymological *e*.
[2] Cf. *supra* 181, II. 3, and 42, note.
[3] Compare *forget forgot forgotten, tread trod trodden*, with *vergessen vergasz vergessen, treten trat getreten*.
[4] Usual in Shakespeare and his contemporaries.

sprechen, stechen, treffen and *pflegen* (*pflag* or *pflog*). The remaining eight introduce the *o* of the participle into the perfect.

(183)   E. Type *see = sehen*.

Excepting as regards the participle the two types D and E are in full agreement: in the present, vowel ĕ, Go. *saíhv-an*; in the pf. sg., vowel ă, Go. *sahv* (cf. E. *see saw* and G. *seh-en sah*); in the pf. pl., the same unexplained ē, Go. *sēhv-um*. The only difference is in Go. *saíhv-an-s* = E. *see-n* = G. *ge-seh-en*, which has the infinitive-vowel.

The reason for this is that type E corresponds to our first class of vowel-gradation, namely to the radical vowel ĕ, standing in any other position but in the four types A–D: such being the case, the ĕ, as noted above, when the syllable becomes reduced, disappears in I.-E. without leaving any vocalic sound to support the neighbouring consonants, so that the syllable ought to disappear altogether; but it has been seen that Pregermanic does not go so far as this. The reduced grade here remains identical with the normal grade, that is, the stem of the participle identical with the stem of the infinitive. Hence there arises a threefold gradation, viz. ĕ ă ē ĕ (Go. *gib-an gaf gēb-um gib-an-s, it-an at ēt-um it-an-s*, etc.), which of course persists in O.E. and O.H.G., but which still, by the process defined above, is confined to two grades, *e a a e*, in the later languages: E. *give gave gave given, eat ate ate eaten*; G. *geben gab gaben gegeben, essen asz aszen gegessen*, etc.

Instead of an ĕ, we may also find in the present, and analogically even in the participle,[1] a metaphonical ĭ, that is, when the verb is formed by means of the I.-E. suffix *-yo-* instead of the simple *-o-*: thus, Preg. *ét-ana-m (to eat), from I.-E. *éd-ō (I eat) = Gr. ἔδ-ω = L. *ĕd-ō*; but Preg. *sit-jana-m (E. *sit* = G. *sitz-en*), from I.-E. *séd-yō; and so also, E. *lie* = G. *liegen*, E. *bid* = G. *bitten* (to beg, to pray) = Go. *bid-jan*.[2]

Briefly, the verbs of this class must have: in the infinitive,

---

[1] In English only, in *bidden* part. of *bid*, whereas German has *gebeten* part. of *bitten*.
[2] In E. *give* = G. *geben*, the sound *i* is caused by the preceding *g* (O.E. *gief-an*, cf. supra 50, II.).

either *e* or *i*; in the perfect, always *a*; in the participle, theoretically at least, always *e*.

This main law holds good in English for six verbs of this class,—which, when its losses are deducted (*stick, tread, weave, get*), becomes reduced to nine in all,—namely: *see saw seen, eat ate eaten*,[1] *give gave given, bid bade* (also *bid*) *bid, spit spat* (also *spit*) *spit*, and *lie lay lain*.[2] In one of them, *sit sat* (*sate*) *sat*, the perfect-vocalism has intruded into the participle. The two remaining have neither a present nor a participle, viz.: *quoth* = O.E. *cwæð*,[3] infinitive *cweðan* = Go. *qiþan* (to say); and *was*, pl. *were*, the only one which, curiously enough, has kept unaltered the regular gradation from the sg. to the pl., together with the regular change of *s* to *r*, though, by being incorporated with the vb. *to be*, it has lost every other tense.[4]

The last verb is in German *wesen* (an infinitive used substantivally), pf. *war* (with the *r* imported from the pl. to the sg.), part. *ge-wes-en*; cf. O.H.G. *wës-an was wār-um gi-wës-an*, and Go. *vis-an vas vēs-um vis-an-s*. And the same triple alternation is reproduced in the fourteen verbs of type E which survive in German: *sehen sah gesehen, essen asz gegessen* (a corrupt form replacing the regular *gessen [5]), *geben, bitten, sitzen, liegen*, etc.; *lesen, genesen, messen, geschehen*, lost in English; *treten, stecken, vergessen*, shifted in English to some other class. Here we cannot but admire the marvellous preservation of the German vowel-change.

(184)   F. Type *slay* = *schlagen*.

With the five types A–E we have completed the five essential classes of I.-E. vowel-gradation [6]; the 6th class has no longer

---

[1] Though a double analogy has produced the pf. *eat* and the part. *ate*, both moreover unusual.
[2] In *lain* = *lein = G. *gelegen*, the vowel may as well be an *e*, as in *way* = O.E. *weg* = G. *weg*, etc., *supra* 50, II. 4.
[3] E. *o* for *a* owing to the influence of the preceding labial consonant.
[4] Cf. *infra* 217, III. But illiterate people often say *you was*, thus effacing the last trace of the traditional accidence.
[5] O.H.G. *gi-ë̆ʒʒ-an*, syncopated to M.H.G. *gëʒʒen*, and this again altered to *gegessen* by receiving anew the half worn-out prefix *ge-*.
[6] Let us state once more, in concluding, the general correspondence:

any representative in Germanic accidence: there remains for examination the 7th class, the characteristic of which has been seen to be a mere alternation between *ă*, in the infinitive and participle, and *ō*, in the sg. and pl. of the perfect; for, as early even as the Pregermanic period, the vowel here had become the same throughout the whole perfect-tense, Go. *slah-an slōh slōh-um slah-an-s*, O.E. *slē-an slōg slōg-on sleg-en*, E. *slay slew* (=*slū*) *slai-n*, O.H.G. *slah-an sluoh sluog-um gi-slag-an*,[1] G. *schlag-en schlug schlug-en ge-schlag-en*.

This type is usually kept without alteration in the verbs which still survive, namely: E. *shake shook shaken*, *take* (borrowed from Scandinavian), *forsake*, *draw drew drawn*= G. *tragen trug getragen*, G. *fahren fuhr gefahren, graben, wachsen, schaffen, laden, backen*, etc.: in all, about ten English and a dozen German verbs, besides the two metaphonical verbs mentioned below. A very few remarks will suffice.

1. Several verbs have passed to some other system: E. *fare* is now a weak verb; so also E. *shave* and G. *schaben*, but the former retains a part. *shaven*; E. *bake* and *lade* are likewise weak verbs, though the latter has a part. *laden*, cf. also the vowel in the substantive *load*; E. *shape* and *wax* preserve the parts. *shapen* and *waxen*, but the pfs. are *waxed* and *shaped*, cf. the G. forms *schaffte geschafft* from the vb. *schaffen* meaning "to work"; and, lastly, E. *awake* has *awoke* and *awaked*, whilst G. *wachen* and E. *wake* are weak verbs.

2. The E. vb. *stand*=O.E. *stond-an* has several peculiarities. The internal nasal, being a present-sign, does not pass to the other tenses[2]: O.E. *stōd* and E. *stood*. Next, the vocalism of the perfect has been transferred to the part., now *stood* instead

Classes: 1st — 2nd — 3rd — 4th — 5th — 6th — 7th

Types: E — A — B — C — D — ,, — F.

[1] Observe the "grammatical alternation," variously levelled in Go., O.E. and Mod. German.

[2] This should be the rule for any verb whatever assuming an interior nasal, supra 82, 3: cf. L. *vinc-ō vīc-ī, find-ō fīd-ī*, etc. But analogy everywhere transferred the nasal of the present into the perfect (as in L. *jung-ŏ junx-i*), and E. *stand* is the only one that remained free from such corruption.

of O.E. regular *gestonden*. The same is the case with *awake awoke awoke*. The G. vb. **standen* is lost,[1] but its pf. *stand* and its part. *gestanden* are in use: the latter is regular (O.H.G. *gistantan*); the former ought to be **stund* (= O.H.G. *stuont*),[2] which is at any rate found in the pf. subj. *stünde*, so that German has certainly undergone the reverse analogy to that of English.

3. Two Anglo-German verbs exhibit, in the present only, instead of an *a*, the metaphonical vowel corresponding to *a*, because they are derived by means of the Preg. suff. *-ja-* = I.-E. *-yŏ-*, namely: Go. *haf-jan* (= L. *cap-iō*), O.E. *hebban* and E. *heave*, O.H.G. *heffan* and G. *heben*; O.E. *swer-ian* and E. *swear*, O.H.G. *swer-ien* and G. *schwören*.[3] Both being identical, in their present-vocalism, with the verbs of the type D, became assimilated to this type, completely in English, and partly in German: E. *heave hove hoven* (also weak), *swear swore sworn*; G. *heben hub* (also *hob*) *gehoben*; *schwören schwur* (also *schwor*) *geschworen*.

§ 2. *Reduplicated Perfects.*

(185)   G. The only Type being *fall=fallen*.

I. The last type we have to study now is merely differentiated from the six preceding,—as the six preceding are differentiated from one another,—by the nature of the alternation in its root-vocalism: in other words, this type appears, no less than the types A–F, to proceed from vowel-gradation. In reality it is nothing of the kind. For the history of the Germanic languages and, in particular, comparison with Gothic accidence show that verbs of this class,—those at least which were primitive and served as patterns for English and German conjugation,—kept the present-vowel both in the perfect and the participle, and that the perfect took no other tense-sign but

---

[1] Replaced by *stehen*, infra 220.
[2] German, less pure than English, has allowed the nasal of the infinitive *stantan* to spread into the whole verb. Compare moreover Go. *standan*, pf. *stōp*.
[3] Spelled *ö* = *e*, cf. *supra* 50, III. 2, and 121, 12; as also in *löschen*, supra 181, II. 3.

the initial reduplication mentioned above: thus Gothic, for instance, answers with *hald-an hai-hald hald-an-s* the verb which is E. *hold held hold-en* (now *held*) and G. *halt-en hielt ge-halt-en*; and, if Gothic had a vb. **fai-fal*, it would likewise oppose a pf. **fai-fal* to O.E. *fēoll* and E. *fell* = O.H.G. *fial* and G. *fiel*.

Hence the perfects of type G were clearly reduplicated in Pregermanic, and adopted an interchangeable vocalism only as late as West Germanic. How the latter fact took place, will be examined further on, though at the outset we may clear the ground, by stating that their leading characteristic is a clearer vowel (E. *e* and G. *ie*) as opposed to the obscurer vowel in the present and participle. This obscurer vowel is not the same throughout the whole class, as it is in the types A–F. Indeed, it is a very capricious one, and here the unity of the class comes by no means from the vocalism of the infinitive, but only from the constant perfect-vocalism, as the whole category admits of no less than nine sub-classes, *fall* = *fallen*, *hold* = *halten*, *blow* = *blasen*,[1] *let* = *lassen*, (*hew* =) *hauen*, (*leap* =) *laufen*, *stoszen*, *heiszen* and *rufen*, all of which, in spite of the differences in their infinitive-stem, assume the same vowel in their perfects *fell* = *fiel*, *held* = *hielt*, *blew* = *blies*, *let* = *liesz*, *hieb*, *lief*,[2] *stiesz*, *hiesz* and *rief*: a remarkable likeness which at first sight betrays a principle of formation common to all these various stems.

And what could this common principle be but reduplication, since the nine corresponding presents and perfects respectively either are or would be Go. **falla *fai-fal*, *halda hai-hald*, *blēsa **bai-blēs*, *lēta lai-lōt*, **hagva *hai-hagv*, *hláupa **hai-hláup*, *stáuta **stai-stáut*, *háita hai-háit* and *hrōpja **hai-hrōp*? The system moreover is of the greatest simplicity: the vowel of the infinitive is always that of the participle, almost always that of the perfect, and the latter always remains unchanged from the singular to the plural. English and German reproduce all

---

[1] More accurately speaking, E. *blow* would be G. *blähen* (weak vb.); but the G. added *s* is reproduced in the E. derivative noun *blas-t*.
[2] Unluckily, these two verbs, with many others, have passed in English to the weak conjugation, cf. *infra* III. 2.

these characteristics with the single exception of the alteration in the perfect-vowel.

II. The whole question, therefore, is how it happened that West Germanic was led to substitute for the primitive reduplication a single syllable with clearer vowel; and this question answers itself; for, since the I.-E. or Preg. reduplication, being always characterized by a vowel $\breve{e}$, necessarily contained a clearer sound than that of the verbal root to which it was prefixed, there can be hardly any doubt that the vocalic change in the E. and G. root is due to the influence of this reduplication. The only difficulty under which we labour is to state the precise circumstances under which this process took place; for we have no historical documents to guide us, and are left to choose between two different though equally plausible and not altogether contradictory ways. Analogy may have followed both at the same time, together with perhaps some unknown paths.

1. Let us restore some Preg. perfects of the Go. type *haihald*, that is to say, perfects of verbs beginning with an *h*, *$h\breve{e}$-hálð-$\breve{e}$* (he held), *$h\breve{e}$-háχw-$\breve{e}$* (he hewed), *$h\breve{e}$-háit-$\breve{e}$* (he called), *$h\breve{e}$-háñχ-$\breve{e}$* (he hung), etc. Nothing is more natural than that, the medial *h* being sounded weakly and then dropped, the two vowels thus brought together should coalesce into one long vowel, whence *$h\bar{e}l\eth\breve{e}$*, *$h\bar{e}\chi w\breve{e}$*, *$h\bar{e}it\breve{e}$*, *$h\bar{e}\tilde{n}\chi\breve{e}$*, etc. (G. *hielt, hieb, hiesz, hieng*). Now the visible relation between such stems as *hálð háχw háit háñχ* and such as *$h\bar{e}l\eth$ $h\bar{e}\chi w$ $h\bar{e}it$ $h\bar{e}\tilde{n}\chi$*, respectively in the present and perfect, being analogically transferred to other verbs, there arose, for instance, *fēl* and *fēñχ* (G. *fiel* and *fing*), created on the stems *fäl* and *fäñχ*, and so forth. Further, when the root contains a *u*, we find the diphthongs O.E. *ēo* and O.H.G. *io* in the perfect stem (O.H.G. *louf-an liof* = G. *laufen lief*); the simple *ē* underwent the O.E. breaking (*feall-an fēoll*), while English still shows it unaltered though shortened (*held, fell*); the same *ē* became diphthongized to O.H.G. *ia* (*fial, hiang*); and, lastly, O.H.G. *io* and *ia* both equally gave G. *ie* or *i* (*lief, fiel, hing*): these are matters of simple inference for any one acquainted with phonetics.

2. We have seen that the root-vowel remained unchanged

throughout the perfect. But it may be doubted whether this was the case in Pregermanic, since it is a well-known fact that in the I.-E. plural of the perfect the root-vowel tended to become reduced, and even occasionally to disappear altogether.[1] Now, it is a curious coincidence that O.E. retains five perfects which clearly show an initial reduplication, together with a root which has lost its vowel, e.g. *he-ht*, from *hāt-an* (to call), and *reo-rd*, from *rǣd-an* (to read); cf. G. *hiesz*, from *heisz-en*, and *rieth*, from *rathen* (to guess). Hence, supposing Pregermanic to have possessed such perfect-stems as *hĕ-ht-, *rĕ-rð-, etc., it was but natural, indeed, almost unavoidable that the medial consonant in these forms should be eliminated, since the speaker, when contrasting them with such present-stems as *háit-, *rēð-, would obtain the misleading view that the interior *h* or *r* (or other consonant) in each was a superfluous growth; and thus he would begin to suppress it, and to form the perfect-stems *hēt-, *rēð- (close *ē*),[2] next analogically *fēl- for *fĕ-fl-, and so on.[3]

III. If however the origin of the phenomenon is lost in the mists of the past, all its present applications are plain, simple and absolutely constant.

1. German keeps fifteen perfects of the reduplicated type,[4] all of them with vowel *ie* (*ī*), and with the same vowel in the infinitive and participle. To those quoted above we need but add *braten briet, schlafen schlief, fangen fing*, and (*gangen*) [5] *ging*.

2. English is far less pure. Besides the four verbs quoted

---

[1] Cf. *supra* 44 and 45, 1.
[2] We may even, in *rēd from *reord*, treat the transition as merely phonetic, inasmuch as we find E. *meed* and G. *miethe* (salary) = O.H.G. *mēta* = O.E. *meord* = Go. *mizdō* = Gr. μσθůs, cf. *supra* 62.
[3] On this difficult and intricate question, the most recent and complete authority is: H. Lichtenberger, *de Verbis quæ in vetustissima Germanorum Lingua reduplicatum Perfectum exhibebant* (Nancy 1891), the work of an acute and well-trained scholar.
[4] O.H.G. had a few more, but some of them have passed to the weak system: thus *salzen* (Go. *salt-an*, pf. *saí-salt*, but G. *salz-te*) still betrays itself as a strong verb through its old part. *ge-salz-en* (but *ich habe ge-salz-t* in conjugating), whilst *mähen, säen*, etc., have lost every survival of the strong type.
[5] Infinitive and present obsolete in German, now replaced by *gehen*. In English the whole verb is lost. Cf. *infra* 219.

above may be mentioned *grow grew, throw*[1] *threw, crow crew, know knew* and *beat beat* (O.E. *bēat-an bēot*). The vb. *hold* replaces its part. *hold-en* by *held* after the analogy of the perfect. The verbs *hew* (= *hauen*), *sow, mow, strow* and *strew, show* and *shew* (cf. G. *säen, mähen, streuen, schauen*, weak verbs) still keep a part. in -*n*, but have a weak perfect. Some others, as *leap* (= G. *laufen*) have become weak throughout their whole accidence. Lastly, the vb. which is quite regularly O.E. **hong-an*[2] *heng ge-hong-en* = G. *hang-en hing ge-hang-en*, is now E. *hang hung hung*, owing to the intrusion of a vowel which has nothing to do with this class and has probably been imported hither from type C.[3]

Section III.

WEAK PERFECT AND PARTICIPLE.

(186) **Weak Verbs,** as already stated, are those in which the perfect and participle are formed, without any vocalic change, by mere addition of a dental element, E. -*d* (-*ed*) or -*t*, G. -*te* (-*ete*) and -*t* (-*et*). The great majority of English and German weak verbs obey this fundamental rule; but a considerable minority, especially in English, are exceptions, whether as apparently lacking the dental element, or as actually undergoing in their root some accidental vocalic shifting. Hence, in order to fully understand the principle of formation, it appears advisable to begin at once with stating all these apparent anomalies and reducing them to the normal form from which they are separated only by an insignificant detail.

§ 1. *Apparent Anomalies.*

(187) In order to analyse the doubtful cases of weak perfect and participle, we must first observe that the unaccented vowel (now *ĕ* mute) which preceded the dental suffix, tended in early times, as it still does, to disappear in rapid

---

[1] G. *drehen* "to turn," weak verb.
[2] The actual O.E. infinitive is *hōn* = Go. *hāhan* = **hănh-an*, supra 24.
[3] For the part. *hang-ed*, see above, p. 148, n. 2, and p. 288, n. 1.

pronunciation. In fact, it vanished in any position, even after a dental consonant, since German regularly has *er sandte* (he sent), *gesandt* (sent), *beredt* (eloquent), so that the fuller forms *send-ete ge-red-et* are obviously refashioned, by a late analogical process, on the basis of the infinitives *send-en* and *red-en*.

Next we must remember the undecided character of the sound *d* as an English final; for, although the consonant here was a true Germanic ð, it could nevertheless become shifted to *t*, either before a voiceless initial consonant in the following word, or when absolutely final at the end of a sentence, or when immediately preceded by a voiceless consonant after the intermediate vowel had been dropped.[1]

No wonder, therefore, if we often find an English final *t*, or if the *d* or *t* appears to be wanting altogether, that is, when the verbal stem itself ends with a dental, so that the two contiguous dentals coalesced after the syncope. Let us now follow, in both languages, the further development of these various processes.

1. Such a form as *pas-t* requires no explanation, being indeed the true transliteration of the pronunciation of the word *pass-ed* with which it alternates. And *durs-t*, instead of the analogical *dare-d*, is hardly more puzzling; for the Preg. root is not *ðĕr-, but *ðĕrs- (I.-E. root *dhĕrs*, cf. Gr. θαρσ-εῖν "to cheer up," θρασ-ύ-ς "bold"), and the present *dare* = O.E. *dearr*[2] merely conceals the *s* by assimilating it to the preceding *r*, whereas it reappears before the *-t* of the perfect. The difference in the vocalism proceeds from *dare* regularly having the deflected grade, while the remarkable archaic form *durst* no less regularly exhibits the reduced grade (O.E. *durs-te*, from an I.-E. root-form *dhr̥s*), which is likewise the case with the Greek words compared above.

2. We can also easily understand the rather rare syncopes which took place, usually in common words, between the final consonant of the stem and the dental of the suffix, and led to a complete absorption of the former: E. *had* = O.E. *hæf-de*, and

---

[1] Remember moreover that the I.-E. suff. *-tó-* of the participle is in some cases represented quite regularly by a Germanic *-t*, *supra* 53 B and 78.

[2] Exactly speaking, this present itself is an old perfect, cf. *infra* 222.

E. had = O.E. ge-hæf-d, cf. E. head = O.E. hĕafod; G. hatte = O.H.G. hap-ta (also hab-ĕ-ta), but part. ge-hab-t = O.H.G. gi-hab-ē-t; E. made = O.E. mac-o-de.

3. Now, whether these two consonants thus become assimilated, or keep their original sound, in any case the loss of the intermediate vowel produces a consonantal group, which again may exert its usual influence over the preceding vowel, that is, may either shorten it, or prevent it being lengthened: we have but to compare the long vowel in G. hāben = O.H.G. hăb-ē-n, with the short one in hatte, gehabt. This is quite an elementary distinction. But in English the phenomenon leads to further consequences: the lengthening or shortening in its turn alters the sound of the radical vowel, whence there arise such alternations as *keep kept* (O.E. cēp-an cēp-te), *weep wept, feel felt, kneel knelt, flee fled*,[1] *lean leant* (also *leaned*), *mean meant, lose lost, shoe shod*, etc., all familiar to the reader.

4. Under the same conditions, if the syncope develops, after a vowel capable of O.E. breaking, a consonantal group capable of causing it (rd, ld), then, the breaking of the vowel produces the alternations *hear heard* (O.E. hēr-an hīer-de), *sell sold* (O.E. sell-an seal-de), *tell told*, etc., so that the verb seems to vary in its stem, whereas the history of the language explains this apparent variation as the result of combined breaking and metaphony, acting on an originally identical vocalism.

5. If the final consonant of the verbal stem happens to be a dental explosive, d or t, like the suffix-consonant, the usual syncope of the intermediate vowel, as a rule, takes place both in O.E. and O.H.G., whereupon, the two dentals being blended into one, the perfect and participle will seem as if they lacked any exponent; and, since English chiefly retains this primitive formation, it inherits and keeps throughout such types as *send sent* (O.E. send-an and sende = *send-de), *rend rent, gild gilt, gird girt*, or *cast cast, cut cut, put put, set set, hurt hurt*, even *cost cost* (borrowed from F.), indeed, even *shed shed* (O.E. scĕad-an scĕad-de), *wed wed*, etc., etc. In the last two cases, the perfect

---

[1] *Supra* 19 and 20. The vb. *flēon* = G. *fliehen* is strong in O.E.: it became weak as a means of differentiation from E. *fly* = O.E. *flēogan* = G. *fliegen*, and assumed a d which closes the syllable, whence the ē is shortened.

and participle have exactly the same relation to the infinitive as in the types of strong verbs *let let, split split*, etc., and it is only the history of the language that allows us to distinguish between these strong and weak forms.[1] Later on, analogy caused the formerly syncopated final to be restored in many verbs of this kind: from *last, blot, wed*, etc., were derived *last-ed, blott-ed, wedd-ed*; and this is almost constantly the case with literary German, *rett-en rett-ete ge-rett-et, red-en red-ete ge-red-et*, etc.; but the surviving forms, *sandte gesandt, wandte gewandt, beredt*, etc., wherein the *d* is spelled but not sounded and might be dropped altogether,[2] still shows in German an early syncopated state, similar in regularity and constancy to the O.E. accidence.

6. Before the double dental group thus obtained in O.E., English naturally undergoes the processes of shortening and vowel-shifting, whence come the well-known alternations *read read* (O.E. *rǣd-an rǣd-de*), *lead led, meet met, light lit*, etc., and even *clothe clad* (O.E. *clǣð-an clǣð-de*). The last shows us that the change of $\bar{æ}$ to $\bar{o}$ is later than the shortening of a vowel in a close syllable. Thus, here too the stem seems to vary, whereas the phenomenon is late and the result of accident.

7. Some variations appear more serious, merely because they are older and carry us back farther into the past of Germanic phonetics. Thus the present sometimes shows a regular metaphony, which has no reason for appearing in the perfect.[3] Taking, for instance, the Go. vb. *vand-jan* (to turn), the pf. of which is *vand-ida*, we find the infinitive to be regularly represented by O.H.G. *wenten*, and the perfect, no less regularly, after syncope has taken place, by *wanta*, after the analogy of which German will replace the old part. *gi-went-it* by a new one *gewandt*. These alternations were quite common

[1] It is quite plain that, reciprocally, this identity must have contributed on a large scale to further the loss of final *-en* in such strong participles as *bid* (for *bidden*), and then, analogically, in a great many others.

[2] The O.H.G. forms are infinitive *went-en*, pf. *wanta*, part. *gi-went-it*; and so also, *rett-en* (to save), pf. *rat-ta* (also *ret-ita*, which shows the work of restoration to have begun very early), part. *gi-ret-it*, nomin. sg. *gi-rat-t-ēr*: a curiously varied, though now altogether uniform accidence, cf. *infra* 7.

[3] This has already been seen above in the types *sell* and *tell*, where the present-metaphony actually combines with the perfect-breaking.

in O.H.G., but the later language has levelled them almost throughout, keeping merely a few survivals in the class of verbs improperly termed "mixed verbs"—intermediate, as it were, between strong and weak—in some grammars, namely: *nenn-en* (= Go. *namn-jan*) *nann-te ge-nann-t, rennen, kennen, brennen, senden* and *wenden*. English, more corrupt in this case, has extended the vocalism of the present to the whole conjugation: *send sent, rend rent, burn burnt* with metathesis.

8. English, notwithstanding, retains some traces of this effect of present-metaphony, namely in verbs in which the present and perfect had diverged too far to be again reconciled by analogy. Nothing could be more unlike, at first sight, than *buy* and *bought*; but, on going back to O.E., we find *bycg-an* and *boh-te*, and we at once recognise the *y* as the metaphony of *o*; in other words, we restore a Preg. *$b\check{u}\mathfrak{z}$-jana-m*, wherein the *ŭ* has been mutated, while it was kept unaltered in the pf. *$b\check{u}h$-ta*, no *i* here being inserted. So also, *seek* and *beseech* are metaphonical forms of *suchen* and *besuchen*, whereas the perfects *sought* and *besought* strictly reproduce the vocalism of *suchte* and *besuchte*. The relation is the same, though combined with metathesis, in *work* and *wrought*, which are O.E. *wyrc-ean* and *worh-te*,[1] and so with others.

9. Lastly, when to these various phenomena is superadded the effect of the well-known and earlier law called Pregermanic compensatory lengthening,[2] we have the curious and rare alternations of the type *bring = bring-en* and *brought = brachte, think = denken* (*dünken*) and *thought = dachte*, upon which we need not dwell further.

10. There remain a couple of English verbs, nearly alike, *teach* and *taught*, *catch* and *caught*. O.E. *tǣc-ean*, contrasted with pf. *tāh-te*, shows in the present a regular metaphony: the sound of the two vowels, which at first scarcely differed, acquired in time the present striking dissimilarity. This explanation, however, cannot hold good for M.E. *caugh-te*, since the M.E. vb. *cacch-en* is not Germanic, but Romance, borrowed from the Picardian *cachier* = M.F. *chacier* (to hunt, to catch,

---

[1] For the interchangeable guttural, see above 53 C.
[2] *Supra* 24, where the applications are enumerated.

now *chasser*): it has been suggested that the perfect was imitated from that of another verb of Germanic origin and similar meaning, which became obsolete after the former had been introduced.[1] Everywhere else analogy worked in a contrary direction; we have, for instance, E. *reached* from *reach* = O.E. *rēc-an*,[2] and many like it.

On summing up results, we find, not only that the forms with dental suffix which appear most irregular agree with the general rule of weak perfect and participle accidence, but even that these are the most regular and primitive, inasmuch as their changes are due to the phonetic laws of the two languages, whereas the specious regularity of others really proceeds from later and artificial restoration.

§ 2. *Principle of formation.*

(188) I. It must now be well understood that the English and German weak perfect and participle are always and everywhere identical, and consequently identical with the Gothic types *sōk-ida* (he sought) and *sōk-iþ-s* (sought). The next question is: what is this dental element? to which I.-E. formation does it correspond? This question has already been asked and answered in the case of the participle: it has been stated that the Preg. suff. -*iða*- is the same, both in form and function, that appears in Sk. *dam-itá-s* (tamed), Gr. δαμ-ατό-ς, L. *dom-itu-s*, Go. *ga-tam-ida*, O.E. **ge-tæm-d* and E. *tame-d*, O.H.G. *gi-zem-it* and G. *ge-zähm-t*; and this identity is too universal to admit of contradiction or even doubt.[3]

II. But the case is quite different in the perfect, though outwardly it looks so like the participle. The first thought, indeed, that occurs to the mind, namely the suggestion of a derivation from the participle itself, proves at once unable to stand the test, since, in a transitive verb, the perfect has always a transitive, and the participle an intransitive meaning, and consequently no precise relation either in meaning or derivation can be perceived between them. But, setting aside

[1] Skeat, *Principles*, II., p. 187.
[2] G. *reichen* and *erreichen* are likewise weak verbs.
[3] Cf. *supra* 78 and 90.

this hasty induction, we are compelled to acknowledge that the Germanic weak perfect occupies a strangely isolated position in comparative grammar; for there is not a single I.-E. tongue, even of the Letto-Slavonic group, which stands so near in many other respects, that can show anything at all related; and, unless we recur to the absurd theory of a creation from nothing, we must suppose Germanic to have somehow developed a previous I.-E. form in which the dental element had nothing to do with deriving the stem of the perfect-tense.

Many intricate processes may have had such an effect. Here we may venture to sketch in rough outline the most plausible of all. In order to understand it, the reader must remember that every I.-E. verb possessed two conjugational systems, the so-called voices, which were differentiated by the nature of their person-endings, and that the so-called middle voice, though it theoretically involved an action returning to the subject, in many cases hardly differed from the active, except for a vague and almost immaterial shade of meaning: thus, Sk. *bhárati* and *bhárate* stand equally well for "he carries," Gr. ἔδω and ἀκούω, actives, have the middle futures ἔδο-μαι and ἀκούσο-μαι, and the L. so-called deponents, *imitor, morior*, etc., though passively conjugated, do not differ in meaning from the active forms *imitō*, *moriō, etc. Nothing, therefore, is more common, and nothing will seem more natural than the use of a middle form in the conjugation of an active verb.[1]

Let us then consider any Gr. vb., for instance τρέφ-ω (to feed), with normal root in the present: with the regular gradations and endings of the active and middle perfect, it forms a pf. active sg. 3 τέ-τροφ-ε (deflected root) and a pf. middle sg. 3 τέ-θραπ-ται (reduced root). Let us now take in the same way an I.-E. root, for instance *skăb* (reduced), the deflected grade of which will be *skōb*: it needs but slight reflection to see that the Pregermanic forms strictly correlative to the Gr. forms above will be pf. act. sg. 3 *skĕ-skōp-e and pf. m. sg. 3 **skĕ-*

---

[1] Particularly in reference to the present remarks, the L. pf. is certainly, in the main, a perfect with middle person-endings, and the anomalies it exhibits, especially when contrasted with the Gr. pf., could by no means be otherwise explained.

skăp-tai. Now, carrying this twofold formation into German, we shall find it to correspond sound for sound with two actual G. forms which have already occurred, viz. the two perfects (*er*) *schuf* and (*er*) *schaffte*, the former strong, the latter weak. Hence, speaking generally, and omitting many accessory elements,[1] we may lay down this main formula: the **strong** and the **weak perfect** look as if they were, respectively, the **active** and the **middle perfect** of the I.-E. conjugation.

But, if this were the case, ought they not both to coexist side by side in any verb, as they actually coexist in Greek, and do here coexist accidentally[2] in the verb *schaffen*, which, owing to this circumstance, has afforded us an appropriate example? Certainly, and it will be seen, moreover,[3] that in fact they do coexist in a larger number of Germanic verbs than we should at first sight expect. In general, however, one of them has disappeared as early as the Pregermanic period; but the loss is attributable to a **principle of economy**, the effects of which are obvious in every language: the memory of the speaking subject has no room for useless words; two exactly synonymous forms, either survive by assuming peculiar shades of meaning, or else, if they remain exactly synonymous, one or the other soon becomes obsolete. So it happened with the Germanic perfect, either strong or weak: wherever a strong perfect was contrasted in its vocalism with the general verbal form, clearly enough to be able to play without confusion the part of past-tense, there was no reason for a weak perfect being retained; elsewhere, its dental element, denoting the 3rd person of the singular, became associated in the speaker's mind with the notion of past time, and thus the form remained indispensable and was secured from decay.

[1] Restricted to these terms, the theory must needs appear superficial, inasmuch as it leaves out of account some phonetic and grammatical difficulties, the details of which cannot conveniently find a place in this work. Should the reader wish to proceed further, he should refer to Collitz' article in either *Amer. Journ. of Philology*, ix., p. 42, or *Bezzenberger's Beiträge*, xvii., p. 227.

[2] Of course, *schaffte* is not primitive, but has been formed on *schaff-n*, after the analogy of some other type; but the twofold pf. of this verb proved convenient for the purpose of the present demonstration.

[3] Under the Preterito-presents, *infra* 222.

III. Our task is not yet over; for, now that we are dealing with a new and complete past-tense, the cause no longer appears adequate to the effect. The Greek exponent -ται is well-known to characterize only the third person singular: now, if the final syllable in *er schaff-te* be the same, how does it come that German says, quite as correctly, *ich schaff-te*, or, in other words, that a whole tense is conjugated on a syllable which really represents one of its person-endings? Here we come to one of the most curious, though by no means rare, phenomena due to **grammatical analogy**, namely, a single and isolated form giving birth to a whole system of forms. Let us briefly state the series of analogical facts.

1. Owing to grammatical and phonetic peculiarities which will be explained below,[1] the two Germanic forms of sg. 1 and sg. 3 of the strong perfect had come to be identical: Go. *bar* "I carried" and "he carried," *nam* "I took" and "he took," etc.; cf. E. *I bare* and *he bare*, G. *ich nahm* and *er nahm*, and so forth, everywhere.

2. On the other hand, as noted above, the form of sg. 3 in the weak perfect was Go. *sōk-ida*, cf. E. *he sough-t* and G. *er such-te*, from vb. *sōk-jan* = *seek* = *suchen*.

3. The identity of sg. 1 and 3 in the strong perfect quite naturally led the speaker to use similarly sg. 3 of the weak perfect for sg. 1, and to say Go. *sōk-ida* "I sought," E. *I sought*, G. *ich suchte*,—a bold transposition, indeed, though so simple in appearance.

4. After these two forms have become levelled, the others must follow: hence, each Germanic language, according to its own genius and to the conjugational resources it is able to display, constructs on the basis of sg. 1 and 3 a new perfect-accidence (Go. *sōkida sōkidēs*, etc.), which, even in O.E. and O.H.G., and still more so of course in Mod. German and English, is entirely modelled on the person-endings of the strong perfect.

5. In this marvellous growth of a single person-ending into a whole tense, and in this new tense again extending throughout almost all the verbs, whether present or future, of the

---

[1] Under the Person-endings, *infra* 208-209.

Germanic family, we ought never to forget that the analogical influence of the weak participle must have played a large and decisive part. It has been already explained that the weak perfect cannot have arisen from it; but these two grammatical categories must have always gone hand in hand, and, by their fortuitous and exact likeness, have protected each other from the risks they ran, inasmuch as every verb which had a participle with a dental suffix would naturally show a propensity to develop a perfect with the same suffix, and *vice versâ*. Hence the actual correspondence, established long ago, with but a few insignificant exceptions, between these two formative currents which, starting from far distant sources, soon flowed together and ended by uniting in a single channel.

§ 3. *Applications.*

(189) I. The formation of the weak perfect being well understood, its applications will appear of the utmost simplicity, the more so because, in the later languages, the progress of analogy, together with the dulness of unaccented finals, greatly contributed to simplify them. Gothic distinguishes mainly three classes of weak verbs, according as the Pregermanic derivative syllable in each was *-ja-*, or *-ō-*, or *-ē-*,[1] viz.:

1. Infinitive *sōk-ja-n*, pf. sg. 3 *sōk-i-da*, part. *sōk-i-þ-s*;
2. „ *salb-ō-n*, „ *salb-ō-da*, „ *salb-ō-þ-s*;
3. „ *hab-a-n*, „ *hab-ái-da*, „ *hab-ái-þ-s*.[2]

II. Old English has the tolerably regular correspondences to these three types, viz.:

1. Infinitive *sēc-ea-n*, pf. sg. 3 *sōh-te*, part. *ge-sōh-t*;
2. „ *sealf-ia-n*,[3] „ *sealf-o-de*, „ *ge-sealf-a-d*;
3. „ *habb-a-n*, „ *hæf-de* „ *ge-hæf-d*.

III. Old High German is either preserved or restored remarkably well, viz.:

---

[1] Besides a 4th class, comprising some intransitive verbs, which does not occur in West Germanic. Cf. *supra* 83 (IV.), 85, 92 and 93.
[2] The derivative vowel of the 3rd class is seen to disguise itself in Gothic. But it appears clearly in O.H.G.
[3] The present-form visibly influenced by the analogy of the 1st class.

1. Infinitive *suoch-e-n*, pf. sg. 3 *suoh-ta*, part. *gi-suoch-i-t*;
2. „ *salb-ō-n*, „ *salb-ō-ta*, „ *gi-salb-ō-t*.
3. „ *hab-ē-n*, „ *hab-ē-ta*,[1] „ *gi-hab-ē-t*.

IV. Now, let the reader contrast the present states:
1. E. *seek sough-t sough-t* = G. *such-en such-te ge-such-t*;
2. „ *salve salve-d salve d* = „ *salb-en salb-te ge-salb-t*;
3. „ *have ha-d ha-d* = „ *hab-en hat-te ge-hab-t*.

Provided he has borne in mind our previous observations (§ 1), he will easily perceive how it happened that, apart from apparent exceptions, the three historical types were blended into one, which may be reduced to the following rules:

(*a*) The English weak perfect and participle are formed by adding to the infinitive a suffix *-d*, which, even when written *-ed*, does not constitute a syllable (*saved* pr. *sēvd*, *pushed* pr. *pušt*, etc.), except when the infinitive itself ends with a dental explosive (*shade shaded, melt melted*, etc.);

(*b*) The German weak perfect and participle are formed by substituting for the *-en* of the infinitive a dental element, respectively *-te* and *-t*, spelled and sounded *-ete* and *-et* when preceded by a dental explosive (*geredet, gestattet*).

V. These rules, without exception, apply: (1) to primary verbs which, as early as the Pregermanic period, were shifted to the weak accidence, especially to those in I.-E. *-sko-*, E. *wish* = O.E. *wȳscean*, G. *forschen* = O.H.G. *forscōn*, etc.; (2) to primary verbs, much more numerous in English than in German, which in Pregermanic still belonged to the strong conjugation, but later passed to the weak [2]; (3) to all secondary, tertiary, etc., I.-E. verbs; (4) to all verbs which in English or German have arisen from later derivation; (5) and, of course, to any late created verbs; (6) lastly, to all verbs in particular which English has borrowed from French, and, generally speaking, to every foreign element imported into English or German;—excluding only the few cases in which a verb of regularly weak conjugation has been compelled, through outward likeness to a strong verb, to obey the laws of strong accidence.[3]

[1] Earlier *hap-ta*, but analogy restored the unsyncopated form, whereupon the syncope again took place in Mod. German.
[2] The most important instances have been quoted under 179–185.
[3] Cf. *supra* 179 (5), 180 (II. 3), etc., etc.

CHAPTER II.

MOODS.

(190) The Indo-European conjugation distinguished four moods, Indicative, Subjunctive, Optative and Imperative, all well preserved in Greek and Sanskrit. But the subjunctive and the optative had a kindred meaning, which was often indistinct and soon became confused: thus, the so-called Latin subjunctive, as a matter of fact, is a mixture of forms borrowed from both the original subjunctive and optative.[1] In Pregermanic, the whole **Subjunctive is** simply **the original Optative**, with perhaps vague traces of the I.-E. subjunctive.[2] Now, as the indicative, from its nature, did not need the use of any exponent, being the stem of the verb itself, the study of Anglo-German moods is confined to two verbal forms, **Subjunctive** and **Imperative**.

SECTION I.

SUBJUNCTIVE.

(191) The two tenses of the Indicative, **Present** and **Perfect**, are both capable of being conjugated in the **Subjunctive**, the form of which is derived for each, by means of a peculiar suffix, from the corresponding form of the Indicative.

§ 1. *Present Subjunctive.*

(192) I. Referring to the Greek optative present, which accurately reproduces the original I.-E. accidence, we find it,—

[1] Cf. *infra* 211, the subjunctive of the vb. "to be."
[2] Immaterial for our present subject: cf. *infra* 192, I.

that is, in the so-called verbs in -ω, as there are no others left in the Germanic conjugation,—to be formed by inserting an element -ι- between the stem in -o- and the person-endings. Thus, a verb, for instance, the stem of which was I.-E. *bhér-ŏ-, formed an optative stem *bhér-ŏ-ĭ-, whence sg. 1 *bhér-oy-m (may I carry), sg. 2.*bhér-oy-s, sg. 3 *bhér-oy-t, etc., as obviously represented by the conjugation of the optative of the Gr. vb. νέμ-ω (I divide), and by the almost identical one of the subjunctive of the Go. vb. nim-a (I take).

    Gr.: sg. 1 νέμ-οι-μι,   2 νέμ-οι-ς,   3 νέμ-οι,
    Go.: „ 1 nim-au,   2 nim-ái-s,   3 nim-ái,
    Gr.: pl. 1 νέμ-οι-μεν,   2 νέμ-οι-τε,   3 νέμ-οι-εν,
    Go.: „ 1 nim-ái-ma,   2 nim-ái-þ,   3 nim-ái-na.

Apart from a slight difference in pl. 3, the agreement is exact; though, only in sg. 1, Gothic has a different diphthong; but this difficulty, however it may be got rid of in Gothic,[1] no longer exists in the later languages, where all the endings have become uniformly obscured. Here, as far as we go back, the whole accidence rests on an identical stem.

    O.E. : sg. 1 nim-e,[2]   2 nim-e,   3 nim-e,
    O.H.G.: „ 1 nëm-e,   2 nëm-ē-s,   3 nëm-e,
    O.E. : pl. 1 nim-e-n,   2 nim-e-n,   3 nim-e-n,
    O.H.G.: „ 1 nëm-ē-m,   2 nëm-ē-t,   3 nëm-ē-n.

The uniformity of the O.E. person-endings being for the present neglected,[3] this single paradigm explains the whole formation of the subjunctive in the modern languages; for it is the same throughout every class of verbs, strong or weak. It is true that the O.H.G. weak verbs of 2nd class still exhibit their characteristic vowel before the endings: sg. 1 salb-ō or salb-ō-e, 2 salb-ō-s or salb-ō-ē-s, etc. But it does not matter for our purpose, since, the final syllables being everywhere obscured, the types nēmēs, farēs, suochēs, salbōs, habēs, etc.,

---

[1] It is probably not a diphthong at all, but the transliteration of a vowel: in other words, nimau ought to be accented nimaŭ and pronounced nimō = Gr. subj. νέμω, a Preg. remnant of the I.-E. subjunctive.
[2] Infinitive niman, with i for e before a nasal.
[3] Cf. infra 212 and 214.

necessarily became blended together in *nehmest, fahrest, suchest, salbest, habest,* etc.

II. These main points being settled, the analysis of the modern subjunctive present is very simple. German keeps it almost unaltered, and English hardly less pure.

1. The Preg. diphthong *ai*, preserved in Gothic, has become G. *e*, more or less distinctly sounded: sg. *nehm-e nehm-e-st nehm-e*, pl. *nehm-e-n nehm-e-t nehm-e-n*; and so everywhere. Since this diphthong could, at no stage of its phonetic evolution, have caused metaphony, and since it was the same for every person, the accidence of the subjunctive always remains free from metaphony, even in strong verbs characterized by the regular metaphony of sg. 2-3 in the indicative: ind. *nehm-e nimm-st nimm-t*,[1] but subj. *nehm-e nehm-e-st nehm-e*; ind. *fahr-e fähr-st fähr-t* = O.H.G. *far-u fer-i-st fer-i-t*, but subj. *fahr-e fahr-e-st fahr-e* = O.H.G. *far-e far-ē-s far-e*, etc. Hence an important rule of practical grammar is accounted for in every detail: verbs of this kind distinguish the subjunctive, in sg. 2 and 3, by the absence of the metaphony of the indicative; the remainder keep it distinct only in sg. 3 by the absence of the person-ending; everywhere else, the present tense is identical in the two moods, except for a slight difference in pronunciation.

2. English not only obscured the final syllables, but also dropped all the person-endings, as will be explained below, both in the singular and plural. But, since the indicative itself has kept no endings except in sg. 2 and 3, the present tense does not differ in the two moods save in these two forms.

§ 2. *Perfect Subjunctive.*

(193) The subjunctive of the perfect, which is often called the imperfect subjunctive, is derived from the perfect indicative by means of a suffix very like the preceding. I.-E. verbal forms which do not end with the conjugation-vowel -*o*-, when conjugated in the optative, add to the stem a syllable which is -*yē*- in the normal, and -*ī*- in the reduced grade: Gr. εἴην = *ἐσ-ίη-ν

[1] Cf. *infra* 204 and 205.

(may I be), τι-θε-ίη-ν (may I place), pl. τι-θε-ῖ-μεν, middle sg. 1 τι-θε-ί-μην, etc. The two grades originally alternated according to a regular law, namely, the normal in the sg. of the active, the reduced in the plural of the active and throughout the middle voice. But in time the conjugation became gradually levelled, so that, for instance, the vocalism of the plural was transferred to the singular: thus, in Latin, the contemporaries of Plautus still conjugated *s-iē-m* (may I be, cf. Gr. εἴην) *s-iē-s s-iē-t s-ī-mus s-ī-tis*, whereas a century later analogy had produced the sg. *s-i-m s-ī-s s-i-t* by extending the plural-vowel throughout the whole tense. This uniform exponent -*i*- is likewise, however far we go back, the general mood-exponent in Pregermanic,[1] so that a Preg. pf. *fĕ-fall-ĕ* (he fell) would show a correlative subj. *fe-fall-i-þ* (might he fall). In the application of this rule, strong and weak perfects must naturally be considered apart.

(194) I. Strong Perfect.—1. Let us start from the double conjugational stem of the perfect in the Go. vb. *nim-an*, thus *nam-* and *nēm-*, and observe, at the outset, that the subjunctive-exponent -*i*- is always added to the reduced stem of the plural, and never to the deflected stem of the singular.[2] The conjugation of the mood thus obtained will be as follows:

Go. sg. 1 *nēm-jau*, 2 *nēm-ei-s*, 3 *nēm-i*,
„ pl. 1 *nēm-ei-ma*, 2 *nēm-ei-þ*, 3 *nēm-ei-na*.

In each of these forms, excluding the first,[3] we recognise at once the suffix -*ī*-, though regularly shortened as final in sg. 3.

2. It would be quite superfluous here to give an O.E. paradigm,[4] for it would lead to no knowledge of the modern accidence, beyond the fact that, at this early period, and for similar reasons, the subjunctive was as poor in endings in the

---

[1] Cf. *infra* 211.
[2] Because the I.-E. suffix -*yē*-, being accented, caused the stem to lose its accent and consequently to be reduced. Compare, for instance, Sk. *va-várt-a* (he turned), optative *va-vṛt-yâ-t*; Gr. τέ-θνη-κ-ε (he is dead), opt. τε-θνα-ίη; L. root *ĕs* (to be), subj. *s-ie-t s-i-t*, etc. Again, in the plural, the accent was shifted to the person-ending: whence the suffix -*yē*- became in its turn reduced to -*ī*-.
[3] Which of course is modelled on sg. 1 of the present subjunctive.
[4] It will occur below (211).

perfect as in the present : sg. -*e* throughout, pl. -*en* throughout. The whole evolution of the E. subj. pf. is contained in the statement of two very simple analogical processes.

(*a*) As shown by the Go. and even the Mod. G. conjugation, the radical vowel of the perfect tended to suffer, and actually suffered metaphony before the *i* of the following syllable. Of this regular metaphony, however, O.E. itself exhibits but scanty traces: it was already effaced almost everywhere by the analogy of the indicative, so that the subjunctive of the perfect had no other stem than that of the indicative plural, viz.: infinitive *bind-an*, pf. sg. 3 *bond*, pf. pl. 3 *bund-on*, subj. sg. 3 *bund-e* (might he bind), pl. 3 *bund-en*, etc.

(*b*) Now, it happened, as seen above, that the E. perfect no longer exhibited two distinct stems, but became entirely conjugated on one of them, thus either *he bound* like *they bound*, or *they drank* like *he drank*.[1] Then, the uniform stem of the indicative became analogically the stem of the subjunctive. The only perfect which keeps the double stem in the indicative, *he was, they were*, is likewise the only one which, according to the historical rule, shows throughout the subjunctive, *he were*, the plural-stem of the indicative. No other English subjunctive perfect differs from the corresponding indicative, except in the loss of the person-ending in the 2nd person singular.

3. German is far purer, and it will be worth while to quote here the paradigm in which either Old or Modern German agrees sound for sound with Gothic:

O.H.G.: sg. 1 *nām-i*,   2 *nām-i-s*,   3 *nām-i*,
G.   : „   1 *nähm-e*,   2 *nähm-e-st*,   3 *näh-me*,
O.H.G.: pl. 1 *nām-ī-m*,   2 *nām-ī-t*,   3 *nām-ī-n*,
G.   : „   1 *nähm-e-n*,   2 *nähm-e-t*,   3 *nähm-e-n*.

Hence we should expect to find, in the G. subjunctive perfect, the radical vowel which regularly ought to appear in the plural of the perfect indicative, though of course metaphonically altered by the influence of the following *i*. Let us now carry the application of the principle throughout the seven classes of strong verbs.

[1] Cf. *supra* 177, 3, and the applications, 179 sq.

A. The vowel of the pf. pl. is not capable of metaphony: so we have, without any difficulty, *trieb-e*, *biss-e*, etc.

B. The vowel of the pf. pl. is *u*, and it is therefore this vowel we find, for instance, in the pf. subj. of the vb. *kios-an*, in the common expressions O.H.G. *ni curi* and *ni curīt*, translating respectively L. *nōlī* and *nōlīte*.[1] But, as the vowel-grade *o* of the sg. finally prevailed in the whole indicative, it was thence transported, with metaphony, to the subjunctive, and consequently the modern formation is *zög-e* (M.H.G. *züg-e*), *frör-e*, *verlör-e*, *kröch-e*, *söff-e*, etc.

C. In the sub-type *trinken*, we should expect *trünk-e* (M.H.G.); but, here also, the stem having once become uniform in the indicative formed the subjunctive with its ordinary vowel, usually *a* (metaph. *tränk-e*, *fände*, *zwänge*), occasionally *o* (metaph. *klömm-e*, and even *begönn-e* in spite of *begann*). The *u* is either preserved or restored in *schünd-e*, *bedüng-e*.—In the sub-type *helfen*, the *u* is, as a rule, unaltered, and *würd-e*, *stürbe*, *verdürbe*, *würbe*, *würfe* are retained, in spite of *starb*, *warf* (though *wärfe* exists also). When corrupted, the vowel hesitates between *a* and *o*, under the influence of the participle (*befähle* and *beföhle*, *gälte* and *gölte*).[2]

D. The perfect-vowel being *ā*, the types *nähm-e*, *käm-e*, *gebär-e*, *bräch-e*, etc., are quite regular; but verbs which have adopted *o* in the indicative, naturally have *ö* in the subjunctive, *scheren schor schöre*.

E. Regular *wär-e*, *gäb-e*, *äsz-e*, without difficulty.

F. Regular *schlüg-e*, *trüg-e*, *führ-e*, without difficulty; but, owing to *stand*, the regular *stünd-e* also admits of a doublet *ständ-e*.

G. The vowel being incapable of metaphony, we have *fiel-e*, *hielt-e*, *liesz-e*, *lief-e*, *rief-e*, etc., without any modification.

(195) II. Weak Perfect.—The Gothic formation rests on the same basis as the plural of the indicative, and both are

---

[1] Literally "choose not to [do this or that]," whence "do not," a general formula of prohibition: cf. the actual use of E. *choose*.—The regular form *ni churis*, which is also met with, had lost its final *-s*, under the influence of sg. 2 of the imperative, as being used here in imperatival function.

[2] Cf. *supra* 181, II. 3 b.

rather difficult to explain.[1] But, fortunately, it is a point we need not deal with, because West Germanic has modelled its subjunctive perfect, as also the plural of the indicative,[2] entirely on the singular forms of the indicative; so that, upon the whole, the result is the same as if the $\bar{\imath}$ of the subjunctive merely replaced the a of sg. 2 and 3 of the indicative.

1. Consequently, owing to the general levelling of the person-endings, which partly took place even in O.E., the English subjunctive bears to the indicative exactly the same relation in the weak perfect as in the strong perfect.

2. O.H.G. for the three classes of weak verbs has respectively *suoh-t-i*, *salb-ō-t-i*, and *hab-ē-t-i*: in the last two, the radical vowel, not being brought into contact with the *i*, could not undergo metaphony, and in fact did not do so; in the first, however, it could undergo it, but the analogy of the other two tended to impede or efface it. Hence Mod. German scarcely shows it,[3] except in the so-called mixed verbs, where the outward likeness to the strong verbs caused it to be kept: O.H.G. *dāhta* and G. *dachte* (he thought), but subj. O.H.G. *dāhti* and G. *dächte*. So also: *brachte brächte*, *that thäte*, next *kennte*, *brennte*, *nennte*, *rennte*, *sendete*, *wendete*, and the archaic *däuchte*; in the preterito-presents,[4] *könnte*, *wüszte*, etc.; lastly, *hätte*, which certainly proceeds from the analogy of the parallel auxiliary *wäre*. Everywhere else, the subjunctive of the perfect, both stem and endings, is identical with the indicative.

SECTION II.

IMPERATIVE.

(196) The **Imperative** Mood, in Germanic, appears **exclusively in the Present** Tense; though, of course, owing to its nature, the mood necessarily involves some idea of future time, either deferred or immediate.

[1] Go. *sōk-idēd-um* (we sought) and *sōk-idēd-jau* (might I seek). Cf. *infra* 233.
[2] Cf. *supra* 188, III. 4, and *infra* 210.
[3] M.H.G. has many more instances of it: *mechte*, *bedrechte*, opposed to indicative *machte*, *bedrachte* " betrachtete."
[4] See below 222 sq.

The I.-E. imperative, generally speaking, is the simplest possible form of the verb; and, in particular, the 2nd person sg. of this mood, which is the genuine and properly so-called imperatival form, in such verbs at least as are characterized by the interchangeable vowel -ĕ-/-ŏ-, is simply the pure and bare verbal stem, always ending in -ĕ-, and without any personal termination: I.-E. *bhĕr-ĕ (carry), *nĕm-ĕ (take), *wĕgh-ĕ (convey); Sk. bhár-a, Gr. νέμ-ε, L. veh-e, etc. Hence the Germanic imperatives of strong verbs, quite regularly, are Go. baír, nim, drigk, tiuh (draw), and so everywhere. In the weak verbs we have sōk-ei (=I.-E. *sāg-yĕ), salb-ō, hab-ái, wherein the final long vowel, being first shortened and then obscured in the later languages, produced O.H.G. suoch-i salb-o hab-e, G. such-e salb-e hab-e, and lastly the Mod. E. form.

The bare **stem** of the verb, altogether **free from the metaphony** we are to meet with in German,[1] and with **no ending whatever**, is what we find without exception in the **English** imperative of verbs either strong or weak:—*drive, drink, bear, give, eat,—seek, salve, have,*—so that the mood requires no further observation.

(197) **German**, on the contrary, as being less affected by phonetic and analogical decay, here retains a primitive distinction, though not between properly strong and weak verbs, but rather between two different classes of strong verbs. For its imperatival formation is well-known to be twofold: in such strong verbs as still retain a vowel *e* in the radical syllable of the indicative, the imperative is usually formed by **metaphony and without** adding any **final vowel**, *nehm-en nimm, geben gieb, essen isz*; whereas, in every other verb, strong or weak, the imperative **ends in** -*e* and the stem is **not metaphonized**, *treib-e, flieg-e, trink-e, fahr-e, lauf-e,* etc.[2] Let us inquire whether the double process is traceable to an original variation.

We must first remember that I.-E. final *ĕ* had become Preg. *ĭ*: thus, to the I.-E. imperatives quoted above, would cor-

---

[1] The metaphony has been eliminated in the same way as the metaphony of sg. 2 and 3 of the indicative, *infra* 204.
[2] Of course, this short unaccented vowel may afterwards be dropped in rapid pronunciation.

respond such Preg. types as *némĭ (take), *ʒĕb-ĭ (give), *fár-ĭ (travel), *hlaup-ĭ (run), etc. On the other hand, the metaphony of ĕ has been seen to be far older, having taken place in Pregermanic, whereas the metaphony of ă is much later, and still more so that of other vowels: hence the first two forms had become Preg. *nĭm-ĭ, *ʒĭb-ĭ, while *făr-ĭ and *hlaup-ĭ remained unaltered; the result, after the loss of the final vowel, was O.H.G. *nim*, *gip*, but *far*, *hlouf*, etc. Shortly, no strong verb had a final vowel in the imperative; in those which had an ĕ in their stem, this mood was differentiated by a stem with metaphonical ĭ; in the remainder, it had no sign at all: such was the ancient and regular state.

Now, the weak verbs, on the contrary, as seen above, showed in the imperative a final vowel, which in M.H.G. had become a uniform and unaccented *e*: to the infinitives *suchen*, *salben*, *haben*, were opposed the imperatives *suche*, *salbe*, *habe*, and the speech only obeyed a logical and obvious tendency, when it restored likewise *fahre*, *laufe*, as opposed to *fahren*, *laufen*, and so also *trage*, *trinke*, *treibe*, *ziehe*, etc.; the more so, because there existed some strong verbs which seemed to exhibit no metaphony in the imperative for the reason that their indicative already had it, *sitze*, *liege*, *hebe*, etc.[1] Thence it followed necessarily that final -*e* became added anew to the imperative, either of verbs in which the imperative was originally like the indicative, or of such as later and analogically had effaced the difference: thus, *schere*, *gebäre*,[2] *räche* (cf. the regular *brich*, *sprich*), even *dresche* in spite of *er drischt*, and *werde* in spite of *er wird*. Here the final vowel is found throughout.

But verbs which had inherited from Pregermanic the metaphony of the imperative, naturally held aloof from the weak verbs with invariable stem and remained free from their influence: wherefore we find them retaining the genuine formation in types C (2nd sub-type, *hilf*, *wirf*, *stirb*, *erlisch*), D (*nimm*, *brich*, *sprich*, *stiehl*), and E (*isz*, *gib*, *tritt*, *vergisz*). The duality in the German imperative may be deemed a very consistent and important survival.[3]

[1] Cf. *supra* 183 and 184 in fine.
[2] Cf. *infra* the metaphony in the present (206 D).
[3] The verbs that still keep it are thirty-five in number.

CHAPTER III.

PERSON-ENDINGS.

(198) The Anglo-German **Person-Endings** constitute a very consistent system, which comprises all verbs, strong or weak, without distinction, though it does not apply, apparently at least, to a few conjugations of anomalous appearance. The latter must be reserved to be dealt with separately. We begin by considering the **ordinary conjugation** of both languages.

Section I.

ORDINARY CONJUGATION.

(199) The I.-E. language distinguished **four classes** of person-endings, which have become more or less altered and blended together in its offspring, namely:—primary or **present-endings**, which in Germanic are those of the indicative present;—**secondary endings**, those of the so-called Gr. augmented tenses, which are also those of the optative, and therefore, in Germanic, **characterize the subjunctive**, either present or perfect[1];—**perfect-endings**, in Germanic (indicative) as everywhere else;—lastly, **imperative-endings**. Though they are much mutilated in the later languages, a thorough analysis will enable us to recognise them.

§ 1. *Present-Endings.*

(200) I. **Primitive Forms.**—Let us conjugate, in the present indicative, the I.-E. stem *$bhér$-$ŏ$- (to carry), together

---

[1] Hence it will prove advisable to study them only after those of the perfect indicative.

PERSON-ENDINGS. 331

with the corresponding forms in the oldest tongues of our family.

	I.-E.	Sk.	Gr.	L.
Sg. 1	*bhér-ō	bhár-ā-mi	φέρ-ω	fer-ō
2	*bhér-ĕ-si	bhár-a-si	φέρεις [1]	fer-(i-)s [3]
3	*bhér-ĕ-ti	bhár-a-ti	φέρει [1]	fer-(i-)t [3]
Pl. 1	*bhér-ŏ-mĕs	bhár-ā-mas	φέρ-ο-μεν	fer-i-mus
2	*bhér-ĕ-tĕ	bhár-a-tha	φέρ-ε-τε	fer-(i-)tis [3]
3	*bhér-o-ntĭ	bhár-a-nti	φέρ-ο-ντι [2]	fer-u-nt.

Two main facts are to be observed at the outset.

First, we note the alternation, as stated above,[4] in the vowel which precedes the termination, being ŏ in sg. and pl. 1 and in pl. 3, ĕ in the three other persons. The I.-E. languages fully agree as to this point, with the single exception of Latin in pl. 1,[5] and this curious variation, which probably proceeds from the effect of primitive accentuation, will be seen to take place in the Germanic group as everywhere else.

Next, we recognise the striking likeness of the person-endings, with but insignificant differences between one language and another.[6] That of sg. 1 is the only one which remains obscure. It has been suggested that the stem *bhér-ŏ- could not have become lengthened to *bhér-ō, unless a vocalic ending had united with the final stem-vowel. But what was this vocalic ending? Perhaps an -ă, as we shall find it in sg. 1 of the perfect.

Further, it must be borne in mind that the I.-E. language

---

[1] These two forms are corrupted, since they ought to be *φέρ-ε-σι and *φέρ-ε-τι. But Gr. shows elsewhere the ending -τι of sg. 3: Doric δί-δω-τι (he gives), Attic δί-δω-σι (because Attic changes τ to σ before ι). Cf. Henry, Gramm. of Gr. and Lat., no. 249.

[2] Doric; but Attic φέρουσι = φέρονσι.

[3] Lest the unity of the L. paradigm should appear to be broken, we have conjugated ferō like legō: the real forms are of course fers fert fertis; but this type is well known to be a unique exception.

[4] Supra 82 (II.), and cf. Henry, Gramm. of Gr. and Lat., no. 269.

[5] We should expect to find *fer-ŭ-mus. But we have s-ŭ-mus, vol-ŭ-mus, quæs-ŭ-mus, and, in a totally different category of words (superlative optimus = optumus), Latin shows a similar, probably phonetic, hesitation between ŭ and ĭ before an m. Then, too, leg-i-mus was furthered by the analogy of leg-i-tis.

[6] All attributable to primitive doublets, infra 203, 1.

had another termination for sg. 1, in verbs which did not form their stem by means of the interchangeable vowel -ĕ- / -ŏ- (Gr. so-called verbs in -μι). This exponent of sg. 1 was -mĭ, which will occur below,[1] and even presently in O.H.G., though it is best seen in Greek: ἵστημι (I place) = *σί-στᾱ-μι, τί-θη-μι, δί-δω-μι, etc. But this ending, although important, only concerns us here as completing the series of forms -sĭ and -tĭ, and in later comparison with the corresponding secondary termination -m. For the Germanic ordinary conjugation consists merely of verbs which in Greek grammar would be called verbs in -ω, and here we have only to deal with the Germanic ordinary conjugation.

(201) II. **Pregermanic Forms.**—Translating now, as it were, into Pregermanic the I.-E. paradigm conjugated above, we obtain a new series of forms, which, apart from unimportant details such as may be reserved for further examination, is rigorously verified in the accidence of the earliest and latest Germanic languages.

	Preg.	Go.	O.E.	O.H.G.
Sg. 1	*bér-ō	bair-a	ber-e	bir-u
2	*bér-ĕ-sĭ	bair-i-s	bir-e-s	bir-i-s
3	*bér-ĕ-þĭ	bair-i-þ	bir-e-ð	bir-i-t
Pl. 1	*bér-ă-měs	bair-a-m	ber-a-ð	bër-a-mēs
2	*bér-ĕ-þĕ	bair-i-þ	ber-a-ð	bër-e-t
3	*bér-a-nþĭ	bair-a-nd	ber-a-ð[2]	bër-a-nt

Let us set apart the obvious metaphony in the O.E. and O.H.G. sg., and the O.E. uniform plural-ending, as both requiring a paragraph for themselves. Considering only the bare outline of the present-accidence, we find it as easy to go back to Indo-European by starting from the earliest Germanic tongues, as to descend from the latter to the contemporary languages.

(202) III. **Modern Forms.**—A. Singular.—1. The final

---

[1] *Infra* 217, I. Cf. sg. 1 -m as a secondary ending, *infra* 211.
[2] The dialects differ, but the principle of conjugation is the same throughout: the type quoted here is the accidence in Wessex, except sg. 2 *birest*, as also *birist* concurrently with *biris* in O.H.G. *infra* 202, 2.

-ō has been shortened, and then variously obscured, down to the dull vowel -ĕ, which again is dropped in English,[1] as also in German when swiftly sounded: *gebär-e, nehm-e, trink-e, fahr-e*, etc. In the weak verbs we have likewise: Go. *sōk-ja, salb-ō, hab-a*; O.E. *sēc-e, sealf-ie, hæbb-e*, whence E. *seek, salve, have*; O.H.G. *suoch-u, salb-ō-m salb-ō-n, hab-ē-m*,[2] whence G. *such-e, salb-e, hab-e*: all the forms having become identical.

2. Final *i* being dropped, there remained -*s*, an ending well preserved in Gothic, but already somewhat obsolete in the sister-tongues, though it occasionally survives even in M.H.G.: *nim-i-s* (thou takest), *fer-i-s* (thou travellest), etc. It will be seen below that the regular Germanic ending of sg. 2 in the perfect was -*t*, and that such perfects as retained it unaltered possessed a decided sense of present-time [3]: from this arose the analogical influence of the perfect on the present-accidence; for, since a West Germanic speaker would say, for instance, *wais-t "thou knowest," *kan-t and even ultimately *kan-s-t "thou canst," it was only natural that he should say likewise *bir-i-st "thou carriest" instead of *bir-i-s. Yet another circumstance must be taken into account: the nominative of the pronoun of sg. 2 *þū was often added to the verbal form of sg. 2, whence proceeded such syntactical complexes as *biris tū,[4] O.H.G. *biris tu*, which the speaker resolved unconsciously into *birist du*, E. *bearst (thou)*, G. *gebierst (du)*. Thus the ending -*st* prevailed, in both languages, either with or without syncope of the preceding vowel: E. *bear-e-st, drive-st, give-st, take-st, drink-e-st*; G. *gebier-st (gebär-st), nimm-st, trink-st, fähr-st*.[5]— The weak verbs require no special remarks.

[1] Even when written: there is no final *e* in *drive, give, shake, take*, any more than in *bear, drink, fall*, etc.

[2] Hence O.H.G., purer in this respect even than Gothic, retains the I.-E. ending -*mi*, which here is quite justified, the verbs of these two classes being stems which did not end in -ĕ- / -ŏ-, supra 85 and 92-93. But M.H.G. effaced the distinction and consequently lost the final *m* (*n*) of sg. 1.

[3] Cf. *infra* 208, 209, and 222.

[4] Do not forget that the *s* preceding a *t* impedes the consonantal shifting.

[5] The syncope was once even more energetic than it is now, cf. *supra* 187: German, for instance, has restored *trägst trägt* after *trage*; but M.H.G. conjugated *trage treist treit*, a syncope which is still kept in *getreide* (corn) = O.H.G. *gi-treg-idi* (product). Compare moreover the syncopated conjugation in E. *have hast hath (has)* and G. *habe hast hat*.

3. The Preg. ending -þi ought to remain -þi after an accented syllable, and become -ði after an unaccented syllable (Verner's law). Now, some I.-E. verbs in -ŏ- were accented on the root, whereas others were accented on the suffix: so that the two terminations -ði and -þi must have coexisted in Pregermanic. But, as already seen above in many other instances,[1] grammatical analogy led to a separate extension of each ending in the two later languages: thus, the latter in O.E. became -ð; in O.H.G. the former became -t: E. *bear-e-th, give-th*, etc.; G. *gebier-t (gebär-t), nimm-t, fähr-t, trink-t*, etc. German retains this state; not so English, though the ending -*th* is still current in scriptural and poetical style. Ordinary speech replaces it by an ending -*s*, which however is quite modern: *bear-s, give-s, drink-s*, etc. The *th* and the *s* both being sibilant sounds, it was easy to pass from one to the other; but this cannot be deemed merely a question of phonetics, since a similar change did not take place anywhere else. It must have arisen from the *s* of sg. 2, which was extended by an unconscious desire to systematise and, as it were, imposed its sound upon the *th* of sg. 3: in other words, because the speaker said *givest*, he took to saying likewise *gives* instead of *giveth*.[2]

(203) B. Plural.—1. I.-E. seems to have had several exponents for pl. 1, viz.: -*mēs*, retained only in O.H.G.; -*mĕs*, Doric -μες; -*mŏs*, L. -*mŭs*; simple -*mĕ*, Gr. -με(ν) and Go. -*m*, an ending originally limited to secondary tenses, but often ultimately extended to the present, as may be seen from Gr. and Go. Thus the latter has everywhere a simple -*m*: *bair-a-m, nim-a-m*, etc. O.H.G. hesitates between the two terminations, that is to say, having primitively -*mēs* for the present (*bër-a-mēs*) and -*m* for the secondary tenses, it extended -*m* into the present (*bër-a-m*), and -*mēs* into the secondary tenses; but the latter form is antiquated and of no interest except from a historical point of view.[3] Thus, O.H.G. still possesses *nëm-a-mēs*,

[1] *Supra* 63, 124 (I.), 139, and *infra* 203 (2–3), 212.
[2] Northumbrian at a rather early date had changed final *th* to *s*, so that here a dialectal mixture is possible.
[3] It has probably proceeded from the very rare cases in which the ending of pl. 1 became attached to the root without any intermediate, thus Preg. *stō-mēs* (we stand), *ɡ̑ō-mēs* (we go), etc.; for this position is the only one

PERSON-ENDINGS.   335

*nëm-e-mēs*¹ and *nëm-ē-m*, *zioh-e-mēs* and *zioh-ē-n*, *far-ē-m* and *far-ē-n*; even M.H.G., *nëm-e-mēs* and *nëm-e-n*²; but the latter type ultimately prevails, and Mod. G. knows no form but *gebär-e-n*, *nehm-e-n*, *zieh-e-n*, *fahr-e-n*, etc. The same is the case with the weak verbs.

2. The termination *-þĕ* was naturally treated like *-þĭ*, whence *-þĕ* after an accented, and *-ðĕ* after an unaccented syllable: the Go. *-þ*, of course, corresponds to both at once; the general exponent of the O.E. pl. comes from *-þĕ*, whereas the G. exponent of pl. 2 represents Preg. *-ðĕ*, either with or without syncope: *gebär-e-t* and *gebär-t*, *nehm-e-t*³ and *nehm-t*, *trink-t*, *fahr-e-t*, etc.

3. The ending *-nþĭ* likewise becomes either *-nþĭ* or *-nðĭ*: Gothic has either; O.E. has *-nþĭ* represented by *-(n)ð*; O.H.G. has *-nðĭ* shifted to *-nt*, O.H.G. *bër-a-nt*, *nëm-a-nt*, *zioh-e-nt*,⁴ *far-e-nt*, M.H.G. *nëm-a-nt* and *nëm-e-nt*, and so forth, without exception. But it will be seen that in the perfect and subjunctive the termination, quite regularly, was simply *-n*: wherefore, during the latest period of M.H.G., *nëment* analogically became *nëmen* (on the pattern of *nāmen* "they took"), so that pl. 3 is the same as pl. 1, G. *gebär-e-n*, *nehm-e-n*, *fahr-e-n*, etc.⁵

§ 2. *Present-Metaphony.*

(204) Our examination has been restricted as yet to the endings, without any regard to the modification which might

that allows the ending to be accented in I.-E., cf. Sk. *i-más* (we go) = Gr. *ĭ-μεν*; and, if it had been unaccented, it could not have preserved its final *s*.
¹ Owing to an encroachment of the vowel of pl. 2 *nëm-e-t*. Cf. the similar process in Latin, *supra* 200, note 5.
² Observe moreover an optional apocope of final *n* when the pronoun subject is placed after the verb: M.H.G. *nëme wir* (we take).
³ M.H.G. (Alamannic) *nëm-e-nt*, pl. 2 having strangely enough adopted the form of pl. 3; still in High Alsatian *ër nāmĕ* "you take" like *sĭ nāmĕ* "they take." But O.H.G. and regular M.H.G. *nëm-e-t*.
⁴ The same vocalic corruption as in pl. 1.
⁵ Let us here, for the sake of completeness, give the paradigm of the three weak verbs, which in the modern languages have reached the same dull vocalic state:

Go.	*sōk-ja*	*sōk-ei-s*	*sōk-ei-þ*	*sōk-ja-m*	*sōk-ei-þ*	*sōk-ja-nd* =
O.H.G.	*suoch-u*	*suoch-i-s*	*suoch-i-t*	*suoch-e-mēs*	*suoch-e-t*	*suoch-ent*;
Go.	*salb-ō*	*salb-ō-s*	*salb-ō-þ*	*salb-ō-m*	*salb-ō-þ*	*salb-ō-nd* =
O.H.G.	*salb-ō-n*	*salb-ō s(t)*	*salb-ō-t*	*salb-ō-mēs*	*salb-ō-t*	*salb-ō-nt*;
Go.	*hab-a*	*hab-ái-s*	*hab-ái-þ*	*hab-a-m*	*hab-ái-þ*	*hab-a-nd* =
O.H.G.	*hab-ē-n*	*hab-ē-s(t)*	*hab-ē-t*	*hab-ē-mēs*	*hab-ē-t*	*hab-ē-nt*.

affect the verbal stem itself. Now the fact is that, while all the English verbs and the German weak verbs conjugate their present indicative on the same invariable stem throughout, the German strong verbs, in general, inasmuch as their radical vowel is capable of **metaphony**, undergo it **in the forms of sg. 2 and 3**, all other persons remaining free from it: *nehm-e nimm-st nimm-t nehm-e-n*, etc.; *fahr-e fähr-st fähr-t fahr-e-n*, etc. This peculiarity of G. accidence we have now to explain.

Referring to Pregermanic, we find the existence of three person-endings capable of producing metaphony, that is to say, containing an *i*, namely, sg. 2 and 3, and pl. 3.

The last, of course, is out of question, for the vowel which precedes it is I.-E. ŏ, whence Preg. ă, in short, a vowel which could not undergo a Preg. metaphony. In other words, such a type as **ném-ă-nŏĭ *făr-á-nṗĭ* remained unaltered in Pregermanic, since *ĕ* was the only vowel capable of metaphony in this early period; whereas later, in O.H.G., when the *ă* in its turn became liable to similar mutation, the *ĭ* which might produce it had long vanished, thus *nëm-a-n-t far-e-nt*, in which metaphony, for another reason, was equally impossible.

Secondly, English also may be neglected, though in its earlier state it exhibits the metaphony precisely under the same conditions as German [1]; but no trace of it survives any more than in the imperative, analogy having extended throughout every verb a uniform vocalism: O.E. sg. 1 *frēos-e cēos-e*, sg. 3 *frīes-ð cīes-ð*, but E. sg. 1 *freeze choose*, sg. 3 *freeze-th choose-th*, without any mutation from one person to another.[2]

Let us now analyse the forms of sg. 2 and 3 in German strong verbs, and then try to account for the fact that the same forms never undergo metaphony in the weak verbs.

(205) **I. Strong Verbs.**—1. Considering in Pregermanic

---

[1] See the O.E. paradigm, *supra* 201; many other similar instances could be mentioned.

[2] E. *ee* being the true representative of O.E. *ēo*, there can be no metaphony in *freeze* as opposed to *choose*, though their vowels are different. Hence the *oo* in *choose* (Chaucer has still *cheese*), *shoot*, etc., probably proceeds from the influence of the preceding consonant. Cf. however E. *lose*=O.E. *lēosan*, where such a reason cannot be given.—For the loss of the metaphony in these types, cf. the same phenomenon in the similar G. *kiesen, frieren*, etc., *infra* 206 B.

any strong verb, but preferably, for convenience of demonstration, a verb containing a radical ă (type F), such as *făr-ana-m (to travel), we know it, as stated and proved above, to have been conjugated, in the present indicative, *făr-ō *făr-ĕ-sĭ *făr-ĕ-þĭ *făr-ă-mĕ *făr-ĕ-þĕ *făr-ă-nþĭ. Now, such an accidence could not persist; for, even as early as Pregermanic, the forms which contained an ĕ followed by an ĭ, namely sg. 2 and 3, metaphonized the ĕ and became *făr-ĭ-sĭ *făr-ĭ-þĭ. Then, in the dialects, final ĭ vanishes, whence Go. far-i-s far-i-þ and O.H.G. *far-i-s *far-i-t. But the two latter forms again become impossible in O.H.G., as soon as in this tongue the a in its turn undergoes metaphony, since, before the i which precedes the ending, the radical a must become e, whence finally sg. 2 fer-i-s (fer-i-st) and sg. 3 fer-i-t, as opposed to sg. 1 far-u.

Let us now pass to the case when the Preg. root contained an I.-E. ĕ. Here the phenomenon will appear at once earlier and more intricate. Though at first sight the two metaphonical processes in far-an fer-i-s fer-i-t and nëm-an nim-i-s nim-it might seem rigorously parallel, this view is incorrect, since the metaphony of ĕ is known to be far earlier than that of ă: hence, it is not to O.H.G., but to Pregermanic itself, that we ought to trace back the vocalic mutation of the latter type: in other words, we have the series *nĕm-ĕ-sĭ *nĕm-ĕ-ðĭ, then *nĕm-ĭ-sĭ *nĕm-ĭ-ðĭ, and lastly *nĭm-ĭ-sĭ *nĭm-ĭ-ðĭ, the whole already in the Pregermanic period. So, on one side, the type nimis nimit refers us to a much earlier Germanic state than the type feris ferit is able to do, though of course both rest on the same principle.[1]

And, on the other hand, the former type shows a wider historical extension than the latter, because in O.H.G. an ĕ is metaphonized under the influence, not only of an i, but also of a following u, and the form of sg. 1 ends with a -u: so that, O.H.G. far-u from far-an being kept unaltered, O.H.G. *nëm-u from nëm-an cannot but become nim-u, and so also bir-u, gib-u, iȝȝu, etc.

---

[1] This is also the reason why the metaphony in the imperative nimm is an isolated form, contrasted with the non-metaphonical imperative fahr-e, supra 197.

Consequently, O.H.G. had a strong present-accidence with metaphony in sg. 2 and 3, *faru ferist ferit*, which is correctly reproduced in Mod. G. *fahre führst fährt*, and another strong present-accidence with metaphony throughout the whole singular, *nimu nimist nimit*, which is only partly reproduced in Mod. G. *nehme nimmst nimmt*. How is it that the modern speaker no longer says *ich *nimme*[1]? The answer is obvious, the analogical process here being as clear as possible: a general levelling has effaced the metaphony of sg. 1. For, in the type *fahren*, sg. 1 *fahre* being free from metaphony in contrast to sg. 2 and 3 *führst führt*, and similar in this respect to the corresponding form pl. 1 *fahren*, it was but natural that, in the type *nehmen*, there should be restored a sg. 1 *nehme*, contrasted with sg. 2 and 3 *nimmst nimmt* and similar to pl. 1 *nehmen*. Even a mathematical proportion could not have a more exact result.

Hence, through a kind of compromise between two types of strong verbs, German has come to its present rule, namely: apart from the rather rare cases in which the vocalism has been entirely levelled by the power of analogy,[2] every strong verb, provided its radical vowel be capable of metaphony, exhibits a metaphony of the root in sg. 2 and 3 exclusively.

(206) 2. Now let us proceed to the applications of the rule throughout the various types of strong verbs.

A. The radical vowel ($\bar{\imath}$) is incapable of metaphony.

B. In O.H.G. we find the regular forms, sg. *ziuh-u ziuh-i-s ziuh-i-t* (metaph.), and pl. *zioh-e-mēs zioh-e-t zioh-e-nt* (nonmetaph.); but Mod. G. has extended the non-metaphonical form, and we have now *zieh-e zieh-st zieh-t zieh-e-n*, etc.,[3] and so in the whole class; apart, however, from such slight traces of metaphony as may still be found, at least in archaic and poetical language, in the verbs *fliehen, fliegen, flieszen, gieszen, schlieszen, kriechen*,[4] etc., but of course only in sg. 2 and 3. In

---

[1] The present is still in M.H.G. *nime nimes nimet*; and down to the present day, in High Alsatian, the regular contrast exists between *i něm* (I take) and *mr̥ nămě* (we take).

[2] A corruption often found in the dialects: Alamannic, for instance, conjugates *er fahrt, er schlagt, er halt* (however *er treit* "he carries"), etc.

[3] The metaphonized stem would be **zeuh-*, supra 29.

[4] Was da *kreucht* und *fleugt*. Schiller, *W. Tell*, III. 12.

one of the four verbs the stem of which exhibits $au = \bar{u}$, we find an analogical metaphony, viz. *sauf-e säuf-st säuf-t sauf-e-n*.

C. The sub-type *trinken* does not here concern us. But the sub-type *helfen* is quite consistent in metaphony: O.H.G. *hilf-u hilf-i-s hilf-i-t, stirb-u stirb-i-s stirb-i-t*; G. *helf-e hilf-st hilf-t, sterb-e stirb-st stirb-t*; further, *schwillt, quillt, befiehlt, erlischt*, and, the two dentals being blended together, after the syncope, *birst* for **birst-i-t, wird* for *wirdit,[1] etc. This violent though regular syncope has been replaced by an ending *-t*, restored anew and preceded by an *ĕ*, whenever sg. 3 happens not to be metaphonic: thus, *binden, gestatten* are conjugated *er bindet, er gestattet*, because the syncopated forms *er* **bint, er* *gestatt are unable to show the exponent of sg. 3 hidden within them. But, if the person is characterized clearly enough by the metaphony, then the restoration is omitted as useless, and the syncope retained: *er gilt, er schilt, er ficht* (from *fecht-en*), etc.[2]

D. The metaphony is constant: O.H.G. *biru biris birit, nimu nimis nimit*; G. *gebäre gebierst gebiert* (also *gebärst gebärt*),[3] *nehme nimmst nimmt*; and likewise, *bricht, spricht, trifft*, even *kömmt* owing to a quite modern analogy. It is effaced, either partly or entirely, in *gebärt, kommt, schert (scheert)* and *pflegt*.

E. The metaphony is constant: O.H.G. *sihu sihis sihit, gibu gibis gibit*; G. *sehe siehst sieht, gebe gibst gibt*; and likewise, *iszt, miszt, liest*; putting aside, of course, such verbs as already have the metaphony throughout their entire accidence (*bitten, sitzen, liegen*).

F. Here, as seen above, the metaphony is identical in O.H.G. and Mod. G.: *faru feris ferit*, and *fahre fährst fährt*; and likewise, *schlägt, trägt, wächst*, etc. But *laden*, once a weak verb, did not adopt it, and *schaffen* has lost it. It stands to reason that *heben* and *schwören* cannot show it at all, since their radical vowel is metaphonical even in the infinitive.

---

[1] Cf. *supra* 187, the syncopes in the weak perfect.
[2] Even in sg. 2 in *wirst* = *wird-i-st. And also in the other classes of strong verbs: *er tritt* = **trit-i-t, er hält* = *helt-i-t*, etc.
[3] The M.H.G. vb. *wëgen* = O.H.G. *wëgan* = E. *to weigh* (weak vb., cf. also G. *wegen* in *be-wegen* "to move"), being conjugated M.H.G. *wige wigest wiget wëgen*, thus gave birth to two synonymous verbs, respectively *wägen* (regular with *ä* = *ë*) and *wiegen* (metaph.).

G. All the verbs of this type, excluding only *hauen*, which have a radical *a*, require the metaphony: *fällt, hält, läszt, läuft*. Indeed, it has been extended to *stöszt* as above to *kömmt*. But *heiszen* could not undergo it, and *rufen* remained free from it.

(207) II. **Weak Verbs.**—The first class of weak verbs being characterized by an infinitive in *-jan* (Go. *nas-jan* "to cure,"[1] *sōk-jan* "to seek), its radical vowel is, constantly and in every form either of the sg. or the pl., followed by a syllable which was able to cause metaphony: now, supposing this to have taken place in earlier days, either in Pregermanic as in *sitzen*, or at least in O.H.G. as in *heben*,—thus, for instance, Mod. G. *nähren* (to feed) = Go. *nas-jan*,—then, of course, the verb is metaphonized everywhere, and cannot appear particularly metaphonized in sg. 2 and 3; the reverse being the case, as in O.H.G. *suochan*, now *suchen*,[2] then the verb can be metaphonized nowhere, for it has no more reason for undergoing metaphony in sg. 2 and 3 than in the rest of its accidence. A type *suochit* (he seeks) could not undergo it in O.H.G., since *uo* is not yet capable of it; and, in M.H.G., when *uo* in its turn became subject to it, the type was already altered to *suochet* and no longer contained an *i*. Hence it is obvious that, in any case, verbs of this class cannot exhibit in sg. 2 and 3 of their present indicative a vocalism in any way different from that of their whole accidence.

Still more so with the other classes; for, in Preg. *salb-ō-ðĭ* *hab-ē-ðĭ*, the *ĭ* is not yet brought into contact with a vowel capable of metaphony, and in West Germanic the *ĭ* is dropped altogether.

Thus we have historically accounted for an important peculiarity which differentiates strong and weak verbs, no less than the difference in the formation of their perfects and participles.

---

[1] The causative of the strong verb which is now Mod. G. *ge-nes-en* "recover."

[2] O.H.G. *suochan* is (regularly) a non-metaphonical form, whereas O.E. *sēcean* (E. *seek*) has been seen to be (no less regularly) a metaphonical one.

[3] With this main restriction, that, in M.H.G., as also in the dialects, the metaphony has often, analogically, spread into the weak verb: there are such conjugations as *mache mächst mächt, sage sägst sägt* (the latter still surviving in High Alsatian); but the literary language has proscribed these forms, keeping only one of them, namely *frägst* (askest) *frägt* (also *fragt*).

§ 3. Perfect-Endings.

(208) It must be understood that the perfect-endings have no primitive character except in the strong perfect, which however has given its accidence to the weak one. Now, starting from the Sanskrit conjugation,[1] *e.g.* the Sk. pf. *vêd-a* (I wot), sg. 1 *vêd-a*, 2 *vêt-tha*, 3 *véd-a*, pl. 1 *vid-mú*, 2 *vid-ú*, 3 *vidúr*, we may state the I.-E. endings of this tense as follows:

sg. 1 *-ă*, 2 *-thă*, 3 *-ĕ*, pl. 1 *-mé*;

the terminations of pl. 2 and 3 being of no interest in Germanic, because there they were borrowed from another series.

(209) I. **Strong Perfect.**—Choosing, for the sake of greater simplicity, such a perfect as, in the Pregermanic period, had already completely lost the vowel-gradation from sg. to pl., we see that its prehistorical and historical endings were as follows:

	Preg.	Go.	O.E.	O.H.G.
Sg. 1	*slôh-ă*	*slōh*	*slōg*	*sluog*
2	*slôh-tă*	*slōh-t*	*slōg-e*	*sluog-i*
3	*slôh-ĕ*	*slōh*	*slōg*	*sluog*
Pl. 1	*slōʒ-ŭmé*[2]	*slōh-um*	*slōg-on*	*sluog-um*[3]
2	*slōʒ-ŭðé*	*slōh-uþ*	*slōg-on*	*sluog-ut*
3	*slōʒ-ŭnþ*	*slōh-un*	*slōg-on*	*sluog-un*

Sg. 1 and 3, after their final vowel had regularly disappeared, became identical: O.E. *slōg* and E. (*I, he*) *slew drove chose drank bound burst bare spoke gave was fell*, etc.; O.H.G. *sluog* and G. (*ich, er*) *schlug trieb erkor trank band barst gebar sprach gab war fiel*, etc. This is the reason why sg. 3 of the perfect never has any ending, whereas sg. 3 in the present always shows E. *-th* (*-s*) and G. *-t*.

Sg. 2 in West Germanic is quite a different form from what it was in I.-E. and even in Gothic: properly speaking, it does not belong to the perfect, but to the primitive aorist,[4] though

---

[1] Controlled and corrected by the testimony of Greek, cf. the accidence of οἶδ-α (I wot), viz. οἶδ-α οἶσ-θα οἶδ-ε ἴδ-μεν ἴσ-τε ἴσ-αντι.

[2] With the regular "grammatical alternation," which everywhere else has become variously levelled.

[3] Also *sluog-umēs*, supra 203, 1.

[4] Thus, for instance, sg. 1 *zōh* (I drew) and sg. 2 *zug-i* (thou drewest) bear

here confounded with the perfect. From this however it does not follow that West Germanic knew nothing of a perfect-ending sg. 2 -*t*, which in Preg. and Go. represents the I.-E. -*thă*; for we have already met with it and shall find it again in the preterito-presents.[1] Next, the analogy of this eventual survival of the ending -*t*, together with the development of a new termination -*st* in the present, actually influenced the perfect, and introduced into it, separately though similarly in both the later tongues, the same ending sg. 2 -*st*: while M.H.G. still conjugates *nam nǣm-e* (=O.H.G. *nām-i*), Mod. G. has now *nahm nahm-st nahm*, and so forth everywhere, E. *slew-est* like *slay-est*, G. *schlug-st* like *schläg-st*, etc.[2]

In pl. 1 the original ending is -*mé*, in which, after a consonant, the initial *m* easily develops its proper vowel, thus -*m̥mé*, whence Preg. -*umé* and Go. -*um*. Later on, final *m* becomes *n*, as may already be seen in the O.E. and even the O.H.G. accidence (also *slᵘog-un*): further E. *slew*, and G. *schlug-en*, so that pl. 1 and 3 are as completely blended together as is the case with sg. 1 and 3.

Like Greek (ἴσ-τε, λε-λοίπ-α-τε), Pregermanic borrows the ending of pl. 2 from the series of the primary or secondary endings, I.-E. -*tĕ*, Preg. -*þĕ*. The *ŭ* developed by a phonetic process in pl. 1 and 3 was analogically transferred to pl. 2, whence a Gothic final syllable -*uþ* (-*uð*), O.H.G. -*ut*, G. (*ihr*) *schlug-et*, etc.[3]

Greek borrows its ending of pl. 3 from the primary series, whence -*ntĭ*; Pregermanic borrows it from the secondary series, whence merely -*nþ*, as in the subjunctive, and consequently, with the vowel-sound *n̥*, an ending -*un* in the later languages

---

to one another exactly the same relation as Gr. (pf.) πέ-φευγ-α (I have fled) to (aor.) ἔ-φυγ-ε-ς (thou fledst). Cf. moreover *supra* 172 and note.

[1] *Supra* 53 A and *infra* 222 sq.

[2] But the ancient aoristic form did not disappear without leaving some traces of its existence: the complete assimilation, either in German or—even more—in English, of the perfect subjunctive to the perfect indicative certainly started from this form of sg. 2, in which both moods were characterized at once by a termination -*i* and the reduced grade of the root.

[3] The uniformity of the E. pl. endings has been reserved for further examination: *infra* 214.

which drop the final consonant. Nothing, therefore, is more regular than the O.E. and O.H.G. contrast between *slōg-on* = *sluog-un* (never **sluog-unt*) " they slew," and *slē-a-ð* = *slah-e-nt* " they slay." But the modern present-accidence has been seen to efface this original difference.[1]

(210) II. **Weak Perfect.**—The weak perfect, as stated above,[2] probably proceeds from a single form of sg. 3: to this form again, West Germanic applied the endings of the strong perfect, so exactly indeed, that it will prove sufficient to quote the modern accidence without entering into any historical details:

E. *sought*   *sought-est*   *sought*   *sought*   *sought*   *sought*
G. *suchte*   *suchte-st*   *suchte*   *suchte-n*   *suchte-t*   *suchte-n*

And so, likewise, E. *salved salved-st, had had-st*, G. *salbte salbte-st, hatte hatte-st*, without either exceptions or difficulty.[3]

§ 4. *Subjunctive-Endings.*

(211) The so-called secondary I.-E. endings, which are those of the I.-E. optative and, consequently, of the Preg. subjunctive, merely differ from the primary endings by dropping the final i wherever it occurs, that is in sg. 1, 2, 3, and pl. 3.[4] Hence we may conceive the two series to run parallel as follows:

Primary : sg. 1 -*mĭ*, 2 -*sĭ*, 3 -*tĭ* ; pl. 1 -*mes*, 2 -*tĕ*, 3 -*ntĭ* ;
Secondary : „ 1 -*m*, 2 -*s*, 3 -*t* ;   „ 1 -*mĕ*₁ 2 -*tĕ*, 3 -*nt*.

As Latin has not only kept, but even transferred to its primary tenses, the secondary endings, it affords us the best means of restoring them. Let us compare, in form and accidence, the subjunctive (optative) of the root *ĕs* (to be):

---

[1] Cf. *supra* 203, 3, and *infra* 211.
[2] *Supra* 188, II. and III.
[3] Gothic conjugates: *sōkida sōkidēs sōkida sōkidēdum sōkidēduþ sōkidēdun*; *salbōda salbōdēs*, etc. ; *habáida*, etc.
[4] Compare, for instance, Gr. pres. λύουσι = λύ-ο-ντι with impf. ἔλυον = *ἔλυ-ο-ντ. The relation is exactly the same in Germanic.

Lat.	:	$s\text{-}\bar{\imath}\text{-}m$	$s\text{-}\bar{\imath}\text{-}s$	$s\text{-}\bar{\imath}\text{-}t$	$s\text{-}\bar{\imath}\text{-}mus$	$s\text{-}\bar{\imath}\text{-}tis$[1]	$s\text{-}i\text{-}nt$;
O.H.G.	:	$s\text{-}\bar{\imath}$	$s\text{-}\bar{\imath}\text{-}s$	$s\text{-}\bar{\imath}$	$s\text{-}\bar{\imath}\text{-}m$[2]	$s\text{-}\bar{\imath}\text{-}t$	$s\text{-}\bar{\imath}\text{-}n$;
Mod. G.	:	sci	sei-est	sei	sei-en	sei-et	sei-en.

It is indeed a marvellous thing to find so striking an agreement, at a distance of so many centuries, between Italic and Germanic.

From a glance at this table, the reader will derive more profit than from any commentary, provided he has borne in mind the essential laws of Germanic phonetics. For, seeing that final *m* and *t* were equally dropped in Pregermanic, he will find that sg. 1 and 3 have become identical even in this period, as they are now. The same loss of final *t* in pl. 3 caused pl. 1 and 3 to be blended together, as soon as O.H.G. pl. 1 $s\bar{\imath}m$ had been changed to $s\bar{\imath}n$. Lastly, the substitution of sg. 2 $s\bar{\imath}st$ for $s\bar{\imath}s$ is a simple and well-known process. Now let us turn to the paradigms, ancient or modern, of both tenses in the subjunctive.

	Present.			Perfect.		
	Go.	O.E.	O.H.G.	Go.	O.E.	O.H.G.
Sg. 1	slah-au	bind-e[4]	slah-e	s'öh-jau	slōg-e	sluog-i
2.	slah-ái-s	bind-e	slah-ē-s	slōh-ei-s	slōg-e	sluog-i-s
3.	slah-ái	bind-e	slah-e	slōh-i	slōg-e	sluog-i
Pl. 1.	slah-ái-ma[3]	bind-e-n	slah-ē-n	slōh-ei-ma[3]	slōg-e-n	sluog-ī-n
2.	slah-ái-þ	bind-e-n	slah-ē-t	slōh-ei-þ	slōg-e-n	sluog-i t
3.	slah-ái-na[3]	bind-e-n	slah-ē-n	slōh-ei-na[3]	slōg-e-n	sluog-ī-n

Whence :

E.	slay	slay	slay	slay	slay	slay,
G.	schlīg-e	schlag-e-st	schlag-e	schlag-e-n	schlag-e-t	schlag-e-n;
E.	slew	slew	slew	slew	slew	slew,
G.	schlü_-:	schlüg-e- t	schlüg-e	schlüg-e-n	schlüg-e-t	schlüg-e-n.

(212) There is but one point left for examination: namely, besides the uniformity in the O.E. pl., a question as yet re-

---

[1] This is the only point of divergence in L., for we should expect *$si\text{-}te$; but -tis is borrowed from the indicative, and L. has lost -te everywhere but in the imperative.

[2] Also $s\text{-}\bar{\imath}\text{-}m\bar{e}s$, which resembles still more the L. form.

[3] These endings with an added vowel do not concern us, since West Germanic knows nothing of them.

[4] It proved convenient to replace here the vb. $sl\bar{e}\text{-}an$ by the vb. $bind\text{-}an$, because the former conceals its person-endings, its subjunctive being contracted to $sl\bar{e}$.

served, we find here a similar uniformity in the O.E. sg.; in other words, E. sg. 2 lacks the ending like all the other persons. But this last difficulty must appear small indeed to any one who remembers that a primitive final *s*, according to the place of the accent, ought either to remain *s*, or to become *z* and then disappear: it is the latter that took place in O.E., with but this additional circumstance, that the cases in which the ending had become -*z* analogically encroached upon those in which the -*s* had been kept, so that the ending vanished altogether, whereas German retained the -*s* (-*st*) everywhere after the analogy of the forms which preserved it quite regularly.[1] Hence, the E. subjunctive is a new instance of a general treatment applicable to every form with final -*s*, as often stated above, and particularly in the contrast between the German and English plural of declined nouns.[2] And thus Modern English has acquired a subjunctive invariable for plural or singular, present or perfect.

§ 5. *Imperative-Endings.*

(213) English and German have lost all the original forms of the imperative, with the exception of sg. 2 and pl. 2. The remainder is simply borrowed from the subjunctive (G. *nehme er, nehmen sie*), or else replaced by a periphrastic locution.

The form of sg. 2 being the stem of the mood,[3] our study is confined to pl. 2, in which the ending is I.-E. -*tĕ*, Preg. -*þĕ* or -*ðĕ*: I.-E. **bhér-e-te* (carry), Sk. *bhár-a-ta*, Gr. φέρ-ε-τε νέμ-ε-τε, L. *leg-i-te dīc-i-te*, etc.; Go. *bair-i-þ* (carry), *nim-i-þ* (take); O.E. *bind-a-ð* (bind), *help-a-ð* (help), *bidd-a-ð* (pray), etc.; O.H.G. *nëm-e-t* (take), *zioh-e-t* (draw), *far-e-t* (travel), and G. *nehmet, ziehet, fahret*, etc., etc., with the occasional syncope of the unaccented *ĕ*.

No remark is here needed, except that, since the syllables

---

[1] As a matter of fact, the -*s* generally follows an unaccented syllable in the optative of the present (Sk. *várt-ē-s*), and an accented syllable in the optative of the perfect (Sk. *va-vṛt-yá-s*), so that in English the present may be said to have influenced the perfect, and *vice versâ* in German.
[2] Cf. *supra* 63, 139 and 143, and also 202, 3, etc.
[3] *Supra* 196 and 197.

which follow the stem are never of such a kind as to require it
to undergo metaphony, the well-known contrast between *nimm*
and *nehmet* is in strict accordance with the history of the
German language from its beginning.

In the weak verbs we find in the same way: Go. *sōk-ei-þ*
salb-ō-þ hab-ái-þ; O.H.G. *suoch-e-t salb-ō-t hab-ē-t*; G. *suchet*
salbet habet.

But in English there is no longer any difference between pl.
2 and sg. 2, that is to say, here, as everywhere else, the plural
has altogether lost its endings. We must now direct special
attention to this strange peculiarity.

§ 6. *The English Verbal Plural.*

(214) I. Having followed up to this point the inferences
which may be drawn, either from the original form of the
person-endings, or from their actual state in Gothic and
German, the reader would expect to find, in the O.E. plural,
five series of regular endings, thus:

(1) Present indicative: **bind-a-n* [1] **bind-e-ð bind-a-ð*
(=**bind-a-nð* [2]); whereas we find only *bind-a-ð* in the three
persons, and in English, also in the three persons, the curtailed
bind;

(2) Perfect indicative: *bund-on *bund-oð bund-on*; whereas
we have *bund-on* everywhere, and in English *bound*;

(3) Present subjunctive: *bind-e-n *bind-e-ð bind-e-n*; but,
actually *bind-e-n* everywhere, and in English *bind*;

(4) Perfect subjunctive: *bund-e-n *bund-e-ð bund-e-n*; but
actually *bund-e-n* everywhere, and E. *bound*.

(5) Imperative **bind-e-ð*, the real O.E. form being nearly
alike (*bind-a-ð*), but in E. merely *bind*.

II. How did such a curious levelling take place? and how
could it happen that an accidence comprising various endings
became uniform in O.E., and completely lost these endings in
English? Of course, phonetic change by itself is unable to

---

[1] More accurately **bind-a-m*, and so likewise in the other tenses; but
remember that the final nasal is of an undecided character, *supra* 29.

[2] With O.E. compensatory lengthening (*supra* 20, 4 A) and later shortening in an unaccented syllable (*supra* 65 and 66).

account for the fact: it must at least have been furthered by several analogical processes, which, plain as they are, would nevertheless require a rather tedious explanation, were we to descend to minute particulars. But they may be briefly summed up as follows.

1. The starting-point of the change is to be found in the two tenses of the subjunctive, where, as explained above, the three forms of the sg. had become the same: since the sg. was indifferently *bind-e* in the present and *bund-e* in the perfect for all three persons, and since, moreover, the plural was indifferently *bind-e-n* and *bund-e-n* in the same tenses for two of their three persons (1st and 3rd), it would seem only natural to say likewise *bind-e-n* and *bund-e-n* in pl. 2. Here, the process is so clear, that it may even be shown in a kind of mathematical proportion, thus: (*gē*) *binden* : (*wē*) *binden* = (ðū) *binde* : (*ic*) *binde*, and (*gē*) *bunden* : (*wē*) *bunden* = (ðū) *bunde* : (*ic*) *bunde*. There can be hardly any scientific problem which admits of a more satisfactory solution.

2. It must be observed, however, that—as our formula clearly suggests—the process is necessarily in strict connection with a new phenomenon of so-called grammatical analytism, namely, the concurrent use of the personal pronoun as a subject to the verb, a pleonastic locution still unfamiliar to Gothic. Thus, for instance, as long as Old French conjugated its present indicative *aim aim-e-s aim-e-t* (= L. *ám-ō ám-ā-s ám-a-t*), distinctly sounding all the vowels and consonants, there was no reason for prefixing to the verb the pronouns *je tu il*; but, as soon as the speaker began to prefix them, there was no longer any reason for distinctly sounding the terminations. Hence, the two facts of uniformity in the endings and analytism in conjugation are seen to go hand in hand and to further one another. If, quite early indeed, Old English was thus allowed to level its accidence, it is because, also quite early, the use of a pronoun subject had secured it from ambiguity.

3. The latter point being well understood, nothing could prevent the uniform ending in *-n*, when fixed in the whole subjunctive, from spreading also in the perfect indicative. It is true that here the three forms of the singular were not

identical; but two of them were alike, and, above all, the perfect indicative and the perfect subjunctive resembled each other very nearly; and, since moreover two persons of the pl. indicative (1st and 3rd) had phonetically become the same, the identical form *bunden* in the pl. subjunctive logically led to a similar identical form *bundon* in the pl. indicative.

4. In the pl. of the present indicative, though the three forms were different, two of them at least, *bindeð and *bindað*, could easily be confounded: both became *bindað*, which passed also to the imperative. This being done, an analogical formula, such as (*wē*) *bindað*: (*gē*) *bindað* = (*wē*) *bundon*: (*gē*) *bundon*, was suggested, the more so as O.E. still preserved a pl. 1 imperative *bindan*, and it seemed convenient to distinguish " we bind" from "let us bind." Consequently, here, the levelling took place at the expense of the 1st person, which became assimilated to the two others.

5. Let us now return to the endings in *n*. Final E. *n*, it is well known, easily disappears. Even as early as O.E. it may disappear from the terminations of the verbal plural when followed by the pronoun subject: in other words, the speaker ought to say *wē bundon* and *gē bundon*, but he may say either *bundon wē* or *bunde wē*, either *bundon gē* or *bunde gē*, etc.[1] From this to the uniform E. type, pf. ind. and subj. *bound*, and pres. subj. *bind*, the transition is merely phonetic.

6. This apocope, being regular as to final *n*, was extended, by an almost uncontrollable analogy, to the final *ð* of the present indicative, whence, likewise optionally, *binde wē* and *binde gē*. Next, M.E. extended the use of this accidence.

7. The curtailed forms having become decidedly prevalent, Mod. E. naturally knows no other form but *bind* in the plural of the present, as also in pl. 2 of the imperative.

8. The same process having run parallel throughout the whole, strong or weak, accidence, the final result is, that the E. **plural**, in any tense or mood, has lost every characteristic except its invariable and **amorphous** state.

[1] A similar phenomenon has been stated in M.H.G., *supra* 203, 1.—Observe, moreover, that the analogical ending *-en* everywhere, even in the present indicative, spread out very early in the Mercian dialect; further, that English is an offspring of Mercian, not of Saxonic.

Section II.

ANOMALOUS CONJUGATIONS.

(215) The apparent anomalies of the Germanic conjugation comprise: (1) **the verb "to be,"** which has retained, almost unaltered, its ancient accidence as a root-stem, that is to say, a conjugation both more primitive and simpler than that of the stems in -ĕ- / -ŏ-; (2) **a few other** verbs, which exhibit at least some traces of the same accidence; (3) **the false presents,** which in reality are genuine perfects and, for this reason, are termed **preterito-presents.**

§ 1. *The Verb " to be."*

(216) It has been already stated[1] that a great many I.-E. verbs could be conjugated without inserting the interchangeable vowel -ĕ- / -ŏ- between the root and the endings, so that the latter were immediately added to the bare root. This is the well-known class of verbs which in Greek Grammar are properly called verbs in -μι, thus, εἰ-μί (I am) = *ἐσ-μί, εἶ-μι (I am going), τί-θη-μι (1 set), etc. It is still tolerably numerous in Greek as well as in Sanskrit. But, in Latin, it was confined to a single verb, namely *sum* (I am), and the same is nearly the case with the Germanic languages.

In one point, however, **the Germanic accidence** is more intricate: it is not a single one, but **confounds several verbs** in one, in such a way that the verb "to be" is conjugated concurrently on **three verbal roots,** which moreover are not the same even in the same persons and tenses of such cognate languages as English and German, though all three are found, with similar or different functions and various shades of meaning, in every other group of the I.-E. family; namely: — ĕs, the proper root for the general sense "to be," cf. Sk. ás-ti (he is), Gr. ἐσ-τί, L. ĕs-t, Russian *jes-tĭ*, etc.;—bhĕw "to become," cf. Sk. *bháv-a-ti* (he becomes, he is), Gr. φύ-ε-ται (he grows), πέ-φῡ-κε (he is grown, he is), L. *fu-i-t* (he was), Russian

[1] *Supra* 81, and cf. 92.

bu-du (I shall be), etc.;—*wĕs* "to dwell," cf. Sk. *vás-a-ti* (he dwells, he finds himself), Gr. ἑστία = *Ϝεσ-τί-ᾱ (hearth), L. *Ves-ta* (hearth-goddess), Go. *vis-a* (I sojourn, I remain), etc.

As early even as Gothic, these three roots possess the common meaning "to be," the third, however, with an accessory shade of durative and permanent state. In Anglo-German they have become entirely synonymous: English shows a decided preference for the second, and German, for the first; but both borrow their perfect-tense from the third.

(217) I. Present indicative.—A. English.—Sg. 1: O.E. *eom eam am* = Go. *i-m*[1] = I.-E. **és-mĭ* (Sk. *ás-mi*, Gr. εἰμί = **ἐσ-μι, Russian *jes-mĭ*, etc.); E. *am*. 2: O.E. *eart* (broken) = **er-t*, which represents Go. *is* = I.-E. **ésĭ *és-sĭ* (Sk. *ási*, Gr. Homer. ἐσ-σί and class. εἶ = **ἔσι, Russian *jesi*, etc.), with the later and analogical addition of the ending *-t* of sg. 2, a process we have already met with; E. *art*. 3: O.E. *is* = L. *es-t*, with secondary termination, whereas Go. *is-t* is equivalent to Gr. ἐσ-τί, with primary termination[2]; E. *is.*—Pl. 1, 2, 3: O.E. *s-ind*, owing to a general extension of the form of pl. 3, as already seen in every other present indicative, this form here being I.-E. **s-éntĭ*,[3] cf. Sk. *sánti*, L. *sunt* (= **s-óntĭ*), Go. *sind*, etc. But Mod. E. has simply *are*, with the form of sg. 2 curtailed of its ending as extended to the plural.[4]

B. German.—Sg. 1: O.H.G. *bi-m*, replacing **biu-m* = I.-E. **bhĕw-mĭ*: whence *bin*, M.H.G. *bin*, G. *bin*. 2: O.H.G. *bi-st*, replacing **bi-s*, the termination *-st*, as explained above, having made its way here as everywhere; G. *bist*. 3: O.H.G. *is-t* = Go. *is-t* = I.-E. **és-tĭ*; G. *ist.*—Pl. 1: O.H.G. *birum birun*,[5] and

---

[1] The O.E. vocalism is clearly corrupt: it has been influenced by the vocalism of the parallel verb *bēo-m* (G. *bi-n*), which was extant in O.E., but has become obsolete in this tense. German, on the contrary, though retaining only **biu-m*, introduced into it the vocalism of *i-m*.—The E. dialects often keep true to *bēom*: thus, we read *I binna* for *I am not* in the first pages of *Adam Bede*.
[2] On this capital distinction, cf. *supra* 199 and 211.
[3] The root *ĕs* is reduced, because the accent rests on the ending.
[4] The approximate formula may be *are* : *art* = *were* : *wast*. As early as O.E. we have *earun* (*aron*), which is obviously refashioned on the double pattern *eart* and *wǣron*.
[5] Also *birumēs*, and *pirum pirumēs*, etc. These strange and obsolete forms are certainly attributable to the analogy of the perfect; since their *u*-vocal-

still M.H.G. *birn*, but also *sīn* borrowed from the subjunctive, and lastly *sint* transferred from pl. 3 ; for, since pl. 1 and pl. 3 had come to be identical in any verb, it seemed only natural to say *wir sint* like *sie sint*, the accidence elsewhere being *sie nëmen* like *wir nëmen*[1]; G. *sind*. 2: O.H.G. *birut*; M.H.G. *birt*, but also *sīt* borrowed from the subjunctive; G. *seid*. 3: O.H.G. *sint* = Go. *sind* = I.-E. **s-éntĭ*; G. *sind*.

II. Present subjunctive.—O.E. *sīe*, etc., as in O.H.G., and *bēo*, pl. *bēo-n*; the former lost in E., the latter changed to invariable *be*.—O.H.G. *sī*, etc. (= Go. *sijau*, etc.), and G. *sei*, etc.[2]

III. Perfect indicative.—The root *wĕs* forms naturally an I.-E. pf. sg. 3 **wĕ-wŏs-ĕ*, whence Preg. **wăs-ĕ*, conjugated Go. *vas vas-t vas vēs-um vēs-uþ vēs-un*. O.E., still purer than Go., shows in the plural the rhotacism, as proceeding from the change of *s* to *z*, after an unaccented syllable: sg. 1 and 3 *wæs*, pl. 1, 2, and 3 *wǣr-on*; to which E. corresponds with sg. 1 and 3 *was* (2 *was-t*), and pl. *were*. Likewise: O.H.G. *was* and *wār-un*; M.H.G. *was* and *wār-en*; but G. *war* (2 *war-st*) and *waren*, the rhotacism and the long vowel having been extended from the pl. to the singular.

IV. Perfect subjunctive: O.E. *wǣre* and E. *were* (sg. 2 also *wer-t* by analogy), O.H.G. *wār-i* and G. *wär-e*; without difficulty.

V. Imperative: E. *be* = O.E. *bēo*; M.H.G. *wis* regular, and also *bis* (instead of **bi*, after the analogy of *wis*) ; G. *sei*, borrowed from the subjunctive.

VI. Infinitive: E. *be* = O.E. *bēo-n*; M.H.G. *wës-en* = Go. *vis-an*, kept only as neuter noun (*das Wesen*, " being, substance," and *ein Wesen*, " a being "), and also *sīn*, G. *sein*, likewise imitated from the subjunctive.

VII. Participles.—Present: E. *be-ing*; G. *wes-e-nd* regular (in such compounds as *abwesend*, etc.), but usually *sei-end* after the analogy of the subjunctive.—Past: E. *been* = O.E. *ge-bēo-n*; G. *ge-wes-en* = O.H.G. *gi-wës-an* = Go. *vis-an-s*.

---

ism and non-etymological *r* cannot come from any other source. They must be imitated from *wārumēs* and *wārum* (G. *waren*).

[1] Cf. *supra* 203, 1 and 3, and 211.
[2] Cf. *supra* 211.

§ 2. *Other Root-Verbs.*

(218) I. E. *do* = G. *thun.*—The I.-E. root *dhē* "to place, to do" (cf. Sk. *da-dhá-ti* = Gr. τί-θη-σι "he places" and L. *fa-c-i-t* "he does" with an inserted *c*), though still conjugated by merely adding the person-endings to the bare root, shows some unusual and even perplexing vowel-gradations, which Gothic, moreover, proves quite unable to account for, since here the verb has the form *tau-jan* and belongs throughout to the weak accidence.

1. The present indicative, by a rare exception, seems to exhibit the deflected grade of the root, thus I.-E. *$dh\acute{o}$-$m\breve{i}$, whence O.E. $d\bar{o}$-*m* = O.H.G *tuo-n* (I do). The metaphonical conjugation O.E. $d\bar{o}$-*m* *dœ-st* (long *œ*) *dœ-ð*, pl. $d\bar{o}$-*ð*, gives us the reason for the present pronunciation of the English forms *dost* and *does* (= *doth*) in contrast with sg. 1 and pl. *do*. But the ending -*m* of sg. 1 is seen to have been dropped in imitation of the corresponding person in the ordinary conjugation. The same is the case with German: O.H.G. *tuo-n*; M.H.G. *tuo-n*, then *tuo*; G. *thue*. The remainder, namely *tuo-st tuo-t tuo-ēn tuo-(n)t tuo-nt*, are rigorously reproduced in the modern accidence *thust thut thun thut thun*.

2. The present subjunctive is regularly derived from the indicative: O.E. $d\bar{o}$, etc., and E. *do*; O.H.G. *tuo-e*, etc., and G. *thu-e*.

3. The perfect indicative is an intricate mixture of two different forms at the least, viz.: a strong perfect-stem with surviving reduplication, thus I.-E. *$dh\breve{e}$-$dh\acute{a}$-, cf. O.H.G. *tëta* "I, he did"; and an originally weak perfect-stem, with normal root and reduplication dropped, thus I.-E. sg. 3 *($dh\breve{e}$-)$dh\bar{e}$- *táy*, whence a Preg. *$\delta\bar{e}\delta a$, G. *that*.[1] But the latter is the only one kept in Mod. German. O.E. again shows a third vocalism, perhaps that of the present, though strangely shortened and undergoing the metaphony which would be regular only in the subjunctive, as though it were a stem of weak pf. subj. $\delta\breve{u}$-δ-$\bar{\imath}$-, whence O.E. *dyde dydes*, etc., E. *did did-st*, etc.

---

[1] For the vocalism is here the same as in the noun denoting action, G. *that* = E. *deed* = Go. *dēþ-s* = Preg. *$\delta\bar{e}\delta i$-*s* = I.-E. *$dh\bar{e}$-*ti-s*, cf. *supra* 26 (II.) and 78, 2.

4. Perfect subjunctive: O.E. *dyd-e dyd-e-n* and E. *did*; O.H.G. *tāt-i tāt-ī-s*, etc., and G. metaph. *thät-e*.

5. Imperative: O.E. *dō*, etc., and E. *do*; O.H.G. *tuo* and G. *thue*.

6. Infinitive: O.E. *dō-n* and E. *do*; O.H.G. *tuo-n*, and G. *thun*.

7. Participles: present, O.E. *dō-nde* (E. *do-ing*) and G. *thu-end*; past, O.E. *ge-dō-n*, and E. *do-ne* with the vocalic shade of *ge-dœ-n*; O.H.G. *gi-tā-n* and G. *ge-tha-n*, with the vocalism borrowed from the perfect.

(219) II. E. *go* = G. *gehen*.[1]—This verb lacks any precise equivalent in the I.-E. family; but there is a general agreement between scholars in considering it a Pregermanic juxtaposition of two I.-E. elements, prefix $\zeta\breve{a}$-, the origin of which has been stated above, and root $\breve{e}y$ $\breve{i}$ (to go) of Sk. *é-ti* (he goes) = Gr. εἶ-σι = L. *i-t*. The vocalism here is still more puzzling than in the preceding type: O.H.G. shows in the present two concurrent vocalisms, *gā-* and *gē-*: O.E. has only the former, *gā-*, changed to E. *go*; Mod. G., only the latter, *gē-*, now spelled *geh-*.[2]

1-2. Present.—Indicative: O.H.G. sg. 1 *gā-m gā-n* or *gē-m gē-n*, and the other persons in keeping. M.H.G. has still *gā-n* and *gē-n*; but Mod. G. has only *gehe* = **gē* with the analogical loss of the ending. The same corruption appears far earlier in English: even O.E. has only sg. 1 *gā*, whence E. *go*, and the rest in keeping with it.—The subjunctive requires no explanation.

3-4. Perfect.—The G. pf. is derived from another root, which, in spite of an outward likeness, has originally nothing to do with *gehen*, namely, from a verb *gang-an* = Go. *gagg-an* (to go) of unknown etymology[3]: it is a strong perfect belonging to type G, thus *gieng ging*. Of this root English has no longer

---

[1] Here, of course, as in *stehen* and similar words, the *h* has no etymological value. It is simply a sign to denote a long vowel.

[2] Without entering into particulars, we may observe that the same double vocalism equally characterizes the following verb (*stān stēn*), and that these two verbs, owing to their obviously contrasted meaning, might very easily have influenced each other.

[3] A tempting comparison is Sk. *jáṅghā* (leg) = I.-E. **ghéṅgh-ā*.

A A

any trace in the conjugation of the verb, though it is kept in the nouns *gang* (cf. G. *gang* "marching") and *gang-way* (cf. Go. *gagg-s* "street"). The pf. of vb. *go* is borrowed from vb. *wend* = G. (*sich*) *wenden* "to turn, apply one's self" [1] = Go. *vand-jan*, causative of Go. *vind-an* = G. *winden* = E. (*to*) *wind*.—The subjunctives *went* and *gienge* offer no difficulty.

5–6. Imperative and infinitive like the present.

7. Participle (pres. *go-ing geh-e-nd*) past: on the stem *gā-*, O.E. *ge-gā-n* and E. *go-ne*; on the stem *gaṅg-*, O.H.G. *gi-gang-an* and G. *ge-gang-en*, according to type G.

(220) III. G. *stehen*, cf. E. (*to*) *stand*.—Here also two conjugations are blended together. English, however, no longer possesses the corresponding verb to G. *stehen*, since (*to*) *stay* is known to be of Romance origin: the whole E. vb. is conjugated on the stem *stand-*, cf. Go. *stand-an*, pf. *stōþ*, and O.H.G. *stant-an* now obsolete. German, on the contrary, retains in the present the bare root-accidence, corresponding to Sk. *á-sthā-t* (he stood) = Gr. ἔ-στη = L. *sta-t*, etc.: O.H.G. sg. 1 *stā-m stā-n* or *stē-m stē-n*, and the rest in keeping; M.H.G. *stā-n* or *stā*, *stē-n* or *stē*; G. only *stehe*. The perfect and participle have occurred under the strong verbs,[2] and the other forms present no peculiarities.

(221) IV. E. *will* = G. *wollen*.—Ordinary grammars usually place this verb in the next following class, with which, in fact, it exhibits a striking though merely outward likeness. The common feature in both, that is to say, the lack of an ending in sg. 3 of the present, is here due to an isolated peculiarity of accidence, *i.e.*, as shown by the corresponding Gothic conjugation, the present of *will* = *wollen* is not an indicative, but a subjunctive, or, in other words, E. *I will* = G. *ich will* = Go. *vil-jau* really means not "I wish," but "may I wish" (optative), though the indicative reappears in the G. plural. The root is I.-E. *wĕl* (cf. L. *vel-le vol-ō vul-t vel-i-m*), which assumes the following regular Preg. vocalisms: normal *wĕl*, whence *wĭl* if metaphony is required; reduced *wŭl wŏl* (= I.-E. *wl̥*); deflected

---

[1] E. *went* bears to G. *wandte* the same relation as *sent* to *sandte*, supra 187, 7. The verb is now obsolete, except in such locutions as *I wend my own way*; but it is still met with twice in Shakespeare.

[2] Type F, *supra* 184, 2.

wăl, whence wĕl with later metaphony. A correct application of these few principles will prove sufficient for the analysis of this verb which is irregular and difficult only in appearance.

1. Present indicative (formerly subjunctive).—Sg. 1: Go. vil-jau, O.E. will-e and E. will, O.H.G. will-u and G. will.[1] 2: Go. vil-ei-s = L. vel-ī-s; O.E. already wil-t, with the intrusive termination -t, and E. wil-t; O.H.G. wil-i = *wil-ī-z,[2] but G. analogically will-st. 3: Go. vil-i = L. vel-i-t; O.E. wil-e wil, and E. will; O.H.G. wil-i and G. will.—Pl. Go. vil-ei-ma vil-ei-þ vil-ei-na, exclusively subjunctive. But the vowel of the O.E. final syllable will-að (E. will) already suggests an intrusion of the indicative-form, which appears even clearer in the root-vocalism of Northumbr. wall-að. The same form becomes prevalent in O.H.G. well-e-mēs well-e-t well-e-nt, which has become G. woll-e-n woll-e-t woll-en, under the influence of the vocalism of the perfect woll-te.[3]

2. Since the present subjunctive had passed to the function of present indicative, a new subjunctive was analogically derived from it: O.E. will-e and E. will; O.H.G. well-e (cf. Northumbr. wœll-a) and G. woll-e.

3–4. The perfect is a regular weak one, with reduced root, thus I.-E. sg. 3 *(wĕ-)wḷ-táy : Go. vil-da has borrowed its vowel from the present; but the vocalism remains pure in West Germanic, O.E. wol-de and E. woul-d, O.H.G. wol-ta and G. woll-te. The subjunctive, being formed here without metaphony, is of course identical.

5–7. Imperative not used. Infinitive: O.E. will-an and E. will, but O.H.G. well-an woll-an, and G. woll-en. Participle ge-woll-t.

§ 3. *Preterito-Presents*.

(222) We have seen that **the I.-E. perfect was not a historical past, but** the tense denoting an achieved action

---

[1] Indicative, or else (rather) subjunctive with analogical indicative-ending; the pure subjunctive form would be *wil-i, supra 193, 194 and 211.
[2] Cf. the regular loss of this ending in O.E., supra 212.
[3] The e of the root is due to metaphony, because the indicative is conjugated on a stem in -yo- with deflected root, thus well-e-nt = Preg. *wäl-ja-nđi. —Even at the present time, in High Alsatian, mr velĕ (e open, ĕ half mute), "we will."

and therefore able to play the part of a **durative present**, and we have already emphasized the difference of meaning between Gr. ἔ-θαν-ε " he died " and τέ-θνη-κε " he is dead." Similarly, λέ-λειπ-ται means not "it was left," but "it has been left," whence "it remains," and such is the case with every Gr. perfect. We have also insisted upon the fact, that the I.-E. pf. *wŏyd-e, literally "he has seen," means "he knows" in almost every language of the I.-E. family[1]: Sk. véd-a, Gr. οἶδ-ε =Ϝοῖδ-ε, Go. váit, etc. Now, the Germanic languages, though currently shifting their perfect to the function of historical past, preserved a trace of its original meaning in about **a dozen perfects**, which down to the present time unite perfect-accidence with **present-meaning**.

The isolated position of this class protected it, as a rule, from the causes which tended to alter the conjugation of ordinary perfects: thus, we shall find in it that vowel-degradation from the singular to the plural, which has been so constantly levelled in the later languages, and even, at least in part, the old ending of sg. 2 -t (=I.-E. -thă) which O.E. and O.H.G. had already forgotten[2]; in regard to the necessary **identity between sg. 1 and sg. 3**, we need scarcely say that it is the leading, specific and regular characteristic of all these verbal forms.[3]

Though every **preterito-present** is really a perfect, each again is provided with a historical past (can could, weisz wuszte, etc.), and the latter always belongs to the type of weak perfects; in other words, the preterito-presents are Germanic verbs which use their active perfect as a present, and their middle perfect as a preterite.[4]

Including will=wollen, ordinary grammars as a rule distinguish nine of them, viz. two exclusively English, one exclusively German, and six common to both languages. There were once

---

[1] Cf. L. nōvi "I have taken notice of" whence "I know," me-min-i "I remember," vixit "he is dead," etc.

[2] Cf. supra 209.

[3] At least in the literary language; for elsewhere analogy may easily have exerted its influence; er weiszt is a current form in several German dialects, and he cans would not be unnatural from an illiterate speaker.

[4] Cf. supra 188, II. in fine.

a few more; but some have become obsolete; some, as for instance E. *dare* and G. *taugen*,[1] were mistaken for real presents and passed to the ordinary conjugation. The best way to study them is to classify them under the familiar heads of our types of strong perfects.[2]

(223) Type A.

I. Go. *váit*[3] (he knows), E. *wot* obsolete, G. *weisz*.

1. Present indicative.—The sg. has regularly the deflected root. 1: Go. *váit* = Sk. *véd-a* = Gr. Ϝοῖδ-α, cf. L. *vīd-ī* (I saw); O.E. *wāt* and E. *wot*; O.H.G. *weiȝ* and G. *weisz*. 2: Go. *váis-t* = Sk. *vét-tha* = Gr. Ϝοῖσ-θα; O.H.G. *weis-t* and G. *weisz-t* (O.E. *wās-t*). 3: Go. *váit* = Sk. *véd-a* = Gr. Ϝοῖδ-ε; O.H.G. *weiȝ* and G. *weisz*.—The pl. has regularly the reduced root. 1: Go. *vit-um* = Sk. *vid-má* = Gr. Ϝίδ-μεν ἴσμεν; O.E. *wit-on*, but E. *wot* with levelled apophony; O.H.G. *wiȝȝ-um* and G. *wiss-en*. 2: Go. *vit-uþ* and G. *wiss-et*. 3: Go. *vit-un* and G. *wiss-en*.

2. Present subjunctive: the root regularly reduced; Go. *vit-jau vit-ei-s*, etc.; O.E. *wit-e*; O.H.G. *wiȝȝ-i* and G. *wiss-e*, etc.

3–4. Perfect (weak): Go. *vissa* (regularly replacing *vis-ta*), etc.; O.H.G. *wissa*, etc.; M.H.G. *wisse*, next *wis-te* with analogical restoration of the ending *-te*, lastly (late) *woste wuste*[4]; G. *wuszte* and subj. *wüszte*.

5. The infinitive, O.H.G. *wiȝȝ-an*, M.H.G. *wiȝȝ-en* and G. *wiss-en*, is formed anew after the analogy of the past participle

---

[1] On *dare*, cf. *supra* 187, 1. As a perfect, *taugen* regularly shows the deflected grade of the same root that appears reduced in *tugend*, cf. Gr. τύχ-η.

[2] The following is an alphabetical list: E. *can, may, must, need, ought, shall, will, wot*; G. *dürfen, können, mögen, müssen, sollen, wissen, wollen*.

[3] This *váit* is clearly the pf. of a vb., the normal infinitive of which would be *veit-an*; cf. also the words, E. *wit* = G. *witz*, E. *wise* (sensible) = G. *weise*, E. *wit-ness*, etc.

[4] The vocalism is corrupted by several influences: the regular subj. *wiste* was partly mistaken for *wüste* (*wöste*), and on these forms, through reversed metaphony, were remade *wuste* and *woste*; but the leading factor, here, was the analogy of such similar forms as *muoste, kunde konde, dorfte*, because the speaker could not but perceive a connection between verbs with both cognate terminations and meanings. This is the reason why in all the vocalism appears rather capricious.—Archaic English has the regular form *he wist* "he knew," *e.g.* Act. Apost. xii. 8.

and present plural, just like the preceding (*wellen wollen*) and following verbs.[1]

6. The past participle is very regular: O.H.G. *gi-wiȝȝ-an* = Go. *vit-an-s = I.-E. *wĭd-onó-s; M.H.G. *ge-wiȝȝ-en* (cf. G. *gewisz* "certain") and *ge-wis-t* (weak); but G. *ge-wusz-t* like the perfect.

(224)   Type C.

II. Go. *kann* (he knows), E. *can*, G. *kann*.—The literal meaning is "he has learnt," whence "he knows," further "he is able, he can," the apparent present being in reality the perfect of the I.-E. root *gen* (to know, Sk. *jānā-ti* "he knows"), which in Greek and Latin appears chiefly in the shape *gnō*, Gr. γι-γνώ-σκω, pf. ἔ-γνω-κα, L. *nō-scō* = *gnō-scō*, pf. *nōvī*, part. *nō-tu-s*, etc.

1-2. Present.—Indicative sg. 1: Go. *kann*, O.E. *con can* and E. *can*, O.H.G. *kan* and G. *kann*. 2: Go. *kan-t* regular, but already O.E. *con-st* and E. *can-st*, O.H.G. *kan-st* and G. *kann-st*. 3: like sg. 1. Pl. 1: Go. *kunn-um*, O.E. *cunn-on*, O.H.G. *kunn-un* and M.H.G. *kunn-en*, regular. But English extends the form *can*, whereas Mod. German, though keeping the apophony, obscures it by borrowing the metaphony from the subjunctive.—For this mood is, quite regularly, M.H.G. *künne* = O.H.G. *kunn-i*. Since however, in the present of the ordinary conjugation, indicative and subjunctive always show the same root-vocalism, a similar correspondence took place here, whence M.H.G. *künnen* and G. *können* in the plural of the indicative as well as in the subjunctive.—So too pl. 2 *könn-t* and 3 *könn-en*.

3-4. Perfect.—Indicative: Go. *kun-þa* = I.-E. (*gĕ-*)*gṇ-táy*; O.E. *cūðe* = *cŭn-ðe, M.E. *coud* and E. *could*[2]; O.H.G. *kon-da*, M.H.G. *kun-de kon-de*, and G. *konn-te*.—Subjunctive: E. *could*, G. *könn-te*.

5-6. The vocalism in the infinitive, E. *can*, G. *könn-en*, is respectively that of the sg. and pl. of the present. The Mod. G. part. *ge-konn-t* is formed from the perfect.[3]

III. Go. *þarf* (he wants), G. *darf* (is allowed, able).—The

---

[1] Though it might also be deemed a primitive form: *supra* 82, 2.
[2] The true spelling changed under the influence of *would* and *should*.
[3] The regular one is the adjective *kund* (known) = Go. *kunþ-s*.

same as Sk. *ta-tárp-a*, pf. of the root *tarp* = I.-E. *tĕrp* (to satisfy, or be satisfied), cf. Gr. τέρπ-ε-ται (he is delighted). Thus, the literal meaning would be " to find one's satisfaction in," whence " to be in want of "[1] and "to have the faculty of," the latter sense now being the only one surviving.

1-2. Present.—Indicative sg. 1 and 3: Go. *þarf*, O.E. *ðearf*, O.H.G. *darf*, G. *darf*. 2: Go. *þarf-t*, O.H.G. *darf-t*, G. *darf-st*. Pl. 1: Go. *þaúrb-um*, with vowel-degradation and consonantal change; O.E. *ðurf-on* and O.H.G. *durf-un*, with degradation, but the *f* extended; M.H.G. *durf-en*, and *dürf-en*, like *künnen*, with the metaphony imported from the subjunctive; G. *dürf-en*. —All the rest in keeping with pl. 1, and similarly G. subj. *dürf-e*.

3-4. Perfect.—Indicative: Go. *þaúrf-ta*, O.H.G. *dorf-ta*, M.H.G. *dorf-te*, but G. *durf-te* influenced by the vocalism of the present.—Subjunctive, likewise, M.H.G. *dörf-te* and G. *dürf-te*.

5-6. Infinitive: *durf-an*, now *dürf-en*. Participle: *ge-dorf-t (in the compound *be-dorf-t*), now *ge-durf-t*.

(225) Type D.

IV. Go. *skal*, E. *shall*, G. *soll*, the pf. of a root which would be I.-E. *skĕl*, but cannot be found outside the Germanic group. The vowel *ŏ* in German is due to the analogy of the plural; but the loss of the *k*, which takes place from O.H.G. to M.H.G., remains as yet unexplained.[2]

1-2. Sg. 1 and 3: Go. *skal*; O.E. *sceal* and E. *shall*; O.H.G. *scal sol*, M.H.G. *sal sol*, and G. *soll*. 2: Go. *skal-t*; O.E. *sceal-t* and E. *shal-t*, unaltered; O.H.G. *scal-t sol-t*, and occasionally even *sol-st*; M.H.G. *sal-t sol-t*, but G. *soll-st*. Pl. 1: Go. *skul-um*; O.E. *scul-on*, but E. *shall*; O.H.G. *scul-un*, M.H.G. *sul-n* or (metaph.) *sül-n*; G. *soll-en*, with the perfect-vocalism, or even (metaph.) *söll-en*. But the non-metaphonical form has

---

[1] The O.E., O.H.G. and still M.H.G. meaning "to want" survives in Mod. G. *be-dürf-en*, whereas the active meaning "to satisfy" and consequently "to thrive" may be seen in the lost primitive *derben*, which, by adding the pejorative prefix (*ver-derb-en*), has acquired the sense "to be corrupted, to corrupt."

[2] Still M.H.G. *er schol* (Bavarian).

decidedly prevailed and even invaded the subjunctive: O.H.G. *scul-i*, M.H.G. *süll-e*, G. *solle*.

3–4. Go. *skul-da*; O.E. *sceol-de* and E. *shoul-d*; O.H.G. *scol-te sol-te*, M.H.G. *sol-te* and G. *soll-te*. The subjunctive is M.H.G. *sol-te* and *söl-te*, but class. G. *soll-te*, like E. *shoul-d*.

5–6. Infinitive *shall* and *soll-en*.—Part. *ge-soll-t*.

(226)   Type E.

V. Go. *mag*, E. *may*, G. *mag*, the pf. of an I.-E. root *mĕgh* (also *mĕg*), which expresses an idea of greatness and might, and is found in Sk. *mah-ánt-* (great), *máh-as* (greatness), Gr. μέγ-α-s (great), cf. O.E. *meah-t* (power) and E. *migh-t*, O.H.G. *mah-t* and G. *mach-t*.

1–2. Sg. 1 and 3: Go. *mag*, O.E. *mæg* and E. *may*, O.H.G. *mag* and G. *mag*. 2: Go. *mag-t*; O.E. *meah-t mih-t*, but E. *may-est*; O.H.G. and M.H.G. *mah-t*, but G. *mag-st*. As early as Pregermanic the plural adopts the singular-vocalism: Go. *mag-um*, O.E. *mag-on* and E. *may*, O.H.G. *mag-un*. But, owing to the analogy of *kunn-un*, *durf-un*, we have also *mug-un*, whence: M.H.G. *mug-en müg-en* (and *meg-en*); G. *mög-en*.—Subjunctive: E. *may*, G. *mög-e*.

3–4. Go. *mah-ta*, O.E. *meah-te mih-te* and E. *migh-t*, O.H.G. *mah-ta* and M.H.G. *mah-te*, quite regular; but also O.H.G. *moh-ta* (like *kon-da*), M.H.G. *moh-te* and G. *moch-te* (*ver-moch-te*). —Subjunctive: M.H.G. *mehte möhte* and G. *möchte*; E. *might*. —The rest present no difficulty.

(227)   Type F.

VI. Go. *ga-mōt* (he finds an opportunity), E. *must*, G. *musz*, pf. of an unknown root.[1] English has lost the strong perfect, and its weak perfect plays at once the part of present and past tense: *he must = er muszte*.[2]

1–2. Sg. 1 and 3: Go. *ga-mōt*, O.E. *mōt* (he can), O.H.G. *muoʒ* (he can) and G. *musz* (must). 2: Go. **mōs-t*, O.E. *mōs-t* and E. *mus-t*, O.H.G. *muos-t* and G. *musz-t*. Pl. 1: Go. **mōt-*

---

[1] Cf. G. *musze* (leisure) = O.H.G. *muoʒa* (possibility, opportunity), lost in O.E.

[2] Excepting, of course, sg. 2 of both tenses, since there is no form **must-est*.

um, O.E. *mōt-on*, O.H.G. *muoʒ-um*, but M.H.G. (metaph.) *müeʒ-en* and G. *müszen*, etc.

3–4. Go. *ga-mōs-ta*, O.E. *mōs-te* and E. *mus-t*, O.H.G. *muosa* (instead of *muos-sa, like *wis-sa*) and *muos-ta* (restored), M.H.G. *muos-te*, G. *musz-te* and subj. *müsz-te*, etc.

(228) Unclassed.

VII. E. *ought*.—A weak perfect: Go. *áih-ta* (he had), from vb. *áih-an*,[1] cf. G. *eig-en* = E. *ow-n*; O.E. *āh-te*; lost in German. According to this etymology, a locution *he ought to do*, either means "he had," or "he should have (subjunctive) to do": whence both the constant construction of *ought* with *to*, and its absolute indifference in use for present and past time.

VIII. E. *need*.—A secondary verb, derived from the substantive *need* = O.E. *nēad* = G. *noth* = Go. *náuþ-s*. But the analogy of *he must not*, *he shall not*, etc., induced the speaker to say likewise *he need not* : the only point in which this verb belongs to the preterito-presents.

IX. E. *will*, G. *will* : is not a preterito-present, *supra* 221.

[1] See the Go. sentence quoted above (128).

CHAPTER IV.

VERBAL PERIPHRASES.

(229) Conjugation being reduced, as seen above, to the utmost simplicity,—a single past tense and no future,—had become unable to express the minute shades of the verbal concept: incomplete as it was, however, it sufficed for Pregermanic, even for Gothic and for the earliest state of English and German; but, as the speech grew more precise and refined, it was led, no less than French and the other Romance languages, to use certain periphrases in order to denote clearly such moods and tenses as could no longer find adequate expression in the forms of the simple verb. **The Verbal Periphrasis**, though it may vary as to particulars, in its main and original structure always and everywhere appears one and the same, namely, a kind of **compounded locution, in which a** so-called **auxiliary verb governs a** verbal noun, whether **infinitive, gerund or participle**, derived from the principal verb. Hence, it is the latter that contains the verbal concept, whereas the auxiliary merely indicates the tense, mood, or aspect, which modifies its general meaning.

I. Our first task will be, therefore, to recall the formation and function of such **Verbal Nouns** as may be met with in a verbal periphrasis.

1. **Infinitive.**—The primitive formation of the infinitive, as originally a neuter noun and, besides, still capable of being used and declined in German in this quality, and further the extension of this grammatical category to all verbs, even non-radical, from the earliest to the latest, and, lastly, the uniformity of its exponent, reduced to *-en* in German, and dropped

altogether in English, have been illustrated in their proper place,[1] and no further details are here required.

2. **Gerund.** — The gerund, though now completely confounded with the infinitive, was originally distinct, not only in that it may be declined, while the infinitive verbal noun never appears but in the accusative neuter, but chiefly because it proceeds from a derivative and amplified stem: for, the infinitive-suffix being I.-E. *-ono-*, the suffix of the gerund is I.-E. *-onyo-*,[2] as shown by the double *nn* (= Preg. *nj*), which everywhere characterizes this form, O.E. dat. *tō sāwenne* (in order to sow), *tō drincenne*,[3] O.H.G. gen. *nëm-anne-s* (of taking), dat. *nëm-anne* (to take), etc. In the later languages, the genitival gerund is extinct,—though, of course, German may decline its infinitive in the gen. sg. (*des nehm-en-s*), like any other neuter noun,—and the datival gerund, owing to the loss of the final syllable, has been blended with the infinitive, E. *to drink*, G. *zu nehmen*, etc.[4]

3. **Participles.—A. Present Active.** The reader need scarcely be reminded of the formation of the I.-E. active present participle,[5] retained in Sanskrit, Greek, Latin, Gothic, Old English, and German, whether Old or Modern, as well as of the artificial and somewhat blundering way in which Middle English has secured a new one [6] : G. *trink-e-nd*, E. *drink-ing*;

---

[1] *Supra* 77 (1), 89 (2), 106 and 107.

[2] In other words, they bear to one another the same relation as Gr. οὐρ-ανό-ς (heaven) and οὐρ-άνιο-ς (celestial), and the gerund is the adjective derived from the noun that plays the part of infinitive.

[3] Cf. *supra* 128, and such sentences as *ic tō drincenne hæbbe* "I have to drink," *ða com hit tō witenne ðam eorlum* "then came it to knowing to the earls," which clearly emphasize both the nature of the gerund, as a noun, and the nature of the form which depends on a verb *have, ought, am* (*he is to do*), and generally on the preposition *to*, as a gerund, and not an infinitive. Hence it is through a rather awkward confusion, and merely for the sake of convenience, that practical grammar uses *to* as the specific exponent of the infinitive.

[4] Already O.H.G. occasionally *ze wësan, za galaupian* (*zu glauben*).— Observe however that, after any other preposition but *to*, E. uses not the infinitive, but the noun of action in *-ing* (*supra* 103, II., 2), which therefore serves for the gerund.

[5] *Supra* 79 (XI.) and 90 (VI.).

[6] *Supra* 103, II., 2. Even passive; for the clear and terse expression, *the tea is a-making* has been replaced only as late as the end of the last century by *is being made*. The passive present participle and the active

and similarly in every verb, strong or weak, primitive or derivative, without exception.

B. **Past Passive.**—This formation has been analysed in its inner structure, the root-form and suffix being different as the verb is strong or weak.[1] The origin of its prefix, which is common, though not obligatory, in O.E.,[2] and of constant use in German,[3] has also been explained, and we have seen how English got rid of it.[4] German, on the other hand, extended it to all its verbs, excluding only such as were already provided with some other inseparable prefix,[5] and even to the latter when the speaker was no longer sensible of the existence of a prefix: *ge-fr-essen, ge-b-lieben, ge-g-laubt*, etc.[6] In fact, no verb remained free from it, but the modern and hybrid formations in *-ieren (-ier-t)*.[7]

C. **Future Passive.**—By blending together, as it were, strangely enough, its gerund and present participle, German has obtained a passive future participle: *das zu lesende buch* "the book which is to be read" (F. shorter *le livre à lire*), *der zu schreibende brief*, etc.; a locution which belongs to the latest period of speech.

II. The verbal periphrases have been said to denote the modifications of the verb, either in **Tense**, or **Mood**, or **Aspect**. Hence the threefold division of this Chapter.

---

past participle are now, in both languages, denoted by peculiar periphrases, respectively: E. *being done*, G. *gethan werdend* (unusual); E. *having done*, G. *gethan habend*. The active future participle does not exist in either.
[1] *Supra* 77 (1), 78 (1), 89 (1), 90 (1), 175 sq., 186 sq.
[2] But unusual in Mercian, a further reason why it should be lost in English.
[3] The current form *worden* is the only surviving example of the faculty of deriving a root-participle without the prefix *ge-*. But compare the use of the infinitive, instead of the participle, in such sentences as *er hat's nicht thun wollen*, etc.
[4] *Supra* 96 (I.) and 97.
[5] And this for a good reason: such forms as *°ge-er-funden, °ge-ver-ziert*, were quite impossible, since there never existed a vb. *°ge-er-finden*, etc.
[6] *Supra* 19 (4), 65 (4) and 183 (twice in *ge-g-essen*).
[7] *Supra* 107 (VI.).

Section I.

PERIPHRASTIC TENSES.

(230) Various tenses, either **Present, Past,** or (in particular) **Future,** either may or must be expressed by a periphrasis.

§ 1. *Present.*

Neither German nor French has a special term for the **Momentary Present.** Thus, a German says, *ich rauche sehr wenig* "I smoke very little" (customary present), like *ich rauche eine gute pfeife* "I am smoking a good pipe"; or, at any rate, it would require a complete change of expression to mark the distinction; whereas English simply says, respectively, *I smoke* and *I am smoking*; and it has been seen that from this very locution English has abstracted its present participle.

The further development of this periphrasis gave birth to a whole conjugation, wherein the principal verb, in the shape of the invariable present participle, serves as a predicate to the verb *to be,* which latter may assume the form of any mood,—though the imperative is unusual,—and, subsidiarily, every tense whatever, viz.: *he was working as I came in; I have been working while you were away,* etc.

§ 2. *Past.*

(231) I. We have already seen, that, in giving the sense of a historical past to the I.-E. perfect which was originally the tense of the achieved action, Germanic deprived itself of any expression for the latter temporal relation[1]: in other words, having lost the aorist, and using *I spoke* and *ich sprach, he died* and *er starb,* etc., with a narrative meaning, English and German, no less than French, missed the simple term corresponding to the precise force of "I have spoken (I have done speaking), he is dead (no longer alive)," etc. Both have filled the gap by means of a very simple device, the same that Low Latin bequeathed to the modern Romance languages.

[1] *Supra* 172 and 222.

1. It is a commonplace fact that an achieved action very often results in either a real or, at least, a metaphorical possession: thus, for instance, the durative consequence of the act of acquiring is the act of possessing,[1] and such locutions as E. *I have bought a house*, G. *ich habe ein haus gekauft*, F. *j'ai acheté une maison*, etc., may be translated word for word "I have (I possess) a house [inasmuch as it is] bought." And so likewise *I have plucked this flower, I have filled this vessel*; further, metaphorically, *I have learnt this science, I have comprehended the fact* (" I *hold* the cause of it"), etc.; and, lastly, such an abusive extension of the use of the verb "to have" as a mere auxiliary, altogether deprived of its genuine and primitive acceptation, that the speaker finds it quite natural to say, in spite of common sense, E. *I have sold my house*, G. *ich habe mein haus verkauft*, F. *j'ai vendu ma maison*.

2. On the other hand, the result of an achieved action may be also very often a durative state, which is therefore conveniently denoted by the use of the verb "to be" followed by a past participle, the latter, like any other adjective, playing in the complex the part of a predicate: thus, such sentences as E. *he is dead*, G. *er ist todt*, F. *il est mort*, are, in their inner and primitive structure, to be put exactly on a level with such as E. *she is pretty*, G. *wir sind stark*, F. *il est grand*, etc.; but the function of the verb "to be" becomes gradually effaced and confined to the meaning of a mere auxiliary and past-exponent; and, the angle of vision, as it were, having slightly changed, such a sentence as G. *er ist gestiegen*, literally "he is mounted (come up)," becomes equivalent to "he has ascended."

3. Of course, it is a matter of pure usage, in French and German as well as English, to decide whether a given verb actually expresses an action or a state,—for the dividing line is often a vague one,—and, consequently, whether it ought to be conjugated with the auxiliary "to have" or "to be." English however, more complete and logical in this respect, may use both at once with the same verb, and, by saying, for instance, either *he has come* or *he is come*, may distinguish two

---

[1] Consequently, Gr. κέ-κτη-μαι "I have acquired" signifies "I possess." Cf. L. *nō-vi* "I have learnt," whence "I know."

delicate shades of meaning, for which both French and German have but one expression, *il est venu, er ist gekommen.*

II. Hence, the tense of achieved action, so-called **Indefinite Past**, in contrast with the historical past (perfect), is expressed, in the indicative or subjunctive, by the present indicative or subjunctive, either of the verb *have=haben*, or *be=sein*, accompanied by the past participle of the principal verb.[1] A further consequence is, that the perfect of these auxiliaries appears well fitted for expressing a new shade of past time, namely the **Pluperfect**, or tense denoting an action achieved as prior even to another action equally achieved: *I had read* (" done reading ") *when he came in*, G. *ich hatte gelesen*, F. *j'avais lu*; E. *he had* or *was come*, G. *er war gekommen*, etc.; and so likewise in the subjunctive (E. *had* or *were*, G. *hätte* or *wäre*).

§ 3. *Future.*

(232) Pregermanic had completely lost the I.-E. **Future**. Gothic translates the future by a mere present, occasionally, though rarely, where more precision is required, using an auxiliary *skal* or *haba* (I have to) with the infinitive. Such being the case, O.E. likewise uses the auxiliary *sceal*, and O.H.G. the auxiliary *sculan* or *wellen*, both however with a decided preference for the simple present indicative as avoiding a tedious periphrasis. Indeed, even at the present day, if the meaning is unmistakable, the present is often used for the future, chiefly in German, as also in French: G. *morgen fahre ich ab*, F. *je pars demain.*

The values involved in the future-meaning being of a somewhat variable character, it is natural that we should find the tense expressed by several periphrases.

1. The most usual value is that of a simple intention, thus

---

[1] It is a curious fact—so great is the tendency, in all languages, to use the well-known paths—that this past of achieved action has often become, in its turn, a historical past: thus, spoken French may be said to have lost the so-called definite past, and a Frenchman will say " j'ai vu " whether he means " I saw " (relating) or " I have seen " (stating); the same is the case with South German (Alamannic), which now knows nothing of *ich sah* and uses only *ich habe gesehen.*

"I *will* do."[1] Hence a verb denoting "will" may be used to indicate a future event in regard to a subject upon whom no outward constraint either is or seems to be exerted. This is the case with English: *I will go* ("because I choose to go"), *you will go* ("but there is nothing that compels you, or at any rate *I* don't"). In German, though a speaker may very well say, with the same meaning, *ich will* and *wir wollen gehen*, the other persons are not used in a similar function, and the verb *wollen* therefore cannot be properly termed an auxiliary or future-exponent.

2. Now, it might also happen that the future involves an accessory idea of obligation or necessity: in which case, an auxiliary denoting duty equally answers the purpose, E. *I shall go*. In this locution, however, the idea of duty is attenuated and nearly effaced,—as it is also in F. *je dois aller*,—though it reappears with great force in the other persons of the tense.[2] German likewise, but with attenuated force in all persons, may say *ich soll* and *du sollst*; but an actual command will require *du muszt*.[3]

3. Exclusively English is another periphrasis, which also contains a sense of obligation, though far less marked, and consists of the verb *to be* combined with the gerund: *he is to go*. It has certainly been furthered by the fact that the imperfect of *will* and *shall* was shifted to the usual meaning of a conditional[4]; for it supplied the speech with an imperfect of the future, which, if expressed otherwise, would have been ambiguous: *the member who was to read the report*, cf. F. . . . *qui devait lire* . . . and G. . . . *der* . . . *vorlesen sollte*.

4. The ordinary German future, although exclusively German, is very like the preceding, only replacing the vb. "to be" by the vb. "to become" and the gerund by the infinitive. Besides, it is a rather late expression, the more so because, the further we trace it back,—and it does not appear before the

[1] Remember that Germanic "I will" was not originally affirmative and peremptory: *supra* 221.
[2] *You shall do it* being, in fact, such an authoritative command that it is rarely used.
[3] Cf. *supra* 225 and 227.
[4] *Infra* 235.

end of the thirteenth century,—the less it shows of a real future meaning, merely denoting, as might be inferred at once from its components, the beginning of an action, thus: *sie wërdent ëȝȝen*, literally "they become [to] eat"; *er wart weinen*, "he began to cry," etc.[1] It was not until Modern German that the speaker took to using this inchoative present in a future sense.

5. By combining each of these locutions with those which denote the past tense, English and German created a future of the achieved action (so-called anterior or past future): *I will* or *shall have done*; *ich werde gethan haben*, etc. Further, in English, a future of the momentary action: *I will be doing*, etc.

SECTION II.

PERIPHRASTIC MOODS.

(233) In the moods, the verbal periphrasis may be applied to the **Indicative**, the **Subjunctive**, the **Conditional**, and the **Imperative**.

§ 1. *Indicative.*

Germanic, at any time, might replace the indicative of a given verb by the indicative of the vb. *do=thun* governing the infinitive of the principal verb,[2] in order to emphasize more strongly either the reality of the action or the intensity of the affirmation. Indeed, in the opinion of some scholars, it is such a verbal agglutination that is to be recognised as the origin of the Go. formation *sōki-dēd-um*[3]*=we did seek*. M.H.G. still possesses this locution, though using it rather rarely: *daȝ sie*

---

[1] Such a sentence would seem to require the gerund rather than the infinitive; but, as early even as M.H.G., the use of either form is a matter of choice and often of caprice. Even now, the use of *zu*, though regulated, is known to be very arbitrary: *ich weisz*, for instance, cannot do without it, whereas *ich kann*, which originally had the same meaning, altogether excludes it, as well as *ich soll* and many others.

[2] The infinitive originally being only the accusative of a neuter noun denoting action, it is clear that a Preg. locution **ďōmi binďanam* (E. *I do bind*, G. *ich thue binden*) must be literally translated "I perform binding," whence "I bind."

[3] *Supra* 195 and 210.

uns tuon bewarn, "that they are aware of us." In Mod. German it is now nearly obsolete, though of course a speaker may still say: *ich thu' es leugnen*, "I deny it expressly." But in English it has been considerably developed, and its use has become an important grammatical principle.

From this a double benefit was derived, namely, the possibility of insisting strongly upon a statement (*I do ask you*), and that of expressing either an interrogation or a negation without being obliged to repeat the verb involved in it (*you mean to go, do you? I don't*). But, since the speaker was accustomed to cast in this mould an abbreviated interrogation or negation, he was naturally led to mistake the words *do you* and *I do not* for the specific exponent of the interrogative or negative force itself; and thus there became gradually consecrated the use, which is now almost obligatory, of the auxiliary *do did* to express **the indicative in an interrogative or negative sentence**,[1] unless the verb is already provided with some other auxiliary: *do you see?* but *have you seen?*

§ 2. *Subjunctive.*

(234) The English **potential** subjunctive, or subjunctive in a final sentence,[2] is really the indicative of the vb. *may*[3] followed by the infinitive of the principal verb: *tell him so, that he may know it*; *I told him so, that he might know it*, etc. The same is the case, if a vague and indefinite eventuality is to be expressed: *I did not believe him, whatever he might say* (G. *was er auch sagen mochte*). Still more so, in the expression of a wish[4]: *God grant, he may succeed!* (G. *es möge ihm gelingen!*). As seen in these instances, German in such cases is likewise always allowed to use the similar *mögen*; but the use of it is never obligatory.

§ 3. *Conditional.*

(235) The Indo-European language had no special mood

---

[1] Of course only when the negative is *not*.
[2] That is to say, expressing a purpose, "in order that."
[3] *Supra* 226.
[4] Here, of course, the auxiliary itself stands in the subjunctive.

for expressing the Conditional: in other words, the conditional eventuality, no less than any other eventuality, was denoted by the subjunctive or by the optative (Sanskrit, Greek, Latin), two moods which in Pregermanic become the same. Even contemporary German, at least in strong verbs, briefly expresses the conditional by the perfect subjunctive: *ich thäte* (I would do), *ich hätte* (I would have), *nähme er* (if he took); cf. E. *were I, were you*, etc. But, in English, and also in German in the great majority of weak verbs and even a small number of strong ones, the perfect subjunctive is scarcely or not at all distinguishable from the perfect indicative. Such a gross ambiguity could not be tolerated in any refined language, and the inconvenience was remedied by recurring to a periphrasis, the main principle of which is, that the conditional is conceived as a past-tense of the future.[1]

1. Consequently, English, together with the infinitive of the principal verb, uses the perfect of its two auxiliaries *will* and *shall*, thus *would* and *should*, respectively with the same shades of meaning as their present may assume in the future-formation: *I would go*; *we should answer*, etc. By means of the auxiliaries *have* and *be*, is further derived a past conditional: *they would have done it*. In the same sense, German may use its verb *sollte*; but this is not its ordinary conditional periphrasis.

2. For, its ordinary future-auxiliary being the present of the vb. *werden*, German naturally uses, as the auxiliary for its conditional, the perfect subjunctive of the same verb: *ich würde gehen, ihr würdet sehen*, etc.; though, of course, in order to avoid such diffuse circumlocutions as *ich würde gekommen sein* and *ihr würdet gesehen haben*, the past conditional is better formed by the simple perfect subjunctive of the auxiliary *sein* or *haben*, thus, *ich wäre gekommen*, and *ihr hättet gesehen*.

§ 4. *Imperative.*

(236) The periphrastic forms of the imperative, E. sg. 3

[1] In French also (and in the other Romance languages) we find *j'aurais*: *j'aurai=j'avais*: *j'ai*.

let him go, pl. 1 *let us go* = G. *laszt uns gehen*, pl. 3 *let them go*, etc., are too plain to require explanation.

Like the negative form of the indicative, the prohibitive form of the imperative, when the negation is *not*, usually introduces in English the auxiliary *do*, thus: *do not steal*, but *never break your word*.

Section III.

PERIPHRASTIC ASPECTS.

(237) It has been seen that every verb is capable of three essential aspects, namely, **Active**, **Reflexive**, and **Passive**. The active aspect having naturally no further expression but the general form of the verb itself, we have only to deal with the two others.

§ 1. *Reflexive*.

(238) The form denoting the reflexive aspect was in Indo-European the so-called middle voice of the verb. But, since the middle voice could also correspond, either to the active,[1] or even, very often, to the passive aspect, there was likely to arise a most inconvenient ambiguity, which is much felt in Sanskrit, Greek and Latin,[2] and would have become quite intolerable in the later and more analytical languages. As early as Pre-germanic, the middle voice was no longer applicable either to the active or even reflexive aspect, but was strictly confined to the passive. Hence, a periphrasis had become necessary for the reflexive function, and nothing could appear better adapted for the purpose than the use of a pronominal complement to the verb, denoting that the action returned to the subject (G. *ich besinne mich*, E. *he asked himself*, etc.), a process which has been already described in the study of the Pronouns.[3]

---

[1] Cf. *supra* 188, II.

[2] In a single conjugation, for instance, *imitor* means "I imitate," *lavor* "I wash myself," and *amor* "I am loved."

[3] *Supra* 167. The reflexive verb ought not to be confounded with the impersonal verb, the neuter subject of which may be either expressed or merely understood: E. *me-thinks* = G. *es dünkt mich* (supra 24) "it seems to me."

§ 2. *Passive*.

(239) Gothic, like Latin, still possesses a passive voice, which, as stated above, is no other but the former middle voice of the Indo-European; that is to say, Gothic expresses in one word what English, German and French are unable to express except by two distinct words: *nimada*[1] "I am taken," *háitada* "I am called (my name is)"[2]; subjunctive *nimáidau háitáidau*, etc. This passive verb, however, has no tenses but the present, and even Gothic, when a past tense was required, was compelled to supply it by a periphrasis, a past participle joined as a predicate to the verb *visan* (to be) or *vaírþan* (to become). Still more so, indeed, in Old English and Old High German, since neither shows a trace of a passive voice, even in the present. The auxiliaries here are the same as in Gothic; but O.E. almost exclusively uses *béon* and *wesan*, which soon become blended into one verb, whereas *weorðan* early becomes obsolete; while, on the contrary, German, from the ninth century, shows a decided preference for *wërdan*, which in fact, as appropriately expressing a **passage from one state to another**, corresponds more exactly than *wësan* to the concept involved in the passive verb properly so-called.

From this it follows that German accurately marks a distinction which is unknown in English as well as in French. These two languages, outwardly at least, confound the true passive verb ("he is wounded," that is "he *becomes* wounded [at this instant], they are wounding him") with the locution formed by the verb "to be" and a past participle serving as a predicate to it, as any other adjective would do ("he is wounded," that is "he has been wounded [and still is so]," thus, in either case, E. *he is wounded*, F. *il est blessé*.[3] In the past tense, the

---

[1] Conjugated: sg. 1 *nim-a-da*, 2 *nim-a-za* (Gr. *νέμ-ε-σαι*), 3 *nim-a-da* (Gr. νέμ-ε-ται), pl. *nim-a-nda* (Gr. νέμ-ο-νται).

[2] A last survival of this lost passive conjugation may be seen in the fact that the G. vb. *ich heisze* means both "I call" and "I am called" (L. *vocō* and *vocor*).

[3] If however the present be not a narrative one, English may adopt the momentary present (*he is being wounded*), whereas French, lacking this form, but possessing an indefinite pronoun *on* (they), preferably uses the active and says *on le blesse*.

inconvenience appears still greater even in English, than it is in French, since *he was wounded* may occasionally mean, either "they wounded him," or "he was hurt." German, on the contrary, expressly distinguishes *ich werde* and *ich ward verwundet*, literally "I become" and "I became wounded," from *ich bin* and *ich war verwundet*, "I am" or "was hurt," and thus possesses, for every tense or mood, whether simple or periphrastic, a passive conjugation which, in meaning, exactly answers the same purpose as the Greek and Latin passive verb.[1]

[1] Cf. L. *volnerātur*, and *volnerātus est* or *fuit*.

CONCLUSION.

(240) We have now come to the end of our task. After having first established, by means of numerous and convincing illustrations, the essential correspondence between English and German sounds, we have studied in detail the grammar of the two languages in regard to word-formation, declension and conjugation, and in all these points we have found them identical. Wherever any violent contrasts have appeared, we have found a reason for them in the fact that each language has extended the use of one of two forms which both originally possessed in common. Further, the analogies we have discovered are not such as strike the eye at the first glance and afterwards prove misleading; they were drawn, as it were, from the heart of the language and have been traced back, step by step, from their present state to the source from which they originally sprang. We have gone beyond Germanic, and have verified them in the classical languages and even in the older eastern tongues.[1] For practical purposes these scientific results may have but little value. A knowledge of them will perhaps encumber rather than smooth the path of those who merely desire the conversational fluency of the courier, and the masterpieces of literature can be equally well understood and enjoyed by students who have not dissected the elements of which these masterpieces are composed, just as a knowledge of botany is not required for the æsthetic appreciation of beautiful flowers.

[1] The subject we have just left is most instructive and suggestive on this point. Nowhere is the likeness clearer and more striking than in the complex structure of the Anglo-German and Indo-European verb; nowhere do the different paths lead us more certainly to the centre from which they diverge.

But the scientific mind, which likes to penetrate into the reason of things, will derive both profit and pleasure from being able to trace in the history and evolution of a language the reasons for its most minute and often apparently contradictory rules. The enthusiastic student—and what is science without enthusiasm?—will find no more fascinating field for his enquiries than among the scientific methods and accurate documents of language. He cannot but admire the unbroken tradition by which our lips still retain the words of ancestors who have left no other trace behind; and he will equally marvel at the genius of those who have re-forged, one by one, the links of a chain which has its beginning in the mists of the past, and which passes on to the future inextricably mingled with the destiny of mankind.

INDEX OF WORDS.

N.B.—This index does not include, as a general rule: (1) secondary and further derivatives, which must be sought under their respective endings in the index of terminations below; (2) such compounds as may be resolved at first sight, though quoted in the Chapter of Composition (112–118); (3) nominal forms other than the nominative singular, and verbal forms other than the infinitive, except in cases which have a special interest.

The references are to the sections (1–240).

I. English.

A... 19, 66, 121, 134	angle 39	awkward 111
a- 50, 96, 98, 103, 229	Angle 23	
abide 179	another 114	Bag 17
above 54	answer ... 96, 139	bake 50, 57, 82, 184
accrue 17	ant 23	balk 17
ache (to) 107	any 31, 134	band 45
acre 30, 34, 50, 57, 76	apple 146	bare 17
adder 49	apron 49	batch 50
ado 96	arbalist 65	bath 17
afford 97	arch- 96	bathe 17
after 117	arise 98	be 217, 230, 231, 232,
again 96	arm 39, 139	239
against 96	as 66	be- ... 17, 19, 65, 99
akin 96	ash 74	bear (to) 26, 82, 174,
alderliefest ... 155	ask 50, 84	182
alike 96	asunder 40	beard 21, 48
all 17, 117	at 96	beat 185
alone 117	aught 96	become 99
along 96	await 103	beech 33, 48, 50, 56,
also 66	awake... 50, 106, 184	139
am (I)... 217	awaken 106	beget 182
an 19, 66, 121, 134	aware 96	begin 181
and 66	away 96	behead 99
angel 39	awful 110	belief 32

ENGLISH AND GERMAN GRAMMAR.

believe ... 19, 32
bellows 146
bend 45
beseech 33, 50, 99, 187
best 80
better 49, 61, 80, 106
better (to)... ... 106
beyond 160
bid 83, 183
bind 26, 28, 45, 48, 49, 56, 82, 181
birch 17
birth 17
bishop... 17
bit 17, 48, 49, 56, 57, 72, 179
bite 27, 48, 49, 56, 57, 82, 179
blast 185
bleed 88
blind 17, 49
blood 33
bloom... ... 33, 75
blossom 33
blot 187
blow ... 48, 56, 185
bolt 17
bond 45
bone 17, 48
book 33, 48, 50, 56, 139
born 182
borough 50, 65, 139
both 31
bottom ... 39, 75
bough... 110
bow 50
bow (to) 1, 50, 110, 180
boy 33
boycott 107
brake (pf.)... 100, 182
breadth 50
break 42, 182
breakfast 117
breed 17, 28
brethren 140
bride 48
bridegroom ... 65
bring 24, 187
broad 90
brood ... 17, 18, 23
brother 18, 33, 41, 48, 49, 51, 53, 54, 139

brow 117
brown... 18
buck 48
buckmast 83
bull 17, 48
burial... 104
burn 187
burst 17, 181
bush 17
bustle... 28
busy 17, 28
but 12, 66
butcher 17
butter... 5
buxom 10, 19, 110
buy 88, 187
by ... 17, 66, 99

Cab 17
calf 48, 56, 139
call 54
can 39, 84, 224
care 18, 189
cast 187
cat 102
catch 187
caterwaul... ... 102
cave 17
chalk 50
chew 36
chide 179
child 18, 139, 140, 147
chill 50
chin 50
choice... 29
choose 29, 50, 57, 61, 82, 180, 194, 204
circle 17
clad 187
clasp 106
clean 17, 77
cleanse 106
cleave (split) ... 180
cleave (adhere) 82
climb 82, 181
cling 181
clothe... 187
co- 67
cold 17, 21, 50, 57, 78
colour... 5
comb 39, 48
come 39, 45, 50, 57, 182
cool 50

corn 50, 57
cost 187
could 224
cow ... 14, 18, 50, 57
coxcomb 114
creed 139
cripple 88
crow (to) 185
cut (to) 187

Daisy... 114
dale 14
danger 65
dare 187, 222
darling 103
daughter 49, 56, 139
day 47, 50, 56, 72, 139, 143
dead 32, 78
deaf 32
deal 96
death 82, 47
deed 26, 45, 47, 78, 218
deem 23, 107
deep ... 29, 57, 90
deer ... 49, 139, 148
defile 28
depth 90
dew 17
die (a)... 145
dig 179
dip 29
dis- 100, 107
dish 50
dive 29
dizzy 17, 28
do 45, 56, 218, 238, 236
doom 23, 75
door 17, 28
dough... 50, 56, 65
dove 32
down 18
drag 50
draw ... 17, 50, 184
dream... 49
drink 117
drink (to) 39, 40, 181
drive (to) 45, 49, 179
due 17
dumb 17, 28
dung 17
durst 187
Dutch... ... 2, 29

INDEX OF ENGLISH WORDS. 379

Ear 32, 61, 74, 139
early 124
earth 13, 17, 20, 21, 78, 139
Easter... 152
eat 26, 183
eatable(s) ... 69, 157
edge 50
egg 50
eight ... 30, 53, 121
either 79
eke 32
elbow 10, 114
elder 80
eldest 80
eleven 121
else 23, 111
'em 66
en- 107
end 22, 139
English ... 23, 91
enough 20, 50, 55, 96
enow 50
ere 124
even ... 10, 17, 48
ever 161
eye 50, 54, 74, 139

Fair ... 13, 50, 76
falcon... 13
fall (to) 17, 21, 83, 84, 185
false 13, 17
falsehood 109
far 17, 21
fare (to) 17, 82, 83, 184
farther 17
farthing 103
fasten 93
father 17, 25, 48, 49, 51, 53, 54, 139
fatherless 10
fathom 39
feather 23, 49, 54
fee ... 34, 50, 54
feed 23
feel 187
feet 144, 145
fell 26
fell (to) 83
fiend 22, 54, 90, 139
fifteen... 48
fifth ... 20, 49, 124
fifty ... 20, 48, 122

fight (to) 181
file (to) 23
fill ... 17, 23, 107
filth .. 23, 70, 90
find 19, 20, 28, 181
fine 12
finger 26, 39, 50, 121
fire 29
first 17, 23, 49, 124
fish 27, 48, 50, 54, 72
fish (to) ... 19, 174
fisher 102
fist 49
five ... 20, 54, 121
flea 139
flee 187
fleet 84
flesh 48, 50
flight 49, 78
fling 181
flood 33, 78
floor ... 17, 76, 139
flower... 33
flutter 106
fly (a)... 50
fly (to) ... 50, 180
fodder... ... 5, 49, 79
fold 110
folk 139
follow... 50
food 23
foot 18, 33, 72, 139, 144, 145
for 99
for- 65, 99
fore 23
fore- 99
foremost 124
forget 182
forlorn 19, 45, 180
form 5
former 124
forsake 184
forth 49
foster 79
foul 23, 28, 50, 70, 76, 90
four 121
fowl 41, 48
fox 23
France 23
freeze ... 61, 180, 204
French 23
fresh 50

fret 99
friend 22, 41, 54, 90, 139
frost 61
fulfil 114
full ... 17, 23, 42, 77
fulness 5
funk 17
furrow 42
further 79

Gander 102
gang 219
gangway 219
garden 30
gardener 102
Gardiner 102
garlic... 32
geese 144, 145
get ... 50, 182, 183
ghost 50, 62
gift ... 48, 50, 78
gild 23, 50, 107, 187
gird 106, 187
girdle... 106
give 45, 48, 50, 188
glass 20, 61
glazier 14, 50, 61
glimmer ... 106, 181
glitter... 106
go 219
God 28, 50
godfather 114
gold 17, 20, 23, 49, 50
good 50
goods... 157
goose 18, 56, 102, 144, 145
gosling ... 18, 103
Gospel 115
grasp 106
great 32
grind 181
groom 65
grow 185
guest 30, 50, 51, 56, 139, 144
guilt 50

Hail 50, 54
hair 50, 143
half ... 21, 48, 124
halm 75
hand 39, 49, 50, 72, 139

handicraft	...	96	hurt	... ...	187	length	... ...	90
handiwork	...	96	husband	5, 18,	114	let	 45,	236
handsome ...	...	110	hussy ...	... ...	65	lick	 27,	50
hang ... 39, 83, 185			hut	... ...	17	lid	... ...	117
hard 17, 20, 50, 54, 72,						lie (a) ...	17, 50,	139
		110	I ...	... ...	164	lie (to)	... ...	180
hare	... ...	61	ice	... ...	145	lie (be laid)	50, 83,	
hark ...	...	20	idle	... ...	110			183
harvest	... ...	41	if ...	... ...	66	lief	 48,	56
haste ...	... ...	17	in	... ...	66	life	... ...	48
hate ...	... 50,	93	in-	... ...	96	light ...	29, 41,	50
hater ...	... ...	102	ink	... ...	13	light (to)	... ...	187
hatred	... ...	109	ink (to)	... ...	107	light (adj.)...	...	50
have 17, 19, 85, 187,			is (he) ...	... 26,	217	like	... ...	96
	189,	231	it ...	... 66,	166	lit	... ...	187
he ...	17, 66,	166	its	... ...	168	little	... ...	88
head ...	19, 32,	187				live	27, 48,	85
headlong ...	...	111	Keep ...	... 20,	187	liver	... ...	27
heal ...	... 90,	93	ken	... 39,	84	load	... ...	184
hear ...	... ...	187	kernel	... ...	88	loaf	 17,	65
heart 20, 21, 49, 74,			kin ...	... 50,	96	loan	... ...	82
		140	kindred	... 5,	109	lone	... ...	117
hearth	... ...	21	king	... 50,	103	long	... 39, 50,	90
heath ...	... ...	137	kiss	... ...	50	loose	 17,	110
heathen	... ...	19	knave ...	... ...	17	lord	... ...	65
heave 54, 83, 182, 184			knee	... 50,	57	lord (to)	... ...	118
hedge ...	... ...	50	kneel ...	... 106,	187	lording	... ...	103
height	... ...	90	knight	... ...	21	lose 20, 45, 61, 180, 187		
heir	... ...	74	know ...	...1, 84,	185			204
help (to)	... 45,	181	knowledge...	50,	109	loss	... ...	45
her ...	... 17,	168				loud 41, 50, 78, 110		
herd ...	... ...	21	Lade (to)	... 50,	184	louse	 144,	145
here ...	... 166,	168	lady ...	... ...	65	love	... 48, 56,	107
hers ...	... ...	168	lamb ...	... 39,	139	low	... ...	50
hew ...	... ...	185	lame ...	... ...	10			
hide ...	... ...	179	land	... 39,	49	Maid ...	17, 19,	50
high ...	50, 54,	90	landscape ...	...	109	maiden	... 19,	114
hill ...	... 50,	88	last ...	... ...	80	make ...	20, 50,	187
hireling	... ...	103	last (to)	... ...	187	man 37, 39, 48, 144,		
his ...	... ...	168	late ...	... ...	80			145
hold 17, 21, 50, 54, 84,			laugh ...	... 36,	50	many ...	... ...	74
		185	laughter	... 50,	79	mare ...	... 10,	65
holy ...	... ...	50	lay (to)	... 50,	83	marshal	... ...	65
home ...	... ...	65	lay (he)	... ...	183	may ... 78, 226, 234		
hoof ...	... ...	17	lead ...	19, 20,	187	me ...	 17,	164
horn ...	... 42,	77	leaf ...	... ...	32	mead ...	... ...	39
horse ...	... ...	143	lean ...	... ...	187	mean (adj.)	...	96
hot ...	... ...	31	leap ...	32, 50,	185	mean (to) ...	...	187
hound...	... 20,	28	learn 20, 21, 31, 61,			meat	... ...	65
house ... 18, 20, 28, 32					106	meed ...	62,	185
hue ...	... 5, 17,	37	lease ...	... ...	61	meet ...	... ...	187
hundred	... 50,	123	leave ...	... ...	20	melt ... 174, 181, 189		
hunger	... ...	50	leek ...	... ...	32	mere ...	17, 19,	72
hunt ...	... ...	103	lend ...	... ...	82	mermaid ...	...	17

INDEX OF ENGLISH WORDS. 381

merry 90	neighbour ... 50, 65	pinafore 117
methinks 238	neither ... 79, 96	pink 13
mice 144, 145	nephew 54	plant 48
mid ... 26, 36, 39, 56	nest 27, 62	play (to) 182
middle 10, 49	net 17	plenty 5
midwife 117	never 96	poison 48
might 50, 78	next 80	pound 18, 48, 143
might (he) 226	nigh ... 50, 80, 110	pretty 110
mild 20	night 21, 39, 50, 54, 79	push 189
mile 17	nightingale ... 114	put 17, 187
mill 42	nine 121	
mine 168	no 134	Queen 72
minster 65	none 96, 184	queer 17
mint 49	nor 96	quick 27, 50
mirth 90	nose 61	quicksilver ... 27
mis- 96	not 96	quite 117
mischief 96	note 10	quoth 183
miss (to) 96	nought 96	
mist 27	nut 50	Radish 23
molten 181		rain 50
Monday 18	Of 54, 66	raise 83
month 90	off 54, 66	rare 10
mood 49	oft 49	rash 50
moon 18, 139	old ... 17, 20, 21, 80	rather 17
more 61, 80	on 96, 103	raven ... 13, 50, 54
morn 50, 54	once 110, 124	re- 67
morning ... 50, 54	one 31, 39, 66, 121, 157	reach 187
most 80	ordeal 96	read 17, 20, 41, 185, 187
mother 18, 19, 33, 49 54, 139	other ... 49, 124, 157	
	ought 96	ready 109
mount 26	ought (he) ... 228, 229	reason 65
mouse 23, 61, 144, 145	our 168	red 41
mouth 40	out 66, 96	reeve 65
move 17	oven 48	relations 5
mow 50, 185	over 54	rend 187
murder 42	own ... 50, 54, 228	rest 73
murther 42	ox 17, 74, 139, 140	rich 50
music 17	Oxford 114	riddle 104
must 227	oxlip 117	ride 41, 179
mutton 5, 65		Riding 68
my 168	Pale (noun) ... 48	right 53, 78
mylady 66	palfrey 48	ring (a) 50
mylord 66	pan 23, 48	ring (to) ... 13, 181
	pass 187	rinse 106
Nail 50	past 187	ripe (to) 107
name 75	path 49, 139	ripen 106
napkin 103	peacock ... 48, 115	rise 83, 179
nation 65	pen (to) 107	rive 179
near 50	pence 145	road 17
need 228	penny ... 23, 145	room ... 17, 28, 39, 75
need (to) 228	people 143	rough 50, 54
needle ... 26, 39, 79	person 17	roundabout ... 117
needs 111	pilgrim 23	rule 17
neigh 50	pillow 17	rummage 17

run 181	ship (to) 107	split 179
	shire 65	spouse 5
Sad 59	shoe 50	spring (to) ... 82, 181
saddle... 49	shoe (to) 187	stand (a) 49
sail 50	shoot 180, 204	stand (to) 53, 184, 220
sailor 102	should... ... 225, 235	star 21
sale 21	shove 50	starch 50
salt ... 30, 49, 59	shovel... 48, 50, 88	stark 50
salve ... 92, 93, 189	show 59, 185	starve... 181
same 110	shrine 59	stay 220
sand 39	shrive 179	steadfast 110
save 189	sight 50, 78	steal 182
say 50	silly 23	steed 33
screw 17	silver 21, 59	stick (to) ... 179, 183
second 124	sin 17	stiff 48
see 17, 45, 50, 54, 183	sing 181	stink 181
seed ... 26, 49, 59	sink ... 39, 82, 181	stitch (to) 83
seek 33, 50, 187, 189, 207	sister 10, 13, 59, 61, 139	stone 105
		stood (he) 184
seethe... ... 53, 180	sit 26, 59, 83, 183	stool 33
seldom 23	six 21, 121	stove 20
self ... 21, 160, 167	slaughter ... 50, 79	stream ... 59, 75
sell 21, 187	slay ... 45, 59, 184	strength 90
send 187	sleep ... 20, 48, 57	strew 185
serve 17	slide 17	stride 59
set 17, 26, 36, 83, 187	slight... 78	strike 50, 179
seven ... 26, 40, 121	slip 59	string 181
sew 59	slow 31	strive 179
shade 189	small 59	strong... 90
shaft 48	smile 59	strow 185
shake 184	smite 179	stud 33
Shakespeare 114, 117	snow 37, 39, 50, 56, 59	sty ... 26, 53, 82
shall 225, 232	so... 66	such 50, 161
shamefaced ... 110	sob 106	suit 17
shape 5	sodden 53	Sunday 117
shape (to) 48, 50, 57, 184	soft 48	swamp 59
	some 40, 134	swart... 59
sharp 20	son 20, 34, 39, 59, 77, 139	swear 182
sharpen 106		sweat ... 49, 57, 59
shave 30, 48, 56, 57, 82, 184	soothly 110	sweet ... 49, 57, 59
	sore 31	swell ... 28, 174, 181
she 133, 166	sorrow 93	swim 17, 39, 59, 181
she- 115	soul 31	swine 27, 59, 89, 143
shear 182	sound (adj.) ... 20	sword 21, 59
shed 187	sour 32, 76	
sheen 77	sow 27	Take 32, 184
sheep 5, 50, 189, 143	sow (to) ... 59, 185	tale 23, 40
shepherd 87	speak 17, 182	tallow... 50
sheriff... 65	spear 48, 139	tame 49
shew 185	spew 48, 53	taught 187
shilling 103	spin 48, 181	teach 187
shine 18, 53, 84, 173, 179	spindle 88	tear (a) ... 30, 76
	spinster 90	tear (to) 41, 82, 182
ship 50	spit 183	teens 121

INDEX OF ENGLISH WORDS. 383

tell ... 23, 49, 187
ten 40, 47, 54, 57, 121
thank 50
that 46, 47, 49, 66, 130, 160, 162
thatch 36, 57, 59
the 47, 49, 66, 133
thee 165
their 49, 168
them 66, 166
there 168
these 160
they 49, 166
thigh 50
thimble 88
thin 47, 54
thine 168
thing 24
think 24, 47, 50, 83, 187, 238
third 124
thirst 42
thirteen 121
thirty 122
this 160
thorn ... 47, 54, 77
those 160
thou ... 47, 49, 165
though 14
thousand 19, 28, 49, 123
thrash 181
three 121
thrice 124
through ... 49, 50
throw 185
thumb 18, 47, 54
Thursday 114
thy 168
tide 49, 139
tight 78
tile 50
timber 47, 57, 76
tin 49
tithe 124
to 66, 100
toe 50
token 77
to-morrow 50
tong 39
tongue 13, 39, 47, 50, 54, 74, 139
too 66
tooth ... 79, 144, 145

tother 66
town 18
tread 182, 183
tree 37
trow 37
true 87
tub 17
Tuesday 17, 37, 114
tune 17
twelve 121
twenty ... 121, 122
twice 110, 124
twig 50
twilight 121
twin 121, 124
twist 124
two ... 37, 49, 121

Udder 28
un- (negative) 17, 40, 96
un- (inversive) 98, 100
uncouth 78
under 40, 49
undo 10, 98
up 66
us 20, 164

Vat 23
very 110
view 17
virgin 17
vixen 23, 87
vouchsafe 118

Wait 103
wake ... 36, 50, 184
Wales 23, 67
wall 139
walnut 115
warm 21, 50, 56, 75
warm (to) 106
warp ... 48, 57, 181
warrant 97
was (he) 17, 20, 61, 183, 217
wash 17, 84
watch (to) 50
water ... 5, 17, 37, 49
wax 50
wax (to) 184
way 50
we ... 17, 63, 164
wear 182

weasel 88
weather ... 17, 49
weave 182, 183
wed 187
wedlock 109
weep 187
weigh 206
Welsh ... 23, 67, 91
wend 219
went (he) 219
were (he) ... 194, 217
were (they) 61, 183, 217
werwolf 27, 115, 117
what ... 50, 54, 161
wheat 50
when 66
where 168
whet 50, 54
which 161, 162
while 17
white ... 37, 50, 54
who ... 17, 161, 162
whole 90, 93
widow 27
width 90
wife 48, 139
wild 17, 49
will 36, 139
will (he) 17, 221, 228, 232
win 97, 181
wind ... 17, 26, 37
wind (to) 17, 181, 219
wine 17, 37
wise (adj.) 223
wise (manner) ... 111
wish 84, 139
wit 223
with 79
witness 223
wolf 34, 37, 42, 48, 54, 139
woman ... 115, 145
womb 48
wood 41
word ... 20, 139
word (to) 107
work 21, 50, 53, 83, 187
world ... 21, 27, 65
worm 139
worship 109
worship (to) ... 118
worth 21
wot (he) 31, 37, 45, 223

would (he)... 221, 235	ye 165	yon 160
wound 78	year ... 36, 76, 143	yonder 160
write 37, 179	yearn... 50	York 54
writhe 179	yellow... 37, 50, 56	you 36, 165
wrought ... 53, 187	yellowhammer... 65	young... ... 28, 36
	yesterday 41, 50, 56	youngster 90
Y- 97	yield 50, 125	your 168
yard 30, 74	yoke 28, 36, 72, 139	youth... 90

II. German.

Ab 54	*aus* 66, 96	*besuchen* 187
abenteuer 6	*ausdruck* 6	*beten* 117
aber 117		*betriegen* 180
aberglaube 117	*Baar* 17	*beugen*... 29
abgott 147	*bachen*... ... 50, 57	*bewegen* ... 182, 206
achsel 76	*backen* 50, 57, 82, 184	*biegen* ... 29, 50, 180
acht (eight) 30, 53, 121	*bad* 17	*biegsam* ... 19, 110
acht (care) 98	*bahre* 26	*bin* 217
achten 98	*balg* 146	*binden* 26, 28, 45, 49,
acker 30, 34, 50, 57,	*balken* 17	56, 82, 181
76, 146	*band* 45, 147	*birke* 17
ader 142	*bart* ... 20, 21, 48	*bis* 96
adler 146	*bauen* 18, 32	*bischof*... 17
afterwort 117	*bauer* (peasant)... 141	*bisthum* 109
all 17	*baum* 10	*bisz* 17, 48, 49, 56, 57, 72
allein 117	*be-* 17, 19, 65, 94, 99	*bitten* 83, 183
allod 115	*beben* 81	*blähen*... 48, 56, 185
als 66	*bedingen* ... 24, 181	*blasen* 185
also 66	*bedürfen* ... 55, 224	*blech* 14
alt ... 17, 20, 21	*befehlen* ... 181, 206	*bleiben* 19, 65, 85, 121,
am 66	*begehren* 28	229
ameise... 23	*begierde* 28	*blind* ... 17, 49, 155
ammer... 65	*beginnen* 181	*blühen*... ... 33, 36
an 96	*begleiten* 19	*blume* 33, 75, 137, 140,
andacht 78	*behaftet* 110	142
ander 49, 124	*behende* ... 22, 99	*blut* 88
anders... 124	*bei* 17, 99	*bluten* 88
anderthalb 124	*beide* 31	*bock* 48
angel 39	*beil* 79	*boden* 39, 75, 141, 146
ant- 96	*bein* ... 17, 48, 143	*bogen* 50
apfel 146	*beiszen* 27, 48, 49, 56,	*bolz* 17
arbeit 142	57, 82, 179	*böse* 109
arm 39, 143	*bekommen* 99	*bösewicht* 147
armbrust 65	*bellen* ... 181, 206	*boshaft* 110
armut 90	*bequem* 65	*bosheit*... 109
asche 74	*beredt* ... 17, 19, 187	*bote* 141
ast 30, 146	*bereit* 109	*braten*... 185
au 142	*berg* 146	*braue* 117
auch 32	*bergen*... 104, 181, 206	*braun* 18
aue 142	*bersten*... 17, 181, 206	*braut* 48
auf 66	*besser* ... 49, 61, 80	*bräutigam* 65
auge 50, 54, 74, 140, 142	*best* 80	*brechen* 42, 182, 206

INDEX OF GERMAN WORDS. 385

brennen 187
brenzeln 106
bringen ... 24, 187
bruder 18, 33, 41, 48, 49, 51, 53, 54, 146
brunnen 141
brut ... 17, 18, 23, 48
brüten ... 17, 23, 107
bube 18, 33
buch 33, 48, 50, 56, 147
buche ... 33, 48, 56
buchstab 33
bucht 136
bulle 17, 48
burg 50, 65
busch 17
butter 5

Chor 146
christ 141, 149
chur 180

Da 168
dach ... 36, 50, 57, 59
dank 50
dar 168
das 130, 162
dasz ... 46, 130, 162
däuchte ... 24, 195
däuchten 24
daumen 18, 47, 54, 141
decken 36, 50, 57, 59
degen 146
dehnen 86
dein 168
denken... 24, 50, 187
der ... 66, 130, 162
deuchte ... 24, 28
Deutsch 23, 29, 91, 141
dicht 78
die ... 66, 132, 162
die (pl.) 181
Dienstag ... 17, 114
dies 160
dieser 160
Dietrich 29
ding 24
dingen... ... 24, 181
dirne 149
doch 14
Donnerstag ... 114
dorn 47, 54, 77, 147
drehen 185
drei 121

dreschen ... 181, 206
dritte 124
du 47, 165
dumm ... 17, 28, 32
dung 17
dünken 24, 47, 83, 187, 288
dünn 47, 54
durch 49
dürfen... ... 55, 224
dürr 42
durst 42
dusel 23
dutzen... 106

Eben 48
eber 54
eck 50
ecke 50
ei... ... 50, 117, 147
eiergelb 117
eigen ... 50, 54, 228
eilf 121
ein 31, 39, 66, 121, 134
ein- 66
einander 114
eindruck 6
einfalt 110
einige 31, 134
einöde 90
einst 124
eis 145
eitel 110
elend 23
elephant 141
elf 121
ellenbogen 114
emp- 98
emsig 28
ende 22, 142
engel 89
ent- ... 95, 96, 98
entgegen 96
er... 166
er- 98, 99
erbe ... 74, 137, 140
erde 17, 20, 21, 73, 137, 142, 152
erklären 180
erlauben 98
erlöschen ... 174, 181
erquicken 27, 50, 107
erschallen 181
erschrecken... 182, 206

erst 124
ersuchen 99
erwägen 182
erz- 96
erzählen 23
es... 166
essen 26, 82, 183, 197, 206, 229
euch 36, 165
euer 168
euter 28, 49
ewig 81

Fach 82, 124
faden 89
fahl 87
fahne 102
fähnrich 102
fahren 17, 82, 83, 184, 204, 205
falb 87
falke 13
fallen 17, 21, 83, 84, 185
fällen 83
falls 111
falsch... ... 13, 17
falte 110
fangen... ... 82, 185
faul ... 23, 28, 32, 76
fäule 23
faust 49
fechten... ... 181, 206
feder ... 28, 49, 54
fegefeuer 50
fegen 50, 76
feind ... 22, 54, 90
fell 26
fels, felsen 141
fern 10, 21
fernsprecher ... 6
fest (fast) 93
fest (feast)... ... 143
feuer 29, 143
finden 19, 20, 28, 181
finger 26, 39, 50, 121
fisch 27, 48, 50, 54, 72, 146
fischen 19, 174
fischer 102
fittich 23
flaum 48
flechten 181
fleck, flecken ... 141
fleisch 48, 50

C C

fliege 50	*ge-* (part.) ... 97, 229	*grab* 147
fliegen 29, 50, 180, 206	*ge-* (nouns) 96, 143	*graben*... 184
fliehen 180, 187	*gebären* 26, 82, 182, 206	*grad* 143
flieszen ... 84, 206	*geben* 45, 48, 50, 183,	*graf* 65, 141
floh 139	197, 206	*greifen* 179
flosz 146	*gebirge* 96	*grosz* 32
flucht 49, 78	*geburt* 17	*gülden*... ... 22, 23
flur 17, 76	*gedeihen* 24	*gusz* 45
flut 33, 78, 136, 142	*gefährte* 96	*gut* 50
folgen 50	*gefallen* 97	
folgern 106	*gefilde*... 96	*Haar* 50, 143
fordern 97	*gegen* 96	*haben* 19, 85, 187, 189,
forschen ... 84, 189	*gehen* ... 185, 219	231
fort 49	*gehl* 37	*hafen* 146
fragen... 207	*geist* ... 50, 62, 147	*haft* (tie) 54
frau 32, 74, 136, 142	*gelächter* 79	*haft* (capture) ... 54
frauenzimmer ... 114	*gelb* ... 37, 50, 56	*hagel* 50, 54
freilich 110	*geleiten* 19	*hahn* 74, 137, 140, 141
fressen... ... 99, 229	*gelten* 50, 125, 181, 206	*halb* ... 21, 48, 124
freund 22, 41, 54, 90,	*gemahl* 96	*hälfte* 43, 124
137	*gemein* 96	*halm* 75, 143
friede, frieden ... 141	*genesen* 97, 183, 207	*hals* 146
frieren ... 61, 180	*genie* 6	*halten* 17, 21, 50, 54.
frisch 50	*genieszen* 180	84, 185, 206
frohndienst... ... 74	*genug* 20, 50, 55, 96	*hammer* 146
frost 61	*gern* 23. 50	*hand* 48, 49, 50, 72
frucht 136	*geschehen* ... 183, 206	137, 146
fuchs 23	*geschweige* 97	*handeln* 106
füchsin ... 23, 87	*geselle* 96	*handhabe* 118
führen... 83	*gesinde* 96	*handhaben* ... 114, 118
füllen ... 17, 23, 107	*gestehen* 97	*hangen* 39, 83, 185
fünf 17, 20, 39, 54, 121	*gestern* ... 41, 56	*hängen* 83
fünfte ... 49, 53, 124	*gestirn*... 23	*hart* ... 20, 50, 54, 72
fünfzehn 48	*gesund*... 20	*hase* 61
fünfzig 48	*getreide* 202	*hassen*... ... 50, 93
funke, funken 17, 141	*gevatter* 96	*hast* 17
für 99	*gewahr* 96	*hauen* 37, 185
furche... 42	*gewinnen* 181	*haupt* 19, 32
fürst 17, 23, 49, 124	*gewisz*... 228	*haus* 18, 20, 28, 32, 147
fusz 18, 33, 72, 144, 146	*gieng* 185, 219	*haut* 146
futter 5, 49, 79	*gier* 23	*heben* 54, 55, 83, 85, 184
	gieszen 45, 84, 180, 206	*hecke* 50
Gabe 142	*gift* ... 48, 50, 78	*heer* ... 41, 137, 143
gähren... 182	*ging* 185, 219	*heft* 54
gang 219	*glas* 20, 61	*heide* (heath) ... 137
gans 56, 102, 144, 146	*glauben* 19, 32, 65, 229	*heide* (heathen)... 19
gänserich 102	*gleich* 96	*heil* 90, 93
gären 182	*gleichen* 179	*Heiland* 90
garten 30, 74, 137, 141	*gleichung* 6	*heilen* 90, 93
gärtner 102	*glimmen* 181	*heilig* 50
gast 30, 50, 51, 56, 137,	*glitzern* 106	*heim* 65
144, 146	*gold* 17, 20, 49, 50	*heimat*... 90
ge- 19, 23, 50, 65, 69,	*golden*... 22, 23, 89	*heischen* ... 50, 84
96, 97, 143, 229	*Gott* ... 28, 50, 147	*heisz* 31

INDEX OF GERMAN WORDS. 387

heiszen... ... 185, 289
helfen 45, 181
henker... ... 13, 83
her 166, 168
herbst 41
herd 21
herde 21, 87
herr 141
herz 20, 21, 49, 74, 137,
   140, 142, 150, 152
herzog... 87, 141, 143
heute 166
hieb 37
hier 166, 168
hin 166
hirte 87, 141
hoch ... 50, 54, 74
hof 53
höhe 50, 74, 136, 137,
   140, 142
hoheit 110
höher 50, 80
holz 147
horchen 20
horn 77
hübsch... 53
huf 17, 143
hügel ... 50, 54, 88
huhn 147
hund ... 20, 28, 143
hundert ... 50, 123
hunger 50
hütte 17

Ich 14, 164
ihr (you) 165
ihr (her) 168
ihr (their)... ... 168
immer... 96
in... 66
irden 89
irdisch 91
irgend... 161
ist 26, 217

Jahr ... 36, 76, 143
jauchzen 106
je 96, 124, 161
jedenfalls 111
jeder 79
jener 160
joch 28, 36, 72, 136, 143
jugend... 90

jung 28, 36
jungfer 117

Kalb 48, 56, 80, 137, 147
kalk 50
kalt 17, 21, 50, 57, 78
kamm 39, 48
kann 39, 224
kater 102
katze 102
kauen 36
kaufen... 99
keck 50
kehren... 105
kehricht 105
kein 134
kennen... 39, 84, 187
kiesen 29, 50, 57, 61,
   82, 180
kind 136, 147
kinn 50
kirche... 142
klauben 32
kleben 82
klein 17, 77
kleinod 17
klimmen ... 82, 181
kloster... 146
knabe ... 17, 36, 141
knappe 36
knecht 21
knie ... 50, 57, 143
knoblauch 32
knobloch 32
kommen 39, 40, 45, 50,
   57, 182
könig 50, 103
können... ... 84, 224
korn 50, 57
kost 142
kosten 29
krächzen 106
kraft 146
kraut 147
kreuz 143
kriechen ... 180, 206
krüppel 88
kuh ... 14, 50, 57, 146
kühl 50
kund 78, 224
kunft 40, 78
kunst 78, 146
kur 180
kürze 74

Lachen ... 36, 50
laden 141, 146
laden (vb.) 17, 50, 184
lahm 10
laib 17
lamm 80, 147
land 39, 49
lang 39, 50
lange 110
länge 74, 142
lassen ... 45, 185, 236
lasz 45
laub 32
lauch 32
laufen 32, 50, 185, 206
läugnen 106
laus 144, 146
laut (sound) 41, 143
laut (loud) 41, 50, 78
lauter 110
leben 27, 48, 85
leber 27
lechzen... 50
lecken 27, 50
legen 20, 50, 83
lehren ...31, 61, 83, 106
leib 147
leiche 110
leicht 50
leiden 179
leier 142
leihen 82, 179
leiten 19
lernen 20, 21, 31, 61,
   83, 106
lesen 61, 183
letzt 80
leuchten 29
leugnen 106
leumund 75
leute 29
leutnant 65
licht 29, 41, 50
lid 117
lieb 29, 48, 56
liebe 48, 56
lieben 107
liegen ... 50, 83, 183
los 17, 45, 110
löschen... ... 174, 181
losen 41
löwe 141
luft 78, 146
lug 139, 180

lüge	...14, 17, 50	münze	 49	Pabst, papst	14, 48
lügen	50, 106, 180	müssen	 227	parlieren	 6
lust	 146	musze	 227	pfad	... ... 49, 143
lützel	 88	muth	 49	pfaffe	 48
		mutter	10, 18, 19, 33,	pfahl	 48
Machen	... 20, 50		49, 54, 146	pfalz	 65
macht	20, 50, 78, 146,			pfanne	... ... 23, 48
	226	Nach	 50	pfau	... ... 48, 149
mag	... 226, 234	nachbar	50, 65, 149	pfennig	 23
magd	... 19, 50, 146	Nachbaur	 65	pferd	... 48, 65, 148
magen	 141	nächst	 80	Pfingsten	48, 65, 152
mähen	... ... 50, 185	nacht	14, 21, 39, 50,	pflanze	... ... 48, 142
mahnen	 83		54, 79, 146	pflaum	 48
mähre	 65	nachtigall	 114	pflegen	 182
maid	... ... 17, 50	nadel	...26, 39, 79	pfund	... 18, 48, 143
manch	 74	nagel	... 50, 146	philosoph	 141
mann	37, 39, 67, 144,	nähe	 50	photographie	... 142
	147	näher	 50	pilgrim	 23
marsch	 6	nähren	 207	planet	 141
marschall	 65	name	75, 141, 142	preisen	 179
marschiren	 6	namen	 141	punkt	 143
maus	23, 61, 144, 146	namhaft	 117		
meer	... 17, 72, 143	narr	 141	Quecksilber	... 27, 50
mehr	... ... 61, 80	nase	 61	quellen	... 174, 181, 206
meiden	 96	natter	 49	quer	 17
meile	 17	neffe	 54		
mein	... ... 10, 168	nehmen	45, 82, 174,	Rabe	...36, 50, 54, 141
meist	 80		182, 197, 204, 205	rächen	 182
meiszel	 88	nein	... 10, 96, 134	rad	 10
melken	 181	nennen	 187	rand	 147
menge	... 74, 140, 142	nest	... ... 27, 62	rappe	 36
mensch	... ... 67, 141	netz	 17	rasch	 50
messen	... ... 183, 206	neun	 121	räsonnieren	... 6
messer	 65	nicht	 96	rast	 78
meth	 39	nichte	... ... 53, 87	rathen	... 17, 41, 185
miethe	... ... 62, 185	nie	 96	räthsel	 104
mild	 20	nimmer	 96	rauchwerk	... 50, 54
mis-	 96	noch	 96	rauh	... ... 50, 54
missen	 96	noth	... 142, 228	raum	...28, 39, 75
mist	 27	nur	 96	recht	... ... 53, 78
misz-	 96	nusz	 50	recht (das)	 148
mit	... ... 73, 117	nutzen	 107	recken	 99
mitte	26, 36, 39, 56, 73	nützen	 107	reden	17, 20, 123, 187
mittel	... ... 10, 49			regen	 50
mode	 6	Oben	 54	reiben	 179
mögen	20, 226, 234	ocean	 65	reich	 50
monat	 90	ochs	17, 74, 140	reich (das)	 109
mond	 18	ochse	 141	reichen	 187
Montag	 18	öde	 90	reifen	 107
mord	 42	ofen	48, 141, 146	rein	 77
morgen	... ... 50, 54	oft	 49	reiszen	... ... 37, 179
mühle	 42	ohr	...32, 61, 74, 142	reiten	... 17, 41, 179
mund	 40	ort	 147	reiter	 102
münster	 65	Ostern	 152	rennen	... ... 181, 187

INDEX TO GERMAN WORDS.   389

retten 187	schieszen 180	sein (his) 168
rettich... 23	schiff 50	sein (to be)... 217, 231,
richtig... 91	schiffen 107	239
rind 147	schilling 103	selb 160
ring 50	schinden 181	selbst 167
rinnen... 181	schlacht 142	selten 23
ritter 102	schlaf 48, 146	seltsam 23
ritz 37	schlafen 48, 57, 185	senden... 187
rohr 146	schlaff 48, 57	setzen 17, 26, 36, 83,174
rosz 143	schlag 72, 146	seufzen 106
roth 32, 41	schlagen 45, 59, 184	sich 167
rufen 185	schlank 13	sicht 50, 78
ruhe 78	schlecht 78	sie 166
	schlitten 17	sieben ... 26, 40, 121
Saat ... 12, 26, 49, 59	schlüpfen 59	sieden 53, 180
Sachse... 141	schmal... 59	sieg 117
säen 59, 185	schmeicheln... ... 59	silber 21, 59
sagen 20, 50	schmelzen ... 174, 181	singen... 181
salbe 92	schmerz 150	singer... 102
salben ... 92, 98, 189	schnauben 180	sinken... 39, 82, 181
salbuch 21	schnee 37,39,50,56,59	sitte 59
salz 10, 30, 49, 59, 143	schneiden 179	sitz 26
salzen 185	schneider 102	sitzen 26, 59, 83, 174,
same 75	schneien 50	183
Samstag 65	schnitter 102	so 66
sand 39	schon 77	sohn 12, 20, 34, 39, 59,
sanft 48	schön 77	77, 137, 146
sang 39, 146	schöpfen 48	solch 50, 161
sänger... 102	schraube 17	soldat 141
satt 59	schrauben 180	sollen ... 225, 232, 235
sattel 49	schreiben 179	sommer 146
sau ... 27, 82, 146	schrein 59	sonder... 40
sauer 32, 76	schreiten ... 59, 179	sonne 142
saufen 32, 180	schuh 50	Sonntag 117
saugen... 180	schwären 182	sorge 93
säule 59, 76	schwarz 59	sorgen... 93
schaben 30, 48, 56, 57,	schweigen 59	spähen... 53
82, 184	schwein 27, 59, 89, 143	spazieren 107
schaf 50, 143	schweisz ...49, 57, 59	speer 48
schaffen 48, 50, 57,	schwellen 28, 174, 181	speien 48, 53
184, 188	schwert ... 21, 59	spielen... 17
schaft 48	schwester 59, 61, 142	spindel 88
schalk 146	schwimmen 17, 39, 59,	spinnen 17, 48, 181
schall 181	181	spleiszen 179
scharf... 20	schwingung ... 13	sprechen ... 17, 182
schärfen 106	schwitzen ...49, 57, 83	springen ... 82, 181
schauen ... 59, 77	schwören ... 96, 184	stand 49
schaufel ...48, 50, 88	sechs 21, 121	stand (pf.) 184
scheiden ... 31, 79	seele 31	stark 50
scheinen 31, 53, 84,	segel 50	stechen... 182
173, 179	sehen ...17, 36, 45, 50,	stecken... ... 179, 183
schelten 181	54, 183, 206	stehen ... 53, 184, 220
scheren 182	sehr 31	stehlen... ... 182, 206
schieben ... 50, 180	sei 211	steif 48

steigen... 26, 82, 179	*treffen*... 182	*wachsen* 184
stein 105	*treiben*... 45, 49, 179	*wägen*... 206
sterben... ... 181, 206	*treten* ... 6, 182, 188	*wahren* 106
stern 21	*tretoir*... 6	*wahrsagen*... ... 118
sticken... 83	*treu* 37	*wald* 41, 147
stinken... 181	*triefen*... 180	*Wälsch* 23
stoszen... 185	*trinken* 89, 40, 181	*wamme* 48
streben... 179	*trittoir*... 6	*wange*... 142
streich... 50	*trügen*... 180	*wann* 66
streiten 179	*tugend*... ... 142, 222	*war* (pf.) 17, 20, 61,
strom 59, 75		183, 217
stube 20	*Über* 54	*wäre* 194, 217
studieren 107	*um* 40	*warm* 21, 50, 56, 75,
stuhl 33, 146	*un-* 17, 40, 96	106
stute 88	*und* 66	*wärmen* ... 106, 107
suchen 33, 187, 189, 207	*universität*... ... 142	*warnen* 106
sumpf... 59	*uns* 20, 164	*was* ... 50, 54, 161
sünde 17, 142	*unser* 168	*waschen* 17, 84, 184
süsz 49, 57, 59	*unter* 40, 49	*was für* 161
	ur- 96	*wasser* 5, 17, 37, 49
Tag ...47, 50, 56, 72,	*urtheil*... 96	*wasserstoff*... ... 6
137, 148		*weben* 182
talg 50	*Vater* ...25, 48, 49, 51,	*wechsel* 104
taub 82	53, 54, 146	*wecken*... 80
taube 82, 142	*ver-* ... 19, 65, 69, 99	*weder* 79
taufen... 29	*verderben* ...174, 181,	*weg* ... 50, 96, 146
taugen... 222	206, 224	*wegen* (vb.) ... 206
tausend 19, 28, 49, 128	*verfaulen* 107	*weib* 48
teig 50, 56	*vergebens* 99	*weichen* 179
Teutsch 29	*vergehen* ... 10, 99	*weigand* 54
thal 14	*vergeigen* 99	*weigern* 54
that 14, 26, 45, 47, 78,	*vergessen* 182, 183, 206	*weile* 17
137, 142, 218	*verhehlen* ... 83, 182	*wein* 17, 37
thau 17	*verkaufen* 99	*weise* (adj.) ... 223
theil 96	*verlieren* 19, 45, 61,	*weise* (manner) 111
thier 49, 148	99, 180	*weisz* (adj.) 87, 50, 54
thiergarten... ... 49	*verlust*... ... 45, 61	*weisz* (vb.) 31, 37, 53,
thor ... 17, 28, 143	*vermögen* 226	223
thräne... 22	*verrecken* 99	*weizen*... 50
thun 14, 45, 56, 218, 233	*versehren* 81	*welch* 161
thür 28	*verwirren* 181	*welt* 21, 27, 65
thürel 88	*verzehren* 41, 82, 182	*wenden* ... 187, 219
tief 29, 57	*vieh* 12, 34, 54	*wenn* 66
tiefe 74	*viel* 12, 84	*wer* 161
tisch 50	*vier* 121	*werben*... 181
toben 82	*vogel* ...41, 48, 50, 146	*werden* 45, 77, 181,
tochter 49, 56, 137, 146	*volk* 189	229, 232, 239
tod 32, 47, 48	*voll* 17, 28, 42, 77, 157	*werfen* 48, 57, 181
todt 32, 78	*vor* 28, 99	*wergeld* 21
tracht 20	*vorder-* ... 79, 97	*werk* 50
tragen 17, 20, 50, 184,	*vorhanden* 146	*werth* 21
205		*werwolf* 21, 27, 115,
trauen... 37	*Wachen* 36, 50, 184	117
traum 49	*wachs* 50	*wesen* ... 61, 183, 217

INDEX OF GERMAN WORDS. 391

wetter 17, 49	
wetzen 50, 54	
wider 79	
wiedehopf 41	
wieder 79	
wiegen ... 14, 180, 206	
wiese 88	
wiesel 88	
wild 17, 49	
will (vb.) 17, 221, 228	
wille 36, 141	
willen 141	
willkürlich 180	
wind 17, 26, 37	
winden 17, 181, 219	
winter 146	
wir 63, 164	
wirken 88	
wirr 181	
wissen ... 45, 82, 223	
wittib 87	
wittwe ... 27, 37, 142	
witz 223	
wo 168	
wolf ... 34, 37, 42, 48, 54, 146	
wölfin 54	
wollen ... 221, 228, 229, 232	

worden 229	
wort 20, 137, 148, 147	
wund 78	
wunde 78	
wünschen 84	
wurde 181	
würde (subj.) 181, 194, 235	
wurf 95, 146	
wurm 147	
Zahl 23, 49	
zählen 23, 49	
zahm 12, 49	
zähmen 49	
zahn ... 79, 144, 146	
zähre ... 80, 76, 146	
zange 39	
zart 20	
zaun 18	
zehe 50	
zehn 40, 47, 54, 57, 121	
zehren 41	
zeichen 77	
zeigen 77	
zeit 49	
zer- 100	
zerren 82	
zeugen 29	

ziegel 50	
ziehen ...29, 53, 55, 82, 180, 206	
zimmer ...47, 57, 76	
zimmermann ... 47	
zinn 49	
zistag 17	
zog (pf.) 32, 55, 180	
zögern 106	
zorn 182	
zu (to) ... 66, 100, 229	
zu (too) 66	
zucht 55	
zug 55	
zunge ...13, 89, 47, 50, 57, 74, 137, 140, 142	
zur 66	
zwanzig ... 121, 122	
zwar 65	
zwei ... 37, 49, 121	
zweifel 121	
zweig 50	
zweite 124	
zwiefach 121	
zwirn 124	
zwirnen ... 121, 124	
zwist 124	
zwo 121	
zwölf 121	

INDEX OF TERMINATIONS.

N.B.—This index does not include the declensional endings of the demonstratives (articles, adjectives, pronouns and possessives), which will be found in their proper place, namely, 128-133, 155-157, 160-162 and 164-168.

The references are to the sections (1-240).

I.—ENGLISH.

-ability 69
-able 69
-age 50
-an 105
-ance 69
-ar 102
-ation 69

-bury 65

-ce (adverbs) 111, 124
-ce (plural) ... 145

-d (participles) 19, 54, 90, 186-189, 229
-d (adjectives) ... 90
-d (weak pf.) 186-189
-d (abstract nouns) 78
-dom ... 67, 75, 109

-e (or no ending at all = infinitive) 19, 77, 89, 107, 229
-e (or no ending at all = past part.) 19, 179-185, 187
-ed (past part.) 19, 54, 90, 186-189, 229
-ed (adjectives)... 90
-ed (weak pf.) 186-189

-en (past part.) 19, 77, 89, 179-185, 229
-en (adjectives denoting material) 89, 105
-en (verbs in) 93, 106
-en (plural) 19, 140
-er (nouns denoting agent) ... 102
-er (nouns denoting instrument) 90
-er (nouns denoting origin) ... 102
-er (nouns denoting males) ... 102
-er (comparatives) 61, 80, 90
-er (verbs in) ... 106
-es (plural) 19, 139
-es (sg. 3) 202
-ese 69
-ess 5, 69, 87
-est (superlatives) 80, 90
-est (sg. 2) 202, 209, 210
-eth (ordinals) ... 124
-eth (sg. 3) ... 202

-fast 110

-fold 110, 124
-ful 110

-ham 65
-head 109
-hood ... 67, 108, 109

-ian 105
-ing (nouns denoting action) 91, 103
-ing (diminutives) 91, 103
-ing (in the first term of a compound) 117
-ing (present part.) 103, 229
-ing (gerund) 103, 229
-ior 102
-ish ... 67, 91, 105
-ism 67
-ist 69

-kin 103

-l (verbs in) ... 106
-le (nouns denoting instrum.) 88
-le (verbs in) ... 106

INDEX OF TERMINATIONS. 393

-ledge 50, 109
-less 110
-ling (derivatives in) 108
-ling (adverbs)... 111
-long 111
-ly (adjectives) 17, 50, 67, 110
-ly (adverbs) 110, 111, 124

-ment 69

-n (past part.) 77, 89, 179-185, 229
-n (adjectives denoting material) 89, 105
-n (verbs in) ... 106
-ness 68, 104

-or 102
-ous 69

-r (nouns denoting agent) ... 102
-r (nouns denoting instrum.) ... 90
-r (comparatives 80, 90
-ric 109
-ry 69

-s (adverbs) ... 111
-s (plural) 19, 63, 139
-s (genitive) 19, 20, 63, 111, 150, 151
-s (sg. 3) 202
-se (verbs in) 93, 106
-sh (adjectives) 67, 91
-ship 67, 109
-som 110
-some 110
-st (superlatives) 80, 90
-st (sg. 2) 202, 209, 210

-t (past part.) 19, 78, 90, 186-189
-t (weak pf.) 186-189
-t (abstract nouns) 78, 90
-t (sg. 2) 202, 217, 222-227
-teen 121
-ter (nouns in) ... 79
-th (abstract nouns) 78, 90
-th (ordinals) ... 124
-th (sg. 3) 202
-ther 79
-ty ... 50, 54, 122

-ward 111
-wards 111
-wise 111
-y (adjectives) 17, 50, 91, 105
-y (nouns) 69
-yer 102

II.—GERMAN.

-at 90

-bar ... 104, 110, 117

-chen 6, 23, 108, 146

-der 79

-e (abstract nouns) 23, 74, 142
-e (plural) 23, 143, 144, 146
-e (dat. sg.) ... 152
-e (pres. subj.) ... 192
-e (pf. subj.) 23, 193
-ei 69
-el (nouns denoting instrum.) 88
-el (diminutives) 23, 88, 103
-eln (verbs in) ... 106
-en (nouns in) 39, 141, 146
-en (infinitive) 19, 23, 77, 89, 107, 229
-en (past part.) 19, 77, 89, 179-185, 229
-en (adjectives de-

noting material) ... 23, 89, 105
-en (plural) 19, 87, 140-142
-en (acc. sg.) 87, 149
-en (gen. sg.) 87, 150
-en (dat. sg.) 87 152
-end (pres. part.) 90, 229
-end (abstract nouns) 90
-ens 124
-er (nouns denoting agent) 102, 146
-er (nouns denoting instrum.) 90
-er (nouns denoting origin) ... 102
-er (nouns denoting males) ... 102
-er (comparatives) 23, 61, 80, 90
-er (plural) 23, 80, 138, 147
-ern (adjectives denoting material) ... 89, 105

-ern (verbs in) ... 106
-es (gen. sg.) 19, 20, 63, 150
-est (superlatives) 23, 80, 90
-est (sg. 2) 202, 209, 210
-et (past part.) 19, 90, 186-189, 229
-et (sg. 3) 202
-et (pl. 2) 203
-ete (weak pf.) 186-189

-fach 124
-falt 110, 124
-fältig 124

-haft 110
-halb 124
-halben 124
-heit 67, 68, 108, 109, 136, 142

-icht 23, 105
-ieren ... 6, 107, 229
-ig 17, 22, 23, 50, 91, 105, 168

-*igen* 107, 109
-*igkeit*... 109
-*in* ... 23, 87, 142
-*ing* 91, 108
-*inn* 87
-*iren* ... 6, 107, 229
-*isch* 22, 23, 67, 91, 105
-*ismus*... 67
-*ist* 69

-*keit* 68, 109, 136, 142

-*lei* 124
-*lein* 6, 23, 108, 146
-*lich* 17, 22, 23: 50, 67, 110, 111
-*ling* 23, 108
-*lings* 111
-*los* 110

-*mal* 124

-*n* (infinitive) 77, 89, 229
-*n* (past part.) 77, 89, 179-185, 229
-*n* (adjectives denoting material) 89, 105
-*n* (plural) 19, 87, 140–142
-*n* (acc. sg.) 87, 149

-*n* (gen. sg.) 87, 150
-*n* (dat. sg.) 87, 152
-*n* (dat. pl.) 39, 152
-*n* (sg. 1) 217
-*n* (pl. 1) 208, 209, 210, 211
-*n* (pl. 3) 208, 209, 210, 211
-*nd* 90, 229
-*nen* (verbs in) ... 106
-*ner* (nouns denoting agent) 102
-*nisz* 68, 104, 136, 143, 146

-*rei* 69
-*rich* 102
-*rn* (adjectives denoting material) 89, 105

-*s* (gen. sg.) 19, 68, 150
-*s* (adverbs) 111, 124
-*sal* 104, 136, 143, 146
-*sam* 104, 110
-*sch* 67, 91
-*schaft* ... 109, 142
-*sel* 104
-*st* (abstract nouns) 70
-*st* (superlatives) 23, 80, 90

-*st* (ordinals) ... 124
-*st* (sg. 2) 23, 202, 209, 210, 211
-*szig* 122

-*t* (past part.) 19, 54, 78, 90, 186-189, 229
-*t* (adjectives) ... 90
-*t* (abstract nouns) 78, 136
-*t* (ordinals) ... 124
-*t* (sg. 2) 209, 222–227
-*t* (sg. 3) ... 23, 202
-*t* (pl. 2) 208, 209, 210, 211, 213
-*te* (weak pf.) 186-189
-*te* (ordinals) ... 124
-*tel* (partitives)... 124
-*ter* (nouns in) ... 79
-*thum*, -*tum* 67, 75, 109, 147

-*ung* ... 91, 108, 142
-*ut* 90

-*wärts*... 111
-*weise* 111

-*zehn* 121
-*zeln* 106
-*zen* 93, 106
-*zig* ... 50, 54, 122

ERRATUM.

P. 236, l. 16, read *Saxonēs*.ᴬ

www.ingramcontent.com/pod-product-compliance
Lightning Source LLC
Chambersburg PA
CBHW022109290426
44112CB00008B/602